SECOND REVIEW OF THE RACE RELATIONS ACT 1976

Being the second review carried out
by the Commission for Racial Equality
pursuant to its duty under
Section 43(1)(c)
of the Act

To the Right Honourable
Kenneth Clarke QC MP
Secretary of State for the
Home Department

© **Commission for Racial Equality**
Elliot House
10/12 Allington Street
London SW1E 5EH

Published 1992
ISBN 1 85442 090 9
Price £5.00

CONTENTS

Foreword by Sir Michael Day	7
INTRODUCTION	11
THE MAIN AREAS OF CONCERN: AN OVERVIEW	16
The coverage of the Act	16
A framework for equality	18
Racial discrimination cases	22
Should there be a separate Commission for Racial Equality?	24
Europe and race relations	25
Northern Ireland	25
Incitement to racial hatred and racial harassment	26
Religion and race relations	26
THE SCOPE OF THE ACT	28
Basic definitions	28
Indirect discrimination	28
■ RECOMMENDATION 1	28
Victimisation	29
■ RECOMMENDATION 2	29
Exemptions from the Act	30
Governmental functions	30
■ RECOMMENDATION 3	30
Criminal justice	31
Seamen recruited abroad	32
■ RECOMMENDATION 4	32
Volunteers	32
■ RECOMMENDATION 5	32
Education	33
■ RECOMMENDATION 6	33

Reserved places in trade unions	34
Registered child-minders	35
■ RECOMMENDATION 7	35

Priority for discrimination law   35

■ RECOMMENDATION 8	35

A FRAMEWORK FOR EQUALITY   37

Ethnic monitoring	37
■ RECOMMENDATION 9	37
■ RECOMMENDATIONn 10	42
Codes of practice	43
■ RECOMMENDATION 11	43
Formal investigation powers	43
■ RECOMMENDATION 12	43
Binding undertakings	45
■ RECOMMENDATION 13	45
Public service duties	46
■ RECOMMENDATION 14	46

RACIAL DISCRIMINATION CASES   48

Ensuring skilled adjudication	48
■ RECOMMENDATION 15	48
Ensuring access to justice	51
■ RECOMMENDATION 16	51
Recognising the difficulties of proof	53
■ RECOMMENDATION 17	53
■ RECOMMENDATION 18	55
The group nature of racial discrimination	55
■ RECOMMENDATION 19	55
Power to order changes	56
■ RECOMMENDATION 20	56
■ RECOMMENDATION 21	57
Adequate remedies	59

Non-monetary	59
■ RECOMMENDATION 22	59
Monetary remedies	60
■ RECOMMENDATION 23	60
Employer's liability	62
■ RECOMMENDATION 24	62

THE COMMISSION 64

■ RECOMMENDATION 25	64
■ RECOMMENDATION 26	65

EUROPE 67

■ RECOMMENDATION 27	67
The position in Europe	67
European Community law	68
The European Human Rights Convention	70
The UN Convention against Racial Discrimination	71
Government action needed	71

NORTHERN IRELAND 72

■ RECOMMENDATION 28	72

INCITEMENT TO RACIAL HATRED AND RACIAL HARASSMENT 73

■ RECOMMENDATION 29	73
■ RECOMMENDATION 30	74

RELIGION AND THE LAW 77

■ RECOMMENDATION 31	77
Blasphemy	78
Identity through religion	79

APPENDIX 1: Results of the 1985 Review of the Act — 81

APPENDIX 2: Organisations and individuals who gave written evidence during the Commission's public consultation — 84

Acknowledgements

The Commission thanks John Whitmore (former head of the Legal Division at the Commission) for the work he did in preparing the consultative paper published last year, and in writing the first draft of this final review.

It is most grateful to all those who took the trouble to convey their views to the Commission during the consultation period and have therefore contributed to the authority of these recommendations.

FOREWORD

Legislation alone cannot create good relations and change attitudes. But it can set clear standards of acceptable behaviour and provide redress for people who have suffered injustice at the hands of others. Race Relations Acts were enacted by Parliament in this country when it was seen that exhortation and protestations of goodwill were not enough to prevent the countless individual acts of discrimination that arose from racial prejudice and hostility, or change the long established patterns of institutional behaviour which effectively denied equality of opportunity.

There are those who claim that legislation has served its purpose and its intrusiveness can become counterproductive. There are others who, while acknowledging the need for a law, see no case for extending it. But racial discrimination remains widespread and 'pernicious', to use the Prime Minister's term, and so far from being redundant the Race Relations Act as at present formulated does not provide a strong enough basis for dealing with it. A Government determined to achieve the standards of fairness and good service promoted by the Citizen's Charter cannot afford to ignore proposals entirely consistent with its aims.

We have learnt a great deal in the 16 years since the 1976 Act was passed. Critical weaknesses and limitations have been exposed, and in some respects the intentions of Parliament have been thwarted by decisions of the judiciary. More recently, the new Fair Employment Act in Northern Ireland has demonstrated how much more can be done through the law to achieve equality of opportunity. That Act, of course, deals with religious discrimination. But there is no good reason why the law against racial discrimination in Britain should be any weaker than the law against religious discrimination in Northern Ireland.

The Commission for Racial Equality has a statutory duty to keep the working of the Race Relations Act under review and where it thinks necessary to submit proposals for change to the Home Secretary. It would therefore be failing in this duty if it did not, from time to time, assess the effectiveness of the Act and indicate where improvements should be made. It submitted its first review in 1985, and remains disappointed by the Government's failure to respond to those detailed proposals. Opportunities have since been taken to introduce certain amendments to the Act through other legislation, bringing planning decisions within the scope of the law, for example, and extending the Commission's code making powers to housing. But the subject deserves more than piecemeal and secondary consideration, and there are many changes that can be effected only by specific race legislation.

For the most part the proposals in this review are a development of those in our first review. But we also address three other issues.

First, we believe that race relations in this country have to be managed within a wider context. We are concerned that neither the Treaty of Rome nor the European Convention makes racial discrimination unlawful. In spite of its weaknesses, our own Race Relations Act is very much stronger than any comparable legislation of our European partners. It is essential for good race relations in Britain that members of ethnic minorities who are established here should not be denied equal opportunity when they move to mainland Europe or Ireland. Freedom of movement will mean very little unless it is backed up by freedom from racial discrimination.

Second, the Race Relations Act does not give protection against religious discrimination as such, and the Muslim communities have been understandably disappointed that the Commission has been unable to translate its concern for their interests into effective law enforcement. We believe that the Government should now give consideration to introducing legislation with enforcement machinery to combat religious discrimination. We do not believe, however, that this would be best achieved by extending the scope of the Race Relations Act or the powers of the Commission.

Nor, third, do we believe that it would be right at this time to combine the Commission for Racial Equality with the Equal Opportunities Commission to form a more comprehensive Human Rights Commission. We judge that race relations require specific attention and legislation and the very focus that we argue for in this review is less likely to be achieved in a more generalist organisation.

The Commission exists to give effect to the will of Parliament. It serves the entire community, for good race relations is in the interests of all. Too often the Commission is depicted as promoting special interests, and enforcing legislation to the disadvantage of the white majority. It needs to be asserted yet again that in presenting these proposals the Commission is seeking to ensure that what Parliament intended is fully realised. The Commission has a crucial role in easing the transition to a thriving multi-racial society. The denial of rights and opportunities to certain groups creates the sense of alienation and injustice which undermines that. As Roy Jenkins asserted in 1966, and as the Prime Minister confirmed last year, our goal is integration, not 'a flattening process of assimilation', but a process based on equal opportunity, mutual respect and understanding, and a celebration of diversity. A strong and effective Race Relations Act is essential if we are to achieve that goal.

Sir Michael Day OBE
Chair, Commission for Racial Equality

INTRODUCTION

This is our second review of the working of the Race Relations Act 1976. We published our first in 1985. Although not statutorily obliged to do so, we consulted widely on both occasions. The present proposals found substantial support during the consultation process we launched in the summer of 1991. Some three hundred responses came from a wide range of organisations and individuals, many of them highly detailed and well informed. Our recommendations are therefore put forward in the confidence that they command wide support.

The results of our first review were sent to the Home Secretary in 1985 (*Review of the Race Relations Act 1976 : Proposals for Change*, CRE, 1985). There was no formal response and little has changed. Concern about this was seen in the points raised with us during the consultation this time round. We were carrying out our statutory duty to review the working of the legislation, and it seems to us that a complementary duty to give proper consideration to our proposals must lie with the Secretary of State. We are sure that these proposals will not be similarly ignored.

The Commission believes that the provision of equality of opportunity and the elimination of discrimination are the foundations on which good relations between persons of different racial groups must be built. The law has an important part to play in this and it is essential that the legal framework is adequate. Experience tells us that at present it is not. Research carried out for the Home Office by the Policy Studies Institute (*Racial Justice at Work*, 1991), and for the Department of Employment by Southampton University (*Measure for Measure*, 1992) supports our view that the law needs substantial improvement.

Research and formal investigation evidence confirms that the level of racial discrimination remains high. Though our concerns are much wider, a clear indication of this can be gained from three main areas of life: employment, education and housing.

Employment

In the employment area, the most detailed survey, using actor testing in London, Birmingham and Manchester, covered the period February 1984 to March 1985 (C. Brown and P. Gay, *Racial Discrimination: 17 Years*

After the Act, PSI, 1986). Controlled testing revealed that over one-third of employers who advertised vacancies in the press discriminated against 'black and Asian' job applicants. This research provided a measure of the extent of direct discrimination only. It gave no indication of the extent to which ethnic minority job applicants were further disadvantaged in the job market by indirect discrimination. The researchers judged that these results, even on a conservative estimate, put the nation-wide figure at tens of thousands of acts of racial discrimination in job recruitment every year. These results related to the first stage of recruitment alone, and, if the candidates had progressed to subsequent stages such as an interview, other forms of racial discrimination would no doubt have occurred.

Although this research is somewhat dated, the latest figures on unemployment levels suggest that not a great deal has changed in the meantime. There is a much higher unemployment rate for ethnic minorities. According to the *Employment Gazette* for March 1992, using data obtained in the 1990 Labour Force Survey:

> Among people with higher qualifications (above A-level) the ethnic minority unemployment rate in 1988-90 was twice that for white people (5 per cent against less than 3 per cent), and among others with qualifications the ratio was almost as high (1.9, reflecting unemployment rates of 12 and just over 6 per cent respectively); among unqualified people, however, the ratio was lower (1.4), although the unemployment rates themselves were higher (17 per cent for ethnic minority groups and 12 per cent for white people).

A brief look at some of the Commission's formal investigations in the employment field suggests less favourable treatment on racial grounds as a cause. For example, in the Leicester Beaumont Shopping Centre investigation, published in September 1985, it was found that, though Asians were adequately represented as applicants for jobs in the shopping centre compared with their proportion in the local job market, they were under-represented amongst those selected. In the major store on the site the success rate for whites was four times that for Asians. The employer could not explain the disparity on non-racial grounds.

These were essentially non-skilled jobs. But a similar pattern was found in a formal investigation into ethnic minority recruitment for Chartered Accountancy Training Contracts, published in April 1987. Across the chartered accountancy profession the success rate for whites, after controlling for qualifications, was still much higher than that of ethnic minorities.

The Commission's *Code of Practice for the Elimination of Discrimination in Employment* came into operation in 1984. Yet the 1991 formal investigation report, *Working in Hotels*, which looked at hotels in many parts of the country, speaks of 'an almost universal disregard' of the Code's recommendations. And in the investigation report, *Employers in Cardiff*, also published in July 1991, two thirds of the major employers examined had no ethnic monitoring scheme in operation. Yet, for reasons which we shall explain later, such a scheme is a prominent feature of the Code.

The Department of Employment has sent out to over 36,000 employers copies of an excellent guide, *Equal Opportunities: A 10-point action plan for employers*, but past experience of voluntarism in equal opportunities so far suggests that most copies will simply be shelved. As researchers in *Measure for Measure*, which was sponsored by that Department, say of employers:

> The majority make no specific efforts to advance equal opportunities practice. A significant minority have issued an equal opportunities policy statement, and pro-active organisations have developed codes of practice, monitoring and positive action programmes. All these practical means of combatting racial discrimination at the workplace are optional rather than required.

Education

In 1988 the investigation report into St George's Hospital Medical School, *Medical School Admissions*, reported that academics' initial selection decisions had been duplicated in a computer programme and had entailed building in a score bias against 'non-Caucasians' (blacks and Asians) and women. The programme then replaced the academics in the initial stage of the selection process.

Computerised racism is probably a rarity. But the academics' decision-making which it mimicked was typical of much decision-making throughout society though, in fact, St George's had an above average number of ethnic minority students. It points to a situation where ethnic minority people may succeed despite their race, but where their race is a significant handicap. It shows how our society requires something extra before it will, at critical points, accept ethnic minority candidates, rather than following the criteria which are supposed to govern selection.

In education there is evidence of significant under-achievement among some ethnic minority groups. It is more difficult in this area to identify and measure the nature and extent of discrimination, but the Commission's formal investigation in Birmingham showed different levels of suspensions which could not be explained by factors other than race; research published in the Swann Report revealed discriminatory patterns of behaviour in the classroom; and the Eggleston Report in 1986 pointed to discrimination in the allocation of pupils to sets, streams, etc. It is also disturbing that ethnic minorities are under-represented among those who hold power in the education system, whether as governors, administrators, inspectors or teachers.

Housing

In housing, ethnic minorities continue to live in poorer accommodation than whites. For example, about 20% of ethnic minority households are over-crowded compared with 3% of white households (*Housing and Ethnic Minorities: statistical information*, CRE, 1988). And ethnic minorities are disproportionately more likely to be homeless, particularly in London, where the figure is proportionately four times as high (*One in Every Hundred: a study of households accepted as homeless in London*, London Housing Unit and London Research Centre, 1989).

Discrimination is clearly a major factor in this, and the Commission's formal investigations continue to reveal discrimination in every type of tenure. In investigations there have been findings of discrimination against local authorities, estate agencies and an estate developer. Our report, *Sorry It's Gone*, looked at accommodation agencies which were tested in 13 areas across the country. A fifth of all accommodation agencies consistently treated the ethnic minority testers less favourably than the white testers.

What has gone wrong?

In all walks of life those in positions of power and authority are in a position to adopt, implement and monitor the kind of comprehensive equal opportunity policies that would help to end discrimination and enable all to realise their potential regardless of ethnic origins. That racial discrimination still exists at substantial levels indicates that few have done so.

It is no longer possible to argue that time is needed to implement policies designed to achieve equality. Time has been allowed in generous measure but with little advantage to the cause of equal opportunity. That time has been at the expense of those who suffer continued discrimination, with consequent misery, indignity, waste of talent and loss of cohesion in society. To achieve a substantial reduction of discrimination within a reasonable timescale, a method must be used which ensures this country takes effective action.

The Commission continues to press for the implementation of the bulk of its 1985 proposals, but developments over the intervening years lead us to advance further proposals for statutory change which emphasise achieving equal opportunity beyond the basic elimination of unlawful racial discrimination.

Changes in the law achieved since 1985

The Commission successfully effected some changes in line with the 1985 Review by the expedient of having amendments put down to legislation and using test cases in the courts. The statutory changes were made in planning, housing and employment legislation. The case-law changes have been of general application to discrimination law covering compensation, the definitions of indirect discrimination and of victimisation, and statutory immunity from race relations law. An account of these changes is to be found in Appendix 1 on page 81. There has been no specific race relations legislation dealing with discrimination and so the chance for wider change has not presented itself.

Although a test case approach aimed at improving parts of the law may be challenging, and may give the impression of a Commission actively fighting to establish rights, it is time-consuming, expensive and piecemeal. It is not a satisfactory substitute for thorough statutory reform. Given the right statutory framework test cases could more fully concentrate on strategically tackling particular areas where equal opportunity is lacking.

THE MAIN AREAS OF CONCERN:
An overview

Particular attention is needed in three areas:

- The coverage of the anti-discrimination provisions of the Act.
- The framework for achieving equality.
- The hearing of racial discrimination complaints.

We also set out our views in relation to a number of other issues:

- The Commission and whether it should be amalgamated with the Equal Opportunities Commission to form a new Human Rights Commission.
- The need for greater protection from racial discrimination elsewhere in Europe.
- The need for protection from racial discrimination in Northern Ireland;
- Whether action is needed in relation to incitement to racial hatred and racial harassment.
- To what extent the law needs to address itself to questions of religion in the interests of good race relations.

We set out the gist of our principal concerns in summary form in this introduction. More detail and further recommendations are to be found in the main body of the text. Not all of these matters are flagged up in this overview.

THE COVERAGE OF THE ACT

Once the idea of equality catches hold, expectations will not be confined within the constraints of the statute which fostered those expectations. Equal opportunities are expected across the board, not just in specific situations, and rightly so, since equal opportunities should, as a matter of principle, apply to the whole of public life. The Race Relations Act 1976, however, is not of general application. It has weaknesses in its basic definitions and allows unacceptable exemptions for some governmental types of activity and acts protected by other statutes, orders and ministerial authority.

Not to tackle these weaknesses is to leave unchallenged areas of activity which the enforcement provisions of the Act cannot penetrate. At the same time it sends out the message that the elimination of racial discrimination is not perceived by the Government to be of fundamental importance since there are other concerns to which it must give way. Society is thus told at one and the same time that equality is important – otherwise there would be no 1976 Act – but not the highest priority.

Our principal areas of concern are:

- **To get the basic definitions right**

    The basic definitions of indirect discrimination and victimisation are inadequate and need major overhaul. They determine the application of the legislation in all the areas to which the Act applies, and it is therefore vital to get them right. There is wide consensus that the law on indirect discrimination is currently defective.

- **To bring exempt areas into the Act**

    Case-law protects many areas of Governmental activity of the controlling sort from the requirements of the 1976 Act. It is strange that officialdom can continue to discriminate on racial grounds unchecked. Government should set an example.

- **To recognise the fundamental importance of racial discrimination law**

    The Race Relations Act 1976 does not have priority over other statutes or acts protected by other statutes, orders and ministerial authority. It is inconsistent with the principles underlying the Act that legislators and ministers should have a free hand to establish systems where racial discrimination can flourish immune from its enforcement provisions. Our concerns in this area have been heightened by the decision of the Court of Appeal in the Cleveland case, which held that parental choice under the 1986 and 1988 Education Acts could be exercised in a discriminatory way. All legislation should include the provision that it is subject to the 1976 Act, unless a specific case for exemption is made. We recognise, for instance, that, if the concept of citizenship is to have any meaning at all, then some discrimination on the grounds of nationality is inevitable.

A FRAMEWORK FOR EQUALITY

The nature of racial discrimination

Any system designed with a determination to achieve racial equality must tackle three distinctive features of racial discrimination:

- It happens to people because they belong to particular racial groups.
- It is not normally practised openly.
- Much of it is perpetrated by people who are unaware that they are racially discriminating.

The importance of ethnic monitoring

The only way in which the presence of racial discrimination, including covert and often unintentional acts, can be routinely revealed is the ethnic monitoring of the relevant decisions. The whole experience of the Commission points to this central conclusion. No organisation can be sure that racial discrimination is not occurring unless it has such a system in place.

We believe that monitoring has now won broad acceptance, and experience in Northern Ireland with the new Fair Employment Act confirms that many of the assumed objections have no substance.

A framework which ensures compliance with the steps necessary to achieve equality is essential, and the Race Relations Act 1976 as it stands does not provide this. Its underlying assumption is that voluntarism is often good enough. The same contradictory message that we have remarked upon before is being sent out here by the legislation: racial equality is important but not especially so. It is important enough to merit action guidelines, but not important enough to require employers to follow them. Action is therefore patchy, as research on the Commission's *Code of Practice in Employment* reveals. In many instances it is very belated and half-hearted – a matter of form rather than directed toward achieving actual change.

Equality targets

Voluntarism has however provided a test-bed for trying out types of action. As a result we now know that taking action following ethnic monitoring can produce positive change.

Ultimately, action on equality will show results. Measuring those results against clear targets or benchmarks establishes the success of equality action. As the Department of Employment's *Equal Opportunities: A 10-point action plan for employers* says: 'You will find it invaluable to develop an overall action plan with targets to help you put it into practice' and 'The success of any policy can be gauged, but only if benchmarks are set and achievements are measured'.

So any new framework for achieving equality needs to incorporate both ethnic monitoring and equality targets.

Equality targets are not the same as quotas. We do not advocate quotas, under which set percentages of a workforce would be reserved for particular ethnic groups. Indeed, there was only minimal canvassing for the use of quotas in the responses to our consultation. Quotas imply accepting the use of race as a criterion for employment or other decisions. Our aim is to reduce the incidence of race being used as a criterion for decision-making in society.

Equality targets can be established on the basis of what might be expected to happen in the absence of decision-making on racial grounds, and taking into account any permitted outreach action. If targets are not met, then searching out the reasons may help to reveal the incidence of racial discrimination, whether direct or indirect, which can then be tackled.

The Northern Ireland experience

Northern Ireland now has 1989 legislation to achieve what Government describes as 'best equal opportunity practice' in relation to religious discrimination in employment. There employers are bound by law to provide religious monitoring data and this has been tied in with their eligibility for public contracts. They are also bound to carry out periodic reviews aimed at fair participation and to draw up affirmative action plans.

The Commission has maintained close contact with the Fair Employment Commission in Northern Ireland and discussed common areas of concern. Solutions to the problems faced will be similar because the nature of the underlying discrimination is similar in relevant respects, even if other closely related factors are different. But our view that equivalent action should be taken here as regards race and employment is based on our analysis of needs in Britain.

Public contracts and grants

We also take the view that public monies in the form of contracts or grants should be used to support equal opportunities as an incidental objective. The White Paper preceding the 1976 Act took that position and the

Institute of Personnel Management reported favourably in a research report, *Contract Compliance – the UK experience* (1987, IPM). We recognise, as IPM's research did, that there needs to be consistency in the use of documentation and standards applied by authorities exercising contract compliance. That is why we produced a document called *Principles of Practice for Contract Compliance* which was, unfortunately, then overtaken by local government legislation.

Not to use contract compliance is to ignore a powerful lever for change. Moreover, in the absence of monitoring the provision of equal opportunities by recipients of contracts, racial discrimination is almost inevitably being sustained by public funds.

Despite this, Government requirements under current local government legislation prevent local authorities and many other public authorities from asking for ethnic monitoring data relating to the workforces of proposed contractors. Government has never monitored the equal opportunity clauses in its own contracts. A wholly new approach is required.

A framework for racial equality

We advocate a more advanced approach in the field of employment, where there has been a code of practice since 1984, than in other areas.

Notwithstanding the Code, major problems persist. Research shows widespread discrimination, and the Commission's formal investigations and individual cases indicate its prevalence in both public and private sectors, and in relation to both skilled and unskilled work. The Department of Employment pack mentioned above says people 'frequently suffer unfair discrimination in employment'. The general picture emerging is that someone from an ethnic minority has to be much better than their white counterpart to receive equally favourable employment decisions.

An adequate framework for equality is needed in employment and elsewhere.

In employment

There should be a statutory requirement imposed on all employers to monitor for ethnic origins. The Commission should be given the power to call for the data. A framework of legislation should be established laying down the objective of achieving equality of opportunity with goals and timetables. This must be backed by appropriate administrative enforcement measures with the Commission having the power to direct that equal opportunity steps are taken, subject to a right of appeal. The economic power of both central and local government should be used in support of this policy.

Both the research for the Home Office by the Policy Studies Institute, and the survey for the Department of Employment by Southampton University referred to above support this approach.

Elsewhere

Outside employment, the code-making power, now extended to housing, should apply also to other areas. The relevant Secretary of State should have the power to prescribe ethnic monitoring.

As a first step ethnic monitoring should be required in respect of housing decisions by those bodies currently subject to Section 71 of the 1976 Act. There is a great deal of evidence from formal investigations and from research that housing allocation decisions are prone to racial bias. This must be a priority area for action. Considerable experience now exists on how to monitor such decisions.

We think it better to proceed here by way of delegated legislation rather than primary legislation because the Secretary of State would need to consult on standards relating to the quality of housing to ensure that meaningful categories are prescribed.

The Commission's role

Apart from the power to call for monitoring data and to issue directions as set out above, some modifications to the Commission's existing powers are needed. To complement requirements to monitor, the limitation imposed by case-law on its power to conduct formal investigations without a suspicion should be removed so that the Commission can undertake an inspectorial role. Powers should also be given to the Commission to accept binding undertakings to carry out good practice. The confrontational role into which case-law casts the Commission in its present use of the formal investigation power in relation to named organisations, is not best calculated to achieve prompt results.

RACIAL DISCRIMINATION CASES

We are concerned about the ineffectiveness of existing provisions for hearing cases under the 1976 Act. Only about 15 per cent of the racial discrimination cases heard by industrial tribunals succeeded in 1990-1991, according to Department of Employment statistics, dipping below the one-in-five level of earlier years. The jurisdiction of the courts in non-employment matters is little used. Moreover the whole system has inbuilt limitations.

Because findings of racial discrimination, and the occasional large settlement, tend to attract publicity, the general perception may well be of a system which is functioning much better than in fact it is. In our view, the persistence of those who do go through with discrimination cases can be explained only by a deep-felt determination to play their part in ending racial discrimination, and not by any rational assessment of their chances of winning, or the personal benefits they might gain. Unhappily, even when they do win, the system is not geared to turning that to the advantage of others, yet by its very nature racial discrimination has group effects.

There are a number of areas requiring attention:

The hearing of cases

In our view, given the level of racial discrimination revealed by research, it is highly improbable that the mere 47 cases which succeeded before the industrial tribunals in 1990-91 were a true reflection of the merits of the whole case-load heard by those tribunals.

Adjudication of disputes concerning racial equality must be in the hands of those with knowledge and experience of the complexities involved. The current system falls short of this. Many industrial tribunals seem to lack training, understanding and experience of dealing with race cases.

The solution we put forward is for specialisation by those adjudicating. This would make special training more cost effective, enable experience to build up rapidly and provide the basis for use of improved remedies. We recommend that a discrimination division should be introduced into the industrial tribunals and should be given jurisdiction over all discrimination cases.

Support for complainants

Access to justice must be adequately provided for, and all research indicates that racial justice is almost impossible without help. Yet legal aid does not exist for employment cases at tribunal level. It should be extended to cover all racial discrimination cases. At present it is confined to non-employment cases and cases in the Employment Appeal Tribunal (EAT) and higher courts. The Commission has helped to provide training to trade unions and encouraged other bodies to give support to complainants, but progress has been slow. Law Centres are failing through lack of funds, and the Commission's plans to establish an independent complainant aid organisation have not yet been fully realised.

Allocation of the burden of proof

The difficulty of proving racial discrimination should be recognised in the statutory provisions. Guidance offered by the Court of Appeal and the EAT on the question of proof has vacillated in recent years and has been less than helpful. If the suggestions in our 1985 Review had been taken up, much confusion would have been avoided and tribunals would have had a clear line to follow. It would have been similar to that which the courts have found acceptable in Northern Ireland and which recognises the difficulties faced by an applicant. Once a complainant establishes circumstances consistent with racial discrimination or victimisation, the evidential burden of establishing a satisfactory explanation should shift to the respondent.

Recognising the group nature of racial discrimination

A peculiar feature of the present system of adjudication is that it entirely fails to recognise the group nature of racial discrimination (except to the extent that similar factual evidence is admissible). It simply deals with the individual. There could be great strides forward if the following were done:

- Rights to bring enforcement proceedings should be widened considerably, in particular so that they can be brought on behalf of groups.

- The remedies in the tribunals to deal with discrimination should be widened beyond those concerned with the individual so as to deal with discriminatory situations.

- The tribunal should have the power, in appropriate cases where discrimination is proved, to order special training or encouragement of members of particular racial groups which are at present permitted as voluntary measures in the Act.

- In any case, the tribunal should have the power to award compensation to any person it finds to have suffered unlawful discrimination either named or otherwise sufficiently identified provided that any such person joins the proceedings within a specified time and seeks the compensation.

Adequate remedies

There is much scope for improving the remedies available. Remedies provided by the system of justice must be adequate and this is not the case at present:

- The limit on compensation for racial discrimination should be removed: it is currently £10,000 in the industrial tribunals. In Northern Ireland the limit for religious discrimination is £30,000.

- There should be no exception for indirect discrimination in the provisions on compensation.

- A minimum figure for compensation for injury to feelings is needed. £25,000 has been awarded in the first case under the new legislation in Northern Ireland. A similar case here might receive £4,000 at best.

- A preventive remedy should be available where a person has stated a directly discriminatory intention.

- Ordinary remedies should apply also to the whole area of education instead of the Secretary of State having powers under Section 19(2) and (3) of the Act.

- Interim relief should be available to preserve a complainant's position pending a hearing in employment cases as well as non-employment.

- In employment cases it should be possible for the tribunal to order appointment, promotion, reinstatement or re-engagement.

SHOULD THERE BE A SEPARATE COMMISSION FOR RACIAL EQUALITY?

In recent years, cooperation between the Commission, the Equal Opportunities Commission (EOC), the Fair Employment Commission in Northern Ireland and the Equal Opportunities Commission in Northern Ireland has significantly increased. We took the view, especially with new grounds of discrimination being suggested, that it was time to question with the public whether there should be one major Commission dealing with all forms of discrimination, or whether the distinctive styles, concerns, and budgets of the separate Commissions confer real advantages.

The weight of opinion in our consultation was that a separate Commission for Racial Equality did offer advantages. There is much to commend an evolutionary approach, based on increasing collaboration on issues of common concern.

EUROPE AND RACE RELATIONS

1992 means that the inhabitants of the UK will be increasingly seeking to work or trade in the European Community while people from other Community countries will be looking to do the same here. While those coming to Britain have the protection of our Race Relations Act, those going the other way will find that protection elsewhere in the domestic laws of other countries is by no means as good. It is a proper area of concern for the Commission that, as a result, the opportunities created in the opening up of Europe may well be less for ethnic minorities than for their white counterparts.

There is no established framework in Community law for protection from racial discrimination; and the protection offered under the European Convention of Human Rights is limited.

Government should be taking a lead to improve the legal position on race in the various European treaties and should also improve Britain's commitment to certain other existing treaties.

NORTHERN IRELAND

There is no law against racial discrimination in Northern Ireland. Several organisations asked that we should press for this. In doing so, we are echoing the call of the Northern Ireland Standing Advisory Commission on Human Rights (SACHR) for such protection.

Though the Commission has no remit in relation to Northern Ireland, we take the view that, even if we concern ourselves with people normally resident in Britain, it cannot be right that, if they travel to another part of the United Kingdom, they should have no protection from racial discrimination. We advance the same argument for protection as we do in relation to Europe generally, but of course the Government is better placed to change things for a part of the United Kingdom.

INCITEMENT TO RACIAL HATRED AND RACIAL HARASSMENT

Undoubtedly the worst feature of race relations in this country in recent years is the terrifying scale of racial harassment. A European Parliamentary enquiry highlighted this shameful aspect of British life.

We call for a review of the enforcement of the incitement to racial hatred provisions (which are now part of the Public Order legislation rather than the Race Relations Act). We take the view that the existence of the Crown Prosecution Service should mean that the statutory involvement of the Attorney-General can be repealed. We make some suggestions for strengthening the law to deal with racial harassment.

RELIGION AND RACE RELATIONS

Our multi-racial society is also a multi-faith society. The two are inextricably linked. The 1976 Act covers discrimination on the grounds of colour, race, nationality or ethnic or national origins. The question of whether religious discrimination should be made unlawful has to be considered because of the impact on race relations.

There was discussion during the passage of the Race Relations Act on whether it should cover religious discrimination, but wide public debate on religious matters in the context of race relations did not start until the *Satanic Verses* issue arose. Protection of religious feelings was then widely seen to be in conflict with the notion of freedom of speech.

An attempt to invoke the blasphemy law, which had itself largely fallen into disuse, revealed that it protected only the established religion. The law was thus perceived as discriminatory. The present position on this is untenable. If the law is not to discriminate, blasphemy as an offence must either be abolished or extended to other religions. Those responding to the consultation were generally in agreement that the present state of the law is unsatisfactory, but divided as to what was the best way forward.

Blasphemy deals only with attacks on religion. There remains the question of the identity which people feel because of their membership of a religious group. This may be much more important to them than their identity arising from their national origins.

Both incitement to hatred against a religious group and discrimination against a person because of membership of that group (unless it is recognised as an ethnic group as in the case of Jews and Sikhs) are lawful in Great Britain, but not in Northern Ireland. Yet, in the international treatment of human rights, religious and racial discrimination tend to be treated similarly.

Neither a law against incitement to religious hatred, nor a law against discrimination on religious grounds poses quite the same problems in respect of freedom of speech as does a law against blasphemy.

THE SCOPE OF THE ACT

BASIC DEFINITIONS

It is of fundamental importance that the basic definitions are correct because they determine the extent to which the law enforcement provisions relate to every field covered by the Act.

Indirect discrimination

RECOMMENDATION 1

A new definition of indirect discrimination is required making unlawful any practice, policy or situation as well as any requirement or condition which is continued, allowed, or introduced and which has an adverse impact on a particular racial group and which cannot be demonstrated to be necessary.

The Court of Appeal in *Perera v Civil Service Commission* [1983] IRLR166 decided that a requirement or condition only exists where it amounts to a complete bar if it cannot be met. This was confirmed by the Court of Appeal in *Meer v Tower Hamlets LBC* [1988] IRLR 399 following which the House of Lords refused leave to appeal.

Thus, if several criteria are used, one of which puts ethnic minority employees or applicants at a serious disadvantage but may be overcome by an individual who has extraordinary compensating qualities, use of that discriminatory criterion is lawful even though it would be impossible to show that it was 'justifiable' (if the preference was exercised with the *intention* of adversely affecting any particular ethnic group it would, however, amount to direct discrimination).

Both SACHR in its 1987 proposals on fair employment in Northern Ireland, and the EOC in its 1988 proposals for amending the sex discrimination legislation put forward proposals similar to the CRE's 1985 proposals. The case for an amendment taking in all the jurisdictions where the law applies is overwhelming. Unhappily what the various agencies see as a major reason for action, Government sees as a reason for inaction. Rather than improve the law across the board it enacted the faulty law in the 1989 Fair Employment Act in Northern Ireland.

The current position on the meaning of 'justifiable' in the law relating to indirect discrimination seems to be that stated by Balcombe LJ in Hampson v DES [1989] IRLR 69 at page 75:

> In my judgment 'justifiable' requires an objective balance between the discriminatory effect of the condition and the reasonable needs of the person who applies the condition.

This falls short of a clear test of necessity, since the qualification 'reasonable' can only mean that a broad view should be taken of what can be put in the balance when arguing for the status quo.

Formal investigations have shown that when a workforce is largely white the practices which most affect ethnic minorities' job prospects are those such as word-of-mouth recruitment, giving preference for apprenticeships to children of existing employees and only trawling for vacancies internally. None of these practices is essential for business efficiency, although there are arguments in their favour.

If the barriers in the way of ethnic minorities are to be removed, the law must ensure that tribunals make decisions which pull down those barriers while permitting only those practices that are really necessary in all the circumstances.

The concept of indirect discrimination must be made to match the task that is required of it.

Victimisation

RECOMMENDATION 2

Protection against victimisation for invoking the Act is at present incomplete. The remedy for victimisation should be redefined so that there is protection against a person suffering any detriment whatever as a result of their doing any of the acts listed in Section 2 1(a)-(d) (involvement in allegations, proceedings, etc, under the Act).

The law on victimisation protects someone from acts only 'in circumstances relevant for the purposes of any provision of this Act'. But it is possible to envisage their being harassed in ways not covered by the Act. There is no sense in protecting a person from some types of harassment and not others.

The case of *Aziz v Trinity Taxis* [1988] IRLR 204, while clarifying the law to some extent, shows that a real problem for complainants lies in proving that the action taken against them followed from their taking action under the Act and not from some other reason. Proving victimisation is very difficult indeed (see pages 53-55, where we make further points concerning the burden of proof).

EXEMPTIONS FROM THE ACT

The general thrust of our argument is that the principle of non-discrimination should be of general application and not shot through with exceptions favouring particular interests.

Governmental functions

RECOMMENDATION 3

At present a wide range of actions, governmental in nature, are outside the ambit of the Act. The definition relating to the provision of 'goods, facilities and services' in the Act should make it clear that it extends to all areas of governmental and regulatory activity, whether central or local, such as acts in the course of immigration control, the prison and police services, and planning control. The non-discrimination duty applicable to the whole criminal justice system under Section 95 of the Criminal Justice Act 1991 should be backed by code-making powers and proper ways of airing grievances.

In *Amin v Entry Clearance Officer, Bombay* [1983] 2 AC 818 the House of Lords by a bare majority (3/2) held that the expression 'provision of goods, facilities and services' in the anti-discrimination statutes applied only to activities or matters analogous to those provided by private undertakings. This position is unnecessarily restrictive.

The result is to raise the question of how many areas of government or government-related activity are entirely outside the enforcement provisions of the Act. Certainly in relation to immigration control, much of the prison system and police activity, there is apparently a wide freedom to discriminate so far as the remedies under the 1976 Act are concerned.

The Commission believes that this is wrong. This lack of remedy occurs precisely where the individual is most vulnerable. In the private sector, if there is discrimination at one source, the individual generally has both the opportunity of going elsewhere to another provider of services and also has a remedy under the Act. There appears to be neither opportunity when the individual is facing an immigration officer, prison officer or police officer prepared to discriminate improperly in exercising control functions.

The same need for change still exists in planning controls except for the limited area which was made subject to the Act by the insertion of a new Section 19A.

As ideas of equality take hold, the exception for the control activities of government deriving from the House of Lords decision in *Amin v Entry Clearance Officer* is so far out of line with the expectations of those seeking protection from discrimination, that the *Amin* decision is bound to come under increasing and sustained attack.

In its 1988 proposals, the EOC also called for an 'amendment to remove the restrictive interpretation ...imposed by the *Amin* decision'.

Criminal justice

As well as arguing for the 'goods, facilities and services' provision in section 20 of the 1976 Act to be freed from the restrictive interpretation of the *Amin* case, the Commission has urged, in the context of the recent criminal justice legislation, that the vague non-discrimination duty applicable to the whole criminal justice system under Section 95 of the Criminal Justice Act 1991 should be made more explicit. It should clearly state the right of everyone to be treated without discrimination on the grounds of race. The duty should be backed by code-making powers together with proper ways of airing grievances. Section 95 goes only part of the way to fulfilling this need.

The Commission has sponsored research into whether there is racial discrimination in crown courts administering criminal justice. The results will be published before the end of 1992. Up to now research has offered conflicting conclusions as to whether or not ethnic minority people receive worse treatment than others. However, it is clear that ethnic minorities believe they do. The huge overrepresentation of ethnic minority people in the prison population – some 16 per cent of prisoners, compared to about 5 per cent in the general population – is very worrying indeed.

Seamen recruited abroad

RECOMMENDATION 4

The present exemption in Section 9 of the Act for seafarers recruited abroad should be repealed by use of the special power provided for that purpose in Section 73 of the Act. Section 8 of the Act should be amended so that the Act applies to employment on board a ship registered at a port of registry in Great Britain wherever the work takes place, and not, as at present, if the work is wholly outside Great Britain. Corresponding provision should be made for employment on aircraft and hovercraft.

This proposal was put forward in our 1985 Review yet there has been no change in the law. In principle this exemption is wrong.

Volunteers

RECOMMENDATION 5

The employment provisions require the existence of a contract for the Act to apply, but there are many volunteers doing work equivalent to that of contracted employees. The Commission recommends that they receive protection under the Act. Where what is volunteered for is not equivalent to employment, we recommend that the Act should cover the situation if volunteers have been called for by advertisement.

The 1976 Act defines employment in Section 78 by the existence of a contract, either of employment or to execute work or labour personally. This caused a problem in the case of the relationship between solicitors and barristers in which, historically, no contract arose. This has been solved by special legislative provision in the courts and in legal services legislation. The case of volunteers in, for example, advice centres or charity shops raises a similar point, unless, unusually, a contract is drawn up or a tribunal finds that it can imply some sort of contract.

There is no reason why volunteers should not be protected from less favourable treatment on racial grounds in recruitment or treatment or in respect of dismissal. Accordingly we recommend that voluntary work be treated as though it is 'employment' to the extent that it is appropriate to do so, having regard to the benefits and conditions the volunteer would have enjoyed as a volunteer but for any discrimination.

When volunteers come forward to do something which is not 'work', but they are called for by some form of advertisement, then they should be protected by law from racial discrimination.

Education

RECOMMENDATION 6

In several ways the enforcement provisions of the Act treat parts of the field of education differently. The Commission recommends that the provisions be brought into line with enforcement in other fields. Moreover, there are doubts about the extension of the Act to functions under recent education legislation, and the Commission recommends that it be made clear that the 1976 Act does apply.

In January 1989 the Commission wrote to the Department of Education and Science setting out what in its view needed to be done to update the Race Relations Act 1976 in its treatment of education. The points made were as follows:

- Section 18(1) of the Race Relations Act 1976 as originally enacted made it unlawful for a local education authority to discriminate racially in carrying out those functions under the Education Acts 1944 to 1975 which do not fall under Section 17 of the 1976 Act. The Education Acts of 1980 and 1981 updated Section 18 so that it covers functions under those Education Acts also. There is no similar reference in the 1986 or 1988 Education Acts and we took the view that there should have been. There is an argument that the words in Section 235(7) of the 1988 Act that it 'shall be construed as one with the 1944 Act' are intended to deal with this point, but the position is far from clear.

- Under Section 57(5) of the Race Relations Act 1976 as amended, complaints against an LEA maintained institution, grant-maintained school, or college falling within the ambit of Polytechnics and Colleges Funding Council (PCFC), must first be referred to the Secretary of State before proceedings can commence in a designated county or sheriff court. We took the view that, instead of helping to avoid an already cumbersome procedure, this was, in many cases, serving to prolong it and delay redress. This is particularly unfortunate in the case of admissions to, and exclusions from, schools and colleges.

- Under Section 58 of the Race Relations Act the Commission may issue a non-discrimination notice where, in a formal investigation, it makes a finding of unlawful discrimination. By virtue of Section 58(6), as amended, this power does not extend to the educational provisions as they apply to the LEA-maintained sector, grant-maintained schools, and institutions under the PCFC umbrella. In those cases the Commission can only recommend to the Secretary of State that they use their powers under the 1944 Education Act to require an LEA, school or college to act reasonably. We took the view that there was no good reason why they should not be amenable to non-discrimination notices. Such notices are subject to appeal and LEAs, schools or colleges can always seek the advice of the Secretary of State in deciding whether to launch an appeal.

- Section 17 of the 1976 Act covers discrimination by educational establishments. During the course of our investigation into St George's Hospital Medical School we noticed a potentially important gap in the wording of the Section. Whereas the employment provision Section 4 covers the arrangements made for determining who should be offered employment, there is no equivalent provision in Section 17. In the particular case of St George's this meant that the adverse racial weightings in the computer program applied to admissions did not give rise to liability *per se* but only in the case of applicants who would otherwise have been called for interview. If Section 17 had been wider, then the lowering of any applicant's score on racial grounds would have constituted less favourable treatment and would have been unlawful.

These points were put to the DES in January 1989. On 12 April 1990 the DES responded to a further prompting saying that their reply would be at least several more weeks. At the time of publishing this Review no response had been received.

Reserved places in trade unions

Several unions pressed on us the need for a provision in the Race Relations Act equivalent to Section 49 of the Sex Discrimination Act. This would permit reserved places for members of ethnic minorities on union bodies. As this issue was not specifically covered by the consultation exercise, we make no recommendation, but we would welcome wider debate on the matter.

Registered child-minders

RECOMMENDATION 7

We recommend that the exception in Section 23(2) of the Act be amended in so far as it is necessary to clarify its non-application to registered child-minders.

Section 23(2), amongst other things, exempts from the Act fostering and anything someone does when taking children into their home and treating them as members of the family. The justification given for this is that the law should not affect private family matters. The exemption is sometimes thought to apply to child minding.

However, child-minding should not be likened to fostering as it is akin to a service or facility as opposed to a private family arrangement. Also, under child care law, children subject to child-minding arrangements can never be regarded as members of the family. In order to remove any confusion it may be necessary to amend Section 23(2). This would be consistent with the Children Act which specifically allows race to be taken into account when considering fostering arrangements but does not in relation to child-minding.

Priority for discrimination law

RECOMMENDATION 8

The Race Relations Act is, by its own terms, subordinated to a wide range of rules, existing or future, with which it conflicts. The basic legislation making discrimination unlawful should be superior to earlier Acts and all subordinate legislation or other forms of rule-making. Where Government requires as a matter of policy that discrimination should be permitted on grounds of birth, nationality, descent or residence, this should be expressly provided for by statute.

Some inroad has been made into this statutory immunity from the Race Relations Act by the House of Lords decision in *Hampson v DES* [1990] IRLR302 which narrowly construed the exception in Section 41. The 1976 Act is still, however, in a subordinate position. This is wrong in principle for a statute which sets out a basic civil right. It ought to be possible to state in advance when derogation from a civil right is permissible in terms which do not give either the legislature, or ministers, such free rein to discriminate on racial grounds.

The Government, it is true, has promoted an 'equal opportunity proofing' policy. All legislative and policy developments are supposed to be vetted according to equal opportunity considerations. However, no public accounting of this is provided for and Government has declined to give reports to the Commission on its implementation. Such an initiative is in any event no substitute for a legal obligation.

The Commission accepts that, if the concept of citizenship is to be at all meaningful, there are bound to be some exceptions for discrimination based on nationality. Even so it is inevitable that Government will have to carry out a review of the exception in Section 75(5) of the Race Relations Act (which allows rules restricting service under the Crown or in any public body by birth, nationality, descent or residence), to ensure compliance with developing EC law. This will narrow the categories of public service not open to other EC citizens, building on Article 48.4 of the Treaty of Rome. While that review is underway it would make sense to reduce the exemptions as far as possible in the light of general equal opportunity considerations.

A FRAMEWORK FOR EQUALITY

Ethnic monitoring

RECOMMENDATION 9

In the field of employment there should be:

1. A statutory ethnic monitoring requirement on all employers.

2. A framework of legislation in which the provision of equality of opportunity becomes the objective with a duty on employers where appropriate to adopt goals and timetables.

3. Appropriate powers in the Commission to issue appealable directions by way of administrative enforcement.

4. The use of the economic power of both central and local government in support of this policy.

In the much more sensitive area of religious discrimination in Northern Ireland, the Standing Advisory Commission on Human Rights considered what action was needed to achieve employment equality (*Religious and Political Discrimination and Equality of Opportunity in Northern Ireland. Report on Fair Employment* Cm 237, HMSO, October 1987). The Report persuaded the Government to introduce compulsory monitoring in the private sector in Northern Ireland.

SACHR relied not on the features of religious discrimination but on a more general experience. In paragraph 7.70 of the report it says:

> Anti-discrimination agencies in every jurisdiction of which the Commission is aware now regard monitoring, both of the composition of the workforce as a whole and of the results of recruitment and promotion, to be an essential tool in controlling discrimination and promoting of equality of opportunity.

After looking at all the arguments they concluded:

> ...there is no compelling practical reason why monitoring ... should not be made a legal requirement for all employers, and a number of reasons why it should. The Commission recommends accordingly.

The reason why ethnic monitoring is essential is that it is the only mechanism that will routinely detect discrimination – often covert, unintentional, and all the while affecting persons because of their membership of particular racial groups.

The collection of ethnic data in the 1991 census will, in time, provide a source of data against which employers can make sense of their own monitoring data.

In March 1983 the Secretary of State for Employment laid before Parliament the Commission's *Code of Practice for the Elimination of Racial Discrimination and the Promotion of Equality of Opportunity in Employment*, making it clear that it would only come into effect a year later. The delay was:

> ... to allow employers and others a reasonable period to consider the Code and its implications for them.

The Code contains ethnic monitoring recommendations. If the assumption was that employers would implement the Code by the end of the year, it was wrong. The research report, *The Race Relations Code of Practice in Employment. Are Employers Complying?* (CRE, 1989), details a survey carried out in late 1985 and early 1986. Only 25 per cent of employers had read through or glanced at the Code. Of those, fewer than 4 per cent had comprehensive equal opportunities policies with adequate systems for monitoring their effectiveness. The overall position might have looked even worse, but for the fact that the survey was skewed towards larger employers. Smaller employers had done even less.

On the other hand, if the Code is fully implemented it can achieve change. The second part of the research study, done in 1987, gave case studies of employers who had taken a great deal of action. The conclusion was:

> For most of the case study organisations the measures introduced had led to positive changes in the overall proportion of ethnic minority staff employed. The initial issue for those organisations had been to attract and recruit more people from ethnic minority groups, and most had succeeded in achieving this. The greatest changes, however, had occurred at the lower grades rather than at the senior levels, so that the main concern of most of these organisations now is to ensure that ethnic minorities progress to middle and senior management positions.

The view of all of the 1987 case study organisations was:

> ... that the Code of Practice needed to have more 'bite'. Some felt the impetus of the Code of Practice had been lost over the past few years and that it needed to be given a higher profile once again.

The researchers concluded:

> In some cases it is likely that the fact that there was a policy, and that it was given a high profile, may have led to complacency.

The best view of the employment Code therefore seems to be that, as a programme for action, it could, if followed, lead to results; but that, being voluntary in nature, it has not had a widespread impact, and what impact it has had is difficult to sustain.

Nevertheless the Code has set standards, even if those standards have not been widely applied. For example, the fact that the Code endorsed the principle of ethnic monitoring led the courts to approve of the use of such data in proving racial discrimination. This was a very important step forward, but it was only a step. The need now is for employers who have so far failed to monitor voluntarily to be made to do so.

In Northern Ireland, with a small population, it is feasible to require employers to make monitoring returns as a matter of course to the Fair Employment Commission. In Britain it may serve little purpose to require returns to be made as a matter of routine to the Commission for Racial Equality. Even a much enlarged Commission could have major problems in handling such a vast accumulation of data.

The primary purpose of monitoring is to put the employer in possession of relevant facts so that the employer can take action. The requirement to monitor therefore should go across the board. The Commission should have the power to require the data on demand, either from an individual employer or by general notice to all employers in a given category, instead of every employer returning the data to the Commission annually. There should also be a requirement for employers to publish a statement, either in their annual report, or in some accessible document referred to in the annual report, as to the designation and address of the person from whom any interested member of the public could obtain the data. For those employers not statutorily bound to produce an annual report there would need to be a separate, equivalent provision made.

Ethnic monitoring, though essential, is but part of progress towards equal opportunity. What incentive do employers then have to go further and pursue an effective equal opportunities programme?

The preface to the Government's publication, *Fair Employment in Northern Ireland* (Cm 380, 1988), says:

> The legislative measures detailed in this White Paper are strong; they are also

fair. They require best employment equality practice from employers, including compulsory monitoring and affirmative action measures where necessary; they provide for strengthened enforcement powers through the criminal and the civil law; and they use the Government's economic strength to support good practice. They are even-handed ...

'Best employment equality practice' is what the Commission for Racial Equality seeks in the British context. Since the White Paper goes on to commend setting equality targets, there is a clear recognition by Government that best employment equality practice includes target-setting.

No government would assert as a matter of policy that it is content to require only second best employment equality practice in Britain. It is also difficult to see how any government could be satisfied with the present rate of progress towards racial equality in Britain.

No doubt the politics of the situation, the level of violence and the divisions between the two communities, could be used to justify legislating earlier for Northern Ireland. They cannot, however, be long-term arguments against treating equal opportunities equally seriously in Britain.

The whole thrust of the Northern Ireland legislation moves away from the narrow notion of eliminating discrimination to the idea of 'more effective practice of equality of opportunity in employment', with the ultimate aim of 'fair participation' by the two communities.

The Race Relations Act 1976 relies entirely on voluntary action to achieve change, provided only that employers avoid actual racial discrimination. Where the Commission carries out a formal investigation and finds discrimination, it can generally issue a non-discrimination notice. But even that cannot prescribe particular changes in practice.

By contrast, employers in Northern Ireland are under a general duty, where appropriate, to draw up affirmative action programmes, and the Fair Employment Commission has powers to issue directions. We believe that the same should apply in Britain and the Commission for Racial Equality should have similar powers.

Finally, the Northern Ireland White Paper referred to use of the Government's economic strength to support good practices. By this is meant the refusal, if necessary, of public contracts or grants to those failing to comply with the legislation.

The emphasis on using its economic strength is not new because in 1981 the Government announced that tenders for its contracts would not normally be accepted from firms unless they held an equal opportunity certificate issued under the Fair Employment Act 1976, and that this was to come into operation from 1 March 1982. The position set out in Sections 38 to 43 of the Fair Employment Act 1989 is merely a development of this thinking, although, in effect, the Government opted for tying the sanction of disqualification from public contracts or grants to failing to carry out the formal requirements imposed on the employer, rather than to a general lack of equal opportunity.

In Britain the contrast could not be greater. Since 1969 there has been a clause in all government contracts requiring contractors to conform to the employment provisions of the Race Relations Act. No attempt has been made to monitor compliance with this clause notwithstanding the fact that the White Paper on *Racial Discrimination* preceding the 1976 Act recognised this as unsatisfactory.

Without any new legislation, a Government could bring its economic power in Britain to bear on the whole question of equal opportunities. Indeed, by not doing so it may be criticised on the moral ground that that power is inevitably being used in many instances to support firms which are not providing equal opportunities, as well as on the practical ground that it is throwing away a chance to influence change for the better.

We believe the economic power of government, both national and local, should be used in support of equal opportunity.

In this context we were disappointed by Government action in relation to the local government legislation of 1988. If it had not been for the existence of Section 71 of the Race Relations Act 1976, the probability is that Government would have banned local authorities altogether from considering equal opportunities in their contracting processes.

Section 71 imposes a statutory duty on local authorities:

> ... to make appropriate arrangements with a view to securing that their various functions are carried out with due regard to the need – (a) to eliminate unlawful racial discrimination; and (b) to promote equality of opportunity, and good relations between persons of different racial groups.

The Sex Discrimination Act contains no similar provision and Government did ban local authorities from considering equal opportunities between men and women in their contracting processes.

Because of Section 71 the Government felt it had to permit some local government action in the area of race, but restricted it. By use of the Approved Questions under the legislation, Government has stopped local authorities obtaining ethnic monitoring data from those they might wish to contract for the supply of goods and services. Yet, in *West Midlands Passenger Transport Executive v Singh* (CA)[1988] IRLR 186 and in the Commission's *Code of Practice in Employment*, the value of that data in determining whether equal opportunities is being provided is recognised.

A wholly fresh approach is now required by Government.

RECOMMENDATION 10

The Secretary of State should be given powers to prescribe ethnic record-keeping of recipients of housing, education or other service provision. The orders prescribing the keeping of records should be capable of limitation by

1. area of the country;

2. types of activity;

3. duration of the record-keeping.

There should be a power in the Commission to require returns to be made where record-keeping has been prescribed. Safeguards against abuse of the information should be enacted.

There is increasing acceptance of monitoring in practice. While we believe the time is right for compulsory ethnic monitoring across the board in the field of employment (with the framework spelt out in primary legislation), in non-employment areas, where there is less experience of monitoring schemes in operation, we advocate a step by step approach.

Public sector housing decisions are, however, an area where unintentional racial discrimination is prone to occur, as revealed in the Commission's investigations of Hackney, Liverpool, and Tower Hamlets councils and research into Liverpool. There is also increasing experience of ethnic monitoring. We advocate that ethnic monitoring be prescribed as soon as possible in respect of housing decisions made by bodies subject to Section 71 of the Race Relations Act: that is local authorities, Housing Action Trusts, the Housing Corporation, Scottish Homes, and Housing for Wales.

The 1991 Census will provide valuable data on housing need in local authority areas. This can be used as a basis for devising realistic targets against which to measure equality, but only if ethnic monitoring is being carried out. A *Code of Practice in Rented Housing* already exists, but some authorities have proved reluctant to establish effective monitoring systems, even after a non-discrimination notice has been issued. A general requirement to monitor is needed if this is to change. There is also no reason why government funding should not be tied to the effective implementation of equal opportunities programmes. The Housing Corporation already does this with Housing Associations in respect of new programme funding.

The reason why we nevertheless feel it appropriate here to proceed primarily by delegated legislation is that there will need to be agreement on standards of assessment for the quality of housing and there may well be the need for different provision according to the type of housing stock in an area.

Codes of practice

RECOMMENDATION 11

The Commission's code-making power under Section 47 should not be restricted to the fields of employment and housing, but should be extended to include other areas.

At the Commission's request its code-making power has been extended by statute to cover housing. Our request that it should also cover education was not accepted. As a result Section 47 Codes have been produced for housing, but only 'quasi-codes' without the same force have been published for education and for primary health care.

While the extension of the code-making power to housing was welcome, we continue to be of the view that it should apply generally.

Formal investigation powers

RECOMMENDATION 12

The effect of the *Prestige* case, [1984] IRLR 166, should be reversed and the Commission's powers 'to conduct a formal investigation for any purpose connected with the carrying out of' its duties under Section 48 should apply whether or not there is a belief that an unlawful act may have occurred.

Paragraph 37 of the 1975 White Paper on Racial Discrimination stated that:

> [The Race Relations Board] has been hampered by its dependence on receiving significant complaints in pursuing the crucial strategic role of identifying and dealing with discriminatory practices and encouraging positive action to secure equal opportunity.

Paragraph 111 said that under the new legislation the successor body would be able to conduct formal investigations on its own initiative into a specific organisation for any purpose connected with the carrying out of its functions. The new body would also be able to compel the production of information/attendance of witnesses, without the sanction of the Secretary of State where the investigation was confined to unlawful conduct which it believed was occurring.

During the passage of the 1976 Act, an amending provision was added, incidentally altering the existing Sex Discrimination Act, in the House of Lords and accepted in the Commons. That provision was sub-section 49(4) which guarantees an opportunity to make representations where discrimination is alleged. It has in fact caused great difficulties.

The rules of interpretation prevent the House of Lords in its judicial capacity from having regard to Parliamentary material in construing an Act of Parliament. Denied this material in interpreting Section 49(4), the Lords construed it in *Prestige* in a way which was not in fact intended by Parliament.

The provision was construed as not merely a *procedural* safeguard but also as a *limit* on the Commission's powers to investigate. The Lords held that the Commission cannot investigate a named person unless it suspects an unlawful act may have occurred or is occurring.

Until Section 49(4) was added to the legislation there was no doubt that the Government understood that the power of the new Commission to investigate the affairs of an individual or particular organisation was not limited to a situation where there was some initial evidence of unlawful activity.

When the Government accepted the House of Lords amendment which became Section 49(4) the effect was stated as being 'to give a person against whom a complaint is made a right to information' (House of Commons Debates 918 c.603). Nothing was said which indicated any belief on the part of Government that it had now accepted a restriction on the Commission's powers to conduct investigations.

A strategic approach to formal investigations is needed. Named person investigations, with or without a suspicion of unlawful acts, should form part of this strategy. Direct discrimination is generally covert. Indirect discrimination is often not recognised as unlawful by those operating the practices involved. Indeed they may not even be applied to any particular member of an ethnic minority, as Section 28 of the Act acknowledges. For example, word of mouth recruiting may be indirectly discriminatory precisely because no one outside the organisation knows the jobs exist. In these circumstances information as to discrimination is unlikely to be brought to the Commission's attention.

The Commission, therefore, needs to be able to look at selected major employers to enable it to identify what practices may be disadvantaging ethnic minorities. In this respect the Commission should be thought of as an inspectorate, bringing technical expertise to bear on identifying the causes of major social problems. We recommend that against this background the intended power taken away by *Prestige* be restored.

As the Policy Studies Institute researchers concluded in their Home Office sponsored research:

> The decision in the *Prestige* case seems to have frustrated the intentions of the legislators. A particularly unfortunate consequence is that formal investigations of specified organisations are bound to be confrontational, since there must be prior belief of unlawful discrimination...Investigations of specified organisations which do not allege unlawful discrimination should be available to the Commission in future, as they are by the Fair Employment Commission.

Moreover, in its 1988 proposals, the EOC also asked for –

> An amendment to make clear that the Commission can carry out an investigation into a named person or organisation for any purpose connected with the carrying out of its duties, and reverse the *Prestige* decision.

Binding undertakings

RECOMMENDATION 13

Where there is agreement between the Commission and a body on specific practices to be adopted, the Commission should have the power to accept legally-binding and enforceable undertakings by that body to adopt those practices. The undertakings should be recorded in a public register.

The Commission's ultimate aim is to bring about good practice which avoids discrimination. The tools it uses can be promotional or law enforcement. If the Commission could be sure that promises to carry out changes in practice would be fulfilled, there would be cases in which the trouble and expense of law enforcement processes could be avoided.

In the Commission's early period of law enforcement it was important to bring to public attention by findings the ways in which discrimination occurs in society. In future this will be less important as much of the groundwork will have been done. The emphasis will then increasingly be on bringing about change in practice. Binding undertakings are ideal for this purpose.

This seems such an obvious way of avoiding many confrontational situations and yet producing a satisfactory outcome, that it is a great pity it has not received legislative sanction. The EOC also recommended in 1988: 'Where there is agreement between the Commission and any person, any undertaking or agreement formally given or made should be recorded in a public register and enforceable under the Act.'

Public service duties

RECOMMENDATION 14

1. **The general statutory duty imposed on local authorities by Section 71 of the Act should be amended to conform to those imposed on the Commission by Section 43 (1) (a) and (b) with regard to each of the various functions of the authorities. Those duties are 'to work towards the elimination of discrimination and to promote equality of opportunity and good relations between persons of different racial groups generally'.**

2. **This duty should be extended to all bodies carrying on a service or undertaking of a public nature (for a definition see Section 75 (5) of the Act).**

3. **Public bodies as above should be required by law to publish, in their annual reports or separately, annual programmes and reports to enable the public to evaluate their work in the field of race.**

Section 71 duties were extended to Housing Action Trusts, the Housing Corporation, Scottish Homes, and Housing for Wales by legislative amendments in 1988. Otherwise the section is restricted to local authorities.

This restriction of Section 71 of the Act to local authorities is illogical when so many functions of providing services to members of the public out of public funds are carried on outside of local authorities. All public bodies should be covered by an improved Section 71 duty.

To enable the public to evaluate the work of public bodies in the field of race relations policy we consider that they should publish, either as part of an annual report or separately, an account of their programme and of the previous year's performance. This will inevitably entail the implementation of proper monitoring schemes. A useful precedent is to be found in Sections 2-4 (inclusive) of the Local Government, Planning and Land Act 1980, where provision is made for authorities to publish annually certain details which are set out in a Code of Recommended Practice which is drawn up by, or on behalf of, the Department of the Environment.

The EOC made a similar recommendation, though there is no Sex Discrimination Act equivalent to Section 71 of the Race Relations Act.

RACIAL DISCRIMINATION CASES

We are concerned about the standard of adjudication, people's access to justice, and the failure of the system to get to grips with the group nature of racial discrimination.

ENSURING SKILLED ADJUDICATION

RECOMMENDATION 15

A discrimination division within the industrial tribunal system should be established to hear both employment and non-employment race and sex discrimination cases. The County Court jurisdiction for non-employment cases should go. The discrimination division should be able to call upon the services of High Court Judges for more complex cases and should have full remedial powers. Personnel of the division should be available to hear other types of industrial tribunal cases when not sitting in the division.

Success rates in race cases in industrial tribunals are lower than in unfair dismissal cases. The Policy Studies Institute found that only 7.6 per cent of all race cases were upheld at a tribunal hearing (with 33 per cent dismissed at a hearing) during the period they studied. That was a success rate of about one in five of the cases that reached a hearing. In 1990-91, according to Department of Employment statistics, it dropped below one in five. It is our view that the industrial tribunals have often failed to face up to the reality of discrimination – that it is highly prevalent in society and occurs in all sorts of subtle, and not so subtle, forms.

Racial discrimination cases form only a tiny proportion of all cases coming before the tribunals. There are not sufficient race cases being heard by particular members to develop a really solid bank of expertise inside the tribunal system. Without that awareness and expertise it is all too easy to regard complainants as over-sensitive or mistaken when the truth is that they *have* been treated less favourably on account of their race. Few tribunal chairs are themselves from ethnic minorities, and only just under 3 per cent of the members are. There is room for improvement here.

The objective therefore must be to build up expertise in discrimination matters and give those with responsibility for adjudicating the opportunity to become familiar with the issues and see the way the law is developing.

The Commission advocates a specialist tribunal division to deal with discrimination cases. This would rapidly develop an understanding of the ways in which discrimination occurs and of ways of dealing with it. The concentration of expertise in the hands of a few people would also make training cost-effective.

The discrimination division should have full remedial powers, including injunctive-type remedies. It should be able to call on a nominated member of the High Court Bench to deal with more complex cases.

The Policy Studies Institute law enforcement study concluded:

> The existing informal specialisation within certain regions of the industrial tribunal system in respect of discrimination cases should be strengthened and formalised. Consideration should be given to the establishment of a more formalised 'equality tier' within the existing tribunal structure. Training should be provided for tribunal personnel to maintain and improve understanding of the legislation and the difficulties thrown up by discrimination cases. The chair and members should not sit in race discrimination cases without having received special training in discrimination law. (*Racial Justice at Work* [1991] 277-8)

If discrimination division personnel hearing both race and sex cases were to hear other sorts of cases when not sitting in the specialist division, the work could be kept sufficiently within the mainstream of law without losing the benefits of greater specialisation. This has the added advantage that it avoids the difficulties which would otherwise be encountered when unfair dismissal is alleged together with discrimination. Thus we advocate specialisation, but not exclusive specialisation.

When the same problem came to be considered in the context of religious discrimination in Northern Ireland, this was the solution adopted.

What is needed is one discrimination tribunal, experienced in the nature of the problem and powerful enough, because it has full remedial powers, to deal with all aspects of discrimination.

We think that a discrimination division should not deal with race cases alone, but with sex discrimination cases also. To set up a separate division dealing with races cases alone would be to run the risk that they would, regardless of the fact that white people allege discrimination from time to time, be regarded as black people's tribunals set up to protect a particular section of society. We cannot think this would serve the interests of race relations, nor would it encourage trade unions to fight discrimination on behalf of their members.

As a separate argument we believe there is a case for saying that the division should deal with both employment cases and non-employment cases. In the Commission's view, familiarity with the ways in which discrimination occurs is more important for those seeking to decide on the facts, in cases which are now subject to the county and sheriff court jurisdiction, than is general familiarity with the subjects covered by Part III of the Act, that is education, housing and the provision of goods, facilities and services.

There are few such cases in the courts. The old Race Relations Board argued powerfully against granting county and sheriff courts jurisdiction in non-employment cases, and it has been proved right. Half of the complaints to the old Race Relations Board concerned non-employment matters. Most of the cases which it took to court were non-employment cases. It was less difficult to prove discrimination in non-employment cases. But, under the present Act, the balance has shifted heavily towards employment cases, without any intention on the legislators' part that this should happen. One solution would be to transfer non-employment cases to the jurisdiction where most cases alleging discrimination are heard, even though this means an extension to the traditional remit of the tribunals. The move would bring with it the advantage of the less daunting procedure of the tribunals. We should only advocate implementing such a change if legal aid continued to be available for these cases.

The delays inherent in the court system and the need for legal assistance, all for a very low potential award of damages, act as a considerable disincentive to pursuing cases there. Most of the issues courts deal with, such as refusal of service in public houses and clubs, tend to be simpler than those dealt with by the tribunals. Where they have dealt with more complex issues, for example, whether Gypsies were an ethnic group, the court system has made very heavy weather of the matter.

ENSURING ACCESS TO JUSTICE

RECOMMENDATION 16

Legal aid should be extended to cover racial discrimination cases in tribunals.

Under section 66 the Commission is able to give support to 'an individual who is an actual or prospective complainant or claimant' 'in relation to proceedings or prospective proceedings' under the Act. This has been an extremely useful power in developing the law.

The Commission can, however, support only some of the cases and has to turn down many applicants. Since there is no other source of public funds to which they can turn for support in having employment cases represented, a large number of aggrieved persons, particularly from ethnic minorities, feel a keen sense of disappointment in the Commission.

In response to the Parliamentary Home Affairs Committee's request for views in 1981-82 (HC 461), the Government argued against extending legal aid to cover tribunal representation in discrimination cases. It is available in the courts. The main objection was that to extend legal aid to discrimination cases 'would be seen as unfairly discriminating between different classes of persons coming before tribunals'.

Whether it is appropriate for legal aid to be applicable to industrial tribunals generally is not for us to say. The Royal Commission on Legal Services thought it should.

If a separate discrimination division were introduced, the basis of the Government's 1982 objection would disappear. Changes simplifying industrial tribunal procedure by the introduction of short-form written decisions excluded discrimination cases and thus recognised that they do stand apart by reason of special complexity from the general run of industrial tribunal cases.

Racial discrimination cases are often more complex than others coming before industrial tribunals. Generally it is necessary to assemble a good deal of comparative evidence to show less favourable treatment in the particular case. Hearings often last several days and sometimes several weeks, unlike most unfair dismissal cases.

The Royal Commission on Legal Services observed that:

> ... our evidence shows that whatever the tribunal and however informal its procedure, representation whether by a lawyer or skilled layman in the majority of cases confers advantage on the represented body.

The Commission's experience is that when a Government Department is itself a respondent in a racial discrimination case, it does not leave the particular branch to deal with the matter unaided by lawyers on the grounds that the proceedings are informal and legal representation is not necessary. In fact it brings in lawyers at a very early stage.

All the research evidence shows that applicants with the benefit of representation in race cases are much more successful than those without, who are rarely successful.

Even at the conciliation stage in tribunal proceedings there is a strong correlation between a successful outcome for the applicant and availability of legal representation. It is not an answer to our arguments in favour of legal aid to say that Section 66 assistance takes its place. A significant proportion of industrial tribunal applicants do not come to the Commission for assistance at all; and, of those who do come, the Commission is only able to provide representation to a relatively small proportion.

We believe that Section 66 by itself is not sufficient to enable individuals to obtain justice and bring racial discrimination to light. Legal aid should be available for all racial discrimination cases.

A Manchester industrial tribunal in the case of *Freeman v Salford Health Authority* said:

> ... this case highlighted the necessity for applicants in discrimination cases to be properly represented. The only way that an applicant's case can be satisfactorily presented is by a properly briefed advocate. So much of an applicant's case depends upon in-depth cross-examination of the respondents' witnesses. Such a cross-examination can in most cases only be conducted by a skilled advocate. Fortunately in this case the applicant's representation was financed by the Commission for Racial Equality. Unfortunately their resources only permit them to represent in selected cases. There must clearly be a case for the availability of legal aid, with proper safeguards, in discrimination cases.

This accords with the view of the Rt. Hon Sir Nicholas Browne-Wilkinson, a judge with great experience of discrimination law, expressed in his Kapila lecture on 27 November 1986.

The same conclusion is also one of the principal points made by the Policy Studies Institute in its Home Office sponsored research into law enforcement in the industrial tribunals:

> Alternative sources of competent representation for individuals cannot be developed unless they can be funded. The best way to do this is to extend legal aid in cases of racial discrimination to applicants in industrial tribunals.
> (*Racial Justice at Work* [1991], page 277)

And even more recently the TUC has gone on record to the same effect. Writing to *The Independent* on 3 February 1992 it said: 'The TUC supports the extension of legal aid to racial discrimination cases in industrial tribunals as these are particularly complex...'. The Chair of the Bar Council has expressed the same view.

RECOGNISING THE DIFFICULTIES OF PROOF

Racial discrimination is difficult to prove for the following main reasons:

- Proof of the state of mind of the discriminator is inevitably difficult.

- The discriminator's own evidence as to the state of their mind is likely to be unreliable because of a wish to avoid liability or because of lack of awareness of the discriminatory influences affecting the decision.

- The evidence which would assist in proving racial grounds is likely to be in the control of the discriminator.

For these reasons it makes sense for a tribunal to look for ways to help respondents.

RECOMMENDATION 17

The Act itself should make clear that in circumstances consistent with less favourable treatment on racial grounds or victimisation, that is, ones which call for an explanation, the alleged discriminator should be required to establish innocent grounds for that treatment, failing which an inference that the grounds were unlawful will be drawn.

We proposed this in our 1985 Review. Several years of confusion in the tribunals would have been avoided had it been acted upon.

In the event, what happened was that there was a back-tracking on the established law set out in *Khanna* [1981] IRLR 331, and *Chattopadhyay* [1981] IRLR 487 by Browne-Wilkinson J, by a later EAT under Wood J.

In *Barking and Dagenham London Borough Council v Camara* [1988] IRLR 373, the EAT appeared to take the view that the earlier formulations were wrong in law.

Basically the point of difference was over whether or not a tribunal should, or may, draw an inference of racial discrimination failing a satisfactory explanation by an employer of circumstances which are consistent with discrimination.

In the sex discrimination case of *Baker v Cornwall County Council* [1990] IRLR 194 the Court of Appeal reasserted the *Khanna* and *Chattopadhyay* formulations but said that, if discrimination takes place in circumstances which are consistent with the treatment being based on grounds of sex or race, the industrial tribunal should be prepared to draw the inference that the discrimination was on such grounds unless the alleged discriminator can satisfy the tribunal that there was some other innocent explanation.

The EAT under Wood J still seemed reluctant to bow to this view (see *British Gas v Sharma* [1991] IRLR101) and the Court of Appeal reasserted it in *King v The Great Britain China Centre* [1991] IRLR 513.

The courts in Britain have rejected as unduly complicated the notion of a shift in the evidential burden to the respondent where the circumstances are consistent with racial discrimination and call for an explanation. However, it may well be that it is the Courts who are being unduly complicated, and that it would be simpler to espouse the notion of shifting the burden.

As the editor of the *Equal Opportunities Review* says:

> We would suggest that the reason why the appeals keep arising on this same narrow (albeit vital) point is because the appellate courts (outside of Northern Ireland) will not accept that it is natural for people to think in terms of a shifting evidential burden of proof and to explain in such terms how they arrived at their decision. To offer 'guidance' which directs tribunal members to find the facts, draw the appropriate inferences, and reach a conclusion on the balance of probabilities, is to set no meaningful standard at all. (*Equal Opportunities Review*, No.41 Jan/Feb 1992, page 46)

In its 1988 proposals, the EOC made a similar recommendation to the CRE's 1985 recommendation:

> Once the applicant proves less favourable treatment in circumstances consistent with grounds of sex or victimisation, a presumption of discrimination should arise which would require the respondent to prove that there were grounds for that treatment other than sex or victimisation.

RECOMMENDATION 18

Where a respondent deliberately and without reasonable excuse either omits to reply, or gives an evasive or equivocal reply, to a questionnaire pursuant to Section 65 of the Act, there should be a duty, rather than a discretion, on the part of the tribunal of fact to draw the inference that it considers just.

Properly used, the questionnaire procedure allows the respondent's reasons for action to be probed and other facts to be uncovered. Very often the response leads to an acceptance by the applicant that the case is not after all racial. But, from time to time, the way the respondent has dealt with the answers, particularly in the light of other evidence, points the other way.

There is still a considerable reluctance on the part of tribunals to draw an inference of racial discrimination from evasive replies. As it stands the statute apparently allows tribunals a discretion not to draw the inference they think is just. If it is just to draw an inference, they should be obliged to draw it.

THE GROUP NATURE OF RACIAL DISCRIMINATION

RECOMMENDATION 19

The Commission should have wider powers to take evidence of discrimination directly to a tribunal seeking a finding that racial discrimination has occurred and appropriate remedies.

At the present time the Commission can bring proceedings before a tribunal in its own name in a very limited range of matters such as discriminatory advertisements or pressure and instructions to discriminate. Otherwise, generally, it has to use the formal investigation processes to deal formally with unlawfulness.

The basic idea of the present system is that the remedy of a non-discrimination notice by the Commission can deal with the likelihood of the recurrence of discrimination of that type, whereas tribunal remedies deal with specific acts and are concerned with the particular complainant.

But the whole formal investigation process can be very lengthy. In the words of Lord Denning MR in *Amari* [1982] IRLR 252, the Commission 'have been caught up in a spider's web spun by Parliament from which there is little hope of their escaping'. 'The machinery is so elaborate and so cumbersome it is in danger of grinding to a halt.'

Essentially the position is that, in an accusatory investigation where a non-discrimination notice is made, a respondent will have had two statutory opportunities to make representations in addition to answering questions in the investigation. Nevertheless, the notice can be appealed and in the appeal the facts on which the notice is based can be reopened.

The Commission needs to keep an investigative fact-finding function and also an involvement in law enforcement. But the system should permit the Commission to put evidence of discrimination forthwith before a tribunal for a decision as to whether discrimination has occurred and the tribunal should have appropriate remedies available. The whole process would thus be shortened.

The EOC in its 1988 proposals also asked for 'a general power to bring legal proceedings in its own name wherever it believes an unlawful discriminatory practice or act exists.'

POWER TO ORDER CHANGES

RECOMMENDATION 20

A non-discrimination notice cannot prescribe particular changes in practice. The notice should be able to do so.

Since the respondent can appeal, there is no reason why the notice should not be able to order particular changes. In practice a draft notice is always sent to respondents so there is an opportunity to negotiate on its contents before it is finalised.

RECOMMENDATION 21

1. Tribunals also should be able to issue orders equivalent to non-discrimination notices to deal with potential future discrimination. The tribunal should be under a duty to consider whether such a remedy is appropriate in any case where discrimination is proved.

2. The Commission should have the power to join in any proceedings in which discrimination is alleged to draw the attention of the tribunal to the potential for future discrimination in the situation.

3. In any case the tribunal should have the power to award compensation to any person it finds to have suffered unlawful discrimination either named or otherwise sufficiently identified provided that any such person joins the proceedings within a specified time and seeks the compensation.

4. The tribunal should have the power, in appropriate cases where discrimination is proved, to order special training or encouragement of members of particular racial groups which are at present permitted as voluntary measures in the Act.

In 1985 we said that there was a gap between what can be achieved by bringing an individual case and what can be achieved as a result of a formal investigation. Individual cases, if successful, result in remedies for the individual; investigations result in changes in practice within the institution investigated. Discrimination should be dealt with in a more coordinated way. This is also a central conclusion of the Home Office sponsored Policy Studies Institute research on law enforcement.

If, in hearing an individual case, and whatever its decision on the case, the tribunal reaches the conclusion that discrimination is occurring which will affect other individuals if it is not curbed, or that further such discrimination is likely, then, as well as dealing with the individual case, it should be able to provide remedies to deal with potential future discrimination.

The best example of the inadequacy of the present law is the case of *Singh v Nottinghamshire Police*. It lasted 82 days in the industrial tribunal. The tribunal had considerable industrial experience and felt able to make a large number of suggestions for avoiding racial discrimination in future. They had been invited by the police to make those suggestions. They did not have the legal power to make recommendations going beyond those 'obviating or reducing the adverse effect on the complainant of any act of discrimination to which the complaint relates' (Section 56(1)(c)), let alone to make orders for changes in practice.

No doubt the particular police force will do its best to implement the suggestions having asked for them. But what of a less accommodating respondent? The Commission should be entitled to join in cases as a party so as to draw attention to these issues, although this should not be a precondition of such remedies being granted.

If necessary, appropriate adjournments could be granted to deal with any general considerations arising out of the evidence presented in the hearing of individual cases.

The tribunal should also have within its armoury of remedies the power to order a discriminator to take those special steps, which at present are purely voluntary under the Act, relating to measures of training and encouragement of members of particular racial groups where they are underrepresented.

Where a tribunal hears evidence of discrimination of a general nature, it should be possible for the tribunal to deal also with any individual cases brought to light. This could be done by some technique, such as making the finding on liability in favour of named persons, or persons defined by reference to a class, and referring the issue of compensation for separate assessment. In these situations, the liability would be conditional upon the people affected joining the proceedings within a specified time to seek compensation.

Such a provision could be of considerable use where, for example, people have been affected by an indirectly discriminatory selection or promotion test, or where individuals could not have known of the discrimination affecting them, but where they could be retrospectively identified. We envisage that trade unions and other representative bodies could make constructive use of such a provision in providing support for cases.

The Standing Advisory Commission on Human Rights in Northern Ireland (SACHR) made a similar recommendation in its 1987 proposals for fair employment in Northern Ireland.

ADEQUATE REMEDIES

Non-monetary

RECOMMENDATION 22

1. In addition to the remedies now available, a full range of mandatory orders should be available to the tribunal.

2. A preventive remedy should be available where a person has stated a directly discriminatory intention to prevent that intention being put into practice.

3. Ordinary remedies should apply also to the whole area of education instead of the Secretary of State having powers under Section 19(2) and (3) of the Act.

4. In employment cases, interim relief should be available to preserve a complainant's position pending a hearing, provided that the relief is sought promptly and the remedy appears appropriate to the tribunal.

5. In employment cases it should be possible for the tribunal to order appointment, promotion, reinstatement or re-engagement, where it appears appropriate to do so.

Any new specialist jurisdiction of the tribunals should have a wide range of remedies available, and there should be greater rights to take proceedings than as at present. The proposals could, however, be implemented without creating a specialist jurisdiction.

A full range of non-monetary orders protecting the individual should be available as remedies. The legislation should not take the stance, as employment legislation generally now does, that such remedies are inappropriate other than in very limited circumstances. It should be for the tribunal to decide in the particular case whether the remedy is appropriate.

Monetary remedies

RECOMMENDATION 23

The provision of compensation should be improved as follows:

1. There should be a prescribed minimum figure by way of compensation for injury to feelings.

2. Compensation should be payable where indirect discrimination is proved and the present exception in Section 57(3) removed.

3. The tribunal should be able to award continuing payments of compensation until a stipulated event such as promotion or engagement occurs.

4. The statutory limit to compensation in employment cases set out in Section 56(2) of the Act should be removed.

1. A prescribed minimum

The cases of *Alexander* [1988] IRLR 190 and *Noone* [1988] IRLR 195 in the Court of Appeal in 1988 increased the level of compensation for injury to feelings. Even so the court did so by reference to the upper limit of compensation in the industrial tribunals (currently £10,000), and this resulted in a lower figure than might otherwise have been achieved.

Since this upper limit is fixed by Government it allows the Government artificially to hold down awards for injury to feelings. This was a wholly unnecessary concession of power to the Government of the day by the courts. They could have simply ignored the upper limit on compensation in industrial tribunals in fixing the appropriate level for damages for injury to feelings.

But since this has happened the remedial step of raising the level of compensation by statute is now needed. The median award in 1990 was £750 (Equal Opportunities Review, Number 41, page 32). Compared to awards in defamation cases, racial discrimination is trivialised.

2. Compensation for indirect discrimination

Under the 1976 Act, a proven case of indirect discrimination does not attract compensation unless the discrimination was intentional. To anyone unlawfully excluded from a job it makes little difference whether the cause was direct or indirect discrimination, save perhaps as to the intensity of hurt feelings if the exclusion is proved to have been deliberate. But that is a matter which goes to the issue of what compensation for injury to feelings should be awarded. Moreover, investigations by the Commission have shown that indirect discrimination plays a major part in excluding members of ethnic minorities from opportunities in various fields. In 1977, when the present Act came into force, the notion of indirect discrimination was new and time was needed to adjust to the concept. There has been more than ample time. Moreover, the Commission's codes of practice draw particular attention to the nature of indirect discrimination and to ways of avoiding it. There are no longer good grounds for employers and others to argue that they did not intend the discriminatory effect. If they do, it means that they have never examined their employment practices properly to see whether they were having this effect and so provided themselves with immunity from liability to compensation. The Commission believes the distinction between intentional and unintentional indirect discrimination is inappropriate. Both arise from a neglect of well-publicised good practices.

3. Continuing payment

When assessing compensation in a case such as discrimination in promotion the tribunal can only estimate how long the complainant will remain at his or her present grade and award compensation within the statutory limits on the basis of that estimate. It cannot order a continuing payment and at the same time say it should continue until actual promotion which may be appropriate if vacancies at that level occur fairly frequently. We recommend that it should be possible for a discrimination tribunal to award continuing payments until a particular event occurs, not just for promotion cases but generally. For example, where an employer with continuing vacancies of the same sort is found to have discriminated against a complainant who would otherwise have been employed, it may well be appropriate to order continuing payments as though the complainant had been engaged until actual engagement, unless employment elsewhere is taken meanwhile. There should be a general liberty to apply to the tribunal to deal with changed circumstances.

4. Removing the statutory limit in employment cases

In Northern Ireland the upper limit is £30,000 for religious discrimination. It is £10,000 for racial discrimination in Great Britain. There is no valid justification for the difference and little reason for a maximum anyway. The higher limit in Northern Ireland came about because of a large settlement occurring at the time of the legislation, but similar large settlements have now occurred in Britain particularly against the police *(Singh £35,000, Asumah £20,000)*. The Policy Studies Institute in their study conclude that:

> ... in addition to providing an incentive to make a complaint, an increase in the scale of damages would achieve a number of other objectives:
>
> - Reflect the seriousness of the wrong done.
> - Re-emphasise the public policy against discrimination.
> - Compensate the individual who has taken a case and others affected by the discrimination.
> - Act as a general deterrent to employers who are discriminating.

If the low maximum remains, there will undoubtedly be concerted efforts to get round it by, for example, arguing that the limit applies to each act of discrimination and, if that line fails in future cases, then by filing several originating applications, each alleging separate incidents between the same parties. A limit designed for the unfair dismissal jurisdiction has been applied without much thought to the race jurisdiction where the applicant may be complaining of many acts. Unless the limit is raised there will be many years of confusion ahead whilst the tribunals and courts sort out the difficulties.

EMPLOYER'S LIABILITY

RECOMMENDATION 24

The special defence provided under Section 32(3) of the Act should be removed. It covers cases where employers can show that they took 'such steps as were reasonably practicable to prevent the employee from doing that act, or from doing in the course of his employment acts of that description'.

Section 32 provides that an employer is liable for the acts of the employee, whether or not the unlawful discrimination occurs with the employer's knowledge. There is a defence under Section 32(3) for the employer if they can show that they have taken 'such steps as are reasonably practicable' to prevent the employee from discriminating.

We can see no reason why discrimination should be treated differently from other civil wrongs by the provision of a separate and special defence. If an individual has been discriminated against by somebody in the

THE COMMISSION

We raised the question in our consultative document whether there should be one equality organisation for Britain instead of a separate Equal Opportunities Commission and one for Racial Equality.

RECOMMENDATION 25

We recommend that the Commission for Racial Equality remains as a separate entity.

We pointed out possible disadvantages that could accrue from the creation of one organisation:

1. The advantages of each separate commission having its own focus of attention or problems, which are rarely similar, would be lost.

2. Quite possibly a new agency would be torn apart by conflicts between the various interest groups.

3. There is a profound difference between racial discrimination and the other forms of discrimination.

4. A considerable loss of experience could occur with the shedding of senior staff in particular.

5. People who are concerned about discrimination in a specific field are not necessarily sensitive to discrimination in other fields.

6. In any amalgamation the race dimension would suffer, as has been the experience in local government.

7. A new agency might be drawn into a wide range of highly controversial peripheral issues.

8. Several years could be lost as a result of reorganisation.

9. The formation of a human rights organisation might be used as an excuse to reduce overall expenditure on equal opportunities without letting the new commission benefit from the resources released by the economies of scale.

We pointed out possible advantages that would accrue from the creation of one organisation.

1. The availability of a single body for advice, research, promotion and law enforcement.

2. The number of Commissioners, senior managers, personnel and finance staff could be slimmed down and more supporting staff recruited for the same expenditure.

3. A Human Rights Commission might command greater public support and perhaps be seen as less partisan than the existing Commissions.

We regarded the question of whether there should be one or separate agencies as one on which consultation could be particularly helpful in offering a perception of our role from outside. The result of our consultation was a clear predominance of views in favour of having a separate Commission for Racial Equality with its own focus of attention and we do not recommend any change. However, we think there is considerable merit in increasingly pursuing cooperative courses of action with the other Commissions and, if that becomes an evolutionary process, we should reconsider the position. The arguments in favour of one Commission, at least in Britain, are sufficiently weighty to warrant the matter being kept under review.

There are a number of matters where minor changes to the Act could make the functioning of the Commission simpler.

RECOMMENDATION 26

We recommend the following:

1. The Commission's accounting year should be brought into line with its reporting year.

2. The Commission should not be required to obtain the approval of the Secretary of State for the arrangements it makes for discharging its functions by committee.

3. Section 66, under which the Commission can give assistance to litigants under the Act, should be altered to achieve two things: to permit costs expended under the section to be recovered where an order for costs in favour of the supported person would otherwise be made in the EAT; and to clarify the freedom from disclosure in proceedings for communications made between the applicant and the Commission in relation to assistance under the Act.

1 & 2: the accounting year and the Secretary of State's approval

These are straightforward changes. Section 46 at present makes the Commission's reporting year coincide with the calendar year, whereas Schedule 1 paragraph 17 makes the accounting year the twelve months ending on 31 March. It would assist the Commission's financial management and planning and enhance its public accountability if the reporting year coincided with the accounting year. Obviously, a transitional arrangement would be needed.

Schedule 1 paragraph 13 requires the Commission to obtain the approval of the Secretary of State for the arrangements it makes for the conduct of its business. This is an unnecessary involvement in the running of the Commission which would be best altered on the assumption that the Commission is capable of acting responsibly in such matters. It would be in line with general Government policy under the Next Steps initiative of devolving greater power to agencies.

3. Section 66

Under the present EAT rules costs are recoverable in certain circumstances where incurred by a successful party, but not where incurred on his or her behalf by the Commission under section 66 of the 1976 Act. This should be remedied to save public funds and avoid benefit to the discriminator.

Although the Commission has been advised that the doctrine of legal professional privilege applies to communications made between applicants and itself in relation to assistance under Section 66, some uncertainty remains over the confidentiality of some information created as a consequence of a Section 66 application – for instance, the report to the Committee. In order to put the matter beyond doubt, a specific provision on confidentiality should be introduced along the lines of that in the legal aid legislation.

EUROPE

The single European market is intended to be completed by the end of 1992, making a reality of the freedom of European Community citizens to work, to establish businesses and to trade in other EC countries. So it is right that the Commission for Racial Equality looks beyond national boundaries to where people may in fact be working.

RECOMMENDATION 27

We recommend that Government takes steps to improve the protection against racial discrimination on a European front, and improves this country's commitment to certain existing international treaties on the subject.

THE POSITION IN EUROPE

When we look to Europe we find:

1. Protection from racial discrimination is not so comprehensively enshrined in the law of other countries as it is in Britain.

2. European Community law has not developed protection from racial discrimination (save in the limited area where a person is discriminated against on the grounds of nationality if they are a citizen of an EC member country).

3. This contrasts with the position of sex discrimination where there is a developed jurisprudence and a treaty provision (Article 119) dealing with the matter.

4. The European Community appears to have legal competence to tackle racial discrimination and the lack of a jurisprudence, therefore, seems to represent a lack of political will.

5. The protection from racial discrimination in the European Convention of Human Rights is only a subsidiary protection coming into play in the exercise of the other convention rights – see Article 14 (save in those circumstances where the racial discrimination is so serious that it can be described as 'degrading treatment' for the purposes of Article 3).

The other countries of the European Community are not without protection from racial discrimination. It exists in a variety of constitutional guarantees, provisions of criminal codes and other measures, but it is nowhere so comprehensively dealt with as in Britain, and no country has an enforcement agency equivalent to that of the Commission for Racial Equality. That is not to say that the Commission believes that all is as good as it could be in Britain; far from it. But in comparative terms Britain has a better framework than elsewhere in Europe. That means three things:

1. People coming here from the rest of Europe fall within the protection of our laws.

2. People going from here to the rest of Europe lose the protection of our laws and are not so well protected.

3. There is the real danger that one day a process of harmonisation of laws might lead, not to an improvement in protection from racial discrimination across Europe, but to a reduction to, as it were, the lowest common denominator. That could all be done in the name of free trade.

EUROPEAN COMMUNITY LAW

European Community law has not developed to protect persons from racial discrimination. There have been reports to the European Parliament in 1985 and 1990 and the Parliament has called for the 'review and amendment of national legislation against political extremism, racism and racial discrimination'. The 1990 report called for a wide range of measures. Moreover, in 1989, the European Commission proposed a resolution on the subject of Racism and Xenophobia which was considered by the Economic and Social Committee when Baroness Flather (as she is now) was the rapporteur and by the Parliament. All of this falls short of what is required: Community legislation against racial discrimination.

European Community law incorporates, as a source of law, rights which are to be found in international human rights conventions to which Member States are party. The clearest recognition of this source of Community law is to be found in the judgement of the European Court of Justice in *Defrenne v Sabena* 149/77 [1978] ECR1365. The question was whether, outside Article 119, sex discrimination was prohibited. The answer was that it was not, but only because at that time no rule of community law had been developed. The clear implication is that there is competence to develop law relating to fundamental human rights outside the treaty provisions, and that this is not limited to sex discrimination:

> The Court has repeatedly stated that respect for fundamental personal human rights is one of the general principles of Community Law, the observance of which it has a duty to ensure.

The European Convention of Human Rights now has an existence within European Community Law. It was treated as a source of Community Law in the *Defrenne* case above. It is also referred to in the Preamble to the Single European Act. Beyond that, however, the Court will look at other conventions and in the *Defrenne* case looked to an ILO convention.

Freedom from racial discrimination is variously protected in international law, for example, by the UN Convention on the Elimination of All Forms of Racial Discrimination (Art. 2 [d]):

> Each State Party shall prohibit and bring to an end, by all appropriate means, including legislation as required by circumstances, racial discrimination by any persons, group, or organisation.

Article 5 obliges States Parties to prohibit and to eliminate racial discrimination in all its forms and to guarantee equality in a wide range of situations. The International Convention on Civil and Political Rights (Art. 26):

> The law shall prohibit any discrimination and guarantee to all persons equal and effective protection against discrimination on any grounds such as race, colour, sex, language, religion, political or other opinion, national or social origin, property, birth or other status.

Our view that the principle of racial equality is a source of Community law is reinforced by an article written by Chris Docksey, a member of the Legal Service of the European Commission, writing in a personal capacity in the *Industrial Law Journal* for December 1991, published after our consultative document. He says that the right of non-discrimination on grounds of race:

> ... undoubtedly exists in inchoate form at Community level, but specific primary and derived Community legislation only exists at present with regard to equal treatment on grounds of nationality. This does not directly cover discrimination in employment on grounds of race. Race is thus a good example of a fundamental right which may be recognised by the Court, an aspect of the general principle of equality which has not yet been specifically legislated into Community law.

Later in the same article Docksey refers to various developments as:

> ... a trend which may one day result in legislation embodying a new form of the principle of equality, at least with regard to discrimination in employment on grounds of race.

It is clear to us that the trend would be much stronger if it had the support of the UK Government.

There is increasingly well-developed Community law against aspects of sex discrimination. There is no principled reason why there should be better protection from sex discrimination than from racial discrimination.

THE EUROPEAN HUMAN RIGHTS CONVENTION

The situation under the European Convention of Human Rights is of the European Commission of Human Rights and the Court endeavouring to make up for the basic failing of the Convention adequately to address itself explicitly to protection from racial discrimination, by recognising that the protection from 'degrading treatment' in Article 3 can also encompass racial discrimination.

The need to do this stems from the fact that explicit mention of discrimination in the Convention comes in Article 14 which simply protects enjoyment of the other rights and freedoms in the Convention free from discrimination. Article 14 does not grant an independent right to freedom from discrimination. It reads as follows:

> The enjoyment of the rights and freedoms set forth in this Convention shall be secured without discrimination on any ground such as sex, race, colour, language, religion, political or other opinion, national or social origin, association with a national minority, property, birth or other status.

As van Dijk and van Hoof say in their leading work, *Theory and Practice of the European Convention of Human Rights* (2nd ed. 1990 Kluwer):

> It may be said that such a right ought not to be lacking in the Convention ... The Convention thus lags behind the development in the United Nations where the elimination of discrimination has received and still receives a good deal of attention, as has been expressed in a number of conventions. (p 532).

Migration News Sheet reports that before the European Parliament on 15 October 1991, Mr Bucquiquio, Head of the Central Division of Legal Affairs of the Council of Europe, spoke of the constant evolution of the European Convention of Human Rights, and said it was possible to envisage in future a new protocol containing a general non-discrimination clause. Again we take the view that this would be all the more likely if there was UK Government support for the idea.

THE UN CONVENTION AGAINST RACIAL DISCRIMINATION

Unhappily for people in the UK, while the Government recognises the individual's right to pursue matters under the European Convention, it does not recognise the individual's right to petition the UN Committee on the Elimination of All Forms of Racial Discrimination where, obviously, freedom from racial discrimination is explicitly recognised in the Convention. The person who has to rely on the European Convention cannot baldly assert such a freedom, but must construct an argument that the racial discrimination they have suffered is sufficiently serious to be regarded as 'degrading treatment' under Article 3. It may also be possible to use Article 6:

> In the determination of his civil rights and obligations ... everyone is entitled to a fair and public hearing within a reasonable time by an independent and impartial tribunal established by law.

GOVERNMENT ACTION NEEDED

There is no good reason why the Government should not declare that it recognises the competence of the UN Committee on the Elimination of All Forms of Racial Discrimination:

> ... to receive and consider communications from individuals or groups of individuals within its jurisdiction claiming to be victims of a violation of that State Party of any of the rights set forth in this Convention. (Article 14).

The Government could go much further and advocate both the taking of measures in the European Community to provide protection from racial discrimination, and an improvement in the European Convention of Human Rights to provide explicitly for full protection from racial discrimination.

There are two major European Courts capable of dealing with human rights, and they should have full powers in this by explicit legislative texts and not need to feel their way there by the adaptation of non-explicit texts.

NORTHERN IRELAND

A number of organisations in Northern Ireland wrote to the Commission in response to our consultative document pointing out that there are visible ethnic minorities in the province, that racial discrimination exists there, and that there is no race relations legislation.

RECOMMENDATION 28

We would endorse the conclusion of the Standing Advisory Commission on Human Rights that there ought to be legislation against racial discrimination in Northern Ireland.

In principle there should be protection from racial discrimination, and in practice it would seem from representations made to us that there is some need for it. We are pressing the Government for action on race in Europe, and it follows that the gap in the UK's own law should be filled. There is good reason to believe that the absence of a law against racial discrimination in Northern Ireland puts the UK in breach of international agreements.

INCITEMENT TO RACIAL HATRED AND RACIAL HARASSMENT

Although the law on incitement to racial hatred is not enforced by the Commission, because of our duty to promote good race relations we clearly have an interest in the way it is enforced just as we do in the areas of racial harassment which fall outside the rubric of less favourable treatment in the fields covered by the Act.

RECOMMENDATION 29

We recommend that an independent review of the working of the law on incitement to racial hatred be carried out, and that the Attorney-General's involvement be ended.

In 1986 the offence of incitement to racial hatred was removed from the ambit of the Race Relations Act 1976 and placed within the Public Order Act. Some improvements were made at the same time.

There has been no change with regard to responsibility for enforcing the law, which lies with the police, but with prosecutions needing to be sanctioned by the Attorney-General. After the Crown Prosecution Service (CPS) was set up there was, however, a change in the way investigations into possible offences were dealt with.

Previously, complaints tended to go to the office of the Director of Public Prosecutions (DPP), and that office asked for the police to investigate matters if they saw fit. Now, the practice is for matters to be referred automatically to the local police to investigate, if they see fit, then to pass back up through the system via the CPS to the Attorney-General. For a prosecution to be got off the ground a lot more people now have to hold the view that it is the right thing to do. There are few prosecutions.

We have previously suggested that the need for the Attorney-General's approval should be ended and the matter left to the DPP. There is no reason why the DPP should not be able to set guidelines for the Crown Prosecution Service to use in deciding whether to prosecute.

The Commission, and others such as the Board of Deputies of British

Jews, are concerned at the way the existing system works. The Commission clearly has an interest in ensuring that race relations are not damaged by the prevalence of inflammatory material. Racial harassment is widespread and incitement must be playing a considerable part.

There should be an independent review of the way the incitement to racial hatred provisions are enforced, and we envisage that at the end of it the Attorney-General's involvement should be abolished and the results of the review used to make any incidental amendments to the law that may be needed and to lay down guidelines for the CPS to follow. The opportunity should also be taken to consider whether the offence should be widened to include vilification of persons because of membership of a racial group, a change which is now being advocated in some quarters.

RECOMMENDATION 30

We recommend that:

1. **Racial harassment become a specific ground for eviction under housing legislation.**

2. **All bodies to which section 71 of the Race Relations Act 1976 currently applies should have a specific statutory duty to monitor complaints of racial harassment and use all available powers to eradicate it.**

3. **Consideration should be given to creating a separate tort of racial harassment.**

4. **Consideration should be given to specifically criminalising racial violence.**

The Home Affairs Committee 1986 report, *Racial Attacks and Harassment*, said with justification that 'the most shameful and dispiriting aspect of race relations in Britain is the incidence of racial attacks and harassment'.

For the most part attacks and harassment do not fall within the Commission's law enforcement remit. But, in pursuance of its duty to promote good race relations, the Commission has published surveys and promoted policies to deal with harassment.

In 1981 the Commission published *Racial Harassment on Local Authority Housing Estates*, a document prepared by the London Race and Housing Forum. In 1988 we published *Learning in Terror*, a survey of racial harassment in schools. In 1987 we published *Living in Terror*, a report on racial violence and harassment in housing. The latter said:

> One thing is clear: racial harassment is a serious and increasing phenomenon.

The Home Office report, *Racial Attacks* (1981), contained the first official estimates of racially-motivated offences, and said Asians were 50 times more likely than whites to be the victims of racially-motivated crimes and West Indians 36 times more likely.

The *Report of the Inquiry into Racism and Xenophobia* to the European Parliament in 1990 has led to Britain being depicted for all Europe to see as a place where:

> Within the four year period under review, there have been year after year reports of systematic and increasingly widespread racial violence which point to increasing ethnic tension.

The report went on:

> Racist attacks have taken the form of hooliganism and terrorising ethnic minority groups: their children have to put up with all sorts of racial harassment and violence and at home, they receive threatening phone calls, excreta and racist literature are pushed through their letter boxes, as well as petrol which is then ignited.

The responses from local authorities to our consultation revealed a measure of support for the proposal we put forward in *Living in Terror* that the Housing Act 1985 should be amended so that racial harassment becomes a specific ground for eviction. In Scotland the equivalent provision is the Housing (Scotland) Act 1987 Schedule 3, and there was support there for amending that also.

We think that there is a case for imposing a specific statutory duty on local authorities and similar housing bodies to monitor the incidence of racial harassment and to use all their available powers to eradicate it. This would ensure that they adopt a strategic approach to the issue.

There was also some feeling in the responses we received that our consultation document had not given enough attention to the whole problem of racial harassment. Where racial harassment constitutes less favourable treatment in those areas covered by the Race Relations Act 1976, there is already a remedy under the Act. But racial harassment is not mentioned specifically in the legislation, consequently it has been decided on occasion that use of racially offensive language has not amounted to detrimental treatment. A court or tribunal so inclined would be likely to find a way round any alternative definition, and we think this is more to do with their attitude than with problems of legal definition.

But there is a general problem of racial harassment, which falls right outside the areas covered by the Act and is not covered by the employment, education, housing or provision of goods, facilities and services sections of the Act.

We recommend further consideration be given in particular to the proposal put forward in Duncan Forbes' book *Action on Racial Harassment* (a work to which readers of the consultative document were referred): that racial harassment should become an actionable tort enforceable by any member of a family or household affected. This would apply where harassment of a person is committed wholly or partly because of the racial origin of that person, or a member of their family, or person living in the same household. There is already some overlap of jurisdictions where racial violence takes place in the workplace, for example, and the person affected can sue for assault, and/or claim less favourable treatment under the Act, so the possibility of different causes of action arising already exists.

The same work recommends that crimes where a racial motive is present should formally be recognised as aggravated offences making the offender liable to a higher penalty. In practice judges may well reflect this line in sentencing policy. The Commission said in evidence to the Royal Commission on Criminal Justice that the use of racially-motivated violence should itself be a separate offence. Either would alert courts and the public alike to the seriousness of a problem which merits particular attention.

RELIGION AND THE LAW

RECOMMENDATION 31

We recommend that a specific law against incitement to religious hatred should be introduced and a law against religious discrimination should be given further serious consideration.

The Commission joined in sponsoring a series of four seminars on these issues. Three were written up as a series of discussion papers and published in February 1990: *Law, Blasphemy and the Multi-Faith Society*; *Free Speech*; and *Britain: A Plural Society*. The final seminar concentrated on legal solutions and was held in October 1990. It is not possible here to cover the full range of issues, and readers are recommended to refer directly to the seminar reports.

As a result of those seminars and of its own deliberations, the Commission feels able to offer comment about three aspects of the current law:

1. The current law of blasphemy protects only the established Christian religion.

2. There is in Britain no law of incitement to religious hatred.

3. There is no law in Britain protecting people from religious discrimination.

The Commission's role includes the promotion of good race relations. For substantial members of the ethnic minorities, their faith, the sense of identity this gives and the reaction of the rest of society to that faith and to them as believers, are of the utmost importance. Indeed, for many, identity through faith is more important than identity through national origins.

Are legal adjustments needed to secure good race relations in a multi-faith society?

BLASPHEMY

It is now generally accepted that the law of blasphemy is unacceptable in principle as it stands. In protecting only one religion, it is discriminatory. The Home Office evidently prefers to leave the law as it is on the grounds that there is no consensus on what to put in its place. Our consultation reinforces the view that the status quo is unsatisfactory. However, there is no clear view as to which of the two alternative options is favoured.

Lord Scarman has given the view that:

> ... there is a case for legislation extending [the offence of blasphemy] to protect the religious beliefs and feelings of non-Christians ... In an increasingly plural society such as that of modern Britain it is necessary not only to respect the differing religious beliefs, feelings and practices of all but also to protect them from scurrility, vilification, ridicule and contempt.

Certainly either the law of blasphemy needs to be abolished or to be extended to protect other religions. Prior to the *Gay News* trial in 1977 the blasphemy law had fallen into disuse for 50 years and since then it has teetered on the brink of abolition, with a majority of the Law Commissioners in 1985 favouring that approach. The *Satanic Verses* issue may have brought to a head what was virtually inevitable in any event.

It cannot be for the Commission to resolve whether ultimately considerations of free speech should triumph and result in the abolition of the blasphemy law, or whether considerations of respect for religion should triumph and result in the extension of the law.

Leaving blasphemy law unchanged sends out the message, to Muslims for example, that their religion is less worthy of protection than the Christian religion. That must affect their commitment to this society.

Extending the blasphemy law as it stands to other religions poses limits on free speech which are bound to be perceived as unacceptable because the present offence can be committed without any intention to outrage, and the chances of committing the offence unintentionally would be much increased by the unlimited extension of the number of religions covered. This was why the minority Law Commissioners considered narrowing the elements of the offence at the same time as extending it to other religions. But does that strike the right balance?

We set out these points in the hope that, when the present law is changed, which we think is inevitable, legislators will give consideration to them.

IDENTITY THROUGH RELIGION

In Northern Ireland, laws exist prohibiting discrimination on religious grounds and incitement to religious hatred. There are no equivalent laws in Britain, where there are laws prohibiting discrimination on *racial* grounds and incitement to *racial* hatred. Yet in international law religion and race are treated similarly.

Indeed there is good reason to suppose that, in not offering any protection in respect of religion, the Government is in breach of international treaty obligations as regards Britain. Article 20.1 of the International Covenant on Civil and Political Rights reads:

> Any advocacy of national, racial, or religious hatred that constitutes incitement to discrimination, hostility or violence shall be prohibited by law.

Whilst blasphemy law is concerned with certain forms of attacks on religion as such, a law of incitement to religious hatred is concerned with stirring up hatred against persons identified by their religion. Arguments that freedom of speech should include the right to stir up hatred against persons inevitably seem limp and the more so when it is done on grounds of religion, since the freedom to practise the religion of one's choice is itself recognised in international law. No country can be said to guarantee the freedom to practise the religion of one's choice if at the same time it permits others lawfully to stir up hatred against those doing just that.

The current law of incitement to religious hatred in Northern Ireland has hardly been used, let alone successfully. In its present form since 1987, it has been based on the incitement to racial hatred provisions in Britain which exist in the Public Order Act 1986. They have been used rather more successfully, though not nearly as often as many would have wished. There is current controversy on this point. But there is a difference between the principle of having a law, and the effectiveness of its enforcement which may depend basically on how judgement is exercised.

In principle, there is a strong case for saying that there should be a law on incitement to religious hatred which is uniform across the whole of the United Kingdom. In practice, there will be an increasing need for such a law if, from day to day, people are identified, both by themselves and by others, by their religion as much as by their national origin. If it is accepted that persons have the right to practise the religion of their choice, it cannot be any more acceptable to stir up hatred against people because they are seen as Muslims than to do so because they are seen as Pakistanis. The UK has accepted that right: it is enshrined in Article 9 of the

European Convention of Human Rights (based on the Universal Declaration on Human Rights).

A law against incitement to religious hatred could be widened to include the intentional vilification of persons because of their membership of the group. We ask for a review of the working of the incitement to racial hatred law, and the same point should also be considered in that context.

By bringing in elements of religion into the definition of 'ethnic group' in the Race Relations Act 1976, the House of Lords in *Mandla v Dowell Lee* [1983] IRLR 209 has, to an extent, made it possible to get round the lack of a ban on religious discrimination as such. Much discrimination against Jews and Sikhs can be dealt with as discrimination against them as members of those ethnic groups. And much religious discrimination is caught by the law on indirect racial discrimination, at least where the exercise of a religion has a particular association with the country of origin. A case of discrimination against Muslims was held by a Sheffield tribunal to be indirect racial discrimination. But, as the law currently stands, compensation would only become payable if intention was proved. Improvements in the general law of indirect racial discrimination, in particular permitting compensation in all cases as we advocate elsewhere in this review, could remove much difficulty.

Even so, a new statutory prohibition on religious discrimination might be better than trying to stretch the Race Relations Act to cover all cases of religious discrimination. Stretching the Act might not work where the religious practice at issue is that of a minority group in the country of origin and that group is not recognised as an ethnic group under the 1976 Act.

It is anomalous that protection against religious discrimination exists in Northern Ireland, but not in the rest of the UK. But we doubt whether it would be appropriate merely to tack onto the Race Relations Act a prohibition on religious discrimination for this Commission to enforce. The whole subject has ramifications going well beyond the area of good race relations.

For that reason, we are keen to see the debate widened and would hope that Government would listen carefully to the views expressed. We can envisage that the principled conclusion might well be to make religious discrimination unlawful, and, if so, it would reflect the considerable measure of public support in our own consultation.

APPENDIX 1
Results of the 1985 Review of the Act

There was no race relations legislation as such following the 1985 Review so the chance of wider change has not presented itself. Equally it did not prove possible to get a Private Member's Bill adopted. The statutory changes there have been have involved specific areas – planning, housing or employment.

While statutory changes have been limited in scope, there have been changes as a result of case-law which have been of general application to discrimination law.

LEGISLATIVE CHANGES:

- Planning control has been brought within the scope of the Race Relations Act (Section 19A).

- The code-making power in Section 47 has been extended to permit the making of Codes of Practice in the area of housing.

- Section 13 has been revamped so that the protection for work-experience trainees has been improved and does not depend on ministerial designation.

- Section 37 has been changed so that positive action training for non-employees does not now require ministerial designation of training bodies.

CASE-LAW CHANGES:

- The level of compensation for injury to feelings has been increased (*Alexander* and *Noone*, both in the Court of Appeal).

- The circumstances under which indirect discrimination may be justifiable have decreased somewhat (the Court of Appeal in *Hampson* restated the law).

- The scope of statutory immunity from racial discrimination law has been reduced (the House of Lords in *Hampson* narrowly construed Section 41).

- Some, but not all, of the difficulties in the law on victimisation have been ironed out (see the decision of the Court of Appeal in *Aziz*).

GENERAL PROPOSALS FOR CHANGE WHICH REMAIN UNFULFILLED:

- The problem caused by the Court of Appeal decisions in *Perera* and *Meer* in the definition of indirect discrimination remains.

- The *Amin* decision still effectively stops the Commission or anyone else from using the 1976 Act to deal with governmental activity.

- The idea of a discrimination division in the industrial tribunals has not been followed up in Great Britain, though such a course was virtually what was taken in Northern Ireland.

- Legal aid has not been extended to cover racial discrimination cases in industrial tribunals.

- The limitation imposed by the *Prestige* decision on the Commission's power to carry out formal investigations still remains. The Fair Employment Commission in Northern Ireland, however, has wider powers than the CRE.

- The Commission's powers to bring law enforcement proceedings are still limited in scope to assisting individuals, dealing with discriminatory advertisements, instructions and pressure to discriminate, persistent discrimination, enforcement of non-discrimination notices and the bringing of judicial reviews. There is no general right to take law enforcement actions or to bring class actions.

- The remedies to deal with discrimination are still limited in the industrial tribunals to those concerned with the individual not the discriminatory situation. After 81 days of hearing giving them ample time to look at systems, the tribunal in the major police case of *Singh v Nottinghamshire Police* could only make *suggestions* for change. It had no statutory power even to make formal recommendations, let alone to order change. Even as they apply to an individual, the remedies available do little about putting that person in the position they would have occupied but for the discrimination.

- There is still an artificially low limit on compensation in industrial tribunals - currently £10,000 - which is imposed by Government and affects the level of compensation for injury to feelings. In Northern Ireland the limit in the Fair Employment Tribunal is £30,000.

- The code-making power, although extended to housing, has not been widened to other areas.

- Ethnic monitoring, though recommended by Codes and approved for use in proving racial discrimination by *West Midlands Passenger Transport Executive v Singh*, has not been given a statutory basis. Indeed, the approved questions under the local government legislation on contract compliance stopped local authorities from asking for such data from proposed contractors. By contrast, in Northern Ireland, the Fair Employment Act is partly directed toward gearing the gathering of religious monitoring data to entitlement to enter public contracts.

- No power has been given to the Commission to accept binding undertakings to carry out good practice.

- Instead of widening the general duties of local authorities imposed by Section 71 to cover other public authorities (other than bringing under it some housing bodies), its application in the area of contract compliance has been limited by local government legislation.

APPENDIX 2
Organisations and individuals who gave written evidence during the Commission's public consultation

ORGANISATIONS

All Nepalese Association
Asian Action Group, Tayside
Association of County Councils
Association of District Councils
Association of Metropolitan Authorities
Avon and Bristol Community Law Centre
Aylesbury Vale District Council
Balham Mosque
Banff and Buchan District Council
Bangladesh Association, Uxbridge
Bangladesh Welfare Trust, Uxbridge
Barking and Dagenham Borough Council
Barnardos North East
Basildon District Council
Bedford REC
Belfast Law Centre
Bexley Afro Caribbean Community Association
Birmingham City Council
Blackburn Council of Mosques
Board of Deputies of British Jews
Bolsover District Council
Borough of Blackburn
Borough of Rossendale
Borough of Thamesdown
Bradford REC
Brent Borough Council
Brent Christian Coalition
Brent CRC
Brighton Borough Council
Brighton Islamic Mission
Bristol City Council
Bristol Muslims Action Committee
Bristol REC
British Shia Muslim Action Committee
Burnley and Pendle REC
Burnley Borough Council
Bury Metropolitan Council
Calamus Foundation
Calderdale Metropolitan Borough Council
Camden Borough Council
Catholic Bishops Conference of England and Wales
Central Regional Council
Central London Law Centre
Charnwood CRC
Cheshire County Council
Chesterfield Borough Council
Children's Society
Christ Church, Uxbridge
Christian Aid
City and District of St Albans
City of Aberdeen
City of Bradford Metropolitan Borough Council
City of Cardiff
City of Dundee District Council
City of Edinburgh District Council
City of Glasgow
City of London Polytechnic
City of Rochester upon Medway
City of Wakefield Metropolitan District Council
City of York
Clackmannan District Council
Cleethorpes Borough Council

Cleveland REC
Committee on the Administration of Justice (Northern Ireland)
Confederation of British Industry
Convention of Scottish Local Authorities
Cooperative Union Ltd
Council of Mosques in South London and Surrey
Council of Religious Freedom
County of Avon
County of Avon Race Equality Forum
Coventry CRC
Committee of Vice-Chancellors and Principals
Darlington Borough Council
Derby REC
Derbyshire County Council
Devon County Council
District of Woodspring
Doncaster Metropolitan Borough Council
Ealing REC
Enfield Borough Council
Enfield REC
Equal Opportunities Commission
Essex County Council
Essex REC
Ethnic Minorities Representatives Council
Falkirk District Council
Fife REC
Fife Regional Council
General, Municipal, Boilermakers and Allied Trades Union
Glasgow Citizens' Advice Bureau
Gordon District Council
Grampian REC
Greater London Action for Racial Equality
Green Party
Greenwich Borough Council
Greenwich CRE
Hackney REC
Hammersmith and Fulham CRE
Haringey Borough Council
Harlow Hindu Sabha

Hertfordshire County Council
Hillingdon Borough Council
Hillingdon CRC
Hounslow Community Police Consultative Group
Hounslow REC
Hull City Council
Humberside County Council
Hyndburn and Rossendale REC
Ickenham United Reform Church
Idara-e-Jaaferiya
Independent Television Association
India Society, Ruislip
Indian Workers Association GB, Uxbridge
Inner City Forum, Newcastle
Institute of Personnel Management
Ipswich and Suffolk CRE
Ipswich Borough Council
Islamic Academy, Cambridge
Islamic Association of North London
Islamic Education and Cultural Society, Hayes
Islamic Education Society, Uxbridge
Islamic Forum, Europe
Islamic Foundation, Leicester
Islamic Medical Association
Islamic Society of Brighton and Hove
Islamic Society of Britain
Jewish Representative Council
Kent County Council
Kilmarnock and Loudoun District Council
Kirklees Metropolitan Council
Kirklees REC
Kshtrya Sabha, London
Kyle and Carrick District Council
Lancashire County Council
Lancashire Polytechnic
Law Centres Federation
Law Society
Leeds REC
Lewisham Borough Council
Lewisham REC

Lincolnshire County Council
London Central Mosque
London Underground Limited
Lothian REC
Manchester CCR
Manchester City Council
Masjid Bilal and Islamic Centre, East London
Medway and Gillingham REC
Memon Association UK
Merseyside REC
Merton Borough Council
Middlesborough Borough Council
Milton Keynes REC
Muslim Aid
Muslim Community Centre, Brighton
Muslim Doctors and Dentists Association
Muslim Information and Welfare Services
NALGO (National and Local Government Officers Association) Hillingdon Branch
National Association of Citizens Advice Bureaux
National Association of Schoolmasters/Union of Women Teachers
National Association of Teachers in Further and Higher Education
National Children's Bureau
National Council of Hindu Temples (UK)
National Pay Equity Campaign
National Spiritual Assembly of the Baha'is of the UK
National Union of Civil and Public Servants
National Union of Public Employees
National Union of Teachers
Neighbourhood Energy Action, Newcastle
Newark and Sherwood District Council
Newcastle upon Tyne Polytechnic
Newham CRE
North Bedfordshire Borough Council
North East Derbyshire District Council
North Yorkshire County Council
Northampton Borough Council

Northumbria Police
Nottinghamshire County Council
Oldham Metropolitan Borough Council
Oldham REC
Orkney Islands Council
Oxford City Council
Oxfordshire County Council
Pakistan Welfare Association, Uxbridge
Parish of St Philip and St Augustine, Newcastle
Park Community Council, Glasgow
Peterborough City Council
Pollockshields Development Association, Glasgow
Polytechnics and Colleges Funding Council
Preston and Western Lancashire REC
Preston Borough Council
Project 10, Newcastle
Q-News International
Reading Borough Council
Reading CRE
Religious Society of Friends, Uxbridge
Renfrew District Council
Resource Unit to Promote Black Volunteering
Richmond upon Thames Borough Council
Rotherham Metropolitan Borough Council
Rotherham REC
Roundabout Centre, Edinburgh
Royal College of General Practitioners
Royal College of Psychiatrists
Ryedale District Council
Sandwell Metropolitan Borough Council
Scottish Asian Action Committee
Scottish Council for Civil Liberties
Scottish Ethnic Minorities Research Unit
Scottish Trades Union Congress
Sefton Metropolitan Borough Council
Sheffield City Council
Sheffield REC
Shromani Akali Dal UK (Supreme Council of Sikhs)
Slough Corporation

Society of Muslim Scholars in the UK
South Glamorgan
South Glamorgan REC
Southampton City Council
Sparkbrook Islamic Centre
St Martin Church, West Drayton
St Mary of the Virgin Church, Harefield
Staffordshire County Council
Stevenage Borough Council
Stirling District Council
Strathclyde CRCC
Strathclyde Regional Council
Sussex Muslim Society
Sutton Borough Council
Sutton REC
Tameside Metropolitan Borough Council
Tayside Regional Council
Trades Union Congress
TSB Group Plc
Tyne and Wear REC
UK Action Committee on Islamic Affairs
UK Islamic Mission, Cardiff
UK Islamic Mission, Leicester
UK Islamic Mission, Walsall
UK Islamic Mission, Wolverhampton
UK Islamic Mission, Glasgow
UK Islamic Mission, North London
Union of Muslim Organisations of UK and Eire
University of London Institute of Education
University of Manchester School of Education
Uxbridge Centre
Walsall REC
Waltham Forest Borough Council
Watford REC
Welwyn and Hatfield Council
West Glamorgan REC
West Lindsay District Council
West Midlands REC Forum
Wolverhamptom Metropolitan Borough Council
Worthing Borough Council

Wycombe District Council

INDIVIDUALS

H A Abdullah
J E Abides
Nimoh Akainyah
P Babbar
Aiyub Bapu
Yusuf I Batan
W Benns
M Bhailoh
Sydney Bidwell MP
Professor Brice Dickson
Jacob Cajer
Michael Carttiss MP
C J Cothe
Issack Desai
D Faulkes
A Faure
M D Francis
Mrs I Gigg
Yusuf M Gurjee
H Hadrena
M M Ibrahim
I M Ismael
E James
Tim Janman MP
W Jenkins
D Johnson
Mary N Jones
Tom Jones
I A Kabir
Dr Q O Khan
Michael Lazzari
M Lulat
Anthony J McCaffry
Mrs McCaffry
Kishan S Mangat
Mrs E Marshall
Salim Musa
T Panes

Dawood Patel
Sebastian Poulter
Mohammed Atiq Quraishy
R Ramskisdoon
S S Rayit
Mrs Jill Rhodes
M Roberts

Mrs J St Louis
Imtiaz Adam Valli
M Vohlal
S Williams
Mr M Zayee-Mellick
Mrs Zayee-Mellick
Umardi I Zinga

GCSE/KEY STAGE 4

GUIDES

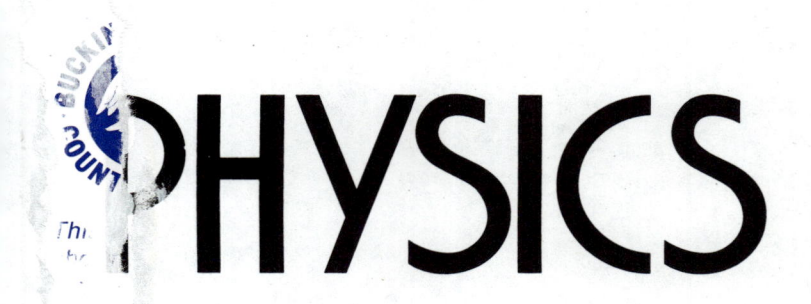

PHYSICS

Keith Palfreyman and Colin Maunder

Longman

LONGMAN REVISE GUIDES

SERIES EDITORS:
Geoff Black and Stuart Wall

TITLES AVAILABLE:
Biology*
Business Studies*
Chemistry*
Economics*
English*
English Literature*
French
Geography
German
Information Systems*
Mathematics*
Mathematics: Higher Level*
Music
Physics*
Psychology
Religious Studies*
Science*
Sociology
Spanish
Technology*
World History

* new editions for Key Stage 4

Addison Wesley Longman Limited,
Edinburgh Gate, Harlow
Essex CM20 2JE, England
and Associated Companies throughout the world.

© Longman Group Limited 1994

All rights reserved; no part of this publication may be reproduced, stored in a retrieval system, or transmitted in any form or by any means, electronic, mechanical, photocopying, recording, or otherwise without either the prior written permission of the Publishers or a licence permitting restricted copying in the United Kingdom issued by the Copyright Licensing Agency Ltd, 90 Tottenham Court Road, London W1P 9HE.

First published 1994
Fourth impression 1996

ISBN 0 582 23774 2

British Library Cataloguing-in-Publication Data

A catalogue record for this book is
available from the British Library

Set by 19QQ in 10/12pt Century Old Style
Produced by Longman Singapore Publishers Pte Ltd
Printed in Singapore

CONTENTS

	Editor's preface	IV
	Acknowledgements	IV
CHAPTER 1.	Science: Physics and Key Stage 4	1
2.	Examination and Assessment Techniques	13
3.	Forces and Structures	22
4.	Energy, Work and Power	41
5.	Forces and Motion	61
6.	Oscillations and Waves	85
7.	Circuits and Direct Currents	105
8.	Electronics: The Components	129
9.	Optics and the Nature of Light	145
10.	Structure of Matter and Kinetic Theory	171
11.	Pressure and Hydraulics	187
12.	Heat Energy	203
13.	Magnetism and Electromagnetism	223
14.	Induced e.m.f. and AC	241
15.	Atomic Structure and Radioactivity	257
16.	Electronics: Systems	279
17.	Earth, Space and Weather	299
	Appendix 1: Equations	323
	Appendix 2: The programme of study	325
	Appendix 3: Circuit diagrams	327
	Index	328

EDITORS' PREFACE

Longman Revise Guides are written by experienced examiners and teachers, and aim to give you the best possible foundation for success in examinations and other modes of assessment. Much has been said in recent years about declining standards and disappointing examination results. While this may be somewhat exaggerated, examiners are well aware that the performance of many candidates falls well short of their potential. The books encourage thorough study and a full understanding of the concepts involved and should be seen as course companions and study guides to be used throughout the year. Examiners are in no doubt that a structured approach in preparing for examinations and in presenting coursework can, together with hard work and diligent application, substantially improve performance.

The largely self-contained nature of each chapter gives the book a useful degree of flexibility. After starting with Chapters 1 and 2, all other chapters can be read selectively, in any order appropriate to the stage you have reached in your course. We believe that this book, and the series as a whole, will help you establish a solid platform of basic knowledge and examination technique on which to build.

Geoff Black and Stuart Wall

ACKNOWLEDGEMENTS

We are grateful to the following Examination Boards for their assistance in the preparation of this book:

    Midland Examining Group (MEG)
    Northern Examinations and Assessment Board (NEAB)
    Northern Ireland Council for Curriculum, Examinations and Assessment (NICCEA)
    Southern Examining Group (SEG)
    University of London Examinations and Assessment Council (ULEAC)
    Welsh Joint Education Committee (WJEC)

Where particular permission to reproduce questions has been granted, further acknowledgement is given in the text. We accept full responsibility for any indication of answers to such questions, and answers or indications of mark schemes have not been approved by any Examination Board.

We are grateful to Stuart Wall and Geoff Black for their help in the publication and in dealing with our problems and enquiries and to our colleagues and students for their help.

Keith Palfreyman and Colin Maunder

I am indebted to Sally Ginns, Elaine Sanderson and Eleanor Wall for their help in typing my part of the manuscript; to Graham Baldry, Geoff Black, and especially to Stuart Wall for their help in the publication, and to Peter Norwood and Liz Hatten for their support and encouragement.

Finally to pupils of Impington Village College for their co-operation with the "Students' Answers".

Colin Maunder

I would like to express my thanks to my two sons for their help, especially Paul for his proof reading and constructive comments on my parts of the text and my wife Angela for yet more of her patience and coffee. I am also grateful to the pupils of Pope Pius X School for their help in preparing answers and review sheets and to its staff for their expertise when help was needed.

Keith Palfreyman

CHAPTER 1

SCIENCE: PHYSICS AND KEY STAGE 4

THE NATIONAL CURRICULUM

PROGRAMME OF STUDY

STATEMENTS OF ATTAINMENT AND LEVELS

THE SYLLABUSES

TIERS OF ASSESSMENT

SPELLING, PUNCTUATION AND GRAMMAR

ATTAINMENT TARGETS FOR SCIENCE: PHYSICS

SCHEMES OF ASSESSMENT FOR SCIENCE: PHYSICS

EXAM GROUP

GETTING STARTED

This book is designed to act as a guide to the whole of your GCSE Physics course, whether as a separate subject (Science: Physics) or as part of GCSE Science. It can be used alongside a conventional textbook throughout your course as well as for help with pre-examination revision. The study of physics requires you to understand ideas and be able to apply them in both familiar and new situations. *Understanding* takes time and effort and it is best to work steadily throughout your course rather than to leave everything to the last minute.

Each chapter refers to a ***particular topic*** or ***area of study***, and contains the ***essential principles*** of that topic which are, in effect, the 'core' materials in the Physics part of the Science National Curriculum.

After covering the essential principles of a topic area, there is a discussion of ***extension materials*** in each chapter. These are the *additional* aspects you need to know on each topic area to gain a separate GCSE in Physics, i.e. Science: Physics.

Examples from GCSE examination papers are provided for practice, together with ***outline answers***. One question is usually selected for ***more thorough treatment*** to give you an idea of what a ***full*** answer should include.

Finally each chapter contains a ***Review Sheet*** to give you the opportunity to check your understanding of the ideas encountered in that chapter.

CHAPTER 1 SCIENCE: PHYSICS AND KEY STAGE 4

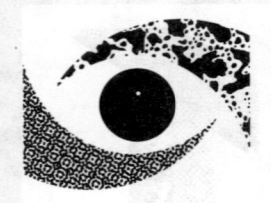

ESSENTIAL PRINCIPLES

This book will be relevant both to those taking Physics as a separate GCSE subject (i.e. Science: Physics) and to those requiring extra help on the Physics part of their Science GCSE. Science is a compulsory subject for all pupils in state schools that must follow the National Curriculum and is, together with Mathematics and English, one of the "core" subjects. This first chapter will try to make the various rules and regulations of the different Examination Groups more clear. If you still need further information their addresses are at the end of the chapter.

Whatever your reason for reading this book remember that regular reading and revision will always lead to a clearer understanding – NEVER leave your revision to the last minute. Always try to plan your work so that you can cope with the demands that it will make on your time. If you have to hand in coursework assignments, find out when they are due and make sure that they are handed in on time. Being behind with work in one subject can mean that you lose time that should be spent on others and all your work suffers – planning avoids the problem and ensures some free time for enjoyment!

1 THE NATIONAL CURRICULUM

❝Separate examination papers in the individual science subjects❞

❝You need to cover core and extension materials for a separate GCSE in Physics❞

❝Attainment Targets for Science❞

❝Science: Physics❞

All pupils in years 10 and 11 (Key Stage 4) of the English state school system have to take either single science (about 12% of total timetable time) or double science (about 20% of total timetable time). An increasing number of pupils are choosing to take this last option by adding to the National Curriculum Science programme of study and taking *separate examination papers* in Science: Physics, Science: Chemistry and Science: Biology. The Examination Boards have provided this option by splitting the Science programme of study between the three subject areas and then adding extra material from the appropriate subject. In the near future this means that all pupils taking this option have to do all three "separate" subjects in order to meet the requirements of the law about National Curriculum but this might of course change. The additional material will of course mean a corresponding increase in the study time required.

It is best to think of the examination syllabus for each separate subject in two parts – the "*core*" that is part of the National Curriculum programme of study and the *extension* material needed to get a separate GCSE in that subject. The *core* materials are set out in the first part of each topic-based chapter; the *extension* materials are separately presented at the end of each topic-based chapter.

The National Curriculum programme of study has four **Attainment Targets** for Science:

- Attainment Target Sc1: Scientific Investigation.
- Attainment Target Sc2: Life and Living Processes.
- Attainment Target Sc3: Materials and their Properties.
- Attainment Target Sc4: Physical processes.

Science: Physics usually covers some of Attainment Target Sc3 and all of Attainment Target Sc4 with suitable extensions. It will also include investigations that allow you to be assessed in Attainment Target Sc1. There is no coverage of any of Attainment Target Sc2 which is mainly biological in content.

Attainment Target Sc1: Scientific Investigation

The National Curriculum divides Attainment Target Sc1 into three strands as follows.
Pupils should carry out investigations in which they

(i) ask questions, predict and hypothesise;
(ii) observe, measure and manipulate variables;
(iii) interpret their results and evaluate scientific evidence.

Attainment Target Sc3: Materials and their Properties

The National Curriculum divides Attainment Target Sc3 into four strands as follows. Pupils should develop knowledge and understanding of:

(i) the properties, classification and structure of materials;
(ii) explanations of the properties of materials;
(iii) chemical changes;
(iv) the Earth and its atmosphere.

The Physics syllabus is usually limited to iv) and parts of ii) but you will also need to know some parts of i) that are about the structure of the atom so that you can understand radioactivity and the operation of nuclear reactors.

Attainment Target Sc4: Physical Processes

The National Curriculum also divides Attainment Target Sc4 into five strands as follows. Pupils should develop knowledge and understanding of:

(i) electricity and magnetism;
(ii) energy resources and energy transfer;
(iii) forces and their effects;
(iv) light and sound;
(v) the Earth's place in the universe

The Physics syllabus would usually include all of this target.

2 > THE PROGRAMME OF STUDY

The National Curriculum gives a **programme of study** which sets out the ground to be covered for each of the Attainment Targets in more detail. It is an account of how you cover the material. The Examination Boards will provide a similar statement for their *extension* material in Physics. There is more detail about this in section 8 about the assessment for individual examination schemes and in Appendix 2 which lists the programme of study for the National Curriculum.

3 > STATEMENTS OF ATTAINMENT AND LEVELS

Levels can give you an idea of what is expected for higher *grades*

The National Curriculum also gives each Attainment Target a set of 10 **levels** going from 1, the simplest level, to 10, the most complex. Each level has a set of **Statements of Attainment** which describe what you should be able to do to reach that level. At Key Stage 4 you will be concerned with the levels from 4 to 10. The Examination Board will also provide statements for the levels within their extension material. Notice that the levels tell you which ideas the Examination Board thinks are hardest – they will be the ones in the higher levels. The level can also be used to give you a clearer idea of what will be expected of you and for this reason most are listed for you in Part 7 of this chapter. It was originally intended that you would be given your examination results in these level numbers but this was changed in 1993 so that you will still get your results as letters (**grades**) from A to G with U for those who do not reach the lowest grade. There will also be a new grade A* which will be awarded to the few who reach the dizzy heights of National Curriculum level 10 in their examination. (If using this book helps you to reach A* please let us know!)

4 > THE SYLLABUSES

Each of the Examination Groups states in a **syllabus** exactly what must be taught for its examination and also the length and style of its examination papers. The main points of ***all*** examination syllabuses for Science : Physics have been covered. The *core* part of the National Curriculum Science is covered in the 'Essential Principles' section of each topic-based chapter. The additional knowledge needed for the award of a separate GCSE in Physics is covered in the 'Extension Materials' section of each chapter. Candidates would be wise to obtain a copy of their syllabus from their own school or college, or by writing directly to their Examination Group, checking their syllabus against the content of each chapter. The main chapter headings and their application to the seven Examination Groups are given in Fig. 1.1.

CHAPTER 1 SCIENCE: PHYSICS AND KEY STAGE 4

Chapter and topic	ULEAC	MEG	NEAB	NISEAC	SEG	WJEC	IGCSE
3 Forces and structure	✓	✓	✓	✓	✓	✓	✓
4 Energy, work and power	✓	✓	✓	✓	✓	✓	✓
5 Forces and motion	✓	✓	✓	✓	✓	✓	✓
6 Oscillations and waves	✓	✓	✓	✓	✓	✓	✓
7 Circuits and direct current	✓	✓	✓	✓	✓	✓	✓
8 Electronics – components	✓	✓	✓	✓	✓	✓	✓
9 Light and optics	✓	✓	✓	✓	✓	✓	✓
10 Structure of matter and kinetic theory	✓	✓	✓	✓	✓	✓	✓
11 Pressure and hydraulics	✓	✓	✓	✓	✓	✓	✓
12 Heat energy	✓	✓	✓	✓	✓	✓	✓
13 Magnetism and electromagnetism	✓	✓	✓	✓	✓	✓	✓
14 Induced EMF and AC	✓	✓	✓	✓	✓	✓	✓
15 Atomic strucure and radioactivity	✓	✓	✓	✓	✓	✓	✓
16 Electronics – systems	✓	✓	✓	✓	✓	✓	✓
17 Earth, space and weather	✓	✓	✓	✓	✓	✓	✓

Fig. 1.1 Syllabus coverage chart

The following Fig. 1.2 gives you an indication of which parts of the *extension materials* in each chapter are relevant to the various Examination Groups.

	MEG	MEG Nuffield	MEG Salters'	NEAB/ WJEC	NISEAC	SEG	ULEAC A	ULEAC B
Chapter 3	1,2,4	1,2,3	1,2,4	1	1,2	1,2,4	2,4	1,2,4
Chapter 4	3	1,2	1,3	1,2,3	1,2,3	1,2	2,3	1,2,3
Chapter 5	4	1,2,4,6	3,4,5	1,2,4	1,2,6	4	3,4,5	4
Chapter 6	1,2		1			1,2	1,2	1,2
Chapter 7	4,5		2,4	2	1,2	1,2,4		2
Chapter 8	4,5,6	5	1,2,4,5,6	5,6	5	4,5	5,6	4
Chapter 9	1,2,3,4, 5,8,10	6,7	1,2,3,4, 5,6,7,10	1,2,3,4 5,7,9,10	1,3,4,5, 6,7,10	1,2,3,4	3,4,6,	3,4,5,7, 10
Chapter 10	1	1	2	1	1	2,3,4	3	
Chapter 11	1,2	1,2	1,2	1,2,3	3	2,4,5	2,3	2
Chapter 12	2,3	1,2,3,4	2,3,4,6	1,2,3,4, 5,7	2,4,6	1,2,3,4	1,2,3,4	1,2,3,4
Chapter 13	1,2	1,2,3	1,2,3	1,2,3	1,2	1	1	1
Chapter 14	1,2,3	1,2	1,2,3	1,2,3	1,2	1,2,3	1,2,3	1,2
Chapter 15	2,3,4	2,3,4	2,3,4	2,3,4	2,3,4	1,2,3	2,3,4	
Chapter 16	1,2	1,2	2,3,4,5	1,2		1,2		1,2
Chapter 17	4,6,7	7	1,2,3,5 6,7,8	3,6,7,8	1,7	4,7,8	2,3,4,5, 7,8	1,7,8

Fig. 1.2 Extension Materials relevant to the various Examination Group syllabuses

Section 8 of this chapter will give you more detail of the ways in which you will be assessed for Science: Physics by each of the examination groups. You can always write to the examination group address given in Section 9 of this chapter to get an up-to-date copy of your syllabus.

AIMS

The *aims* are a description of the purpose of the syllabus. They may be long-term goals that cannot be assessed in the final examination but they should give you good reasons why you should follow this particular course. The *aims* for Science: Physics will follow those for the National Curriculum and are broadly the same for all of the Examination Boards. They are:

Aims of the syllabuses

1. To give you sufficient knowledge and understanding to:
   - become confident citizens in a technological world, able to take or develop an informed interest in matters of scientific importance;
   - recognise the usefulness, and limitations, of scientific methods and appreciate their applicability in other disciplines and in everyday life;
   - be encouraged to pursue and be suitably prepared for further studies in physics;

2. To develop abilities and skills that:
   - are relevant to the study, practice and application of physics;
   - are useful in everyday life;
   - encourage safe practice.

3. To stimulate:
   - curiosity, interest and enjoyment in physics and its methods of enquiry;
   - interest in and care for, the environment.

4. To promote awareness that:
   - the study and practice of science are co-operative and cumulative activities and are subject to social, economic, technological, ethical and cultural influences and limitations;
   - the applications of physics may be both beneficial and detrimental to the individual, the community and the environment;
   - the concepts of science are of a developing and sometimes transient nature.

ASSESSMENT OBJECTIVES

These are a list of the abilities and skills which you will develop and on which you will be assessed. The attainment targets can be divided into two main groups of objectives; one group involves *investigations* under Attainment Target Sc1 (assessed by coursework) and the other group involves *knowledge and understanding* of physics (assessed in the examination). Again they are broadly the same for each of the Examination Boards:

1. Scientific investigation Sc1 (usually 25% by coursework)
   Use your knowledge, skills and understanding of physics to plan and carry out investigations in which you:

Two broad groups of assessment objectives

   - ask questions, predict and hypothesise;
   - observe, measure and manipulate variables;
   - interpret your results and evaluate scientific evidence.

2. Attainment Targets Sc3, Sc4 and extension material (a total of 75% by examinations)
   Through your knowledge, skills and understanding you show an ability to:
   - communicate scientific observations, ideas and arguments effectively;
   - select and use reference materials and translate data from one form to another;
   - interpret, evaluate and make informed judgements from relevant facts, observations and phenomena;
   - solve qualitative and quantitative problems.

5. TIERS OF ASSESSMENT

You can enter for the examination in one of three "tiers". The tiers ask questions of different difficulty and can lead to the grades in the following table. You should be entered for a tier that lets you answer as much as possible so that you can get your best possible grade. There is no point in entering for a level that is beyond your ability so that you get a lower grade than you would on the next level.

You need to be entered for the correct tier

Tier	GRADES
Further	A* A B (C,D)
Central	(A) B C D E (F)
Basic	(C) D E F G (U)

Note
(i) A on central tier and C on basic tier are only awarded in very exceptional cases.
(ii) A* is a grade that matches the requirements of level 10 of the Science national curriculum and is therefore above grade A.
(iii) The central tier is now very wide in its coverage and will probably be the level for which the majority of candidates are entered.
(iv) Some Boards give these tiers letters rather than names.
(vii) You might find it helpful to see how the grades given at the end correspond with the level statements of the National Curriculum. They are approximately as follows:

> For Key Stage 4, it is the *grades* which will be reported in your GCSE results

Grades	Level
A*	10
A	9
B	8
C	
	7
D	
	6
E	
F	5
G	4
U	3

6 > SPAG

Spelling, Punctuation and Grammar must all carry marks towards your final grade. The total will be 5%. In written examinations this will be assessed by the examiners. In coursework such as your practical investigations for Sc1 the assessment may be carried out by your teacher. To help teachers and examiners the following levels have been agreed by the Examination Boards:

> Don't forget to be as accurate as possible in spelling, punctuation and grammar

- **Threshold performance.** Candidates spell, punctuate and use the rules of grammar with reasonable accuracy; they use a limited range of specialist terms appropriately.
- **Intermediate performance.** Candidates spell, punctuate and use the rules of grammar with considerable accuracy; they use a good range of specialist terms with facility.
- **High performance.** Candidates spell, punctuate and use the rules of grammar with almost faultless accuracy, deploying a range of grammatical constructions; they use a wide range of specialist terms adeptly and with precision.

Out of a total of 100 marks you should expect that the following marks would be awarded:

- Threshold performance: 1 mark allocated.
- Intermediate performance: 2–3 marks allocated.
- High performance: 4–5 marks allocated.

7 > THE TARGETS AND ATTAINMENT LEVELS FOR SCIENCE: PHYSICS

These are the National Curriculum targets that will apply to **Science: Physics** as it is examined by each Examination Board. All of the Boards will use Sc1 and Sc4. Most of the Boards will use the sections of Sc3 that are shown. Each Board will also have a set of levels for its own extensions to the core syllabus. Remember to check yours with an up to date copy as the exact wording can change from one year to another.

ATTAINMENT TARGET Sc1: SCIENTIFIC INVESTIGATION

Strand (i) Ask questions, predict and hypothesise

Pupils should carry out investigations in which they:

Level 4: ask questions, suggest ideas and make predictions, based on some relevant prior knowledge, in a form which can be investigated.

Level 5: formulate hypotheses where the causal link is based on scientific knowledge, understanding or theory.

Level 6: use scientific knowledge, understanding or theory to predict relationships between continuous variables.

> *An outline of what you must attain to achieve various levels in GCSE in physics as a single subject*

Level 7: use scientific knowledge, understanding or theory to predict the relative effect of a number of variables.
Level 8: use scientific knowledge, understanding or theory to generate quantitative predictions and a strategy for the investigation.
Level 9: use scientific theory to make quantitative predictions and organise the collection of valid and reliable data.
Level 10: use scientific knowledge and an understanding of laws, theories and models to develop hypotheses which seek to explain the behaviour of objects and events they have studied.

Strand (ii) Observe, measure and manipulate variables;

Pupils should carry out investigations in which they:

Level 4: carry out a fair test in which they select and use appropriate instruments to measure quantities such as volume and temperature.
Level 5: choose the range of each of the variables involved to produce meaningful results.
Level 6: consider the range of factors involved, identify the key variables and those to be controlled and/or taken account of, and make qualitative or quantitative observations involving fine discrimination.
Level 7: manipulate or take into account the relative effects of two or more independent variables.
Level 8: select and use measuring instruments which provide the degree of accuracy commensurate with the outcome they have predicted.
Level 9: systematically use a range of investigatory techniques to judge the relative effects of the factors involved.
Level 10: collect data which are sufficiently valid and reliable to enable them to make a critical evaluation of the law, theory or model.

Strand (iii) Interpret their results and evaluate scientific evidence

Pupils should carry out investigations in which they:

Level 4: draw conclusions which link patterns in observations or results to the original question, prediction or idea.
Level 5: evaluate the validity of their conclusions by considering different interpretations of their experimental evidence.
Level 6: use their results to draw conclusions, explain the relationship between variables and refer to a model to explain the results.
Level 7: use observations or results to draw conclusions which state the relative effects of the independent variables and explain the limitations of the evidence obtained.
Level 8: justify each aspect of the investigation in terms of the contribution to the overall conclusion.
Level 9: analyse and interpret the data obtained, in terms of complex functions where appropriate in a way which demonstrates an appreciation of the uncertainty of evidence and the tentative nature of conclusions.
Level 10: use and analyse the data obtained to evaluate the law, theory or model in terms of the extent to which it can explain the observed behaviour.

ATTAINMENT TARGET Sc3: MATERIALS AND THEIR PROPERTIES

Some of Sc3 will not be examined in Science: Physics but will be examined in Science: Biology or Science: Chemistry. The following are included in the schemes of most Examination Boards.

Strand (i) Properties, classification and structure of materials

Most physics schemes require an understanding of

Level 8: understand the structure of the atom in terms of protons, neutrons and electrons and how this can explain the existence of isotopes.

Strand (ii) Explanations of the properties of materials.

Pupils should:

CHAPTER 1 SCIENCE: PHYSICS AND KEY STAGE 4

Level 6: understand the physical differences between solids, liquids and gases in particle terms.
Level 7: understand changes of state, including the associated energy changes, mixing and diffusion in terms of the proximity and motion of the particles;
understand the relationships between the pressure, volume and temperature of a gas.
Level 8: understand radioactivity and nuclear fission and the harmful and beneficial effects of ionising radiations.
Level 9: understand the nature of radioactive decay, relating half life to the use of radioactive materials.

Strand (iv) The Earth and its atmosphere

Pupils should:

Level 4: know how measurements of temperature, windspeed and direction describe the weather.
Level 5: understand the water cycle in terms of the physical processes involved.
Level 6: understand how different airstreams give different weather related to their recent path over land and sea.
Level 7: understand how some weather phenomena are driven by energy transfer processes.
Level 9: be able to use appropriate scientific ideas to explain changes in the atmosphere that cause various weather phenomena.

ATTAINMENT TARGET Sc4: PHYSICAL PROCESSES

Strand (i) Electricity and magnetism

Pupils should:

Level 4: be able to construct circuits containing a number of components in which switches are used to control electrical effects.
Level 5: know how switches, relays, variable resistors, sensors and logic gates can be used to solve simple problems.
Level 6: understand the qualitative relationships between current, voltage and resistance.
Level 7: understand the magnetic effect of an electric current and its application in a range of common devices.
Level 8: be able to explain charge flow and energy transfer in a circuit.
Level 9: be able to use the quantitative relationships between charge, current, potential difference, resistance and electrical power.
Level 10: understand the principles of electromagnetic induction.

Strand (ii) Energy resources and energy transfer

Pupils should:

Level 4: understand that energy transfer is needed to make things work.
Level 5: understand that energy is transferred in any process and recognise energy transfer in a range of devices;
understand the difference between renewable and non-renewable energy resources and the need for fuel economy.
Level 6: understand that energy is conserved;
understand that the Sun is ultimately the major energy source for the Earth.
Level 7: understand how energy is transferred through conduction, convection and radiation;
be able to evaluate methods of reducing wasteful transfers of energy by using a definition of energy efficiency.
Level 8: be able to use the quantitative relationship between change in internal energy and temperature change.
Level 9: be able to evaluate the economic, environmental and social benefits of different energy sources, using quantitative secondary sources of information.

Level 10: understand that in many processes energy is spread out into the surroundings and shared amongst many particles, so reducing the possibility of further useful energy transfers.

Strand (iii) Forces and their effects

Pupils should:

Level 4: know that more than one force can act on an object and that forces can act in different directions.

Level 5: know that the size and resultant direction of a force on an object affects its movement.

Level 6: understand the relationship between an applied force, the area over which it acts and the resulting pressure;
understand the relationship between speed, distance and time.

Level 7: understand the quantitative relationships between force, distance, work, power and time;
understand the law of moments.

Level 8: understand the quantitative relationship between force, mass and acceleration.

Level 9: be able to use the quantitative relationships between mass, weight, potential energy, kinetic energy and work.

Level 10: understand the concept of momentum and its conservation.

Strand (iv) Light and sound

Pupils should:

Level 4: know that light travels faster than sound.

Level 5: understand how the reflection of light enables objects to be seen;
know that sound is produced by a vibrating body and travels as a wave.

Level 6: be able to relate loudness and amplitude, pitch and frequency of a sound wave.

Level 7: be able to use the wave model of light to explain refraction at a plane surface.

Level 8: understand the quantitative relationship between speed, frequency and wavelength;
be able to explain resonance in oscillating systems and how this can be advantageous or disadvantageous.

Level 9: be able to relate the physical properties of the main areas of the electromagnetic spectrum to their uses and effects.

Level 10: be able to relate an understanding of the nature of electromagnetic radiation to its behaviour in the processes of interference, diffraction and polarisation.

Strand (v) The Earth's place in the Universe

Pupils should:

Level 4: be able to explain day and night, day length and year length in terms of the movements of the Earth round the Sun.

Level 5: be able to describe the motion of the planets in the solar system.

Level 6: know that the solar system forms part of a galaxy which is part of a larger system called the Universe.

Level 7: know that gravity acts between all masses and the magnitude of the force diminishes with distance.

Level 8: be able to use data on the solar system or other stellar systems to speculate about the conditions elsewhere in the Universe.

Level 9: be able to relate the theory of gravitational force to the motion of satellites.

Level 10: be able to relate current theories about the origin and future of the Universe to the astronomical evidence.

SCHEMES OF ASSESSMENT

New schemes are still being published and there is some change from year to year. Check with your teacher or your examination group for the details of your particular scheme and make sure that you know exactly what you need to achieve.

CHAPTER 1 SCIENCE: PHYSICS AND KEY STAGE 4

> How the exam groups will assess Physics as a single subject in the GCSE

MEG SCIENCE: PHYSICS (NUFFIELD)

Terminal examination 75%. Not more than 25% for fact recall.
One paper per option (tier) as follows

Paper 1 – hr 30 min – (Basic) Short structured questions, some of which will require more extended responses.
Paper 2 – 2 hrs – (Central) Structured questions, some of which will require more extended responses
Paper 3 – 2 hr 15 min – (Further) Structured questions, some of which will require more extended responses

Coursework 25% assessed internally (by the school) for the three investigation skills of Sc1.

Main extensions: Kinematics, density, vector addition, cooling curves, energy stored in springs, communications, digital data, am radio transmission.

MEG SCIENCE: PHYSICS

Terminal examination 75% Within each paper 85% of the marks will be for core material and the rest for extensions.
One paper per option (tier) as follows

Paper 1 – 1 hr 30 min – (Basic) Short answer structured questions.
Paper 2 – 2 hrs – (Central) Short answer structured questions, some of which will require more extended responses
Paper 3 – 2 hr 15 min – (Further) Structured questions, some of which will require more extended responses

Coursework 25% assessed internally (by the school) for the three investigation skills of Sc1.

Main extensions: Spectra and photons, effect of ionisation on living material, photoelectric effect.

MEG SCIENCE: PHYSICS (SALTERS')

Terminal examination 75%. Not more than 25% for recall of facts.
One paper per option (tier) as follows

Paper 1 – 1 hr 30 min – (Basic) Section A Short answer (multiple choice, sentence completion, matching pairs); Section B: Structured questions.
Paper 2 – 2 hrs – (Central) Section A: Short answer, structured questions; Section B: Structured questions, some of which will require more extended responses.
Paper 3 – 2 hr 15 min – (Further) Section A: Short answer structured questions; Section B: Structured questions which will require more extended responses.

Coursework 25% assessed internally (by the school) for the three investigation skills of Sc1.

Main extensions: Electronics including logic gates, digital and analogue signals, semiconductors and their function in terms of charge carriers, op amps.

NEAB AND WJEC SCIENCE: PHYSICS

Terminal examination 75%. Approx. 60% from core and 15% from extensions.
One paper per option (tier) as follows

Option P – 1 hr 30 min – (Basic) Short answer and structured questions.
Option Q – 2 hrs – (Central)
Option R – 2 hr 30 min – (Further)

The papers for P and Q will be comprised of structured questions. All papers will provide an opportunity for extended writing and calculations.

Coursework 25% assessed internally (by the school) for the three investigation skills of Sc1.
Main extensions: Kinematics, density, expansion and thermometry, ray optics, colour.

NISEAC SCIENCE: PHYSICS

Terminal examination 76%. Two examination papers for each tier.
Options P (Basic) and Q (Central):

Paper 1 – 1 hr. – 20 objective questions and 20 short answer questions.
Paper 2 – 1 hr 30 min. – 4 structured questions

Option R (Further):

Paper 1 – 1 hr 30 min. – 5 structured questions
Paper 2 – 1 hr 30 min. – 4 structured questions and 1 free response question.

Coursework 24% assessed internally (by the school) for the three investigation skills of Sc1.

Main extensions: Kinematics, Hooke's law, resistivity.

SEG SCIENCE: PHYSICS

Terminal examination 75%. Two examination papers for each tier. Core content 60% and extension material 15%. Candidates have a first paper which examines Sc4 and is the same as the Sc4 paper taken by those candidates doing Double Award Science from the same Examination Board. It counts as 60%. The second paper examines the content from Sc3 and the extension material. It counts as 25%

Foundation Tier:	Component 2	1 hr 30 min assessing Sc4
	Component 3	1 hr assessing Sc3 and extensions
Intermediate Tier:	Component 4	1 hr 30 min assessing Sc4
	Component 5	1 hr assessing Sc3 and extensions
Higher Tier:	Component 6	1 hr 30 min assessing Sc4
	Component 7	1 hr assessing Sc3 and extensions

Component 1 is the coursework assessment on Sc1.
Possible combinations are Components 1,2,5 or 1,3,6 or 1,4,7.

Coursework 25% assessed internally (by the school) for the three investigation skills of Sc1.

Main extensions: Fluids. This includes work on surface tension, fluid flow and the principles of flight.

ULEAC SCIENCE: PHYSICS A

Terminal examination 75%. "Paper 1" in each case is the teacher assessment of coursework.

Foundation Tier:	Paper 2F	1 hr 30 min assessing Sc4
	Paper 3F	1 hr assessing Sc3 and extensions
Intermediate Tier:	Paper 2I	1 hr 30 min assessing Sc4
	Paper 3I	1 hr assessing Sc3 and extensions
Higher Tier:	Paper 2H	1 hr 30 min assessing Sc4
	Paper 3H	1 hr assessing Sc3 and extensions

There will be a variety of questions on each paper, including structured questions involving both short answer and extended prose responses.

Coursework 25% assessed internally (by the school) for the three investigation skills of Sc1.

Main extensions: Electrons including electron guns and oscilloscopes, Semiconductors and the effect of resistance on temperature, Communication and the transmission of information including centripetal force and the orbits of satellites.

ULEAC SCIENCE: PHYSICS B

Terminal examination 75%. Core material 60% and extensions 15%. "Paper 1" in each case is the teacher assessment of Sc1.

Foundation Tier:	Paper 2F	1 hr 30 min: Structured questions.
	Paper 3F	1 hr: 25 multiple choice questions plus questions on specified topics.
Intermediate Tier:	Paper 2I	1 hr 30 min: Structured questions.
	Paper 3I	1 hr: 25 multiple choice questions plus questions on specified topics.
Higher Tier:	Paper 2H	1 hr 30 min: Structured questions.
	Paper 3H	1 hr: 25 multiple choice questions plus questions on specified topics.

The specified topics for 1995 are Space exploration since 1957 and Sensing, responding and controlling.

Coursework 25% assessed internally (by the school) for the three investigation skills of Sc1.

Main extensions: these are the "specified topics listed above.

9 EXAMINATION GROUP ADDRESSES

MEG Midlands Examining Group
1 Hills Road
Cambridge
CB1 2EU
Tel. 01223 61111   Fax. 01223 460278

NEAB Northern Examination and Assessment Board
Devas Street
Manchester
M15 6EX
Tel: 0161 953 1180   Fax. 0161 273 7572

NICCEA Northern Ireland Council for Curriculum, Examinations and Assessment
Beechill House
42 Beechill Road
Belfast
BT8 4RS
Tel. 01232 704666   Fax. 01232 799913

SEG Southern Examining Group
Stag Hill House
Guildford
Tel. 01483 506505   Fax. 01483 300152

ULEAC University of London Examinations and Assessment Council
Stewart House
32 Russell Square
London
WC1 5DN
Tel. 0171 331 4000   Fax. 0171 631 3369

WJEC Welsh Joint Education Committee
245 Western Road
Cardiff
CF5 2YX
Tel. 01222 561231   Fax. 01222 571234

CHAPTER 2

EXAMINATION AND ASSESSMENT TECHNIQUES

MULTIPLE CHOICE QUESTIONS

STRUCTURED QUESTIONS

FREE-RESPONSE QUESTIONS

INSTRUCTION WORDS IN EXAMS

DIAGRAMS

GRAPHS

EQUATIONS

NUMERICAL TECHNIQUES

WRITING UP INVESTIGATIONS

EXAMPLE INVESTIGATION AND MARKING SCHEME

FINAL GRADES

GETTING STARTED

As the exam approaches, you will *already* have contributed to your final mark by your coursework assessments over the past months and years. The exam itself will still, however, represent a considerable hurdle, and you should realise that just as assessments were conducted over a period of time, so too should your revision be a continuous process. No matter how good your memory is, physics cannot be 'learned' in a short time, and questions in GCSE are likely to test both your understanding and your ability to analyse and apply data, rather than to simply test your recall of facts.

This book can help as you *approach your exam*. It can also help *throughout your course* if you use it to revise a whole topic area shortly after you have covered it in your class. The past examination questions and answers should give you confidence in using and applying your knowledge. You should try all the questions on each syllabus topic – they have been selected from several Examination Boards and are representative of the standard which is common to *all* the Boards.

Having completed a question, check your answer with the one supplied. Look carefully to see whether you have missed any important points in developing your answer. Check that numerical work is clearly laid out, and that answers are given with the appropriate unit.

You will also find student answers with examiner comments at the end of each chapter. These will help you to see what the examiner is looking for. Each chapter concludes with a Review Sheet which you can use to check your understanding of what you have read in that chapter.

EXAMINATION QUESTIONS

1 ▸ MULTIPLE CHOICE QUESTIONS

These are designed to test knowledge and understanding across the **whole** syllabus. They are 'computer marked' and your answers will need to be written in pencil. If you make an error, your original response must be carefully rubbed out and a new, clear response made. A question which has more than one response on the answer paper is rejected by the computer.

Look carefully at **all** the possible responses and in making your selection try to ensure that you are clear in your mind **why** you rejected all the other possible responses. Even if you are not quite sure of the **single** correct response, you can usually eliminate some of the other responses as clearly wrong. At the end, go through the whole paper and check each answer.

2 ▸ STRUCTURED QUESTIONS

These are intended to test **more detailed** understanding of **particular areas** of the syllabus. Such questions usually have several parts or sections, each part following on from the previous part, i.e. there is a clear *structure* to the question. Most Examination Boards give an indication of the maximum mark to be awarded for each part of such a question – or imply the required length of answer by providing a number of lines below each question. The important thing to bear in mind is that where a mark is stated, e.g. (3), then it broadly reflects the number of significant points the examiners regard as relevant in answering that question. You must think carefully to ensure that your answer contains **sufficient** points to satisfy the examiner's idea of a 'good' answer. A six-mark question will obviously require a more detailed answer than a three-mark question. The answers to structured questions in this book give an indication of the likely requirements in this part of your examination.

3 ▸ FREE-RESPONSE QUESTIONS

These are only likely to be met in the **optional** papers for candidates expected to gain the higher grades awarded in GCSE. They typically require the candidate to present an answer which is organised, without having the benefit of the 'structure' contained in the previous type of question. Essay, data analysis and comprehension are common types of question within this paper.

ESSAY QUESTIONS

Essay questions need **planning**. Spend time in thinking about what you wish to say, and in making sure that you are responding to the statements **in the question**. You can draw up a **list** of points that you wish to make in your answer; perhaps each major point can have its own paragraph. Try to arrange the points so that they have a **logical** order, i.e. one point follows on 'naturally' from the previous point. An essay should have a brief **introduction** telling the examiner the points you are about to make. It should also have a brief **conclusion** where you comment on the major findings of your analysis.

DATA ANALYSIS

Data analysis should show **how** an answer is arrived at. Do not rely on your calculator to provide the answer, but show on your exam paper how you get to your answer. Where a graph has to be analysed, draw appropriate lines to show how you arrived at values, intercepts or gradients. The main point here is to try to make your **method of working** clear to the examiner.

COMPREHENSION

Your ability to deal with this kind of question will depend on how much reading you have done. You may be asked to comment on part of an article, or some other piece of written work. Look for science-based articles in newspapers or magazines. Use your library to read about the background to a topic area in physics. Ask questions in class when you find an area of the subject which is difficult to understand.

4 > INSTRUCTION WORDS IN EXAMS

The examiner will try to help you to give the correct information by the words used in the questions. You need to remember what these 'key words' mean.

Look carefully at words used in the question

- **State** means that a short fact is needed.
- **Define** means give a short but accurate meaning for the word or phrase in the question.
- **Calculate** means work out the answer and show the working. This is usually best done as shown under 'Numerical Techniques'.
- **Describe** means write about the item in the question. Try to give accurate facts in reasonable detail. General statements that lack accuracy or evidence don't usually get many marks. The examiner will have a list of fairly exact items that do get marks.
- **Explain** means that you must give reasons. Stating that something will happen is not enough – you must say WHY it happens.

5 > DIAGRAMS

Diagrams are important. Make them clear to the reader and remember to use labels

- Always draw a clear labelled diagram that fills the space that you are allowed on the examination paper. If you are writing on 'loose' A4 paper most diagrams will be about a third to a half of a page in size.
- Read the question carefully and make sure that you include the detail that is specially asked for.
- Always label your diagram clearly, spacing the labels as well as possible and joining the label to the correct point on the diagram with a neat straight pencil line.
- Always use a sharp HB pencil and a ruler with a good straight edge. Carry a spare sharp pencil with you.
- Check the marks available if you can. This will give you some idea of the level of detail needed. There is not much point in spending 20 minutes on a work of art that carries only 2 marks for a simple sketch!

6 > GRAPHS

If you are asked to draw a graph or if you do graphs as part of your coursework then you will need to do the following to obtain the best marks:

Some useful hints when drawing graphs

- If the question gives you axes and scales you MUST use them.
- Always use the largest possible scale. You will lose a lot of marks if your graph is all in one corner of the graph paper and cannot be used accurately.
- Do make sure that your scales are uniform, i.e. that the number increases by the same amount across every square.
- Make sure that your axes are labelled clearly with both the quantity and its units, e.g. a cooling graph might have its axes labelled temperature/°C and time/s.
- Make sure that all of the points are plotted as accurately as you can.
- The x-axis is along the bottom or horizontal and the y-axis goes up the side or vertical.
- Put the variable that you changed, the one that goes up in regular steps, on the x-axis; e.g. this variable is often time.
- If all the points are on a straight line, or very close to one, fit the best straight line that you can as near as possible to all the points.
- If all the points are on or very close to a curve then draw the nearest smooth curve that you can – DON'T just 'join up the dots'!
- If one point is a long way out check that you have plotted it correctly. If it is correctly plotted but is not on the same line as the others then ignore it when you fit your best line. It may have been put in to see how you would deal with a 'rogue result' caused by an error in an experiment for example.

7 > EQUATIONS

From the examination year of 1994 the government has decided that there are certain equations that you may not be given in National Curriculum Science examinations.

8 NUMERICAL TECHNIQUES

Your calculator is your greatest friend and may well prove to be your worst enemy! Make sure that you write your 'instructions to the calculator' on your exam paper.

For example, in calculating a value for a fuse to be used with a 2 kW kettle from mains supply:

State   Power = $I \times V$

Show $I = \dfrac{\text{Power}}{V}$

Substitute $I = \dfrac{2000}{240}$

Calculate $I = \underline{8.3 \text{ A}}$ including units

State   Suitable fuse is 13 A

Equally, be aware of problems involving π. Your calculator will show a large number of decimal places in its answer. You need to be aware of the number of significant figures which are *sensible* for a *particular question*. A question giving values to one decimal place only requires an answer to that number of decimal places – and no more.

Be aware of likely errors. You will be under stress in an exam and a slip of the hand can give a very silly answer. Try to *estimate* what a sensible answer will be like. A light bulb would not carry a 60 A current; a person cannot run at 20 m/s and so on. Check your numerical answers by applying common sense.

9 WRITING UP INVESTIGATIONS

All of the assessment schemes award about a quarter of all the marks for work on **practical investigations**. This is to satisfy Sc1 of the National Curriculum and it is marked by your teachers in school. The teachers have a set of standards (attainment targets) and they will decide which of these your work matches best. This gives you a grade in each of the three strands of this target. The details of this are in section 7 of chapter 1. Samples of your work will be sent to a moderator who works for the Examination Board and ensures that all of the work from the different schools is being judged at the same standards. Your work is therefore an important part of the final grade and it is important to present it in the best way that you possibly can. Be neat, clear and accurate and give full details. Don't hand in a piece of work that you could have improved with a little more time!

The following are words that are often used in investigations. Some of them are new or are not used a lot in other parts of the course. Try to understand them so that you can get the best possible marks from your investigation.

“Some important words often used in questions involving investigations”

- **Hypothesis.** This is what you think is going to happen. You should always follow it with carefully thought out reasons why you think it is true.
- **Fair Test.** In this test you have changed ONE variable to check its effect. You will have made sure that everything else is kept the same or compared your test with a 'control'.
- **Variable.** This is something that changes during your experiments. You will observe it carefully and try to make accurate measurements of it.
- **Constant.** This is something that you do *not* allow to change during your experiments.
- **Independent variable.** This is the variable that you choose to change in steps during your experiment, e.g. the weight that you put onto a rubber band that you are stretching.
- **Dependent variable.** This is what changes when you alter the independent variable. You will usually be hoping to find a link between the independent variable and its dependent variable, e.g. the distance that a rubber band stretches when you hang a weight on it.

- **Discrete variable.** This is a variable that can only change in fixed steps, e.g. the colour of a metal container that is absorbing heat.
- **Continuous variable.** This is a variable that you can change as much or as little as you like without fixed steps, e.g. the force pulling on a trolley.
- **Proportional.** If two variables are proportional then doubling one will also double the other and so on, e.g. the extension of a rubber band is proportional to the weight that is hung from it.
- **Inversely proportional.** If two variables are inversely proportional then doubling one of them will halve the other, e.g. the time taken to lift a load is inversely proportional to the power of the motor that is lifting it.

The work is assessed in three stages and the following sections should help you see what an examiner will look for. Following these is a sample investigation that has been used to assess the middle levels of Sc1 called 'Science investigation – Energy'. Different schools will do different investigations but the marking schemes and comments on the example (called 'Cooling Off') is typical of how teachers mark these investigations. The examples in the next sections refer to the Energy investigation that follows them.

Strand (i)

In this section you will be presenting your ideas about what the investigation will show to be correct. Always:

- read the problem carefully, making sure that you know what to test.
- state clearly exactly what you are going to test.
- state your *hypothesis* – predict what you think will happen and give good scientific reasons. This may involve you in doing some revision or some reading about the topic in your library. Let the examiner know that you have thought it through fully and understand the science involved, e.g. *'Larger masses of liquid in the same tanks will cool more slowly. This is because each kilogram of the liquid can release the same quantity of heat energy when it cools by one degree.'*
- Carefully choose the variable that you are going to change. You will get much better grades if you choose one that can be varied continuously and you will be able to plot a graph of your results, e.g. choosing mass is better than choosing to change the material that the tank is made from. You can steadily increase the mass in a series of tests, finding the time taken for a 5°C temperature fall each time. Changing the material that the container is made from is a discrete variable which can only be put on a bar chart.
- try to be as exact as you can in your prediction. It is much better to say *'I think that the time that it takes for a liquid to cool is directly proportional to its mass'* than to say "*more liquid takes longer to cool.*'

Strand (ii)

In this section you will design and then carry out a fair test for your hypothesis.

- make sure that your test is fair. It is important that you only change one variable and then observe what happens. If you change more than one thing at a time you will not know which one causes the effects that you observe. e.g. Change the mass of water each time but always use the same container and start measuring at the same temperature with the same surroundings.
- plan your experiment carefully before you do it. Include details of all the apparatus you will use, e.g. 250 ml beaker, 0–100°C thermometer marked in 1°C intervals, electric balance to read to 1 g accuracy.
- prepare a results table and state what the steps in the independent variable will be. e.g. *'I will do the first test with 100 g of water and then repeat the test with an additional 25 g of water each time'*.
- repeat any results that look obviously wrong and don't fit the pattern of the others.
- repeat the experiment with a new variable. Predict what will happen as before and also try to predict which of the factors that you test will have the largest effect. e.g. A second variable might be the starting temperature for the cooling. You might predict before you do this that it will have a smaller effect that the change in mass did in the first experiment.

- investigate your variables as thoroughly as possible and take your readings with as much accuracy as possible.

NOTE: The predictions and experimental plans should be assessed by your teacher BEFORE you carry out the tests. You may find that you change some things when you actually carry out the experiment. Include these changes in your written work just before the results, e.g. to get more results you might decide to increase the mass of water by 10 g each time instead of 25 g. If you do additional checks such as repeating parts of the experiment then say so and record all the results.

Strand (iii)

In this section you carefully analyse your results and come to reasonable conclusions.

- show all the results clearly by tables and graphs or bar charts.
- discuss any patterns in the results for each experiment and say whether or not they support your hypothesis. e.g. *'My graph of time taken against mass of the water is almost straight and shows that the time taken is directly proportional to the mass which was what I predicted'*.
- say which of your variables had the greater effect and whether you were correct in your prediction.
- go back over your reasoning and whether it was supported by the experiment. Don't be afraid to discuss what you find. Was your experiment a success? Could it be improved? Should you have changed your variable more? Would the results still be the same as your model if the changes were made on a larger scale? (e.g. large tanks of water instead of beakers).

NOTE: Your original prediction does NOT have to be correct to get good grades. As long as your prediction was sensible and based on scientific reasons it will be OK to prove yourself wrong. This does often happen in the real world of industry!

The final page gives you some idea of how a teacher might mark this exercise. Go down each strand until you find the best match for the work that is being marked and the level is at the left hand end of the row.

Try planning this 'Energy' investigation and see for yourself what sort of grade you get.

10 EXAMPLE INVESTIGATION AND MARKING SCHEME

SCIENCE INVESTIGATION: ENERGY – COOLING

THE PROBLEM:

An engineer is designing part of a factory production line in which a row of tanks contains some liquid. The chemists have told her that the liquid must not cool by more than 5°C in each of the tanks. She needs to know how long the liquid can stay in a tank but decides that she doesn't really understand what affects the cooling. She asks you to design some simple experiments to find out what happens.

Plan an experiment to investigate one of the factors that affects how the liquid cools. So that the results from all the experiments can be compared you should find the time taken for the liquid to **cool** by **5°C**.

There are lots of factors that you can investigate but you must be careful and make a **fair test.** Look at your task sheet and choose your variables carefully as some will carry more marks than others. You will need to read and revise conduction, convection and radiation before you make your hypothesis.

Check your idea with your teacher before you do a detailed plan and again before you carry out the experiment.

Make sure that your results and conclusions are clear. If you find that you can improve your experiment when you do it, make sure that you write down the changes.

You will get best marks for a **clear plan** that says **what** you will **measure, how** you will measure it, **when** you will measure it and **lists all the apparatus** that you will need.

CHAPTER 2 **EXAMINATION QUESTIONS** 19

Fig 2.1

POPE PIUS INDUSTRIES

> **The steps you should take**

THE TASK
1. **Read** the problem sheet carefully. Decide on a title.
2. **Make a list** of all the variables that you think will have an effect.
3. Use the headings below to **design an experiment** that will test ONE of the variables that you think will have an effect. Remember that you will need to keep all of the other variables the same so that you make a fair test.
4. **Variable being tested.** Name the variable that you have chosen to test.
5. **Hypothesis.** Write down what you expect to happen. Be as exact as possible, giving a mathematical relationship if you can.
6. **Reason.** Write about why you expect your hypothesis to be true. You will probably need to do some reading or revision to do this well.
7. **Diagram.** Draw a labelled diagram of the apparatus that you are going to use.
8. **Method.** Write about what you are going to do. Remember that you will probably need to do more than one test during your experiment and collect quite a lot of results. Prepare a table to put the results in.

Your method should include answers to the following questions:
    (i)   What are you going to do?
    (ii) What are you going to change and what will the steps be?
    (iii) What else will you measure? How much do you expect it to change?
    (iv) What will you use to do the measuring and when will you do it?
    (v) What will you take care NOT to change?
    (vi) How are you going to record your results?

READ YOUR METHOD CAREFULLY AND MAKE SURE THAT YOU HAVE NOT LEFT ANYTHING OUT.

GET YOUR TEACHER TO CHECK AND MARK YOUR WORK

9. **Do** the experiment and put your **results in the table** that you designed.
   If you change anything in the experiment make sure that you write about it and explain why it was changed.
10. Make your results as clear as possible – graphs are a great help here.
11. Look at your results and write down **conclusions**. Was your hypothesis correct? Why? If it wasn't correct what do you think now?
12. **Repeat** the whole process for a different variable.
13. Which variable did you find had the most effect? Compare the sets of results.

THE MARKING SCHEME
COOLING OFF

AT1 LEVEL	STRAND (i)	STRAND (ii)	STRAND (iii)
3	States at least one testable idea/prediction. e.g. The mass of the liquid affects the time for it to cool.	Measures both variables with appropriate instruments to get a set of results. e.g. Measures time taken (using stopwatch) and mass of water (balance). Note: series of results should be obtained if the variable is continuous.	Simple conclusions based on results obtained (ref. to hypothesis not needed). e.g. When there was more water it took longer to cool.
4	As 3 with simple reason based on everyday knowledge. e.g. If there is less hot water it cools faster like less tea in a cup.	As 3 but ensures that a fair test is carried out and writes down what is controlled. e.g. As 3 and states starting temperature is always same.	Uses table of results or graph to draw conclusions about original hypothesis. e.g. My table of results shows that a bigger mass of water took longer to cool, which was what I predicted.
5	As 3, Prediction based on scientific knowledge (such as on info sheet). e.g. A bigger tank of hot water will cool faster because it has a bigger surface area to radiate the heat to its surroundings.	Carries out fair test as in 4. Chooses a suitable range of values for the independent variable. e.g. As 4 and selects suitable range of masses.	Student offers an alternative explanation of the results. e.g. The results show that a bigger mass of water took longer to cool but it could be caused by more heat trying to escape through the same surface at the top of the beaker.
6	Predicts relationship between two continuous variables. e.g. As 5 and doubling the surface area (independent) will halve the time taken (dependent) for the cooling.	Carries out good fair test with detailed observations and careful control of other factors. More than one other factor must be stated and controlled. e.g. As 5 and states starting temperature, beaker, surrounding temp all constant.	Uses results to obtain a valid relationship between the variables AND refers to the 'model' for an explanation. e.g. The graph shows that the larger mass takes longer to cool. This is because the bigger mass contains more heat energy.

Table 2.1

How you will be assessed

11 FINAL GRADES IN Sc1

Your teacher will set several of these investigations during the course and record your achievements in each strand on each occasion. The best level for each strand will then be sent to the Examination Board to count for the 25% of total marks. These best levels may come from different investigations. Although all the strands may carry a different level you cannot do a part of an investigation and be assessed on one strand alone; e.g.

you cannot do just the planning and be assessed on strand (i) alone – you must carry out the entire investigation.

There is a lot of discussion at the moment about the difficulty of the top levels in Sc1 and the statements may eventually be changed. In the meantime you will not need to get levels 9 and 10 to get your grade A result – but do perform the best that you can!

IN THE EXAMINATION

Make sure that you have *adequate equipment*. You will certainly need a calculator, a ruler, writing materials and, in the multiple choice paper, a pencil and a rubber. You may also need a protractor and a compass.

Read the question paper carefully, and be aware of the way in which examiners phrase their questions:

State – means 'say what you understand by _____'.
Explain – means 'add more information to what has already been said'.
Discuss – means 'we expect quite a lot of information about this topic'.
Show – means 'put down, numerically, how this idea applies to a particular situation'.

Some questions add 'show, using clear diagrams', which means you must *both* write and draw. Check, using past papers, whether you have a clear understanding of *what* the examiner is asking.

Check everything. Make sure that you have answered each question and that you have written exactly what you intended.

A FINAL WORD

Good luck, in your exam and in your studies. Use this book to help you, and use your own notes to amplify the basic information given. Remember that understanding physics is a long-term process and not something which you will be able to "cram" into a short period. Use the book as intended, as a guide through the time of your study and as a help at the time of your exam.

CHAPTER 3

FORCES AND STRUCTURES

TENSION AND COMPRESSION

FRICTION

MASS AND WEIGHT

NORMAL FORCES (OR REACTION FORCES)

FIELDS

VECTORS AND SCALARS

EQUILIBRIUM

MOMENTS

CENTRE OF MASS

FORCE AND ACCELERATION

BEHAVIOUR OF MATERIALS

HOOKE'S LAW

PARALLELOGRAM OF FORCES

TERMINAL VELOCITY

GETTING STARTED

The idea of a *force* is fundamental to physics, and to engineering. The simplest way of thinking of a force is to describe it as a "push" or a "pull", but this is not very satisfactory. We cannot see a force but we can see its *effect* on an object, so we describe forces in terms of what they *do*. Forces tend to cause changes in an object's:

1 Shape or size;
2 Speed in a straight line;
3 Direction.

Forces are measured in newtons (N), using a "force-meter" (sometimes called a "newton-meter").

When several forces act on an object, they can either combine to give an *overall force* – which will change the object's shape or motion – or they could cancel each other out, giving no overall force. In this last case we would say that the forces are "balanced". If there is no force acting, or if all the forces acting on an object are balanced, then there will be no change taking place. An object at rest will remain at rest, and a moving object will continue to move, keeping the same speed and travelling in the same direction.

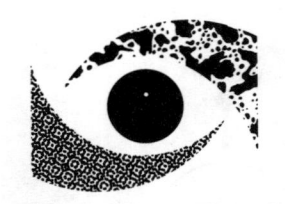

ESSENTIAL PRINCIPLES

1 TENSION AND COMPRESSION

Tension and compression are forces which increase or decrease the dimensions of an object or structure. In Fig. 3.1 an object under *tension* (or stretching force) has been *extended*. Its original length has been *increased*. Under *compression* the original length is *decreased* (Fig. 3.2).

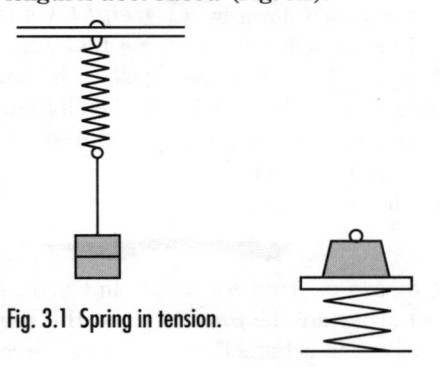

Fig. 3.1 Spring in tension.

Fig. 3.2 Spring in compression.

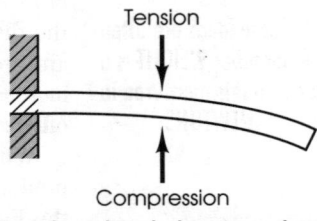

Fig. 3.3 A cantilever shows both tension and compression.

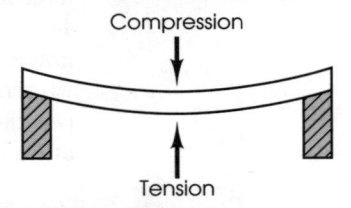

Fig. 3.4 Simple bridge structure.

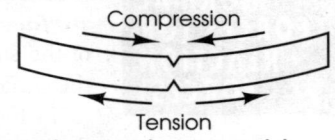

Fig. 3.5 Cracks open under tension and close under compression.

In many situations, both tension and compression exist at the same time. A simple beam or balcony will bend under its own weight (Fig. 3.3). So will a bridge or a simple doorway (Fig. 3.4). Materials such as brick or concrete are *weak under tension* but *strong when compressed*. Cracks form easily when tension is applied, but the cracks close under compression (Fig. 3.5).

Reinforcing concrete makes it stronger and able to resist tension forces. The designing and building of bridges needs a careful consideration of tension and compression forces, and the use of materials in construction which can withstand tension forces.

2 FRICTION

Friction is a force which opposes the movement of an object. It acts in the *opposite* direction to the way the object is being pushed or pulled (Fig. 3.6).

Friction between *solid surfaces* depends on:

1. The type of surface;
2. The size of the normal (or *reaction*) force.

It does *not* depend on:

3. The contact area;
4. The velocity of movement.

The force needed to *just start an object moving* is equal to the *static friction value* for the surfaces. The force needed to *keep an object moving steadily* (with constant velocity) on a surface is equal to the *dynamic friction value* for the surfaces. Static friction is always greater than dynamic friction.

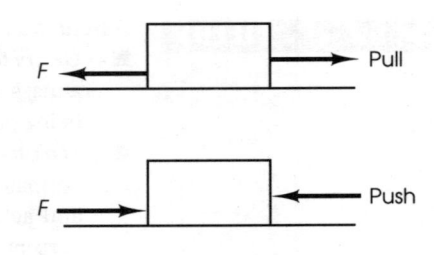

Fig. 3.6 Friction opposes the direction of motion.

Objects moving through liquids or gases (*fluids*) also have friction acting on them. This *fluid friction* does depend on the contact area and the velocity of movement. Fluid friction becomes greater as the object's surface area or its velocity increases. A reduction of surface area, or streamlining, reduces friction in planes or cars, whereas lubrication reduces friction between solid surfaces.

3 MASS AND WEIGHT

❝ These ideas are often confused. Remember WEIGHT is a force so it is measured in NEWTONS. **❞**

The **mass** of an object tells us how much *matter* it contains and is measured in kilograms (kg). **Weight** is a *force* caused by the pull of a planet (Fig. 3.7). All masses exert a *pull* on each other. This is one of the properties of mass. The force gets smaller as the distance between the masses increases, and gets bigger as the size of the masses increases. This effect is called **gravity** and we often refer to the "pull of gravity".

When a planet pulls on a mass the force produced is called **weight**. Near the surface of the Earth, 1 kg of mass is pulled down by a force of approximately 10 N (exactly 9.81 N). The size of the "pull on 1 kg" is called the **gravitational field strength** of a planet and is written as g. For the **Earth** g = 10 newtons per kilogram (10 N/kg). Other planets have other field strengths. These determine the pull on a mass – or in other words, its *weight*. On the **moon** 1 kg weighs 1.6 N, so g = 1.6 N/kg. In **space**, away from a planet's pull, each kilogram has no weight. There is no pull on it from any planet and the mass is now weightless.

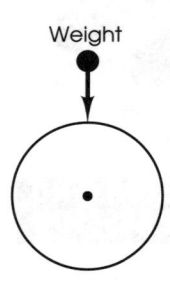

$$\text{weight} = \text{mass} \times g$$

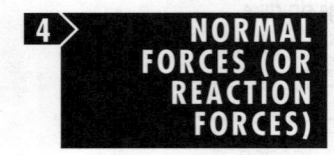

Fig. 3.7 Weight is the pull of a planet on a mass.

4 NORMAL FORCES (OR REACTION FORCES)

Normal forces are forces exerted *by a surface on an object*. They are the *push* of the surface on the object and act at 90° to the surface.

In Fig. 3.8 the *weight* of the object and the *normal force* are *equal and opposite* if the object is *at rest*.

In Fig. 3.9 the object is no longer "at rest". Here the **weight** of the object and the **normal force** are **not** equal and opposite. Unless there is another force acting, such as friction, the object will begin to move. Note that **weight** acts towards the centre of the Earth and the **normal force** acts at 90° to the surface.

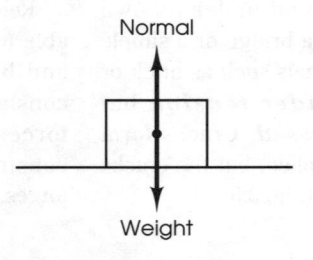

Fig. 3.8 Normal force at 90° to a surface.

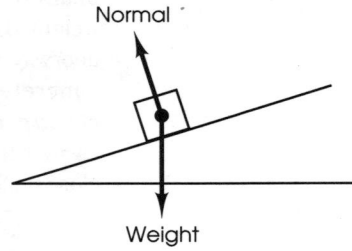

Fig. 3.9

5 FIELDS

A **field** is a region in which a force is felt.
- *Gravitational field.* This is caused by a mass and acts on a mass, e.g. the moon being pulled by the Earth (Fig. 3.10).
- *Magnetic field.* This is caused by a permanent magnet or a current in a wire and acts on another magnet or another current (Fig. 3.11).
- *Electric field.* This is caused by charged objects and acts on charged objects.

In all cases the *strength* of the field *reduces* as the *distance* from the source of the field *increases*. For example, a particular object on the Earth *weighs less* up a mountain than it does at sea level; it also weighs less at the Equator than it does at the North Pole. This is because the Earth "bulges out" at the Equator and is flattened at the poles.

The strength and direction of each sort of field can be represented by *field lines*. These are rather like contour lines on maps.

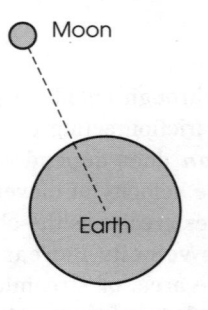

Fig. 3.10 Gravitational field of the Earth extends to the moon.

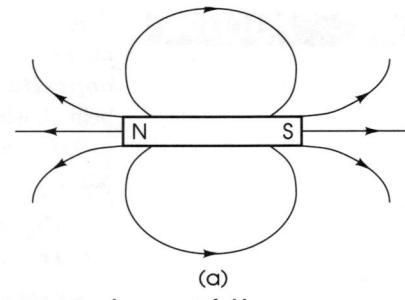

Fig. 3.11(a) Simple magnetic field;

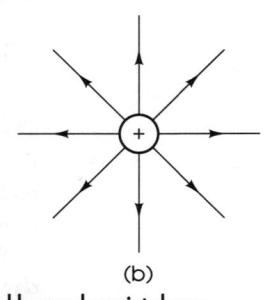

(b) electric field around a point charge.

6 VECTORS AND SCALARS

Forces are *vector* quantities. They have direction *as well as* size. Quantities which *only* have size and where direction is not important (e.g. temperature, mass, volume) are called *scalars*. Force directions need care. It is important to sort out what object the force is *acting upon*. In Fig. 3.12 the forces acting on the *picture* are its weight (*W*) and the tensions (*T*) in the strings. Figure 3.13 shows the forces acting on the *hook* from which the picture is hung.

The effect of *more than one* force acting on an object depends on the *force directions*. In Fig. 3.14 these forces have the same effect on the object as a single 7 N force acting to the right. In Fig. 3.15 the two forces have the same effect as a 1 N force acting to the left. The *single force* which can *replace several forces* on an object, and still have the *same effect*, is called the **resultant force**.

❝ Remember to choose a large but easy scale like 5 cm = 1 Newton, and to STATE the scale in your answer. ❞

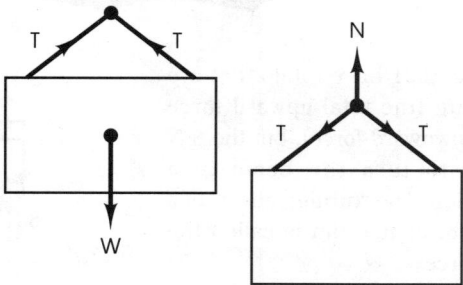

Fig. 3.12 Forces acting on the picture.

Fig. 3.13 Forces acting on the hook.

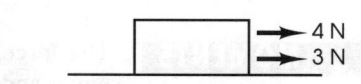

Fig. 3.14 Resultant 7 N to the right.

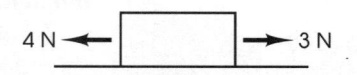

Fig. 3.15 Resultant 1 N to the left.

7 EQUILIBRIUM

If an object remains at rest, although acted on by several forces, it is in *equilibrium*. The resultant force acting on the object is zero. The two forces in Fig. 3.16 have a resultant *R*. The body would be in equilibrium if a third force equal to *R*, but in the *opposite direction*, was also acting.

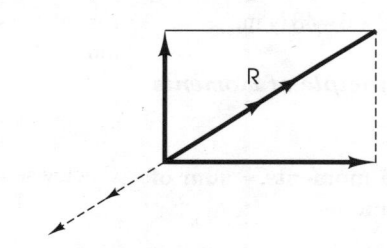

Fig. 3.16 Condition for equilibrium.

A diagram such as Fig. 3.17 is called a *space diagram*. If forces act to produce equilibrium then a scale diagram of them, taken in order, will form a *closed figure*. This is the case in Fig. 3.18. The force between two surfaces is the **contact force** between two solids. It is the *resultant* of the *normal force* and the *friction force* (Fig. 3.19).

If the forces are **coplanar** (acting in the same plane) there are two requirements for equilibrium. One is that the forces must obey the **Principle of Moments** (see next section) and secondly the resultant of all the forces in any direction must be zero. The commonest case of this last requirement is when the forces are parallel. The total of the forces in one direction is then equal and opposite to the total in the opposite direction. Fig. 3.20 shows a bridge where the forces are the **weight W** acting downwards and the two **normal reaction forces N_1 and N_2** acting upwards. Clearly

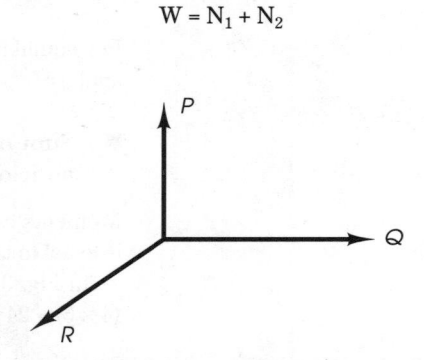

$$W = N_1 + N_2$$

Fig. 3.17 Space diagram for three forces in equilibrium.

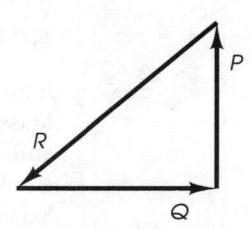

Fig. 3.18 Force diagram for three forces in equilibrium.

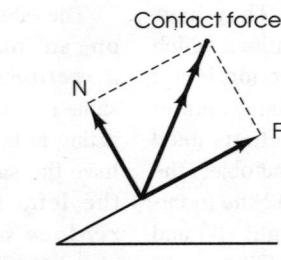

Fig. 3.19

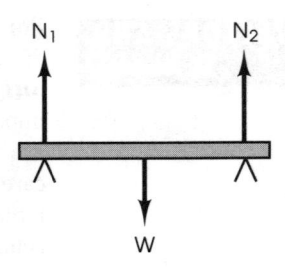

Fig. 3.20 Coplanar forces in equilibrium.

8 > MOMENTS

The forces in Fig. 3.21 have totals that are equal and opposite (the total upward force equals the total downward force), but the 8 N force will tend to turn the beam in a *clockwise* direction. The "turning effect" of a force about a pivot or fulcrum is called the *moment* of the force.

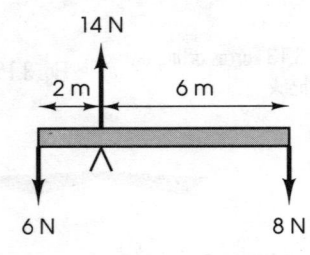

Fig. 3.21

66 Be careful with distance measurements. The distance is FROM the force TO the pivot 99

- **Moment = Force × Distance at 90° from the line of the force to the pivot.** Moments are measured in newton metres (N m) or newton centimetres (N cm). The moment of the 8 N force in Fig. 3.21 would be 8 × 6 = 48 N m.

For equilibrium, the *principle of moments* applies:

- **Sum of clockwise moments = sum of anticlockwise moments.**

Moments can be taken about any point, but it is usual to take them about the *pivot*.

In Fig. 3.22 the moment of the 4N force is (4 × 6) = 24 Nm (clockwise) and that of the 8N

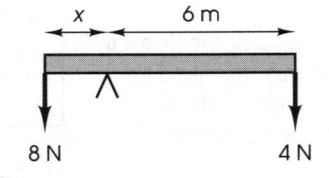

Fig. 3.22

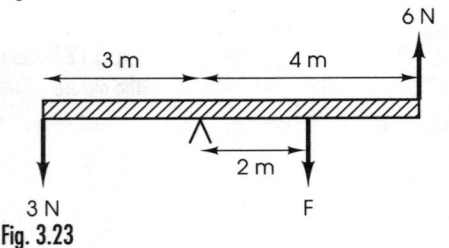

Fig. 3.23

force is 8 × x) = 8x Nm (anticlockwise).
For equilibrium

$$24 \text{ Nm} = 8x$$
$$3 \text{ m} = x$$

Without force F, both the 6 N and the 3 N forces have an anticlockwise moment about the pivot (Fig. 3.23). To obtain equilibrium, force F is needed. Total anticlockwise moment about the pivot

$$= (6 \times 4) + (3 \times 3)$$
$$= 33 \text{ N m}$$

Clockwise moment $= (2 \times F)$
$$2F = 33 \text{ N m}$$
$$F = 16.5 \text{ N}$$

Remember that the distance to be used is measured from the force to the pivot in each case.

VERIFYING THE PRINCIPLE OF MOMENTS

A metre rule is balanced on a pivot (fulcrum). Masses are hung from thin strings as shown, and their positions adjusted to achieve equilibrium, with the metre rule horizontal. Repeat for several values (Fig. 3.24).

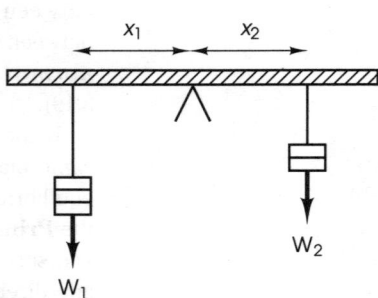

Fig. 3.24

MEASUREMENTS

Weight added to each side
(100 g weighs 1 N) = W_1 and W_2
Record W_1 and W_2
Distance from each weight to the pivot
= x_1 and x_2

TREATMENT OF RESULTS

Tabulate as shown (Fig. 3.25) recording W_1, x_1, W_2 and x_2. Calculate the clockwise and anticlockwise moments.

PRECAUTIONS

Ensure that the metre rule is initially balanced horizontally, and that it is horizontal when all other readings are taken.

Anticlockwise		
W_1(N)	x_1(cm)	Moment

Clockwise		
W_2(N)	x_2(cm)	Moment

Fig. 3.25

9 > CENTRE OF MASS

The mass of an object acts as if it is concentrated at a single point called the **centre of mass**. The object will also behave as though all its weight acts at the same place which is therefore also called the **centre of gravity** in some cases. For a regular object the *centre of mass* is the same as the *geometric centre* (Fig. 3.26).

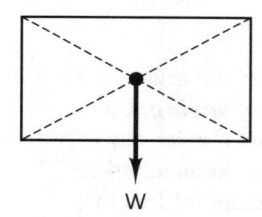

Fig. 3.26 Centre of mass.

The centre of mass of an object need **not** lie on the object. For a ring it is the centre of the ring – so the centre of mass is in space (Fig. 3.27).

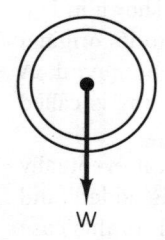

Fig. 3.27 Centre of mass.

For an object to be in *equilibrium* and to be *stable* the weight, acting vertically from the centre of mass, must pass through the *base* of the object (Fig. 3.28). So to design a *stable* object, it should have a *low centre of mass* and have a *large base area*. Double-

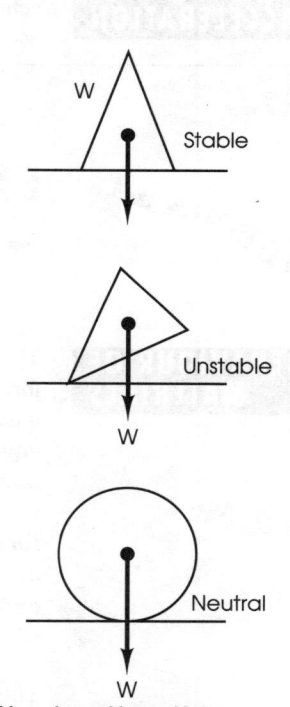

Fig. 3.28 Stable and unstable equilibrium.

decker buses are very stable – the heavy parts, such as the engine, are on the lower level. However, people are asked not to stand upstairs, because the raised centre of mass would make the bus less stable.

The first cone in Fig. 3.28 is stable because a small displacement to one side produces a moment that tips it back onto its base.

The second cone is unstable when balanced on its point because a slight push to one side produces a moment that topples it over. The third part of Fig. 3.28 shows a ball that is in the same state after a small push as it was before, so its equilibrium is neutral.

CENTRE OF MASS OF A PLANE LAMINA

A lamina is a thin shape – usually a piece of card. Drill holes in it and suspend it from a pin held in a clamp (Fig. 3.29).

Connect a plum-line to the pin. Draw a line on the card showing the position of the plumb-line. The centre of mass lies along this line. Repeat with the card suspended from Y then Z. The centre of mass is the *intersection* of the three lines.

PRECAUTIONS

Make sure that the lamina is freely suspended. In drawing the lines mark two points behind the plumb-line carefully and join them after removing the lamina from the pin.

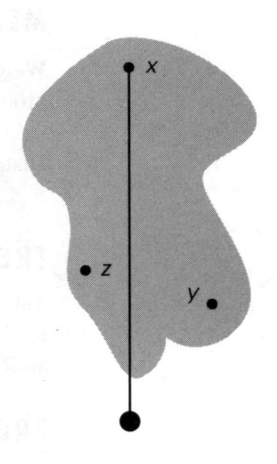

Fig. 3.29

10> FORCE AND ACCELERATION

This is dealt with fully in the chapter on motion. However, remember that if a resultant force acts on a mass, it causes it to accelerate:

Force = Mass × acceleration

EXTENSION MATERIALS

11> BEHAVIOUR OF MATERIALS

The simplest behaviour under the action of a force is perhaps that of a *steel spring*. Up to a point the spring extends in a regular way as equal forces are added to it. Remembering that *extension* means "change of length", this can be written as *equal increases in force gives equal changes of extension* or as *force (F) is proportional to extension (x)*, i.e. mathematically:

$$F \propto x$$

The graph for this behaviour is shown in Fig. 3.30. The spring would return to its original length when the forces are removed. A material which behaves in this way is called an *elastic material*.

However good the spring is, it eventually "gives" when too much force is added, and becomes permanently stretched. In this case it no longer returns to its original length. The graph now becomes like that in Fig. 3.31. Point E on the graph is the point where the force and extension *stop* going "hand in hand", i.e. where they are no longer proportional. This is called the *limit of proportionality* or the *elastic limit*. Up *to this point* the spring's behaviour is described by Hooke's law: *"Force is proportional to extension"* (provided the elastic limit is not reached).

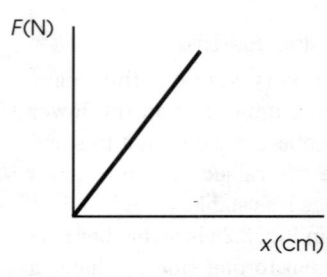

Fig. 3.30 Force-extension graph for a spring

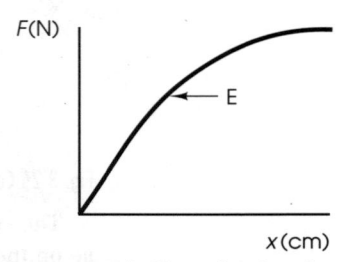

Fig. 3.31 Spring stretched beyond its elastic limit.

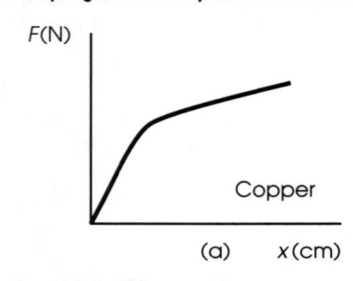

Fig. 3.32(a) Elastic behaviour of copper;

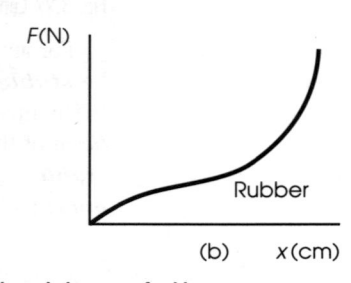

(b) Elastic behaviour of rubber.

Many materials follow Hooke's law to some extent. Two *extremes* of behaviour are shown by copper wire and a rubber band (Fig. 3.32). **Copper** suddenly gets easier to stretch and begins to flow (***plastic yielding***) until it breaks. **Rubber** gets harder and harder to stretch and finally snaps (***brittle fracture***) when it breaks.

The size of force to give a particular extension depends on the ***dimensions*** of the material (Fig. 3.33). A ***large area*** of cross-section gives a ***small extension*** for a ***particular force*** (F). Again longer samples extend more than short samples for a fixed force. However, the ratios

$$\frac{\text{Force}}{\text{Area}} = \text{Stress}$$

and

$$\frac{\text{Extension}}{\text{Original length}} = \text{Strain}$$

would be the same for *all* samples at their breaking points.

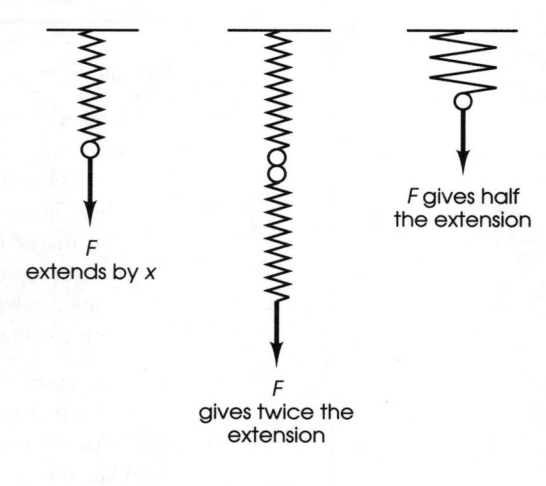

F extends by x

F gives twice the extension

F gives half the extension

Fig. 3.33

12 HOOKE'S LAW

A steel spring is hung from a retort stand (Fig. 3.34). A ruler is clamped vertically near the spring. Weights are added to the spring to extend it.

MEASUREMENTS

Original length of spring = L
Weight added (100 g mass weighs 1 N) = W
New length of spring = l

TREATMENT OF RESULTS

Record weight added W
Record extension $x = (l - L)$

GRAPH

Plot W (horizontally) against x (vertically) (Fig. 3.35).

PRECAUTIONS

Make sure the ruler is vertical. Measure l using the same points on the spring each time. Eliminate parallax errors by keeping the eye level with the spring when taking measurements.

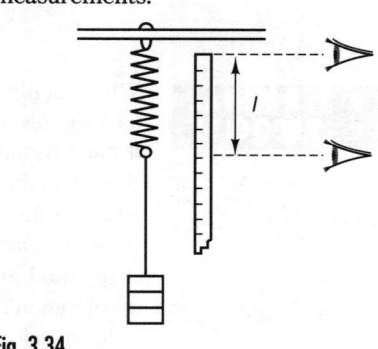

Fig. 3.34

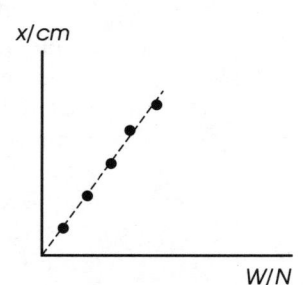

Fig. 3.35

13 THE PARALLELOGRAM OF FORCES

This is a method of adding vectors that are not in the same direction. To add together **vectors** you must add their directions as well as their sizes. This is usually done by using the parallelogram of vectors. It will probably help to think of + as meaning "followed by". Draw a scale diagram as follows:-

(i) Choose a suitable scale for the vectors and draw one of them v_1 as a line of the correct length. At its end draw the second vector v_2, also to its correct scale length and at the correct angle to the first one.

(ii) The line from the start of the first vector to the end of the second vector now represents the answer that you need (in both size and direction) and is called the **resultant** R.

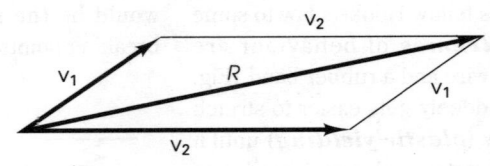

Fig. 3.36

(iii) You will make sure that your answer is correct if you "complete the parallelogram" by repeating the first two steps but use the second vector first. As the order of adding vectors does not matter, you should end at exactly the same place and therefore have a check on your resultant.

In some cases, especially the ones where the vectors are at 90°, it may be easier and more exact to draw a sketch diagram and then calculate the answer.

EXAMPLE

A boat is following a compass bearing of 090° at 8 knots but is also in a current moving north at 6 knots. What is its true speed and direction?

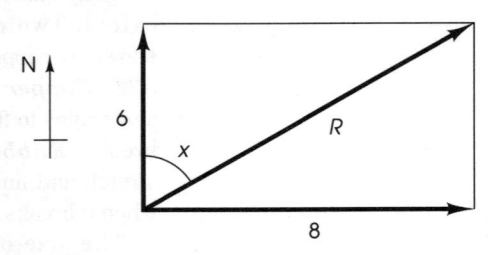

Fig. 3.37

You can check the following answer by doing a scale drawing with a scale of 20 mm = 1 knot. Remember that this is NOT a graph and you must use the same scale in all directions.

Using Pythagoras' rule

$$R^2 = 6^2 + 8^2$$
$$R^2 = 36 + 64 = 100$$
$$R = 10 \text{ knots}$$

also $\tan x = \frac{8}{6} = 1.333$

$$x = 53.1°$$

So the boat is actually moving at 10 knots on a bearing of 053.1°

14. TERMINAL VELOCITY

When an object falls in a gas or a liquid (such as a sky diver in air or a marble in a jar of oil) it has two forces acting on it. It is accelerated downwards by weight and slowed by the **drag** of the fluid through which it is passing. As it falls faster the drag force increases until it is equal and opposite to the weight. The acceleration then stops and the object falls at a uniform velocity called **terminal velocity**.

A sky diver can change the terminal velocity by altering his/her shape and therefore the air resistance but may still have a terminal velocity of 55 m/s! A parachute will produce a greater air resistance and therefore the equilibrium between the forces is achieved at a lower terminal velocity.

When a marble falls through a liquid it will accelerate at first and then fall at its terminal velocity. You can measure the terminal velocity by timing the fall over a known distance as shown in the diagram. Make sure that you only time a section *after* the acceleration has stopped. The experiment will show that the terminal velocity depends on the radius of the marble that is dropped, the viscosity of the liquid and the weight of the

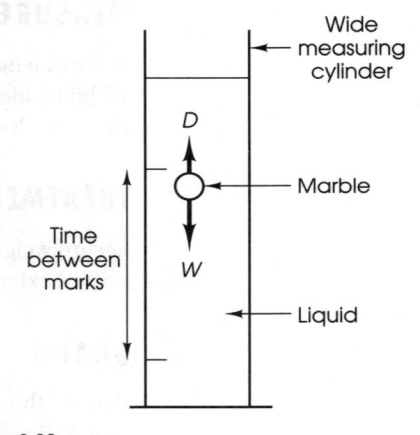

Fig. 3.38

marble. The viscosity is a measure of the "stiffness" of the liquid. A liquid with a bigger viscosity will flow more slowly (like treacle). The terminal velocity in water is sometimes high and oil or glycerol will give better results with ball bearings. Results may be improved if you coat the ball in some of the liquid before it is dropped to avoid air bubbles which cause errors. A longer glass tube will also improve the results.

EXAMINATION QUESTIONS

MULTIPLE CHOICE QUESTIONS

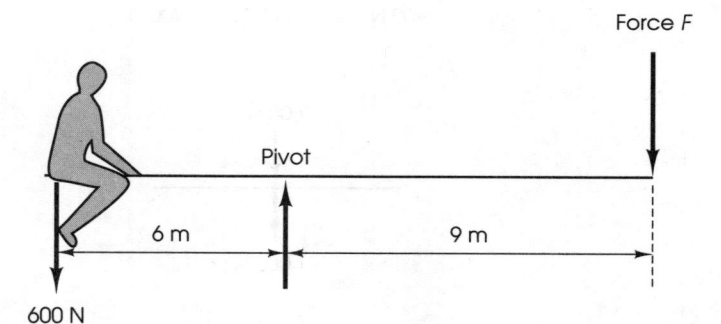

Fig. 3.40

QUESTION 1

Three similar elastic bands are tied as shown (Fig. 3.39). One end is fixed and the other end is pulled. Which one of the following describes the new lengths of the bands?

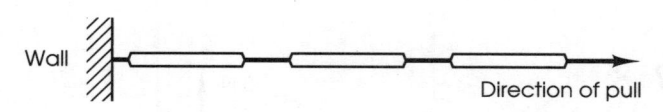

Fig. 3.39

- A Their lengths are all equal.
- B The band nearest the wall is stretched most.
- C The middle band stretches more than the other two.
- D The band nearest the wall stretches twice as much as the other two.
- E Only the band furthest from the wall stretches.

QUESTION 2

The force of gravity on a body is a *vector* quantity because it

- A Has size and direction
- B Acts in a vertical direction
- C Is a force of attraction
- D Has a direction but no size   (SEG)

QUESTION 3

A steel spring obeys Hooke's law. A force of 8 N extends the spring by 40 mm. A force of 10 N will extend the spring by

- A 10 mm   C 50 mm
- B 20 mm   D 90 mm   (SEG)

QUESTION 4

A boy, weighing 600 N, sits 6 m away from the pivot of a balanced see-saw, as shown (Fig. 3.40). What force F, 9 m from the pivot, is needed to balance the see-saw?

- A 300 N   D 600 N
- B 400 N   E 900 N
- C 450 N   (ULEAC)

QUESTION 5

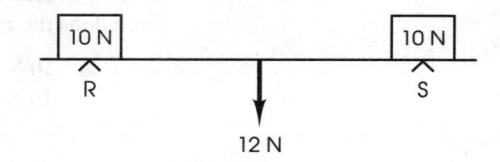

Fig. 3.41

Figure 3.41 shows two 10 N weights resting on a board of weight 12 N supported at R and S. The total upward force acting on the board is

- A 10 N   C 20 N
- B 16 N   D 32 N   (SEG)

QUESTION 6

The diagram (Fig. 3.42) shows a man of weight 800 N standing in the middle of a uniform, rigid, horizontal plank. The plank weighs 1000 N. Which of the diagrams in Fig. 3.43 shows the forces on the plank?

(ULEAC)

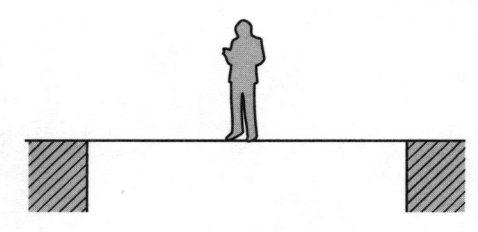

Fig. 3.42

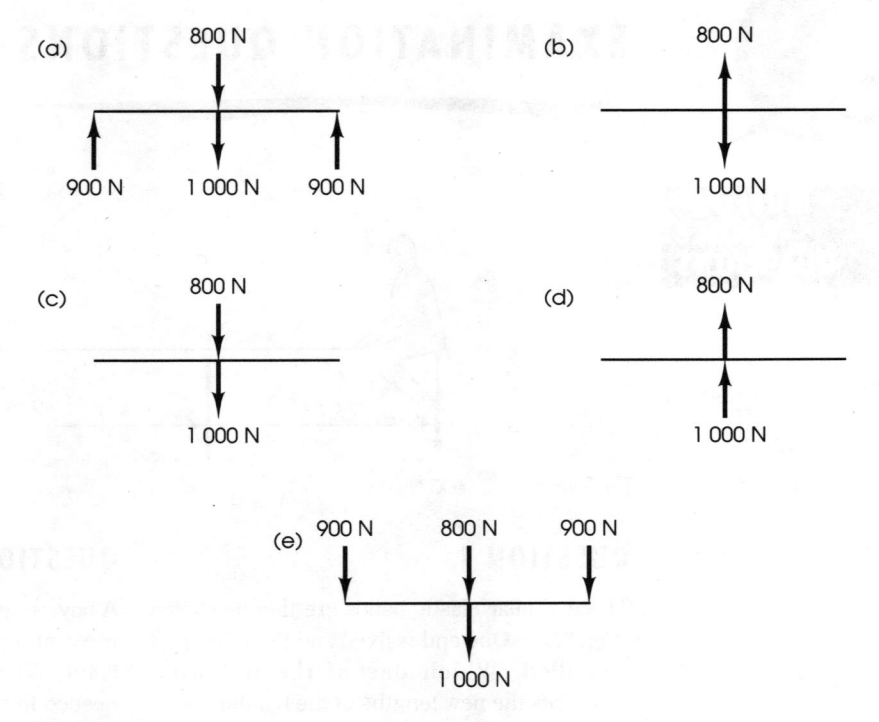

Fig. 3.43

QUESTION 7

As it nears the moon's surface, a lunar probe of mass 10 000 kg is accelerated by the moon's gravitational field at 1.5 m/s². What force does the moon exert on the probe?

    A 10 N   C 1000 N
    B 15 N   D 15 000 N

(SEG)

QUESTION 8

A force of 3 N and a force of 4 N act at right angles to each other at a point (Fig. 3.44). The magnitude of the resultant of the two forces will be

    A 3 N   D 7 N
    B 4 N   E 12 N
    C 5 N

(ULEAC)

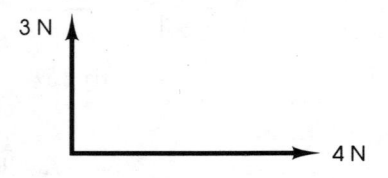

Fig. 3.44

QUESTION 9

Which of the following is not a force?

    A Tension   C Weight
    B Mass   D Friction

QUESTION 10

Figure 3.45 shows designs for a double-decker bus. The symbol ⊘ represents the centre of mass. Which design will be the most stable?

(ULEAC)

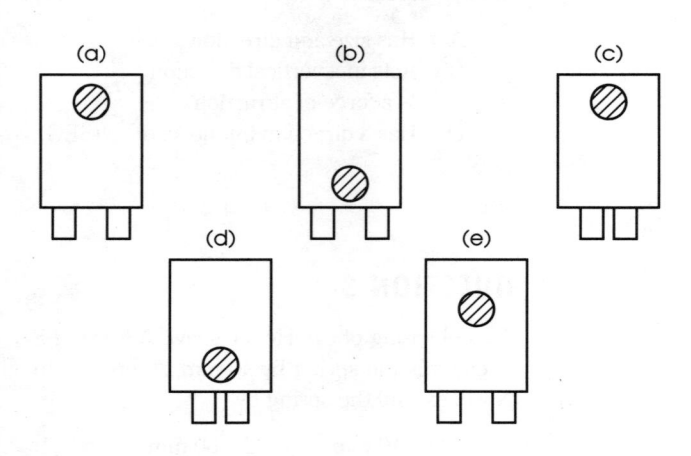

Fig. 3.45

STRUCTURED QUESTIONS

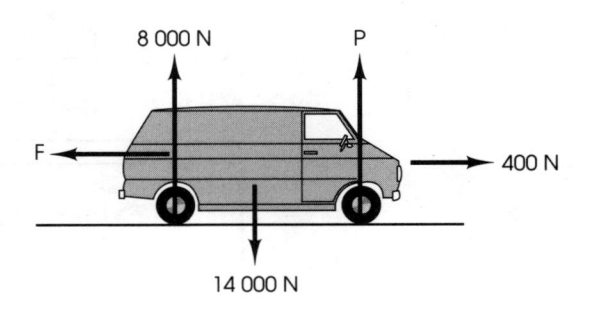

Fig. 3.46

QUESTION 11

A front-wheel-drive car is driven at constant velocity. The forces acting on the car are shown in the diagram (Fig. 3.46). *F* is the push of the air on the car, and *P* is the total upward force on both front wheels.

(i) Name the 400 N force to the right.
(ii) Taking the weight of 1 kg to be 10 N, calculate the mass of the car.
(iii) The 400 N force to the right is suddenly doubled.
 (1) At the instant this happens, what is now the net (i.e. resultant) force moving the car forward?
 (2) Explain how this causes the car to accelerate.
 (3) Calculate this acceleration.

(ULEAC)

QUESTION 12

An experiment is carried out to see how a steel spring stretches with the load applied. The readings are given in Table 3.1.

Table 3.1

Load (N)	Extension (mm)
1.0	1.3
2.0	2.7
2.5	3.3
3.0	4.0
3.5	4.7
4.0	5.3
5.0	7.0
6.0	8.0
8.0	10.7

(a) On graph paper, plot a graph with extension on the vertical axis and the load on the horizontal axis. Use the points you have plotted to draw what you think is a suitable line to show how the spring behaves when it is stretched.

(b) What does the gradient of the graph tell you about the spring?

(ULEAC)

QUESTION 13

This question is about stretching a spiral spring. A loaded spring is mounted vertically as shown in Fig. 3.47; *h* is the height of the bottom of the load above the bench.

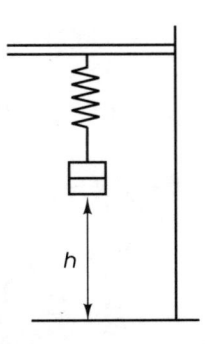

Fig. 3.47

(a) Describe how you would use a metre rule to measure *h*. Include the precautions you would take to make your results as reliable as possible.

(b) A student measures values of *h* for several values of load. The results are shown in Table 3.2.

Table 3.2

Load (N)	Height h (mm)
1	184
2	172
3	162
4	150
5	141

(i) Plot a graph of *h* (*y*-axis) against load (*x*-axis).
(ii) Draw the best straight line.
(iii) Use your graph to find the load which gives a value of *h* of 180 mm.
(iv) Use your graph to find the value of *h* at a load of 1.50 N.
(v) Use your graph to find the change of load which gives a change in *h* of 1.00 mm.

(SEG)

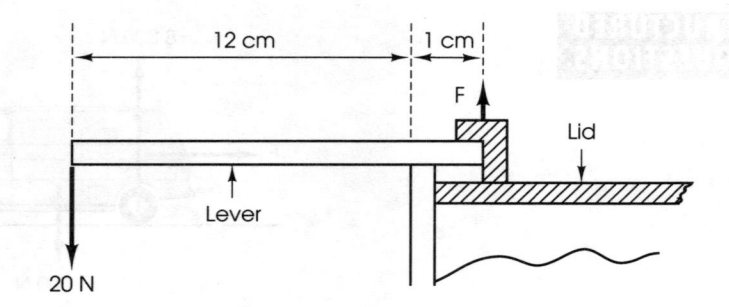

Fig. 3.48

QUESTION 14

Figure 3.48 shows a lever being used to lift a lid from a paint can.
(a) State the principle of moments.
(b) Use the principle of moments to help you calculate the force F exerted by the lever on the lid. Show your working clearly.
(c) What are the size and direction of the force exerted by the lever on the pivot?
(d) State two changes which could be made to increase the size of the force F if it proved to be too small to lift the lid.

(SEG)

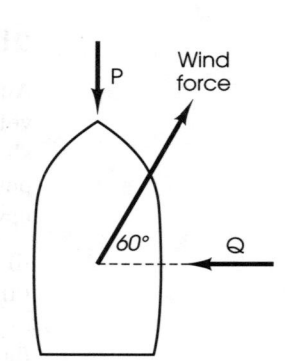

Fig. 3.49

QUESTION 15

(a) (i) State the difference between a vector quantity and a scalar quantity.
 (ii) Name two vector quantities.
 (iii) Name two scalar quantities.
(b) Explain in simple language the difference between adding two vector quantities and adding two scalar quantities.
(c) A sailing boat is steered due north through the water at a steady speed. The force exerted on the boat by the wind has a magnitude of 1200 N in a direction 60 north of east. This force is balanced by two frictional forces, force P opposing the forward motion of the boat and force Q opposing the sideways motion of the boat (Fig. 3.49). Find by scale drawing or calculation the magnitudes of forces P and Q.

(d) Suggest why the resistance of the water to the motion of the boat in a forward direction is likely to be much smaller than the resistance to motion in a sideways direction. The diagrams showing the shape of the boat (Fig. 3.50) may help you in your explanation.

(SEG)

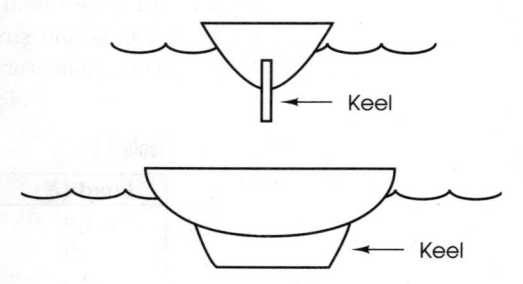

Fig. 3.50

OUTLINE ANSWERS

MULTIPLE CHOICE QUESTIONS

Question	1	2	3	4	5	6	7	8	9	10
Answer	A	A	C	B	D	A	D	C	B	B

STRUCTURED QUESTIONS

ANSWER 11

(i) The force to the right is the force provided by the engine of the car. It would be named the "tractive force" or "force due to the engine".

(ii) Weight of car = 1400 N. If 1 kg weights 10 N,

$$\text{Mass of car} = \frac{14000}{10} = 1400 \text{ kg}$$

(iii) (1) For the car to move with constant velocity, there is no resultant forward force.

$$F = 400 \text{ N}$$

At the *instant* the tractive force is doubled, F is still 400 N.
Resultant forward force =
(800 − 400) = 400 N.

(2) There is now a resultant force. Since $F = ma$, the car will accelerate.

(3) $F = ma$, therefore

$$a = \frac{F}{m} = \frac{400}{1400} = 0.286 \text{ m/s}^2$$

ANSWER 12

The important point here is to draw the best straight line through the points, i.e. to show the "pattern" of the experimental values. The slope shows how "stiff" the spring is. A large slope is a weak spring – one which extends a lot for a small force applied. A strong spring would give a small slope – a lot of force would be needed to stretch the spring by a small amount.

ANSWER 13

Graph drawing is important as stated above.
(a) **Precautions**: (1) Rule placed vertically; (2) zero of rule on bench; (3) position of load read without parallax and read at bottom of load.
(b) (iii) 1.1–1.5 N
    (iv) 176–179 mm.
    (v) 0.09–0.095 N

ANSWER 14

(a) For equilibrium,

Sum of clockwise moments =
    Sum of anticlockwise moments
    about any point

(b) Moments taken about edge of tin:

Clockwise = (F × 1) N cm
Anticlockwise = (20 × 12) N cm
20 × 12 = F × 1
F = 240 N

(c) 220 N vertically downwards.
(d) (1) Increase force 20 N; (2) use longer lever.

ANSWER 15

(a) (i) Vector – described by magnitude and direction; scalar – magnitude only.
(ii) Examples of *vectors* – force, velocity, displacement, momentum, etc.
(iii) Examples of *scalars* – mass, volume, temperature, distance, speed, etc.

(b) Scalar addition – add numbers – no direction needed; vector addition – add direction numbers or use scale diagrams.

(c) Scale diagram needed (Fig. 3.51).

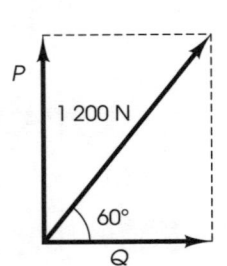

P = 570–630 N
Q = 1000–1100 N

Fig. 3.51

(d) The forward direction is streamlined, but not the sideways direction. There is a bigger area sideways so more water to push.

TUTOR'S QUESTION AND ANSWER

1› QUESTION

Theory suggests that, when a beam is loaded at the centre, the deflection x is directly proportional to the cube of l, the distance between the supports, provided that the same force W is applied for each value of l (Fig. 3.52). In other words, $x = kl^3$ where k is constant.

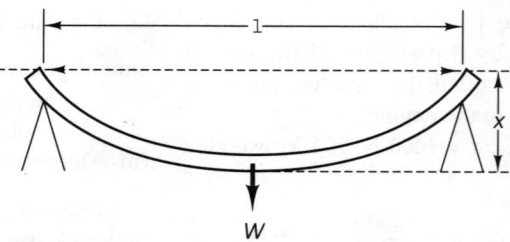

Fig. 3.52

You are required to carry out an experiment to confirm that $x = kl^3$ using a metre rule as a beam. From initial checks you know that when a metre rule rests on edge supports 0.90 m apart, its centre is deflected by about 1 cm when a load of 8 N is hung from the centre. Describe:

(a) How you would set up the apparatus.
(b) How you would make your measurements.
(c) The number and range of measurements you would make.
(d) How you would use your measurements to test the theory.

2› ANSWER

(a) Lay the metre rule on movable supports. Load with 8 N (800 g mass) at the centre of supports. Make sure the unloaded rule is horizontal. Measure distance using a vertical rule, eye level with the lower side of the "beam" each time.

(b) Change l by moving the supports and measure the distance between the top sides of the pivots. Eye above the beam and directly over the edges of the pivots.

(c) Since a graph must be drawn, at least five sets of values of l must be made. Repeat each set and take a mean value if necessary. Vary l between about 0.5 and 0.9 m.

(d) There are several possibilities:

(i) Check numbers from tabulated results. If $x = kl^3$, then doubling l would give 2^3 times the value of x, i.e. 8 times the value of x.

(ii) Plot a graph. If $x = kl^3$, a graph of x against l^3 will give a straight line. Presumably there will be a degree of experimental error so if there appears to be such a pattern, then $x = kl^3$.

STUDENT'S ANSWER WITH THE EXAMINER'S COMMENTS

STUDENT ANSWER TO QUESTION 12

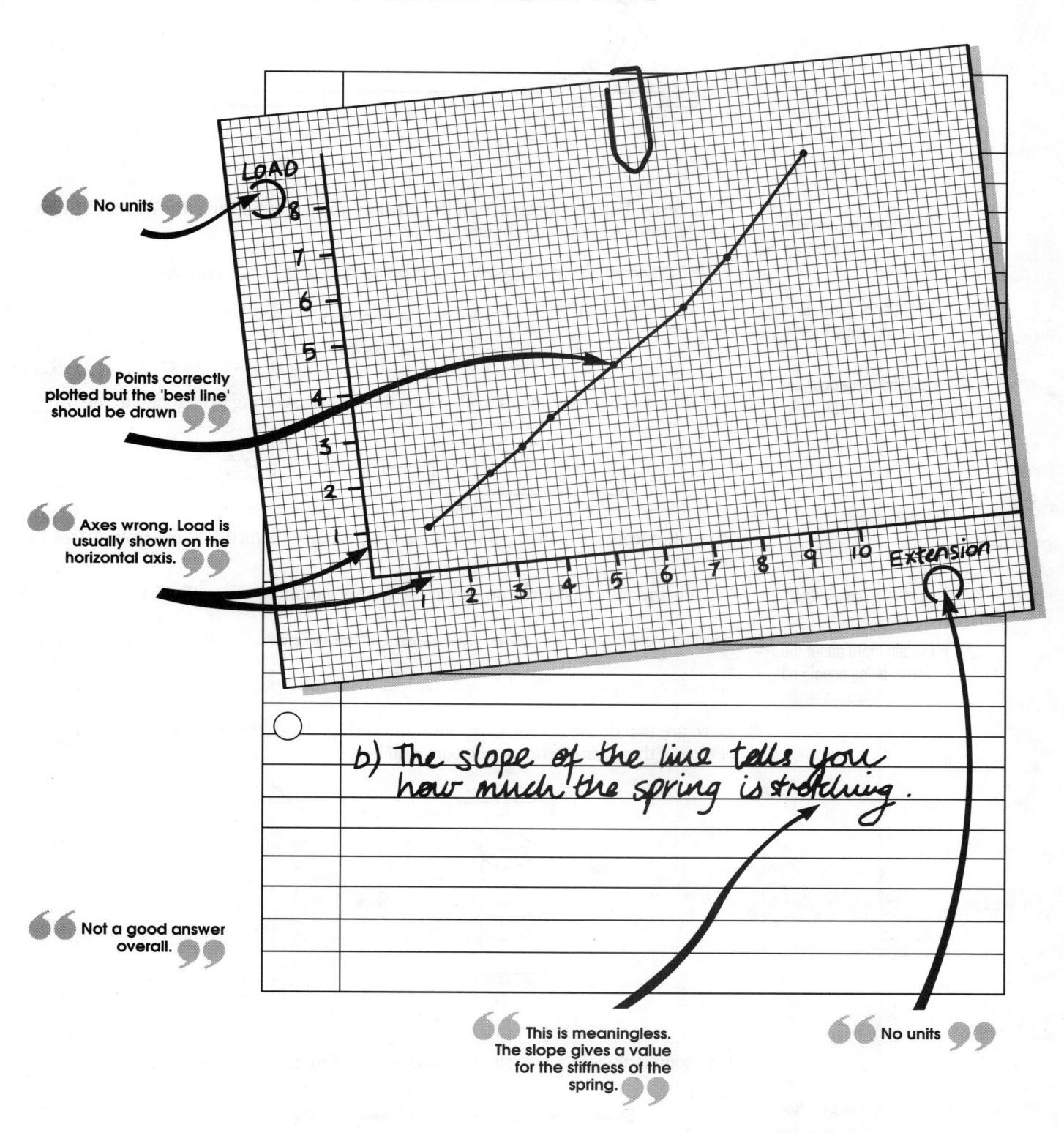

"No units"

"Points correctly plotted but the 'best line' should be drawn"

"Axes wrong. Load is usually shown on the horizontal axis."

b) The slope of the line tells you how much the spring is stretching.

"Not a good answer overall."

"This is meaningless. The slope gives a value for the stiffness of the spring."

"No units"

MORE EXAMINER'S COMMENTS FOUNDATION AND CENTRAL TIER

1. A girl weighing 600 N sits 2 metres away from the pivot of a uniform see-saw. The see-saw is pivoted at its centre of mass.

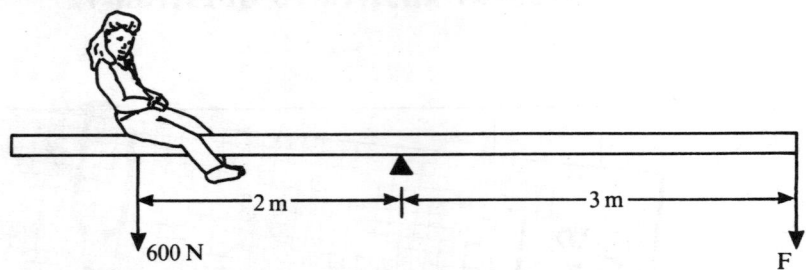

   What force, F, three metres from the pivot, is needed to balance the see-saw? Show clearly how you get your answer.

   ❝ Say that moment = Fd ❞

   ❝ Using 'Principle of Moments'? ❞

   Moment of girl = 600 × 2 = 1200
   F × 3 = 1200
   F = 400

   ❝ Could be more clear but probably gets 2 marks ❞

   Force F = ...400..... N (2)

2. The diagram below shows a trolley on a flat bench. A string is attached to the trolley and to a spring balance as shown.

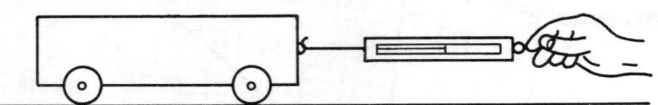

   When the trolley is pulled, so that the spring balance reads 0.5 N, the trolley does not move.

   ❝ 1 mark ❞

   What is the frictional force opposing the trolley's motion? ......0.5 N..........

   Explain your answer ...The forces balance..............

   ❝ Explain more about the forces being equal and opposite ❞

   ....(2)

3. Here are two diagrams showing the same spring. In each case when the load is removed the spring returns to its original length.

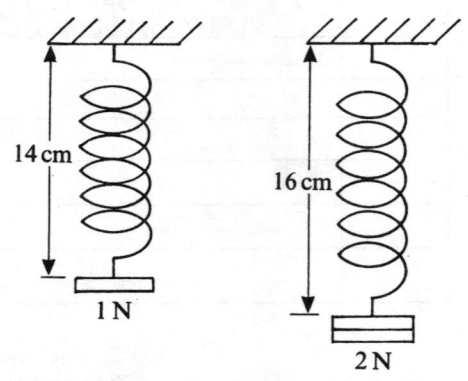

   How long is the spring when no load is attached to it?

   2N = 16   1N = 14
   So 1 extra N = 2cm
   So it starts at 12

   ❝ Probably 2 marks. Not very clear but does give the correct answer. Don't be afraid to use words ❞

   Length = ...12........ cm
   (2)

REVIEW SHEET

- The side of a beam that is under tension is _____ .

- Forces can change objects in three different ways. These are

    1. _____ .
    2. _____ .
    3. _____ .

- The force needed just to start an object moving is equal and opposite to the force called _____ .

- The force needed just to keep the object moving is less than the force to start it moving and is called _____ .

- When an object rests on a surface a force is produced that acts at _____ to the surface and is called a _____ .

- The three main types of Field are _____ , _____ and _____ .

- A vector is a quantity that has both _____ and _____ .

- The turning effect of a force about a pivot is called its _____ .

- A stable racing car will have a _____ centre of mass.

- The total of two forces is called their _____ .

- Two vectors can be added by using a scale diagram called the _____ __ _____ .

- Springs obey _____ law when they stretch until they reach the _____ .

- A girl pulls on a door handle with a force of 20 N. If the door is 1.2 m wide the moment of the force is _____ .

- Two boys push a box in opposite directions with forces of 100 N and 250 N. The size of the resultant is _____ .

- A teacher has a weight of 700 N. When he stands still the force of the floor on him is _____ .

- Complete the following equation

    weight = _____ .

- If your teacher weighs 600 N her mass is _____ kg.

- The gravitational force between two objects depends directly on their _____ and inversely on _____ .

- When a falling object reaches terminal velocity its weight is equal and opposite to the _____ .

- A quantity with size but no direction is a _____ .

- A 10 N force stretches spring by 4 cm. A 5 N force will stretch the same spring by _____ cm.

- The point where the extension of a stretched wire stops being proportional to the load on it is called _____.

- The force F that will balance the beam is _____.

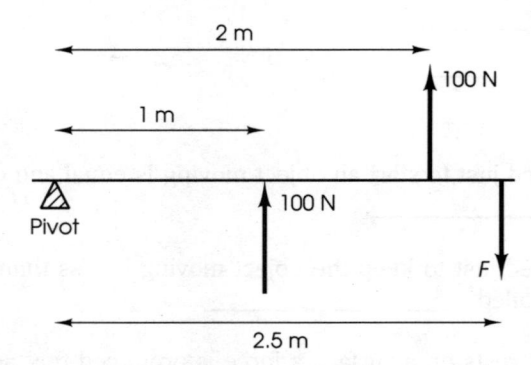

Fig. 3.53

CHAPTER 4

ENERGY, WORK AND POWER

GETTING STARTED

Energy is a basic idea in physics; in fact you could explain what "physics" is by saying that it is a study of *energy* forms, and their relationship with each other and with matter. So an understanding of energy is essential to an understanding of physics.

The idea of **work** is inseparable from the idea of energy, because whenever work is done, energy is transformed and if an energy change takes place work is done.

Power is a measure of how quickly work is done (the rate of doing work, or the rate of transfer of energy).

- FOOD, FUELS AND ENERGY
- KINETIC ENERGY
- POTENTIAL ENERGY
- CONSERVATION OF ENERGY
- WORK AND ENERGY
- POWER
- MACHINES
- EFFICIENCY
- ALTERNATIVE ENERGY
- PRIMARY AND SECONDARY SOURCES
- STORING ENERGY
- LEVERS AND PULLEYS
- ENERGY ARROWS AND CHAINS

ESSENTIAL PRINCIPLES

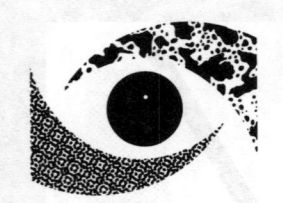

1 FOODS, FUELS AND ENERGY

Living things need energy simply to be alive! Most plants obtain their energy directly from the sun and are able to "manufacture" food using a process called **photosynthesis** (Fig. 4.1). Many animals obtain their food by eating the *cells of plants* where energy is stored as chemical energy. Flesh-eating animals obtain their food by eating the *cells of other animals* which again are a store of chemical energy. The food in each case is not itself energy, but *energy can be released from the food during respiration*.

from the refining of *oil*. The fuel in each case is not itself energy — it is a **store** of chemical energy — but as we shall see *energy can be released from the fuel during burning*.

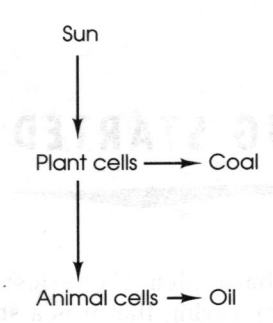

Fig. 4.2

Fig. 4.1 Our energy comes originally from the sun.

In the long run all living things derive energy ultimately from the sun. This is even the case, indirectly, with non-living things which rely on *fuel* to make them run. A steam engine may need *coal*, which is a store of chemical energy. A car of a bus may need petrol or diesel, i.e. fuel products which result

Coal and oil were formed over millions of years by the action of pressure and heat on the decaying remains of plants and animals (Fig. 4.2). So the chemical energy in the plant and animal cells became trapped in the final products of coal and oil. These are called *fossil fuels*. The energy released today when coal or oil is burned originated from the sun millions of years ago.

We have already seen that when food is taken in by a living thing the process of *respiration* converts chemical energy to *other energy forms*. Similarly, when a fuel is *burned* the chemical energy stored in it is changed to heat *(thermal energy)*.

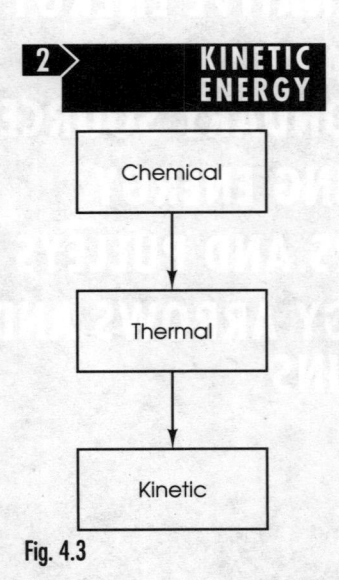

2 KINETIC ENERGY

The release of energy in the human body or in a vehicle can enable it to move. An object which is *moving* has **kinetic energy** (kinetic just means "movement"). To make a car move the energy originally in the fuel has undergone a number of changes; these can be summed up in an energy-flow diagram as in Fig. 4.3. The greater the speed required of a person, the more "fuel" has to be burned, so that a person running has more kinetic energy than when walking (Fig. 4.4).

A greater fuel consumption is needed to get a large-mass car moving at the same speed as a small-mass car. Therefore the *larger the mass* the *more kinetic energy is needed* for the same speed to be produced

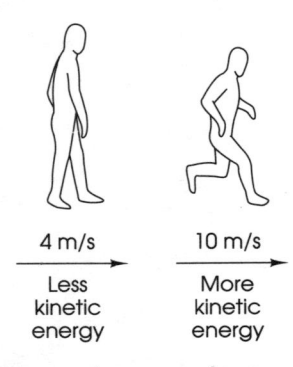

Fig. 4.3

Fig. 4.4 Faster speed means more kinetic energy.

(Fig. 4.5). This can be summed up as:

Kinetic energy = ½ (mass) × (velocity)²

or

$$KE = \tfrac{1}{2}mv^2$$

(See also Ch. 5.)

A dynamo can change **kinetic** energy into **electrical** energy. Electrical energy can also be obtained directly from **chemical** energy using a torch battery or a car battery. Electrical energy is a very useful form (a) because it can easily be **transported**, and (b) because it can easily be **converted** to other energy forms.

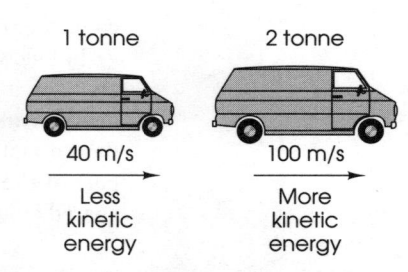

Fig. 4.5 More mass means more kinetic energy.

3 > POTENTIAL ENERGY

❝ Avoid describing potential energy as "stored" energy. This can cause confusion with other stored forms like the chemical energy stored in food. ❞

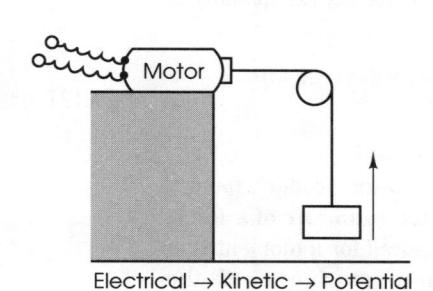

Fig. 4.6
A motor converts **electrical** energy into **kinetic** energy. It can then be used to lift a mass off the ground (Fig. 4.6). Now if the mass **falls back** to the ground, the motor would run like a dynamo, turning kinetic energy back into electrical (Fig. 4.7).

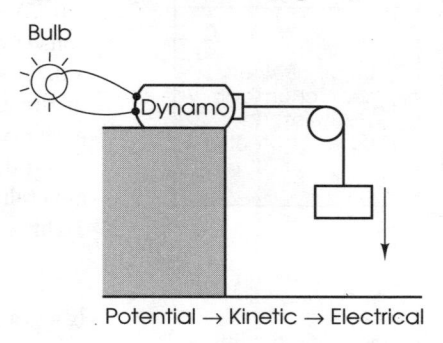

Fig. 4.7

While the mass was above the ground, it also had energy simply because it **was** above the ground. This energy is available for conversation into kinetic energy and then into electricity. The energy of an object because of its **position** (usually above the ground) is called **gravitational potential energy**.

"Potential" energy is "energy-in-waiting"; waiting to be converted to kinetic energy. It could also be described as the maximum energy reclaimable from a system.

A different type of system with potential energy is one with a **stretched** or **compressed elastic material**, like a rubber band, spring or animal muscle. A stretched catapult elastic has energy "waiting" to be released as kinetic energy (Fig. 4.8).

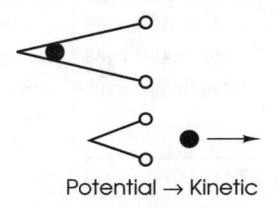

Fig. 4.8

A mass on a stretched spring will obtain kinetic energy when the spring is **released** (Fig. 4.9). This energy form is called **strain** (or elastic) **potential energy**.

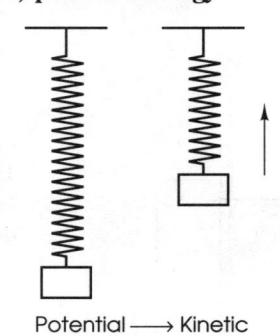

Fig. 4.9

4 > CONSERVATION OF ENERGY

A number of **forms** of energy can be identified: chemical, electrical, kinetic, potential (both gravitational and strain), thermal (or internal energy), light, sound and nuclear.

Any one of these can be changed into another energy form, but it is found that whatever change takes place the total energy available at the start is **equal** to the total at the end (taking everything in the system into account). This is called **energy conservation** and is sometimes stated as "energy cannot be created or destroyed".

In following through a sequence of energy changes it sometimes seems, however, that energy *has* been "lost". This is often due to the unwanted production of heat or sound in part of the system, where energy becomes shared among many particles, including those of the atmosphere.

Whenever we do work we change energy from one form to another. Whenever we use energy it ends up more spread out than when it started, often in the form of heat. This is called **energy degradation**.

5 WORK AND ENERGY

Many laboratory examples of energy conversion involve an object moving at some time (even if the movement is the drift of electrons in a wire to give an electric current). When a force moves, it is said that *work* is being done. The greater the force, and the larger the distance, the greater the quantity of work.

Work = Force (F) × distance (d)
$W = F \times d$

Work is measured in *joules* (J).

(Notice that in Ch. 3 the product, force × distance, measures the *moment* of a force, but the distance measured for a moment is at 90° to the force. In measuring *work* the distance is measured in the *same direction* as the force acts.)

If a system has energy, it can do work. If *work is done, energy is converted*. So measuring work is the same as measuring energy converted (Fig. 4.10).

66 An important point. The words "Work done" and "Energy converted" mean exactly the same thing. 99

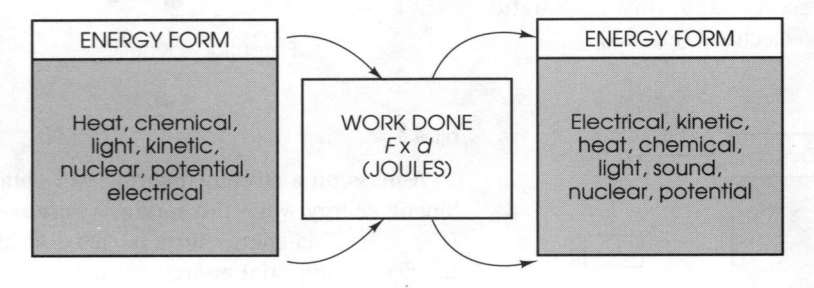

Fig. 4.10

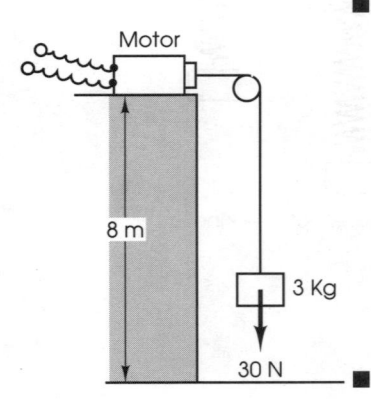

Fig. 4.11 Work done = energy converted.

■ *Example (a)* Suppose a motor lifts a 3 kg mass 8 m off the ground (Fig. 4.11). The *force* acting on the mass = 30 N (since g = 10 N/kg). Therefore the *work done* is

$30 \times 8 = 240$ J

and the *energy converted* to potential energy = 240 J. If the mass now falls freely to the ground it will also have 240 J of kinetic energy just before it hits the ground.

■ *Example (b)* A football weighing 5 N dropped 2 m from the ground will have (5 × 2) = 10 J of kinetic energy just before hitting the ground. It would have 10 J of potential energy before being dropped, and 10 J of work would have to be done to lift it up in the first place (Fig. 4.12).

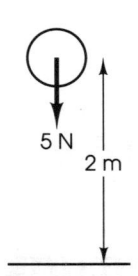

Fig. 4.12 Potential energy kinetic energy

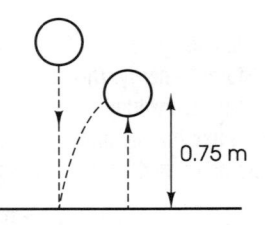

Fig. 4.13 Energy is converted to heat when a ball bounces.

However, if the ball bounces it may only rise 0.75 m (Fig. 4.13). Its potential energy at the top of the bounce is now (5 × 0.75) = 3.75 J. According to the laws of conservation of energy the "missing" (10 − 3.75) = 6.25 J, must be present as heat in the ground and the ball, and some perhaps as sound when the ball hits the ground. This type of example can be generalised (Fig. 4.14).

To lift a mass m up to a height h:

Force moved = mg

(g = gravitational field strength)

Work done = mgh.
and **potential energy** = mgh.
Or, in words,
potential energy = weight × height.

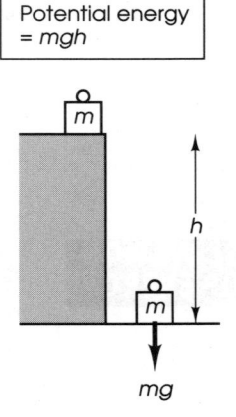

Fig. 4.14

6. POWER

Motors, engines and people can do work at different *rates* (i.e. some do the job more quickly than others). Suppose motor A lifts the weight of 40 N in 5 s and B lifts the same weight in 3 s, both through the same distance of 3 m (Fig. 4.15). Then B is more *powerful* than A, although both do the same work.

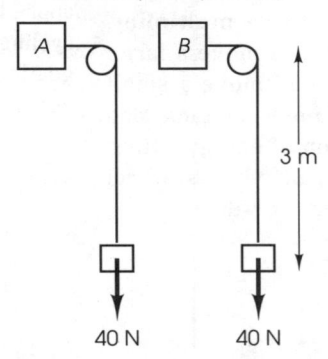

Work = (40 × 3) = 120 J

Fig. 4.15 Comparison of two motors.

Power is the work done in 1 s; it is therefore measured in joules per second or watts (W):

$$\text{Power A} = \frac{120}{5} = 24 \text{ W}$$

$$\text{Power B} = \frac{120}{3} = 40 \text{ W}$$

Since *work* is equivalent to *energy transferred*, we can say:

A transfers 24 joules of energy per second
B transfers 40 joules of energy per second

More formally, ***power is the rate of doing work or the rate of transfer of energy***, i.e.

$$\text{Power} = \frac{\text{Work done}}{\text{Time}} = \frac{\text{Energy transfer}}{\text{Time}}$$

■ **Example (c)** If a person has a mass of 70 kg and climbs a flight of stairs 3 m high in 4 s, then

70 kg weighs (70 × 10) newtons

Work done = Energy transferred
= 70 × 10 × 3 = 2100 J

$$\text{Power developed} = \frac{2100}{4} = 525 \text{ W}$$

POWER OUTPUT OF A MOTOR

The motor is connected in series to a 12 V DC supply and a rheostat (Fig. 4.16). The load is attached to a line-shaft unit coupled to the motor. In a preliminary run the rheostat is adjusted to give a suitable running speed for the motor. The motor is switched on, and a stop-clock started as the load passes a point X marked on a rule, and stopped as it passes point Y. The load is weighed and the distance XY measured with a metre rule.

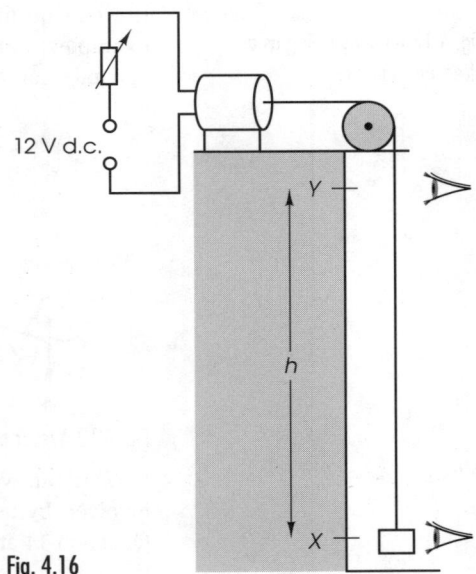

Fig. 4.16

RESULTS

Weight of load = W (N)
Distance XY = h (m)
Time = t (s)

CALCULATION

$$\text{Power} = \frac{\text{Work done}}{\text{Time}} = \frac{W \times h}{t}$$

PRECAUTIONS

The time is likely to be short, so the distance XY should be as large as practically possible and the motor speed as slow as possible. Several runs should be made and a ***mean value*** of time taken.

7. MACHINES

The word "machine" has become a very general one – but in science it has a special meaning. An engine is a system which enables an energy conversion to take place, e.g. tractor, dishwasher, record player. A machine causes a *change* in the way the forces involved in energy conversions act. So a machine does not itself convert energy in a strict sense. The change in the way forces act can be:
1. Direction change;
2. Force increase;
3. Force reduction.

(A) A SINGLE PULLEY

The weight W being lifted is called the ***load force***. The pulling force F is called the ***effort*** *force* (Fig. 4.17). With this machine the load and effort forces are equal. But to lift this load *upwards* the effort acts *downwards*. This machine is a **direction changer**.

(B) SIMPLE LEVER

With this arrangement a small effort force F can be used to lift a larger load force W (Fig. 4.18). This machine is a **force multiplier**. However, the effort has to move a large distance to make the load move a small distance, so the **work done** is the same, and there is no multiplication of energy. Other examples: nutcrackers, pulley hoists, wheel and axle, car jack, spanner, screwdriver.

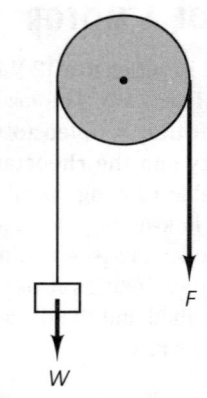

Fig. 4.17 A pulley acting as a direction changer.

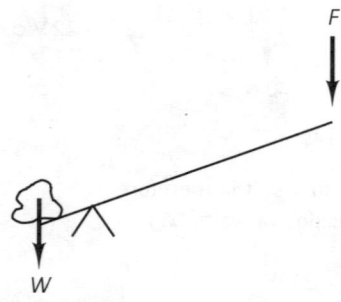

Fig. 4.18 A lever acts as a force multiplier.

You can work out the size of the forces involved by using the principle of moments. Question 14 at the end of chapter 3 illustrates this.

It is also useful to have a measure of how good a force multiplier is and this is called the **mechanical advantage** where:

$$\text{Mechanical advantage} = \frac{\text{Load force}}{\text{Effort force}}$$

(C) GEAR SYSTEMS

As bicycle owners will realise, a gear system can act as a **force multiplier**, i.e. a small force applied gives a larger force output – this is like cycling in low gear. The "pedal" side of the gearing would need a large number of teeth and the wheel side a small number (Fig. 4.19).

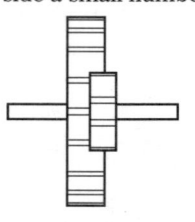

Fig. 4.19 A gear wheel acting as a distance multiplier.

However, if the reverse is used (high gear) then a large force is applied and a small force results, but the distance travelled by the wheel side is increased. This is now acting as a **distance multiplier**.

A distance multiplier will change the speed that forces move at. The load usually moves more slowly than the effort. We can measure how good a distance multiplier is by its **velocity ratio**.

$$\text{Velocity ratio} = \frac{\text{distance moved by effort}}{\text{distance moved by load}}$$

8 > EFFICIENCY

Energy is always conserved, but when energy is put into a system, like a pulley or a motor, not all the available energy turns into the energy form you require. A motor is designed to convert electrical energy into kinetic energy, but of course some heat and sound will be produced – so less kinetic energy is available at the end than there was electrical energy at the start.

$$\text{Efficiency} = \frac{\text{Energy output}}{\text{Energy input}}$$
$$= \frac{\text{Work output}}{\text{Work input}}$$

And since power is energy change per second, then efficiency is also

$$\frac{\text{Power output}}{\text{Power input}}$$

Efficiency has no units. It is a *ratio*. It can also be expressed as a percentage: e.g. if a motor is supplied at 60 W and the power output is 40 W, then its efficiency is 40/60 = 0.66 or 66 per cent.

CAUSES OF INEFFICIENCY

HEAT

Electrical devices must be inefficient because when a current flows a wire becomes hotter. It follows that no motor or dynamo can be 100 per cent efficient for its particular purpose. However, an immersion heater in water is close to 100 per cent efficient for its particular purpose.

FRICTION

Friction is a force, *not* an energy form. However, friction is responsible for converting kinetic energy to heat. A rope moving over a pulley does *work* against friction – so not all the energy input is available to give potential energy to a load.

LOADING

This is particularly true of mechanical systems. A pulley system has its own weight, so to lift a load, some energy is used in lifting the pulley system itself. It would be silly to push a single brick in a wheelbarrow because most of your energy would be given to the barrow and little to the brick. The effect of the weight of the barrow becomes smaller, in proportion, as the weight of the bricks becomes larger.

9 ALTERNATIVE ENERGY

Chemical energy

Chemical energy is contained in many chemicals by the way that their atoms are bonded together. If you react chemicals together so that their atoms are joined in a different way then the new chemicals may contain a different amount of energy. If the new chemicals need less energy to hold them together than before then the extra energy is released. This is an **"exothermic"** reaction and the energy is usually released as heat. Most fuels that we burn release chemical energy as heat in this way.

e.g. If you light a candle then the wax (which is the fuel) burns with oxygen from the air and makes carbon dioxide and water. These need less energy than the more complicated wax and the spare energy is released as heat and light energy.

e.g. Our bodies take in chemical energy as food (and store some of it as fat!). When the cells need energy they can burn some of this fuel by combining it with the oxygen that is transported by the blood stream. The new chemicals from the reaction are carbon dioxide and water vapour which need less energy. They are taken away by the blood stream and the cells get the "spare" energy.

i.e. We use an **exothermic** reaction.

$$\text{Glucose} + \text{oxygen} \longrightarrow \text{carbon dioxide} + \text{water} + \text{energy}$$

Chemical energy can be both renewable (sugars grown in plants) or non-renewable (oil products).

NON-RENEWABLE RESOURCES

Fossil fuels

Fossil fuels such as coal, oil and natural gas are the remains of plants and animals that have been trapped between layers of rock. They are a valuable source of many chemicals as well as fuels such as diesel, petrol (gasoline) and paraffin (kerosine). They are only present in the earth's crust in limited quantities and are running out as we use more and more. Since we cannot make more of these fuels – the natural process that formed them took millions of years – they are called **non-renewable** resources. Chemical energy in the fuel is changed into heat energy when the fuel is burned.

Another main disadvantage is the production of air pollution including carbon dioxide which increases the **"greenhouse effect"** and is therefore slowly changing the temperature of the earth's surface and its climate. Some coal and oil contains small quantities of sulphur which forms sulphur dioxide when it is burned. This dissolves in moisture in the air and leads to **acid rain** that is believed to damage plants and can accumulate sufficiently to kill plant and animal life in lakes and rivers. The plants and animals that these fossil fuels were made from got their energy from the sun – so the sun is the original source of all this energy.

Nuclear Energy

Nuclear energy comes from the energy released when atoms of uranium or plutonium are split into smaller pieces. The smaller pieces need less energy to hold them together and the "spare" energy is released as heat energy. This is much cleaner to use and creates much less air pollution than using fossil fuels but the new atoms created are usually radioactive. This means that some of the waste from the power station can be dangerous for many years into the future. The original fuel, uranium, is mined as uranium ore and will eventually run out like the fossil fuels although far less fuel is actually used. The sun is **not** the source of this particular type of energy as the uranium was made in the earth at the time of its formation. Many industrialised countries now produce quite a large fraction of their electrical energy from nuclear power stations.

RENEWABLE RESOURCES

These can be put into two main groups:

Solar energy, wind power, wave power, hydroelectric power and biomass all derive their energy from the sun whereas tidal energy and geothermal energy do not.

Solar energy

This is the wide range of electromagnetic radiation that comes to us from the sun. When the radiation hits a suitable surface the energy is turned into heat energy. **Solar energy** can be used to heat water in solar panels. In some hot countries mirrors have been used to focus enough energy into one place to create a solar furnace. The energy can also be used to produce a small electric current from a solar cell. Banks of these solar cells can then be used to charge batteries and provide electrical energy. The energy per m^2 in colder countries is not sufficient to make large scale use practical and the weather makes it unreliable but it does have some applications in electronics where the energy required is small – calculators and radios work well on solar power with a storage or back-up battery. Solar energy is used to power satellites and a 50cm square panel should produce enough energy to run a light.

> Hydroelectric power is also a well established form in some regions, and could be included. Problems are siting and land use.

■ EXAMPLE

If the solar energy reaching the earth is 1250 W/m^2, what power can be obtained from a solar cell that measures 50 cm × 50 cm and is 12% efficient?

Area of panel = 0.5 × 0.5 = 0.25 m^2
power output = area × solar power × efficiency
= $\frac{0.25 \times 1250 \times 12}{100}$
= 37.5 W

■ Wind power

Wind power can be derived from modern windmills which have rotors that are rather like the propellers of an aeroplane in shape. Large rotors can produce enough electricity by driving a generator to be economical, especially for charging batteries, but there can be problems with lack of wind – or too much – some of the time! If these windmills are to provide an alternative energy source on a large scale there would have to be a lot of them on hills facing the wind and many people would find the effect on the landscape unacceptable. The original source of energy is the sun. The kinetic energy of the wind is turned into the kinetic energy of the rotors and then into electrical energy by the generator. Denmark plans to generate 10% of its electricity from wind turbines by the year 2000. California already generates 1500 MW in this way. To give some idea of the size that a modern generator might be, there is an experimental one in England which is 45 m high, has blades 55 m in diameter and can generate 1 MW. A smaller one seen on a farm near my home has blades about 1 m in diameter and charges a 12V car battery. Several sites in the north of England, on the Pennines and the west coast are at present being set up as wind farms with between 4 and 15 large generators on each site.

■ Wave power

Sea waves can carry large quantities of energy as a large mass of water is being moved up and down. To exploit **wave power** involves strings of machines on the surface of the sea. As the waves go by they drive part of the machine up and down and this drives a hydraulic pump. The fluid driven by the pump in turn drives a generator. The waves emerge smaller than before meeting the machine. The main problems have been the large variation in size of the waves and the damage done by bad weather. A lot of machines are needed and suitable sites can be difficult to find. The original source of this energy is the sun – NOT the moon which produces tidal energy!! The kinetic energy of the water in the waves is turned into electrical energy by these machines.

■ Hydroelectric power

Hydroelectric power is used in many countries where there are rivers large enough to provide the energy required. In some countries the rivers do not fall through enough height or have a large enough rate of flow to produce large quantities of energy but many are used on a smaller scale. The important factors are the mass of the water and the height that it falls through. The gravitational potential energy of the water is converted into kinetic energy as it falls and then into electrical energy by turbines. The original source of the energy is the sun which drives the water cycle, producing the rain that fills the rivers.

There are important hydroelectric schemes at several places where there are big waterfalls, e.g. Niagara Falls on the Canada–USA border and at the Victoria Falls (Zimbabwe–Zambia). In other countries large dams have created the necessary water pressure.

■ Biomass

Biomass involves using the sunlight to grow quick-growing plants with a high chemical energy content, usually in sugars. The energy is then extracted from the chemicals produced in the plants. In Brazil sugar is extracted from plants and fermented to produce alcohol. This can then be used to power engines in cars instead of petrol. In the USA a lot of the petrol has alcohol added to it (about 9%). The process is only renewable if you keep replanting the land. Burning wood is using the same process but the wood can take much longer to replace as trees are quite slow growing. If the land is poor it may be difficult to grow more trees before the soil is eroded by wind or rain, making replanting difficult and leaving the land barren. Forests used in this way must be replaced as they are part of the natural cycle that balances carbon dioxide and oxygen in the air. The original source of energy is the sun. The energy in the sunlight has been used by the green chlorophyll in plant leaves to build up more complex chemicals from carbon dioxide and water. These new chemicals therefore contain more energy. (The process is called photosynthesis.)

Carbon dioxide + water + sunlight ⟶ glucose + oxygen

We then reverse the process by burning the chemicals to get the energy back out as heat energy.

A gas known as **biogas** is produced when bacteria break down the waste from farms, especially cow dung and pig slurry. For good production the bacteria need to be warm – at about 35°C – and the gas is then about 60% methane and 40% carbon dioxide. Biogas produced in this way provides energy for more than 30 million people in China.

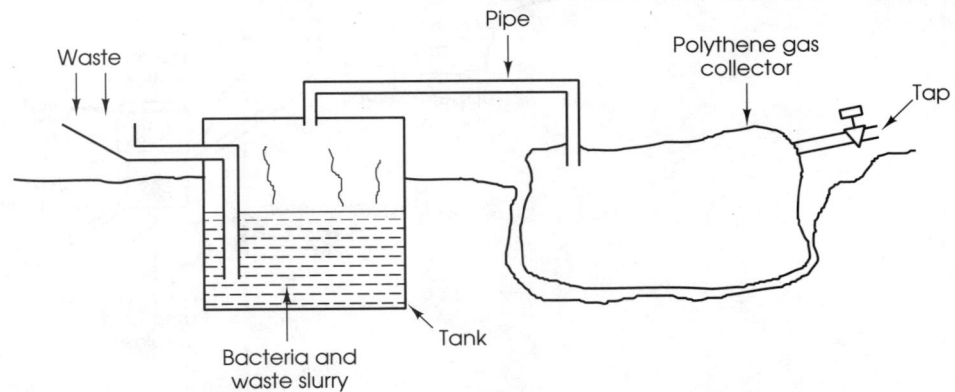

Fig. 4.20

■ Tidal energy

Ocean currents contain a very large mass of moving water and so they have a lot of kinetic energy. In some countries the tides are being used as an energy source. Tidal energy is produced by the relative motion of the moon around the earth. We can use it by making the tide flow through barriers across bays or narrow straits, driving turbines as it does so. The main problem is in finding suitable sites and the large initial building costs. There are also worries about the ecological effects of the reduced tide after the barrier and visual impact of the barrier on coastal sites. The kinetic energy of the water is turned into electrical energy by the turbines driving generators.

■ Geothermal energy

Geothermal energy is used by pumping water under pressure down to hot rocks below the earth's surface. The water returns heated and the heat energy can be used as the alternative resource. The centre of the earth has a temperature of about 4500°C and the temperature increases by about 20°C per 100 m as you drill down into a thermally active area. The original source of the energy is radioactive decay within the earth's core which keeps the interior of the earth molten. The process is being trialled in a number of areas of the world, especially those that have volcanic areas where natural hot springs already exist. In Iceland about half of the population live in houses heated by natural hot water and there are 9 power stations of this type in Japan. About 8% of New Zealand's electricity is produced in this way from natural steam wells in the North Island.

10> PRIMARY AND SECONDARY SOURCES

The renewable and non-renewable resources in the previous section are all regarded as **primary sources** of energy as they are used as the fuel at the start of a series of energy changes. *Electrical energy* is different because it must always be made from one of these other sources. It is an example of a **secondary source**. The main reason why we all like to use electricity is that it is quick and easy to "transport" once a connecting cable system (a national grid) has been built to connect towns and villages. Places where there is a greater demand can be given energy almost instantly from places where the demand is less. The user also sees electricity as cleaner and more pollution free than other sources but this can be an illusion as you only see the final product and not the power station that produces it.

11> STORING ENERGY

The most common way to **store** energy is as electrical energy in rechargeable batteries. These work by having a chemical reaction that goes in one direction when they are used but which can be reversed when the battery is recharged. The coiled spring in a clock or watch contains potential energy that can easily be restored. Weights are sometimes lifted so that the energy is stored as gravitational potential energy and is released as the weight is allowed to fall. This was used for many years as a way to power clocks but the same principle is now used in some power stations where it is possible to build a water reservoir both above and below the station. The system is called *pumped storage*. It is more efficient to run the generators in a power station continuously. Unfortunately we do not use the electrical energy at a constant rate and the power stations sometimes produce more energy than we require and sometimes less. When too much electrical energy is being produced it is used to pump water up into the higher reservoir where it has a lot of gravitational potential energy.

When we require more energy the water is allowed to flow back down again and the energy is converted back into electrical energy by turbines that drive generators.

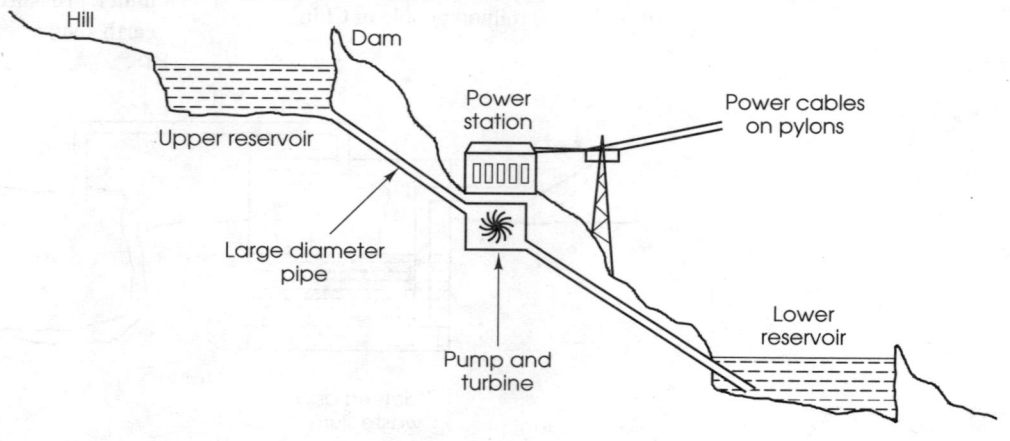

Fig. 4.21

EXTENSION MATERIALS

12> MORE MACHINES

LEVERS

You can find the connection between the load and the effort by assuming that the forces just balance and then using the **principle of moments**. This will then tell you the **mechanical advantage**. Most levers belong to one of three types as shown in the examples in the diagram.

In each case think of the distance from the effort to the pivot as l_1 and the distance from the load to the pivot as l_2. If the effort just balances the load then, using the principle of moments

$$\text{load } l_2 = \text{effort } l_1$$

$$\text{M.A.} = \frac{\text{load}}{\text{effort}} = \frac{l_1}{l_2}$$

Type 1

In the case of the crow bar, l_1 is bigger than l_2 and you have a very useful M.A., i.e. the force that you put in (effort) is multiplied by quite a large number so it can move a large load. Levers often come in pairs in simple tools. A pair of scissors or pliers will have two of the first type of lever so that a small effort can act on quite a large load.

Type 2

In the wheelbarrow the load and effort are on the same side of the pivot but the distances still make the M.A. larger than 1 (because the effort is farther away from the pivot than the load). It will be easier to move the wheelbarrow if the load is at the front, close to the wheel, so that the M.A. is as large as

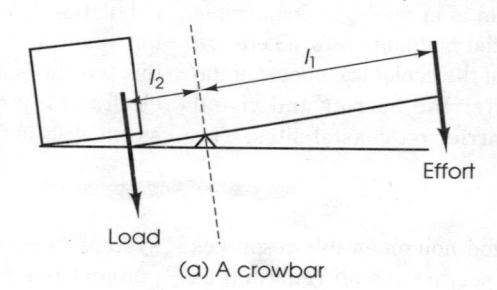

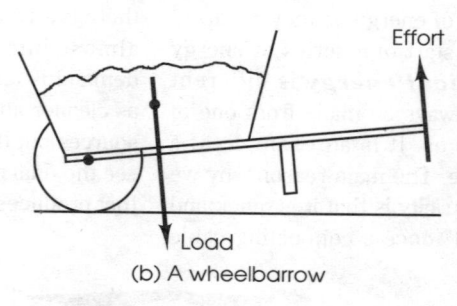

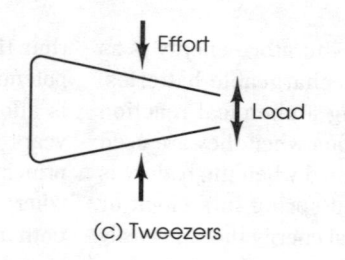

(a) A crowbar
(b) A wheelbarrow
(c) Tweezers

Fig. 4.22

possible. Both of these first two types are **force multipliers**.

Type 3
In the tongs or tweezers the load is at a greater distance from the pivot than the effort so the M.A. is less than 1. This pair of levers is for convenience rather than for making a large force. When the muscles that we call the biceps pull on the forearm, the load in the hand is further away from the pivot (elbow) than the effort and the lever is one of the third type. This third type of lever are **distance multipliers**.

Many simple machines use levers. Some other examples are a spanner, the pedal of a cycle, a door handle and nut-crackers.

PULLEYS

There are two common ways of using a pulley.

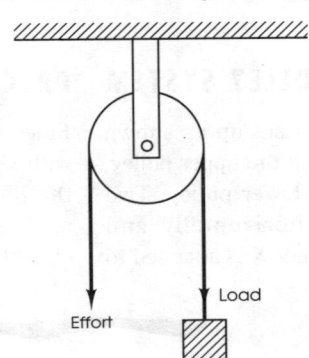

Fig. 4.23

A *fixed pulley* is only able to rotate on its axle and the axle is kept firmly in place usually on an overhead beam (see Fig. 4.23). The load hangs on the rope on one side and is supported by the effort on the other side of the pulley. The effort and the load must move through the same distance so

V.R. = velocity ratio = 1.

The tension in the rope will be the same on both sides of the pulley so that the load = effort and

M.A. = mechanical advantage = 1.

In a real case the effort has to be larger than the load so that it can overcome friction in the pulley and this will mean that the M.A. is a bit less than 1 and the efficiency is less than 100%. You might be able to improve the M.A. and the efficiency by oiling the bearings on the axle – but you will never reach M.A. = 1. In spite of this the system is often used because it is easier to use your weight to pull downwards than to pull or lift upwards.

A *moving pulley* will move up and down with its load (see Fig. 4.24). The load will only move half as far as the effort moves. Imagine pulling up the rope at the effort by 1 m. The rope on each side of the pulley will shorten by 0.5 m

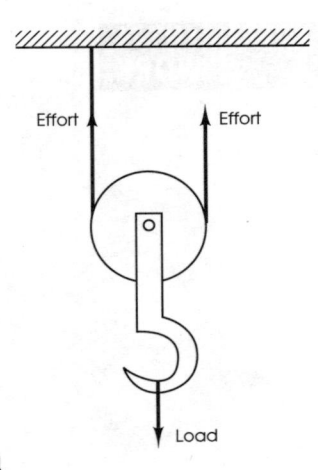

Fig. 4.24

and the load rises by 0.5 m. This will mean that

V.R. = velocity ratio = 2.

If the tension in the rope on each side of the pulley is the same then there will be a force equal to the effort pulling upwards on each side of the pulley. A load can be lifted that is twice as large as the effort and

M.A. = mechanical advantage = 2.

In a real moving pulley there is friction to be overcome and the pulley also has to be lifted along with the load. Each of these increase the effort needed and the real M.A. will be less than 2 so that the efficiency is less than 100%. Oil, good bearings and a lightweight pulley will all improve the M.A. The snag is that the effort may be difficult to apply because it is upwards. The two types of pulley can be combined to produce a working system with a small but useful gain in the force applied, by passing the effort rope from the moving pulley over a fixed pulley. There will still be friction in both pulleys and the moving pulley has to be lifted with the load. More pulleys can be introduced to improve the machine further.

A *block and tackle* uses one rope with several fixed and moving pulleys to produce a bigger M.A. (see Fig. 4.25). This system is often used in factories to move heavy loads and in smaller systems such as those used to lift engines out of cars.

In the system in the diagram each of the 5 lengths of rope supporting the lower pulleys and the load will have a tension equal to the effort. This means that the maximum possible M.A. is 5.

Remember that you are not getting "something for nothing" – you have produced a force larger than the effort but it will move through a distance that is smaller. In a real system the pulleys in each of the two sets would be the same size and side by side to save space and weight. The maximum M.A. will be the same as the number of ropes supporting the moving pulleys.

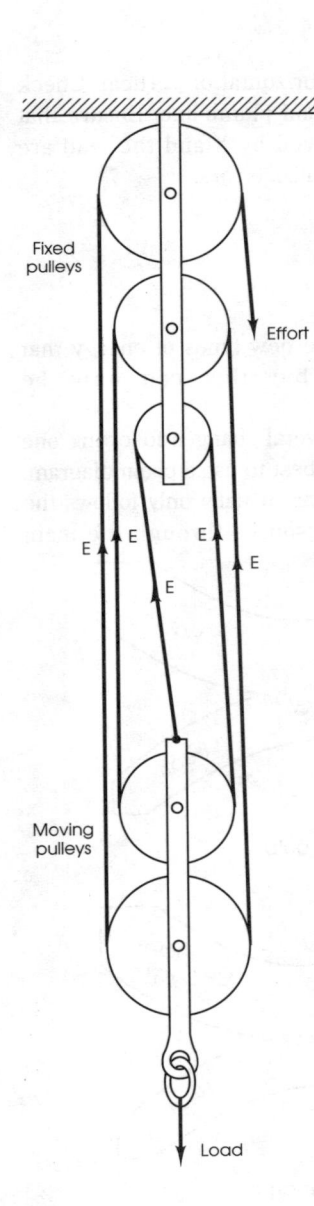

Fig. 4.25

13 EXPERIMENTAL WORK

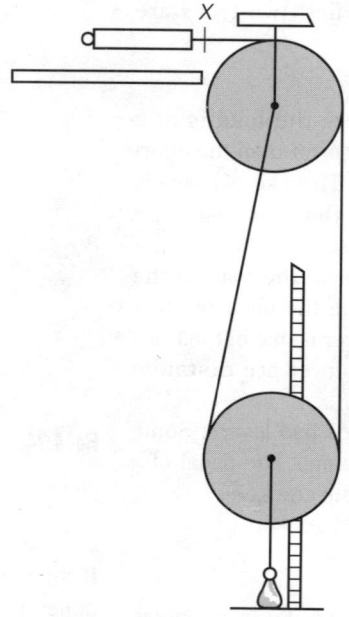

Fig. 4.26

EFFICIENCY OF A PULLEY SYSTEM

A simple pulley system is set up as shown (Fig. 4.26) clamped firmly at the upper pulley. A load is attached to the lower pulley. Two metre rules are fixed horizontally and vertically as shown. A marker X is attached to the string leaving the upper pulley. The force-meter is used to raise the load, say 50 cm.

RESULTS TAKEN

Weight of load $= W$ (N)
Force-meter reading $= F$ (N)
Distance moved by load $= h$ (m)
Distance moved by point X $= d$ (m)

CALCULATION

Work (*input*) done by effort $= F \times d$
Work (*output*) on load $= W \times h$

$$\text{Efficiency} = \frac{\text{Work output}}{\text{Work input}}$$

$$= \frac{(W \times h)}{(F \times d)} \times 100\%$$

PRECAUTIONS

Rules must be horizontal or vertical. Check with set square and plumb-line. Ensure that the distance moved by X and the load are made without parallax errors.

14 ENERGY ARROWS AND CHAINS

Energy changes are often shown best by a diagram. If the change is a single one it is best shown by an **arrow diagram**. Begin with the original energy form and clearly label the parts of the arrow as the new forms are produced. You can try to make the width of the new parts of the arrow show the proportions of the new types of energy that are produced but this can only be approximate.

If there are several changes following one another then it is best to use a chain diagram. This sort of diagram usually only follows the energy from the source through the main

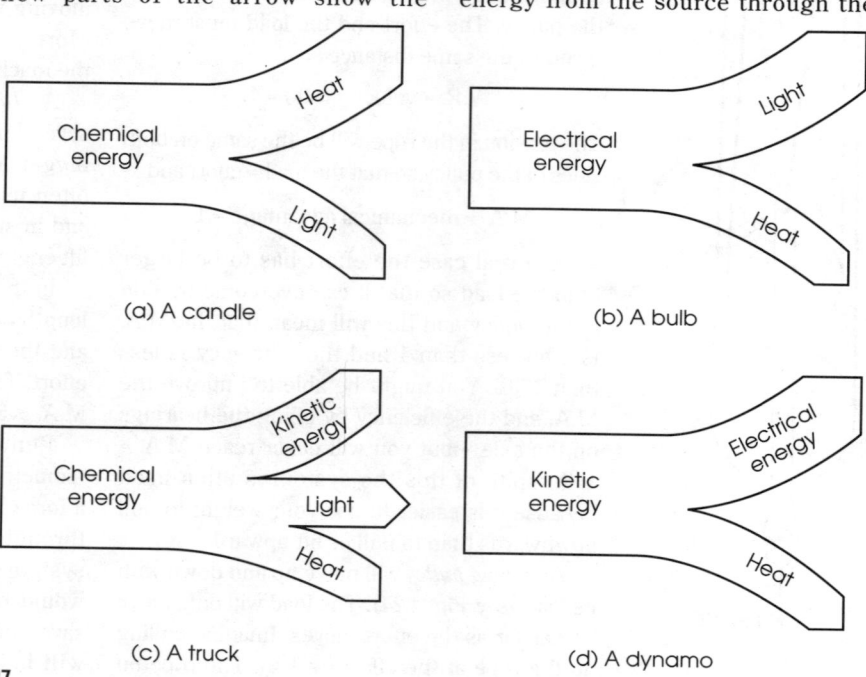

(a) A candle

(b) A bulb

(c) A truck

(d) A dynamo

Fig. 4.27

changes and ignores the energy "lost" into other forms on the way.

In the chain diagram for the car, energy lost as heat etc. is not shown but the overall pattern of a more complicated system would be clearer when shown this way. You can fit side arrows to show important losses if you wish.

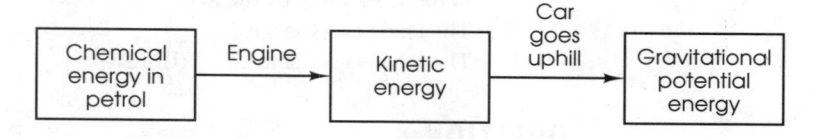

Chemical energy in petrol → Engine → Kinetic energy → Car goes uphill → Gravitational potential energy

Fig. 4.28

EXAMINATION QUESTIONS

MULTIPLE CHOICE QUESTIONS

QUESTION 1

Which of the following is *designed* to convert electrical energy into sound energy?

- A Mains transformer
- B Loudspeaker
- C Crystal microphone
- D Telephone mouthpiece
- E Recording tape   (ULEAC)

QUESTION 2

Which of the following best describes the energy changes which take place when a steam engine drives a generator which lights a lamp?

- A Thermal–Light–Sound–Kinetic
- B Kinetic–Light–Thermal–Electrical
- C Thermal–Kinetic–Electrical–Thermal and Light
- D Electrical–Kinetic–Thermal–Light
- E Thermal–Sound–Kinetic–Electrical

(ULEAC)

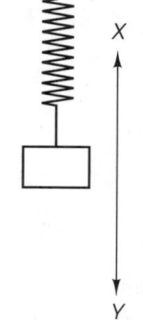

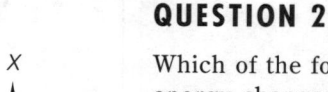

QUESTION 3

A bullet strikes a fixed target and is brought to rest. The main energy changes when this happens are

- A Kinetic to potential and sound
- B Kinetic to sound and internal energy
- C Potential to sound and internal energy
- D Kinetic to sound and light   (SEG)

QUESTION 4

Which one of the following statements is *untrue*?

- A Hydroelectric power stations use water to drive turbines.
- B In a power station turbines drive generators.
- C Generators produce electricity.
- D A nuclear power station generates electricity which flows as a direct current.
- E Some energy is wasted as heat in the power station.

QUESTION 5

Figure 4.29 shows a mass moving up and down on the end of a spring. X and Y are the highest and lowest positions of the mass. Which one of the statements in the table is true when the mass is at its highest point X?

(SEG)

	Kinetic energy of the mass	Potential energy of the mass
A	Maximum	Minimum
B	Maximum	Zero
C	Zero	Maximum
D	Same	Same

QUESTION 6

Which one of the following is the meaning of power?

- A Work done per second
- B Velocity per kilogram
- C Force per metre
- D Acceleration per newton   (SEG)

QUESTION 7

A machine such as a pulley system will have an efficiency of 100% if

- A The load is equal to the effort.

Fig. 4.29

B   The distance moved by the effort is equal to the distance moved by the load.
C   The work done by the effort is equal to the work done by the load.
D   The load is very large.
E   The load is very small.   (ULEAC)

QUESTION 8

A force is applied to an object and causes it to move a certain distance in the direction of the applied force. The amount of work done is

A   Force × distance moved
B $\dfrac{\text{Force}}{\text{Distance moved}}$
C   Weight of object × distance moved
D $\dfrac{\text{Weight of object}}{\text{Distance moved}}$
E   Weight of object × force   (NISEAC)

QUESTION 9

A boy whose weight is 400 N climbs a flight of stairs 4 m high in 5 s. His power output is

A $\dfrac{5 \times 4}{400}$ W   D $\dfrac{400 \times 4}{5}$ W

B $400 \times 5 \times 4$ W   E $\dfrac{400 \times 5}{4}$ W

C $\dfrac{400}{5 \times 4}$ W

QUESTION 10

Which of these quantities has the same units as energy?

A   Mass   C   Work   E   Velocity
B   Power   D   Weight

STRUCTURED QUESTIONS

QUESTION 11

This question is about **forces, work** and **energy**. A worker on a building site raises a bucket full of cement at a slow steady speed, using a pulley like that shown in the diagram (Fig. 4.30). The weight of the bucket and cement is 200 N. The force F exerted by the worker is 210 N.

(a) Why is F bigger than the weight of the bucket and cement?
(b) The bucket is raised through a height of 4 m.
   (i)   Through what distance does the worker pull the rope?
   (ii) How much work is done on the bucket and cement?
   (iii) What kind of energy is gained by the bucket?
   (iv) How much work is done by the worker?
   (v)   Where does the energy used by the worker come from?   (SEG)

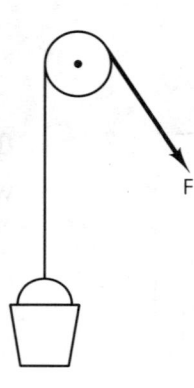

Fig. 4.30

On the diagram, show clearly the main energy changes in the system.

(b) Write down the names of *three* different sources of energy which are used for driving an electrical generating system.   (SEG)

QUESTION 12

In a hydroelectric generating station, water falls through pipes from a high reservoir to a turbine. The turbine drives a generator.

(a) On the block diagram (Fig. 4.31), label the three parts of the system.

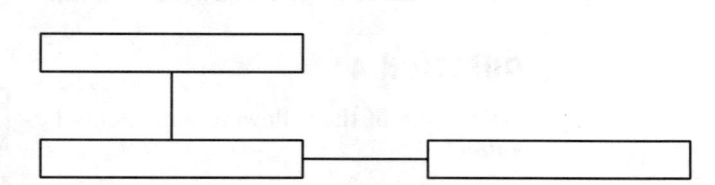

Fig. 4.31

QUESTION 13

(a) The pie chart shows five sources of energy used by a country.

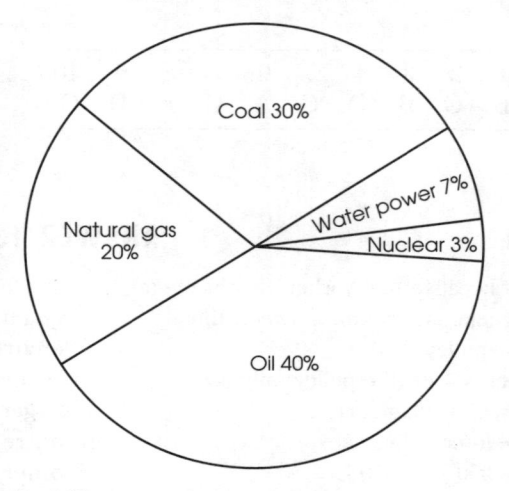

Fig. 4.32

Coal 30%
Natural gas 20%
Water power 7%
Nuclear 3%
Oil 40%

The table shows the proportional use and estimated reserves of coal, oil and natural gas.

	Relative estimated reserves	Relative quantity used/year
Coal	500	1.25
Oil	100	3
Natural gas	90	1.5

(i) Explain why it is always difficult to make accurate predictions of how long reserves will last.
(ii) Why will the pie chart be different in about 20 years time?
(iii) Explain the economic, environmental and social benefits of using nuclear energy as the main source of providing electrical power.

(b) Pumped storage power stations are used to produce electricity during periods of peak demand. Water is stored in one reservoir and allowed to fall through a pipe to another reservoir at a lower level. The falling water is used to turn turbines which are linked to generators.
In one such power station 400 kg of water passes through the turbines every second after falling through 500 m. The gravitational field strength is 10 N/kg.
Assume that no energy is wasted.

(i) What is the weight of 400 kg of water?
(ii) Calculate the decrease in gravitational energy when 400 kg of water falls 500 m.
(iii) What is the power delivered to the turbines by this falling water?
(iv) If the generator is perfectly efficient calculate the current it produces if the output voltage is 20 000 V.
(v) Why are pumped storage power stations used to produce electricity for a few hours and not for continuous generation of electricity? (SEG)

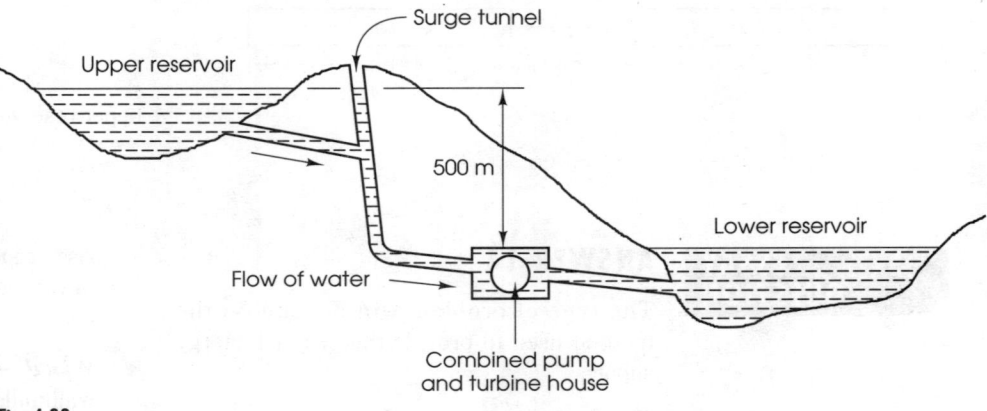

Fig. 4.33

Upper reservoir
Surge tunnel
500 m
Flow of water
Lower reservoir
Combined pump and turbine house

ESSAY QUESTION

QUESTION 14

Write a short account of the possible dangers to the environment arising from large electricity generating stations. (SEG)

OUTLINE ANSWERS

MULTIPLE CHOICE QUESTIONS

Question	1	2	3	4	5	6	7	8	9	10
Answer	B	C	B	D	C	A	C	A	D	C

STRUCTURED QUESTIONS

ANSWER 11

(a) *F* is bigger because the worker also has to do work against friction between the rope and the pulley.

(b) (i) Distance = 4 m (the pulley only acts as a direction changer).
    (ii) Work = force × distance
              = 200 × 4 = 800 J.
    (iii) The bucket and cement gain gravitational potential energy.
    (iv) Work = 210 × 4 = 840 J.
    (v) Energy comes from his food (chemical energy).

ANSWER 12

(a) See Fig. 4.34.

(b) There are many possibilities: burning coal or oil; nuclear fuel; wind, solar or tidal energy sources.

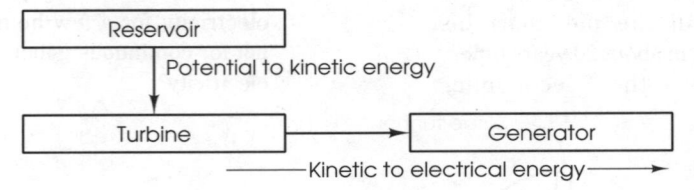

```
┌───────────┐
│ Reservoir │
└─────┬─────┘
      │ Potential to kinetic energy
      ▼
┌───────────┐         ┌───────────┐
│  Turbine  │────────▶│ Generator │
└───────────┘         └───────────┘
       Kinetic to electrical energy
```

Fig. 4.34

ANSWER 13

(a) (i) any four of – Reserves are estimated, quantity used each year can vary, environmental considerations, reserves depleted, more use of larger reserves, change of costs etc.
    (ii) oil reaching low reserves, use of other fuels/renewable sources of energy.
    (iii) Economic (large capital investment), electricity "cheap" to produce.
Environmental – no greenhouse gases/acid rain/ ash (waste problem).
Social – more use of electrical power in future, "clean" atmosphere.

(b) (i) weight = mass × g
              = 400 × 10 = <u>4000N</u>
    (ii) energy change = weight × height (= grav. pot. energy)
              = 4000 × 500 = 200 000 J = <u>2 MJ</u>
    (iii) 2 MJ per second = 2 MW
    (iv) Power (watts) = volts × amps
        2 000 000 = 20 000 × I
        I = 2 000 000 / 20 000 = <u>100A</u>

(v) More power used in raising water to upper reservoir hence not efficient/economic.

ESSAY QUESTION

ANSWER 14

The type of problem will depend on the method used to provide the original energy supply.

- **Coal or oil** – waste gases from burning giving rise to atmospheric pollution. Coal burning gives sulphur dioxide as by-product, which is responsible for acid rain. Both give carbon oxides with the possibility of "greenhouse effect" in the long run.

- **Nuclear** – needs siting near the sea for optimum free cooling. Sea temperature rises causing a shift in ecology. Problem of disposal of waste, of leakage, and of control.

- **Wind** – requires large clusters of windmills with vanes about 20 m radius. Land use and unsightliness are the main problems.

- **Solar** – similar to wind. Land use is the main environmental consideration.

- **HEP** – unless harnessing a natural fall, hydroelectric power may require the flooding of arable land to make the necessary reservoirs.

(*NB*. The question carries eight marks. One mark for each valid point made.)

TUTOR'S QUESTION AND ANSWER

QUESTION

A student requires a small electric motor for a model crane. The crane load is raised on a single cord attached to a shaft driven by the motor through reduction gearing. At the start of the lift, one revolution of the shaft raises the load through a vertical height of 10 mm. At the end of the lift one revolution of the shaft raises the load through a vertical height of 20 mm.

(a) Assuming that the lifting shaft rotates at a constant rate of 3 rev/s, estimate the power used in raising a load of 2 N.
   (i) At the beginning of the lift;
   (ii) At the end of the lift.

(b) The rated characteristics of three possible motors, A, B and C are given in Fig. 4.35.
   (i) What is the power output of each motor?
   (ii) The motor is to be powered from a DC source giving output voltages of 3, 6 or 9 V. Given that the efficiency of the gearing system is 0.40 (40%), which motor would you recommend? Explain how you make your decision. (SEG)

Motor	Voltage (V)	Load current (A)	Speed (rev/s)	Efficiency
A	3	0.5	60	0.10 (10%)
B	6	0.5	60	0.10 (10%)
C	9	0.4	60	0.12 (12%)

Fig. 4.35

ANSWER

(a) (i) At the start, 1 rev raises the load by 10 mm (0.01 m). Since the shaft rotates at 3 rev/s, the time for 1 rev = ⅓ s.

$$\text{Power} = \frac{\text{Work done}}{\text{Time}}$$

$$= 2 \times 0.01 \times 3 = \underline{0.06 \text{ W}}$$

(ii) Similarly, at the end of the lift,
Power = $2 \times 0.02 \times 3$ = 0.12 W

(b) (i) Input power = Current × voltage
Output power = Input power × efficiency

Therefore

Power A = $3 \times 0.5 \times 0.1$ = 0.15 W
B = $6 \times 0.5 \times 0.1$ = 0.30 W
C = $9 \times 0.4 \times 0.12$ = 0.43 W

(ii) The power output required is that calculated in (a) (ii), i.e. 0.12 W. With gearing efficiency of 0.40, the overall output powers of the motor and gear system become

Total power = Motor output × gear efficiency

Therefore

Power A = 0.15×0.4 = 0.06 W
B = 0.30×0.4 = 0.12 W
C = 0.43×0.4 = 0.17 W

The calculation of power required assumed that the lift occurred at 3 rev/s for the required lifting rate, so the following factors influence the decision:

A   The output power is too small. Therefore the speed will also be too small.

B   The output power matches that required. Therefore the speed will also match and B should be selected.

C   The output power and speed are too great, so while it can do the job it would be wasteful to use C.

STUDENT'S ANSWER WITH THE EXAMINER'S COMMENTS

STUDENT'S ANSWER TO QUESTION 14

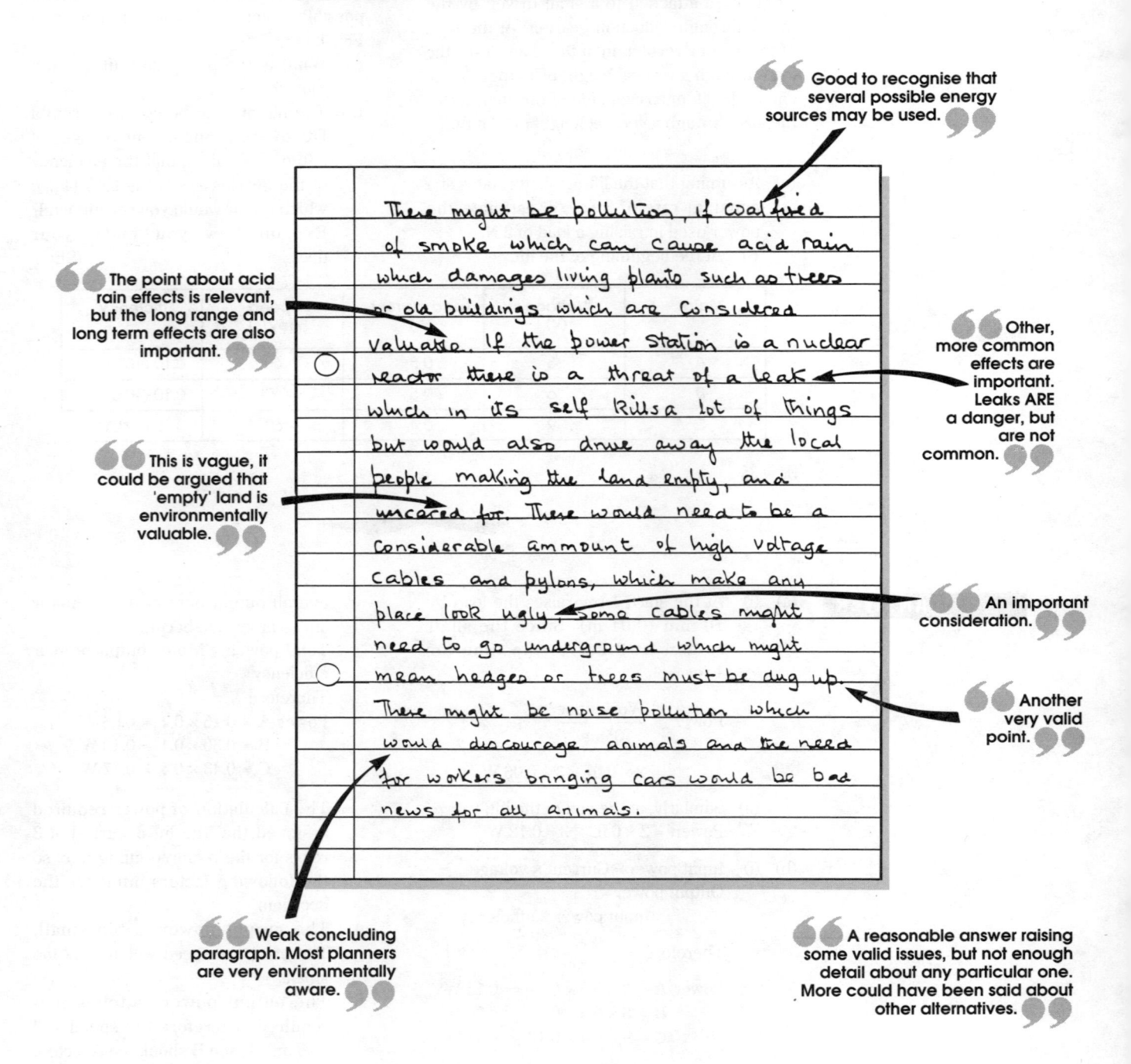

> **Good to recognise that several possible energy sources may be used.**

> **The point about acid rain effects is relevant, but the long range and long term effects are also important.**

> **This is vague, it could be argued that 'empty' land is environmentally valuable.**

> **Other, more common effects are important. Leaks ARE a danger, but are not common.**

> **An important consideration.**

> **Another very valid point.**

There might be pollution, if coal fired of smoke which can cause acid rain which damages living plants such as trees or old buildings which are considered valuable. If the power station is a nuclear reactor there is a threat of a leak which in itself kills a lot of things but would also drive away the local people making the land empty, and uncared for. There would need to be a considerable ammount of high voltage cables and pylons, which make any place look ugly. Some cables might need to go underground which might mean hedges or trees must be dug up. There might be noise pollution which would discourage animals and the need for workers bringing cars would be bad news for all animals.

> **Weak concluding paragraph. Most planners are very environmentally aware.**

> **A reasonable answer raising some valid issues, but not enough detail about any particular one. More could have been said about other alternatives.**

REVIEW SHEET

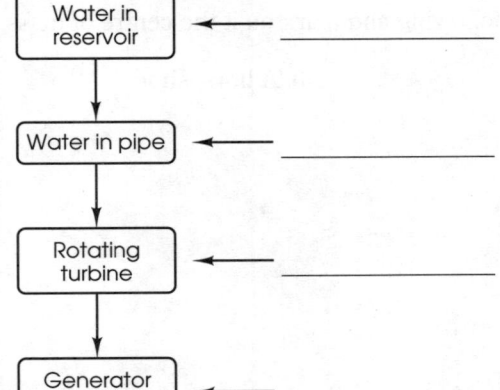

- If you lift a mass upwards it gains _____ energy

- Every moving object has _____ energy

- Name six different forms of energy

    1. _____   2. _____

    3. _____   4. _____

    5. _____   6. _____

- A simple lever lifts a 250 N load when the effort put in is 100 N. Its mechanical advantage is _____ . A lever like this is a _____ multiplier.

- Draw an energy arrow for a ball that is dropped, bounces and rises to a lower height.

- Fill in the labels on the energy diagram for a hydroelectric power station to show the energy type at each stage.

    Water in reservoir ← _____

    Water in pipe ← _____

    Rotating turbine ← _____

    Generator output ← _____

Fig. 4.36

- Complete the following equations

    1. Power =   2. Efficiency =

    3. Kinetic Energy =   4. Gravitational P.E. =

- State the units for each of the following

    1. Work _____   2. Power _____

    3. Energy _____   4. Force _____

- The most common type of energy "wasted" is _____

- Name a renewable source of energy that does NOT originate from the Sun.
  _____

- State two sources of energy that are suitable for development in hot third world countries with a few natural resources.

    1. _____   2. _____

- State two advantages and two disadvantages for the use of wind power to generate electricity.

Advantages:

   1. _____

   2. _____

Disadvantages:

   1. _____

   2. _____

A lever can be used to increase *force*. Why does the lever not increase *energy* at the same time?

_____

_____

Draw a simple diagram of each of the following and mark on it the centre of mass.

1. A ball   2. A brick   3. A horseshoe

Fossil fuels are non-renewable. Explain the meaning of each of the following words:

Fossil: _____

Fuel: _____

Non-renewable: _____

CHAPTER 5

FORCES AND MOTION

DISTANCE, DISPLACEMENT
SPEED & VELOCITY
TICKER-TAPE MEASUREMENTS
INFORMATION FROM GRAPHS
ACCELERATION
COMPUTER MEASUREMENTS
***g* AND ITS MEASUREMENT**
NEWTON'S LAWS OF MOTION
CONSERVATION OF MOMENTUM
PROJECTILES
CIRCULAR MOTION
ROCKETS AND JETS
VELOCITY – TIME GRAPHS
EQUATIONS OF MOTION
IMPULSE AND SAFETY
SATELLITES
INERTIA
DETERMINATION OF *g*

GETTING STARTED

The analysis of moving objects and the way that **forces** affect movement leads to the three ***laws of motion*** suggested by Newton. In their turn they help to explain how satellites and planets move and how jets and rockets will behave. They also help unify the motion of planets into a theory of **universal gravitation**.

To start, however, as is often the case in physics, a careful look at vocabulary (definitions) is needed. You need to be quite sure that you understand exactly what is meant when words are used in a "scientific" manner.

Most Examination Groups state that any questions set on this topic can be solved by graphical methods, but in the harder papers algebra may be needed. Both types of example are included in this chapter.

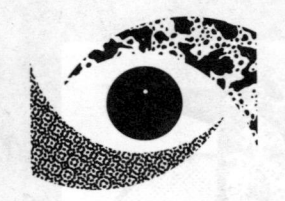

ESSENTIAL PRINCIPLES

1. DISTANCE, DISPLACEMENT, SPEED AND VELOCITY

The distance from A to B in Fig. 5.1 depends on the route taken. You could travel the "long way", AXYZB, take a short cut, AXB or go directly AB. Whichever way you go the measurement would still be "the distance from A to B". **Distance** then is the total length of the journey, and it clearly depends on the route taken.

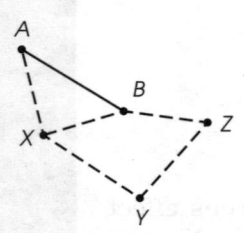

Fig. 5.1 Distance is route-dependent.

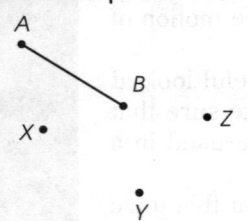

Fig. 5.2 Displacement is route-independent.

The **displacement** of B from A is the "distance as the crow flies" (Fig. 5.2). It does *not* depend on the route because there is only **one** route possible, and only **one** direction in which to travel. Displacement is the distance between two points in a fixed direction.

Distance, like mass, is a **scalar** quantity; displacement, like force, is a **vector** quantity.

To find out how "fast" you are travelling, you need to measure two things: "How far is the journey?", and "How much time did it take?". "How far?" can mean either **distance** or **displacement**, so we use two more definitions to make the meaning clear, dividing by **time** in each case.

$$\text{Speed} = \frac{\text{Distance}}{\text{Time}}$$

$$\text{Velocity} = \frac{\text{Displacement}}{\text{Time}}$$

So speed is a **scalar** quantity and velocity is a **vector** quantity. Both speed and velocity are measured in metres per second (m/s) or centimetres per second (cm/s), but velocity is measured in a *particular direction*.

2. TICKER-TAPE MEASUREMENTS

The problem in measuring speed or velocity is that both a length and a time are needed. In a laboratory the lengths are likely to be no more than a few metres and times will be only a few seconds or less. A **ticker-timer** is often used because it gives **both** pieces of information at once and can time to 1/50 s when run from a mains power pack. The timer taps out 50 dots on to a piece of paper tape in 1 s. So the interval between dots is 1/50 s or 0.02 s.

In Fig. 5.3 the time to travel from X to Y is (5 × 0.02) = 0.10 s. Simply pulling a tape by hand can tell you a lot about the way you moved. In Fig. 5.4:

- A Travelled with a steady speed. This is called **constant velocity** (velocity because it is in a fixed direction).
- B Started slowly and became faster and faster. This is called **accelerating**.
- C Became slower as the time went on. This is called **decelerating**.

But more information is available. Since the time interval between dots is 0.02 s, we can say *how long* it took to pull each tape:

Fig. 5.3

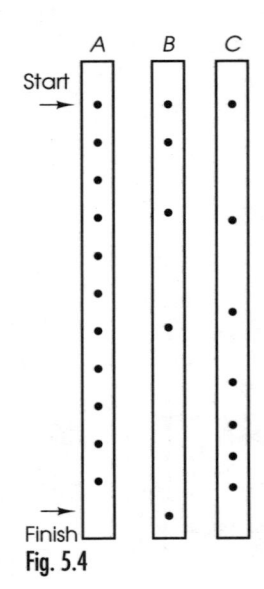

Fig. 5.4

CHAPTER 5 ESSENTIAL PRINCIPLES

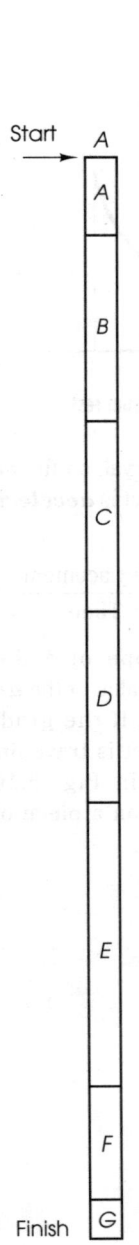

A took $10 \times 0.02 = 0.20$ s
B took $4 \times 0.02 = 0.08$ s
C took $6 \times 0.02 = 0.12$ s

All are pulled in a fixed direction so we can measure the displacements with a ruler and find the velocities. In this case the lengths were as shown in table 5.1. Apart from A there is no single time when the other tapes were travelling at a fixed value for velocity, so we need to say "average" velocity, as in Table 5.1.

Table 5.1

Tape	Displacement (cm)	Time (s)	Average velocity (cm/s)
A	8	0.20	40
B	9	0.08	112.5
C	8	0.12	66.6

This gives another, more exact definition:

$$\text{Average velocity} = \frac{\text{Total displacement}}{\text{Total time}}$$

or

$$v_{av} = \frac{s}{t} \text{ and } s = v_{av} t$$

where s = displacement and t = time.

Now imagine a length of tape, as in Fig. 5.5, made in the same way, but cut into shorter lengths to make a bar chart. If each tape piece has five intervals on it, then **each piece** represents a **time** of 0.10 s.

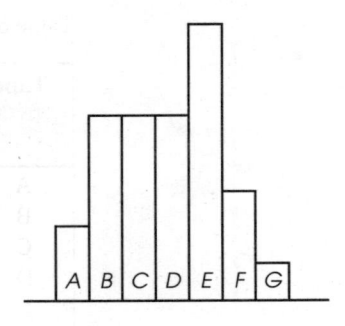

Fig. 5.5

Fig. 5.6 A tape chart constructed from Fig. 5.5.

The information given by this type of chart is:

(i) The **type of motion** (i.e. how the pulling object moved Fig. 5.6). We can say that it began slowly, increased velocity, which then stayed constant for a while, increased velocity again and at the end rapidly slowed down.

(ii) **Total time** for the journey. Each piece has five intervals on it, i.e. 0.10 s; total time = 7×0.10 s = 0.70 s.

(iii) **Total displacement** (Fig. 5.7). Measuring each piece we have (2 + 4 + 4 + 4 + 6 + 3 + 1) = 24 cm.

(iv) **Average velocity**:

$$v_{av} = \frac{\text{Total displacement}}{\text{Total time}}$$

$$= \frac{24}{0.7} = 34.28 \text{ cm/s}$$

(v) **Average velocity** in each 0.1s (Fig 5.8) found by dividing displacement by 0.1 see table 5.2.

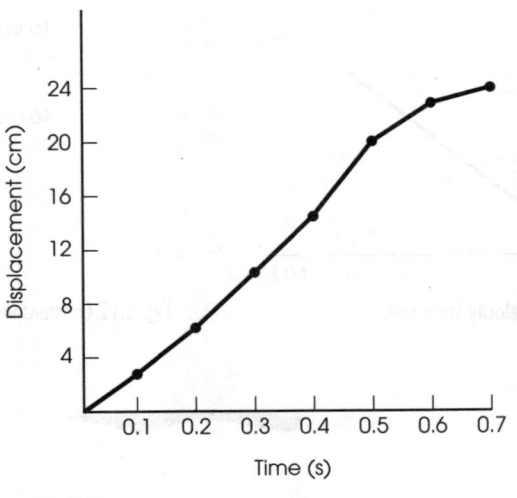

Fig. 5.7

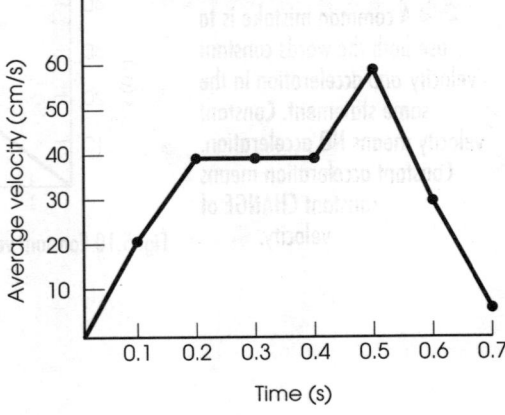

Fig. 5.8

3 > INFORMATION FROM GRAPHS

The tape in the last section can be analysed and the data presented as a graph. Taking each individual piece of tape the average velocity for each 0.10 s time interval can be found (Table 5.2).

The same information is available:

1. Type of motion;
2. Total time;
3. Total displacement;
4. Average velocity in each time interval.

Table 5.2

Tape	Total time from start (s)	Total displacement (cm)	Average velocity (cm/s)
A	0.1	2	20
B	0.2	6	40
C	0.3	10	40
D	0.4	14	40
E	0.5	20	60
F	0.6	23	30
G	0.7	24	10

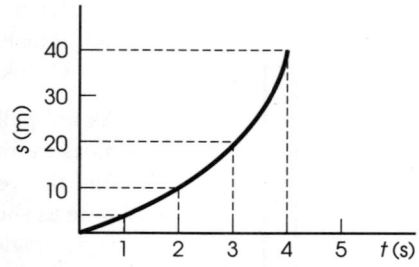

Fig. 5.11 Constant acceleration from rest.

Some graphs of displacement against time can easily be understood. The object in Fig. 5.9 is *at rest*, since its displacement is the same all the time. It remains 6 m from the observer.

In Fig. 5.10 the **displacement increases in a steady way** as time goes on. So the **velocity is constant.** The displacement is 8 m after 1 s, 16 m after 2 s and so on. The velocity is constant at 8 m/s.

In Fig. 5.11 the displacement has become greater in each time interval, so the **velocity is increasing**. The object is **accelerating**.

Since

$$\text{Average velocity} = \frac{\text{Displacement}}{\text{Time}}$$

the **gradient**, or slope of a displacement/time graph, is the value of the **average velocity** at that time. If the gradient is constant, then the object is travelling with constant velocity, as in Fig. 5.10. The equivalent information on a piece of *tape* would look like Fig. 5.12.

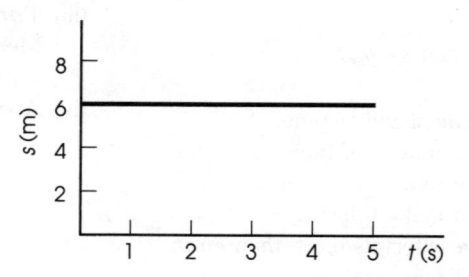

Fig. 5.9 Object at rest.

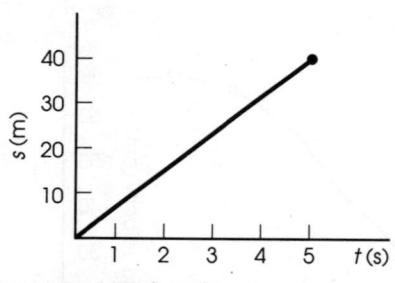

Fig. 5.10 Constant velocity from rest.

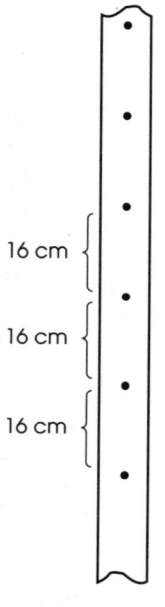

Fig. 5.12 Constant velocity.

> A common mistake is to use both the words constant velocity *and* acceleration in the same statement. Constant velocity means NO acceleration. Constant acceleration means constant CHANGE of velocity.

4 > ACCELERATION

"Accelerating" means "getting faster". A *tape chart* for acceleration would look like that of Fig. 5.13 or Fig. 5.14. Figure 5.13 represents a **constant** acceleration. The increase in velocity is the same after each time interval. There is also acceleration in Fig. 5.14, though here the velocity changes are *not* the same from one time interval to the next. This represents **non-uniform** acceleration. The same information in **graph form** is shown in Figs 5.15 and 5.16.

$$\text{Acceleration} = \frac{\text{Change in velocity}}{\text{Time}}$$

In Fig. 5.15

$$\text{Acceleration} = a = \frac{(8-0)}{5} = 1.6 \text{ m/s}^2$$

The **units** of acceleration must be units of

$$\frac{\text{(Velocity change)}}{\text{Time}} \quad \text{or} \quad \frac{\text{metres per second}}{\text{seconds}}$$

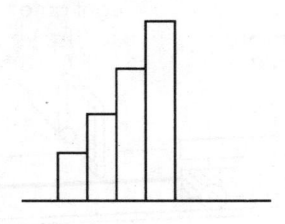

Fig. 5.13 Constant acceleration.

Fig. 5.14 Non-uniform acceleration.

which is written **metres per second per second** or **m/s²**.

Figure 5.17 also represents **constant acceleration**, but not in this case starting from rest.

$$a = \frac{\text{Velocity change}}{\text{Time}} = \frac{(40-10)}{8} = \frac{30}{8}$$

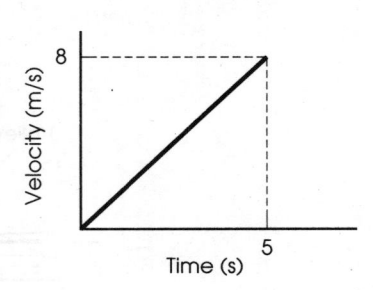

Fig. 5.15 Constant acceleration: graph.

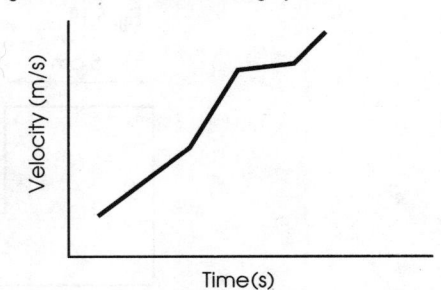

Fig. 5.16 Non-uniform acceleration: graph.

$a = 3.75 \text{ m/s}^2$

Figure 5.18 represents **constant deceleration**

$$a = \frac{10-30}{8} = \frac{-20}{8} = -2.5 \text{ m/s}^2$$

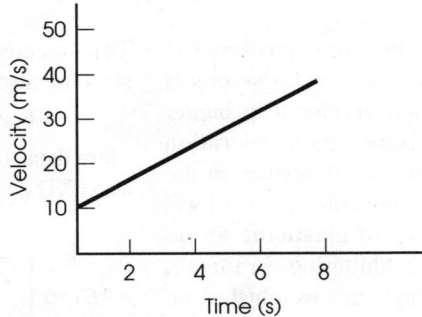

Fig. 5.17 Constant acceleration.

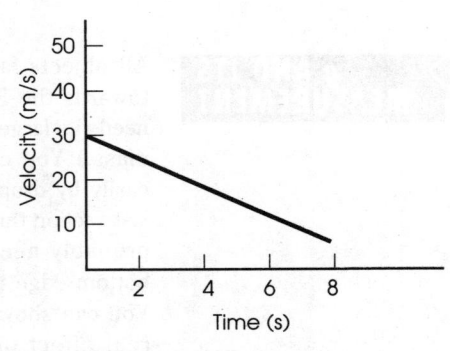

Fig. 5.18 Constant deceleration.

> Note that in a **velocity-time graph**, the **acceleration** is the **value of the gradient** or slope of the graph. Note also that the **deceleration** is given a **negative** sign.

5 COMPUTER MEASUREMENTS

All of the measurements that were described in the section on the ticker timer can also be done very quickly using a computer connected to a light gate sensor. This sensor will measure the time taken for a piece of card to pass through it. The computer can usually do this to at least 1/100 s accuracy. If you measure the length of the card all that is needed is to put the two numbers into the equation for velocity. In most cases you can type the length of the card into the computer and the software will work out the velocity for you.

This makes measuring the velocity of a trolley easy – all you do is attach the card to the trolley and send it through the light gate as in Fig. 5.19.

If you have two of the gates and the program to match you can measure two velocities v_1 and v_2 for the trolley as it passes down the track. The computer will also measure the time t taken between the two velocities and can then calculate the acceleration from the acceleration equation:

$$\text{acceleration} = \frac{v_2 - v_1}{t}$$

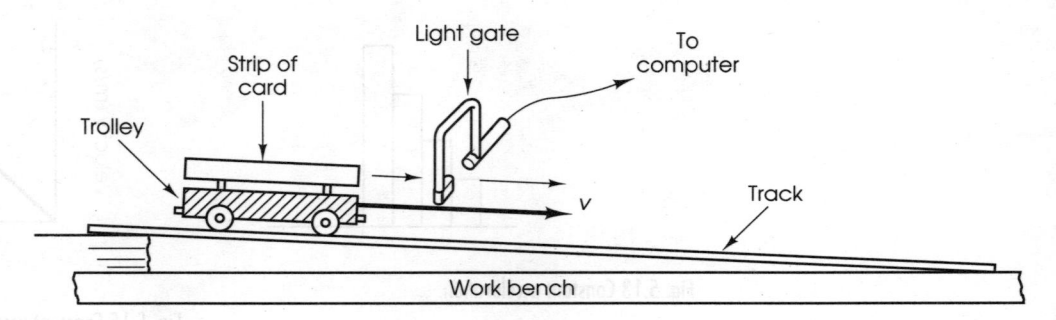

Fig. 5.19

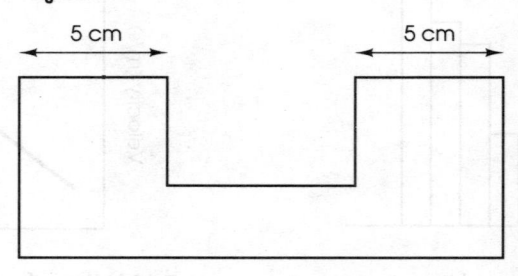

Fig. 5.20

This process can appear quite mysterious when all that appears is the answer on a screen. Do note that all the computer does is the same calculations that you could do by pencil and paper! There is a better way to measure the acceleration. All that the computer is doing is finding the time for the card to go through each light gate. If you use a card shaped like the one in Fig. 5.20 and attach that to the trolley you can tell the computer to measure both times on one light gate. You will then find the average acceleration as the trolley passes through the light gate instead of the average acceleration down quite a long length of track. Note that the width of the gap between the two parts of the card need not be measured. The computer measures the *time* between the two velocities and not the distance.

6 > g AND ITS MEASUREMENT

All objects fall with the same acceleration towards the Earth. (A more massive object needs its larger weight to accelerate its bigger mass.) You can measure this acceleration easily by dropping the card described in the last section through a light gate. The card will probably need a piece of plasticine on its bottom edge to stop it "fluttering" in the air. You can show that this extra weight has no real effect on the acceleration by using different sized pieces of plasticine. Although simple this method often gives better results than more complicated mechanical apparatus. *g* was described as the gravitational field strength in Chapter 3 so that

$$\text{Weight} = \text{mass} \times g$$

This acceleration is exactly the same as *g* since we also know that

$$\text{Force} = \text{mass} \times \text{acceleration}$$

More detail on this law in the next section! (See also EXTENSION MATERIAL SECTION 17)

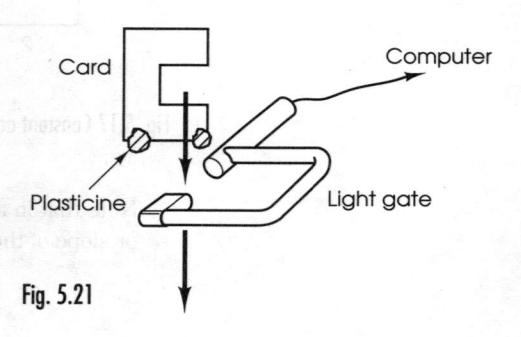

Fig. 5.21

7 > NEWTON'S LAWS OF MOTION

LAW 1

This explains what a force is. We know that forces cause changes. Newton's first law clarifies this by saying that:

▶ **Any object will continue to do what it is already doing unless a resultant force is acting on it.**

We are used to the idea that an object on the ground which is given a push to start it moving will come to rest quickly. Of course once it is moving, friction is a force which acts upon it to cause a change, in this case a reduction in velocity until the object stops.

Without friction, as in space, an object given a push will continue to move in a straight line with the velocity it had at the end of the push. You may show this "constant velocity" behaviour using an air track (Fig. 5.22) or some other method of reducing friction.

66 To summarise – constant velocity is only possible if there is NO RESULTANT FORCE. 99

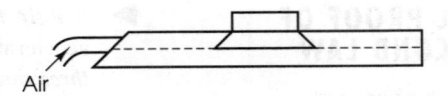

Fig. 5.22 A linear air track gives almost frictionless motion.

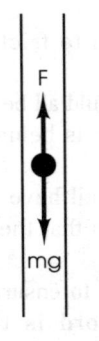

Fig. 5.23 Balanced forces produce constant velocity.

Notice that Newton's first law refers to **resultant force**. So the other way in which an object can remain in a constant state is if the resultant force acting on it is zero, i.e. all forces are "balanced". A ball-bearing in a tube of viscous liquid soon begins to travel with constant velocity, when its weight acting down is balanced by fluid friction upwards (Fig. 5.23). A free-fall parachutist experiences the same effect. On leaving the aircraft he will accelerate towards the ground. Air resistance increases as his velocity increases so while he continues to accelerate the acceleration is *less* than before. As his velocity increases so does air resistance until his weight and the resistive forces **balance**. He can accelerate no more and has reached his terminal velocity (Fig. 5.24).

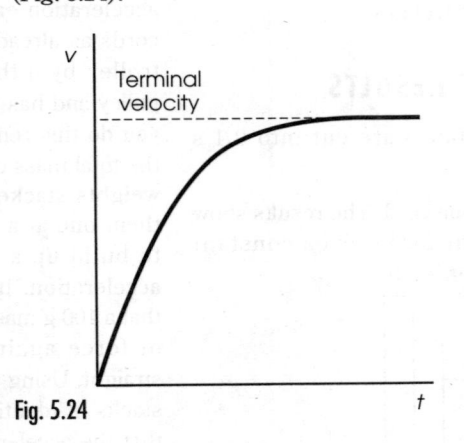

Fig. 5.24

LAW 2

This defines a force. It can be shown experimentally (see Pg. 68) that a *constant force causes constant acceleration*. The *greater the force, the greater the acceleration* for a particular body. Therefore:

Force is proportional to acceleration

So

$$F \propto a$$

If a particular acceleration is to be achieved, the force required to achieve it is also dependent on the mass to be moved.

So

$$F \propto m$$

Then

▶ $$F = ma$$

If we define the unit of force such that 1 unit of force will accelerate 1 kg by 1 m/s², we have the definition of the **newton**.

It also helps to think about what mass means; $m = F/a$ so the bigger the mass the less the acceleration that could be produced. One way of thinking about mass is to regard it as the "lack-of-willingness-to-move" of an object. This property is sometimes called *inertia*. The F in the equation $F = ma$ is the resultant force acting on an object.

A car has a forward force due to its engine of 900 N. Friction acting while it moves is 600 N. If the car's mass is 1000 N, its acceleration is

$$F = ma$$

$$a = F/m = \frac{(900 - 600)}{1000} = 0.3 \text{ m/s}^2$$

LAW 3

This is about *pairs of forces*. Newton maintained that:

- **When an object is acted on by a force, then somewhere another object is also acted on by an equal force, but in the opposite direction.**

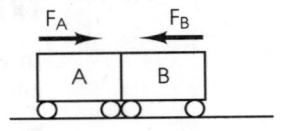

Fig. 5.25

If truck A hits truck B, then A exerts a force on B (Fig. 5.25). At the same time B exerts an equal and opposite force on A. If a tennis racquet is used to hit a ball, the racquet exerts a force on the ball, but the ball also exerts an equal and opposite force on the racquet. Note that Newton's third law refers to *pairs of forces* acting on *different objects*.

A book resting on a table has *two* pairs of Newton forces acting (Fig. 5.26):

1. Push of book on table, P;
   Push of table on book, N.
2. Weight of book W (pull of earth on book);
   Pull of book on earth W^1.

These are all equal if the system is at rest, but not if the table were in, say, an accelerating lift!

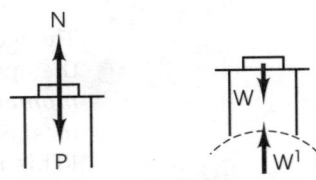

Fig. 5.26 Newton "pairs" of forces for a book at rest on a table.

EXPERIMENTAL PROOF OF NEWTON'S SECOND LAW

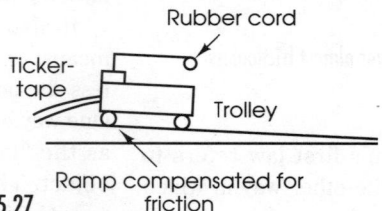

Fig. 5.27

This needs a "frictionless" surface. A wood plank, slightly tilted, can be used to "compensate" for friction (Fig. 5.27). The trolley, given a push, should move along it with constant velocity. The force is provided by a rubber cord, the end of which is kept always above the end of the trolley. This means the extension of the cord is the same all the time and so also is the tension in the cord. The ticker-tape passes through a timer making 50 dots per second. The trolley is accelerated using first one rubber cord, then two cords in parallel at the same extension. Then use two similar trolleys, one on top of the other, then three trolleys.

TREATMENT OF RESULTS

In each case the tapes are cut into 0.1 s intervals.

▶ Single trolley, one cord. The results show that a constant force gives constant acceleration (Fig. 5.28).

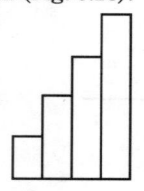

Fig. 5.28

▶ Single trolley, two cords – twice the acceleration.
  three cords – three times the acceleration.
▶ Two trolleys, one cord – half the acceleration obtained initially.

PRECAUTIONS

1. Care must be taken to friction compensate the slope.
2. The rubber cords should all be similar to ensure that the force is being doubled and trebled.
3. The trolleys should all have the same mass, or be loaded so that their masses are equal.
4. Care should be taken to ensure that the extension of the cord is the same throughout the experiment.

The law can also be demonstrated by using a computer and a light gate as in section 5 "computer measurement". Use the special double card and a single gate to determine the acceleration each time. You can use elastic cords as already described or accelerate the trolley by a thin string that passes over a pulley and has weights hanging on the end. If you do this remember that you need to keep the total mass constant – so begin with all the weights stacked on the trolley and transfer them one at a time to the end of the string to build up a set of results for force and acceleration. It may also help to remember that a 100 g mass weighs close to 1 N. A graph of force against acceleration should be straight. Using the same accelerating force on stacks of identical trolleys should also show that the acceleration is inversely proportional to the mass.

8 > CONSERVATION OF MOMENTUM

Momentum ideas are mainly required by Nuffield-based courses.

Newton's second and third laws combine to produce an important principle, namely, **conservation of momentum**. From law 2

$$F = ma$$

$$F = m\frac{(v-u)}{t}$$

$$F \times t = mv - mu$$

The quantity $(F \times t)$ is called **impulse** and the quantity mass × velocity is called **momentum**. The unit of momentum is kg m/s. So impulse = change of momentum. (This is only another way of stating the second law.) The units for impulse will be either kgm/s or Ns.

Now imagine again a collision process. Truck A hits truck B (Fig. 5.29).

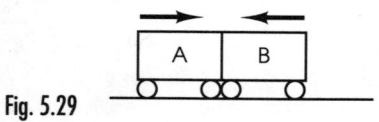

Fig. 5.29

From the third law A exerts a force F on B and B exerts the same force on A. The forces must both act for the same time.

Impulse A on B
 = Impulse B on A

Change of momentum of A
 = Change of momentum of B

Before

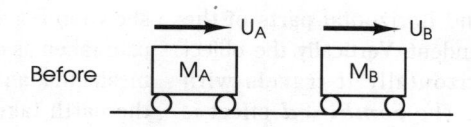

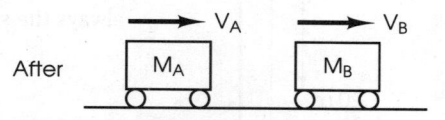

Fig. 5.30 Conservation of momentum

Suppose A and B have masses m_A and m_B (Fig. 5.30). **Before colliding** they travel with velocities u_A and u_B ($u_A > u_B$). **After colliding** the velocities are v_A and v_B ($v_A < v_B$). Then

$$m_A(v_A - u_A) = m_B(v_B - u_B)$$

▶ $$m_A u_A + m_B u_B = m_A v_A + m_B v_B$$

i.e. the total momentum before the collision is equal to the total momentum after the collision.

Note that momentum is a vector. It is usual to use a + sign for objects travelling from left to right and a − sign if they travel in the opposite direction.

WORKED EXAMPLES
WORKED EXAMPLE 1

A 2 kg trolley is travelling at 4 m/s (Fig. 5.31). It collides with a 3 kg trolley at rest. The two trolleys become coupled together and continue to travel together. What is their velocity?

Total momentum before collision:
$$(2 \times 4) + (3 \times 0) = 8 \text{ kg m/s}$$

Total momentum after collision:
$$(2 \times v) + (3 \times v) = 5v \text{ kg m/s}$$
$$5v = 8$$
$$v = \underline{1.6 \text{ m/s}}$$

This is an example of an **inelastic collision**.

WORKED EXAMPLE 2

A billiard ball of mass 0.3 kg hits another stationary ball of mass 0.4 kg head on. The first ball initially travels at 3 m/s and after colliding it travels at 1 m/s. What is the velocity of the second ball?

Before collision total momentum
$$= (0.3 \times 3) + (0.4 \times 0)$$
$$= 0.9 \text{ kg m/s}$$

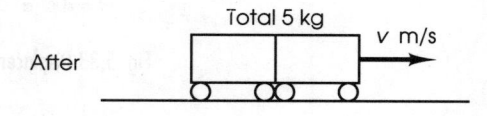

Fig. 5.31

If the second ball then travels at v metres/second:

After collision total momentum
$$= (0.3 \times 1) + (0.4 \times v)$$
$$= 0.3 + (0.4v) \text{ kg m/s}$$

i.e. $\quad 0.9 = 0.3 + (0.4v)$
$\quad\quad 0.6 = 0.4v$
$\quad\quad\;\; v = \underline{1.5 \text{ m/s}}$

9> PROJECTILES

Any mass falling vertically near the surface of the earth has an acceleration of 10 m/s². This acceleration does not depend on the mass.

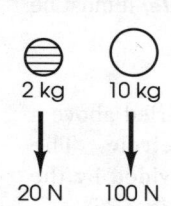

Fig. 5.32

In Fig. 5.32 the larger mass has a larger force acting on it (100 N compared with 20 N) but the force has to accelerate more mass, so the accelerations are the same.

▶ $$a = F/m = \frac{100}{10} = \frac{20}{2} = 10 \text{ m/s}^2$$

(This applies as long as air resistance is negligible.)

A vertically falling mass travelling at 10 m/s² will cover distances from rest of 5 m in 1 s, 20 m in 2 s, 45 m in 3 s and so on (from $s = \frac{1}{2}at^2$). This is shown in Fig. 5.33. A mass projected "horizontally" in space will continue to move with the same velocity all the time (Newton's first law). If projected horizontally on earth, provided there is little air resistance, the same applies, and it will continue to travel equal **horizontal** distances in equal times.

The vertical and horizontal parts of the motion are independent. Vertically the object accelerates; horizontally it travels with constant velocity. The **combined** effect is shown in Fig. 5.34. The dotted line shows the path taken as a result of the two motions. This means that an object projected horizontally on the earth takes the same time to reach the ground as one dropped vertically. Change in horizontal velocity only changes the horizontal displacement. The time of flight is always the same.

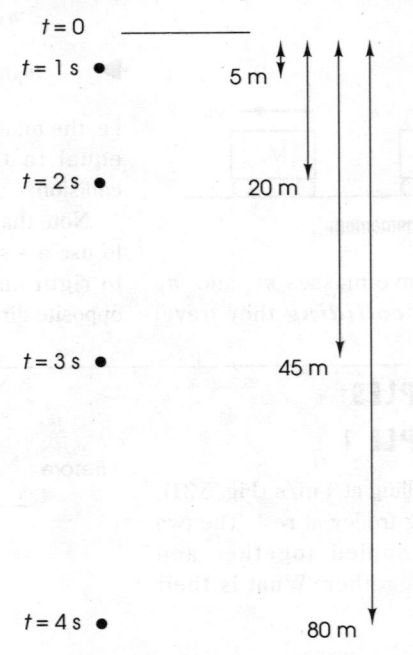

Fig. 5.33 Displacements from rest in a 1:49:16 ratio.

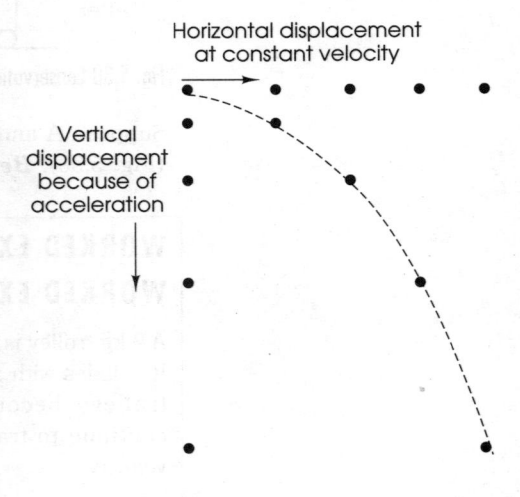

Fig. 5.34 Horizontal and vertical motions are independent.

WORKED EXAMPLE

Fig. 5.35

A ball is kicked from a cliff top with a horizontal velocity of 20 m/s. It hits the ground after 3 s. (a) How far from the base of the cliff does it land? (b) How high is the cliff?

(a) Horizontal velocity is 20 m/s and the ball travels for 3 s. Since

Distance = Velocity × time
Distance $d = 20 \times 3 = $ <u>60 m</u>

(b) Vertically the ball is falling under gravity for 3 s.

Use $s = \frac{1}{2}at^2$

$s = \frac{1}{2} \times 10 \times 9 = $ <u>45 m</u>

10. CIRCULAR MOTION

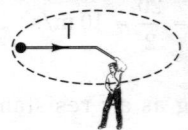

Fig. 5.36 Tension provides the centripetal force.

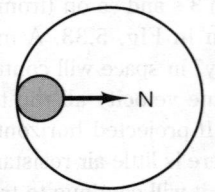

Fig. 5.37 The normal force provides the centripetal force.

For an object to move in a circle, a force must be acting on it, directed **towards the centre** of the circle. Such a force is called a **centripetal force**. The name centripetal is simply a "group name" for any force acting **towards the centre of a circle**; it must be provided by some real agency.

1. A stone on a string is whirled above a person's head in a circle. The **centripetal force** is provided by the **tension** (T) in the string (Fig. 5.36).
2. A ball-bearing is moved around a ring in a horizontal circle. The **centripetal force** is provided by the **normal (reaction) force** (N) of the walls of the circle on the ball (Fig. 5.37).
3. A car cornering – the **centripetal force** is provided by **friction** (Fig. 5.38).
4. Motion of the moon around the earth. The **centripetal force** is provided by the **gravitational pull** of the earth on the moon.

Experience of such forces can lead to some confusion. In whirling a stone on a string you will feel an "equal and opposite" force acting outwards on you. But **you are not moving in a circle**. The inward force on the stone **keeps it in a circle**.

In driving a car around a corner, you will start to move out, away from the centre of the circle. This is because while friction is acting on the car inwards and moving the car in a circle, you are still moving in a straight line – until either friction between you and the seat, or the reaction of the car body on you, provides you with the centripetal force needed to *move you in a circle*.

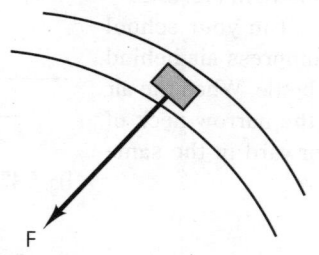

Fig. 5.38 Friction provides the centripetal force.

When an object is moving in a circle its speed (a scalar) in orbit is constant, but its velocity (a vector) is changing. The force towards the centre is not changing the speed

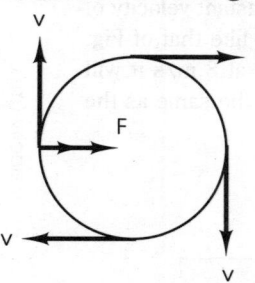

Fig. 5.39 The velocity vector changes because the object is accelerating.

at any time, but it *is* changing its *direction* – the force is causing acceleration (Fig. 5.39).

Remember that acceleration means "change of velocity" and velocity refers to speed in a fixed direction. In a straight line, acceleration can only mean "getting faster" since the direction is fixed. In *circular motion, acceleration* means *changing direction*. The force is still causing a change, but the change is now *a direction change*.

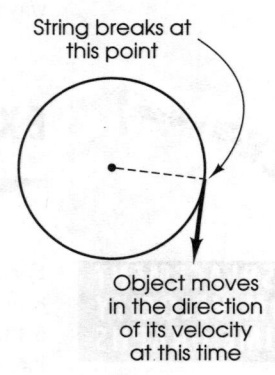

Fig. 5.40

If the force is suddenly removed (in the stone example the string may break) then the object continues to move according to Newton's first law in the direction of its velocity *at that time*, which will be at a tangent to the circular path (Fig. 5.40).

11> ROCKETS AND JETS

In section 7 we found that Newton's third law stated that for every force there would be an equal but opposite reaction force. If water is squirted from a hosepipe there is a reaction force pushing the pipe backwards that is equal to the force pushing the water forward. This can be a problem with large fire hoses which can be difficult to hold and direct.

A **rocket** carries with it all the fuel and oxygen that it needs. When this is burned the hot expanding gases can only leave at the back of the engine. This is then the same situation as the hosepipe and the rocket is driven forward by the reaction force which is equal to the force driving the hot gases backwards (remember that the molecules of hot gases will be moving very quickly). If a lot of fuel is being burned rapidly the force will be large.

A **jet engine** works on exactly the same principle as the rocket where hot (very fast) gases leave the rear of the engine and cause the engine to be forced in the opposite direction. The difference is that it is only designed to work in the Earth's atmosphere and does not need to carry a supply of oxygen with it. The air is taken in at the front of the

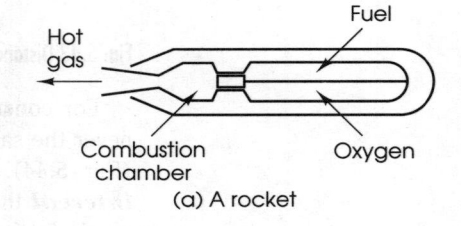

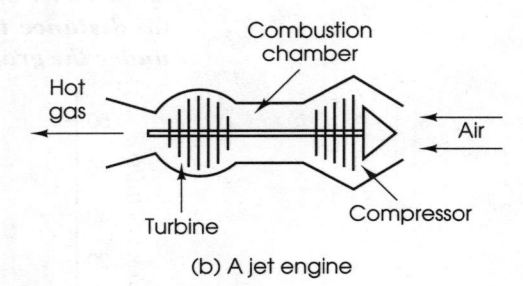

Fig. 5.41

engine and compressed before being burned with the fuel. The compressor can be driven by a turbine placed in the path of the hot gases just before they leave the engine.

▶ NOTE Rockets and jet engines (and hosepipes!) will produce this force when obeying the third law. They do NOT need

72 CHAPTER 5 **FORCES AND MOTION**

something to push against – a rocket, for example, will work just as well in a vacuum.

You can show the principle with a simple balloon driven vehicle as shown in Fig. 5.42.

You may also have a kit in your school which uses a pump to compress air behind water in a half full plastic bottle. When the air pushes the water out of the narrow neck of the bottle it is pushed forward in the same way as a rocket.

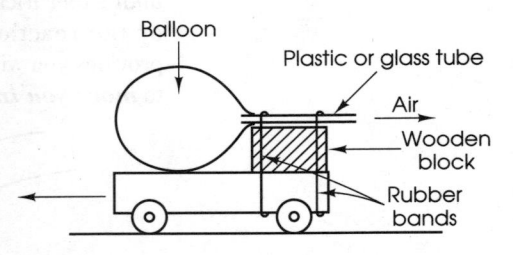

Fig. 5.42

EXTENSION MATERIALS

12> DISPLACEMENT FROM VELOCITY – TIME GRAPHS

For an object moving with constant velocity of 8 m/s, the graph would look like that of Fig. 5.43. After travelling for 20 s at 8 m/s it will have travelled 160 m. This is the same as the **area under the graph**.

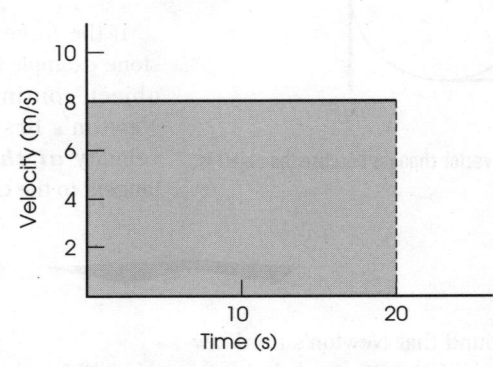

Fig. 5.43 Distance travelled is the area under the graph.

For constant acceleration the velocity is never the same from one second to the next (Fig. 5.44). But over a **very small time interval** the velocity would not change too much. So for the small interval around 10 s, the **distance travelled** is again the **area under the graph**.

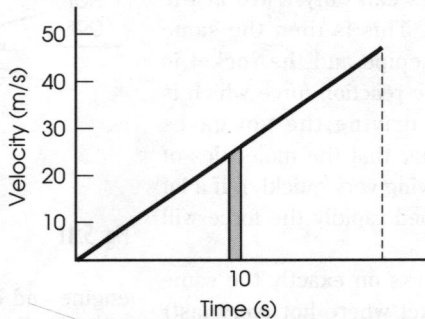

Fig. 5.44 Velocity is almost constant over a short time interval.

Adding up all such small areas is like adding up many small displacements, so the **total displacement** is also the area under the graph (Fig. 5.45).

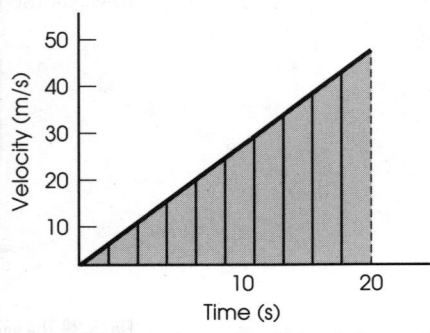

Fig. 5.45 Displacement is the area of the whole triangle.

Area = Area of triangle

= ½ (base × height)

Displacement = ½ × 20 × 50 = 500 m

It is **always** true that the **distance travelled** is the **area under a velocity–time graph**. In Fig. 5.46 you would have to "count squares" on graph paper to find the area. For a more complex journey, a number of pieces of information are available (Fig. 5.47):

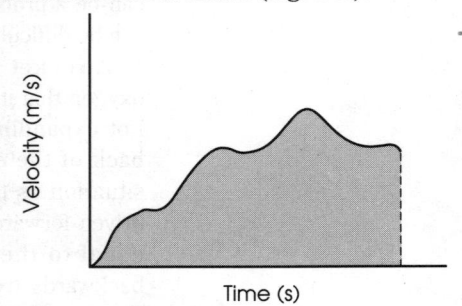

Fig. 5.46 Displacement is the area under the curve.

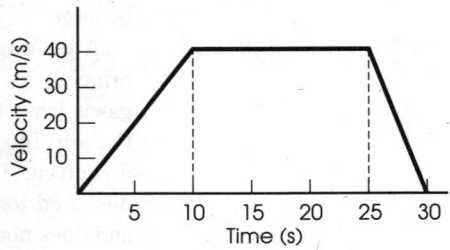

Fig. 5.47

1. **Description of motion.** Constant acceleration from rest for the first 10 s to a velocity of 40 m/s for a further 15 s and constant deceleration to rest in the last 5 s.
2. **Acceleration values.** Initially

$$a = \frac{40}{10} = \underline{4 \text{ m/s}^2}$$

Finally

$$a = \frac{-40}{5} = \underline{-8 \text{ m/s}^2}$$

3. **Total distance travelled.** This is the total area below the graph.

(a) Area of first triangle = ½ × 10 × 40
    = 200 m
(b) Area of rectangle = 15 × 40
    = 600 m
(c) Area of last triangle = ½ × 5 × 40
    = 100 m
Total = (200 + 600 + 100) = 900 m

The acceleration due to gravity near the surface of the earth is fairly constant at 9.81 m/s², so that 10 m/s² represents a reasonable approximation. (See Pg. 76 for a method to determine this.) For an object falling from rest, and accelerating at 10 m/s², a graph of velocity against time will be like that in Fig. 5.48.

By using the areas under the graph, for an object falling freely from the rest, we have:

In 1 s, displacement from rest = 5 m
In 2 s, displacement from rest = 20 m
In 3 s, displacement from rest = 45 m
In 4 s, displacement from rest = 80 m

and so on. These numbers, 5, 20, 45, 80, are in the ratio 1:4:9:16, i.e. $1^2:2^2:3^2:4^2$. *The displacement from rest is proportional to the squares of the times.* (See $s = ½at^2$ below).

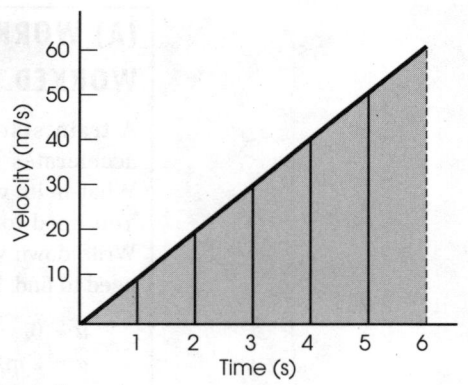

Fig. 5.48

13 > EQUATIONS OF MOTION

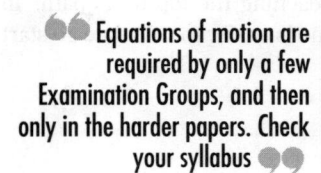

The calculations using graphs in the last two sections can be generalised into a set of equations. In each of them the following symbols are used:

> *Equations of motion are required by only a few Examination Groups, and then only in the harder papers. Check your syllabus*

s = displacement a = acceleration
u = initial velocity t = time
v = final velocity

From the definition of acceleration we already have

$$a = \frac{v - u}{t} \quad \therefore \quad \underline{v = u + at} \quad [5.1]$$

For constant acceleration from initial velocity u to final velocity v over a time t, the **displacement** is the area under the graph, i.e. area of rectangle plus triangle in Fig. 5.49.

$$s = (ut) + ½(v - u)t$$

but from eq [5.1]

$$v - u = at$$
$$s = ut + ½(at)t$$
$$\underline{s = ut + ½at^2} \quad [5.2]$$

For an object accelerating uniformly from rest, this simplifies because $u = 0$, so that $s = ½at^2$.

Combining eqs [5.1] and [5.2] gives [5.3]:

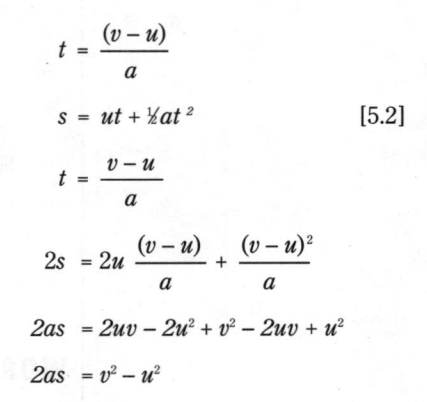

$$\underline{v = u + at} \quad [5.1]$$

$$t = \frac{(v - u)}{a}$$

$$s = ut + ½at^2 \quad [5.2]$$

$$t = \frac{v - u}{a}$$

$$2s = 2u\frac{(v - u)}{a} + \frac{(v - u)^2}{a}$$

$$2as = 2uv - 2u^2 + v^2 - 2uv + u^2$$

$$2as = v^2 - u^2$$

$$\underline{v^2 = u^2 + 2as} \quad [5.3]$$

It is also true that, with constant acceleration the average velocity is $(u + v)/2$ so that

$$s = \frac{(u + v)t}{2} \quad [5.4]$$

To summarise, the four equations for constantly accelerated motion are

$$v = u + at \quad [5.1]$$
$$s = ut + ½at^2 \quad [5.2]$$
$$v^2 = u^2 + 2as \quad [5.3]$$

$$s = \frac{(u + v)t}{2} \quad [5.4]$$

You do not need to memorise how to obtain these. You *do* need to be able to use them.

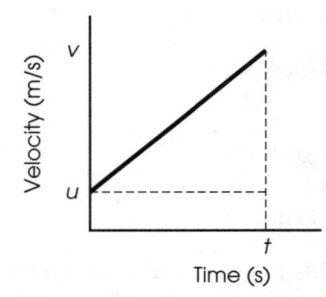

Fig. 5.49

(A) WORKED EXAMPLES
WORKED EXAMPLE 1

A train starts from rest in a station and accelerates uniformly at 2 m/s² for 1 min. What is its velocity at the end of that time? You need to decide which equation to use. Write down what you are given and what you need to find. Here

$u = 0$ $t = 1$ min $= 60$ s
$a = 2$ m/s² $v =$ unknown

▶ So use

$$v = u + at$$

Then

$$v = 0 + (2 \times 60)$$
$$= \underline{120 \text{ m/s}}$$

WORKED EXAMPLE 2

An object is dropped down a deep pit from rest. The pit is 50 m deep. How long will it take to reach the bottom of the pit? ($g = 10$ m/s²). Here

$u = 0$ $s = 50$ m
$a = 10$ m/s² $t =$ unknown

▶ Use

$$s = ut + \tfrac{1}{2}at^2$$

Since

$u = 0$ $s = \tfrac{1}{2}at^2$
$50 = \tfrac{1}{2} \times 10 \times t^2$ $50 = 5t^2$

$$t^2 = \frac{50}{5} = 10$$

$$t = \sqrt{10} = \underline{3.2 \text{ s}}$$

WORKED EXAMPLE 3

A car is travelling with a constant velocity of 30 m/s. In order to overtake a lorry, the driver accelerates at 0.5 m/s² for 0.5 s. What is his velocity at the end of that time? How far did he travel while accelerating?

For the first part

$u = 30$ m/s $t = 0.5$ s
$a = 0.5$ m/s² $v =$ unknown

▶ So use

$$v = u + at$$
$$v = 30 + (0.5 \times 0.5) = \underline{30.25 \text{ m/s}}$$

▶ To find the *distance* use

$$s = ut + \tfrac{1}{2}at^2$$
$$s = (30 \times 0.5) + \tfrac{1}{2}(0.5 \times (0.5)^2)$$
$$= 15 + \tfrac{1}{2}(0.125) = \underline{15.06 \text{ m}}$$

▶ Alternative solution could use

$$v^2 = u^2 + 2as$$

then

$$(30.25)^2 = (30)^2 + 2(0.5)s$$

giving

$$s = \underline{15.06 \text{ m}}$$

Many problems using these ideas involve projecting an object **upwards,** i.e. throwing a ball vertically in the air. The things to remember in these cases are:

1. The acceleration due to gravity is acting **down.** So the "acceleration" becomes **negative.**
2. At the top of the path, before the object starts to return, its velocity is **zero.**
3. The time to go **up to** the top of the path is the same as the time to **come down**.
4. Whatever velocity the object had on leaving the ground, it will have the **same** on returning. (This follows from conservation of energy since there is (almost) no energy changed to heat through work done against friction.)

WORKED EXAMPLE 4

A stone is thrown vertically upwards leaving a person's hand at 30 m/s. (i) How high will it travel before coming to rest? (ii) How long will it take before reaching the top of its path? In this case the time is easier to calculate so start with part (ii).
You are told

$u = 30$ m/s
$a = 10$ m/s² (acceleration due to gravity)
$v = 0$ (top of path)
$t =$ unknown

So use

$$v = u + at \quad 0 = 30 + (-10)t$$

(*NB.* (–10) since decelerating.)

$$30 = 10 t \quad t = \underline{3 \text{ s}}$$

For distance travelled use

$$s = ut + \tfrac{1}{2}at^2$$
$$s = (30 \times 3) + \tfrac{1}{2}(-10(3)^2)$$
$$s = 90 + \tfrac{1}{2}(-90)$$
$$= 90 - 45 = \underline{45 \text{ m}}$$

It is again possible to use $v^2 = u^2 + 2as$ which would give the distance first, then use $s = ut + \tfrac{1}{2}at^2$. You may wish to try the solution this way.

(B) PROOF OF FORMULA FOR KINETIC ENERGY

In Chapter 4 a formula for kinetic energy was stated as

Kinetic energy = $\tfrac{1}{2}mv^2$

This can be proved using the equations of motion. In Figure 5.50 a vehicle is travelling at

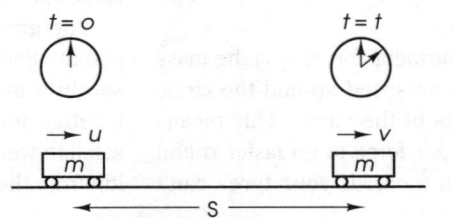

Fig. 5.50 Calculating kinetic energy change.

a velocity u when a stop-clock is started. After t seconds it is travelling at a greater velocity v. The distance between observations is s. The mass of the vehicle is m. If the vehicle accelerates uniformly then

$$a = \frac{v-u}{t}$$

In order for it to accelerate a **resultant force F** must be acting and

$$F = ma \qquad F = \frac{m(v-u)}{t}$$

The *work done* to move the vehicle causes a change in kinetic energy, so

Change in kinetic energy = $F \times s$

i.e.

Change in kinetic energy = $m \dfrac{(v-u)}{t} s$

but s/t is the average velocity, v_{av}. Average velocity is the average of the starting velocity u and the final velocity v, i.e.

$$v_{av} = \frac{(v+u)}{2}$$

So

Change in kinetic energy

$$= m(v-u)\frac{(v+u)}{2}$$
$$= \tfrac{1}{2} m(v-u)(v+u)$$
$$= \tfrac{1}{2} m(v^2 - u^2)$$
$$= \tfrac{1}{2} mv^2 - \tfrac{1}{2} mu^2$$

If this is the *change* in kinetic energy then each term represents the kinetic energy at a *particular time*. So

Kinetic energy at velocity $v = \tfrac{1}{2} mv^2$

This is the usual formula, namely **kinetic energy** = $\tfrac{1}{2} mv^2$

14> IMPULSE AND SAFETY

Section 8 showed that

Impulse = F × t = change of momentum

In many cases where the change of momentum is large you need to make the *force* involved as *small* as possible: e.g. if an egg is dropped you will have a change of momentum when the egg hits the floor. If the egg is to be unbroken the force must be as small as possible and, looking at the equation, this means that the *time* that the force acts for should be as *long* as possible. This is done by putting eggs in boxes that *can* be crushed so that the stopping force lasts longer.

Crumple zones in cars have the same effect. The car is designed to crumple in an impact so that the force stopping the car lasts longer and is reduced. Seat belts, apart from restraining the passengers within the car, also stretch a little and the "inertia reels" helps to make the force on your body last longer and therefore be smaller. Crash helmets and cycling helmets work on the same principle. Once such items have been deformed in an accident they will not work effectively again and should be replaced.

15> SATELLITES AND CIRCULAR MOTION

All satellites stay in their orbit because of a **centripetal** force provided by gravity. This includes the moon in its orbit around the Earth and, although their orbits are not circular, the planets rotating around the Sun.

Satellites round the Earth are of two principal types. **Polar** orbital satellites take an orbit that passes over the north and south poles. As the Earth rotates beneath the orbit can pass over a different part of the Earth on each orbit. This can be useful for weather observation, spy satellites and for gathering information on a range of subjects from climatic changes to crop growth. The second type is called **geostationary** and rotates round the Earth once in 24 hours. Since the Earth also rotates on its axis in this time the satellite appears to be stationary when viewed from the Earth. This is especially useful in telecommunications for retransmitting telephone calls or television pictures to particular areas and for more "local" weather forecasting.

The centripetal force for any object moving in a circle is given by

$$F = \frac{mv^2}{r}$$

where F is the centripetal force, m is the mass of the object, v is its speed around the circle and r is the radius of the circle. This means that it needs a larger force to go faster round the same bend in a car. If your tyres can't provide a large enough friction force because of ice or gravel then you cannot go round the arc and you will start to go straight on, hitting the outside of the bend. A "tighter" bend has a smaller radius and therefore also requires a greater centripetal force to get you round the bend at the same speed. A heavier (and therefore more massive) lorry will also need a greater force than a light car travelling at the same speed.

The gravitational force between a satellite and the Earth also depends on the mass of the satellite and by putting the two equations together it can be shown that a geostationary satellite will need to orbit in a radius of 42 000 km from the centre of the Earth.

16 INERTIA

Inertia is a measure of how difficult it is to change the motion of a body. If an object has more inertia it will be more difficult to start or stop it moving or more difficult to change its direction. This depends on the amount of matter that the object contains, so mass is a good measure of inertia. (We have already seen in Newton's second law that the force needed to produce an acceleration depends on the mass of the object.)

17 DETERMINATION OF g BY A FREE-FALL METHOD

The time of the fall will be small and must be measured as precisely as possible. A millisecond or centisecond timer is needed. A steel ball-bearing is held on to an electromagnet (Fig. 5.51). The electromagnet is connected to the timer so that when the supply to the electromagnet is switched off, the timer starts. Several metres below the electromagnet is a trapdoor made of metal. Two contacts connect the trap to the timer. When the ball hits the trap it breaks the contacts and the timer stops.

RESULTS

Time of fall

(average of several runs) = t seconds
Distance fallen = s metres

CALCULATION

$$s = \tfrac{1}{2}gt^2 \qquad g = 2s/t^2$$

PRECAUTIONS

1. Measure distance s from the bottom of the ball-bearing to the top of the trap, using a plumb-line and a metre rule.
2. On switching off the supply to the electromagnet, the timer immediately starts, but the electromagnet may retain some magnetism and the ball may not release immediately. Use a soft iron core for the electromagnet and place a small piece of tissue paper between the ball and the electromagnet core.
3. Take several readings of time and use an *average* in the final calculation.

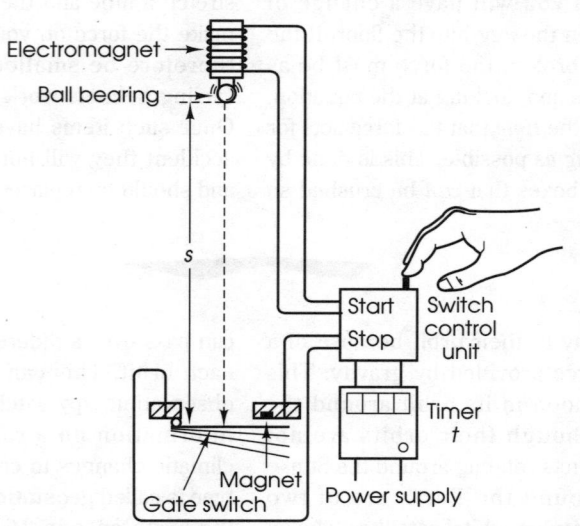

Fig. 5.51

EXAMINATION QUESTIONS

MULTIPLE CHOICE QUESTIONS

QUESTION 1

Which of the following is constant for an object falling freely towards the earth?

- A Velocity
- B Potential energy
- C Acceleration
- D Kinetic energy
- E Momentum

QUESTION 2

The force of gravity on a body is a vector quantity because it

- A Has size and direction
- B Acts in a vertical direction
- C Is a force of attraction
- D Has direction but no size (SEG)

QUESTION 3

The graph (Fig. 5.52) shows how the speed of an object varies with time. The object is

- A Falling freely
- B Moving with constant speed
- C Moving with constant acceleration
- D Moving with constant deceleration (SEG)

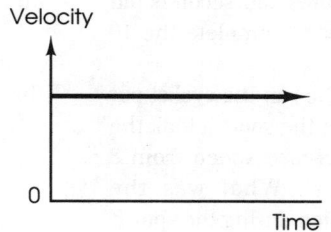

Fig. 5.52

QUESTION 4

The force on a 10 kg mass is 25 N. The acceleration is

- A 0.4 m/s^2
- B 2.5 m/s^2
- C 25 m/s^2
- D 250 m/s^2 (SEG)

QUESTIONS 5–8

The following are five physical quantities:

- A Force
- B Power
- C Pressure
- D Acceleration
- E Work

5. Which one requires a knowledge of area?
6. Which has the same units as weight?
7. Which has the same units as energy?
8. Which would be measured in newton metres per second? (ULEAC)

QUESTION 9

As it nears the moon's surface, a lunar probe of mass 10000 kg is accelerated by the moon's gravitational field of 1.5 m/s^2. What force does the moon exert on the rocket?

- A Zero
- B 1500 N
- C 10000 N
- D 15000 N
- E 100000 N (ULEAC)

QUESTION 10

Which of the following velocity-time graphs (Fig. 5.53) represents constant, positive acceleration?

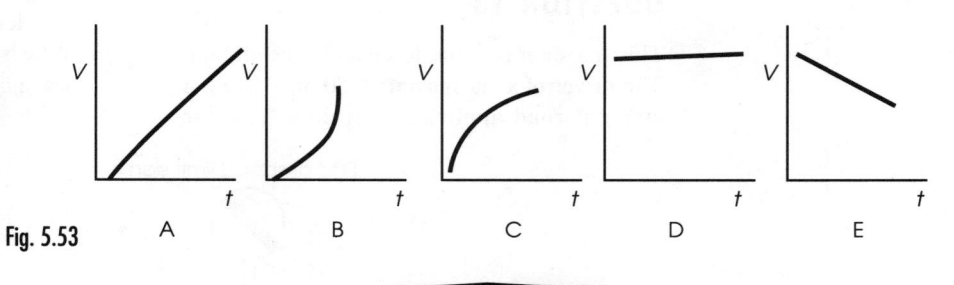

Fig. 5.53   A   B   C   D   E

STRUCTURED QUESTIONS

QUESTION 11

A runner and a dog of similar mass had a race. The graph (Fig. 5.54) shows how they moved during the race.

(a) Over what distance was the race run?
(b) How long did it take the dog to overtake the runner?

(c) How far had the dog travelled after 8 s?
(d) Describe the motion of the runner after point X on the graph.
(e) Describe the motion of the dog after point Y on the graph.
(f) Which gained the most kinetic energy during the race? Explain your answer.
(NEAB)

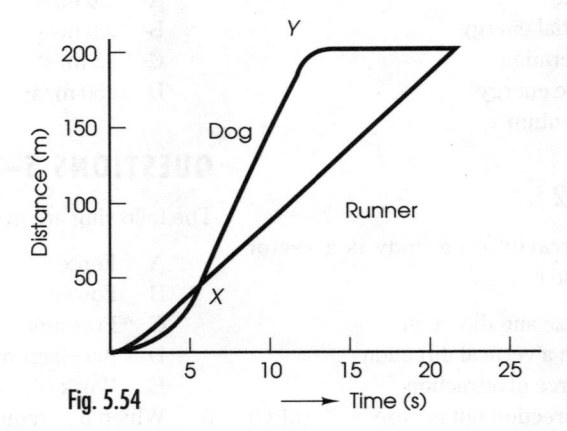

Fig. 5.54

QUESTION 12

This question is about speed and acceleration. A cycle track is 500 m long. A cyclist completes 10 laps (that is, rides completely round the track 10 times).

(a) How many kilometres has the cyclist travelled?
(b) On average it took the cyclist 50 s to complete one lap. What was the average speed of the cyclist?
(c) How long in minutes and seconds did it take the cyclist to complete the 10 laps?
(d) Near the end of the run the cyclist put on a spurt. During the spurt it took the cyclist 2 s to increase speed from 8 m/s^1 to 12 m/s^1. What was the cyclist's acceleration during the spurt?
(SEG)

QUESTION 13

This question is about force and acceleration. The driver of a car moving at 20 m/s^1 along a straight road applies the brakes. The car decelerates at 5 m/s^2.

(a) How long does it take the car to stop?
(b) What kind of force slows the car down?

QUESTION 14

A car engine is leaking oil. The drops hit the ground at regular time intervals, one every 2.5 s. Figure 5.55 shows the pattern of drops it leaves on part of the journey.

(a) What can you say about the speed of the car before it reaches the signs?
(b) If the car is travelling at 10 m/s^1 calculate the distance between the drops on the road before it reaches the signs.
(c) How can you tell the car is accelerating after it reaches the signs?
(d) After the car passes the signs, the fourth drop falls at a distance of 300 m past the signs. Calculate the acceleration using the formula
$s = ut + \frac{1}{2}at^2$.
(ULEAC)

QUESTION 15

Slow-motion photography shows that a jumping flea pushes against the ground for about 0.001 s during which time its body accelerates upwards to a maximum speed of 0.8 m/s.

(a) Calculate the average upward acceleration of the flea's body during this time.
(b) If the flea then moves upward with an acceleration, assumed constant, of 12 m/s^2, calculate:
  (i) How long it will take after leaving contact with the ground at a speed of 0.8 m/s to reach the top of the jump?
  (ii) How high it will jump after leaving contact with the ground?
(c) Why is the acceleration of the flea after leaving the ground not equal to g?
(ULEAC)

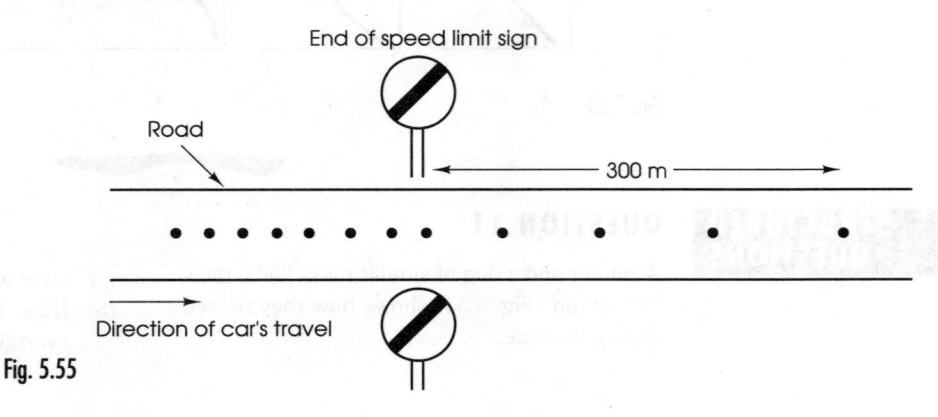

Fig. 5.55

…

OUTLINE ANSWERS

MULTIPLE CHOICE QUESTIONS

Question	1	2	3	4	5	6	7	8	9	10
Answer	C	A	B	B	C	A	E	B	D	A

STRUCTURED QUESTIONS

ANSWER 11

(a) 200 m (from graph).
(b) 6 s (from graph).
(c) 100 m (from graph).
(d) Runner is travelling with constant velocity (equal distances in equal times).
(e) The dog is at rest (200 m, and stays there all the time after Y).
(f) The dog. Kinetic energy = ½mv^2. Both have the same mass. The dog has the greatest velocity shown by the greater gradient of the graph.

ANSWER 12

(a) $500 \times 10 = 5\,000$ m = 5 km

(b) Average speed = $\dfrac{\text{Total distance}}{\text{Total time}}$

   = $500 \div 50 = 10$ m/s^{-1}

(c) $50 \times 10 = 500$ s

   1 m = 60 s $\dfrac{500}{60}$ = 8 min 20 s

(d) Acceleration = $\dfrac{\text{Velocity change}}{\text{Time}}$

   = $\dfrac{(12-8)}{2} = \dfrac{4}{2} = 2$ m/s^2

ANSWER 13

(a) Use $v = u + at$ but remember he is decelerating so the acceleration is (−5) m/s². Final velocity $v = 0$ m/s since he is at rest

   $0 = 20 + (-5)t$

   $5t = 20$ $t = 4$ $\underline{t = 4\text{ s}}$

(b) The force is friction.

ANSWER 14

(a) Before reaching the signs the car is travelling with constant velocity.
(b) One drop every 2.5 s. At 10 m/s the distance is $(10 \times 2.5) = 25$ m.
(c) The distance between dots is greater, so the velocity is increasing and the car is accelerating.
(d) Four intervals means $(4 \times 2.5) = 10$ s to travel 300 m. Velocity before reaching the signs is 10 m/s.

$$s = ut + \tfrac{1}{2}at^2$$
$$300 = (10 \times 10) + \tfrac{1}{2}a(10)^2$$
$$300 = 100 + 50a$$
$$200 = 50a$$
$$a = \underline{4\text{ m s}^2}$$

ANSWER 15

(a) Acceleration = $\dfrac{\text{Velocity change}}{\text{Time}}$

   = $\dfrac{0.8}{0.001}$ = $\underline{800\text{ m/s}^2}$

(b) In this part remember that although the question uses the word "acceleration" it is negative – pulling the flea back to the ground.

   (i) Use $v = u + at$; v = final velocity at the top of the jump = 0 m/s.

   $0 = 0.8 + (-12)t$ $12t = 0.8$
   $t = 0.06$ s

   (ii) Use $s = ut + \tfrac{1}{2}at^2$.

   $s = (0.8 \times 0.06) + \tfrac{1}{2}(-12)(0.06)^2$
   $= 0.048 - 0.022 = 0.026$ m
   $s = \underline{26\text{ mm}}$

(c) The acceleration due to gravity is 10 m/s². If the flea is experiencing a greater downward acceleration of 12 m/s² there is an extra downward force – this can only be air resistance pushing down as the flea jumps upwards.

TUTOR'S QUESTION AND ANSWER

QUESTION

(a) A trolley starts from rest and runs along a straight track, about 3 m long. Describe, with the aid of a suitable diagram, how you would make measurements from which you could work out the speed of the trolley at different times from the start. Explain carefully how you would calculate the values of the speed.

(b) A car of weight 7000 N is travelling along a level road at a speed of 20 m/s when it comes to a hill which rises vertically 100 m and is 1.0 km long, the driver increases the power output of the engine to keep the speed constant at 20 m/s.

 (i) How much time does it take the car to climb the hill?

 (ii) How much work does the car do against gravity as it climbs the hill?

 (iii) What power is needed to do the work.

 (iv) On the return journey the car crosses the top of the hill in the opposite direction at 20 m/s and the driver then disconnects the engine. Explain, in terms of energy changes, why the speed of the car increases. Include the effects of air resistance in your explanation.

ANSWER

(a) The track should be set up and levelled. Check using a spirit level. A 50 Hz ticker-timer is connected to a suitable power supply and tape fed through it and attached to the trolley. The trolley is started at the same time as the timer and it travels 3 m pulling the tape (Fig. 5.56).

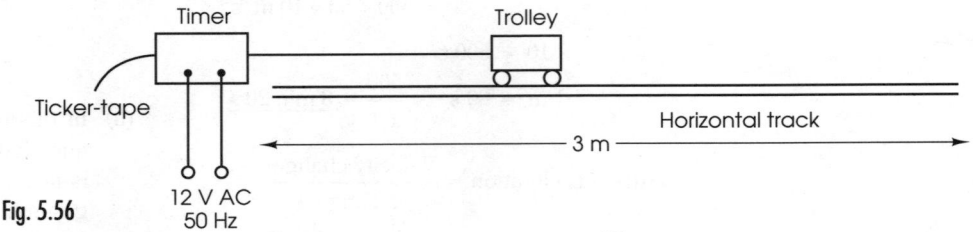

Fig. 5.56

CALCULATIONS

The tape carries both distance and time information. If the timer is working at 50 Hz then a piece of tape with five intervals represents a time of 0.1 s. For the first 0.1 s interval measure the tape length. Suppose it is 3 cm long as shown (Fig. 5.57). Then the velocity is 3/0.1 = 30 cm/s. This can be repeated as required along the whole tape.

(b) (i) Time taken to climb the hill is the same as the time to travel horizontally at 20 m/s^{-1}.
Horizontal distance travelled = 1 km = 1000 m.

$$\text{Time} = \frac{\text{Distance}}{\text{Velocity}} = \frac{1\,000}{20} = \underline{50\ s}$$

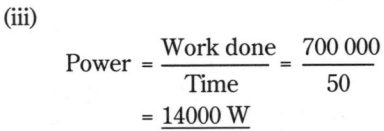

Fig. 5.57

(ii) Work done against gravity is the same as the change in potential energy in rising 100 m above the ground.

$$\text{Work done} = mgh = 7000 \times 100 = \underline{700\,000\ J}$$

(iii)
$$\text{Power} = \frac{\text{Work done}}{\text{Time}} = \frac{700\,000}{50} = \underline{14000\ W}$$

(iv) At the top of the hill the car has kinetic energy (because it is travelling at 20 m/s) and potential energy (because it is 100 m above the ground). On cruising downhill the potential energy will be converted to kinetic energy, so the velocity will increase above 20 m/s. However, not all the potential energy will convert to kinetic energy since work will be done against various friction forces, including air resistance, which will convert some kinetic energy into heat.

STUDENT'S ANSWER WITH THE EXAMINER'S COMMENTS

STUDENT ANSWER TO QUESTION 15

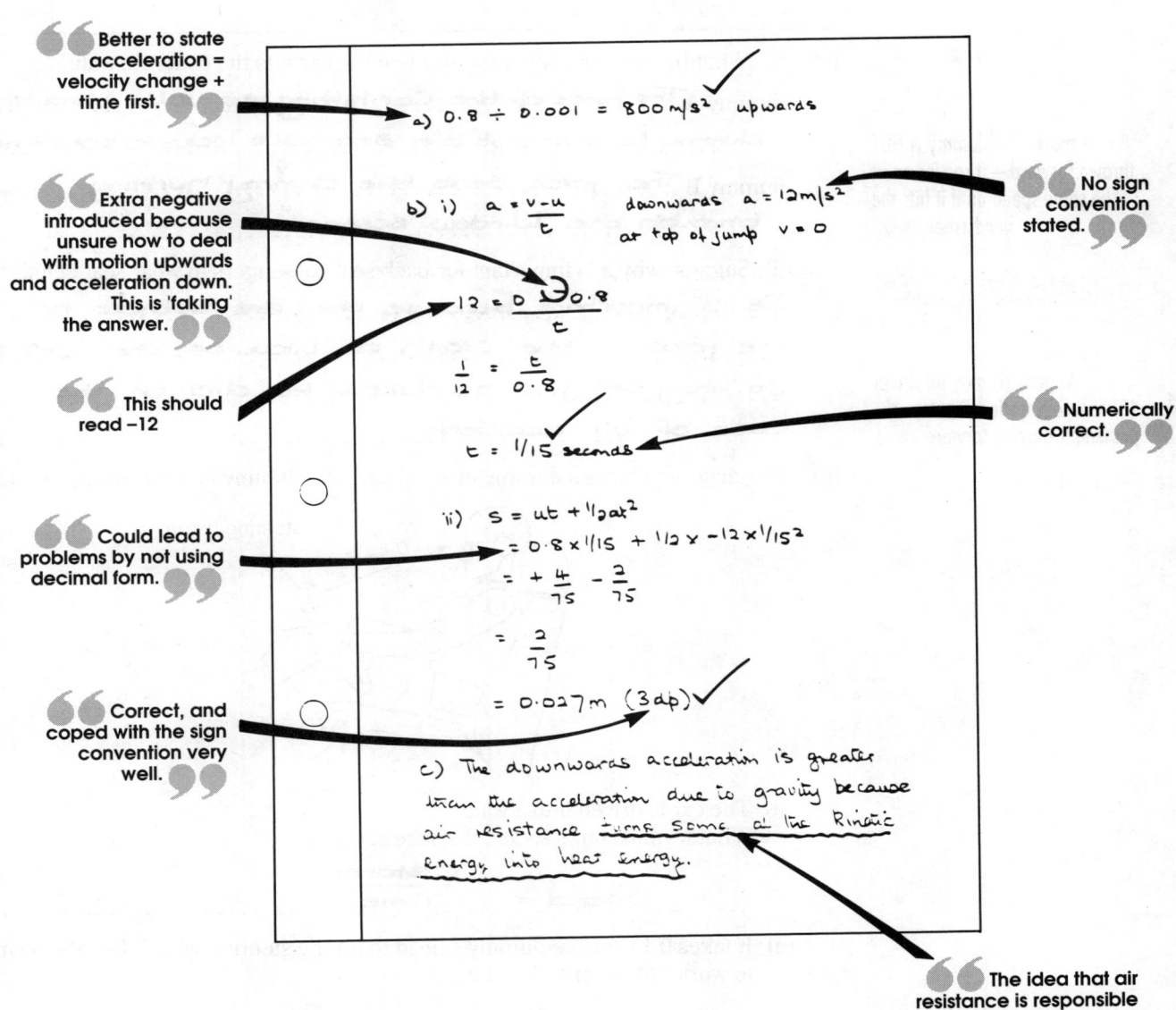

> **Better to state acceleration = velocity change ÷ time first.**

a) $0.8 \div 0.001 = 800 \text{ m/s}^2$ upwards ✓

> **No sign convention stated.**

b) i) $a = \dfrac{v-u}{t}$ downwards $a = 12 \text{ m/s}^2$
at top of jump $v = 0$

> **Extra negative introduced because unsure how to deal with motion upwards and acceleration down. This is 'faking' the answer.**

$12 = 0 - 0.8 \over t$

> **This should read −12**

$\dfrac{1}{12} = \dfrac{t}{0.8}$

$t = 1/15$ seconds ✓

> **Numerically correct.**

> **Could lead to problems by not using decimal form.**

ii) $s = ut + \tfrac{1}{2}at^2$
$= 0.8 \times 1/15 + 1/2 \times -12 \times 1/15^2$
$= +\dfrac{4}{75} - \dfrac{2}{75}$
$= \dfrac{2}{75}$
$= 0.027 \text{ m}$ (3 dp) ✓

> **Correct, and coped with the sign convention very well.**

c) The downwards acceleration is greater than the acceleration due to gravity because air resistance turns some of the kinetic energy into heat energy.

> **The idea that air resistance is responsible is correct, but Energy ideas do not relate to the acceleration change.**

MORE EXAMINER'S COMMENTS CENTRAL TIER

In road safety tests cars are crashed into walls.

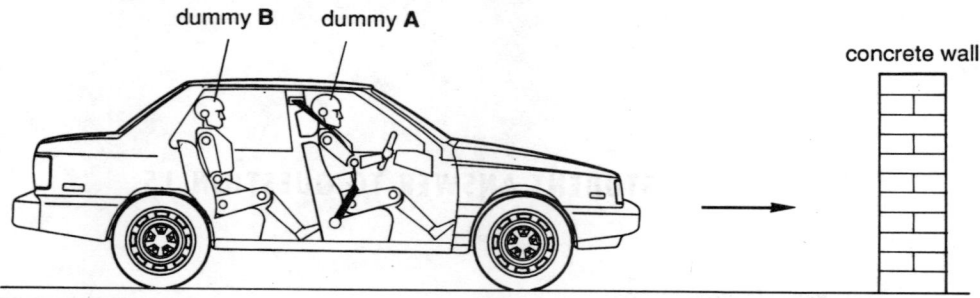

(a) (i) What happens to each dummy when the car hits the concrete wall?

dummy A *The force of the Car hitting the wall throws the dummy forward but the seatbelt locks to keep him in place*

dummy B *The force sent the dummy hurtling through the Window screen* ...(2)

> **1 mark. The dummy is NOT thrown forward – it carries on at the same speed until it hits the windscreen**

(ii) Suggest why it is important for back seat passengers to wear seat belts.

It is important because they are subject to the force of the crash as well as the driver. So they are just as likely to die in the case of an accident ...(2)

> **Vague? (i) may hit driver (ii) reduces injuries (iii) stops the passenger moving forward**

(b) The diagram shows a dummy in a test car. The dummy is not wearing a seat belt.

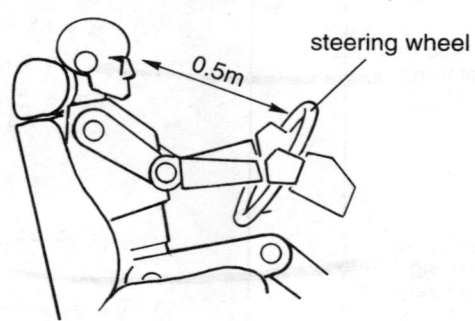

(i) The car is driven into a wall. What formula links speed, distance and time?

$$\text{Speed} = \frac{\text{Distance}}{\text{Time}}$$ ...(1)

(ii) It takes 0.1 s for the dummy's head to hit the steering wheel. Use the formula to work out the speed of the car.

$$\text{Speed} = \frac{D}{T} \quad \text{Speed} = \frac{0.5}{0.1} = 5 \text{ m/s}$$ ...(2)

> **Calculations done clearly and well, getting full marks**

(iii) In a crash at 10 m/s, the driver must be stopped in 0.05 s to avoid hitting the steering wheel.

Calculate the average deceleration of the driver.

$$\text{Deceleration} = \frac{\text{Change in velocity}}{\text{Time Take}}$$

$$\text{Deceleration} = \frac{-10}{0.05} = -200 \text{ m/s}^2$$ ...(3)

it will be Decelerating at 200 m/s²

REVIEW SHEET

Define the newton by completing the following sentence.

- A newton is a force that can _____
  _____.

- Displacement is the distance moved in a _____ .

- Complete the following equations

    1. Average velocity = _____   2. Speed = _____

    3. Acceleration = _____   4. Momentum = mass × _____

    5. Force = _____   6. _____ = Force × time

- To keep an object moving in a circle there must be a _____ force acting _____ the centre of the circle.

- A geostationary satellite is one which _____
  _____.

- A car accelerates from 0 m/s to 30 m/s in 10 s. Its acceleration is _____.

- The weight of a 1 kg mass at the Earth's surface is 10 N. A 2 kg mass will have a weight of _____ and if it is dropped its acceleration will be _____ _____ that of the 1 kg mass.

- A satellite is kept in orbit round the Earth by a _____ force that is caused by _____.

- A car of mass 100 kg moving at 5 m/s has a momentum of _____.

- Newton's first law says that _____
  _____
  _____.

- A rocket engine is an application of _____ law.

- A ball has a mass of 0.2 kg and is thrown with an acceleration of 25 m/s^2. The force of the throw is _____ N.

- Cars have crumple zones to make the _____ of a crash longer so that the _____ on the passengers is smaller.

- In a collision the total _____ is conserved.

- On a velocity–time graph the area under the graph is the same as _____.

- On a displacement–time graph the gradient is the same as the _____.

CHAPTER 5 FORCES AND MOTION

■ Draw small sketch graphs to show the movement of each of the following objects as a velocity–time graph.

   1. constant velocity   2. constant acceleration

   3. increasing acceleration   4. stopped

■ The three equations of motion are

   1. $v =$ _____   2. $s =$ _____   3. $v^2 =$ _____ .

■ A car of mass 1000 kg moves at 9 m/s. Its kinetic energy is _____

■ A 1000 N force acts for 0.10 s. What is the impulse? _____ .

■ Write down the units for each of the following quantities:

   Force _____ Acceleration _____ Momentum _____

   Impulse _____ Weight _____ Mass _____ Energy _____ .

■ A passenger has a mass of 60 kg and is travelling at 25 m/s in a car.

   (i) What is the momentum of the passenger? _____

   (ii) The car stops. What is the momentum of the passenger now? _____

   (iii) What is the impulse applied to the passenger? _____

   (iv) If the car took 20 s to stop, what was the force on the passenger? _____

   (v) If the car had an accident and stopped in 1 s what force is needed to keep the passenger in her seat? _____

       How might this be done? _____

       What would happen otherwise? _____

CHAPTER 6

OSCILLATIONS AND WAVES

GETTING STARTED

Waves are a way of transferring *energy* from one place to another, and are also a means of transferring information. This is clearly important in modern communications systems.

The way in which energy is transferred relies on **oscillations** taking place. Water waves spread out through the oscillation of water particles. Sound is transferred by the oscillation of particles in whatever material the sound is travelling, and electromagnetic waves, like radio or TV, are propagated by oscillating fields. Waves and oscillations are clearly ideas which are connected.

OSCILLATING SYSTEMS

VARIATIONS IN PERIOD

NATURAL FREQUENCY AND RESONANCE

WAVES

SOUND WAVES

SPEED OF SOUND AND ECHOES

WAVE BEHAVIOUR USING WATER WAVES

ELECTROMAGNETIC WAVES

HEARING AND THE HUMAN EAR

HARMONICS AND OVERTONES

A SIMPLE OSCILLATOR

ESSENTIAL PRINCIPLES

1 > OSCILLATING SYSTEMS

Any system which carries out a repeated "to and fro motion" is described as an **oscillator**. Simple examples are a mass on the end of a vertical spring, a pendulum, or a trolley tethered between two springs (Fig. 6.1). The **amplitude** of an oscillation is the *maximum displacement of the system from its rest position*.

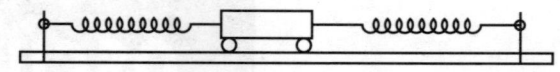

Fig. 6.1 A trolley oscillator.

Once started, oscillations gradually die away. The kinetic energy of the oscillation is transferred to heat through friction, so that the amplitude gets smaller and smaller (Fig. 6.2). However, for many oscillators, the time for one complete oscillation, T, remains constant regardless of the amplitude. They behave like "clocks". The time T is called the **period** of the oscillation. The *frequency*, f, of an oscillation is the number of complete oscillations in 1 s. It is measured in **hertz** (Hz) (1 Hz means one oscillation per second).

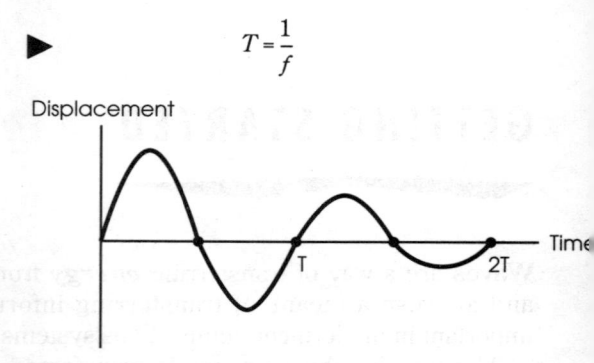

$$T = \frac{1}{f}$$

Fig. 6.2 Damped oscillations.

2 > VARIATIONS IN PERIOD

For the simple mass and spring system (Fig. 6.3), the period can be altered in two ways:

1. **Increasing mass increases T.**
2. **A stiffer spring decreases T.**

However, **mass** has **no effect** on the **period of a pendulum system**, although the longer the pendulum, the greater the period. Pendulum swings should be measured through a small angle. Large angle swings do **not** keep constant time until the angle is less than about 15°.

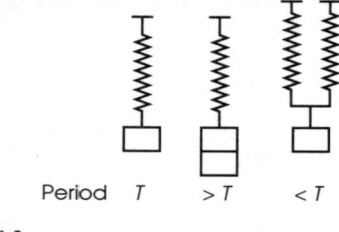

Fig. 6.3

3 > NATURAL FREQUENCY AND RESONANCE

An oscillating system once started and left to oscillate keeps constant time. The frequency of its oscillation is called the **natural frequency**. If, now, a small force is applied at the end of each swing, any energy converted during the oscillation is replaced and added to. This causes large amplitude oscillations to build up. A typical example is a child on a swing. A small push at the end of each swing builds up a large amplitude.

The **mass** on a spring behaves in the same way, if connected to a vibration generator driven at a range of frequencies (Fig. 6.4). When the frequency of the generator (**the driver**) matches the natural frequency of the system (**the responder**) then the mass makes large-amplitude vibrations. This is called **resonance**.

A car, or a large piece of machinery, has many moving parts, each with its own natural frequency. When designing such machines, it is important to take resonance into account since at particular engine frequencies some

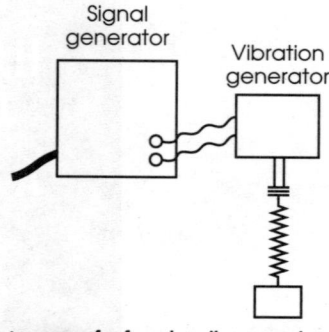

Fig. 6.4 Apparatus for forced oscillations and resonance.

4 WAVES

parts of the machine may begin large-scale vibrations, with possibly dangerous results.

The human body also has a sequence of natural frequencies, for example the stomach and the diaphragm. It is thought that resonance of these may be responsible for sea- or travel-sickness, the nausea being induced by strong vibrations at particular frequencies. Similarly, the eyeball is suspended in its socket like a mass on a spring. Resonance of the eyeball is a dangerous problem often experienced by helicopter pilots.

Perhaps the most famous example of resonance is the collapse of the **Tacoma Narrows Bridge** in the USA. Wind gusts at the natural frequency of the bridge caused the whole bridge to oscillate, and as the amplitude increased, the oscillations led to the eventual and spectacular collapse of the bridge.

We have already met the idea that a **wave** carries *energy* from one place to another, and that oscillating particles or fields enable this to happen. There are two types of wave, *transverse* and *longitudinal*.

A **transverse wave** is like a wave along a string or a rope. In Fig. 6.5 the energy is being transferred from left to right, but the particles of the rope are only moving up or down. This is a transverse wave. The direction of the particle oscillations is at 90° to the direction of energy transfer. Other examples are water waves and electromagnetic waves (though for electromagnetic waves it is fields not particles which oscillate).

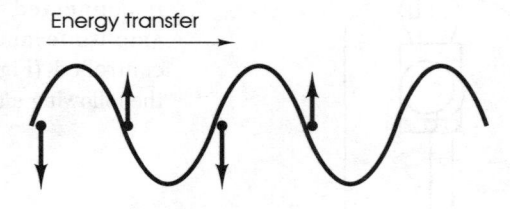

Fig. 6.5 Transverse wave.

A spring like a "slinky" can be used to demonstrate a longitudinal wave. Here the particles oscillate about fixed points from left to right, and the energy is also transferred from left to right. Sound waves are also longitudinal waves (Fig. 6.6).

66 It is worth noting that these are the only two common examples of longitudinal waves. All the rest are transverse. 99

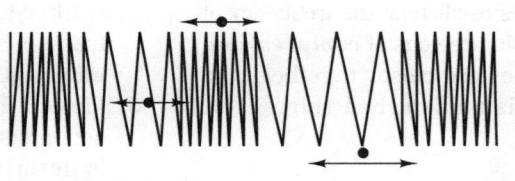

Fig. 6.6. Longitudinal wave.

The **amplitude** (A) of a **wave** has the same meaning as it has for an oscillation. It is the ***maximum displacement of a particle from rest*** (Fig. 6.7).

The ***wavelength*** is the ***distance between wave crests*** or ***wave troughs***. It is given the symbol λ and is measured in metres (Fig. 6.8). Many other points on a wave are also a wavelength apart, and some are marked in Fig. 6.9. Notice that at such points the particles are moving in the ***same direction***, and with the ***same speed***. They are described as being ***in phase***. So ***wavelength*** can also be defined as the ***distance between adjacent particles in phase***.

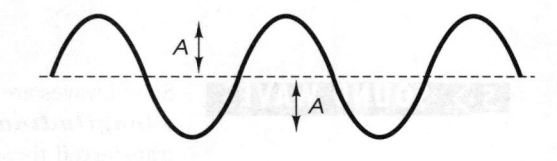

Fig. 6.7 Wave amplitude.

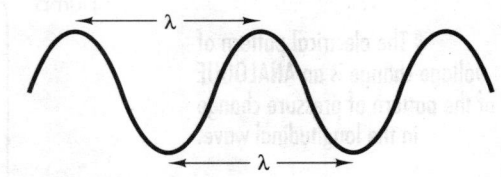

Fig. 6.8

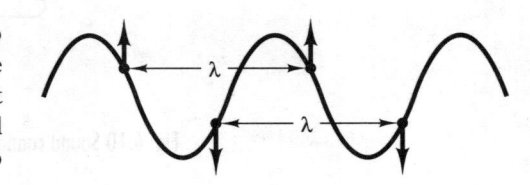

Fig. 6.9 At points one wavelength apart, particles are in phase.

The ***frequency*** of a wave is the ***number of complete cycles of disturbance each second***. It is measured in Hertz (Hz)

If a wave has a wavelength of 2 m and a frequency of 20 Hz then it will make 20 complete cycles of movement each second. Each cycle carries wave energy forward by one wavelength (2 m). So at the end of 1 s the energy has travelled $(20 \times 2) = 40$ m, and the wave velocity is 40 m/s.

In general if the velocity is v, the frequency f and wavelength λ then

$$v = f\lambda$$

> **EXAMPLE 1**
>
> Sound travels at 330 m/s in air. If a note of 150 Hz is struck on a piano, what is the wavelength of the sound wave? Using
>
> $$v = f\lambda$$
> $$330 = 150\lambda$$
>
> Therefore
>
> $$\lambda = \frac{330}{150} = \underline{2.2 \text{ m}}$$

> **EXAMPLE 2**
>
> Water waves are generated at 20 Hz. If their wavelength is 2 cm what is the wave speed? From
>
> $$v = f\lambda$$
> $$v = 20 \times (0.02) \text{ (note } \lambda \text{ in metres)}$$
> $$v = \underline{0.4 \text{ m/s}}$$

5 > SOUND WAVES

Sound waves are the only common example of a *longitudinal* wave. Sound can only be transferred through a material (medium). It cannot travel through space (a vacuum). This is usually demonstrated with a bell inside an evacuated jar (Fig. 6.10). The bell can be seen to be ringing but no sound can pass through the vacuum. If air is let into the jar, the sound can be heard again.

> ❝ The electrical pattern of voltage change is an ANALOGUE of the pattern of pressure change in the longitudinal wave. ❞

Fig. 6.10 Sound cannot pass through a vacuum.

Sound is transferred through air by the oscillation of molecules. Near a source of sound, molecules oscillate at the frequency of the source, causing regions of *compression*, where molecules are closer together than when the gas is undisturbed (Fig. 6.11).

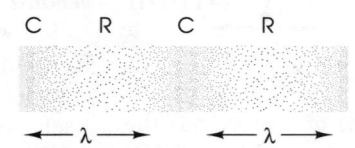

Fig. 6.11 Compressions (C) and rarefactions (R) in a sound wave.

Equally there are regions where molecules are further apart than usual. These are called *rarefactions*. The sound is transferred by this sequence of compression and rarefactions. The wavelength (λ) is the *average distance* from one compression to the next, or from one rarefaction to the next.

Because it is difficult to represent a longitudinal wave, sound waves are often studied using a microphone connected to a cathode ray oscilloscope (CRO). The microphone converts the longitudinal signal into an electrical signal, which is displayed on the CRO as an equivalent transverse wave. However, the original wave was longitudinal.

A signal generator can produce the sound, if connected to a loudspeaker, so that amplitude and frequency can be easily controlled (Fig. 6.12). Using this apparatus the following effects can be seen and heard:

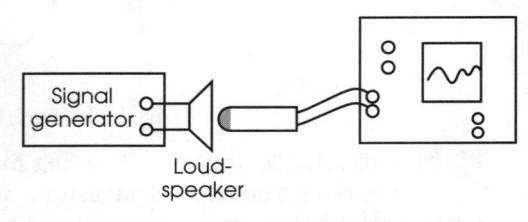

Fig. 6.12 A microphone gives an electrical signal corresponding to pressure changes.

1. A loud sound produces a large-amplitude wave (Fig. 6.13).
2. Higher-pitch sounds have higher frequencies and therefore shorter wavelengths (Fig. 6.14).
3. Musical instruments playing the same note produce different waveforms. This is described as producing notes of *different quality* (Fig. 6.15).

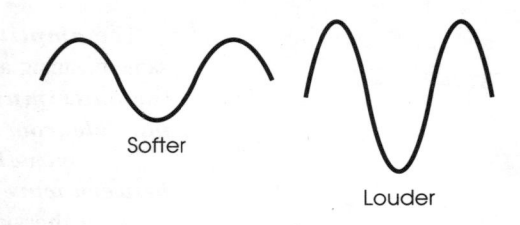

Fig. 6.13

> All sounds start from a vibratioon

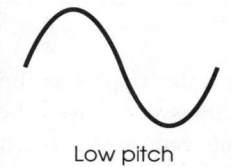

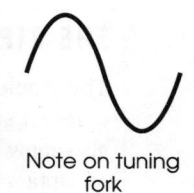

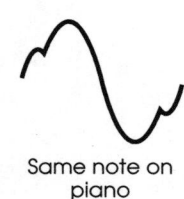

Low pitch   High pitch

Fig. 6.14

Note on tuning fork   Same note on piano

Fig. 6.15

6 SPEED OF SOUND AND ECHOES

Sound, like all waves, can be **reflected**, and the reflected wave is heard as an **echo**. This can be used as a means of finding the **speed** of sound in air.

Standing as far as possible from a smooth wall, a regular sequence of clapping noises is made. If the sequence is of low frequency, it will be followed by a sequence of echoes:

Clap—Echo—Clap—Echo—Clap

If the rate of clapping is increased, there comes a time when no echo is heard. This takes place when each echo corresponds to the next clap, i.e. in the time between one clap and the next, sound has travelled to the wall and back, a distance $2d$ (Fig. 6.16).

If, say, 20 such claps are timed, then the time between one clap and the next is known.

Time for 20 claps   = T seconds
Interval between claps   = $T/20$ seconds
Distance travelled by sound   = $2d$

Velocity of sound $= \dfrac{2d}{T/20}$

$= \dfrac{2 \times 20 \times d}{T}$

This type of method is used in echo-sounding. The speed of sound depends on the material through which it travels. The greater the density of the material the greater the speed. Typical values for the same frequency are given in Table 6.1.

Table 6.1

Material	Frequency (Hz)	Wave-length (m)	Velocity (m/s)
Air	300	1.1	330
Sea-water	300	4	1200
Steel	300	8.3	2500

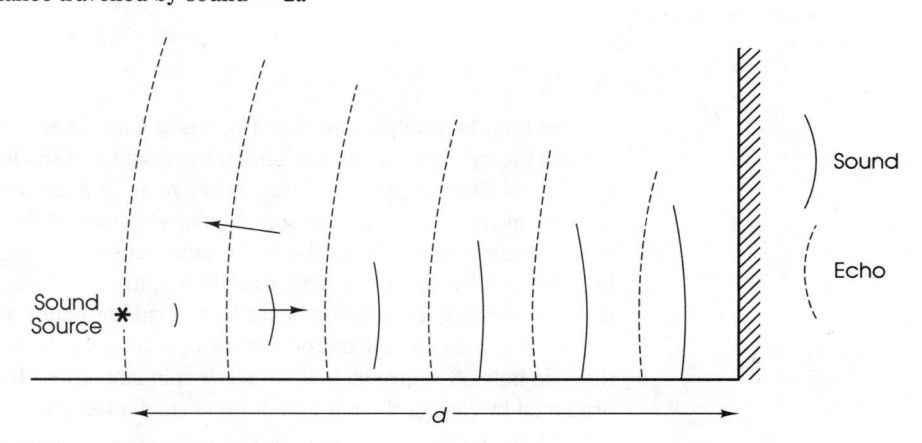

Fig. 6.16 Echo method for the speed of sound in air.

7 WAVE BEHAVIOUR USING WATER WAVES

Water waves are often used to examine the more general behaviour of waves because they can be seen easily, and because the velocity is small and the wavelength large for a fixed frequency. A ripple tank is normally used for this. When single water drops are pulsed regularly into a tank, a pattern is produced as in Fig. 6.17. The circular lines are called **wavefronts** and the lines with arrows show the **direction** of energy transfer (at 90° to the wavefront).

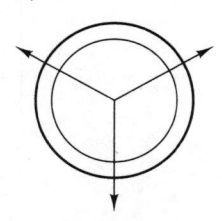

Fig. 6.17 Wavefronts and wave direction.

THE RIPPLE TANK

The ripple tank shows what happens to water ripples as they are reflected or refracted at different surfaces. Since these are simple transverse waves, the patterns and properties shown also apply to other types of wave. You should compare the results seen with those in the chapter on Optics and the nature of light.

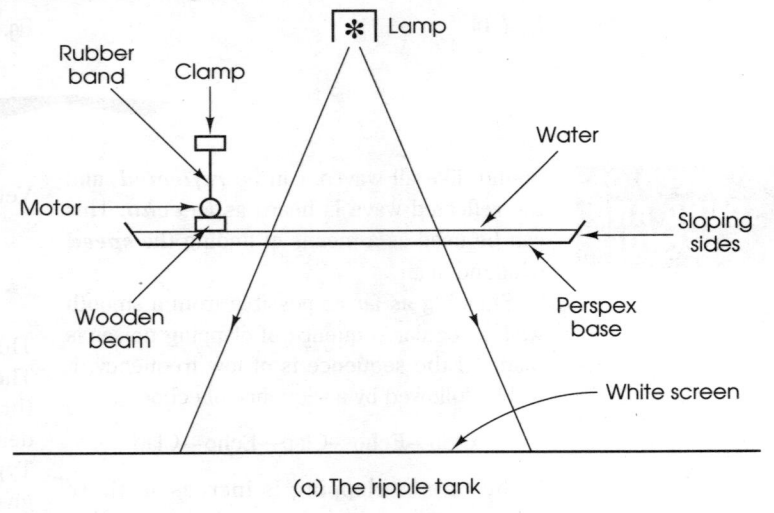

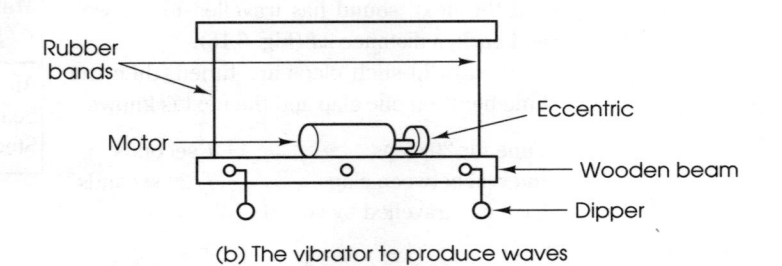

(a) The ripple tank

(b) The vibrator to produce waves

Fig. 6.18

The tank is shallow and has a perspex base with sloping sides. As a ripple crosses the surface the light above the tank shows the ripple as a shadow on the screen below. (You can see this sort of shadow pattern on the bottom of an ordinary sink or bath —if you dip your finger in and out of the water you can see circular shadows of the ripples.) The sloping sides stop the waves being reflected from the sides and complicating the pattern. Straight (plane) waves can be produced by dipping a short straight length of wood in and out of the water. This is usually done by hanging the wooden beam on two rubber bands and making it vibrate up and down by means of a small electric motor driving an eccentric. (An eccentric is a small metal cylinder with the axle hole off centre so that it doesn't spin smoothly.) If circular ripples are required they are produced by raising the bar and fitting a small plastic ball as a "dipper" to it so that the ball just touches the surface.

The patterns can be made to appear stationary by viewing them through a spinning disc with a slot cut in it. If the disc spins at the correct speed the waves will have moved on by one wavelength each time the slit comes round so that the pattern always looks the same. This is the **"stroboscope effect"**. Another method is to replace the lamp with a flashing light (stroboscopic lamp) and adjust the flash rate until it is the same as the frequency at which the beam is bouncing up and down. Each time that you see the pattern it will be in the same place and looks stationary.

To make reflectors, strips of aluminium about 30 mm wide can be bent into the appropriate shape and used as mirrors by standing them in the path of the waves in the tank. You will produce patterns that show that the laws of reflection and the images produced by curved mirrors are all properties of waves.

To make the water shallower to change the speed of the ripples and get refraction you can put pieces of perspex of the correct shape into the bottom of the tank so that the perspex is only just covered by the water.

A straight-edged barrier oscillating in water in a ripple tank gives *plane* wavefronts, with the direction of energy transfer at 90° to the wavefront as before (Fig. 6.19). Continuous waves of either type can be produced using a small motor, and the waves then need to be viewed with a stroboscope (see "Applied Materials"). Just as sound can be reflected, so can any wave.

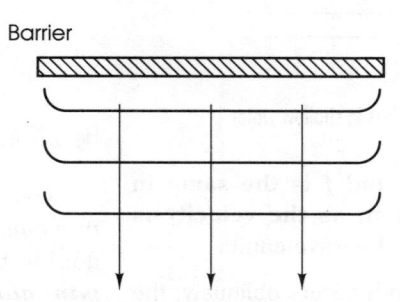

Fig. 6.19 Plane wavefronts.

In a ripple tank, a *circular wavefront* approaching a flat barrier is reflected as in Fig. 6.20. The reflected wave *appears* to have come from a point *behind* the barrier. This point is an *image* of the original source of waves and lies as far behind the barrier as the source lay in front of it (Fig. 6.21). A *plane wave* hitting a flat barrier is reflected as a plane wave. In both cases there is no change of velocity, wavelength or frequency on reflection (Fig. 6.22).

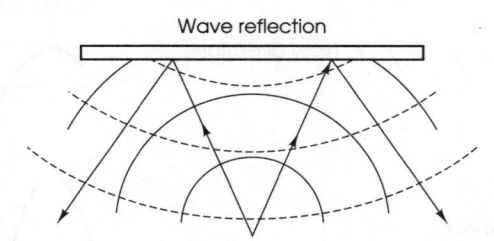

Fig. 6.20 Reflection of a barrier.

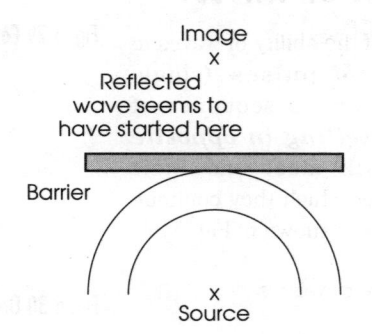

Fig. 6.21

If a plane wave approaches a barrier obliquely (i.e. at an angle) the wave *direction* follows the usual reflection rule, in that *the angle between the direction and barrier before reflection is the same as after reflection*. Again the wavefronts are at 90° to the wave direction, and there is no change of velocity, wavelength or frequency (Fig. 6.23).

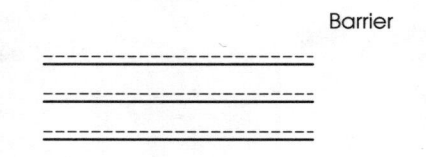

Fig. 6.22 Reflection of plane wavefronts.

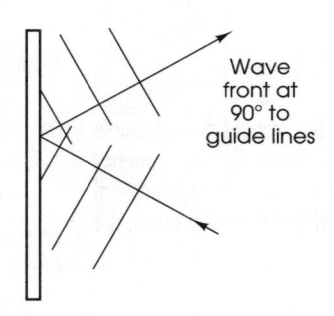

Fig. 6.23

When the waves are reflected you will often see both the incident and reflected waves. If you reflect plane waves from a straight barrier you will be able to see a pattern of parallelograms as the two sets of waves cross. If the waves hit the barrier at 45° the pattern becomes squares. At any other angle the pattern becomes parallelograms as shown in Fig. 6.24.

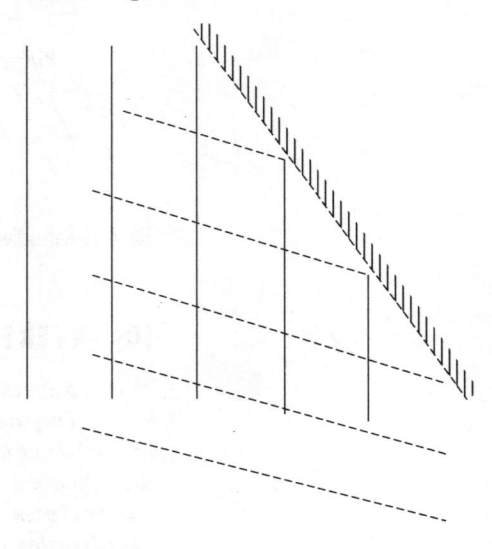

Fig. 6.24

(A) REFRACTION OF WAVES

Refraction is an effect concerned with a *velocity change*. Sound waves change velocity in moving from one material to another; so does light in passing from air to glass. Water waves change velocity on moving from deep to shallow water. The effect is clearly seen in a ripple tank and the ideas can be applied to other waves.

In shallow water, waves generated at a particular frequency travel more slowly than in deep water (Fig. 6.25).

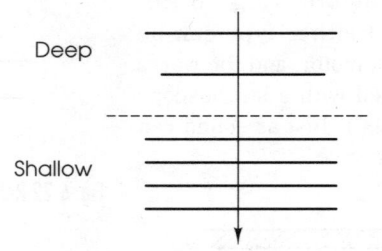

Fig. 6.25 Wave velocity is less in shallow water.

> The frequency is of course fixed by the oscillation frequency of whatever causes the original disturbance to produce the wave.

▶ Since $v = f\lambda$ and f is the same in both cases then, as the velocity is reduced, so is the wavelength.

If the change of depth occurs obliquely, the change in velocity also results in a change in direction (Fig. 6.26). As the wavefronts are successively slowed down, the new fronts travel at an angle to the original fronts. See also Chapter 9.

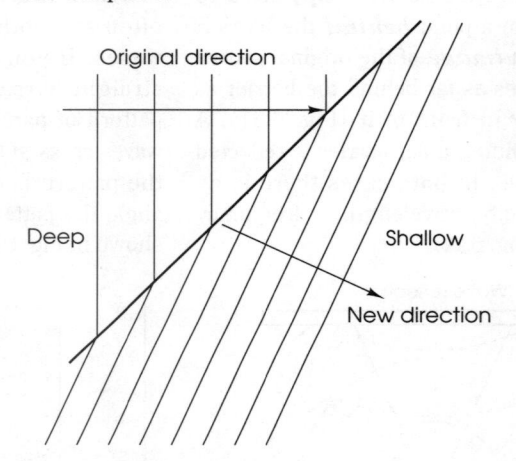

Fig. 6.26 Refraction of waves.

(B) INTERFERENCE OF WAVES

This is a special case of the ability of waves to *superimpose*. If two **pulses** (single disturbances rather than a sequence of disturbances) are *travelling in opposite directions* they will meet and their *amplitudes add*, after which they continue as before. The sequence is shown in Fig. 6.27.

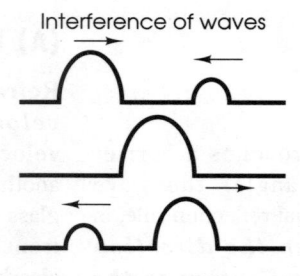

Fig. 6.27 Constructive superposition.

Similarly, if their *amplitudes were in opposite directions*, when they meet their *amplitudes subtract* (Fig. 6.28).

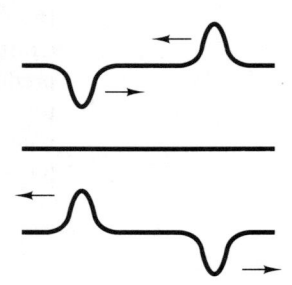

Fig. 6.28 Destructive superposition.

In the special case of **equal amplitudes**, they **combine** to give either a **maximum** of double the amplitude of one pulse or a **minimum** of zero amplitude.

Waves also combine in this way. If the two waves meet, and are of equal wavelength, frequency and amplitude, and are *in phase*, they combine to give a single wave of maximum amplitude 2A (Fig. 6.29). This is called **constructive interference**. If, however, they are *out of phase* they combine to give zero resultant amplitude. This is described as a wave minimum (Fig. 6.30). This is **destructive interference**.

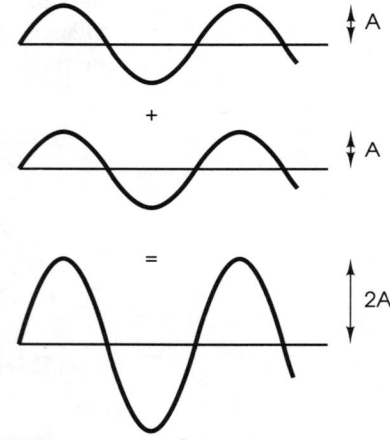

Fig. 6.29 Constructive interference.

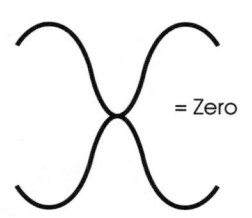

Fig. 6.30 Destructive interference.

This behaviour can again be seen in a ripple tank with two connected vibrating sources, ensuring waves of the same amplitude, frequency and wavelength. The resulting pattern is viewed through a stroboscope.

At points like X in Fig. 6.31, two wave crests (maxima) are meeting. These will at

> All points along a line of maximum interference are oscillating, but points along a minimum line are always at rest.

some time give the maximum amplitude of 2A, and all points along the lines of maxima will also at some time be a maximum. The waves at a "maximum" point **combine** to give a greater value of (+2A) and a least value of (−2A). They will vary periodically between these values.

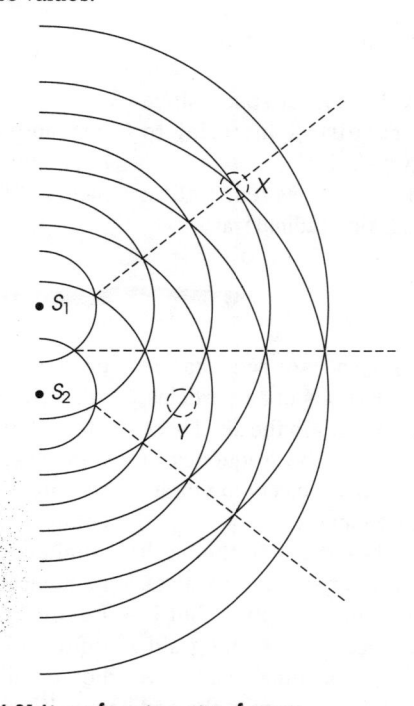

Fig. 6.31 Lines of maximum interference.

At a point like Y a maximum (crest) and a minimum (trough) are meeting. These points will always be at zero amplitude — so there is no disturbance of water, because at all times they are out of phase. The sequence is shown in Fig. 6.32. The minima are lines of zero disturbance in an otherwise moving pattern.

This can be demonstrated for sound waves using two matched speakers in a large room (Fig. 6.33). If the speakers are connected to the same signal generator then, moving parallel to the speakers, areas of "sound" and "silence" will be obvious ("silence" will not be total because of added waves caused by reflection from the walls and ceiling of the room).

Fig. 6.32 The sequence of events at a minimum point.

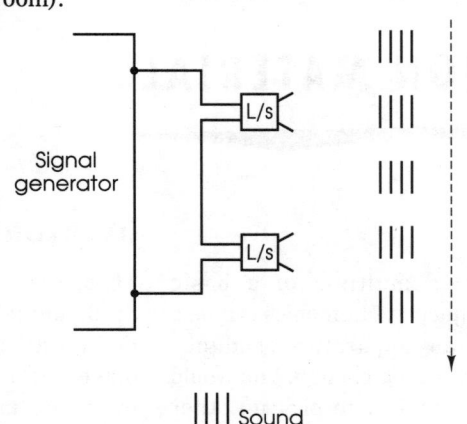

Fig. 6.33 Interference of sound waves.

(C) DIFFRACTION OF WAVES

Waves can *change the shape* of their wavefront on moving past the edge of an object or on passing through a gap in an object. They do not change velocity, frequency or wavelength. This is easily observed in a ripple tank. If plane waves approach a barrier, they spread beyond its edges. This effect is called **diffraction** (note that as in Fig. 6.34 part of the wave is

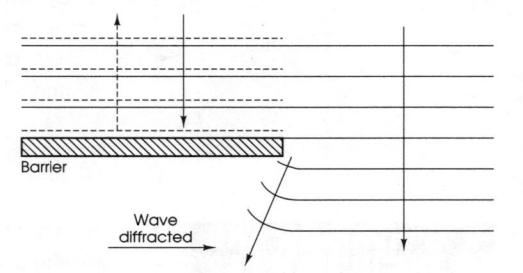

Fig. 6.34 Edge diffraction.

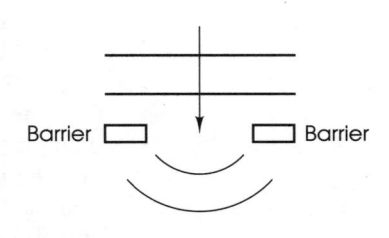

Fig. 6.35 Slit diffraction.

reflected). Similarly, diffraction also takes place on approaching a gap in a barrier with the wave being found beyond the edges of the barrier (Fig. 6.35). The amount of diffraction depends on the *size of the gap* and the *wavelength of the wave*.

▶ The *wider the gap*, as compared with the wavelength, *the less the observable diffraction* (Fig. 6.36). The gap needs to be about a few wavelengths wide for diffraction to be appreciable.

▶ The *smaller the wavelength for a fixed gap, the less the amount of diffraction*. This effect is especially important with electromagnetic waves.

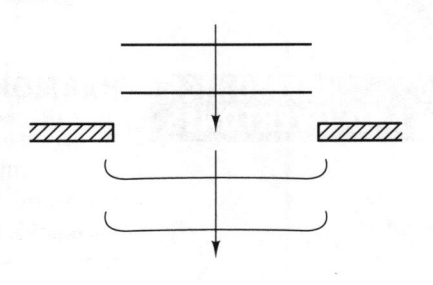

Fig. 6.36 Larger gaps give less diffraction.

8 ELECTROMAGNETIC WAVES

These will also be discussed in Chapter 9 since light is a particular example of an electromagnetic wave. Here it is enough to point out the following facts about **electromagnetic waves**:

1. They are produced and propagated by changing fields and not by particles. The fields originate in accelerating charges.
2. They can travel through space since they do not require a material to transfer energy.
3. They are transverse waves, unlike sound which is a longitudinal wave.
4. They all travel at the same velocity (3×10^8 m/s) in a vacuum.
5. They have no single wavelength. They occupy a wide band of wavelengths from 10^{-14} m (gamma waves) to 10^4 m (radio waves).
6. They include visible light, which consists of a range of wavelengths from 3.3×10^{-7} m (violet) to 6.6×10^{-7} m (for red).

For more information on the electromagnetic spectrum see Chapter 9, "Optics and the nature of light".

9 HEARING AND THE HUMAN EAR

Sound waves from a source cause compressions and rarefactions of air particles, resulting in pressure changes in the air. These pressure changes occur at the frequency of the source, causing flexible objects to vibrate strongly at the same frequency.

The human ear is based inside the skull (Fig. 6.37). The external gristle and cartilage flap (the pinna) may "collect" sound, but is thought to be a directional or warning aid. The "outer" ear is a tube leading inside the skull, and is air-filled. The ear-drum at the end of the outer ear vibrates at the frequency of pressure changes applied to it. These vibrations are passed along an interconnecting sequence of bones, the hammer, anvil and stirrup, which act as "distance multipliers" in a level system. They connect to the "oval window" which, being smaller than the ear-drum, gives a "force multiplication" rather like a car-brake system. Beyond the oval window the inner ear is liquid-filled. Vibration of fine hairs in the liquid causes nerve stimulation resulting in impulses passed to the brain and the response of "hearing".

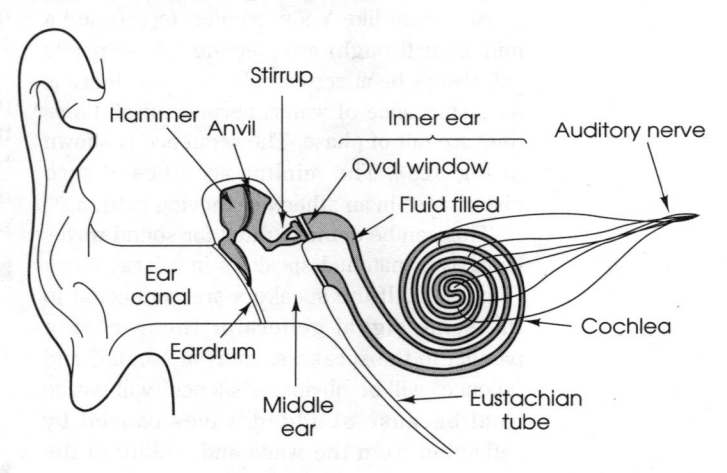

Fig. 6.37

EXTENSION MATERIALS

10 HARMONICS AND OVERTONES

HARMONICS

A **harmonic** is a multiple of a basic (fundamental) frequency. Harmonics can be a problem when an apparatus produces harmonics that are strong enough. You would not want a radio receiver to pick up other stations transmitting on harmonics of the one that you are listening to!

OVERTONES

These are the multiples (harmonics) of the fundamental frequency of a note that are mixed with the fundamental when the note is played on a particular instrument. These **overtones** give the note its particular quality or "timbre". Different instruments produce different overtones or different amounts of the same overtones and therefore don't sound the same, even when playing the same note. Some instruments can produce all the harmonics, some only the odd or even multiples. The overtones closest to the original fundamental frequency will be loudest.

You can display the waveshapes from different instruments by playing the instrument close to a microphone that is connected to an oscilloscope through an amplifier. You will be able to see that different instruments playing the same note display a different waveshape because of the different overtones. The wave still repeats in the same time with the same underlying wavelength and frequency. Some computers will now let you record a sound and then display its wave on the screen. This is another useful way of seeing the different shapes. Analysing the different shapes of the same basic sound is the basis for voice recognition which is starting to be used on some computers.

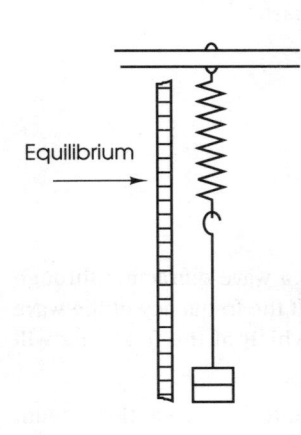

11 THE MOTION OF A SIMPLE OSCILLATOR

Fig. 6.38

This example can be applied to the investigation of any oscillator. The chosen apparatus is the mass and spring oscillator. A spring is firmly fixed to a rigidly held retort stand and clamp. A mass and holder (total 100 g) are connected as shown and the equilibrium position marked on a vertical fixed metre rule (Fig. 6.38). To investigate the motion a number of repeated timings needs to be taken.

DOES THE PERIOD DEPEND ON AMPLITUDE?

The mass is displaced from rest by, say, 2 cm and the time for five oscillations recorded. This is repeated at least three times and a *mean* taken.

The procedure is repeated for displacements of 4, 6, 8 cm, each time recording the mean of three sets of five complete oscillations.

RESULTS

Table 6.2

Amplitude (cm)	Time for five oscillations (s)	Mean time for five oscillations (s)
2		
4		
6		

DOES THE PERIOD VARY WITH THE MASS ADDED?

The amplitude is initially fixed, perhaps 4 cm, and the mass is changed in equal multiples of 100 g. Timings are as before.

RESULTS

Table 6.3

Mass (g)	Time for five oscillations (s)	Mean time for five oscillations (s)	Period, T (s)
100			
200			
300			

DOES THE PERIOD VARY WITH THE STRENGTH OF THE SPRING?

This is more difficult to investigate. The amplitude and mass should be kept constant, and a number of springs which are similar should be available. Two springs in *parallel* double the overall *spring constant* (stiffness). Two springs in *series* have half the overall *spring constant*. The results should be recorded as before.

PRECAUTIONS

1. Take care not to overload the spring or otherwise to exceed its elastic limit.
2. Repeated timings will reduce uncertainty in the value of the time period.

EXAMINATION QUESTIONS

MULTIPLE CHOICE QUESTIONS

QUESTION 1

Which one of the following is an example of a longitudinal wave?

A Ripples in water in a ripple tank
B VHF radio waves
C Visible light
D Waves along a stretched rope
E Sound from a guitar   (ULEAC)

QUESTION 2

Which one of the following would change the period of oscillation of a pendulum?

A Increase the length of the pendulum.
B Increase the mass of the pendulum.
C Change the thickness of the string on the pendulum.
D Change the density of the pendulum bob.

QUESTION 3

A child stands some way from a high flat wall. She claps her hands and half a second later hears an echo. How far from the wall is she standing? (Take the speed of sound in air to be 320 m/s.)

A 80 m
B 160 m
C 320 m
D 670 m
E 720 m

QUESTION 4

Which of the following statements about waves is incorrect?

A The speed of a wave is how far the front of a wave travels in one second.
B The frequency of a wave is the time that it takes a wave to pass a point.
C The wavelength is the distance from crest to crest.
D Waves can carry energy from one place to another.
E Waves can carry information from one place to another.

QUESTION 5

Figure 6.39 shows a water wave travelling in the direction of the arrow. As the wave moves forward which of the following will happen?

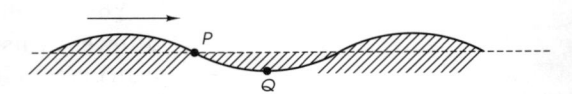

Fig. 6.39

A P and Q move from left to right.
B P will go down, Q will go up.
C P will go up, Q will go up.
D P will go down, Q will go down.

QUESTION 6

In which of the following materials will a sound wave travel fastest?

A A vacuum
B Air
C Water
D Steel

QUESTION 7

Figure 6.40 shows a wave diffracting through a slit in a barrier. If the frequency of the wave is made greater which of the following will happen?

A The wavelength increases; the amount of diffraction increases.
B The wavelength decreases; the amount of diffraction decreases.
C The wavelength increases; the amount of diffraction decreases.
D The wavelength decreases; the amount of diffraction increases.
E Both wavelength and amount of diffraction stay the same.

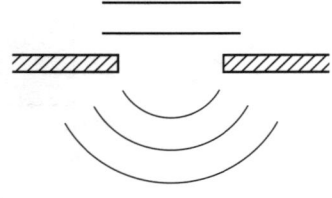

Fig. 6.40

QUESTION 8

When water waves in a shallow ripple tank move from a shallow region to a deeper region which of the following will happen?

A The wavelength stays the same; the velocity stays the same.
B The wavelength increases; the velocity increases.
C The wavelength decreases; the velocity

decreases.
D The wavelength increases; the velocity decreases.
E The wavelength decreases; the velocity increases.

QUESTION 9

Which of the following is not an electromagnetic wave?

A X-rays
B Ultrasound
C Light
D Radio
E Ultraviolet   (ULEAC)

QUESTION 10

Which of the following is not possible for a sound wave?

A Reflection
B Interference
C Travelling through space
D Changing speed in different materials
E Diffraction

STRUCTURED QUESTIONS

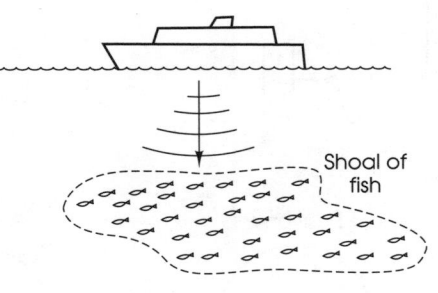

Fig. 6.41

QUESTION 11

Figure 6.41 shows a fishing boat using sonar to detect a shoal of fish. A short pulse of sound waves is emitted from the boat, and the echo from the shoal is detected $1/10$ s later. The sound waves travel through sea-water at 1500 m/s.

(a) How far has the pulse travelled in $1/10$ s?
(b) How far below the boat is the shoal?
(c) The reflected pulse lasts longer than the emitted pulse. Suggest a reason for this.   (NISEAC)

QUESTION 12

A microphone is connected to a cathode ray oscilloscope. Three sounds are made in turn in front of the microphone. The traces A, B and C produced on the screen are shown in Fig. 6.42. (The controls on the oscilloscope are not altered during this experiment.)

(a) Which trace is the loudest sound? Explain your answer.
(b) Which trace is due to the sound with the lowest pitch? Explain your answer.
         (NISEAC)

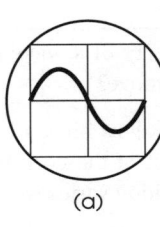

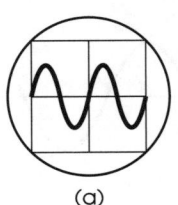

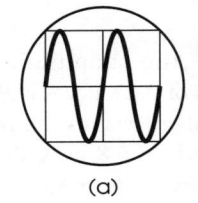

Fig. 6.42

QUESTION 13

Figure 6.43 represents a wave on a rope.

Fig. 6.43

(a) Show clearly on the diagram what is meant by:
(i) The wavelength of the wave;
(ii) The amplitude of the wave.
(b) State in words the equation which relates the speed of a wave to its wavelength and frequency.
(c) Use the equation to find the speed of a water wave which has a wavelength of 4 cm and a frequency of 6 Hz.
         (ULEAC)

QUESTION 14

Sonar waves are emitted from a surface vessel which is determining the depth of the sea. The emitted signal and its reflection from the sea-bed are displayed on the screen of an oscilloscope as shown in Fig. 6.44.

The speed of sound in water is 1200 m/s and the horizontal speed of the oscilloscope trace is 8 cm/s. Calculate the depth of the sea at this point.

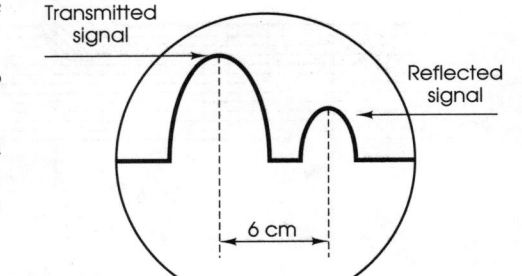

Fig. 6.44

QUESTION 15

Figure 6.45 shows an arrangement to observe the interference of sound waves of a single frequency from loudspeakers A and B. The microphone is placed at position P, a point at which constructive interference occurs, and then at Q at which destructive interference occurs.

Show on the diagrams (Fig. 6.46) what will be seen on the oscilloscope screen when one loudspeaker is switched on and when both are switched on. (The oscilloscope is adjusted so that the amplitude due to each wave is about 0.5 cm on the screen and so that one complete waveform may be displayed.)

(ULEAC)

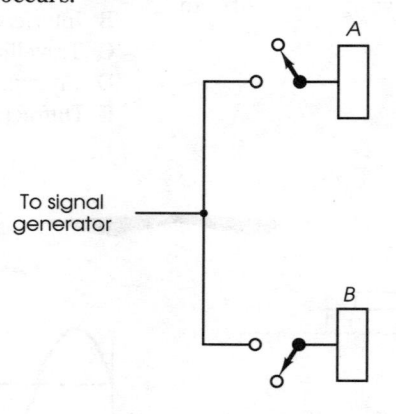

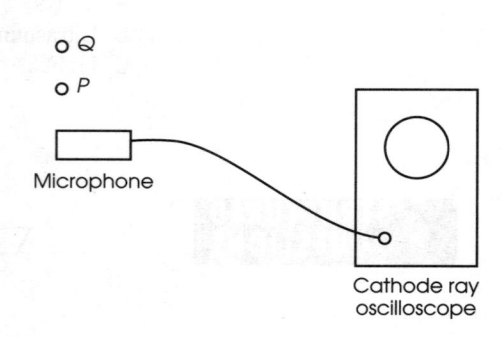

Fig. 6.45

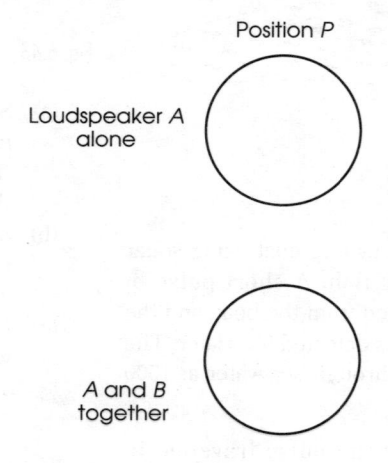

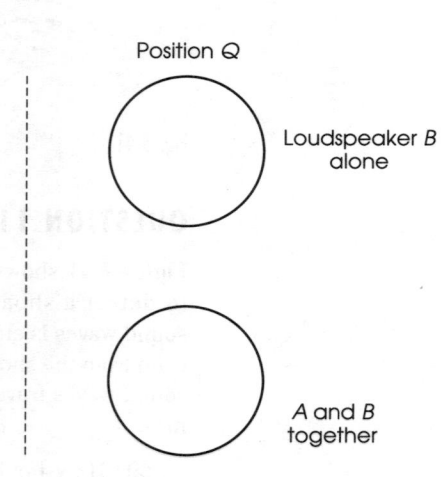

Fig. 6.46

QUESTION 16

(a) A cork is floating on water. A stone is dropped into the water.

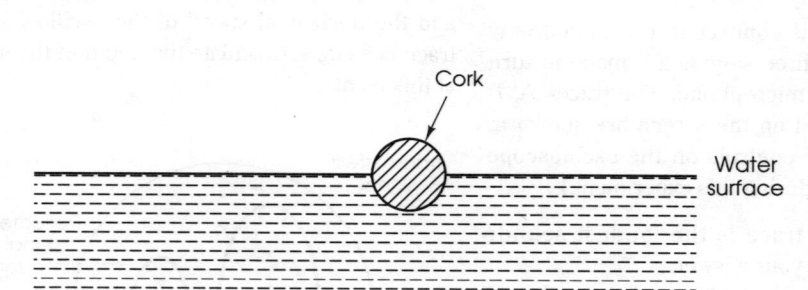

Fig. 6.47

(i) After a short time the cork begins to move. Describe how the cork moves.

(ii) What property of a wave causes the cork to move?

The graph below shows how the displacement of the cork from its original position varies with time.

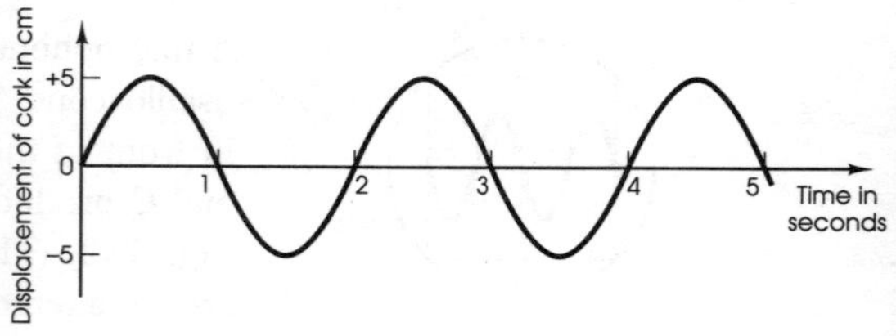

Fig. 6.48

(iii) What is the amplitude and frequency of the water wave?
(iv) The water waves have a wavelength of 0.8 m. Calculate the velocity of the water waves. Show clearly how you obtain your answer.

(b) One method of finding the velocity of sound is to use a cathode ray oscilloscope (CRO), a loudspeaker and a microphone.

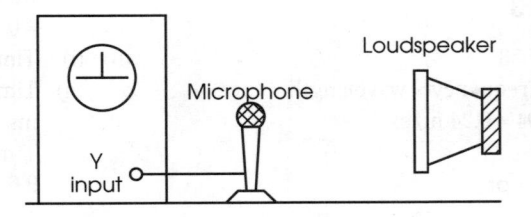

Fig. 6.49

The loudspeaker makes a clicking noise which is detected by the microphone and displayed on the CRO.
The diagram below shows what is seen on the CRO.

For the *x* axis
1 cm = 2 milliseconds (ms)

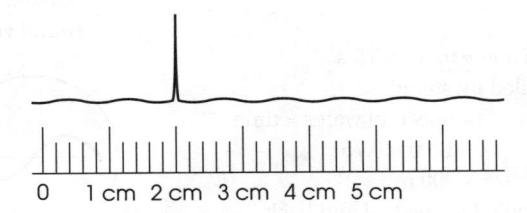

Fig. 6.50

(i) The spot on the CRO starts to move across the screen from 0 just as each click is made.
How long does it take the sound to reach the microphone?
Show clearly how you obtain your answer.

When the loudspeaker is moved a FURTHER 2 m from the microphone the trace below is seen. The settings on the CRO are the same as before. Again the spot started at 0 when the first click was made.

For the *x* axis
1 cm = 2 ms

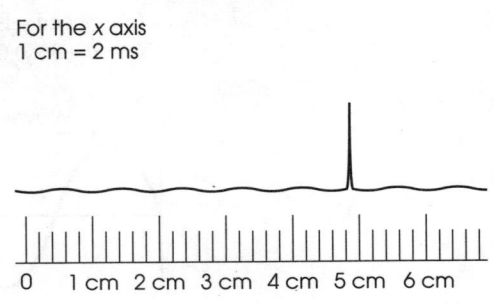

Fig. 6.51

(ii) Use the information in (b) (i) to find the velocity of sound. Show clearly how you obtain your answer.

(c) Loudspeakers used in theatres are arranged vertically as shown in the diagram 1 below. Explain why this is better than arranging them horizontally as shown in diagram 2.
(NISEAC Central tier)

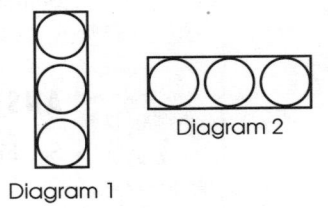

Fig. 6.52

OUTLINE ANSWERS

1 MULTIPLE CHOICE QUESTIONS

Question	1	2	3	4	5	6	7	8	9	10
Answer	E	A	A	B	C	D	B	B	B	C

2 STRUCTURED QUESTIONS

ANSWER 11

(a) Sound travels at 1500 m/s. In $^{1}/_{10}$ s the pulse travels 150 m.
(b) The pulse has travelled to the shoal and back. The shoal is 150/2 = <u>75 m</u> below the boat.
(c) The pulse will reflect off several "layers" of fish in the shoal, so that the collected reflection will have parts which have travelled further than others and will therefore last longer.

ANSWER 12

(a) Trace C. Loudness is related to wave amplitude.

ANSWER 13

(a) See Fig. 6.53.
(b) Speed = Frequency × wavelength.
(c) $v = 6 \times 0.04 = 0.24$ m/s.

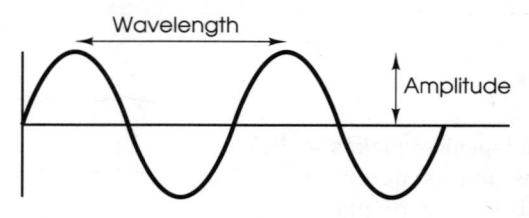

Fig. 6.53

ANSWER 14

Time between pulses: dot on screen travels 6 cm at 8 cm/s

Time = 6/8 = 0.75 s
Distance travelled by sound
  = Speed in water × time
  = 1200 × 0.75
  = 900 m
Sound has travelled to sea-bed and back
Depth = 900/2 = <u>450 m</u>

ANSWER 15

See Fig. 6.54.

ANSWER 16

(a) (i) The cork moves up and down.
(b) Trace A. Pitch relates to frequency. Lowest frequency also means longest wavelength.
    (ii) The waves carry energy
    (iii) Amplitude = 5 cm frequency = 0.5 Hz
    (iv) Velocity = frequency × wavelength
         = 0.5 × 0.8 = 0.4 m/s
(b) (i) Time = 2 × 2 ms = 4 ms
    (ii) Time in second diagram = 4.8 × 2 ms = 9.6 ms
         Time to cover additional 2 m = 9.6 – 4 = 5.6 ms

$$\text{Velocity} = \frac{\text{distance}}{\text{time}} = \frac{2 \times 1000}{5.6} = 357 \text{ m/s}$$

(Note that the time is in milliseconds which gives the 1000 in the final equation)

(c) The sound will be diffracted more through a narrower gap. The vertical speakers will therefore diffract the sound more horizontally to reach more of the audience whereas the horizontal speakers would diffract the sound vertically.

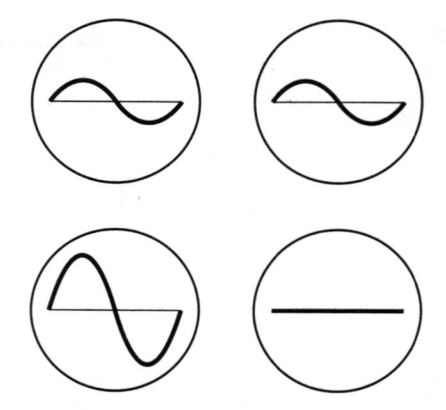

Fig. 6.54

TUTOR'S QUESTION AND ANSWER

QUESTION

Figure 6.55 shows a large-diameter steel pipe 80 m long (not drawn to scale). An experimenter at E bangs the pipe and his assistant at O listens for the sound reaching him.

(a) Explain why the assistant will hear two sounds, one arriving after the other.
(b) In an experiment to measure the time needed for sound to travel through air from E to O five values were recorded: 0.20, 0.28, 0.25, 0.27 and 0.23 s. Find
  (i) The mean time;
  (ii) The mean speed of sound in air.
(c) Suggest how you would attempt to measure the time needed for the sound to travel from E to O through the air.
(d) Further experiments were conducted by:
  (i) Hitting the pipe harder, producing much louder sound.
  (ii) Using a different pipe which gave the sound a considerably increased pitch. What would you expect to be the effect on the velocity of sound in air in each case? (UCLES)

Steel pipe

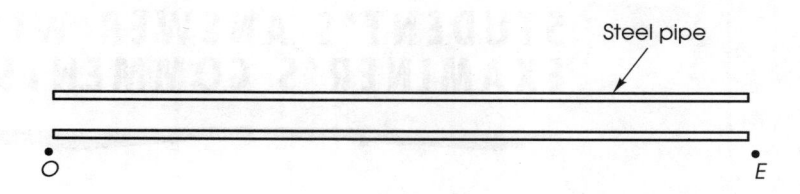

O · ———————————————————— · E

Fig. 6.55

ANSWER

(a) Sound travels fastest on the most dense material. The assistant will hear the sound wave transmitted through the steel pipe before the wave which travels through the surrounding air.

(b) Values are 0.20, 0.28, 0.25, 0.27, 0.23 s.
Sum of values = 1.23 s

$$\text{Mean} = \frac{1.23}{5} = \underline{0.25 \text{ s}} \quad (0.246)$$

$$\text{Speed} = \frac{\text{Distance}}{\text{Time}} = \frac{80}{0.25}$$

$$= \underline{320 \text{ m/s}}$$

(c) A signal must be arranged between the experimenter E and the assistant O. At the signal, E strikes the rod and O starts a clock. When O hears the **second** sound (i.e. through air) the clock is stopped. This is clearly a crude method and many attempts would be needed to reduce the uncertainty in measurement.

(d) (i) No change;
(ii) No change.
Reason not required but velocity of a wave is a function of the **medium** not the mechanism by which it is produced.

CHAPTER 6 OSCILLATIONS AND WAVES

STUDENT'S ANSWER WITH THE EXAMINER'S COMMENTS

STUDENT'S ANSWER TO TUTOR'S QUESTION

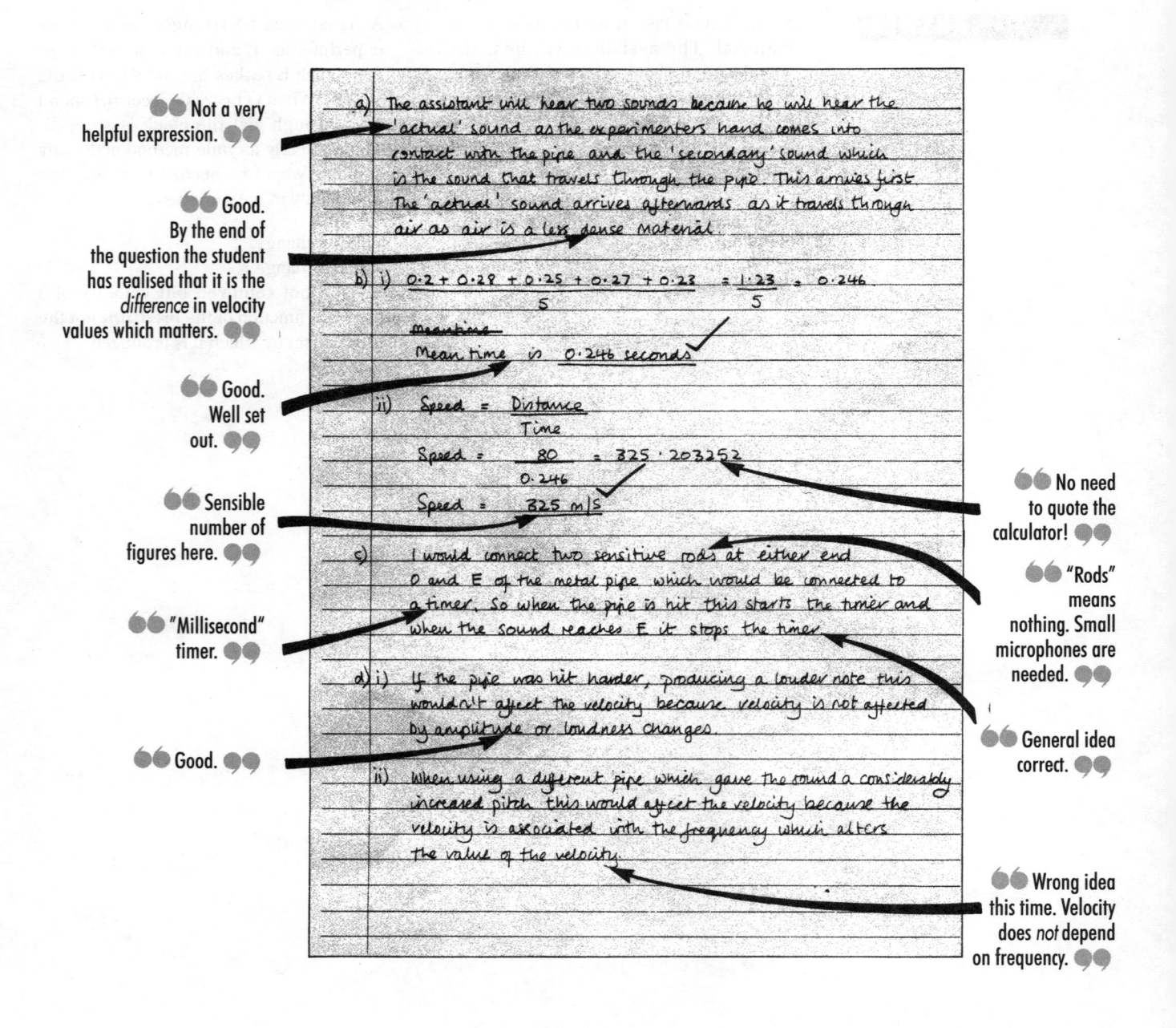

a) The assistant will hear two sounds because he will hear the 'actual' sound as the experimenters hand comes into contact with the pipe and the 'secondary' sound which is the sound that travels through the pipe. This arrives first. The 'actual' sound arrives afterwards as it travels through air as air is a less dense material.

> *Not a very helpful expression.*

b) i) $\frac{0.2 + 0.28 + 0.25 + 0.27 + 0.23}{5} = \frac{1.23}{5} = 0.246$

Mean time is 0.246 seconds ✓

> *Good. By the end of the question the student has realised that it is the difference in velocity values which matters.*

ii) Speed = $\frac{Distance}{Time}$

Speed = $\frac{80}{0.246}$ = 325.203252

Speed = 325 m/s ✓

> *Good. Well set out.*
> *Sensible number of figures here.*
> *No need to quote the calculator!*

c) I would connect two sensitive rods at either end O and E of the metal pipe which would be connected to a timer. So when the pipe is hit this starts the timer and when the sound reaches E it stops the timer.

> *"Millisecond" timer.*
> *"Rods" means nothing. Small microphones are needed.*
> *General idea correct.*

d) i) If the pipe was hit harder, producing a louder note this wouldn't affect the velocity because velocity is not affected by amplitude or loudness changes.

> *Good.*

ii) When using a different pipe which gave the sound a considerably increased pitch this would affect the velocity because the velocity is associated with the frequency which alters the value of the velocity.

> *Wrong idea this time. Velocity does not depend on frequency.*

REVIEW SHEET

- Sound is an example of a _____ wave.

- All the electromagnetic waves are _____ waves.

- Sound always starts at something that is _____ .

- The units for frequency are _____ .

- Complete the wave equation

    Velocity = _____ .

- Sound cannot travel through a _____ .

- Sound waves travel faster in _____ dense materials.

- In the spaces draw a sketch of the wave pattern that you would see on a ripple tank set up as described.

    1. Plane waves hit a plane barrier at an angle.   2. Plane waves hit a concave barrier.

    3. Plane waves are refracted in shallower water.   4. Plane waves diffract through a narrow gap.

- A radio wave of frequency 200 kHz has a wavelength of 1500 m. What is its velocity?

- Two similar waves that arrive at the same place out of phase will _____. This is called _____ interference.

- If longer waves arrive at a narrow gap they will be diffracted _____ than shorter ones. Blue light will therefore be diffracted _____ than red light at a narrow slit.

- Fm radio waves have a higher frequency than those on the medium waveband. Their wavelength is _____ so when they pass over hills or past other barriers they are diffracted _____ This can make them more difficult to receive.

CHAPTER 6 OSCILLATIONS AND WAVES

- A ripple tank has sloping sides so that _____
  _____.

- If a wave has a frequency of 256 Hz its first harmonic will have a frequency of _____.

- The frequency of a pendulum depends only on its _____ .

- A brighter light wave has a greater _____.

- A sound with a greater frequency has a greater _____.

- When a system vibrates at its own natural frequency because of vibrations of the same frequency from outside it is called _____. It is important to avoid this in the design of _____ (several possible answers for this last word!).

- Check that you can

   (i) Describe an experiment to find the speed of sound.

   (ii) Label the parts of a human ear on the following diagram and explain how it works.

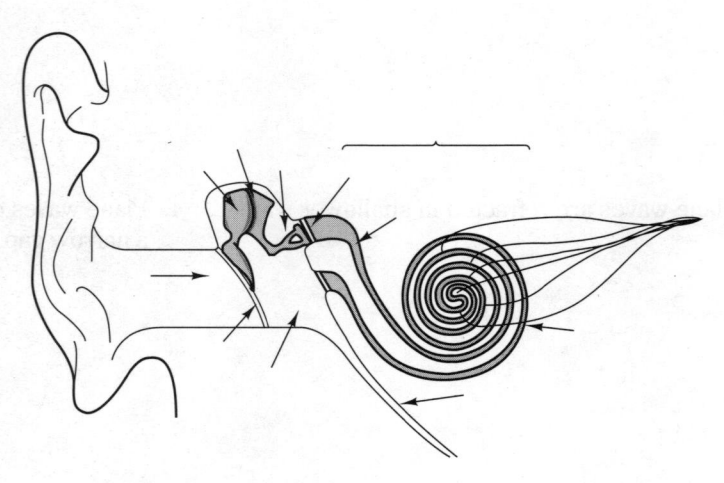

Fig. 6.56

CHAPTER 7
CIRCUITS AND DIRECT CURRENTS

GETTING STARTED

We all use electrical equipment, at home, at school, in offices and factories. Electricity is the most adaptable energy form, because it is easily converted into other forms which simply make life easier – light to turn "night into day", heat to change winter cold at home into all-year comfort, kinetic energy to move motors in washing machines, food mixers, vacuum cleaners. The availability of electrical energy has caused a revolution in social habits; and we take it for granted.

However, few people really understand how "electricity" **works**, many are frightened of it through their lack of understanding, and even more are confused by the terms used to describe what is going on. The aim of this chapter is to clear up some of these confusions and to deal with simple **circuits** where currents flow in one direction only.

A list of the circuit symbols that are used is in appendix 3 at the end of the book so that you can easily find and check them all.

CIRCUITS AND CONDUCTORS

CURRENTS

CURRENT AND CHARGE

ENERGY AND CHARGE – THE VOLT

ELECTRICAL POWER

MAINS ELECTRICITY, SAFETY AND FUSES

RESISTANCE

CURRENT AND VOLTAGE RELATIONSHIPS – OHM'S LAW

EMF

CELLS AND RESISTORS

CURRENT CHARACTERISTICS

C.R.O. AS A VOLTMETER

RING MAINS AND HOUSE WIRING

RESISTIVITY

USING METERS

INTERNAL RESISTANCE

DOUBLE INSULATION

TWO-WAY SWITCHES

ESSENTIAL PRINCIPLES

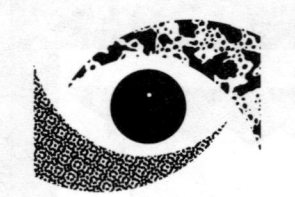

1 > CIRCUITS AND CONDUCTORS

To make an electric current *flow*, an *energy supply* is needed – a battery, a power pack, the mains supply or some other energy source like a dynamo on a bicycle. The energy supply can cause a current flow if there is a complete route of **conducting** material for the current. All *metals* are good conductors, but carbon is exceptional because it is a non-metal and yet still conducts very well; liquids can conduct if they are ionic solutions.

Materials which do *not* conduct electricity are called **insulators**. A good insulator is usually a non-metal or a non-ionic material, like plastics, rubber and wood (Fig. 7.1).

Conductor	Insulator
Copper	Wood
Iron	Sulphur
Aluminium	Polythene
Carbon	Rubber
Sea-water	Paraffin
Sulphuric acid	Propanone

Fig. 7.1

This division into "conductors" and "insulators" is in fact a little too simple – for instance, glass conducts well near its melting-point, and even polythene allows a tiny current to flow through it. In general we shall use the term "conductor" to refer to very good current conductors and "insulator" to refer to very bad conductors.

Symbols are a useful way of drawing how a circuit is constructed. The diagrams in Fig. 7.2 show the symbols used in this chapter. Currents are assumed to flow from the ⊕ side of a battery or cell to the ⊖ side. (This is sometimes called the ***conventional flow of current***.) The two lamp symbols are used to distinguish between a light deliberately used to give illumination and one simply placed in a circuit to let you know if everything is working (indicator).

A **resistor** reduces current flow. A **variable resistor** can *change* current flow in a circuit.

Switches can direct *where* currents are able to flow. A switch is described as "open" when drawn like Fig. 7.3. No current will flow until it is closed (Fig. 7.4).

Single cell

Group of cells (battery)

Lamp as indicator

Lamp for illumination

Resistor

Variable resistor

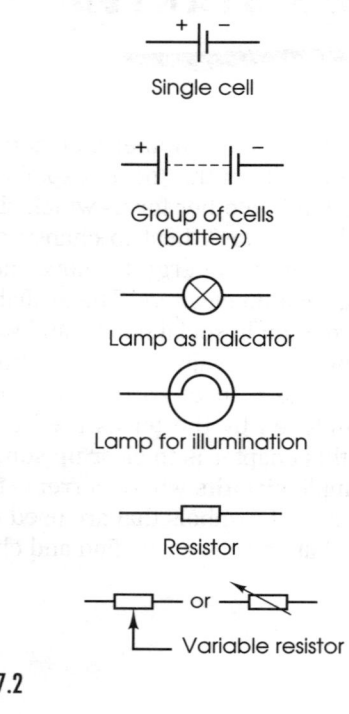

Fig. 7.2

Fig. 7.3 Open switch.

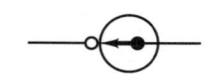

Fig. 7.4 Closed switch.

2 > CURRENTS

> ❝ This point cannot be stressed too much. It is a common error to state that CURRENT is used in a bulb. Energy is converted but the flow of charge (current) remains the same all round the circuit. ❞

An electric current is a *flow* of charged particles. In a metal conductor these charges are **electrons**, which are part of the metal atoms and are able to move if they are given energy from a power supply. An **ammeter** is used to *measure current*, and the unit of current is called an **ampere** or amp (A).

The circuit in Fig. 7.5 illustrates an important point about currents in circuits. A simple "loop" for current flow, with no branches, is called a **series** circuit. The current readings on all the ammeters will be the same, so ***no current is used up*** in flowing round the circuit. The current flowing into the bulb is the same as the current flowing out of it.

The **branching** circuit (Fig. 7.6) is called a ***parallel*** circuit, and the same rule applies.

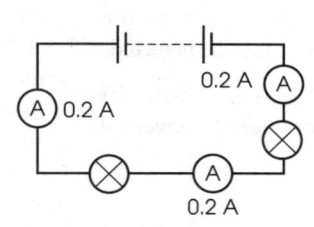

Fig. 7.5 Current in a series circuit.

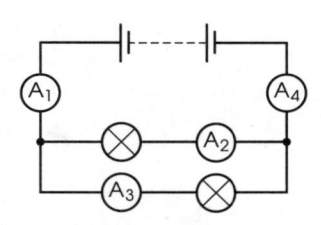

Fig. 7.6 Currents in a parallel circuit.

The currents in ammeters 1 and 4 are the same. The currents in ammeters 2 and 3 add up to the same as 1 or 4. Current is not "lost". It is only a flow of charges drifting slowly around a circuit, rather like water flowing through a group of connected pipes.

The "rule" is that the current, measured in amps, flowing *into* a point in a circuit is the *same* as the total current flowing *out* (Fig. 7.7).

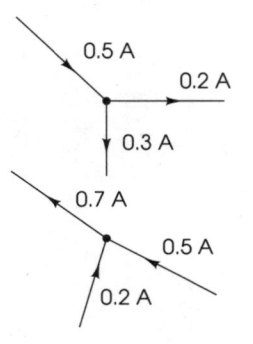

Fig. 7.7

3 > CURRENT AND CHARGE

All materials are made up of **atoms**, and all atoms are made up of **charges**. The number of charged particles needed to make a current flow of 1 A is very large; 6.2×10^{18} charged particles (electrons) need to flow in 1 s. So a "group word" is used to describe this large number; 6.2×10^{18} charges is called 1 **coulomb** (C). This is like saying

12 objects = 1 dozen
20 objects = 1 score
144 objects = 1 gross

So (6.2×10^{18}) electrons charges = 1 C

When a current of 1 A registers on an ammeter it means that 1 C of charge passes through the ammeter in 1 s. So 0.5 A means 0.5 coulombs per second (C/s), 10 A means 10 C/s, and for a current of 2 A to flow for 10 s means that $(2 \times 10) = 20$ C have passed through a point in a circuit.

If charge is given the symbol Q, current is given the symbol I, and time is called t, then

$$Q = I \times t$$

or

Charge = Current × Time

This is another way of saying 1 amp means 1 coulomb per second.

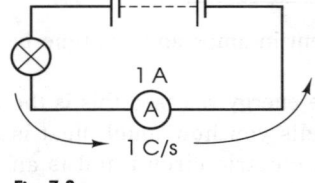

Fig. 7.8

4 > ENERGY AND CHARGE – THE VOLT

In the circuit of Fig. 7.9, as we have seen, the current (flow of charge) is the same when it flows *into* a lamp, as when it flows *out*. Clearly, though, there is an **energy change** taking place as the current flows through a bulb, but this is *not* indicated by the value of the current shown on the ammeters.

If lamps X and Y were of different power, e.g. 60 W and 24 W, they would be seen to convert different amounts of energy – the 60 W lamp will be brighter than the 24 W lamp. So current, or flow of charge, is *not* the only important thing happening in a circuit. The *energy changes* matter too.

A **voltmeter** records the **energy converted** as each coulomb (6.2×10^{18} electrons) of charge moves from one point to another. Since voltmeters measure energy

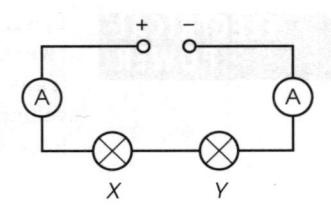

Fig. 7.9

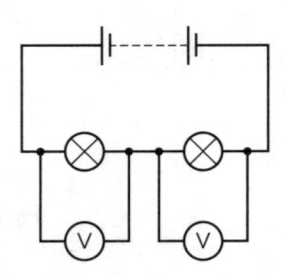

Fig. 7.10

changes between two points, they are connected *in parallel* across the points where the change in energy of a coulomb is to be detected.

▶ Just as 1 A means 1 C/s so 1 volt (V) means 1 *Joule* (J) of energy converted for each coulomb.

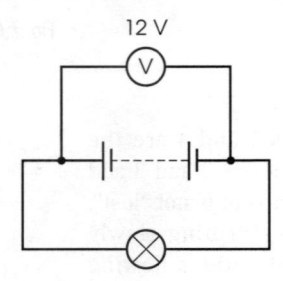

Fig. 7.11

The "voltage" across points in a circuit can measure two types of energy conversion. In the circuit of Fig. 7.11 the voltmeter is connected across the battery. Suppose it reads 12 V. This means 12 J of chemical energy from the battery are given to each coulomb, and converted to electrical energy.

A voltmeter connected across a bike dynamo may read 6 V. This means 6 J of energy are given to each coloumb and converted to electrical energy.

When a voltmeter records a change from some energy form to electrical, the "voltage" is described as the EMF (electromotive force) of the supply.

The circuit of Fig. 7.12 shows the voltmeter across a *lamp*. The energy change per coulomb is *from electrical to heat and light*. A voltmeter across a *motor* would record the change *from electrical to kinetic energy*.

When a voltmeter records a change from electrical energy *to another form*, the "voltage" is described as the p.d. (*potential difference*) between two points in the circuit.

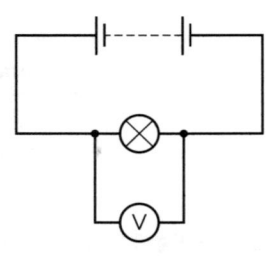

Fig. 7.12

The energy equation
If the p.d. in volts is the energy per coulomb then

$$V = \frac{E}{Q}$$

where p.d. = V, E = energy in joules, Q = charge in coulombs
so

$$E = V \times Q$$

and we already know that $Q = I \times t$ which means that

$$E = V \times I \times t$$

where I is current in amps and t is time in seconds.

Since E is the energy released this is the equation that tells you how much heat is produced in an electric circuit and is an important equation!

---

5 ELECTRICAL POWER

Power has already been discussed as meaning "work done per second" or "energy transferred per second". Ammeters and voltmeters combined in a circuit can give this information about the *rate* of energy transfer.

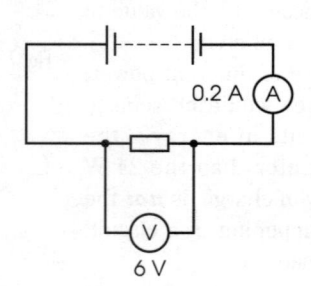

Fig. 7.13

In the circuit of Fig. 7.13 the current = 0.2 A = 0.2 C/s. The p.d. = 6 V = 6 joules per coulomb (J/C).

The *energy converted per second* is

$6 \times 0.2 = 1.2$ joules per second (J/s)

$= 1.2$ W

i.e.

Current × voltage = Power

or

▶ $$P = I \times V$$

and since power is energy converted in 1 s, then

▶ $$\text{Energy} = I \times V \times t$$

where t = time in seconds.

The power equation

You can also get this equation from the energy equation.

If power is the energy converted in 1 second then, putting $t = 1$ into the $E = V \times I \times t$ equation,

Energy per second = $V \times I$

so

Power = $V \times I$

the power will be in watts if the p.d. is in volts and the current is in amps.

EXAMPLE

A lamp running normally needs a p.d. of 12 V and the current through it is 2 A.
1. What is the power of the bulb?
2. How much energy is converted in 2 minutes (min)?

1. $P = IV = 2 \times 12 = 24$ W
2. Time = 2 min = 120 s
   Energy = $IVt = 2 \times 12 \times 120$
   = 2880 J

When the Electricity Board sends out a bill for your electrical consumption, it is basically a bill for the energy you have used. If you run a 60 W lamp for 1 hour (h), you would use

$60 \times 60 \times 60 = 216\,000$ J

Clearly the energy measured in joules for an ordinary household would be a very large number each day. So for household or industrial measurements a *larger* energy unit is used – the *kilowatt-hour* (kWh). This is the energy converted by a 1 kW device running for 1 h. The Electricity Board calls this "1 unit"; each "unit" costs about 8p. To work out costs, then, you calculate the number of kilowatts and multiply by the number of hours, giving the number of "units". From this you can work out the cost (see Table 7.1).

Table 7.1

Device	Power rating	Running time (h)	Units	Cost (p)
Fire	3 kW	2	6	48p
TV	400 W = 0.4 kW	3.5	1.4	11p approx.
Reading lamp	100 W = 0.1 kW	0.5	0.05	0.4p approx.

6. MAINS ELECTRICITY, SAFETY AND FUSES

The mains supply is at 240 V and is an *alternating current* (AC). The wires carrying the supply are called *live* and *neutral* and wiring is colour-coded; live = *brown*; neutral–*blue*. All switches are fitted into the *live* side of a circuit. Fuses are also fitted into the live side. Power appliances are fitted with a three-pin plug (Fig. 7.14). The third wire is the *earth* wire, colour-coded *green/yellow*.

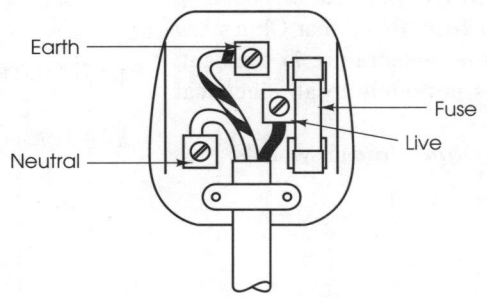

Fig. 7.14 Wiring in a mains plug.

❝ Live = brown
Neutral = blue
Earth = green/yellow ❞

The purpose of the *fuse* is to protect wiring from overheating because of dangerously high currents. If the current rises *above* a safe level the thin wire in the fuse melts, causing a break in the circuit, like an automatic safety switch. It is important that the correct fuse is fitted to each appliance. Fuses are generally available as 3 A, 5 A and 13 A fuses. To find the *correct* value, you need to know the *power* of the appliance (this is marked on it by the manufacturer). For example, if a 2 kW fire is plugged into the mains (240 V): since

▶ $P = IV$

then

▶ $I = P/V$

So the working current $I = 2000/240 = 8.3$ A. The nearest fuse value would be 13 A. (3 A or 5 A would "blow" every time you switched on.)

For a 100 W table lamp, the working current is only $100/240 = 0.4$ A. And here the nearest fuse value is 3 A.

The *earth* wire is to protect you from

7 RESISTANCE

A **resistor** is used to **control or reduce the current in a circuit**. The simplest form of resistor is a thin wire placed in a circuit (Fig. 7.15). The greater the **resistance** of the wire, the **smaller the current flow**.

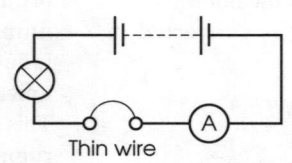

Fig. 7.15

If the dimensions of the wire are changed, it is found that:

- The **longer** the wire, the **greater** its resistance.
- The **thicker** the wire, the **less** its resistance.

The **type** of wire also matters; for example, identical lengths and thicknesses of iron wire and copper wire can be compared.

- **Copper** wire has a **lower resistance than iron**.

Resistance is also affected by

- **temperature**. The resistance of metals is **increased** if the temperature **rises**.

Resistance is measured in **ohms** (Ω); 1 Ω means that 1 V would be needed **across** the wire to drive 1 A **through** it. 100 Ω would require 100 V to drive 1 A. So in general

$$R = \frac{V}{I}$$

or

$$\text{Resistance} = \frac{\text{"Voltage"}}{\text{Current}}$$

Most resistors used in laboratories are convenient, manufactured resistors, consisting usually of carbon granules.

A **variable resistor (rheostat)** enables **different lengths of wire to be added into a circuit**, so that current can be controlled (Fig. 7.16).

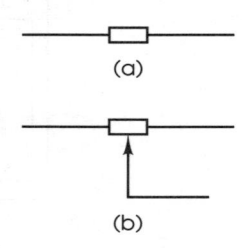

Fig. 7.16(a) Resistor; (b) variable resistor.

8 CURRENT AND VOLTAGE RELATIONSHIPS – OHM'S LAW

Using a circuit such as Fig. 7.17, an important **general relationship** can be seen. The variable resistor is used to control the current in the circuit and the voltmeter measures how the p.d. across the resistor varies. Provided the temperature does not change significantly, the results give a graph like that in Fig. 7.18. This means that the **current is proportional to the p.d.** The relationship is called **Ohm's law**. (Note that Ohm's law only applies if the temperature is constant, and that it does not apply to all electrical components.)

We can write **Ohm's law** in symbols:

$$V \propto I$$

or

$$V = IR$$

where R is the resistance of the resistor.

> There is often confusion here. $R = V/I$ DEFINES resistance at *all times*
>
> $R = V/I$ AND IS CONSTANT is a statement of Ohm's Law, and is only SOMETIMES true.

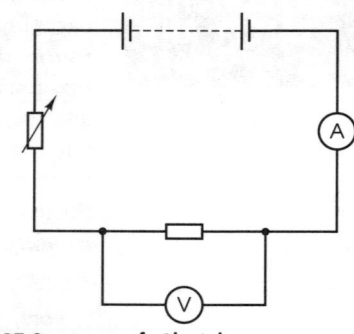

Fig. 7.17 Circuit to verify Ohm's law.

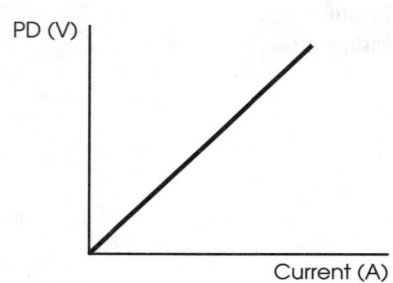

Fig. 7.18 Current/voltage for a resistor.

EXAMPLE

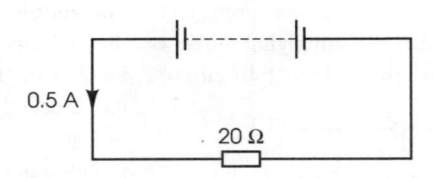

Fig. 7.19

In Fig. 7.19 the p.d. across the resistor would be

$$V = IR = 0.5 \times 20 = 10 \text{ V}$$

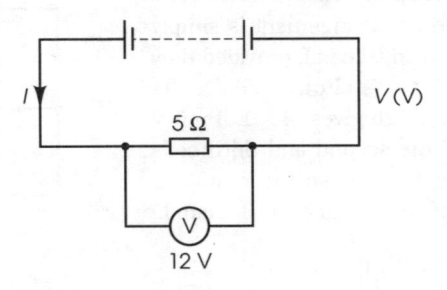

Fig. 7.20

In the circuit of Fig. 7.20 the current can be found. Since

$$V = IR$$

then

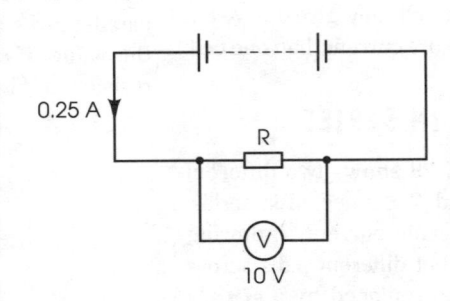

$$I = V/R$$
$$I = 12/5 = \underline{2.4 \text{ A}}$$

Fig. 7.21

Finally, in the circuit of Fig. 7.21, the unknown resistance R can be calculated. Since

$$V = IR$$
$$R = V/I$$
$$R = 10/0.25 = \underline{40 \text{ }\Omega}$$

The graph obtained (Fig. 7.22) showing current and voltage changes for a resistor is a useful way of finding an **unknown** resistance experimentally. Since $R = V/I$ it is also the slope or gradient of the graph.

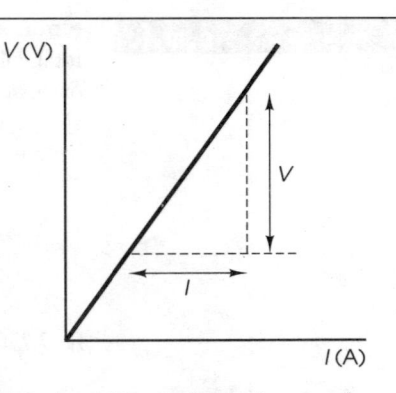

Fig. 7.22 Gradient of the graph gives the value of resistance.

▶ The *larger the resistance,* the *greater the gradient* will be.

Ohm's law **does not always apply**. A light bulb in place of the resistor in the circuit (Fig. 7.23) gives a different pattern for the current and voltage relationship, as shown in the graph (Fig. 7.24). Here the current and voltage are **not** proportional. The bulb obviously gets hotter and hotter. Since "resistance" is measured by the gradient of the graph, we have here an example where the resistance is *increasing*.

A heat-dependent resistor or thermistor gives the **opposite** pattern. Its resistance **decreases** as the **temperature rises**.

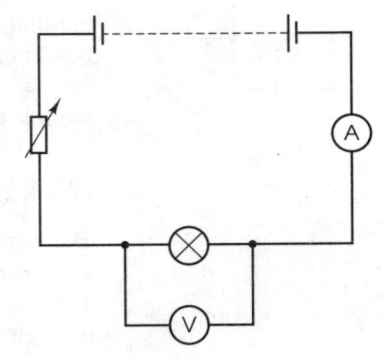

Fig. 7.23

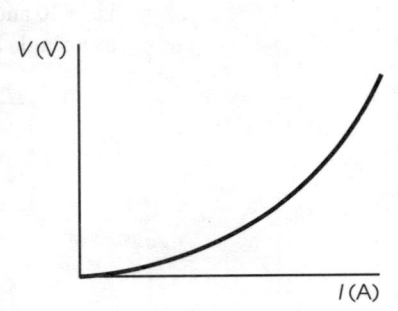

Fig. 7.24 Current/voltage for a bulb.

9 > e.m.f.

e.m.f. stands for *electromotive force*. It is the total voltage that is produced by a cell, battery or power supply. If you want to measure it you should do so when it is not supplying current i.e., not connected in a circuit because otherwise some of the e.m.f. is used in driving current though the supply itself and you will only measure what is left. e.m.f. will usually be divided among the components of the circuit so that each component has a share of the e.m.f. called its p.d. One way to find the e.m.f. of a supply is to add all the p.d.s in a complete circuit that includes the supply.

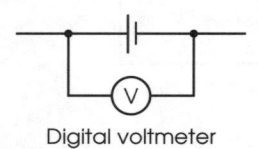

A modern digital voltmeter will usually take so little current that the reading is very close to the e.m.f.

Fig. 7.25 — Digital voltmeter

10 > CELLS AND RESISTORS IN SERIES AND PARALLEL

A "battery" is a group of cells in series. The total e.m.f. of such an arrangement is simply the sum of each individual e.m.f, provided they are connected ⊕ to ⊖. Four 1.5 V cells connected as in Fig. 7.26 gives (4 × 1.5) = 6 V e.m.f. In Fig. 7.27 the second and third cells are *opposing* each other so the resulting e.m.f. is only that of cells 1 and 4, i.e. 3 V e.m.f.

Fig. 7.26

Fig. 7.27

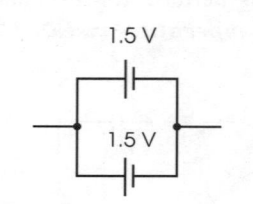

Where *equal* value cells are connected in parallel, there is no increase in e.m.f. The resulting value is only that of *one* cell. The cells in Fig. 7.28 will still only give 1.5 V, but are able to produce more current than one cell.

Fig. 7.28

(A) RESISTORS IN SERIES

The circuit of Fig. 7.29 shows two different value resistors R_1 and R_2 connected in series. They will have the same current, I, flowing through them both, but different p.d.s across them. They could be replaced by a *single* resistor R, without changing the current or total energy change in the circuit, if

▶ $$R = R_1 + R_2$$

i.e. a 10 and 20 Ω resistor in series is the same as a single 30 Ω resistor.

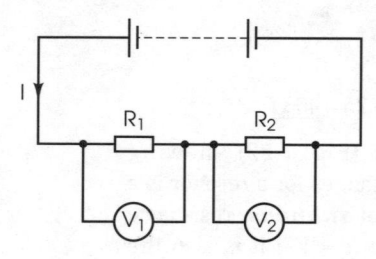

Fig. 7.29

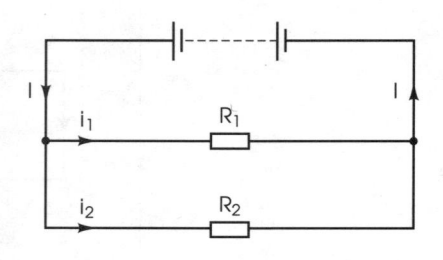

Fig. 7.30

(B) RESISTORS IN PARALLEL

The current now splits up (Fig. 7.30). The voltage across each resistor is the same. The two parallel resistors could be replaced by a *single* resistor R if

▶ $$\frac{1}{R} = \frac{1}{R_1} + \frac{1}{R_2}$$

The effect of two equal value resistors in parallel gives a total resistance equal to *half* the value of *one* of them. For the two 5 Ω resistors in Fig. 7.31,

$$\frac{1}{R} = \frac{1}{5} + \frac{1}{5}$$

$$\frac{1}{R} = \frac{2}{5}$$

$$R = \frac{5}{2} = \underline{2.5\ \Omega}$$

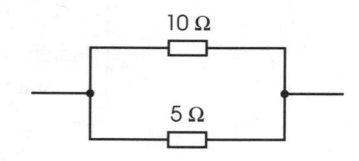

Fig. 7.31

Where the resistors do *not* have equal values (Fig. 7.32), the formula is needed to find their effect. Here

$$\frac{1}{R} = \frac{1}{10} + \frac{1}{5}$$

$$\frac{1}{R} = \frac{1}{10} + \frac{2}{10}$$

$$\frac{1}{R} = \frac{3}{10}$$

$$R = \frac{10}{3} = \underline{3.3\ \Omega}$$

Fig. 7.32

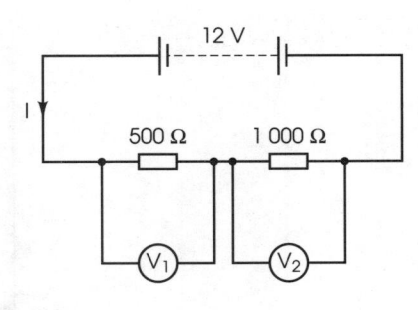

Fig. 7.33

So *more resistors in series increase the total resistance in a circuit*, and *more resistors in parallel decrease the resistance in a circuit*.

If a voltmeter is placed across each of a group of resistors *in parallel*, it reads the same across each of them.

However, if voltmeters are placed across resistors *in series*, the individual voltage readings depend on the resistor values. For example, the current, I, is the same through both resistors (Fig. 7.33).

Since
$$V = IR$$
then in series
$$V \propto R$$

Therefore the larger resistor has the greatest p.d. across it. The e.m.f. of the cells (12 V) is equal to the sum of the p.d.s ($V_1 + V_2$). The values are in proportion to the resistances, so

$$V_1 \text{ reads } \frac{500}{1500} \times 12\ \text{V} = 4\ \text{V}$$

(See also Chapter 8.)

$$V_2 \text{ reads } \frac{1000}{1500} \times 12\ \text{V} = 8\ \text{V}$$

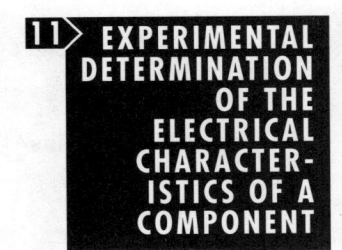

11 EXPERIMENTAL DETERMINATION OF THE ELECTRICAL CHARACTERISTICS OF A COMPONENT

"Characteristics" means the way in which current and voltage are related for a particular piece of apparatus. The usual practical examples are:

1. A resistor;
2. A lamp;
3. A thermistor;
4. A diode.

In each case a circuit must be set up containing an *ammeter in series* with the component, a *voltmeter in parallel* with it, and some means of varying the current and voltage. Two possibilities are shown. In Fig. 7.34 a variable resistor is used as a rheostat (current variation). In Fig. 7.35(a) it is used as a potential divider (voltage variation). The appropriate circuit is set up, and values of full-scale deflection of the ammeter and voltmeter are chosen (usually 0–5 A and 0–15 V).

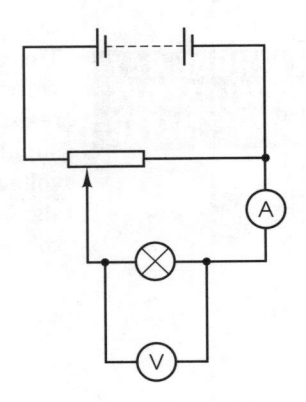

Fig. 7.35(a)

MEASUREMENTS

Either the current is varied in suitable steps of about 0.2 A or the voltage is varied in, say, steps of 0.5 V. Readings should be tabulated.

Current (A)	PD (V)

If resistance variations are to be noted, the most suitable graph to plot would be V (vertical) against I (horizontal) since $V/I = R$, so the *gradient* of the graph gives a *resistance value*. See Fig. 7.35(b).

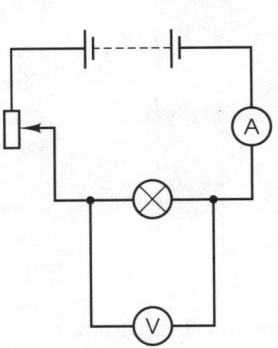

Fig. 7.34

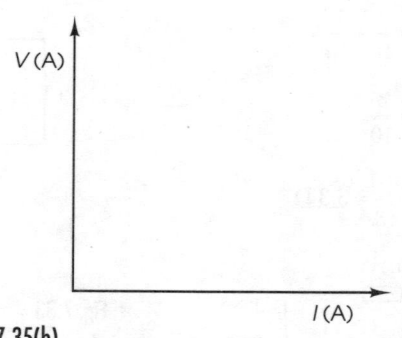

Fig. 7.35(b)

PRECAUTIONS

1. Check that both the ammeter and voltmeter are reading zero when the circuit is not switched on. Use a small screwdriver to adjust zero if necessary.
2. If the meters are fitted with a mirror below the indicator, use it to reduce parallax error in taking a reading.
3. Check each reading and if necessary take a *mean* value.

Some of the expected results are shown in Fig. 7.36.

Only one of these has a straight line graph and therefore the others do not obey Ohm's law as their resistance is not remaining constant. To get a full graph for the diode you will need to reverse the voltage applied to it and show that the current remains zero – there are practical limits to this and the diode will eventually fail, so take care and keep the applied p.d. down to less than 12 V.

(a) A bulb   (b) A thermistor   (c) A diode

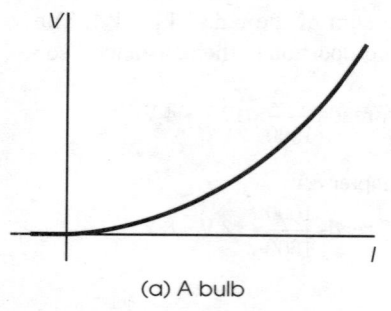

Fig. 7.36

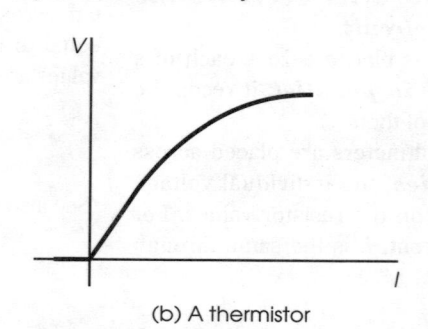

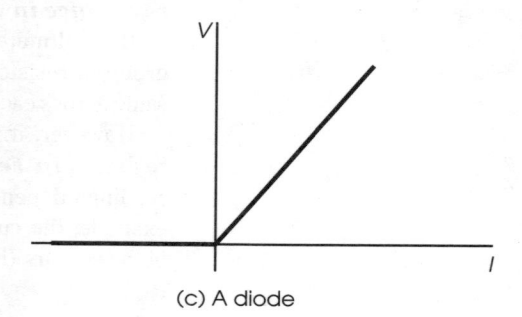

12. CATHODE RAY OSCILLOSCOPE AS A VOLTMETER

The CRO is increasingly used in place of a voltmeter. It has an infinitely high DC resistance, and so draws no current from a supply (Fig. 7.37). It is also able to show voltage variations as time goes on – and to show the variation on a screen. It is a visual voltmeter.

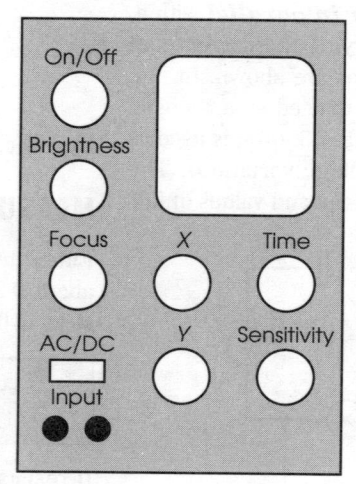

Fig. 7.37

The positions of the controls will vary from one model to another, but you should be able to identify the following:

1. ON/OFF – connecting to the mains supply:
2. Brightness.
3. Focus.

Turning on should produce a bright dot on the screen. It should be focused, and bright enough to see easily, but not so bright that the screen could be damaged.

4. X-shift will move the dot from left to right.
5. Y-shift moves the dot up and down.

To use an oscilloscope with direct current the AC–DC switch is turned to DC.

At the start of a measurement, then, the dot on the screen looks like that in Fig. 7.38. Since the oscilloscope is a *voltmeter*, any change in the position of the dot can only be caused by a voltage across the CRO. The CRO is connected *in parallel* between two points – just like a voltmeter. The dot will be moved *up* or *down*, depending on whether the applied voltage is in the *positive* or *negative* direction.

6. Use "sensitivity" to adjust the number of centimetres movement for each volt of

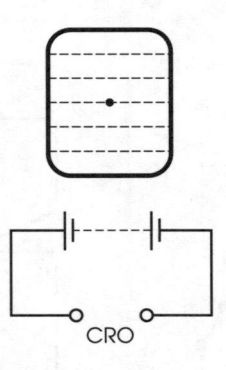

Fig. 7.38

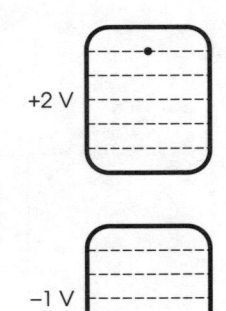

Fig. 7.39

p.d.. Typical examples are shown in Fig. 7.39.

7. Finally, to show how the voltage varies with time, turn on the "time base". This will make the dot move horizontally and draw a visual graph of volts against time (Fig. 7.40).

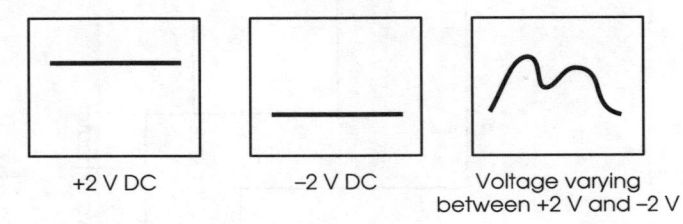

+2 V DC   −2 V DC   Voltage varying between +2 V and −2 V

Fig. 7.40

13 RING MAINS AND HOUSEHOLD WIRING

Cables entering the home have three insulated wires within an insulated exterior sheath. The cable can be overhead or underground. On entering your home, or your place of work, the main cable is connected to:

1. The Electricity Board's main fuse;
2. The electricity meter.

These are the property of the Electricity Board, so you are hiring property from the Board.

3. The fuse box (consumer unit) contains a switch to turn off all circuits. It will switch off both live and neutral connections by breaking the circuits. It also contains fuses to protect each circuit.

The ring main for power sockets consists of a double loop of cable beginning and ending at the consumer unit. The current therefore reaches any socket through two loops, and because the wire gauge can be reduced, it reduces the risk of overloading the circuit.

The ring main is not a series circuit. Current can only flow from live to neutral if connected with an appliance.

The fuse in the ring main will usually be 30A so that several devices can be supplied from the different sockets at the same time. A house will usually have a separate ring main for each floor. There will also be a lighting circuit for each floor, usually fused at 5A and a separate "spur" that goes directly to the cooker point in the kitchen. Since this is likely to supply more power (carry more current) than the other circuits it has its own fuse on the consumer unit.

The consumer unit may be earthed by connecting it to metal buried in the ground. An alternative (also used in caravans) is a residual current circuit breaker (**RCCB**) which detects any difference in current between that supplied on the live and that returning on the neutral and switches off the circuit. Modern consumer units have miniature circuit breakers (**mcb**) instead of fuses. These react faster and can be reset by pushing in a button (after finding the fault of course!).

Fig. 7.41

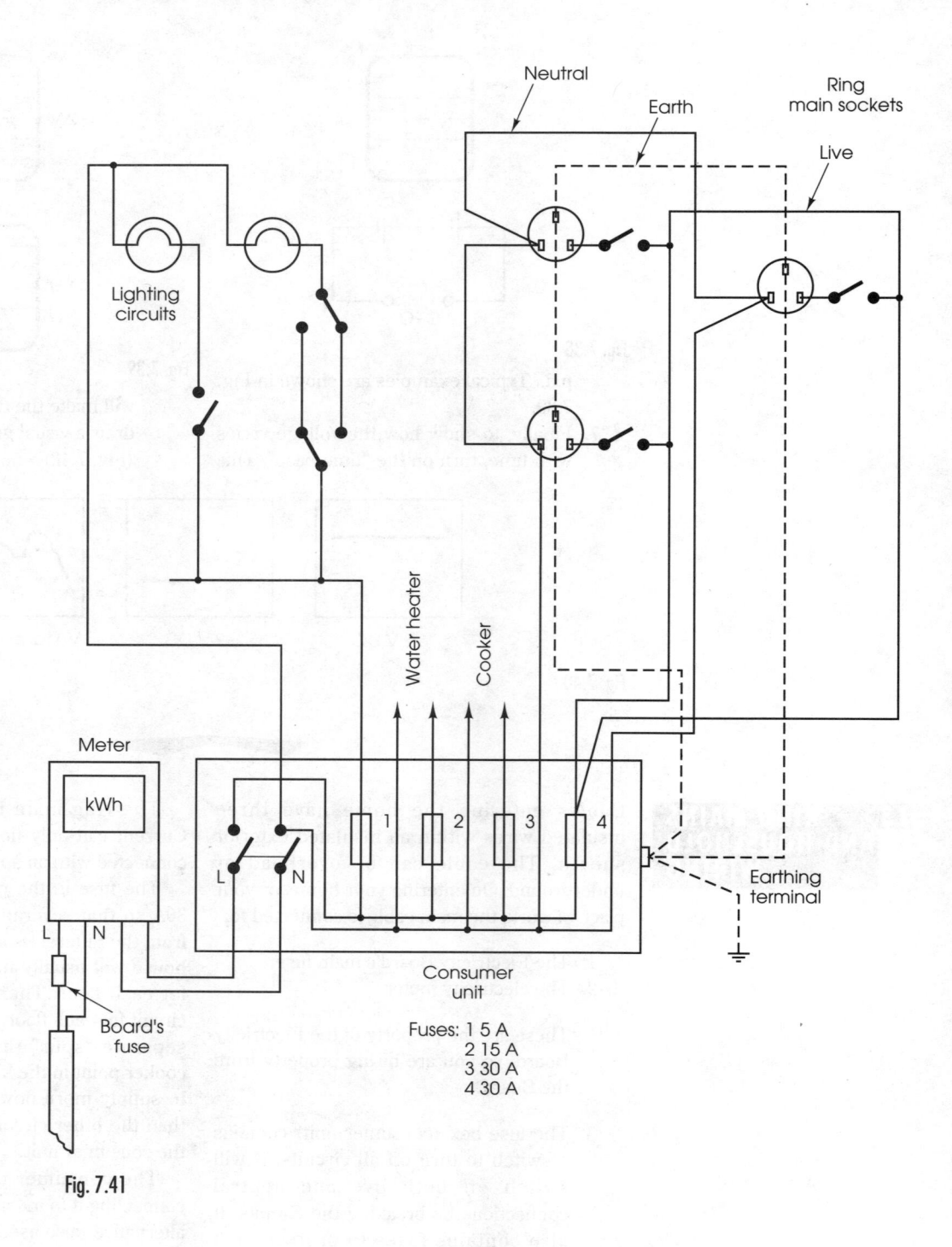

EXTENSION MATERIALS

14> RESISTIVITY

The resistance of a metallic conductor is proportional to the length of the conductor and is inversely proportional to the cross-sectional area of the conductor: i.e. long thin wires have more resistance than short thick ones made from the same material. (The wire should be metallic and at constant temperature or it doesn't obey OHM'S LAW anyway). This is written as

$$\text{resistance} \propto \frac{l}{A}$$

where l is the length and A is the cross-sectional area. This can be changed into an equation if we include a suitable constant.

$$\text{resistance} = p \times \frac{l}{A}$$

If you put $l = 1$ and $A = 1$ in the equation then

resistance = p. This means that the constant is really the resistance of a piece of the material 1 m long and 1 m² in cross-sectional area. This constant is called the resistivity of the material and it will obviously be a small number as a piece of metal that size would have a very small resistance. Some examples are shown below. Note the units are Ω m.

Metal	Resistivity in ohm metres
copper	0.000 000 018
aluminium	0.000 000 03
invar	0.000 000 75

EXAMPLES:

1. What is the resistance of a piece of copper wire 3m long and 0.5 mm in diameter? Resistivity of copper = 1.8×10^{-8} Ω m.

$$\text{resistance} = p \times \frac{l}{A}$$

$$= \frac{0.000000018 \times 3}{\pi \times 0.00025^2}$$

$$= 0.28 \, \Omega$$

2. A piece of wire has a resistance of 4 Ω. What would be the resistance of another wire made from the same material that was twice as long and twice as thick?

Making the wire twice as long would double its resistance. Making it twice as thick will make its cross-sectional area four times as big and quarter the resistance. When both effects are put together the resistance is halved.

15) USING METERS

▶ AMMETERS

Since ammeters are connected in series with the circuit (so that the current to be measured goes through the meter), the resistance must be as small as possible. A perfect ammeter would have no resistance at all so that when you put it into the circuit it wouldn't make the current smaller and give a slightly wrong reading.

▶ VOLTMETERS

Voltmeters are connected across the part of the circuit where you are measuring the p.d. The meter must have the largest possible resistance so that current doesn't by-pass part of the circuit by going through the meter. Modern digital meters can have a resistance of millions of ohms so that they are very accurate.

▶ GALVANOMETERS

A galvanometer is a sensitive meter designed to show very small currents. You may use one to detect the small currents produced in simple electromagnetic induction experiments. (See Chapter 14.)

▶ A galvanometer can be made into an **ammeter** by connecting a **low** resistance called a **shunt** in parallel with it.

▶ A galvanometer can be made into a **voltmeter** by connecting a **high** resistance called a **multiplier** in parallel with it.

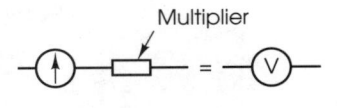

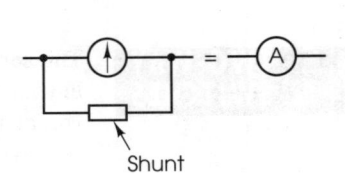

Fig. 7.42

16) INTERNAL RESISTANCE

This topic is only required by a few Examination Groups. Check your syllabus

So far we have only considered a battery or other supply as an energy "provider". However, every supply has itself got some resistance (called *internal resistance*) so it is also an energy "converter".

A voltmeter connected directly across a supply draws very little current from the supply, since voltmeters have *very* high resistance. In these circumstances the voltmeter is recording the supply e.m.f. (Fig. 7.43).

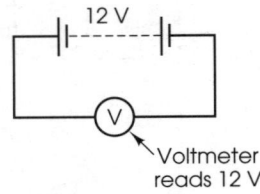

Fig. 7.43 e.m.f. on open circuit.

However, if a lamp is also connected, the supply provides a lot of current, and the voltmeter reading falls (Fig. 7.44a). The reason is that the current also has to flow back through the supply – and the supply itself has some resistance; so energy is converted into heat in the supply and not all the "available" 12 V is converted at the lamp.

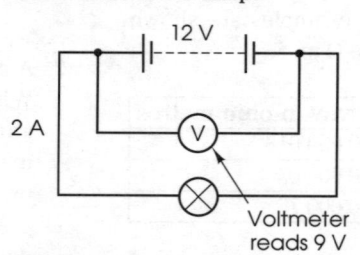

Fig. 7.44a Voltmeter reads terminal p.d.

Since energy is conserved, then

Energy available = Energy converted externally
+ Energy converted internally

or

$$E = V_{\text{in bulb}} + V_{\text{internal}}$$

The same current I flows in the bulb of resistance R as in the supply of resistance r:

$$E = IR + Ir$$

or

$$E = I(R + r)$$

The factor (Ir) is sometimes called "lost volts" since it represents energy which is **not** converted usefully in the circuit.

Using the data in Figs 7.43 and 7.44, the lost volts = (12 − 9) = 3 V. Current flowing = 2 A.

$$2 \times r = 3$$

and

$$r = 1.5\ \Omega$$

Most power packs and batteries have low internal resistance, and it is usually ignored in simple calculations.

17 DOUBLE INSULATION

You may have noticed that some appliances only have two wires – the live and neutral – and are not "earthed". Mains appliances that can be connected safely in this way will be double insulated and will carry a special symbol.

The appliance will be totally enclosed in an insulating plastic body so that there is no possibility of an internal electrical component making contact with any exterior metal part. Hair driers, electric drills and vacuum cleaners are all made like this.

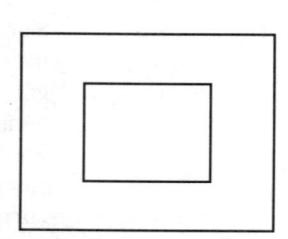

Fig. 7.44b Double insulation symbol.

18 TWO-WAY SWITCHES

The sort of lighting circuit that you may have in your hall at home with a switch at each end (or at the top and bottom of the stairs) requires a different sort of switch. The switch does not turn on and off but connects to either of two wires. Two of these switches connected as shown mean that you can turn the circuit on or off at either switch.

The circuit is shown off but can be put on by setting switch 1 to A or setting switch 2 to B. Check that you can then understand how to turn the circuit off again.

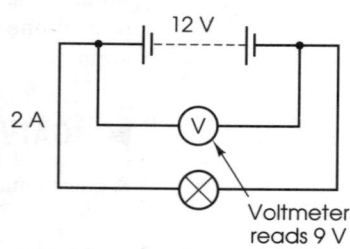

Fig. 7.44c Two way switch.

EXAMINATION QUESTIONS

MULTIPLE CHOICE QUESTIONS

QUESTION 1

In a correctly fused plug, the cartridge fuse is connected between the

- A Neutral lead and live lead
- B Live lead and live pin
- C Neutral lead and earth lead
- D Live lead and earth pin
- E Neutral lead and neutral pin   (ULEAC)

QUESTION 2

Which of the circuits (Fig. 7.45) would be suitable for measuring the resistance of a lamp?   (ULEAC)

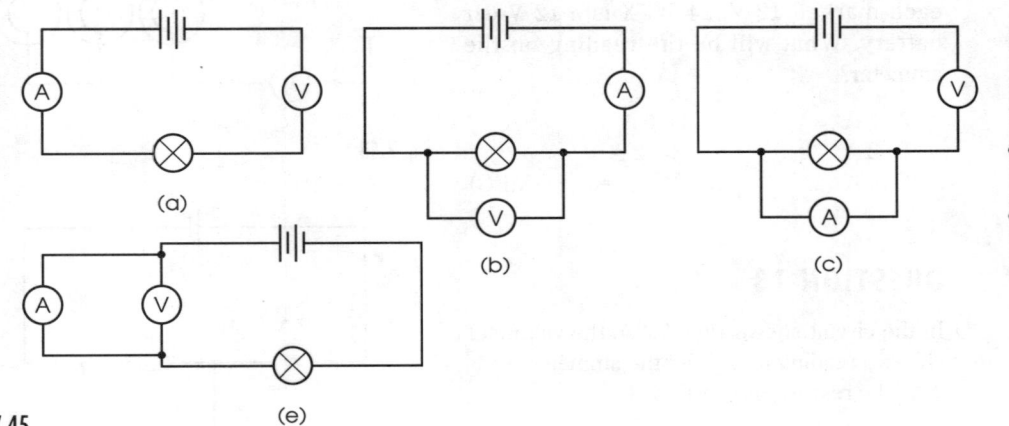

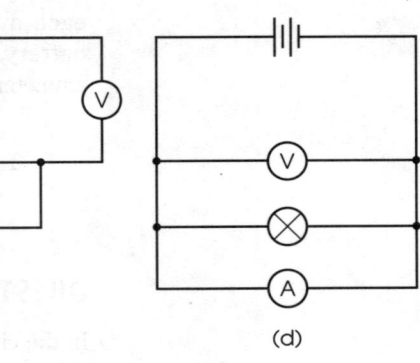

Fig. 7.45

QUESTION 3

Two resistors, one of 3 Ω and one of 6 Ω are connected in parallel in a circuit. Which of the following is their effective resistance?

- A 2 Ω
- B 3 Ω
- C 6 Ω
- D 9 Ω
- E 18 Ω   (ULEAC)

QUESTION 4

When wiring a house, switches and fuses should be connected in one (and only one) arrangement. This one arrangement has

- A Switches in the live side and fuses in the neutral
- B Switches in the neutral side and fuses in the live
- C Switches and fuses both in the live wire
- D Switches and fuses both in the neutral wire
- E Switches and fuses both in the earth wire   (ULEAC)

QUESTION 5

A three-core cable is connected to a three-pin plug. The colour of the cable which should be connected to the live terminal is

- A Brown
- B Black
- C Blue
- D Green and yellow
- E Green   (ULEAC)

QUESTION 6

Electrical appliances have voltage and power ratings as listed below. Which has the largest electrical resistance?

Appliance	Voltage (V)	Power (W)
A Washing machine	250	3000
B Television	240	160
C Kettle	240	1500
D Hair curler	250	20
E Car headlamp	12	36

(ULEAC)

QUESTIONS 7–9

- A Ampere
- B Coulomb
- C Joule
- D Watt
- E Volt

7. Which one of the above is a unit of energy?
8. Which one of the above is a unit of current?
9. Which one of the above is a unit of power?

QUESTION 10

In the circuit shown (Fig. 7.46), the p.d. between X and Y is 6 V. What is the current through the resistors?

A 1⁄6 A
B ½ A
C 1 A
D 1½ A
E 6 A

(MEG)

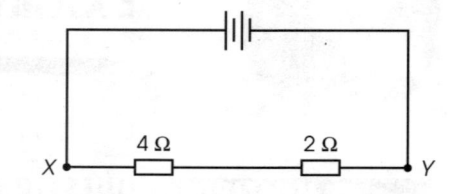

Fig. 7.46

QUESTION 11

In the circuit shown (Fig. 7.47) the p.d. between X and Y is 10 V. What is the p.d. between P and Q?

A 5 V
B 10 V
C 50 V
D 100 V
D 210 V

(MEG)

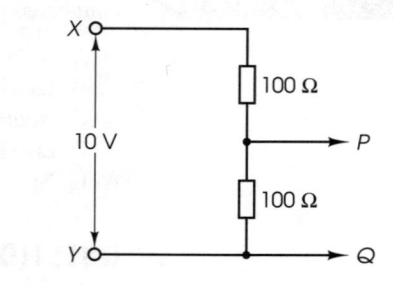

Fig. 7.47

QUESTION 12

In the circuit shown (Fig. 7.48), the lamps are each marked 12 V, 24 W. X is a 12 V car battery. What will be the reading on the ammeter?

A 1 A
B 2 A
C 4 A
D 6 A
E 12 A

(MEG)

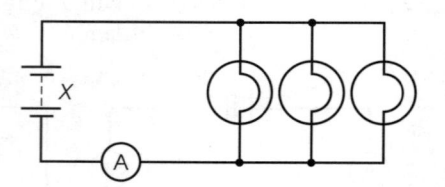

Fig. 7.48

QUESTION 13

In the circuit shown (Fig. 7.49), the voltmeter shows a reading of 5 V and the ammeter reads 2 A. The resistor has a value of

A 0.4
B 2.5
C 4.0
D 10.0

(SEG)

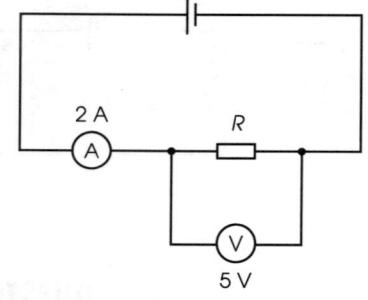

Fig. 7.49

QUESTION 14

The graph (Fig. 7.50) shows how current I changed with voltage V when applied to a sample of the material. The shape of the graph shows that

A The resistance of the material decreases as the current applied to it increases.
B The resistance of the material is constant.
C The current decreases as the voltage increases
D The resistance of the material increases as the voltage increases.

(SEG)

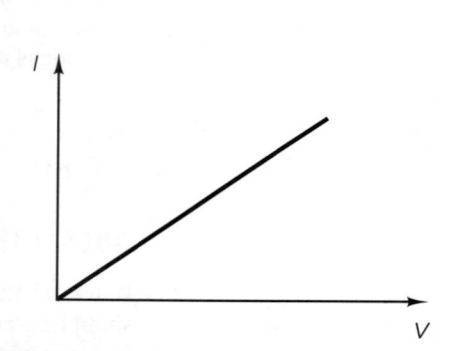

Fig. 7.50

QUESTION 15

Two 3 V batteries are connected as shown in Fig. 7.51. The voltage between X and Y is

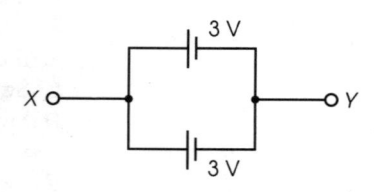

A Zero
B 1½ V
C 3 V
D 6 V

Fig. 7.51

STRUCTURED QUESTIONS

QUESTION 16

The ammeters in this circuit (Fig. 7.52) have negligible resistance. Using the values shown in the circuit, calculate:

(a) The p.d. across the 6.0 Ω resistor.
(b) The current through ammeter A_2.
(c) The current through ammeter A_1.
(d) The reading of the voltmeter across the cells. (UCLES)

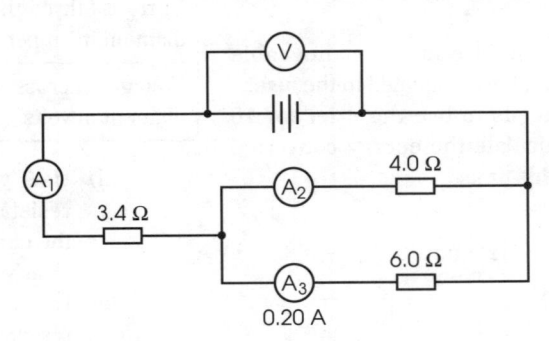

Fig. 7.52

QUESTION 17

In an experiment to measure the current through a component for different potential differences across it, the following readings were obtained.

Table 7.2

Potential difference across X (V)	Current through X (A)
0.0	0.0
1.2	0.6
2.0	1.0
3.0	1.0
4.2	2.1
4.8	2.4

(a) There seems to be a mistake in one of the readings. Draw a circle around the reading.
(b) What reading would you have expected?
(c) In doing the experiment the following meters were available:

0–1 A ammeter 0–5 V voltmeter
0–5 A ammeter 0–15 V voltmeter

Which meters would you choose? Explain your answers.
(d) Why is it that teachers often ask you to repeat your readings in an experiment? (ULEAC)

QUESTION 18

Diagram (1) of Fig. 7.53 shows the inside of a mains-operated hair drier. The fan can either blow hot or cold air. Diagram (2) is a circuit diagram of the same drier, showing how it is wired up for use.

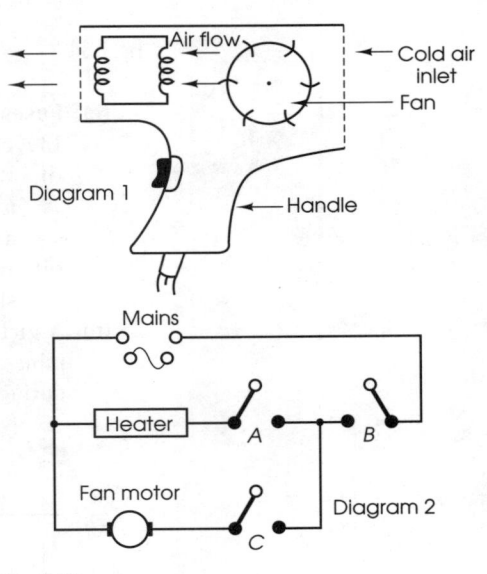

Fig. 7.53

(a) Show, by placing ticks in columns in the table which switches need to be ON to get the results shown. (You may use each switch once, more than once or not at all.)

Table 7.3

Result	Switch A	Switch B	Switch C
A blow of hot air			
A blow of cold air			

(b) The heater must not be on without the fan.
  (i) Which of the switches A, B, or C must always be ON to achieve this?
  (ii) Explain carefully what you would expect to happen if the heater was on, and the fan failed to work.
(c) The manufacturer wishes to include a two-speed fan. This can be done by connecting a suitable resistor across one of the switches as shown.
  (i) Draw a resistor across the correct switch in the diagram (Fig. 7.53) in order to make a two-speed fan.
  (ii) When this switch is open (Fig. 7.54), will it give a fast or slow speed? Explain your answer.
(d) The details of the fan are 250 V, 500 W. Calculate the current from the supply when the drier is working at its stated power.

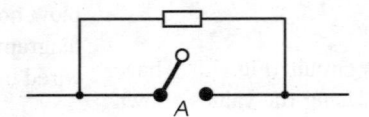

Fig. 7.54

(e) Fuses for the mains of 3 A, 5 A and 13 A are available.
  (i) Which fuse would you choose for use in a plug attached to the drier?
  (ii) Which wire in the mains cable should be connected to the fuse?
(f) A girl needs to use the drier for 10 min. Calculate the energy converted during this time.

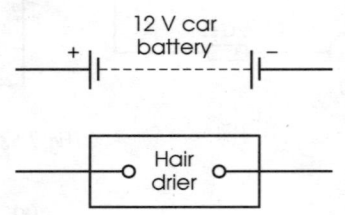

Fig. 7.55

(g) The manufacturer makes a different drier which will work from a 12 V car battery. You are required to find the energy taken by this new 12 V drier. Complete the circuit diargam (Fig. 7.55) to show how you would connect an ammeter and a voltmeter to do this.
(ULEAC)

QUESTION 19

Alan was asked to set up an experiment to investigate how the current through the filament of a lamp changed with the potential difference across its ends. Alan was provided with connecting wire and five pieces of equipment.

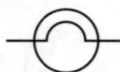

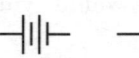

Fig. 7.56

(a) (i) using the symbols above draw a circuit diagram of the apparatus Alan might use in carrying out this investigation.

(ii) Mark with an arrow on your diagram the direction in which electrons flow through the lamp.

(b) (i) Some of the results of this experiment are shown in the table below. Plot the graph of current I against voltage V and draw a suitable curve through the data points.

Current I through filament in amperes	0.10	0.25	0.30	0.35
Voltage V across filament in volts	0.10	0.40	0.60	1.00

(ii) Use your graph to find the resistance of the filament when the current flowing is 0.3 A. Show clearly how you get your answer.
(iii) In what way, if any, does the resistance of the filament increase as the current through it increases?
(iv) The lamp is at normal brightness when the current flowing through the filament is 0.3 A. Calculate the normal power of the lamp.
(v) Does the lamp obey Ohm's law? Give a reason for your answer.

(c) (i) When a house is wired it is often necessary to wire a light in such a way that it can be switched on or off from two separate switches. Draw a diagram of a bulb connected to a two way switch circuit.
(ii) The diagram shows a fused three pin plug. Label the THREE wires correctly on the diagram.

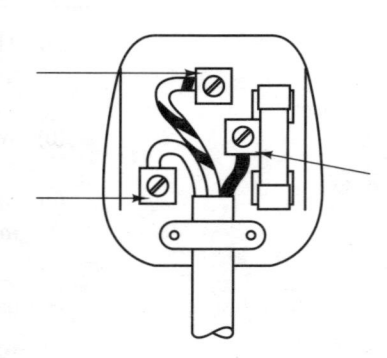

Fig. 7.57

CHAPTER 7 ANSWERS TO EXAMINATION QUESTIONS

ANSWERS TO EXAMINATION QUESTIONS

MULTIPLE CHOICE QUESTIONS

Question	1	2	3	4	5	6	7	8	9	10	11	12	13	14	15
Answer	B	B	A	C	A	D	C	A	D	C	A	D	B	B	C

STRUCTURED QUESTIONS

ANSWER 16

(a) p.d. across 6 Ω resistor is given by $V = IR$. Current in the resistor is 0.2 A.

$$V = 0.2 \times 6.0 = \underline{1.2 \text{ V}}$$

(b) The p.d. across all parallel branches is the same. p.d. across 4 Ω resistor is also 1.2 V. Resistance is given and $I = V/R$.

$$\text{Current} = 1.2/4 = \underline{0.3 \text{ A}}$$

(c) Current into a junction is the same as the current flowing out.

$$A_1 = A_2 + A_3 = (0.2 + 0.3) = \underline{0.5 \text{ A}}$$

(d) Voltage across cells (if no internal resistance) = Total in circuit.

p.d. across 3.4 Ω = IR = 0.5 × 3.4 = 1.7 V
p.d. across total parallel part of circuit = 1.2 V
Total available from cells = $\underline{2.9 \text{ V}}$

ANSWER 17

(a) Likely mistake is the <u>second 1 A value at 3 V</u>.
(b) Resistance = V/I = 1.2/0.6 = 2 from all other values. Expect current I at 3 V to be $V/R = 3/2 = \underline{1.5 \text{ A}}$
(c) Ammeter 0–5 A; voltmeter 0–5 V (in order to give greatest sensitivity within the range of readings).
(d) To eliminate uncertainty, both in terms of experimental error (the person making the readings) and inherent errors in the apparatus itself.

ANSWER 18

(a)

Result	A ON	B ON	C ON
A blow of hot air	✓	✓	✓
A blow of cold air		✓	✓

(b) (i) B must always be ON to make either part of the circuit work. C must be ON to make the fan work.

(ii) If the fan is not working, no air from outside is drawn over the heater so the temperature inside the drier rises and there is fire risk.

(c) (i) Resistor would have to be across C.
(ii) Open switch gives slow speed. Increased resistance in the circuit will reduce the current to the motor.

(d) Power = IV
$I = P/V = 500/200 = \underline{2 \text{ A}}$

(e) (i) With 2 A "safe current" a 3 A fuse is advisable.
(ii) Fuses *must* be connected into the live side.

(f) Energy = Power × time in seconds
Time = 10 × 60 = 600 s
Energy = 500 × 600 = $\underline{300000 \text{ J}}$

(g) Circuit should have a voltmeter in parallel with the drier and an ammeter in series.

ANSWER 19

(a) (i)

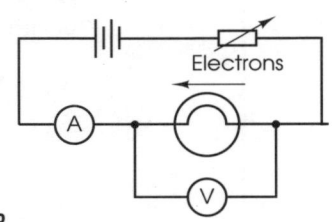

Fig. 7.58

(ii) on the diagram – but note that electrons flow in the opposite direction to conventional flow.

(b) (i) the graph will show a smooth curve.
(ii) Using the graph voltage = 0.6 V when current is 0.3 A

$$R = \frac{V}{I} = \frac{0.6}{0.3} = 2 \, \Omega$$

(iii) Resistance increases.
(iv) Power = $V \times I$ = 0.60 × 0.30 = $\underline{0.18 \text{ W}}$
(v) No – because the graph is curved. Increasing the voltage in equal steps does not always produce the equal increases in current.

(c) (i) See Fig 7.59
(ii) The plug will be wired as shown on Fig. 7.14 in the text.

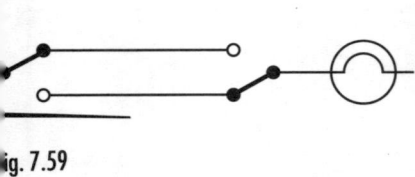

TUTOR'S QUESTION AND ANSWER

THIS IS A PRACTICAL INVESTIGATION QUESTION

You are given 100 cm of wire. How would you find the length of wire to make a 2.0 Ω resistor? You should write down details of the experiment that you wish to carry out, showing clearly what apparatus, chosen from that supplied, you wish to use. Show all results and any calculations you make to obtain your answer. (SEG)

ANSWER

The apparatus needs to be: a suitable power supply 0–12 V DC; an ammeter 0–5 A; a voltmeter 0–15 V; leads and crocs clips; 100 cm of wire provided; metre rule.

In all measurements it is important that the wire is laid straight – it is likely to be uninsulated, so a short circuit could develop leading to inconsistent results.

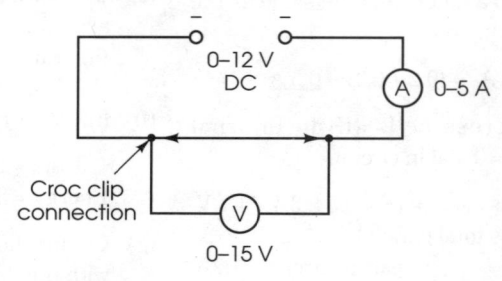

Fig. 7.60

The apparatus is set up as shown (Fig. 7.60), initially using the whole length of wire. Length is checked with a metre rule. Readings of current (ammeter) and potential difference (voltmeter) are taken. The power is turned off and the croc clip positions adjusted to give a wire length of 80 cm, and the current and p.d. are again recorded. The procedure is repeated at 20 cm intervals (10 cm intervals may be better if time is available).

The resistance is calculated from the relationship

$$\text{Resistance} = \frac{\text{Voltage (p.d.)}}{\text{Current}}$$

A graph is then plotted of resistance against length (Fig. 7.61). Draw the best straight line through the points plotted. (The examiners' instruction for this question specifies that the required 2 Ω value should need a length of wire *greater* than that provided – so the graph should look as shown.)

To obtain the "2 Ω length" the graph is extrapolated (shown by a broken line) and the required value read from the graph.

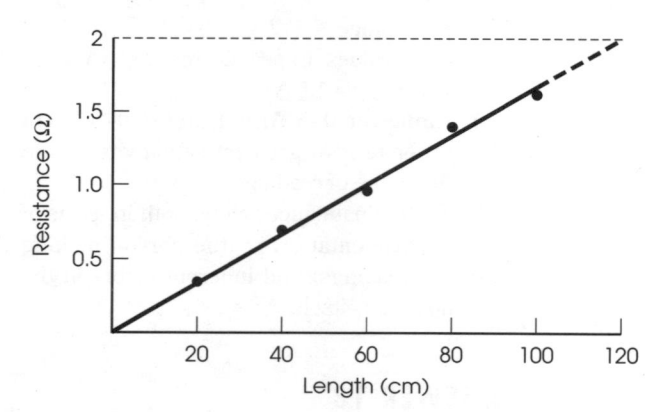

Fig. 7.61

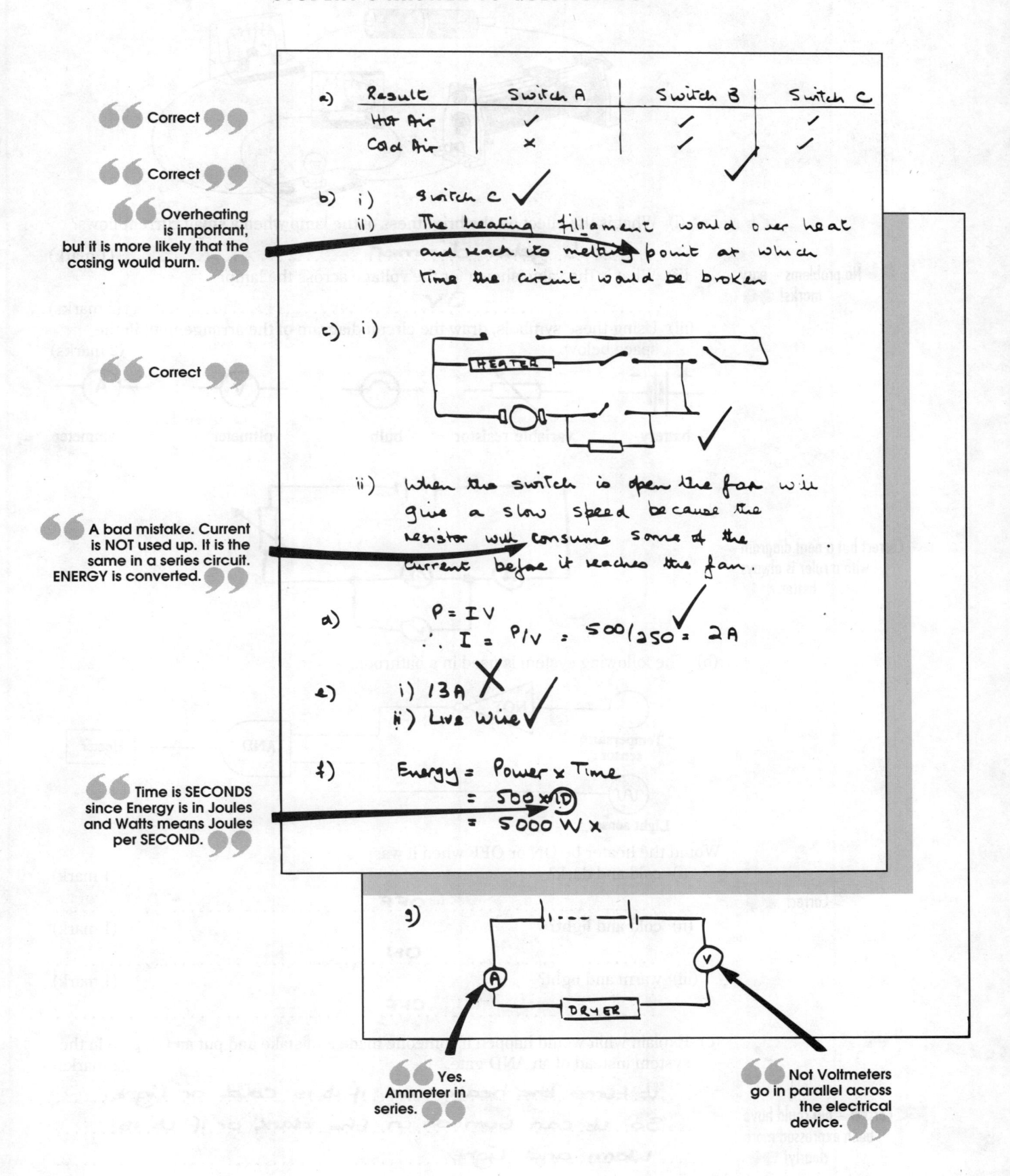

STUDENT'S ANSWER – EXAMINER'S COMMENTS

STUDENT'S ANSWER TO QUESTION 18

a)

Result	Switch A	Switch B	Switch C
Hot Air	✓	✓	✓
Cold Air	✗	✓	✓

> *Correct*

b) i) Switch C ✓

> *Correct*

ii) The heating filament would over heat and reach its melting point at which time the circuit would be broken.

> *Overheating is important, but it is more likely that the casing would burn.*

c) i) [circuit diagram with HEATER] ✓

> *Correct*

ii) When the switch is open the fan will give a slow speed because the resistor will consume some of the current before it reaches the fan.

> *A bad mistake. Current is NOT used up. It is the same in a series circuit. ENERGY is converted.*

d) $P = IV$
$\therefore I = P/V = 500/250 = 2A$ ✓

e) i) 13A ✗
ii) Live Wire ✓

f) Energy = Power × Time
= 500 × 10
= 5000 W ✗

> *Time is SECONDS since Energy is in Joules and Watts means Joules per SECOND.*

g) [circuit diagram with DRYER, ammeter A, voltmeter V]

> *Yes. Ammeter in series.*

> *Not Voltmeters go in parallel across the electrical device.*

MORE EXAMINER'S COMMENTS CENTRAL TIER

(a) The diagram below shows an electrical circuit correctly set up to measure the current going through the lamp and the voltage across it.

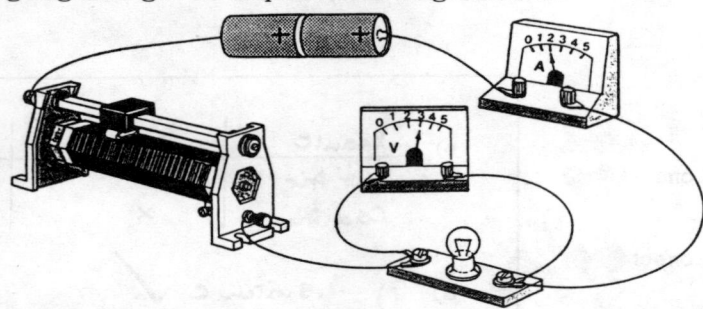

(i) What is the effect on the brightness of the lamp when a small current flows?
..........it gets dimmer..........(1 mark)

> No problems – easy marks!

(ii) What is the value shown for the voltage across the lamp?
..........3v..........(2 marks)

(iii) Using these symbols, draw the circuit diagram of the arrangement in the space below. (2 marks)

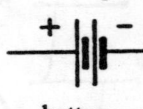

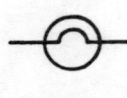

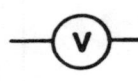

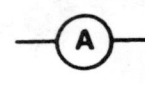

battery   variable resistor   bulb   voltmeter   ammeter

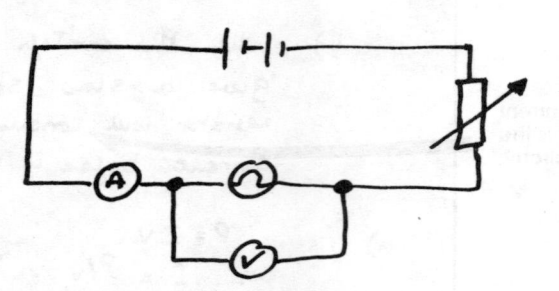

> Correct but a neat diagram with a ruler is always better

(b) The following system is used in a bathroom.

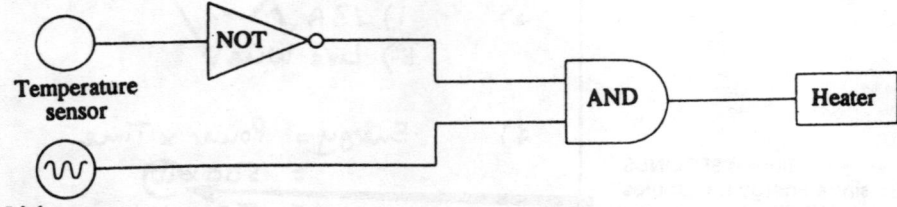

Temperature sensor → NOT → AND → Heater
Light sensor ↗

Would the heater be ON or OFF when it was:
(i) cold and dark? (1 mark)
..........OFF..........

> Correct

(ii) cold and light? (1 mark)
..........ON..........

(iii) warm and light? (1 mark)
..........OFF..........

(c) Explain what would happen if someone made a mistake and put an OR gate in the system instead of an AND gate. (2 marks)

..........It turns the heater on if it is cold or light.
So it can turn on in the dark or if it is
warm and light..........

> Correct – but could have been expressed more clearly!

REVIEW SHEET

- Components that follow one another in a circuit are in _____.

- Charge is measured in _____.

- Draw the circuit symbols for a battery, bulb, two wires that join, switch, ammeter, voltmeter, variable resistor.

- Complete the following equations:

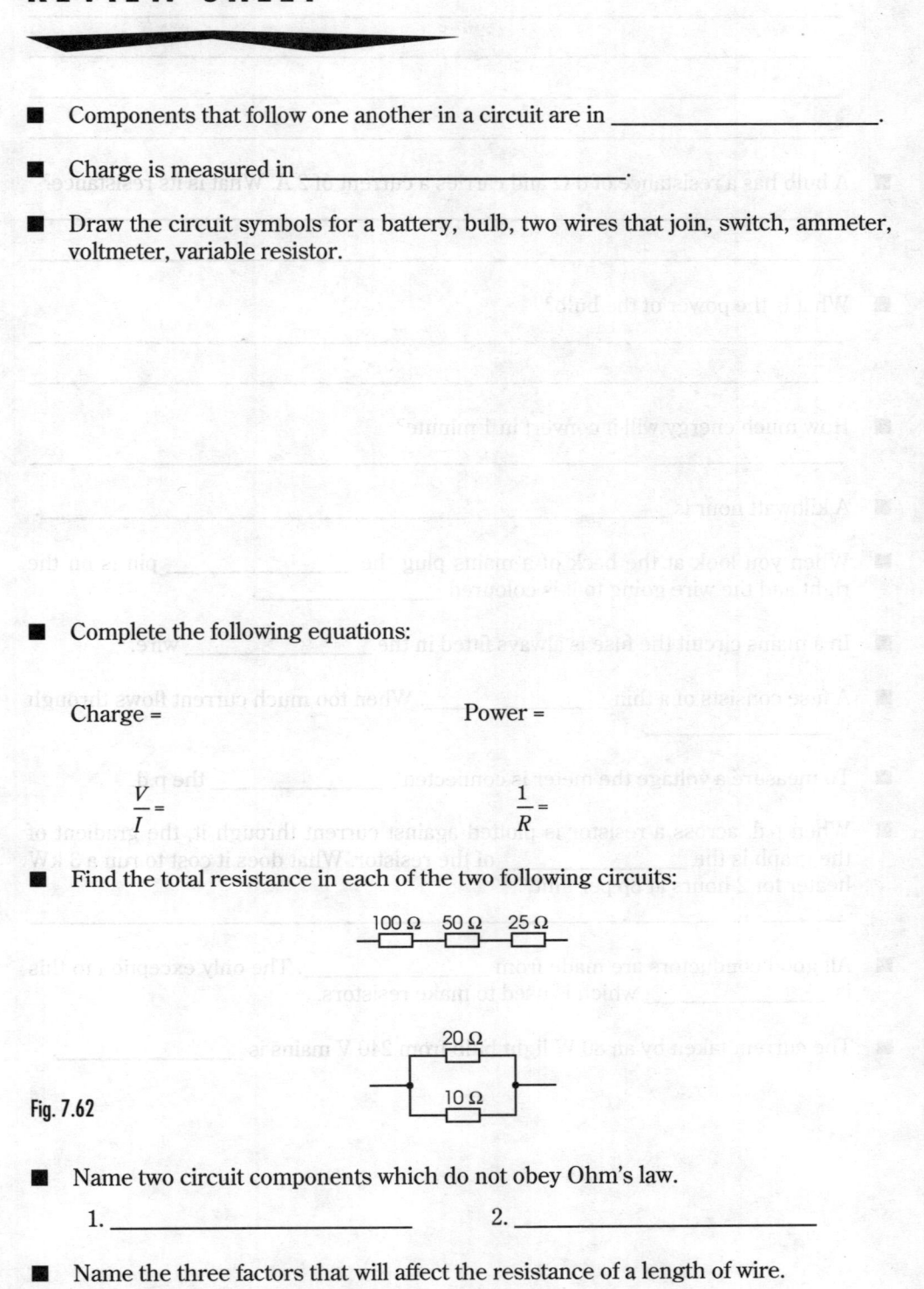

    Charge =   Power =

    $\dfrac{V}{I} =$ $\dfrac{1}{R} =$

- Find the total resistance in each of the two following circuits:

    100 Ω   50 Ω   25 Ω

    20 Ω
    10 Ω

Fig. 7.62

- Name two circuit components which do not obey Ohm's law.

    1. _____   2. _____

- Name the three factors that will affect the resistance of a length of wire.

    1. _____   2. _____   3. _____

- Draw a suitable circuit, including the meters, that you could use to measure the resistance of a bulb.

- State Ohm's law
  _____
  _____
  _____

- A bulb has a resistance of 6 Ω and carries a current of 2 A. What is its resistance?
  _____
  _____

- What is the power of the bulb?
  _____
  _____

- How much energy will it convert in 1 minute?
  _____

- A kilowatt hour is _____.

- When you look at the back of a mains plug the _____ pin is on the right and the wire going to it is coloured _____.

- In a mains circuit the fuse is always fitted in the _____ wire.

- A fuse consists of a thin _____. When too much current flows through it _____.

- To measure a voltage the meter is connected _____ the p.d.

- When p.d. across a resistor is plotted against current through it, the gradient of the graph is the _____ of the resistor. What does it cost to run a 3 kW heater for 2 hours at 8p per unit?
  _____

- All good conductors are made from _____. The only exception to this is _____ which is used to make resistors.

- The current taken by an 80 W light bulb from 240 V mains is _____.

CHAPTER 8

ELECTRONICS: THE COMPONENTS

GETTING STARTED

Everyone must be aware of the importance of **electronics** in modern life, and of the way in which the so-called "new technology" has changed industry and society over the past few years. Calculators, watches, digital sound systems, the operation of industrial plant in factories . . . the list of changes caused by electronics is seemingly endless. However, despite the fact that the applications of electronics are diverse, the individual **components** involved are few, and fairly simple.

A system designed to control traffic lights and a system designed to count high-energy particles in radioactive decay will consist of essentially *similar* components. These include power supply, transistors or printed circuits with a similar function, capacitors, resistors, and some kind of indicator display. Here we consider the individual components and the way in which they operate in simple circuits.

> 66 There is great variation in the coverage of electronics in the different syllabuses. The chapters in this book cover the needs of *all* candidates so you must check your own requirements. 99

RESISTORS
VARIABLE RESISTORS
DIODES
CAPACITORS
LED
TRANSISTORS
SIMPLE SWITCHING CIRCUITS
A TIME-DELAY CIRCUIT
IMPROVING THE SWITCH
FULL WAVE RECTIFIER
CAPACITOR SMOOTHING
A POWER PACK CIRCUIT
POTENTIAL DIVIDERS
TRANSDUCERS AND DRIVERS
USING AN LED

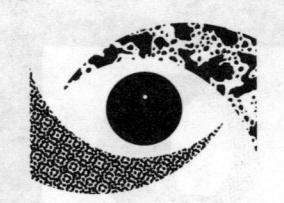

ESSENTIAL PRINCIPLES

1> RESISTORS

A **resistor** is designed to *limit* the current in a circuit or in part of a circuit (Fig. 8.1).

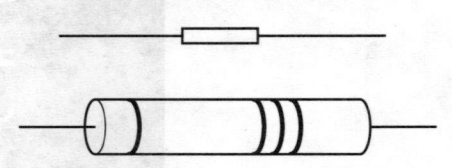

Fig. 8.1 Resistor.

The value of a resistor is indicated by a colour code printed in bands around the resistor, or as a value printed on its side. The resistance to current is measured in ohms (Ω) and is defined as the ratio (V/I), so that $R = V/I$ where R = resistance in ohms; I = current in amps; V = potential difference (PD) in volts.

Bearing in mind that $R = V/I$ this means that a 1 Ω resistor would pass 1 A of current of 1 V PD was applied. A 10 Ω resistor would need 10 V across it to allow a 1 A current, and so on. (See Chapter 7 for Ohm's Law.)

Commercial resistors obey **Ohm's law** provided they do not become too hot, so that their resistance is constant, as in Fig. 8.2 (see also the direct current section, Pg. 73).

Two types of resistor which are designed *not* to maintain constant resistance are the *light-dependent resistor* (LDR) and the *thermistor*. The **LDR** (Fig. 8.3) is a resistor whose resistance *decreases* as the *intensity of light falling on it*

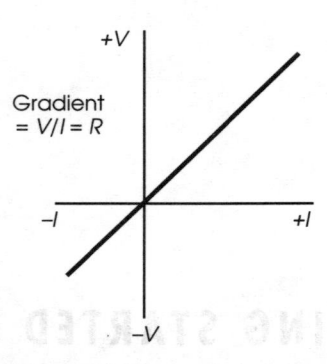

Fig. 8.2 Characteristics of a resistor.

increases. The **thermistor** is a heat-dependent resistor whose resistance *decreases* as the *temperature increases* (Fig. 8.4). Notice that two symbols are in common use for a thermistor. The upper symbol is the "approved" one, though the lower one is often still used.

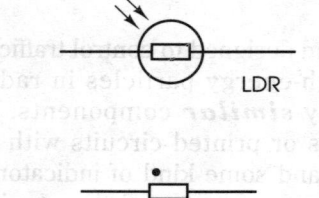

Fig. 8.3

Fig. 8.4

2> VARIABLE RESISTORS

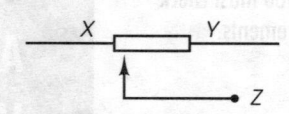

Fig. 8.5 Variable resistor.

A **variable resistor** has three connections (Fig. 8.5); X and Y connect the whole resistance into a circuit, and a sliding contact Z can allow varying amounts of resistance to be used. There are *two* ways of connecting a variable resistor into a circuit – either as a *rheostat* or as a *potential divider*.

The **rheostat** is connected as shown in Fig. 8.6. As the slider Z moves from X to Y, more and more resistance is incorporated into the circuit. The lamp becomes dimmer, and both the current and the voltmeter reading are reduced. When the slider is at Y the current is a minimum but it is not zero.

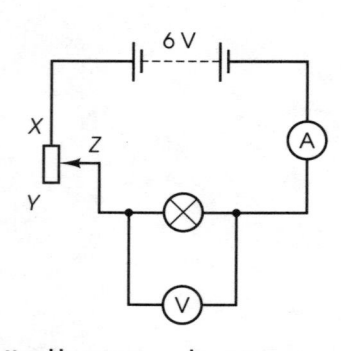

Fig. 8.6 Variable resistor as a rheostat.

The **potential divider** circuit is shown in Fig. 8.7. If the battery voltage is 6 V, then the PD across XY will be 6 V since they are in parallel. With the slider at X, the bulb is itself in parallel across the whole of the resistor, so the PD across the bulb is also 6 V and the ammeter reading will show maximum current. If Z is then moved half-way between X and Y, the PD between Z and Y will be only 3 V, so the current through the bulb will be halved. When Z is at Y there is no PD across the bulb and the current will be zero. The potential divider can therefore give *continuous variation of current and p.d. across the whole range from 0 to maximum*.

A rheostat provides variation by controlling the current in a circuit. A potential divider provides variation by controlling the voltage available across a component.

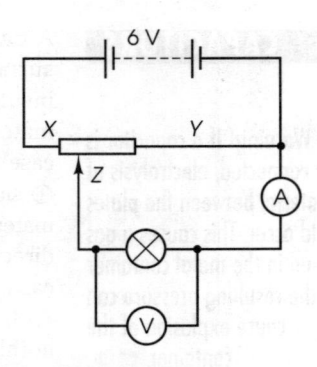

Fig. 8.7 Variable resistor as a potential divider.

3> DIODES

A **diode** consists of two semiconductor slices which have low resistance in one direction, and high resistance in the other.

Fig. 8.8 Diode.

The diode symbol is shown in Fig. 8.8. The arrow in the diagram points in the direction of *low* resistance to conventional current (i.e. ⊕ to ⊖). This means that in a circuit such as Fig. 8.9 one lamp will be ON and the other OFF.

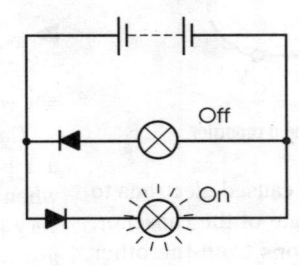

Fig. 8.9

If an ammeter and voltmeter are used to measure the current/voltage relationship for a diode, the low "forward" resistance and the high "reverse" resistance are clearly demonstrated (Fig. 8.10). The "forward" current is of the order of milliamps and the "reverse" is a few microamps. Because larger voltages result in a very rapid current rise, diodes are usually connected in series with a high-value resistor, to protect them from the surge of current which could easily cause overheating, and the diode to burn out.

If an AC supply is connected across a circuit containing a diode, the diode will only conduct during the part of the cycle when the current flows in the positive ("forward") direction. Oscilloscopes across the supply and across the series resistor show this effect, as in Fig. 8.11. The flow of current is now in **one direction only**. This is called "half-wave rectification".

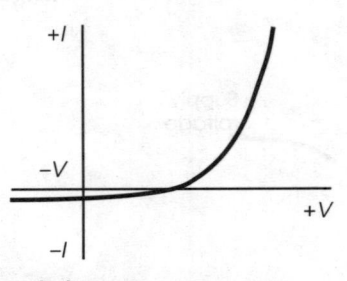

Fig. 8.10 Diode characteristics.

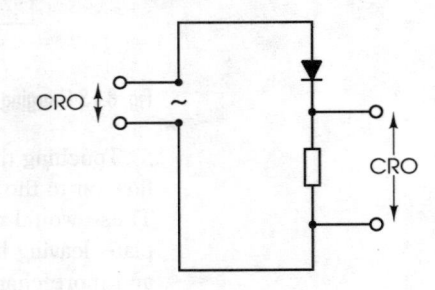

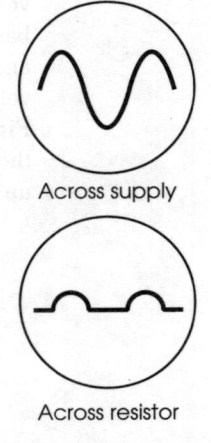

Fig. 8.11 Half-wave rectification

4 CAPACITORS

> **Warning!** If a capacitor is wrongly connected, electrolysis of the material between the plates could occur. This causes a gas build-up in the metal container and the resulting pressure can cause explosion of the container.

A **capacitor** consists of two conducting surfaces, separated from each other by an insulating layer (Fig. 8.12). The insulating material may be a polar material (in which case the capacitor must be connected with its ⊕ side to the ⊕ of the circuit) or it may be a material such as waxed paper or air where the direction of connection does not matter. If a capacitor is connected as in the circuit of Fig. 8.13, and the "flying lead" is connected to X, nothing appears to happen. However, if the lead is now touched at Y, the bulb will light briefly.

Electrolytic capacitor

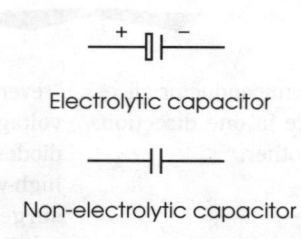

Non-electrolytic capacitor

Fig. 8.12

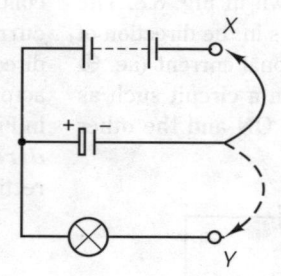

Fig. 8.13 Charging and discharging a capacitor.

Touching the lead at X caused electrons to flow on to the negative plate of the capacitor. These would repel electrons from the other plate, leaving it *positively* charged. As more and more charge builds up on the capacitor, so does the voltage across it. When the voltage across the capacitor is *equal* to the battery voltage, no more electrons will flow and the capacitor is charged to the supply voltage. It is now storing energy. The graph in Fig. 8.14 shows how the voltage, and therefore the charge in the capacitor, builds up as time goes on.

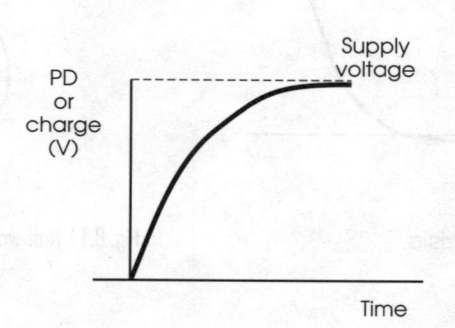

Fig. 8.14 Capacitor charging.

When the lead is then touched at Y, the capacitor voltage is able to push charges around the completed circuit. As more and more charge leaves the capacitor, the p.d. across it drops, until eventually there is no longer any charge on the capacitor plates, and therefore no p.d. across it. The capacitor has **discharged**.

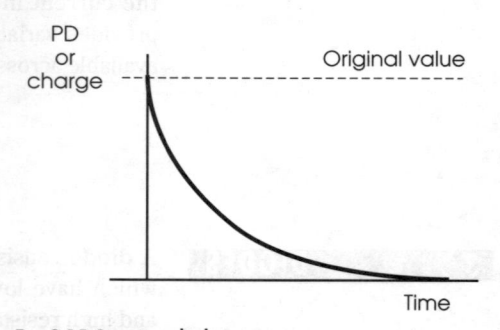

Fig. 8.15 Capacitor discharging.

The graph of Fig. 8.15 shows how the voltage, and therefore charge, decays away with time. The time taken to charge or discharge depends on the value of resistance in the circuit, and the "size" of the capacitor. The **more charge** a capacitor can store at a given supply voltage, the **greater its capacitance**.

Capacitance is defined as

$$C = \frac{Q}{V}$$

where Q = charge and V = voltage.

Capacitance is measured in **farads** (F) so a 1 F capacitor would store 1 C of charge when connected to a 1 V supply. The farad is a very large unit, and practical capacitor values are usually expressed as microfarads (µF) where 1 µF = 10^{-6} F.

The charge and discharge graphs shown in Fig. 8.16 illustrate the effect of varying the values of resistance and capacitance. A *large-value capacitor* and a *large resistance* cause a *slow charge build-up* and a *slow discharge*. In contrast, small values of resistance and capacitance cause a rapid charge build-up and a rapid discharge.

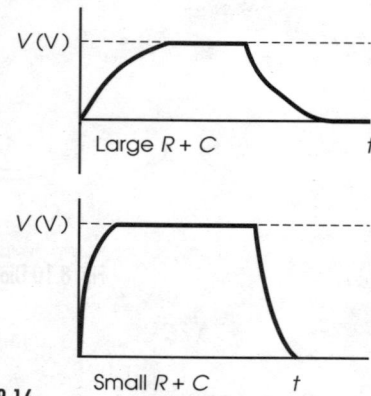

Fig. 8.16

5 LIGHT EMITTING DIODE

A light emitting diode (LED) gives out light when a current flows in a positive (forward) direction (Fig. 8.17). As with a diode, the LED must be connected with a protective resistor in series with it. LEDs are often used in electronics circuits because they require less power than an ordinary indicator lamp.

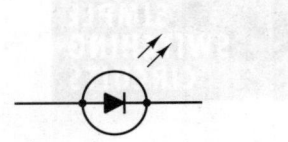

Fig. 8.17 LED.

6 TRANSISTORS

This semiconducting device has three connections. They are called the **base**, **collector** and **emitter** (Fig. 8.18). Currents in a transistor circuit are likely to be small, so an indictor should be either a low-power lamp (e.g. 6 V, 0.06 A) or an LED.

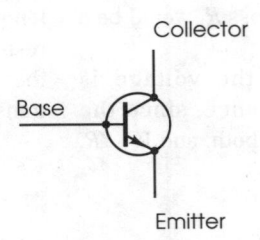

Fig. 8.18 Transistor.

In the circuit of Fig. 8.19 there is a complete path for current flow through the collector to the emitter, but the lamp will not light. This suggests that the route from collector to emitter is a high-resistance route. If, however, a second battery is connected between the base and the emitter, and a large-value resistor is incorporated, as in Fig. 8.20, the lamp will light. The flow of current in the "base" circuit (through the base to the emitter) appears to change the resistance in the collector-emitter path and a larger current can now flow, enough to light the lamp.

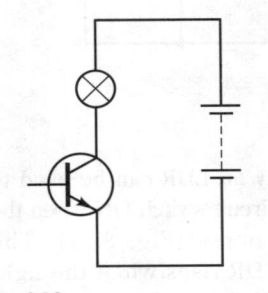

Fig. 8.19

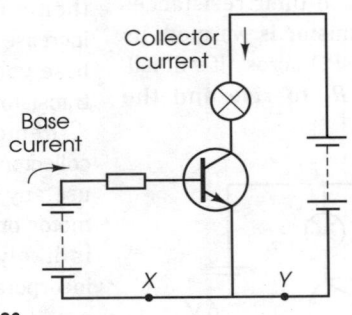

Fig. 8.20

Placing ammeters in the circuit at X and Y shows that the base current is very small (usually microamps) compared with the collector current (milliamps). So a small base current controls the larger collector current. The current in the base circuit must be in the direction shown in Fig. 8.20. This is called "*forward biasing*"! The base current must also be limited by using the large-value series resistor in the base to protect the transistor from over-heating.

❝ 1 microamp = 10^{-6} amp
1 milliamp = 10^{-3} amp
i.e. 1 million microamps in 1 amp.
1000 milliamps in 1 amp. ❞

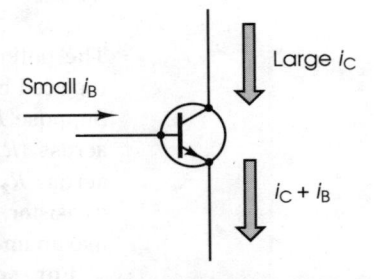

Fig. 8.21(a) Small base current controls large collector current;

When a current flows in the collector, the transistor is described as being "ON" or "OPEN". It is effectively an electronic switch, with the base current acting as the switch operator. It is not necessary to use two sets of batteries as in Fig. 8.20. In Fig. 8.21(b) there will be a PD of 6 V between X and Y and this can be used to provide the voltage necessary to give the base current.

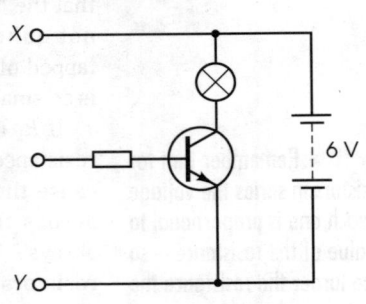

Fig. 8.21(b)

A potential divider circuit, Fig. 8.22, could be incorporated. The PD across XY is then 6 V and the slider Z can vary the voltage between the base and the negative side. A voltmeter in the base circuit will show that a minimum voltage between the base and the negative side of 0.6–0.7 V is needed for the transistor to "switch" ON.

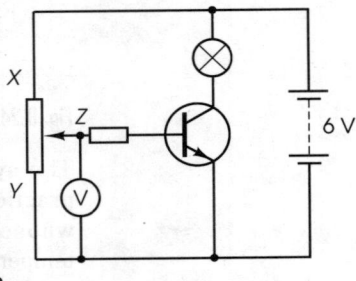

Fig. 8.22

7 SIMPLE SWITCHING CIRCUITS

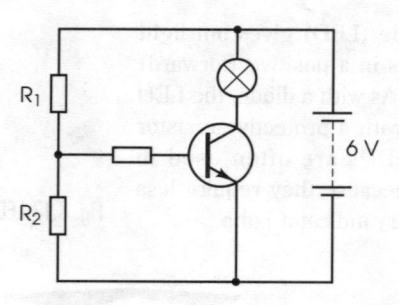

Fig. 8.23

The potential divider in Fig. 8.22 could be replaced by two fixed resistors as in Fig. 8.23. Suppose R_1 is a 1 kΩ resistor and the PD across $(R_1 + R_2)$ is 6 V. A minimum voltage across R_2 of 0.6 V is needed to switch the transistor, so the voltage across R_1 would be a maximum of 5.4 V.

For series resistors, the voltage is proportional to the resistance, since the current is the same through both, and $V = IR$. Therefore, $V \propto R$.

$$\frac{R_1}{R_2} = \frac{5.4}{0.6}$$

$$R_2 = \frac{0.6 R_1}{5.4} = \frac{0.6 \times 1000}{5.4} = \underline{111 \, \Omega}$$

If R_2 is any smaller than this value the transistor would remain OFF. (The statement that the "current in R_1 is the same as in R_2" is not quite correct. A small current (µA) is tapped off through the base resistor – but this is so small it can be ignored.)

If R_1 is now replaced with a thermistor of resistance 1 kΩ and R_2 is 90 Ω the circuit will cause the transistor to be OFF. The voltage across the thermistor and R_2 together is always 6 V, and this is shared between the two resistors in proportion to their resistances (Fig. 8.24). If the thermistor is warmed, its resistance falls, and the PD across it will fall, causing that across R_2 to rise and the transistor to switch ON.

> **Remember that for resistors in series the voltage across each one is proportional to the value of the resistance – so that the larger the resistance the bigger the voltage across it.**

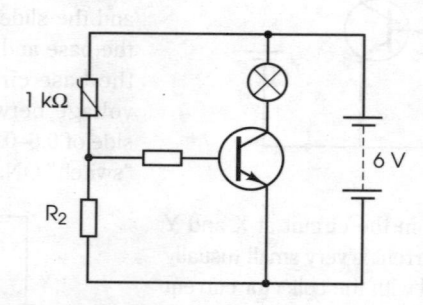

Fig. 8.24

The system could act as a fire alarm. In practice R_2 is usually a variable resistor, whose value is adjusted so that at room temperature the transistor is OFF, but with switching occurring when the temperature rises beyond an acceptable level (Fig. 8.25).

Reversing the positions of the two resistors (Fig. 8.26) would cause the system to switch ON when the temperature *drops* significantly, like an "icing-up" warning device. When the temperature falls the thermistor has a bigger resistance and therefore gets a larger share of the voltage. When this is equal to 0.7 V the transistor is switched on.

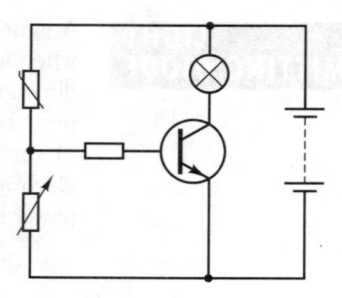

Fig. 8.25

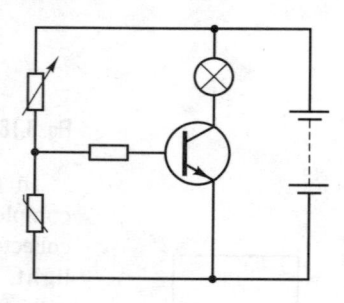

Fig. 8.26

In the same way an LDR can be used to make a transistor circuit switch ON when the level of light changes (Fig. 8.27). The resistance of an LDR rises when the light intensity drops. If the resistance of R is adjusted so that the circuit is OFF in daylight, then a reduction in intensity of light will increase the resistance of the LDR, raising the base voltage above 0.7 V and switching the transistor ON.

Remember that in these circuits the collector current is only a few milliamps, so to use any circuit practically to operate a bell, motor or other device using large currents, it is likely that a *relay* would have to be incorporated (see P. 231).

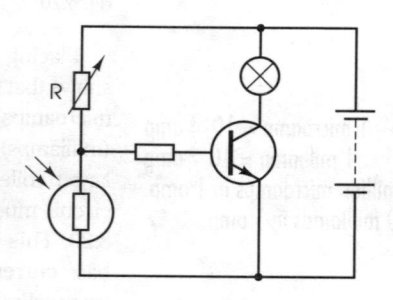

Fig. 8.27

8 > A TIME-DELAY CIRCUIT

When the switch is open there is no PD between the base and the negative line, so the transistor is closed (OFF). On closing the switch, charge flows on to the capacitor, building up a voltage across it. When this exceeds 0.7 V the transistor "switches ON" and the lamp lights (Fig. 8.28). The delay before this happens will be increased if the resistor R has more resistance so that the current charging the capacitor is smaller and it takes longer to reach the 0.7 V.

If the manual switch is opened again the lamp remains ON for a time. The capacitor is discharging and maintains the base voltage above 0.7 V for some time (Fig. 8.29). The delay is increased if the capacitance or the base resistor are increased in value.

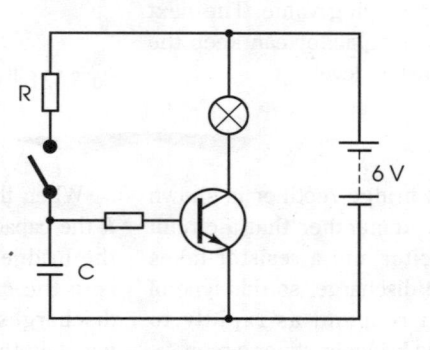

Fig. 8.28 Capacitor delay circuit.

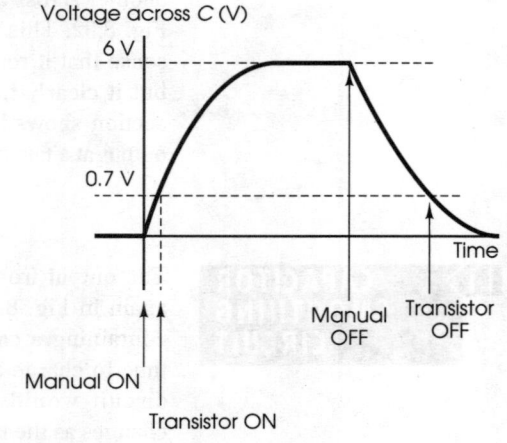

Fig. 8.29

9 > IMPROVING THE SWITCH

The circuits so far only turn on a low power lamp or an LED (with a series resistor). Putting a relay (see Chapter 13) in the collector lead enables the circuit to switch much larger currents on or off. The circuit in Fig. 8.30 will switch on a "mains" lamp when it gets dark.

The NO on the relay symbol shows that it is "normally open" –off until current passes through the coil – and the box represents the coil of the relay. There are hidden dangers when using relays and a diode may be needed to protect the transistor – see Chapter 14.

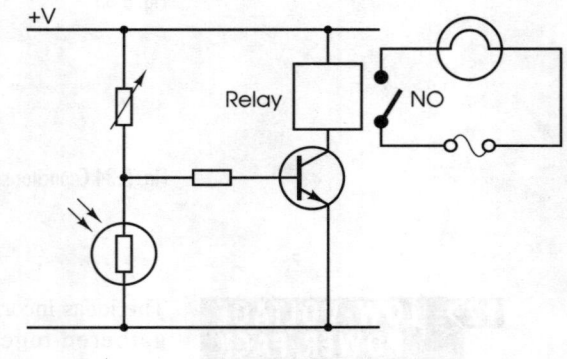

Fig. 8.30

EXTENSION MATERIALS

10 > FULL WAVE RECTIFICATION – THE BRIDGE RECTIFIER

A single diode in an AC circuit gives a **half-wave rectified output**, since the dioide will only conduct when the current flow is ⊕ to ⊖ (conventional current flow). Clearly energy supplied to the input is not made available at the output for half of the time for one cycle of AC. A more useful circuit to deliver "one-direction" current would need to produce current **over the entire cycle of energy delivery**. The circuit requires a bridge

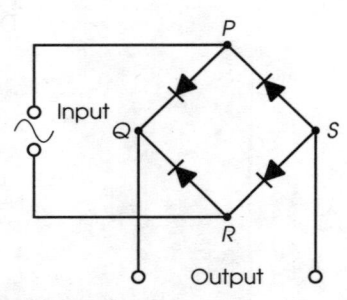

Fig. 8.31 Bridge rectifier.

rectifier and is shown in Fig. 8.31. On the positive part of the cycle, current flows in the direction P → Q. On the negative part, the flow is R → Q. Point Q is always at the start of positive current flow, so the output is always in the same direction.

An oscilloscope across the input and another across the output show the patterns of Fig. 8.32. This gives "direct" current in the sense that it remains in the positive direction but it clearly has a varying value. The next section shows how a capacitor can keep the output at a fairly constant level.

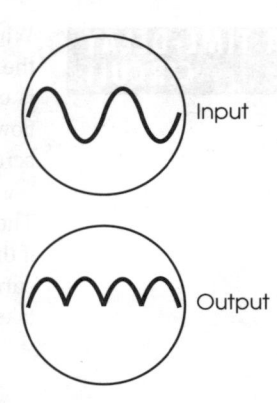

Fig. 8.32 Full wave rectification

11> CAPACITOR SMOOTHING CIRCUIT

The output from a bridge rectifier is shown again in Fig. 8.33. Remember that a circuit containing a capacitor and a resistor takes time to charge and discharge, so this type of circuit would not respond as rapidly to changes as the basic bridge rectifier circuit.

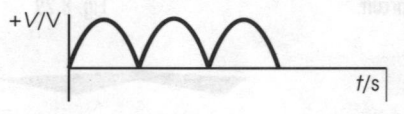

Fig. 8.33

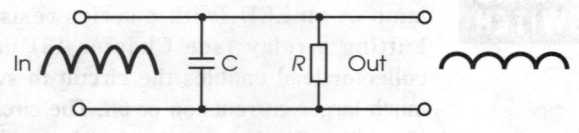

Fig. 8.34 Capacitor smoothing circuit

When the voltage rises across both C and R the capacitor is charging (Fig. 8.34). When the bridge rectifier output drops rapidly to zero the capacitor, which is fully charged, discharges slowly, supplying the energy to maintain the current at a fairly constant value until the bridge output is high again.

The *greater the value of capacitance and resistance, the longer the effect lasts* and the *smaller the reduction of voltage from the maximum value*.

12> LOW-VOLTAGE POWER PACK CIRCUIT

The ideas incorporated in this section can be gathered together to explain how a low-voltage power pack works (Fig. 8.35). You have probably used a power pack many times and will be aware that either AC or DC is available. The requirements of the pack are as follows:

1. Mains AC at 240 V and 50 Hz are transformed to 2–12 V AC or DC. This clearly needs a step-down transformer.
2. If DC is required the low-voltage AC must be made into a "one-direction" supply – a bridge rectifier will do this.
3. The output should be as "smooth" as possible giving a fairly constant DC voltage.

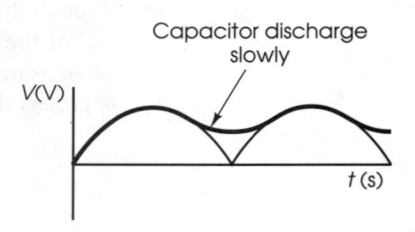

Fig. 8.35

4. Safety needs consideration since the original supply is from the mains. The circuit is shown in Fig. 8.36. The transformer has a fuse and switch in the live side and the core is earthed.

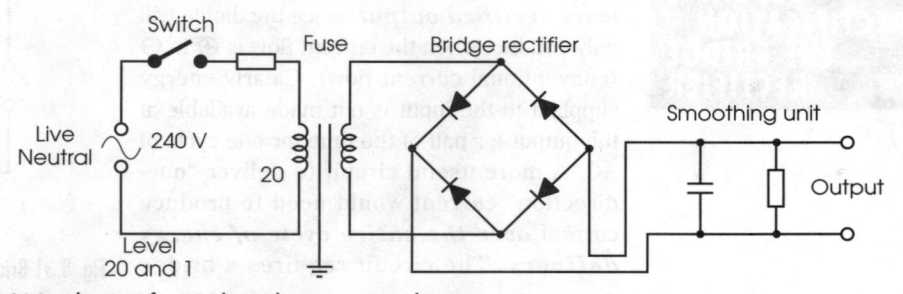

Fig. 8.36 Simple circuit for a DC low-voltage power supply.

13> MORE ABOUT POTENTIAL DIVIDERS

It is possible to calculate the output voltage from a voltage divider provided that the current taken is very small; i.e. you can assume that the current through both resistors is the same. The voltage across each resistor is then proportional to its resistance, and for Fig. 8.37:

$$V_{out} = V_{in} \times \frac{R_1}{(R_1 + R_2)}$$

where the symbols represent the values shown in the diagram.

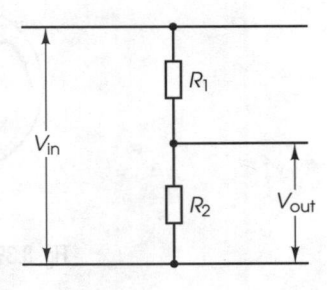

Fig. 8.37

14> TRANSDUCERS

Devices that change energy from one form to another are called **transducers**. Bulbs are transducers, as are heaters, fans, loudspeakers and microphones. You might want to switch one of these transducers by the transistor switch but the current needed is often too large for the simple transistor to carry. One way is to use a relay as shown in section 9. The voltage at the collector could also be connected to the base of a transistor that *can* carry a larger current and this will in turn switch your transducer. This transistor is known as a transducer driver. It is often used so that the low-power transistor circuits in logic gates can switch transducers (see chapter 16).

15> USING AN LED

An LED can only pass a small current of about 10 or 20 mA. You must fit a series resistor to protect it.

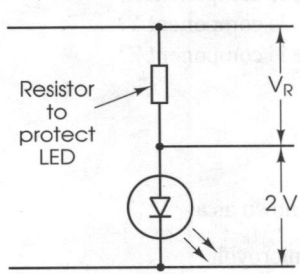

Fig. 8.38

If you can use Ohm's law you can find the size of the resistor needed.

The diode will work with a p.d. across it of about 2 V. If the supply is from a 9 V battery then the voltage across the resistor

$$V_R = 9 - 2 = 7 \text{ V}$$

The LED will be quite bright if it carries a current of about 15 mA. This same current flows through the resistor. Applying Ohm's law:

$$R = \frac{V_R}{I}$$

$$R = \frac{7}{0.015}$$

$$R = \underline{467 \, \Omega}$$

The nearest value to this that you can buy is 480 Ω. Larger supply voltages will require larger value resistors. The resistors can be very small (low power) because they carry so little current.

EXAMINATION QUESTIONS

MULTIPLE CHOICE QUESTIONS

QUESTION 1

The trace on an oscilloscope is shown in Fig. 8.39(a). A student then alters one of the oscilloscope controls and obtains the trace in Fig. 8.36(b). Which one of the controls did the student alter?

A The Y gain
B The Y shift
C The X shift
D The time base frequency   (SEG)

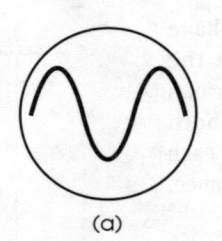

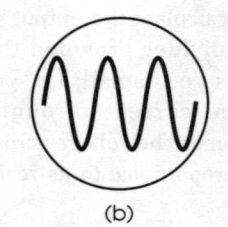

Fig. 8.39

QUESTIONS 2–4

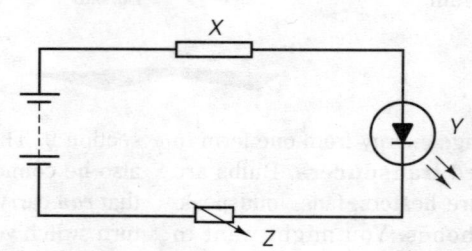

Fig. 8.40

Figure 8.40 refers to questions 2–4. The answer code is:

A Resistor
B Transistor
C LED
D Capacitor
E Variable resistor

2. Which one of the above is component X?
3. Which one of the above is component Y?
4. Which one of the above is component Z?

QUESTION 5

One-millionth of a volt is known as a

A centivolt   D microvolt
B kilovolt   E millivolt
C megavolt   (ULEAC)

QUESTION 7

When a capacitor is charged from a battery, which of the following cannot take place?

A Electrons move in the circuit.
B Energy is stored in the capacitor.
C The capacitor acquires a steady voltage across it.
D The current in the circuit is constant.

QUESTION 6

In which one of the circuits (Fig. 8.41) will the lamp light?

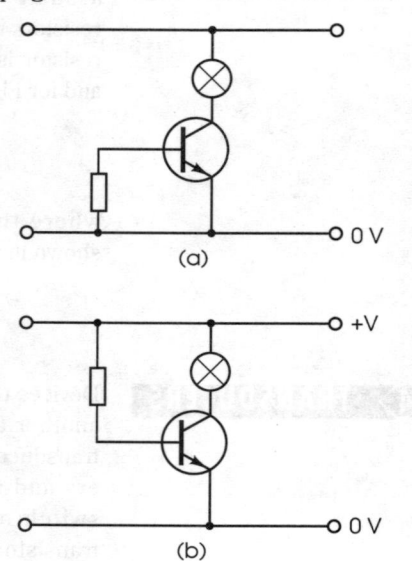

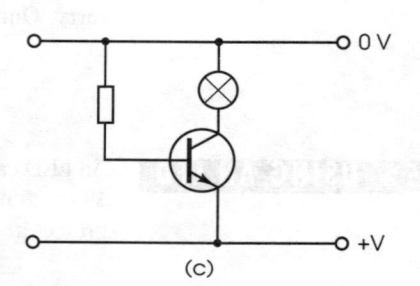

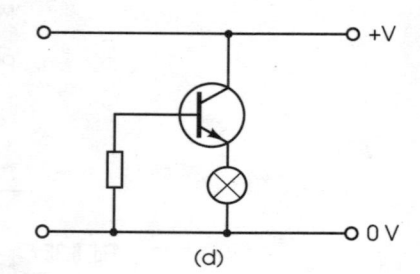

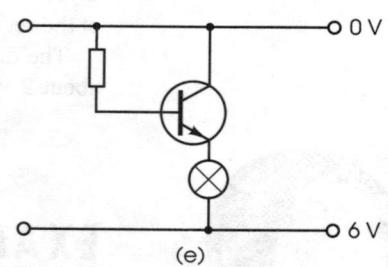

Fig. 8.41

STRUCTURED QUESTIONS

QUESTION 8

This question is about the voltages across devices connected in series.

(a) Figure 8.42 shows a 500 Ω resistor and a 1000 Ω resistor connected in series across a constant 3 V DC supply.

(i) What is the total resistance across the supply?
(ii) What is the current through the circuit?

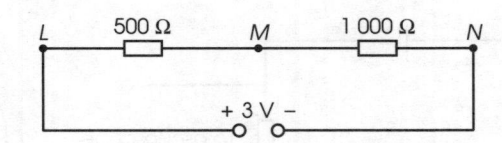

Fig. 8.42

(b) When a voltmeter is connected across LN as in Fig. 8.43 it shows a voltage of 3 V. The voltmeter is then connected across MN as shown in Fig. 8.44. What voltage will it now show?

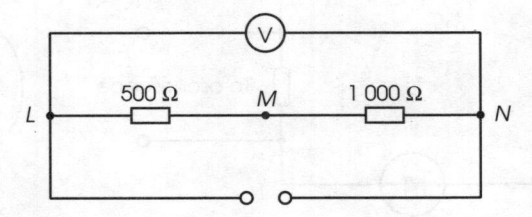

Fig. 8.43

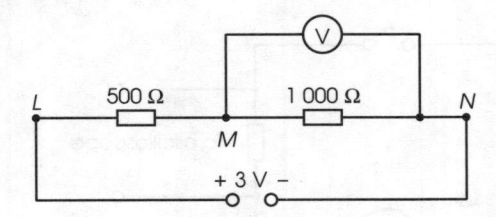

Fig. 8.44

(c) The 1000 Ω resistor is then taken out of the circuit and a well-lit light dependent resistor (LDR) is put in its place, as shown in Fig. 8.45.

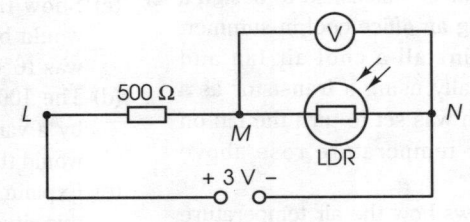

Fig. 8.45

(i) The voltmeter now shows a reading of 1.5 V. What is the resistance of the LDR?
(ii) What would happen to the voltmeter reading if no light were allowed to fall on the LDR (by wrapping it in black cloth for example)?
(iii) Explain why this would happen.

(SEG)

QUESTION 9

The circuit diagram (Fig. 8.46) shoes how a transistor may be used to make a lamp come on in the dark.

(i) Complete the circuit (Fig. 8.46) by

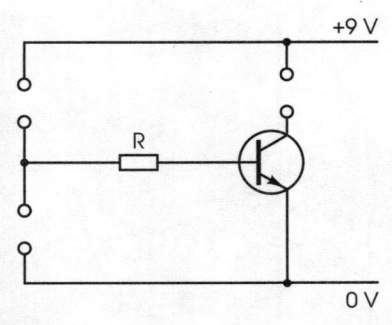

Fig. 8.46

adding in the spaces the symbols and labelling as Fig. 8.47:

A A light-sensitive resistor;
B A variable resistor;
C An electromagnetic relay.

(a) A light sensitive resistor

(b) A variable resistor

(c) An electromagnetic relay

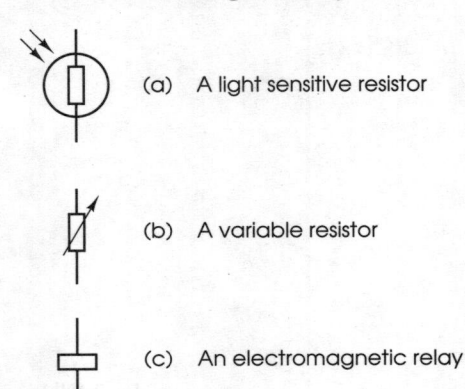

Fig. 8.47

(ii) Explain how the circuit will operate the relay, and hence switch a bulb on in the dark.
(iii) Why is a variable resistor preferable to a fixed resistor?
(iv) Why is a relay preferred to inserting a bulb directly into the circuit?
(v) What is the purpose of resistor R?

(ULEAC)

QUESTION 10

Name the component whose circuit symbol is shown in Fig. 8.48.

Fig. 8.48

(i) Name _____
(ii) The trace on an oscilloscope with the time base turned on and no input to the Y plates is shown in Fig. 8.49(a). For each of the circuits in Fig. 8.49(b), use the blank circle on its right to sketch the trace that would be seen on the oscilloscope screen.

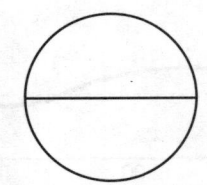

Fig. 8.49(a)

CHAPTER 8 ELECTRONICS: THE COMPONENTS

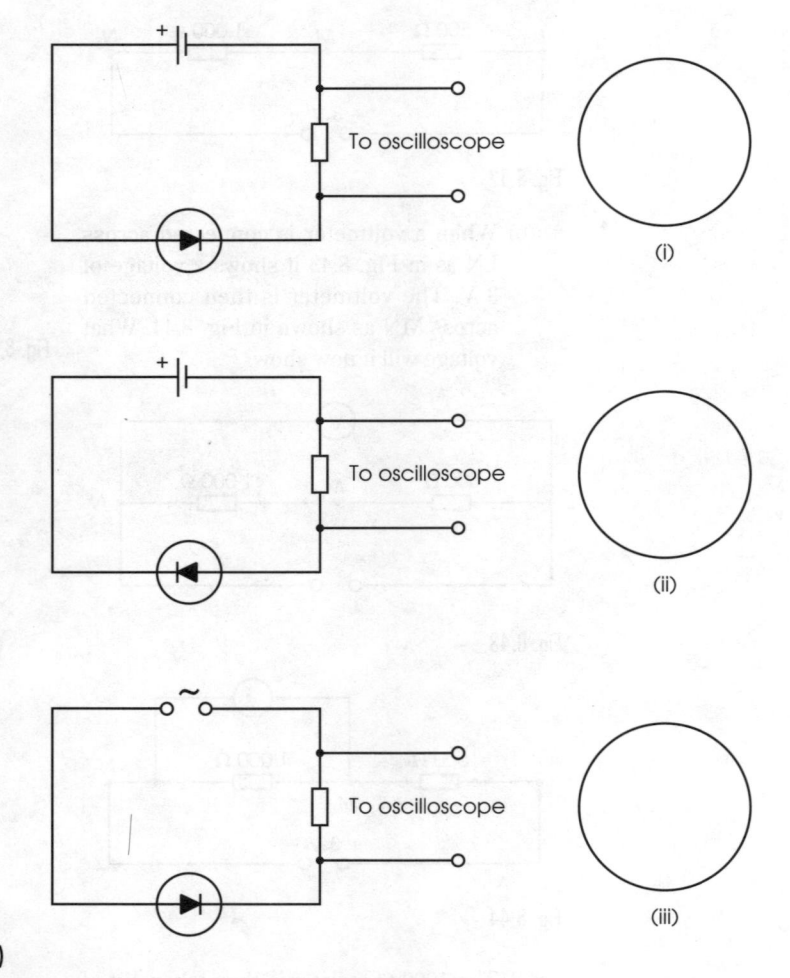

Fig. 8.49(b)

QUESTION 11

Sensing, responding and controlling.

A building engineer was asked to design a system for keeping an office cool in summer. She decided to install a cool air fan and control it electrically using a transistor as a switch. The switch was set to turn the fan on when the sensor temperature rose above 23°C.

The graph shows how the air temperature in the room changed during an hour at midday.

(a) Explain what the fan was doing at the following times.

   (i) 11.00
   (ii) 12.00

(b) Explain why the air temperature did not rise far above 23°C.

The thermistor was connected to a 1000 Ω resistor and a 6 V battery as shown. The resistance of the thermistor is 1000 Ω when its temperature is 16°C.

(c) Show that the input to the transistor would be 3 volts when the temperature was 16°C.

(d) The 1000 Ω resistor was then replaced by a variable resistor. What advantage would this have?

(e) Explain how feedback was achieved in this situation. (ULEAC)

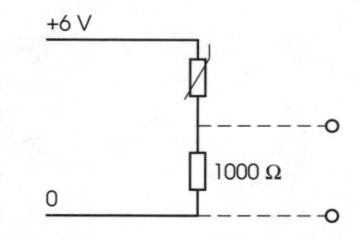

Fig. 8.51

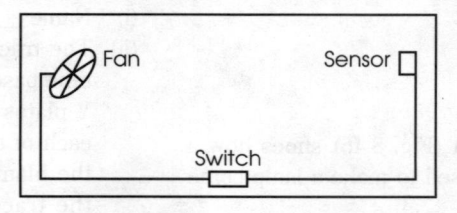

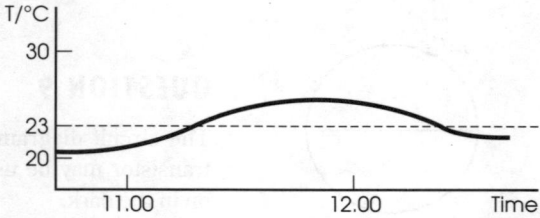

Fig. 8.50

OUTLINE ANSWERS

MULTIPLE CHOICE QUESTIONS

Question	1	2	3	4	5	6	7
Answer	D	A	C	E	D	B	D

STRUCTURED QUESTIONS

ANSWER 8

(a) (i) Total resistance $R = R_1 + R_2 = 1500\ \Omega$.
(ii) Current = $V/R = 3/1500 = 0.002$ A.

(b) Voltage divides in proportion to resistances

$$V = \frac{1000}{1500} \times 3 = 2\ \text{V}$$

(c) (i) Since there must be 1.5 V across each resistor, they must be of equal value:

Resistance of LDR = 500 Ω

(ii) Voltmeter reading increases.
(iii) The resistance of the LDR is greater in the dark; voltage across it is greater.

ANSWER 9

(i) See Fig. 8.52.

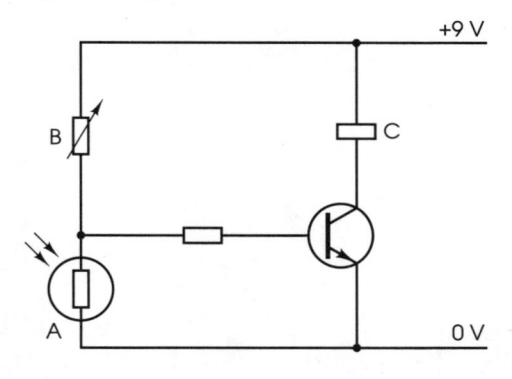

Fig. 8.52

(ii) B is adjusted so that in bright light the transistor is OFF. When it gets dark, the resistance of the LDR increases and the voltage between the base and 0 volts rises, switching the transistor ON. This energises the relay coil and a second circuit is switched causing a light to turn ON.
(iii) The variable resistor will give greater sensitivity.
(iv) The current in the collector is too small to power a large lamp. The relay will control a circuit with a high-power lamp in it.
(v) Resistor R is to limit the current to the base, protecting the transistor.

ANSWER 10

(i) The component is a diode.
(ii) See Fig. 8.53.

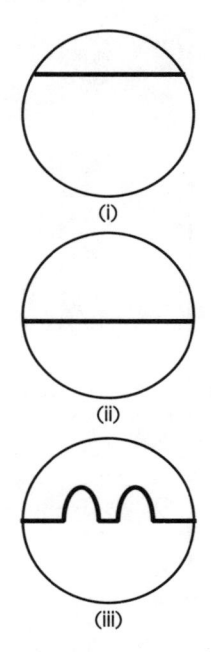

Fig. 8.53

ANSWER 11

(This is an intermediate level question.)

(a) (i) fan off.
(ii) fan on.

(b) As room temperature goes greater than 23°C the sensor switches the fan on and the room cools. As room temperature goes less than 23°C the sensor switches the fan off and the room warms up.

(c) The two equal resistors in the potential divider will each have the same share of the voltage – i.e. 3 V each.

(d) Feedback happens when the fan blows cold air across the room to the sensor and changes its state.

REVIEW SHEET

- Draw the symbols for

    1. LED   2. LDR   3. Thermistor

    4. Transistor   5. Electrolytic capacitor

- A diode only allows current to flow _____.

- A LED will only light when it is _____ biased and takes a _____ current from the circuit.

- A circuit that connects across an a.c. supply so that current can only leave it flowing in one direction is called a _____.

- The simple type uses one _____ to control the current flow.

- Write down the equation that connects charge, capacitance and voltage.

- The unit for capacitance is the _____.

- Name a use for a capacitor _____.

- When two resistors of equal value are put in series across a supply voltage the voltage at the junction of the two is _____.

- A 900 Ω resistor and a 100 Ω resistor are connected in series across a 24 V supply. The p.d. across the smaller resistor is _____.

- Write down the names of the three connections to a transistor.

    1 _____.   2 _____.   3 _____.

- A time delay circuit uses a capacitor charged through a resistor. What could you change to make the time delay longer?

    _____
    _____
    _____
    _____

- A transistor uses a small current through its _____ to switch on a larger current that flows through its _____ and _____. The voltage at the base must be at least _____ before the transistor turns on.

- Draw a transistor switch circuit that will turn on a small warning lamp if the temperature outside falls to freezing point. (Use a thermistor as the sensor and make sure that you put it in the correct place!)

- A 200 µF capacitor is charged up to 9 V. Use the equation to work out the charge on it. If it is discharged in 0.5 s what is the *average* current that flows? (You will find the equation for charge in chapter 7 if you have forgotten it! Note that the current will be bigger than this at the start and zero at the end.)

_____
_____
_____
_____

CHAPTER 9

OPTICS AND THE NATURE OF LIGHT

GETTING STARTED

This chapter is closely linked to the earlier one about oscillations and waves (Ch. 6). **Light**, in common with the whole electromagnetic wave spectrum, is a *transverse wave*, consisting of oscillating electric and magnetic fields. The wavelength of light is so small that the effects normally associated with waves are only apparent under very carefully controlled conditions.

It is convenient to discuss light in terms of "rays" emitted from a luminous object. A light ray as such does not really exist. It is a *guideline* drawn to indicate the direction of travel of a wavefront. However, the use of the ray idea is simpler than drawing wavefronts and still leads to correct predictions.

RAYS OF LIGHT
REFLECTION
REFRACTION
TOTAL INTERNAL REFLECTION
LENSES
DISPERSION
LIGHT AS A WAVE
POLARISATION
THE ELECTROMAGNETIC SPECTRUM
RAY DIAGRAMS FOR LENS IMAGES
VIRTUAL IMAGES
SIMPLE PROJECTOR SYSTEM
LENS CAMERAS
THE HUMAN EYE
YOUNG'S SLIT EXPERIMENT
COLOUR
THE PHOTOELECTRIC EFFECT
LENS FORMULA
VISION DEFECTS

1 RAYS OF LIGHT AND STRAIGHT LINES

ESSENTIAL PRINCIPLES

Around a small light source, waves travel out as spherical wavefronts. The **direction** in which the wavefront travels (or the "ray" of light associated with it) is at 90° to the wavefront. We therefore say that light "rays" travel from a source in straight lines (Fig. 9.1). This idea is useful in explaining the behaviour of light in a simple pinhole camera experiment.

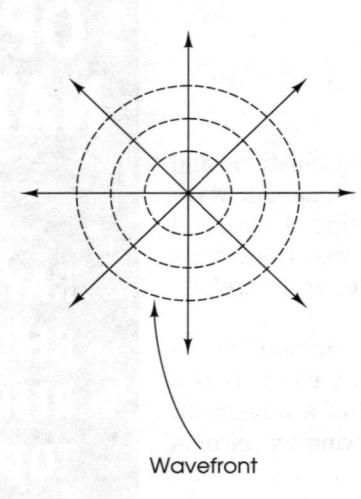

Fig. 9.1

The pinhole camera is a light-proof box with a translucent screen at one end, made of tracing paper. The other end has a small pinhole made in the otherwise light-proof front. Observations are made from behind the screen (Fig. 9.2). Since little light enters the "camera" a source of light, like a bright filament in a lamp, must be observed.

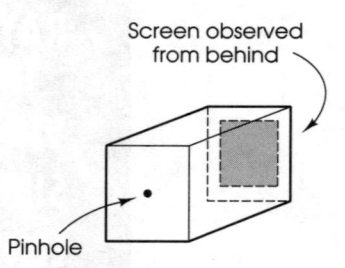

Fig. 9.2 Pinhole camera.

The following are typical observations and results:

1. With a small pinhole, and observing a filament lamp "object", an inverted image is seen on the screen (Fig. 9.3). The image is sharply focused for all distances of the object from the camera. The image is larger when the camera is moved closer to the object.

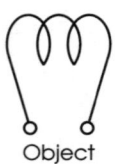

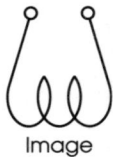

Fig. 9.3 Image in a pinhole camera.

2. If the single hole is made larger, the image remains the same size for a given camera distance, but it is brighter (since more light can enter) and blurred (Fig. 9.4).

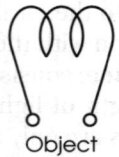

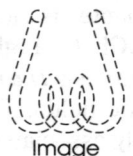

Fig. 9.4

3. A number of small pinholes give an equal number of images, all inverted, and overlapping if the original holes are close together (Fig. 9.5).

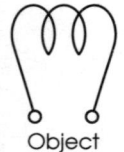

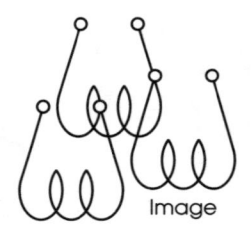

Fig. 9.5 Overlapping images with three pinholes.

The image is inverted because of the straight line path taken by the light rays. A ray leaving the top of the object carries that information to the bottom of the screen and vice versa (Fig. 9.6).

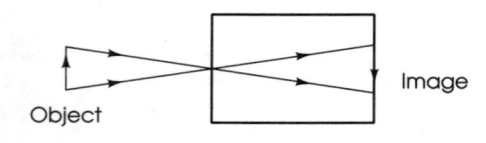

Fig. 9.6 Ray diagrams for a pinhole camera.

In drawing ray diagrams, it is important to show the **ray direction** by putting an **arrow** on the ray. For the pinhole camera, rays leaving the object and forming the image all across at the pinhole.

2 > REFLECTION OF LIGHT

Most objects can only be seen because they reflect light into the eye, since they are not themselves luminous. A plane mirror reflects in a special way (***specular reflection***). A simple experiment with light rays illustrates this (Fig. 9.7). The arrangement of the lamp with a single slit and a lens enables a narrow single parallel beam of light to be used, and this arrangement should be used in all such experimental arrangements where rays are

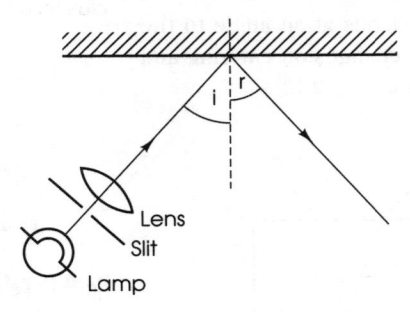

Fig. 9.7 Reflection at a plane mirror.

being studied. If the positions of the two rays are marked on paper, and a reference line called the ***normal*** is marked at 90° to the reflecting surface, the following rule is apparent:

▶ **The angle of incidence (i) = the angle of reflection (r)** where the angles are the angles between the rays and the normal (Fig. 9.8).

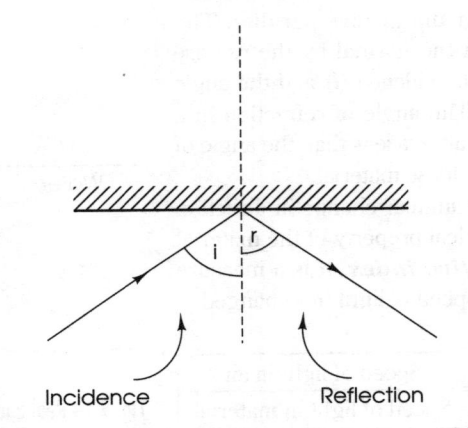

Fig. 9.8 Law of reflection $i = r$

Reflection at any surface follows this rule, even when the surface is not smooth (***diffuse***

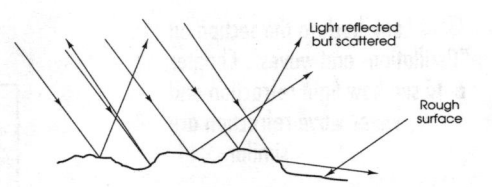

Fig. 9.9

reflection). It is because of its smooth surface that an image can be seen in a plane mirror. Experiment shows that the image lies ***as far behind the mirror as the object is in front of it***. The reason for this is shown by the geometry of the rays reflected in Fig. 9.10.

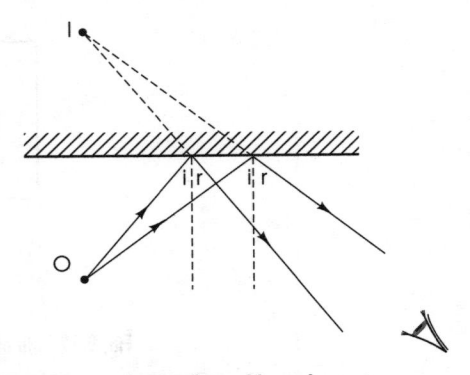

Fig. 9.10 Virtual image formed by a plane mirror.

All rays leaving the object and hitting the mirror are reflected such that their angles of incidence (i) are equal to their angles of reflection (r). Rays entering the eye are therefore diverging and are seen as coming from a point behind the mirror. The ***image*** is the point from which the rays ***appear*** to have come; only two rays are shown in the diagram. There are of course many of them, all appearing to have started at the image I.

The image in a ***plane mirror***, unlike that in a pinhole camera, cannot be put on a screen, since it does not exist in space. It is a ***virtual image***. However, the image in a ***pinhole camera*** is called a ***real image***. A real image can always be formed (***focused***) on a screen.

The image in a plane mirror is also the ***right way up (erect)*** but it is ***laterally inverted (left and right are interchanged)***.

3 > REFRACTION

Light travels at a unique speed of 3×10^8 m/s in a vacuum. It travels slightly more slowly in air, and much more slowly in glass, water or other transparent materials. It is because its speed changes that it also changes direction if it enters a transparent material at an angle.

This change of direction is called ***refraction***. This is a property of waves and is also described in Section 7 of Chapter 6.

A ray of light entering a glass block at 90° to a surface passes straight through with no direction change, as in Fig. 9.11.

CHAPTER 9 OPTICS AND THE NATURE OF LIGHT

> Look back to the section on "Oscillations and waves", Chapter 6, to see how light refraction and water wave refraction are similar

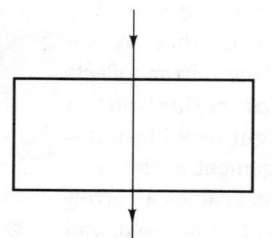

Fig. 9.11 No refraction for light normal to a surface.

But if the ray approaches at an angle to the normal, its direction changes on entering and leaving the glass block (Fig. 9.12).

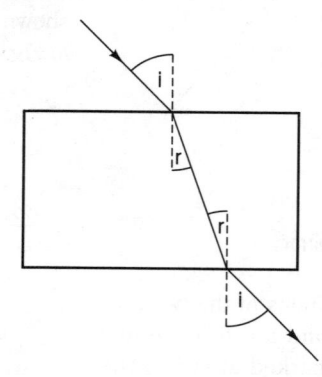

Fig. 9.12 Path of a light ray through a glass block.

On moving from air to a more dense material, the ray refracts towards the normal. It refracts away from the normal on moving from the denser material to a less dense one. Notice that for a parallel-sided block the incident and emerging rays in the air are parallel. The angles made with the normal by the ray are called the angle of incidence (*i*) and the angle of refraction (*r*). The angle of refraction in a denser material is always less than the angle of incidence in a less dense material.

The amount of angular change in direction depends on an optical property of the material called the ***refractive index***. It is a measure of how much the speed of light has changed.

$$\text{Refractive index} = \frac{\text{Speed of light in air}}{\text{Speed of light in material}}$$

Refraction can also be seen in a glass prism and follows the same rules for direction change, though the path of light looks very different (Fig. 9.13). Light refracts towards the normal on entering the prism and away from the normal on leaving the prism. (This is best shown using single-colour light, not white light, to avoid complications with spectra.) It is because of refraction that objects viewed below a glass block or under water, appear closer to the surface than they really are.

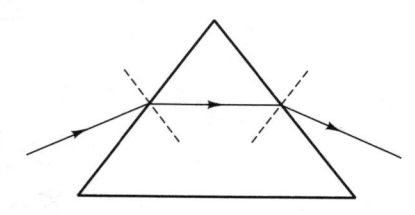

Fig. 9.13 Refraction with a prism.

Rays from an object, O, under a water surface (Fig. 9.14) are refracted away from the normal when they leave the water and enter the air. An observer sees an image, I, where the rays appear to have come from. This again is a ***virtual*** image and cannot be put on to a screen.

The distance from the surface of the water to the object is called the ***real depth*** (RD) and the distance from the surface to the image is called the ***apparent depth*** (AD).

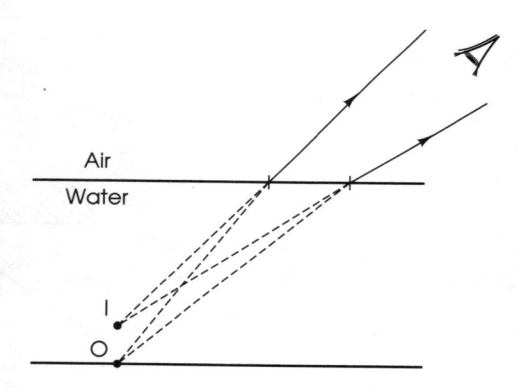

Fig. 9.14 Real and apparent depth

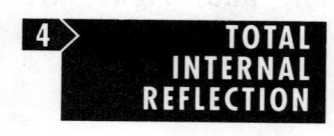

---

4 ▸ TOTAL INTERNAL REFLECTION

> Remember to send the ray along a radius to the centre of the straight side

This is an effect which can occur when light travels from a denser material to a less dense one. To illustrate it experimentally a semicircular glass block is used, because any light ray travelling along a radius of a semicircle will cross the boundary circumference at 90° and will not therefore be refracted. This enables angles such as *r* inside the block to be measured.

The block is placed on paper and its position is marked by drawing around it. The ***incident ray*** and ***refracted ray*** are also marked, so that when the apparatus is removed the drawing on the paper shows the block and the ray directions, as in Fig. 9.15. The diagram has added to it the usual arrangement of a lamp, slit and lens which give a single parallel ray of light.

If angle *r inside* the block is gradually increased, then angle *i outside* will also increase until eventually the emerging ray just grazes the edge of the block (Fig. 9.16).

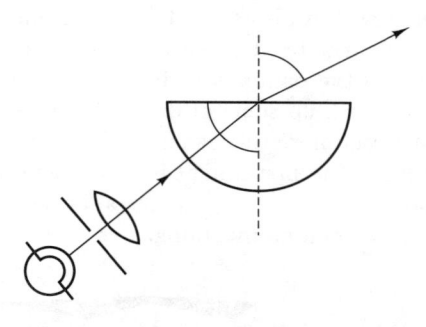

Fig. 9.15 Refraction with a semicircular block.

Eventually, if *r* is made bigger, the light can no longer escape from the far surface, but is reflected, and the usual law of reflection applies (Fig. 9.17). This is called ***total internal reflection***. The position of the ray between refraction and total internal reflection occurs at a particular angle for each material. It is called the ***critical angle*** (Fig. 9.18) and depends on the ***refractive index*** of the material. The *larger the refractive index*, the *smaller the critical angle*. For glass the critical angle is about 42° and for water it is about 48°.

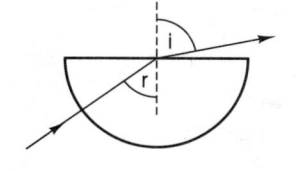

Fig. 9.16

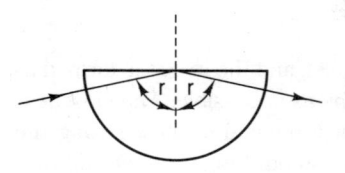

Fig. 9.17 Total internal reflection.

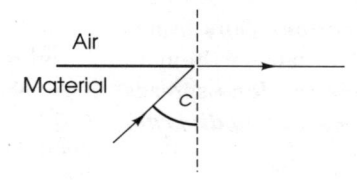

Fig. 9.18 Critical angle.

To summarise: Total internal reflection can only take place if light travels from a denser to a less dense material, and if the angle it makes with the normal inside the denser material is ***greater than*** the critical angle. With water, and a critical angle of 48°, light could only leave an underwater lamp through a narrow cone, since any light rays hitting the water surface at greater than 48° will be reflected back again (Fig. 9.19).

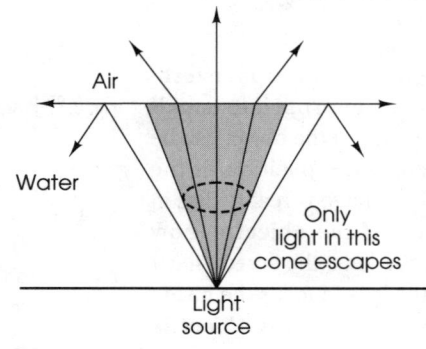

Fig. 9.19

With glass, and a critical angle of 42°, the effect can be made use of with the help of prisms. If the prism angles are 45°, 45°, 90° then, as in Fig. 9.20, light entering one face at right angles will hit the opposite face at ***more than*** 42°, and reflect internally, turning the ray through 90°.

A second prism can be used to make a ***prism periscope***. This is often used in preference to mirrors because there is no lateral inversion (left and right on the image are the same as on the object) and because there are no problems with poor silvering of glass surfaces. An internal reflection acts as a perfect reflector. Notice that the image in Fig. 9.21 is the same way up (erect) as the object.

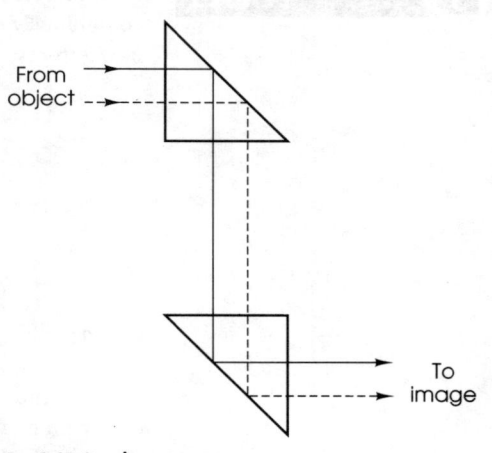

Fig. 9.21 Simple periscope.

Used in a different way, a 45° prism can be used to erect an inverted image. This is used in ***binoculars*** (Fig. 9.22).

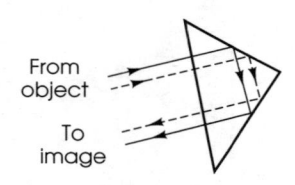

Fig. 9.22 45° prism as an inverter.

While it has been stated that light rays travel in ***straight lines***, there are certainly times when it would be useful to see around corners. This is particularly so in internal surgical operations. Optical fibres overcome this problem by using total internal reflection (Fig. 9.23).

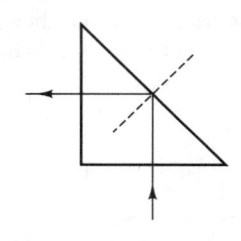

Fig. 9.20 Internal reflection with a 45° prism.

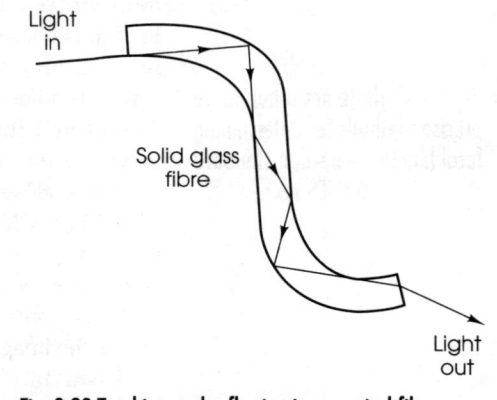

Fig. 9.23 Total internal reflection in an optical fibre.

5 ⟩ LENSES

A bundle of the very thin fibres can be used. Some of these carry light down to illuminate the inside of the patient's body whilst the others each pick up some of the reflected light so that each fibre carries one dot of the final picture. The instrument is called an **endoscope**.

Another use is in telecommunications. Telephone calls can be sent down a fibre by converting the signal into a digital signal so that it can be sent as a series of light flashes. The fibres are lighter and cheaper and less liable to corrosion than copper wires. Computer networks can also be connected in a similar way.

Lenses refract light, but because of their continuously curved surfaces they show some new effects. The most common lenses are convex and concave (Fig. 9.24). A simple experiment with a "fan" of rays shows the effect of each type. A **convex lens** brings rays of light together (causes them to **converge**) while a **concave lens** spreads them further apart (causes them to **diverge**) as in Fig. 9.25.

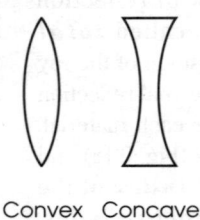

Convex   Concave

Fig. 9.24

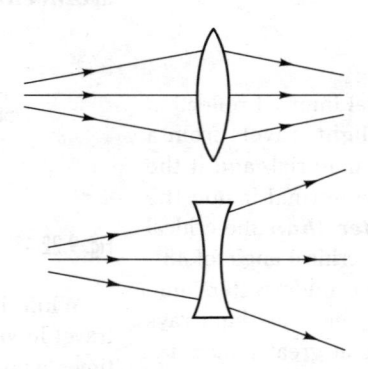

Fig. 9.25 Action of lenses on a beam of light.

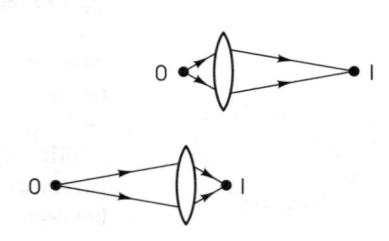

Fig. 9.26 The further the object is from the lens, the closer the image.

If a convex lens is set up several centimetres from an appropriate small luminous object, an image of the object can be focused on a screen, if the position of the screen is adjusted. The image is real (exists in space) and inverted. If the object is now moved further from the lens, the screen must be moved closer to the lens to focus the image again (Fig. 9.26), i.e. the **closer an object is to a convex lens, the further away from the lens is the image**. The further an object is from a convex lens, the closer to the lens is the image.

When an object is very far away from a lens, the rays arriving at its surface are effectively parallel, and the image is formed as close to the lens as is possible. The closeness of the image will depend on how strong the lens is (i.e. how good it is at converging rays of light).

If the "distant" rays are also parallel to the main axis of the lens (called the **principal axis**) the image will lie **on** this axis. This point is called the **principal focus** (F) of the lens. The distance from the centre of the lens to the principal focus is called the **focal length** (f) of the lens. These are marked in Fig. 9.27.

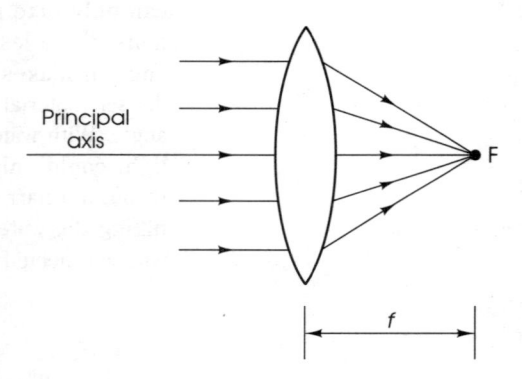

Fig. 9.27 Principal focus and focal length.

All parallel rays are focused at a distance away from the lens **equal** to the focal length (Fig. 9.28). This is so whether or not they are parallel to the lens axis, but they only focus at F if they are parallel to the axis.

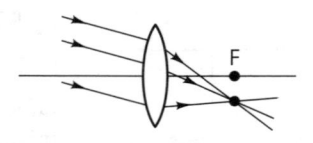

Fig. 9.28 Focusing in the focal plane.

❝ There are other, more precise methods for determining focal length. (Consult a standard OPTICS text.) ❞

The focal length of a convex lens can easily be measured using a "distant object". In a laboratory an object outside the window is far enough away for rays leaving it to be parallel at the lens surface. If the image is "caught" on a paper screen, the distance from the lens to the screen can be measured and this is the focal length (Fig. 9.29).

A powerful lens has a short focal length because it can converge rays more readily than a weaker lens.

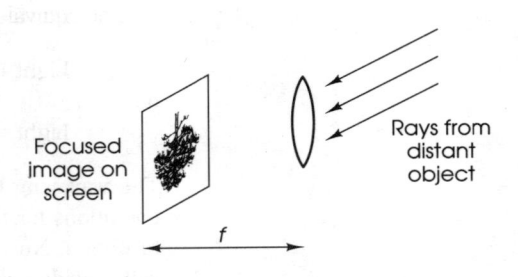

Fig. 9.29 Measurement of focal length.

6. DISPERSION

A prism has been shown to refract light of one colour (red, green or blue – Fig. 9.30). If white light is shone in a similar way on to a 60° equilateral prism, a spectrum of coloured light will be seen on a screen on the far side of the prism. Seven colours have been identified; starting at the top of the screen they are: red, orange, yellow, green, blue, indigo, violet. This effect, where white light is split into a sequence of colours, is called *dispersion*. When the colours are mixed in the right proportion and enter the eye, they give a white impression.

Each colour corresponds to a different wavelength of light – and since refraction depends on velocity changes, this suggests that each wavelength travels through the prism at a different speed – blue being slower than red since its refraction is greater.

A white light source also emits invisible waves – infra-red which is detectable because it produces heat when absorbed, and ultraviolet which causes fluorescence of certain chemicals.

A heat-sensitive detector placed at X in Fig 9.31 will show that despite visible light being present, there is a heating effect due to the infra-red waves. Fluorescent paper will fluoresce at Y through interaction with the invisible ultraviolet waves at Y.

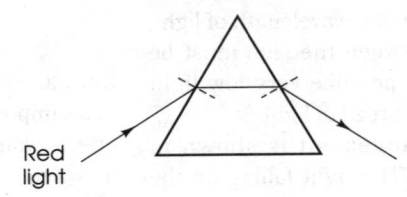

Fig. 9.30 Effect of a prism on monochromatic light.

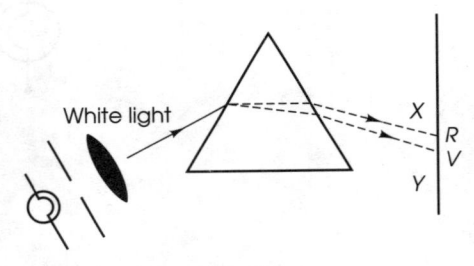

Fig. 9.31 Prism disperses white light.

7. IS LIGHT A WAVE?

Light can be reflected *and* refracted. White light can be dispersed into a *spectrum*. This is not, however, evidence that light actually *is* a wave, though in this chapter a wave picture has been used to explain these effects. The only properties which distinguish waves from particles like electrons or ions are interference and diffraction. So if light is a wave, then, like sound, it should give situations where *interference* occurs (see Ch. 6). Interference takes place when waves of equal amplitude, frequency and wavelength, and which are initially in phase, superimpose to give regions of maximum and minimum intensity. This was illustrated with water waves earlier (Fig. 9.32).

66 Such waves are described as arriving from COHERENT sources. 99

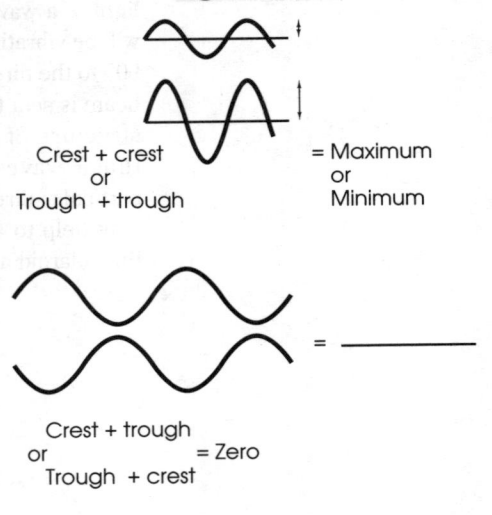

Crest + crest or Trough + trough = Maximum or Minimum

Crest + trough or Trough + crest = Zero

Fig. 9.32 Constructive and destructive interference.

The equivalent statement for light would be

Light + light = Extra intensity

or

Light + light = Darkness

The wavelength of light is very small, so the conditions for this to be observed are difficult to obtain. No two individual sources of light will provide exactly the same amplitude or be exactly in phase. To overcome this problem experimentally **one** source of light is used which is split into two sources by a finely ruled pair of slits on a blackened glass slide. A lens in front of the source provides parallel plane wavefronts, and diffraction at the slits causes a spread of light from the two sources (Fig. 9.33). The width of each slit must not be too much greater than the wavelength of light, and the distance between the slits must be small, so there is in practice very low light intensity and a small spread of light.

The optical arrangement is shown in diagram (Fig. 9.34). The light falling on the screen is viewed from behind with an eyepiece and dark and bright bands are seen spread over a few centimetres.

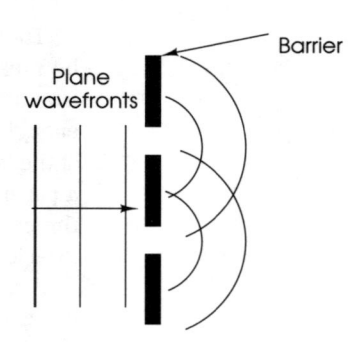

Fig. 9.33 Interference between two diffracted wavefronts.

The spreading is caused by diffraction at the slits and the dark areas are caused by destructive interference where

Light + light = Darkness

i.e. a wave crest and trough have superimposed to give zero amplitude. These effects would not be possible unless light was a wave. (For further discussion see "Extension Materials", p. 157.)

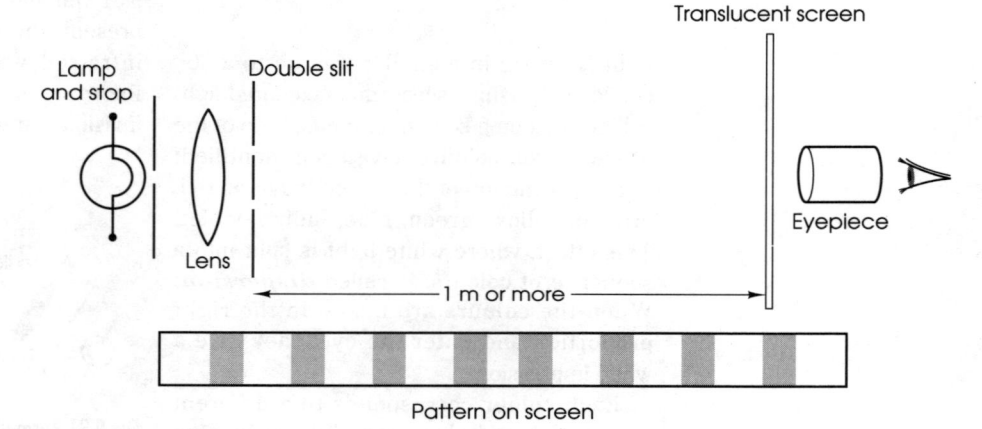

Fig. 9.34 Young's double slits.

8 > POLARISATION

This is another property which shows that light is a wave. The waves in a beam of light will be vibrating in all the directions that are at 90° to the direction of travel of the wave. If the beam is sent through a sheet of *polaroid* the structure of the solid only allows through those waves that have a vibration in a particular direction and blocks the others. (It may help to think of the crystal structure of the polaroid as being like the parallel bars of a grille. Only the waves vibrating parallel to the bars can get through the gaps between them.)

If two pieces of polaroid are used, the light can get through both if their structures are parallel. If one is then turned through 90° the waves are all blocked by one sheet or the other and no light gets through. Rotating one of the sheets takes you steadily from light to dark and back again. This effect is used in polaroid sun-glasses.

Fig. 9.35

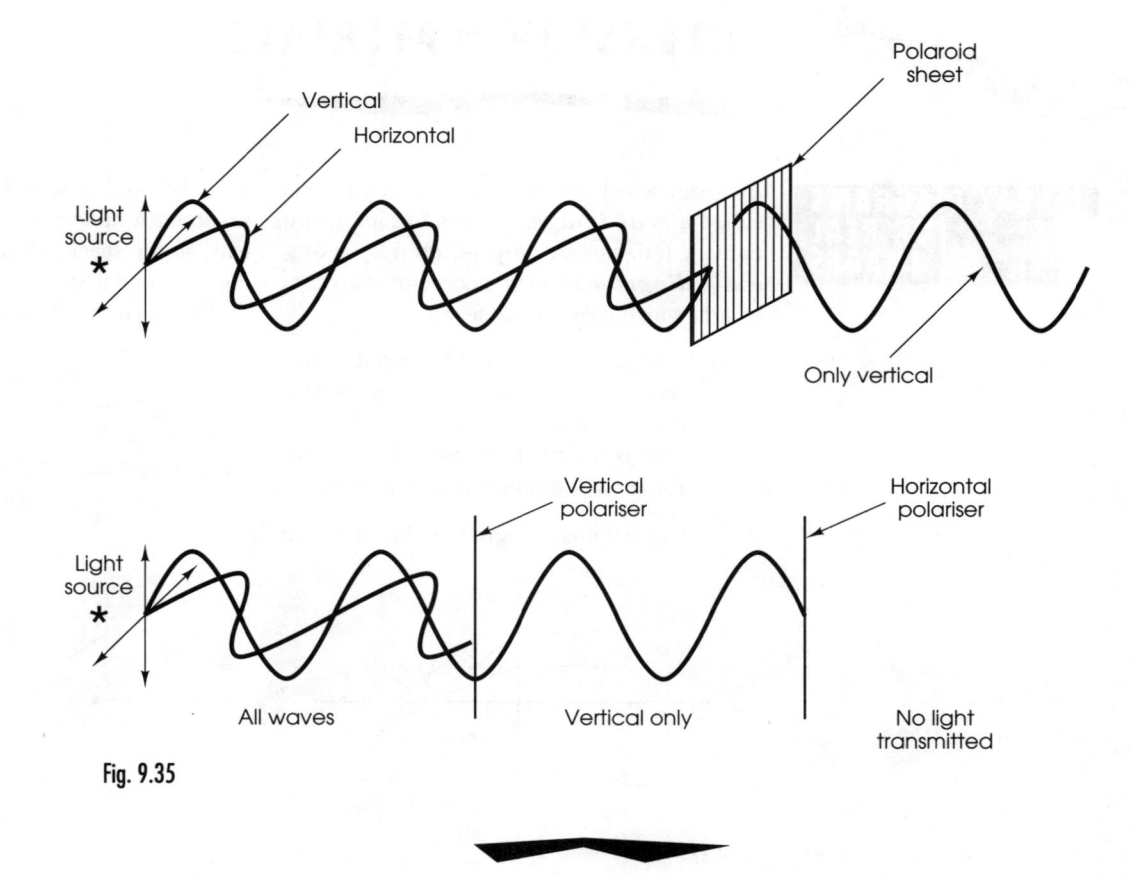

9 › THE ELECTROMAGNETIC SPECTRUM

Light is only one part of a family of waves called **electromagnetic waves**. They are similar in that they all travel at the same speed in a vacuum, and all are transverse. The only difference is in the wavelength. Their characteristics are outlined in Fig. 9.36.

Name	λ (m)	Effect
Radio	0.01–3 000	Cause electrical oscillation in circuits
Infra-red	7×10^{-6}	Cause heating on absorption
Visible	5×10^{-7}	Response of human eye
Ultraviolet	$<3 \times 10^{-7}$	Fluorescence
X-rays	10^{-10}	Affect photographic plates. Penetrate some materials
γ-waves	10^{-14}	Cause ionisation

Fig. 9.36

EXTENSION MATERIALS

1. RAY DIAGRAMS FOR REAL IMAGES

An image which can be focused on a screen is called a **real image**. Images formed using convex lenses can be predicted by using **scale diagrams** which incorporate two rays of light which have special features:

1. A ray **parallel to the principal axis** always passes through the principal focus, F.
2. A ray **passing through the centre of a lens** does not change direction.

In drawing ray diagrams the thickness of the lens is not included. The changes are assumed to take place at the **centre** of the lens, so the special rays would be drawn as in Figs 9.37 and 9.38.

The **principal focus** is marked on both sides of the lens. Since the lens is symmetrical, it does not matter if the light is travelling from right to left or left to right. So by knowing the focal length of the lens, the position and size of the image can be found from a suitable scale diagram.

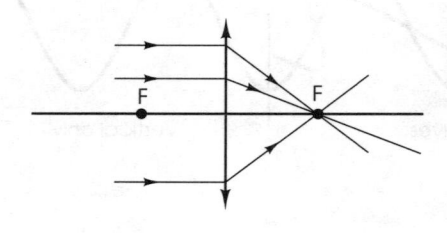

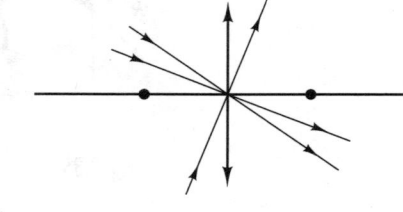

Fig. 9.37

Fig. 9.38

The following diagrams (Figs 9.39, 9.40, 9.41(a)) are drawn to scale. The lens has a focal length of 10 cm.

> Lenses must be thin. They can be shown as a line. The "arrow heads" show convex or concave lenses

Object at 15 cm (between F and 2 F)

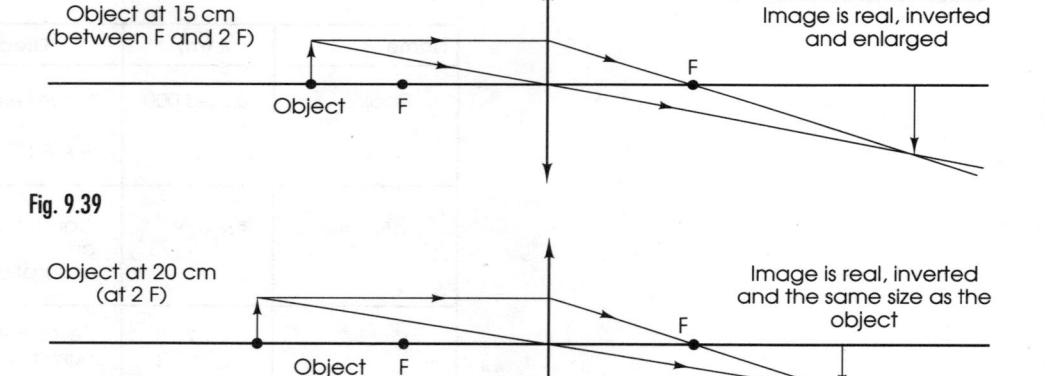

Image is real, inverted and enlarged

Fig. 9.39

Object at 20 cm (at 2 F)

Image is real, inverted and the same size as the object

Fig. 9.40

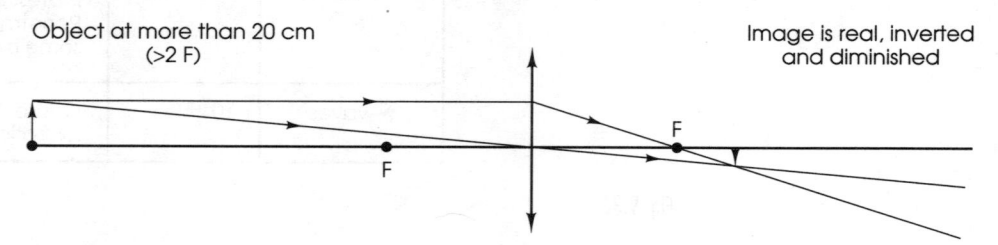

Object at more than 20 cm (>2 F)

Image is real, inverted and diminished

Fig. 9.41(a)

For an object placed at F no image is formed (Fig. 9.41(b)). Light rays become parallel and do not converge to form an image.

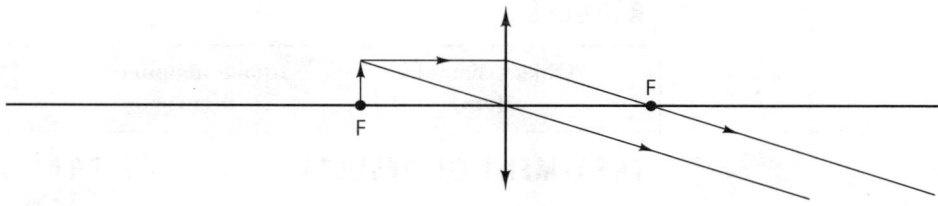

Fig. 9.41(b)

The **magnification** of the image can also be found if the diagrams are drawn to scale.

$$\text{Magnification} = \frac{\text{Height of image}}{\text{Height of object}}$$

Notice also in the previous group of diagrams that as the **object distance decreases** the **image distance increases**, and **so does the magnification**.

In a camera, the image is often a **diminished one** (magnification less than × 1). This happens if the object is further away from the lens than twice the focal length. A projector, on the other hand, is designed to give an enlarged image so the object film or slide must be as close as possible to the lens but not closer than the focal length or no real image will be formed.

2 > VIRTUAL IMAGES WITH CONVEX LENSES

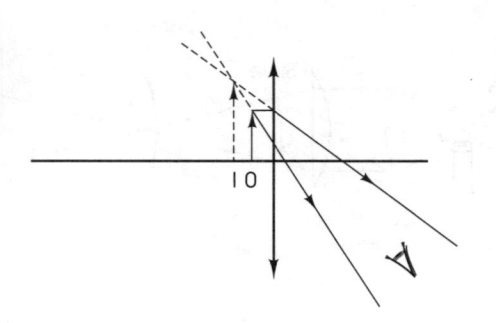

Fig. 9.42 Convex lens as a magnifying glass.

A convex lens will always give a real image when the object is **further** from the lens than its focal length. The same lens can be used as a magnifying glass if the object is closer to the lens than the focal length (Fig. 9.42). Rays entering the eye are now diverging rather than converging and the image is seen as the point where the rays appear to come from.

The image in this case is **virtual, erect** and **enlarged**. Notice that in this diagram, the same two rays have been used; the "parallel" one which passes through F and the one passing through the centre which is not deviated. Once these two are established and the image is located any other rays can be drawn since any ray from any point on the object has to arrive at the point on the image as in Fig. 9.43.

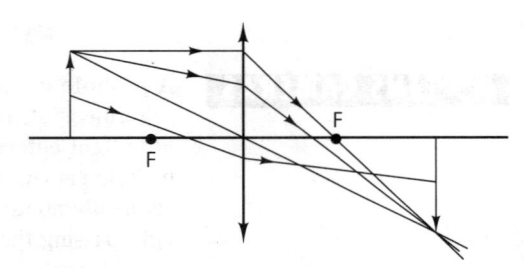

Fig. 9.43

3 > EXPERIMENTING WITH A SIMPLE PROJECTOR SYSTEM – MAGNIFICATION

METHOD

The apparatus is set up as shown in Fig. 9.44, carefully lined up using a metre rule, and with each component in a suitable holder to give vertical alignment. The lens position is initially adjusted to give a sharp image of the slide on the screen. The distance from the object to the lens (object distance, u centimetres) is measured, as is the image distance (v centimetres). The original height of the slide is measured with a millimetre scale and the corresponding height of the image recorded. This is repeated for a number of object distances, the screen being moved each time till a focused image is obtained.

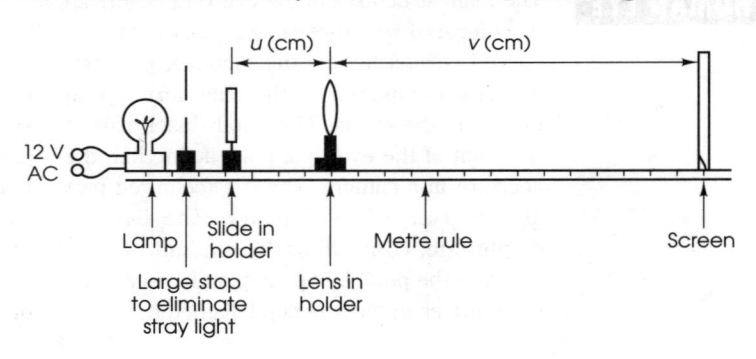

Fig. 9.44

RESULTS

Object distance u(cm)	Image distance v(cm)	Height of object	Height of image

TREATMENT OF RESULTS

Magnification is calculated in each case as

$$\frac{\text{Image height}}{\text{Object height}}$$

It is also found that magnification is

$$\frac{\text{Image distance}}{\text{Object distance}}$$

So in practical projector, image distances are large and the distance of the object from the lens must be small (but not smaller than the focal length of the lens).

A PRACTICAL PROJECTION SYSTEM

The slide or film is placed upside down so that the final image is erect (Fig. 9.45). The projection lens and slide are slightly further apart than the focal length of the lens, fine focusing is obtained by screwing the projection lens in and out of the projector casing. The condenser lens converges light evenly over the whole of the slide. The mirror reflects all light leaving the lamp towards the condenser lens.

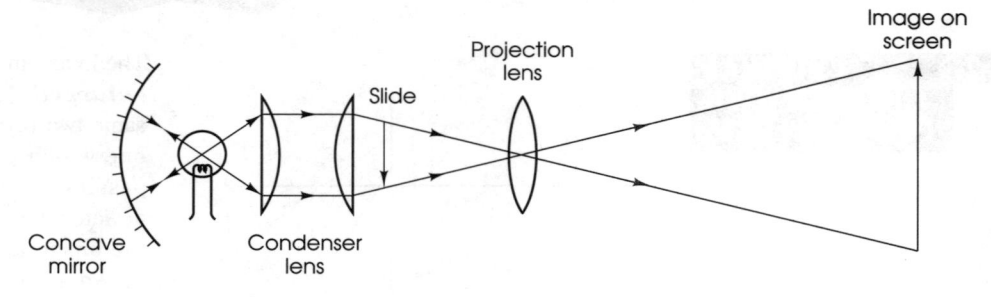

Fig. 9.45

4. LENS CAMERAS

A pinhole camera gives a focused image regardless of the object distance, but since little light enters, the exposure time using a pinhole camera with film in it would be long (typically about 15 min). A lens focuses all light passing through it, but it will only focus on a fixed screen for one particular object distance. A lens camera needs to give a lot of light intensity on a screen and to focus at many distances.

The following are some features of a **lens camera**:

1. The shutter is a spring-loaded blind covering the film, except when a photograph is taken. The shutter speed can change the exposure time and affect how much light reaches the film.
2. The diaphragm adjusts the size of the aperture, which also affects the light reaching the film. Since small apertures (as in pinhole cameras) give sharp focusing for all distances, the aperture also has an effect on focus.
3. The lens converges light to the film forming an image. The lens position relative to the film can be changed with the focusing ring, moving the lens further from the film for a close-up object and towards the film for a distant object.

5. THE HUMAN EYE

The main structures of the eye (Fig. 9.46) can be compared with those in a lens camera. The curved cornea begins the focusing process, which is completed by the lens, forming an image on the retina. The pupil (black part at the front of the eye) is a hole, acting like the aperture in a camera. The iris (coloured part at the front of eye) is like the camera diaphragm, controlling the amount of light entering the pupil by opening and closing and therefore changing the pupil diameter.

When light falls on the retina, nerve endings are stimulated and a "message" is sent along the optic nerve to the brain which interprets the message into a sensation of seeing. The lens cannot move in and out to give fine focusing as in a camera. Instead it is made of a flexible material, and muscles surrounding it change its shape, making it more powerful to focus on near objects and less powerful for distant objects. This change of lens power is called **accommodation**.

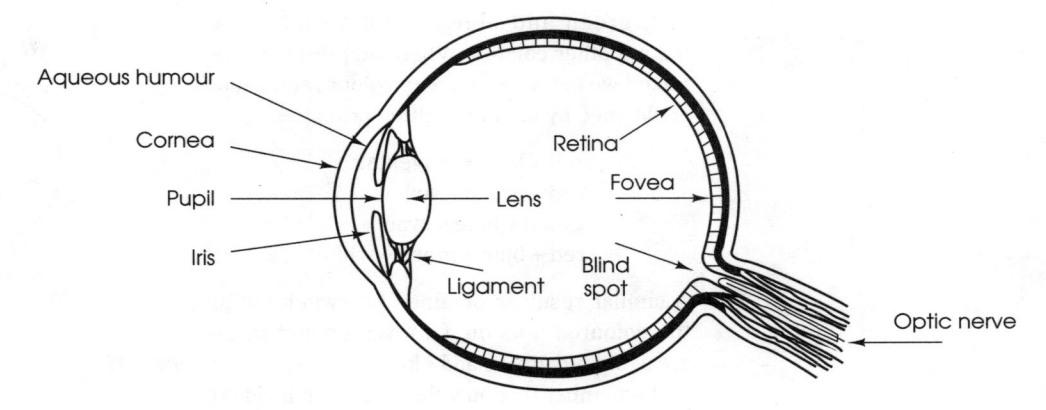

Fig. 9.46

6) YOUNG'S DOUBLE SLIT EXPERIMENT – SOME THEORY

The experiment and result were discussed under "Essential Principles", p. 152. Light emerges from the double slit and a pattern of light and dark "fringes" is seen on a screen. The fringes are evenly spaced (Fig. 9.47). The two slits are arranged to give coherent light, same phase, wavelength, amplitude and frequency.

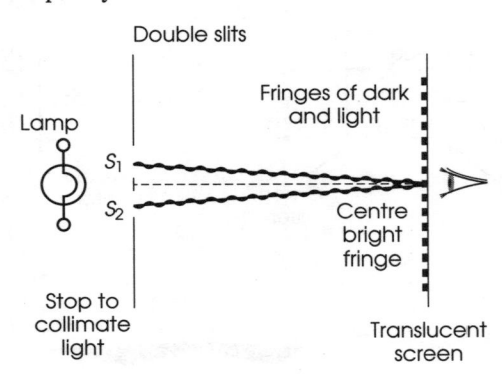

Fig. 9.47

At the centre bright fringe: waves from S_1 and S_2 have travelled the same distance. If they leave in phase they will arrive in phase, giving a maximum response. There is no path difference between them (Fig. 9.48).

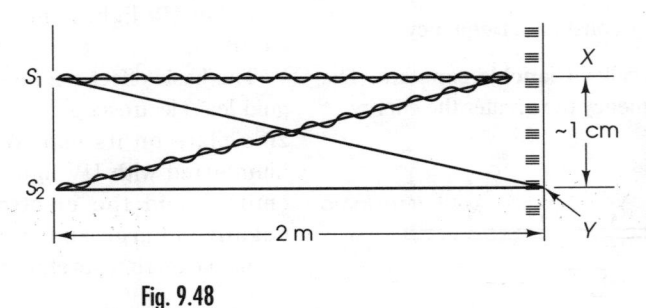

At some other maximum position the wave from S_2 has travelled further to point X than the wave from S_1. There is a path difference of $S_2X - S_1X$. If the point X is a maximum the waves must be in phase at X. This can only occur if the path difference is a whole number of wavelengths:

$$S_2X - S_1X = (\text{whole number} \times \lambda)$$
$$= n\lambda$$
(n = any whole number)

For a point Y which is a minimum, the path difference must have an odd half-wavelength in it, so that the waves arrive exactly out of phase:

$$S_1Y - S_2Y = (n + {}^1/_2)\lambda$$

The geometry of the situation gives the following equation which can be used to obtain the value of the wavelength of light:

$$\frac{\text{Separation of fringes}}{\text{Wavelength}} = \frac{\text{Distance from slits to screen}}{\text{Distance between slits}}$$

The fringes separation is therefore wavelength dependent (smallest for blue and greatest for red), so the experiment is best done with single-colour light. The greater the distance from slits to screen, and the smaller the distance between slits, the bigger the fringe separation.

Fig. 9.48

7) COLOUR

We have already found that light of a different wavelength is seen as a different colour. Surfaces look coloured because they reflect those colours and absorb the others. A red rose reflects red light but absorbs the other colours of the spectrum. A white surface will reflect all the colours of the spectrum and a black surface will absorb them all and reflect none.

When different colours of light are shone onto a white screen we see their addition as they are all reflected. The ***primary colours*** red, green and blue cannot be made by mixing other colours. When the primaries are mixed we get the secondary colours and white is obtained by mixing all three primaries.

red + blue = magenta
red + green = yellow
green + blue = cyan
red + blue + green = white

A similar result is obtained by switching on the coloured dots on a TV screen and these are again red, green and blue.

Remember that only the colours in incident light can be reflected. Reflecting surfaces don't produce their own light. A red rose in white light or in red light will appear red. In blue light it will appear black because it absorbs the blue and there is no red light to reflect.

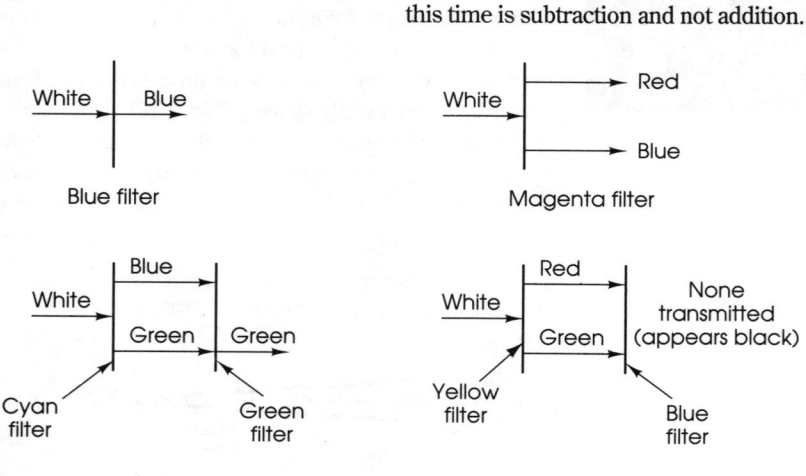

Fig. 9.49

Colour filters also work by absorbing some colours and transmitting the ones that we can see. A blue filter transmits blue light but absorbs all the other colours. If filters follow one another you should remember that the process this time is subtraction and not addition.

Fig. 9.50

8 THE PHOTOELECTRIC EFFECT

Light is emitted from atoms in short bursts of waves called *photons*. Each photon carries an exact amount of energy that depends on the frequency of the light.

Energy = constant × frequency.

The constant is called **Planck's constant.** The greater the frequency the greater the energy.

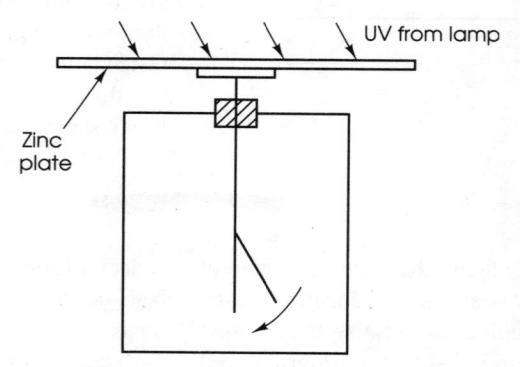

Fig. 9.51

Some of the evidence for this comes from the *photoelectric effect*. When you shine light on the surface of some metals electrons are released. This can be done with a zinc plate but UV light is needed to release the electrons.

The basic effect can be seen by charging a gold leaf electroscope negatively with a clean zinc plate on its cap. When the plate is illuminated with UV light the electrons are emitted and the electroscope loses its negative charge and the leaf falls. More detailed experiments show that:

- A *brighter* light does NOT give more energy to the electrons.
- A brighter lamp does release *more* electrons with the *same energy*.
- Light with a *greater frequency* gives *more energy* to the electrons.
- There is a **threshold frequency** f_0. Light below this frequency cannot release electrons from the metal, no matter how bright the light source.

EXPLANATION

The light arrives in photons. *All* the energy from *one* photon is absorbed by an electron when it is emitted. For the electron to leave the metal a certain amount of energy called the **work function** is needed. If the photon energy is less than the work function the electron is not emitted. If the photon energy equals the work function then its frequency is the threshold frequency f_o and the electron is just able to leave the surface. If the photon energy is greater than the work function the electron emitted has the "extra" energy as its kinetic energy. Making the light brighter doesn't change the energy of the individual photons; there are more of them but their energies can't be added to reach the threshold energy as they all behave individually.

For most materials visible light does not have sufficient energy to cause ionisation in this way. X-rays do have the energy needed and are usually absorbed when a photon causes ionisation of an atom of the absorber. In cell tissue the ejected electron might have sufficient energy to cause further damage. Remember that the photons are either absorbed or pass through unchanged. The energy of the individual photons is fixed and cannot be partly reduced.

9 > THE LENS FORMULA

To find the position of an image more accurately than by using scale drawing you can use the lens formula.

$$\frac{1}{f} = \frac{1}{v} + \frac{1}{u}$$

f = focal length, v = distance of image from lens. u = distance of object from lens. This equation uses the "***real is positive***" sign convention:

- All distances to real objects, images and focuses are positive.
- All distances to virtual objects, images and focuses are negative. The focal length of a convex lens will be + and the focal length of a concave lens will be –.

You can also find **linear magnification**.

$$\text{Magnification} = m = \frac{\text{object size}}{\text{image size}} = \frac{v}{u}$$

EXAMPLES

1. Find the position, size and nature of the image produced by an object 5 mm high placed 200 mm in front of a convex lens of focal length 150 mm.

From the question, f = +150 mm
u = +200 mm

$$\frac{1}{f} = \frac{1}{v} + \frac{1}{u}$$

$$\frac{1}{150} = \frac{1}{v} + \frac{1}{200}$$

$$\frac{1}{v} = \frac{1}{150} - \frac{1}{200}$$

$$= \frac{4-3}{600} = \frac{1}{600}$$

$$v = 600 \text{ mm}$$

$$\text{magnification} = \frac{v}{u} = \frac{600}{200} = 3$$

size of image = size of object × magnification
= 5 × 3 = 15 mm

Looking at the signs of the answers you should be able to see that the image is real, inverted, 600 mm from the lens on the opposite side to the object and 15 mm high. You will always find it helpful to draw a sketch diagram to ensure that you have got the correct answer and not made an arithmetic mistake.

2. An object is placed 40 cm from a diverging lens of focal length 10 cm. Find the position, nature and magnification of its image.

From the question, f = –10 cm
u = +40 cm

$$\frac{1}{f} = \frac{1}{v} + \frac{1}{u}$$

$$\frac{-1}{10} = \frac{1}{v} + \frac{1}{40}$$

$$\frac{1}{v} = \frac{-1}{40} - \frac{1}{10}$$

$$= \frac{-1-4}{40} = \frac{-5}{40}$$

$$\underline{v = 8 \text{ cm.}}$$

$$\text{magnification} = \frac{v}{u} = \frac{8}{20} = \underline{0.4}$$

The image is 8 cm from the lens on the same side as the object, virtual, and erect. Compare this with the expected answer from a sketch diagram.

10 DEFECTS OF VISION

A normal eye can focus objects from infinity (its **far point**) down to about 25 cm (its **near point**) without being strained. The distance from the eye to its near point is also called the **least distance of distinct vision**. As we grow older the ciliary muscle becomes less able to change the shape of the lens and many older people are unable to focus on objects that are either very far away or very close. Bifocal lenses in spectacles correct this, the lower part of the lens for the near objects and the rest, with a different lens shape, for those farther away.

■ SHORT SIGHT (MYOPIA)

In this case the eyeball is too long or the lens is too powerful and the image is focused in front of the retina so that it is not clear – Fig. 9.52(a). The far point of this eye is not at infinity but is closer to the lens.

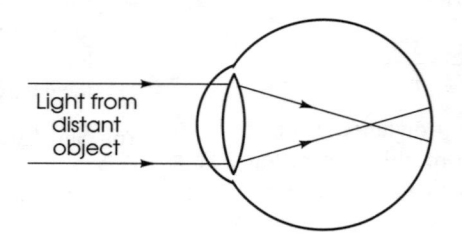

Fig. 9.52(a)

The light from an object close to the eye can be focused. The correction is therefore to wear a diverging lens so that the light from the distant object appears to come from the far point of the eye – Fig. 9.52(b) – and can be focused.

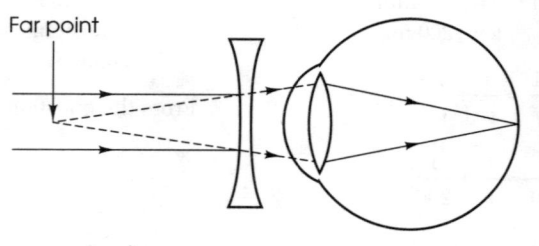

Fig. 9.52(b)

■ LONG SIGHT (HYPERMETROPIA)

In this case the eyeball is too short or the lens is not powerful enough and the image is focused behind the retina – Fig. 9.53(a). The near point of this eye is farther away than is normal. Light from a more distant object can be focused.

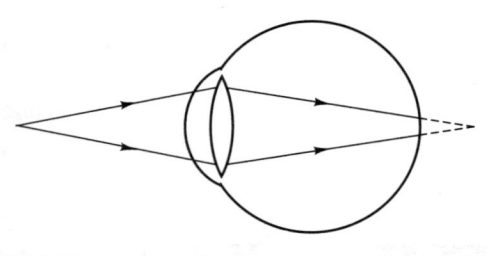

Fig. 9.53(a)

The correction is to wear a converging lens to help the eye lens focus the light. The lens makes the light seem to come from the near point of the eye so that it can be focused – Fig. 9.53(b).

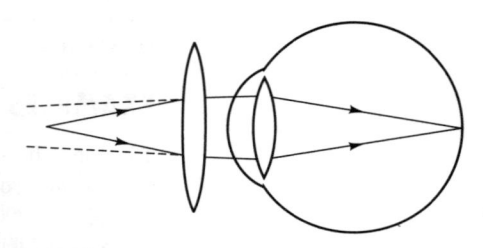

Fig. 9.53(b)

■ ASTIGMATISM

In this case the eye lens is slightly cylindrical instead of being spherical. This makes one plane of vision less clear. The correction is a cylindrical lens to help the eye lens in its "weak" plane. It is not possible to use contact lenses to correct for this as they rotate on the eye when in use.

EXAMINATION QUESTIONS

MULTIPLE CHOICE QUESTIONS

QUESTION 1

A ray of light is incident on a plane mirror. The mirror is then turned through an angle of 30°. The reflected ray will be turned through

A 15° C 60° E 90°
B 30° D 75°   (ULEAC)

QUESTION 2

A clear erect image can be obtained from a prism periscope only if the prisms are correctly positioned. Figure 9.54 shows five possible arrangements of two prisms, with rays of light drawn. Which is the correct arrangement for prisms and light? (ULEAC)

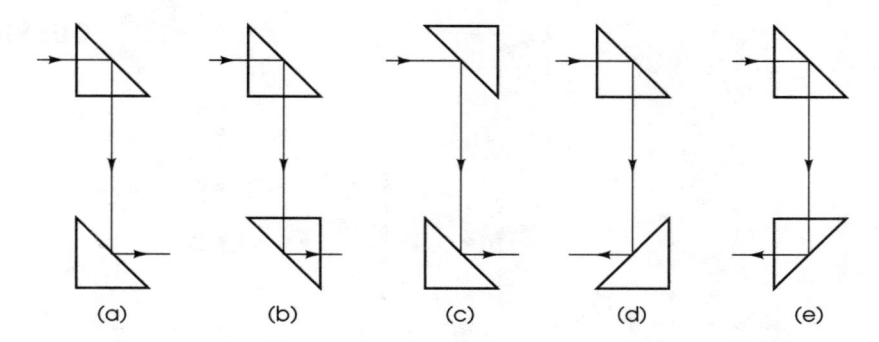

Fig. 9.54

QUESTION 3

A magnified and inverted image is obtained by placing an object in front of a converging lens. The distance of the object from the lens must be

A Less than one focal length
B Equal to one focal length
C Between one and two focal lengths
D Equal to two focal lengths
E Greater than two focal lengths

QUESTION 4

Which one of the diagrams in Fig. 9.55 correctly shows the path of a ray of light through a glass block? (ULEAC)

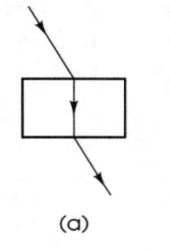

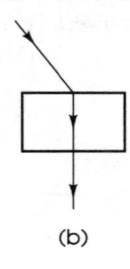

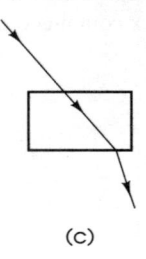

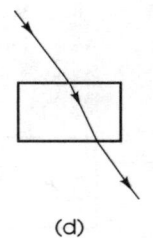

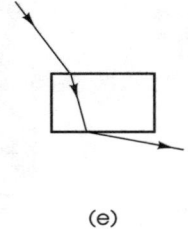

Fig. 9.55

QUESTIONS 5 AND 6

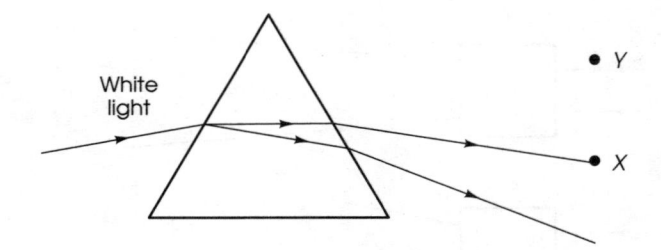

Fig. 9.56

Figure 9.56 represents a narrow beam of white light passing through a glass prism and forming a spectrum on the screen. The points X and Y are on the screen and the rays drawn show the limits of the visible spectrum.

5. The colour of light appearing at X will be

    A Red
    B White
    C Violet
    D Blue
    E Green
    (ULEAC)

6. A thermometer placed at Y records a rise in temperature from the radiation produced. The correct name for this radiation is

    A Ultraviolet
    B X-rays
    C Gamma rays
    D Alpha particles
    E Infra-red
    (ULEAC)

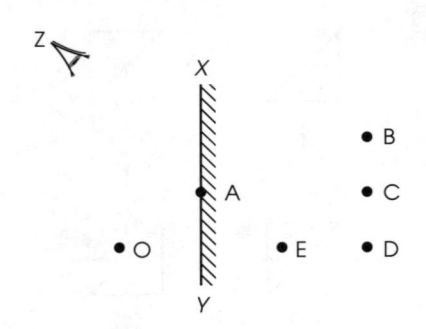

Fig. 9.57

QUESTION 7

An object O is placed in front of a plane mirror XY (see Fig. 9.57). At which of points A–E will an observer at Z see an image of the object?
(ULEAC)

QUESTION 8

In each of the diagrams in Fig. 9.58, two parallel rays of light enter the left-hand side of a box and leave the right-hand side as shown. Which box contains the most powerful convex lens? (MEG)

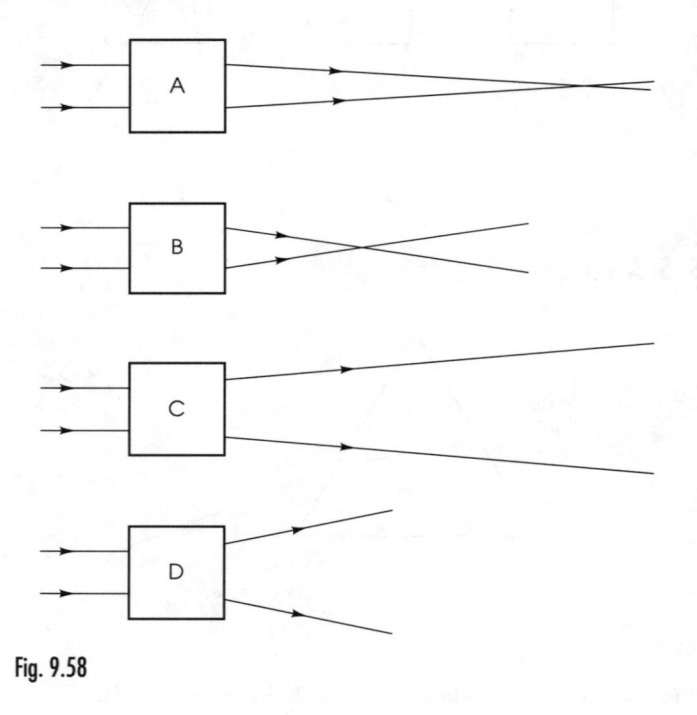

Fig. 9.58

QUESTION 9

A ray of light is incident on a thin convex lens as shown in Fig. 9.59. In which of the directions A–E will the ray emerge? (ULEAC)

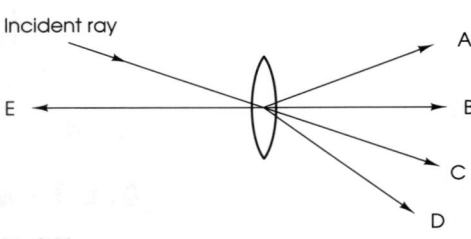

Fig. 9.59

QUESTION 10

A lamp 6 cm high is placed 24 cm in front of a small hole in a pinhole camera. The distance from the hole to the screen is 8 cm (Fig. 9.60). What is the size of the image on the screen?

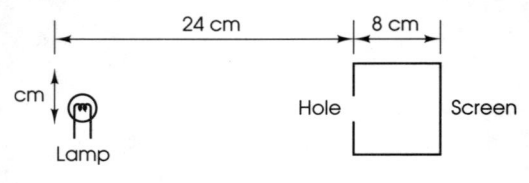

A 24 cm
B 8 cm
C 3 cm
D 2 cm
E 1 cm

Fig. 9.60

STRUCTURED QUESTIONS

QUESTION 11

(a) The diagrams in Fig. 9.61 show four lenses made from glass. Complete the ray paths through the lenses.
(b) In this part of the question you are going to compare a pinhole camera and a lens camera. Each is to be used to photograph a tree.
  (i) Complete the paths of any rays which go through the pinhole in Fig. 9.62(a). Mark on the film the "image" produced by the pinhole camera.

(ii) Name the type of lens used in the lens camera.
(iii) Complete the paths of any rays hitting the lens in Fig. 9.62(b). Mark on the film the image produced by the lens camera.
(iv) State two ways in which the images produced on the film in these cameras are different from the tree itself. (2 lines) (ULEAC)

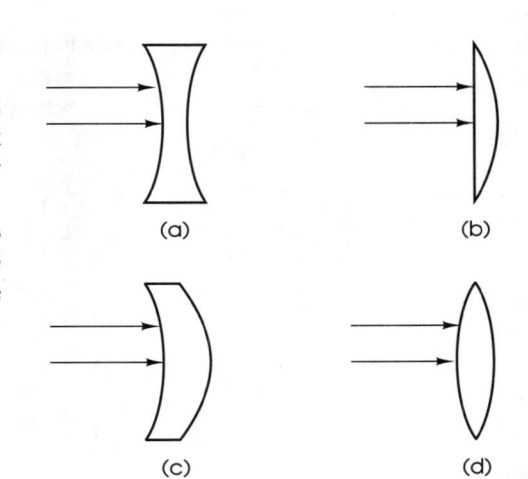

(a) (b)
(c) (d)

Fig. 9.61

(a)

(b)

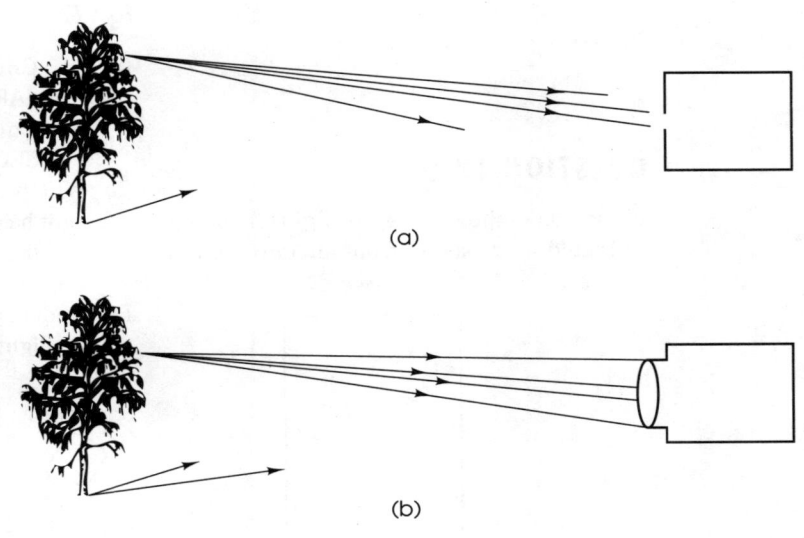

Fig. 9.62

QUESTION 12

(a) Figure 9.63 shows a narrow beam of light, incident on a 90°– 45° glass prism. Complete the diagram showing the path of the ray in and out of the prism.

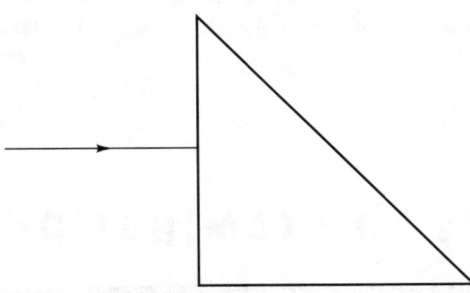

Fig. 9.63

(b) Figure 9.64 shows plane waves of light incident on the same prism. (Let 2.0 cm represent the wavelength of light.)
(i) Make an exact copy of the diagram, and complete it to show the path of the waves into, and out of, the prism.

(ii) What, if anything, happened to the wavelength and frequency of the light waves as they enter the prism?

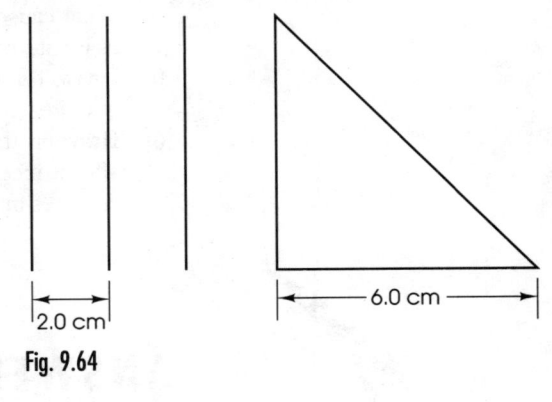

2.0 cm   6.0 cm

Fig. 9.64

(c) Figure 9.65 refers to an optical dipstick which causes an alarm to operate when the level of liquid in a tank is below F.
(i) By referring to the diagram describe in words how the light reaches the photocell when the liquid level is below F.
(ii) Explain, with the aid of the diagram, why the photocell will not operate when the liquid level is above GE.

(iii) Explain whether or not the detector will work when the liquid level is between GE and F. (ULEAC)

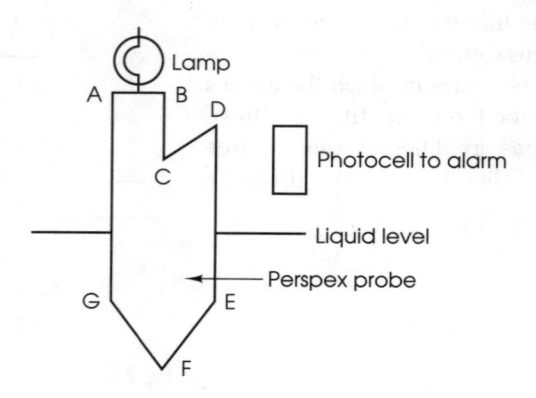

Fig. 9.65

QUESTION 13

Figure 9.66 shows a ray of light, A, being refracted as it passes from air into a glass block.

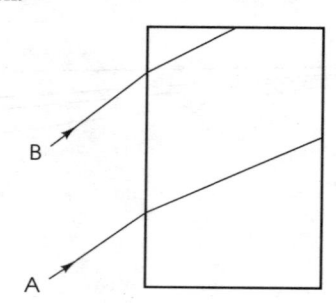

Fig. 9.66

(i) What causes the ray to change direction as it enters the glass?
(ii) Draw on the diagram the ray as it emerges from the glass.
(iii) Draw on the diagram the path of ray B, after it meets the top of the block until it emerges into the air.

QUESTION 14

Some students are preparing spotlights for the school play. Fig. 9.67 shows the spotlight arranged in two groups: PRIMARY colours and SECONDARY colours.

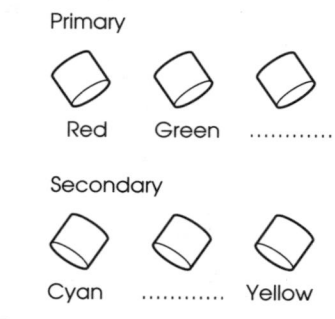

Fig. 9.67

(a) (i) Complete the labelling of the PRIMARY colour spotlights.
   (ii) Complete the labelling of the SECONDARY colour spotlights.
(b) Which of the three primary colours of light has
   (i) the shortest wavelength.
   (ii) the longest wavelength.

The students set up the three primary colour spotlights as shown in Fig. 9.68.

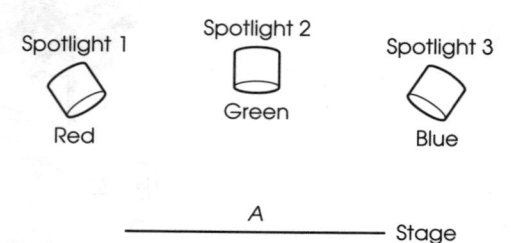

Fig. 9.68

(c) What colour of light is seen on the stage at A when
   (i) spotlights 1 and 2 are switched on.
   (ii) spotlights 2 and 3 are switched on.
   (iii) all three spotlights are switched on.
(d) What is
   (i) a primary colour?
   (ii) a secondary colour?

ANSWERS TO EXAMINATION QUESTIONS

MULTIPLE CHOICE QUESTIONS

Question	1	2	3	4	5	6	7	8	9	10
Answer	C	B	C	D	A	E	E	B	C	D

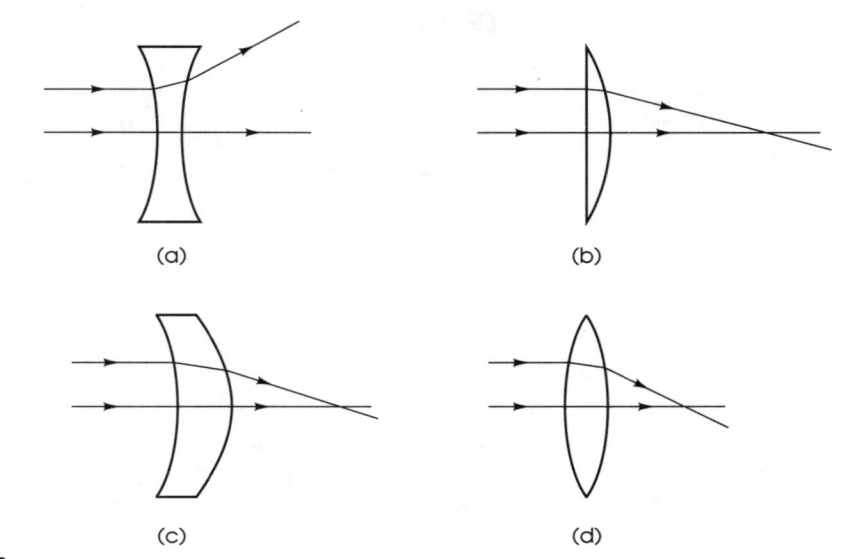

STRUCTURED QUESTIONS

Fig. 9.69 (a) (b) (c) (d)

ANSWER 11

(a) See Fig. 9.69. Explanation: The lower ray in each case hits the lenses at 90°, so there is no change of path. (A is a diverging lens; B has less curvature than D so it is weaker, less converging; C is a concave lens at one surface and convex at the other.)

(b) All rays from a point on an object which pass through the lens contribute to the same point on the image. Rays 1 and 2 pass through the centre of the lens, placing the positions of the top and bottom of the image.

(i) See Fig. 9.70.
(ii) The lens is a convex (converging lens).
(iii) See Fig. 9.71. Pinhole cameras require a long exposure time since they allow only a little light to enter. Pinhole cameras cannot take good photographs of anything likely to move a little – it would result in several blurred images. A lens camera has a short exposure time so this is possible.
(iv) Image is diminished and inverted.

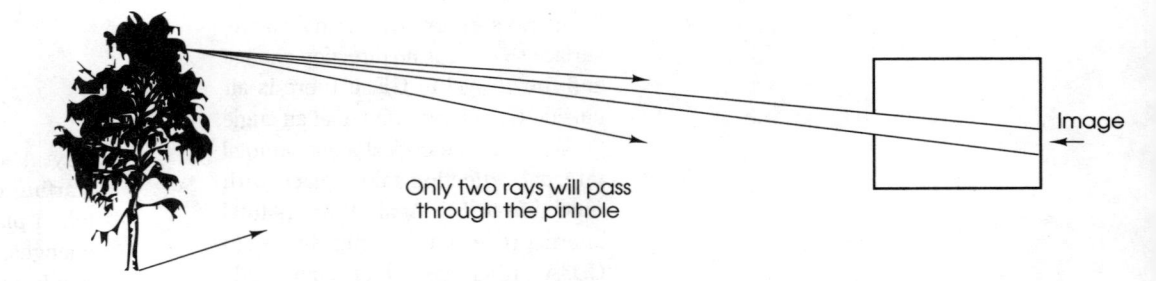

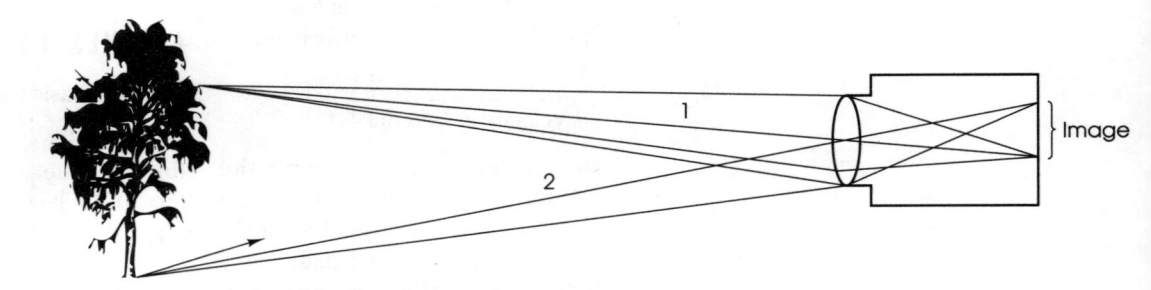

Fig. 9.70 — Only two rays will pass through the pinhole

Fig. 9.71

ANSWER 12

(a) See Fig. 9.72.

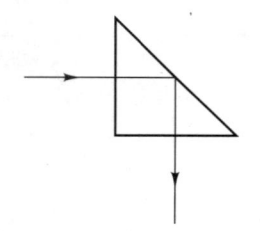

Fig. 9.72

(b) (i) See Fig. 9.73. Explanation: "Rays" in Fig. 9.72 are the line at 90° to the wavefronts.

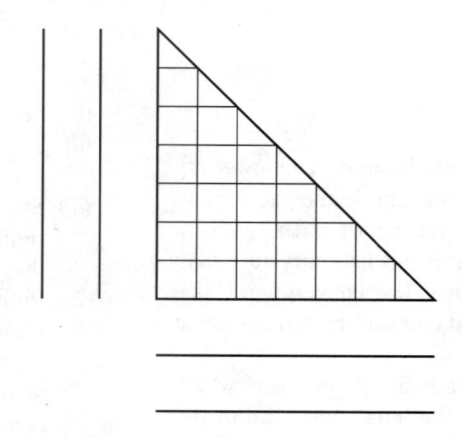

Fig. 9.73

    (ii) As shown in Fig. 9.73, wavelength is reduced in the prism and frequency remains the same.

(c) (i) Light rays enter AB normal to the surface so there is no direction change and they travel to GF. If there is air outside GF the rays hit GF at an angle greater than the critical angle so total internal reflection takes place with reflection to FE. Again there is total internal reflection sending the ray to CD. A further internal reflection sends light out normally to the photocell.

    (ii) With liquid outside GF the refraction relationship is changed, and so is the critical angle. The refractive index is.

$$\frac{\text{Velocity in material 1}}{\text{Velocity in material 2}}$$

so with liquid in place of air the refractive index is less, the critical angle is greater and light hitting GF is refracted out into the liquid.

    (iii) If the liquid level is very close to F, internal reflection will take place; if very close to G it will not. So a small, and gradually increasing amount of light will reach the cell as the level falls from G to F.

ANSWER 13

(i) Light changes direction because it enters the block at an angle, and it then changes speed. The wavefront as a whole changes direction because of this.

(ii) and (iii) See Fig. 9.74, and 9.75.

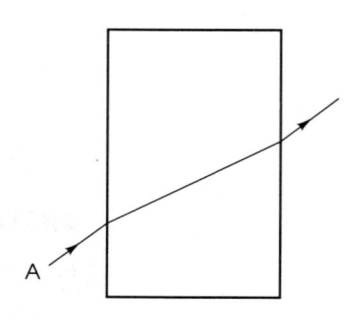

Fig. 9.74

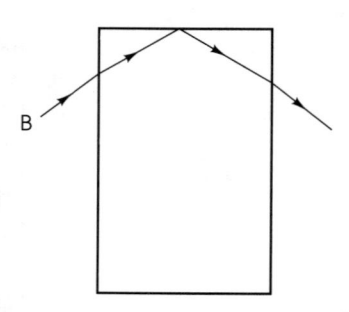

Fig. 9.75

Ray A emerges parallel to the starting direction, refraction having taken place each time the medium changes.

Ray B hits the top surface at an angle greater than the critical angle, so total internal reflection occurs.

ANSWER 14

(This is a basic level question)

(a) (i) Blue   (ii) Magenta
(b) (i) Blue   (ii) Red
(c) (i) Yellow (ii) Cyan   (iii) White
(d) (i) one that cannot be made by mixing other colours
    (ii) one that is made by mixing two primary colours

TUTOR'S QUESTION AND ANSWER

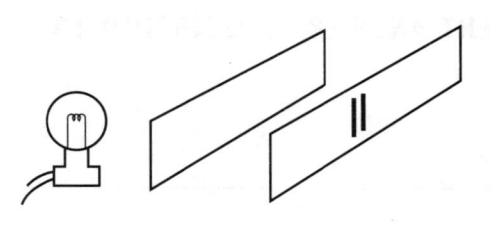

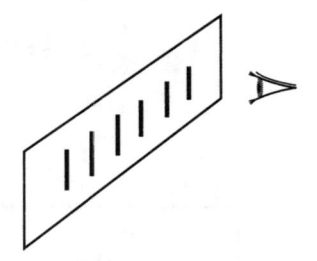

Fig. 9.76

QUESTION

To observe Young's fringes, a blackened microscope slide with two slits ruled close together is placed between a lamp and a screen in a dark-room (Fig. 9.76). Bright and dark bands (fringes) are seen on the screen.

(a) What property of waves does this experiment demonstrate?
(b) Explain, with aid of diagrams, what causes the bright bands on the screen.
(c) Why are there several bright bands?
(d) Explain the cause of the dark bands.
(e) Describe what measurements you would make to find the wavelength of light.
(f) Blue light has a shorter wavelength than red light. What would happen to the fringe separation if a blue filter were used instead of red? Explain your answer.
(g) What would happen to the fringe width if the slits were replaced by two slits closer together? (ULEAC)

ANSWER

(a) Interference.
(b) Waves spread out at the slits (Fig. 9.77). When they reach the screen there are regions of overlap. If waves meet in phase a bright patch is produced. This happens when the path difference between the two sets of waves is a whole number of wavelengths.

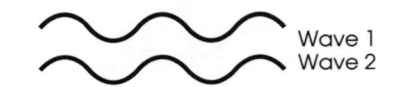

Wave 1
Wave 2

Fig. 9.77

(c) There are several bands because constructive interference is possible for path differences of $0, \lambda, 2\lambda$, etc.
(d) Dark bands happen where waves arrive out of phase and amplitudes are equal and opposite causing destructive interference (Fig. 9.78). It happens if the path difference is $(n + \frac{1}{2})\lambda$.

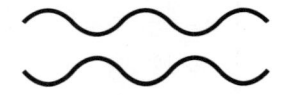

Fig. 9.78

(e) $$\frac{\text{Fringe separation}}{\text{Wavelength}} = \frac{\text{Distance from slits to screen}}{\text{Distance between slits}}$$

Need to measure separation – use several fringes – say 10. Mark the start and end of 10 fringes on the screen. Measure the separation of 10 fringes with a millimetre scale and divide by 10. Measure distance from slits to screen with a metre rule. Measure slit distance using a microscope with a scale.

(f) The fringes would be closer. Smaller path difference is needed to get a wavelength difference.
(g) The pattern is wider. Greater separation of fringe.

STUDENT'S ANSWER – EXAMINER'S COMMENTS

STUDENT ANSWER TO QUESTION 13

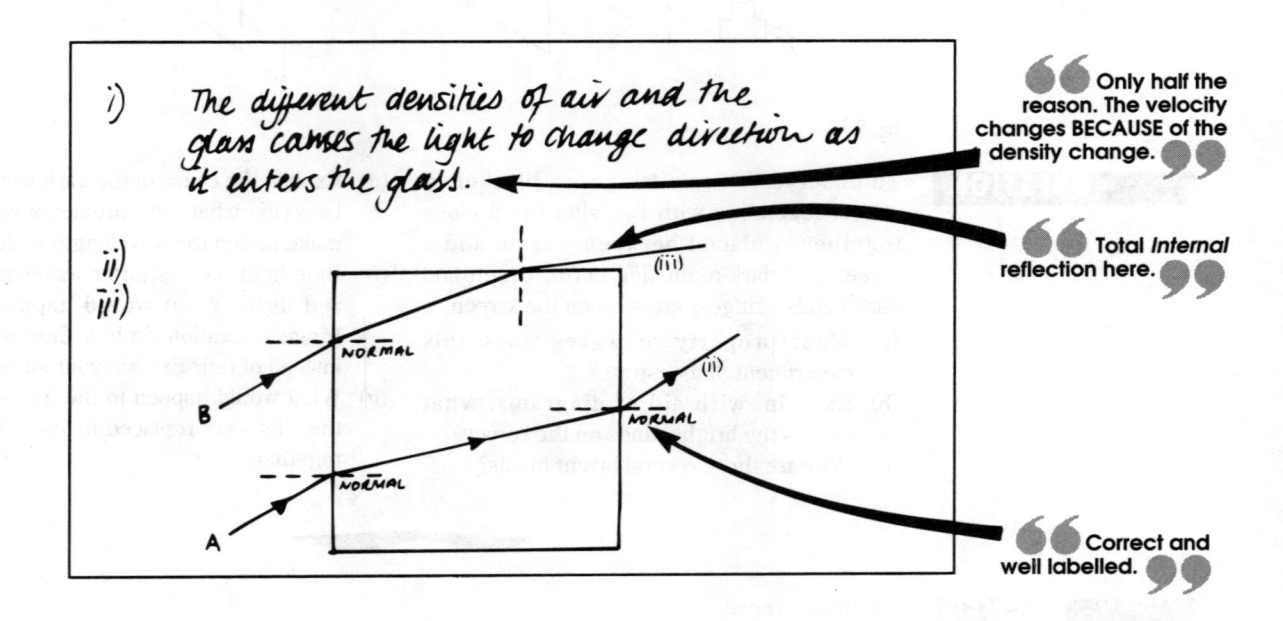

i) The different densities of air and the glass causes the light to change direction as it enters the glass.

> *Only half the reason. The velocity changes BECAUSE of the density change.*

> *Total Internal reflection here.*

> *Correct and well labelled.*

REVIEW SHEET

- All angles of incidence, reflection and refraction are measured from the _____.

- All waves reflect so that the angle of reflection = _____.

- An object is placed 20 cm in front of a mirror. The image will be _____ from the mirror and will be _____ inverted.

- An image which cannot be found on a screen is a _____ image.

- Waves refract when their _____ changes as they go from one material into another.

- When a ray of light inside a more dense material meets the surface at more than the _____ _____ it is _____ reflected.

- Name two uses for optical fibre.

   1. _____. 2. _____.

- A lens that is thicker in the middle is a _____ lens and will make parallel light converge to a _____.

- A lens used as a magnifying glass will be a _____ lens and the object will be _____ to the lens than the focus. The image that is produced is magnified, _____, and erect.

- The distance from the centre of a lens to its focus is called the _____.

- Name the colours the spectrum formed from white light in order of their wavelength.

   _____

- In a projector the two lenses that make sure that the slide is evenly illuminated are called _____.

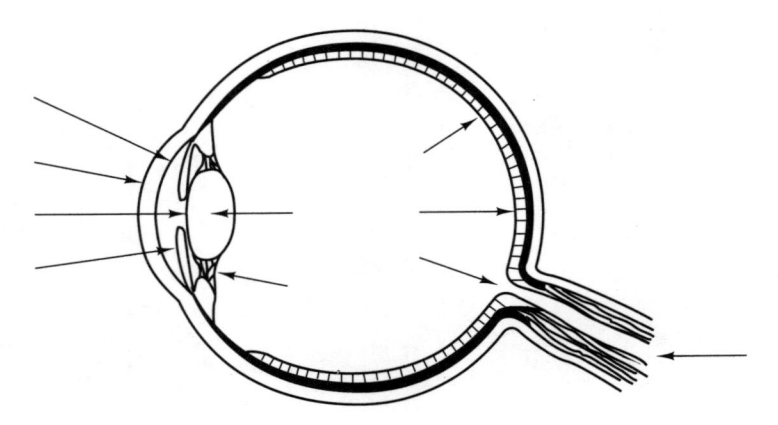

- Label the parts of the eye in the following diagram.

Fig. 9.79

- If two waves arrive at the same place at the same time they will _____.
  If the two waves are in phase they will cause _____.

- Briefly explain what is meant by "in phase".
  _____
  _____
  _____

- Light can be seen to cause interference patterns. What does this tell you about the nature of light?
  _____
  _____

- Describe the difference in the ways in which the eye and the camera focus on objects at different distances.
  _____
  _____
  _____

- Complete the paths of the light rays in the following diagrams.

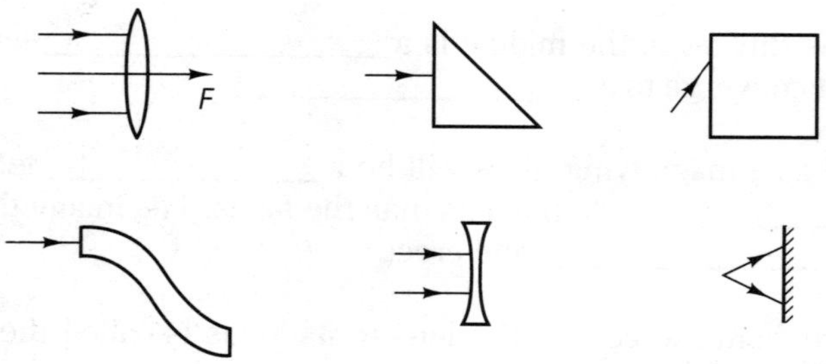

Fig. 9.80

- Name the three primary and the three secondary colours.
  _____
  _____

CHAPTER 10

STRUCTURE OF MATTER AND KINETIC THEORY

STATES OF MATTER
DENSITY
A MODEL FOR MATTER
DIFFUSION
BROWNIAN MOTION
KINETIC THEORY AND KINETIC ENERGY
CHANGE OF STATE
EVAPORATION
THE BEHAVIOUR OF GASES
DETERMINING DENSITIES
REFRIGERATORS
BOILING POINTS
SURFACE TENSION

GETTING STARTED

One of the questions which concerns a scientist is "Why do materials behave in a particular way?" There is often no conclusive answer to the question, because the particles which make up the material are very small, and cannot be observed directly. We can, however, see *large-scale effects* and it is these that are often used as the basis for a "model". To a physicist a *model* is a mental picture of what is actually going on. It is an attempt to explain how small-scale interactions can combine to cause large-scale behaviour. The model is sometimes expressed in words or pictures or by using the language of mathematics. This chapter considers the ways in which *solids, liquids* and *gases* behave and tries to explain the *differences* in their behaviour in terms of *atoms* and *molecules*.

The word "particle" will be used throughout this chapter, with no attempt being made to distinguish atoms, molecules or ions.

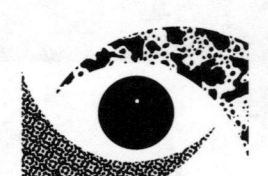

ESSENTIAL PRINCIPLES

1 > STATES OF MATTER

Matter is a general word used to describe any piece of material. The material could be a solid, a liquid or a gas, and these are described as the *states of matter*.

Any substance can, under the right conditions of temperature and pressure, exist in *any* of the three states. For example, we are used to seeing mercury at room temperature as a liquid metal. However, if mercury is cooled enough it becomes a silvery solid, and it vaporises easily to become a gas. In a similar way water can exist as ice or as steam.

The obvious differences between the three states are:

1. *Solids* have a fixed volume, and a fixed shape. They are not easily expanded or compressed by mechanical means.
2. *Liquids* have a fixed volume, but no fixed shape. They take up the shape of their container. They pour easily and are not easily compressed.
3. *Gases* have neither fixed volume nor fixed shape. They can take up any volume available to them. They flow easily and are easily compressed.

Because both liquids and gases can *flow* they are sometimes referred to as *fluids*, so "fluid" can mean either a liquid or a gas.

2 > DENSITY

Solids, liquids and gases show very different *densities*. The **density** of a material is large if a *large mass* of it occupies a *small volume* (e.g. lead, mercury, steel). A small density means that a large volume of material has a small mass (e.g. all gases at normal temperatures and pressures, cotton wool, expanded polystyrene).

Density is calculated using the ratio

■ Density = $\frac{\text{Mass}}{\text{Volume}}$ or $D = \frac{M}{V}$

It is measured in kg/m^3 or g/cm^3. It sometimes helps to remember that a material can only float on top of a *more* dense material – so oil is less dense than water!

EXAMPLE 1

A piece of glass has a mass of 40 g and a volume of 16 cm³. Calculate the density of the glass.

$$D = \frac{M}{V} = \frac{40}{16} = 2.5 \text{ g/cm}^3$$

or

$$D = \frac{M}{V} = \frac{40 \times 10^{-3}}{16 \times 10^{-6}} = 2500 \text{ kg/m}^3$$

EXAMPLE 2

Expanded polystyrene has a density of 1.6 kg/m³. What volume does it occupy of its mass is 400 g?

400 g = 0.4 kg

$$D = \frac{M}{V} \quad \text{so} \quad V = \frac{M}{D}$$

$$\text{Volume} = \frac{0.4}{1.6} = 0.25 \text{ m}^3$$

The densities of some common materials are given in Table 10.1. It is worth noting that air and other gases have values of density which are much less than those of solids and liquids.

Table 10.1

Material	Density (kg/m³)	Material	Density (kg/m³)
Water	1000	**Turpentine**	1362
Air	1.2	**China**	2800
Mercury	13 600	**Iron**	7860
Concrete	2400	**Hardboard**	900
Lead	11 340	**Helium**	0.09

3 › A MODEL FOR SOLIDS, LIQUIDS AND GASES

If we assume that all matter is made up of particles, then the density data suggest that the particles are packed more closely together in solids and liquids than in gases. It follows that a larger mass of particles is occupying a smaller volume in solids and liquids than in gases.

(a) SOLIDS

High-density materials such as metals, must have a **closer packing** arrangement than low-density materials such as expanded polystyrene. The closest packing of all would be achieved if the particles were arranged as in Fig. 10.1 with each particle **stacked** in three dimensions.

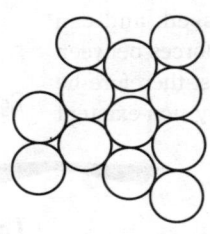

Fig. 10.1 Close-packed particles in a high-density solid.

However, since all materials show different densities, the arrangement must vary slightly from material to material. There may, for example, be gaps in the close-packed structure, and the particles of some material may vary in size, e.g. for alloys such as steel. The idea of an orderly arrangement does, however, seem to fit the large-scale density data for metallic solids.

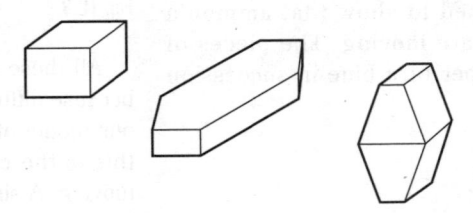

Fig. 10.2 Crystal shapes.

Compounds which form **crystals** also show an orderly arrangement (Fig. 10.2). Typical crystals have a regular **geometric** shape, which suggests that the internal arrangement of particles may also be an orderly one. Metallic solids tend to have high-density values. High density, therefore, suggests a close packing of particles.

Non-crystalline and low-density solids are thought to show little orderliness. Their particles might be arranged in a more **random** way (Fig. 10.3).

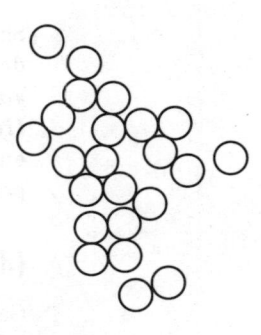

Fig. 10.3 Low-density solid or liquid.

(b) LIQUIDS

Liquids must also be arranged in this random way. Liquids and solids both reveal low-density values, and both are difficult to compress. Although the arrangement of particles is similar for liquids and solids, there remains a basic difference. Liquids can flow and pour, so their particles must have greater freedom to move. The models have, up to this point, taken no account of the **forces** holding the particles together.

(c) FORCES AND PARTICLES

Forces between particles are **electrical** in nature, because within each particle there are positive and negative charges. Two types of forces are therefore possible, **attraction** and **repulsion**. A picture of this would be along the lines of Fig. 10.4, where two trolleys are linked by a **spring** (**attraction**) but mounted with repelling **magnets** (**repulsion**). They will stay at rest, separated from each other, when the two sets of forces are in **equilibrium** (**balance**).

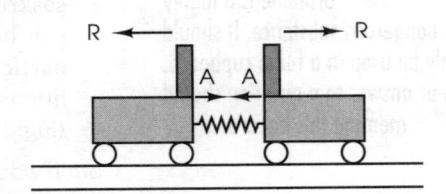

Fig. 10.4 Forces of both attraction and repulsion.

The following provides some evidence of the nature of these two sets of forces:

1. Solids are difficult to pull apart – this suggests that there are attracting forces holding the particles together.
2. Solids are difficult to compress – there are repelling forces stopping the particles from getting too close together.
3. Liquid droplets hold together – attracting forces.
4. Liquids are difficult to compress – repelling forces.

Since solids maintain their shape and liquids do not, this suggests that the **forces in a solid are stronger than those in a liquid**. The forces in liquids are weak enough to allow some movement of the particles.

(d) GASES

Gas densities are about 1000 times less than solid or liquid densities. This suggests than on average gas particles are further apart than solid or liquid particles. 1 cm³ of water will expand to give about 1000 cm³ of steam. This gives a figure of about 10 times the particle distance in a gas compared with solids or liquids (since 10³ = 1000). A particle model for a gas would therefore look something like Fig. 10.5.

Gases are easily compressed, and can expand to fill any volume. The forces between particles at these distances must therefore be very weak. They are effectively non-existent except when a gas is greatly compressed and the particles are moved closer together.

Fig. 10.5 Model for a gas.

4 DIFFUSION

(a) GASES

Gases like ammonia and hydrogen sulphide, which have unpleasant smells, can be quickly detected at one end of a room after a little has escaped at the other end. This strongly suggests that gas particles are moving.

Clearer evidence for this can be provided by the following experimental demonstrations:

1. **Ammonia** is an alkaline gas. It will turn damp red litmus paper blue. A long tube containing pieces of damp red litmus paper and with an ammonia-soaked piece of cotton wool in one end can be used to show that ammonia particles are moving. The pieces of litmus paper turn blue in succession (Fig. 10.6).

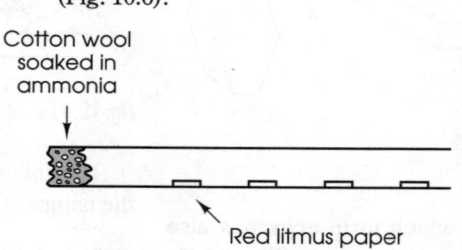

Fig. 10.6 Diffusion of ammonia.

2. **Bromine** liquid vaporises easily at room temperature. If bromine liquid is introduced into a gas jar, the brown gas colour slowly moves up the jar (Fig. 10.7).

3. **Carbon dioxide** placed in the lower tube can be detected in the upper tube after several minutes, despite being denser than air (Fig. 10.8).

(b) LIQUIDS

Liquids also show diffusion. A large copper sulphate crystal, placed in a gas jar of water, dissolves slowly. The blue colour of the solution gradually develops throughout the jar over the course of a few days (Fig. 10.9).

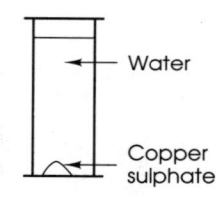

Fig. 10.9

All these diffusion experiments take time, because diffusion is a random process. Indeed our model of gases and liquids explains why this is the case. In a gas, the particles are moving. A single bromine particle in a gas jar has around it many air particles. It is **not** simply able to move from one end of the jar to the other by a **direct route**. It will collide

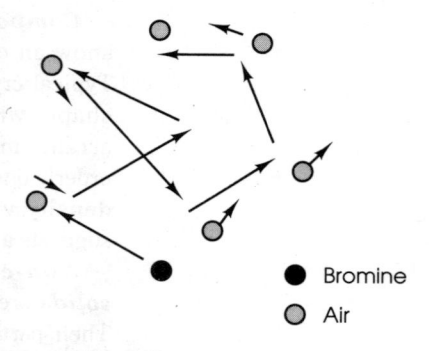

Fig. 10.10 Diffusion of bromine.

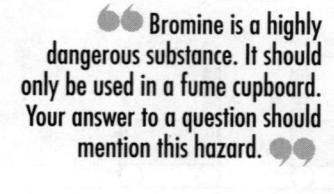

> 66 Bromine is a highly dangerous substance. It should only be used in a fume cupboard. Your answer to a question should mention this hazard. 99

Fig. 10.7 Bromine diffusion.

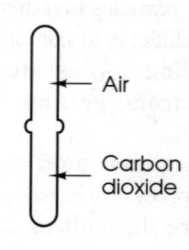

Fig. 10.8

many times with air particles and make a ***random journey*** (Fig. 10.10). The distance between collisions is called the "mean free path". A typical particle may experience 10^9 collisions per second!

Liquid particles, because of their weak forces, are also able to move. However, they are unable to escape from the total liquid volume unless they have a lot of extra energy (see ***evaporation***).

Applying these ideas to a ***solid*** suggests that even in a solid some movement is possible, but that the movement is confined by the strong forces. Particles in solids can only move by vibrating about fixed positions, so that the solid shape is maintained. The theory which suggests that particles in solids, liquids and gases are in constant motion is called the ***kinetic theory.***

5 BROWNIAN MOTION

This is a much more direct piece of evidence for the movement of particles. It is best observed using a smoke cell. The smoke cell is a small container, like a test-tube, about 1 cm high (Fig. 10.11). Smoke can be poured into it using a burning piece of string or a drinking straw. A cover slide placed on top of the cell prevents the smoke from escaping.

Light from a strong light source can be focused with a lens into the cell. The light is scattered by the smoke particles. When viewed with a microscope the smoke particles appear as bright specks against a darker background. They are seen to be in ***continuous random*** motion.

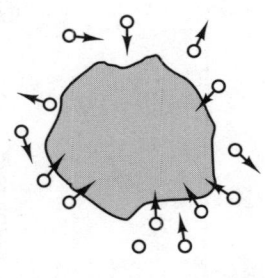

Fig. 10.12 Smoke particle is bombarded by air molecules.

Smoke particles are very large (as particles go) and in the cell they are surrounded by small (invisible) air particles in motion. Air particles hit the smoke particles on all sides and at random. If enough air particles hit in one particular direction, thereby providing a large enough resultant force on the massive smoke particle, it will move (Fig. 10.12).

The movement of the smoke particles, caused by the random movement of the air particles, is called Brownian motion. Brownian motion can be observed using any fluid (liquid or gas) with suitable particles. The original discovery was with pollen grains in water. It can also be seen with Indian ink in water, and with milk (fat globules) in water. However, the movement is seen most clearly with smoke in air.

> ❝ Randomness is a recurring idea in Physics. It refers to a process which seems to occur only by chance. Check that you understand which other processes are random, and list them. ❞

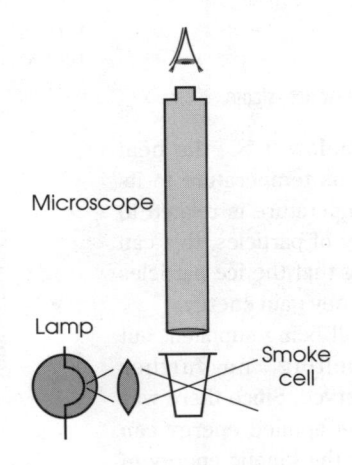

Fig. 10.11 Smoke cell to show Brownian motion.

6 KINETIC THEORY AND KINETIC ENERGY

The hotter a gas becomes, the greater the internal energy of its particles. We can interpret this in the model for matter if we assume that the greater the internal energy of a material, the greater the average kinetic energy of its particles. So the hotter a gas becomes, the faster, on average, is the movement of its particles.

Temperature is directly linked to the kinetic energy of particles. It can be looked on as a rough measure of kinetic energy. This raises the important point that at the same temperature the average kinetic energy of all particles is the same, regardless of whether the particles are in the form of a solid, a liquid or a gas. The effect of having a particular amount of kinetic energy will, however, depend on the mass of each particle and the forces restraining them.

7 CHANGE OF STATE

If ice is taken from a deep freeze so that its temperature is well below 0 °C and heated with a constant and controlled energy supply, like a small immersion heater, its temperature gradually rises to 0 °C (melting-point). We continue to supply heat at the same rate until all the water obtained when the ice melts, boils and turns to steam. The temperature is recorded at one-minute intervals during this process. A graph similar to that in Fig. 10.13 would be obtained.

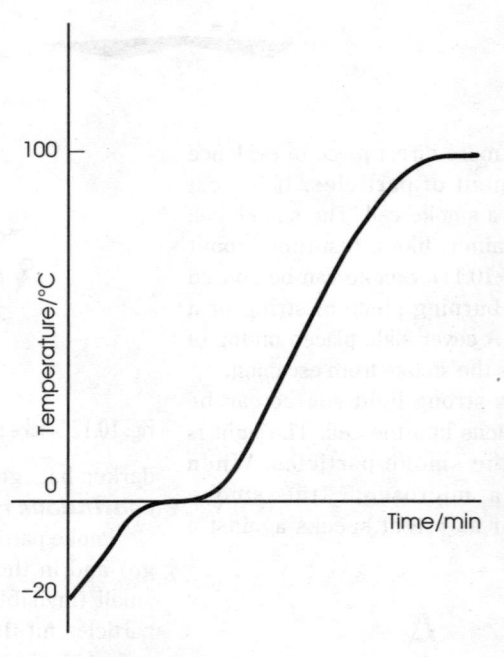

Fig. 10.13 Change of state: ice–water–steam.

While the ice was below 0 °C, the heat energy supplied raised its temperature to its melting-point. Since temperature is related to the mean kinetic energy of particles, this can be interpreted as saying that the ice particles vibrate more rapidly as they gain energy.

At 0 °C, heat was still being supplied, but while the ice is melting, no further temperature rise is observed. Since there was no temperature rise, the applied energy can no longer be increasing the kinetic energy of the particles. Instead it is being used to do work, namely to break the bonds holding the particles in the solid state.

Once the bonds are broken, and the ice has turned to water, the temperature rises again, and the heat supplied increases the kinetic energy of the particles in the liquid.

The energy applied to cause a change of state without a change of temperature, is called the **latent heat** of the material (see Ch. 12). There is a similar effect when water boils. The temperature remains steady, with the energy provided now being used to do work in removing particles from the liquid to the gas state. Once all the particles are in the gas state the temperature rises again. The energy has been used in separating the particles against their attracting forces. The same quantity of latent heat is released when the gas condenses back to a liquid.

In a laboratory demonstration, the reverse process is usually shown, where a hot liquid is allowed to cool and solidify. Stearic acid crystals are suitable for this with a melting-point around 40 °C. A hot solution will give a cooling curve like that in Fig. 10.14.

As the liquid begins to solidify the temperature remains steady. Bonds are reforming as the particles join together in the solid state, and in the process energy is released. This release of energy maintains the temperature, until the whole of the mass is solid and then cooling takes place. The kinetic energy of the particles drops, and the temperature is again seen to fall.

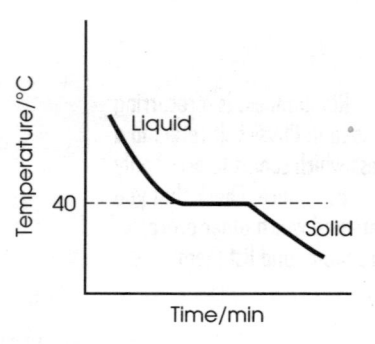

Fig. 10.14 Cooling curve for a liquid changing to a solid at 40° C.

8 EVAPORATION

Unlike boiling, evaporation of a liquid can take place at any temperature. The **rate of evaporation** depends on a number of factors. It can be **increased** by the following:

1. Increased temperature;
2. Decreased pressure on the surface;
3. Increased surface area;
4. Draughts over the surface.

In terms of kinetic theory, increased temperature means an increased average kinetic energy of the particles. The term "average" has been used throughout since not all particles have the same kinetic energy at a particular temperature. Some have above-average energies, some below average. The overall picture follows a **normal distribution curve** (Fig. 10.15).

If a particle has above-average kinetic energy, it has a greater chance of removing itself from the forces holding it in the liquid and therefore of entering the gas state. This

CHAPTER 10 **EXTENSION MATERIALS** 177

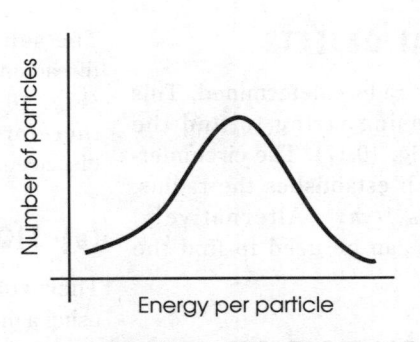

Fig. 10.15 Normal distribution of energy among particles.

change is further increased if it is also at the **surface** of the liquid. So greater temperatures and larger surface areas give greater rates of evaporation.

The surface is, of course, being bombarded by gas particles which can collide with an escaped liquid particle, forcing it back into the liquid. Reduced pressure or a draught across the surface helps prevent this taking place.

If the rest of the liquid loses "above-average kinetic energy" particles, then the remaining particles in the liquid have now a reduced average kinetic energy, and the liquid temperature falls. So evaporation results in the cooling of the original liquid.

9 THE BEHAVIOUR OF GASES

Gases, because their particles are much further apart than in liquids and solids, have extremely small forces acting between the particles. For this reason, gases respond more noticeably to changes in pressure and temperature. These changes can be explained in terms of gas particles using kinetic theory.

The following are explanations of typical gas behaviour, using the kinetic theory model.

> 66 The ideas have often formed the basis of examination questions. It is worth checking that you understand and can remember all the points raised here. 99

(a) GASES EXERT A PRESSURE

Gas particles are in constant, random motion. They collide with other particles and with the walls of their container. Each collision exerts a force on the container. Since many collisions take place, a fairly constant force is exerted. A constant force on an area is described as a constant pressure since pressure is defined as force ÷ area.

(b) FOR A GAS AT CONSTANT VOLUME, AN INCREASE IN TEMPERATURE CAUSES AN INCREASE IN PRESSURE

Increased temperature increases the average kinetic energy of the particles, so the average velocity increases. Therefore in a fixed volume, the time between each collision is reduced, and there are more collisions with the walls per second. This increases the average force exerted and therefore increases the pressure.

(c) A VOLUME REDUCTION AT CONSTANT TEMPERATURE INCREASES THE GAS PRESSURE

A reduced volume means smaller distances between collisions and therefore more collisions per second. This increases the average force exerted and again increases the pressure. There is more detail about the gas laws in Chapter 12.

EXTENSION MATERIALS

1 EXPERIMENTAL DETERMINATION OF DENSITY

Density is defined as mass/volume. Modern electronic balances present no problem in measuring masses very precisely to about 0.1 g or less, but measuring volume is more difficult.

(a) REGULAR SOLIDS WITH A CUBOID SHAPE

These can be directly measured using a ruler with a millimetre scale (Fig. 10.16). Volume = $a \times b \times c$.

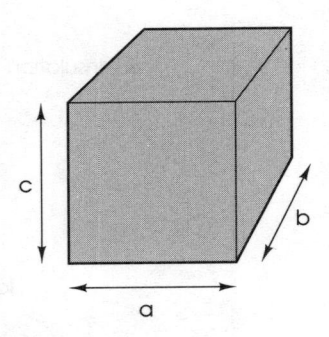

Fig. 10.16

(b) SPHERICAL OBJECTS

These need their radius determined. This could be done using string to find the circumference (Fig. 10.17). The circumference is $2\pi r$, which establishes the radius. Then volume is $\frac{4}{3}\pi r^3$. Alternatively, vernier callipers can be used to find the diameter.

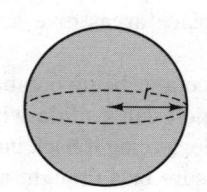

Fig. 10.17

(c) CYLINDRICAL OBJECTS

These need their length and radius determined (Fig. 10.18). A millimetre scale on a ruler can be used for the length and vernier callipers for the radius. Volume = $\pi r^2 l$.

(d) IRREGULAR SOLIDS

Volumes have to be found indirectly by displacement of water. A measuring cylinder is filled to a known volume with water, e.g. 25 cm³. The volume is read with the eye level with the bottom of the meniscus (Fig. 10.19).

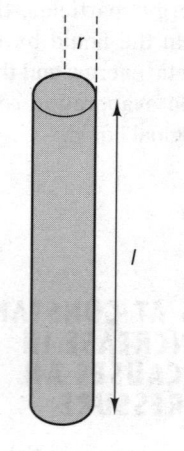

Fig. 10.18

The solid is lowered into the liquid on a thread and the water-level rises to say 35 cm³ (Fig. 10.20). The volume of the solid is therefore 10 cm³. For larger solids a displacement can is used.

(e) LIQUIDS

Their volumes can be determined directly using a measuring cylinder.

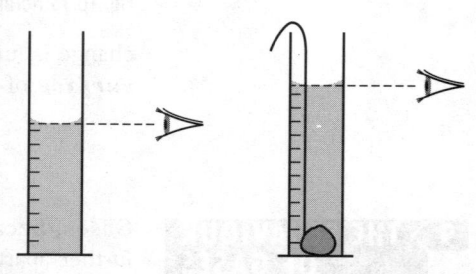

Fig. 10.19 Volume measurement: the eye is level with the bottom of the meniscus.

Fig. 10.20 Volume of an irregular solid by displacement.

2 > REFRIGERATORS

The inside of a refrigerator is cooled by evaporation. A liquid called **Freon** is circulated inside the refrigerator through a system of pipes by a pump. Evaporation of the Freon occurs inside the refrigerator, which has several loops of pipe inside the freezer cabinet. The pump helps evaporation by pumping vapour out of the "evaporator" pipes and reducing pressure. The latent heat for the Freon to evaporate is removed from the air and food inside the refrigerator, making them cold (Fig. 10.21).

The compressor pump compresses the freon vapour inside the condenser pipes which are at the back of the refrigerator and surrounded by air. Pressurising the vapour helps it condense, and causes it to give up its latent heat of vaporisation to the surrounding air.

The refrigerator is an example of a heat pump, removing heat energy from the air and food inside the cabinet and transferring it to the air outside.

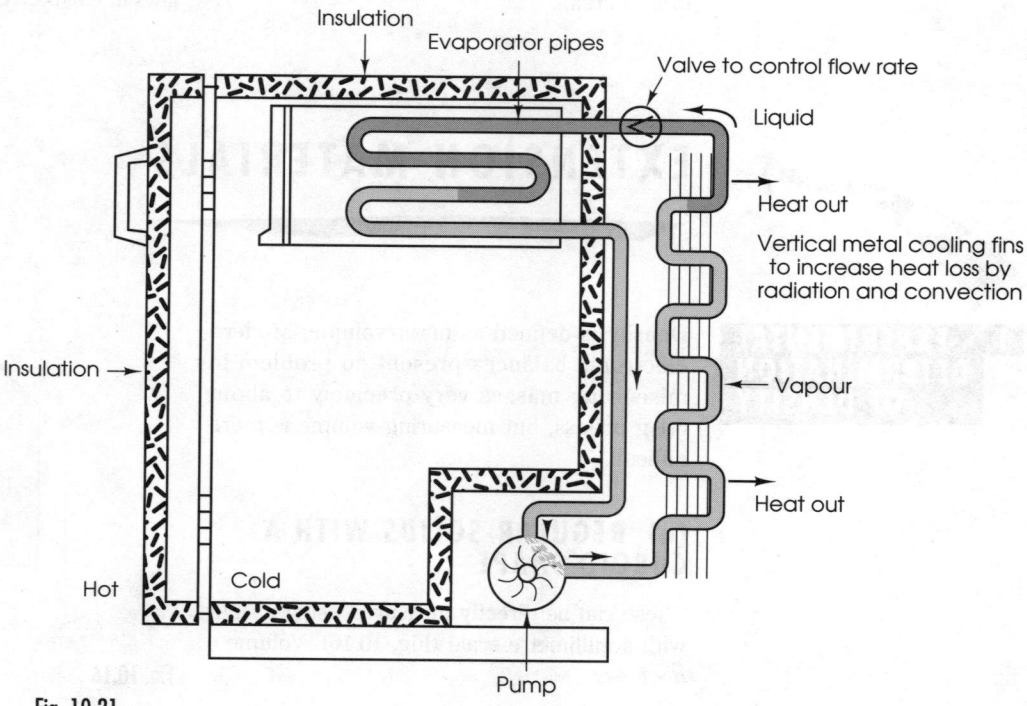

Fig. 10.21

3 > BOILING POINTS

A liquid will boil when the pressure of its vapour is the same as the pressure in the space above it. Standard **boiling point** is measured when the pressure is one standard atmosphere (760 mm mercury pressure). The vapour that is formed is then able to form bubbles in the liquid. Water will normally boil at about 100 °C because that is the temperature at which the vapour pressure of water becomes equal to the pressure of one atmosphere. A liquid can therefore boil at almost any temperature depending on the pressure above it. A modern car will have a pressurised cooling system where the vapour is not released so that the water will not boil even though the temperature rises above 100 °C.

A pressure cooker also works on this principle. The steam can only escape through the valve when its pressure has been raised. Since the pressure is greater than one atmosphere the boiling point is raised and the food cooks faster. Reducing the pressure above a liquid will enable it to be boiled at a lower temperature. Dissolved substances will also change boiling point (salt raises the boiling point of water). Chemists use this to check the purity of chemicals.

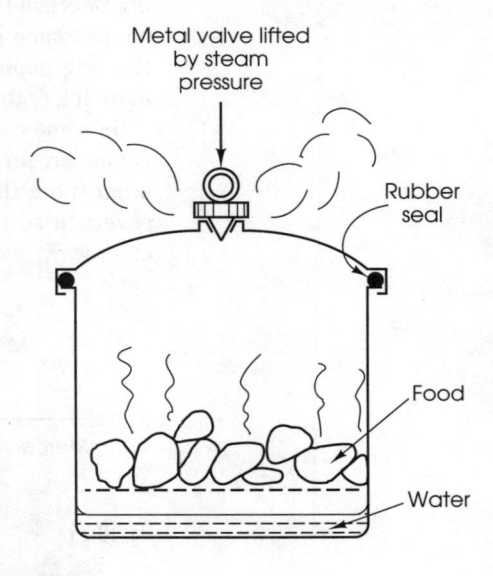

Fig. 10.22

4 > SURFACE TENSION

We have already seen that the particles of a liquid attract each other. A particle in the liquid will be attracted in all directions by the surrounding particles and the forces will therefore cancel leaving it free to move. This is not true for a particle at the surface where there are no particles above it and the particle will need quite a lot of energy to move out above the surface because of the downward attraction of the other particles (as we found in the section on evaporation). The *sideways attraction of the particles at the surface* produces the surface tension effect. (Note that there is NOT a "skin" on the surface!)

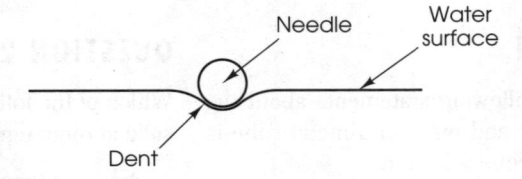

Fig. 10.23

If a needle is placed gently on the surface of water its weight will not be sufficient to push apart the surface particles and it will rest *on* the surface. If you look closely you can see that it makes a dent in the surface. Note that the needle is NOT floating. If you put the needle onto the water point first its weight will be acting on fewer particles and it can push them apart and sink. Detergents make the forces between the particles smaller. If you add a drop of detergent to the water the needle will break through the bonds and sink.

In a glass container water molecules are attracted more to the glass than to each other and are pulled up the side of the glass. We see this as a **meniscus**.

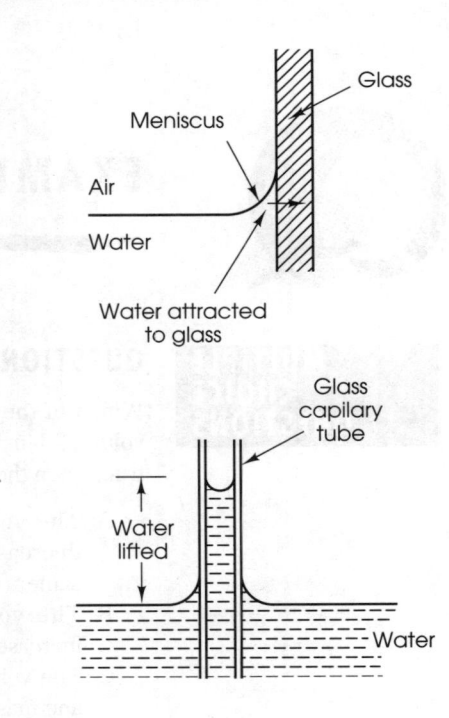

Fig. 10.24

If the container is narrow (a capillary tube) the liquid will be pulled up the tube until the attractive force from the glass is balanced by the weight of water being lifted. The same effect is the reason why water soaks up through your bath sponge or tea soaks up through a sugar cube. This is known as **capillary action**. Damp will rise through brickwork in this way and is stopped by a non-porous damp proof layer between the bricks. Blotting paper and wicks use the effect to move ink or the fuel upwards.

In some cases, such as mercury in a glass container, the liquid molecules attract each other more than the glass and the effect is reversed so that the meniscus curves the other way.

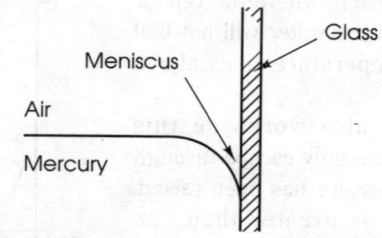

Fig. 10.25

Water molecules attract each other but are repelled by some other materials such as waxes. Water will therefore "bead" on a waxed surface rather than soak in. This is why we polish coffee tables and car bodywork. When the polish wears off the water is attracted to the surface and spreads out into a large thin layer. This same attraction between molecules can make two wet microscope slides or two wet plates difficult to separate.

The attraction of the molecules in soap film will make it take up the smallest possible area (spherical bubbles have the smallest possible area for their volume). This can be investigated by making soap bubbles in a wire frame crossed by a cotton loop. When the bubble is burst on one side of the loop the cotton is pulled into an arc by the remaining soap film.

A soap film formed at the wide end of a clean glass funnel will move towards the narrower end so that it has a smaller area.

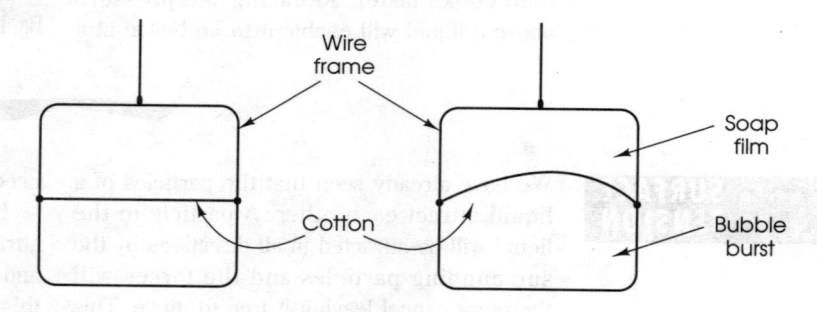

Fig. 10.26

EXAMINATION QUESTIONS

MULTIPLE CHOICE QUESTIONS

QUESTION 1

Which of the following statements about the volume, density and mass of a metal cube is true, when the cube is heated?

A The volume decreases, the density decreases, but the mass remains the same.
B The volume, density and mass all increase.
C The volume increases, but the density and mass remain the same.
D The volume increases, the density decreases, but the mass remains the same.
E The volume remains the same, but the density and mass both increase.
(ULEAC)

QUESTION 2

Which of the following describes particles in a solid at room temperature?

A Close together and stationary
B Close together and vibrating
C Close together and moving about at random
D Far apart and stationary
E Far apart and moving about at random
(ULEAC)

QUESTION 3

A material has a density of 2 g/cm³. What would be the mass of a block of it 3 cm × 2 cm × 1 cm?

CHAPTER 10 **EXAMINATION QUESTIONS** 181

A 2 g
B 3 g
C 6 g
D 8 g
E 12 g
(NISEAC)

QUESTION 4

When air in a closed container of fixed size is heated, which of the following statements is true?

A The molecules move more slowly.
B The pressure of the air increases.
C The velocity of the molecules stays the same.
D The molecules expand.
E The force between the air molecules increases.

QUESTION 5

A cube has a side of 2 cm, a volume of 8 cm³ and a density of 8 g/cm³. The mass of the cube is

A 1 g
B 16 g
C 32 g
D 64 g
(SEG)

QUESTION 6

Small particles of smoke in air in a well-lit glass box are seen making small jerky movements. These movements are due to

A Energy from the light source making the particles expand
B Energy from the light source causing convection currents in the box
C Static electricity on the particles
D The motion of molecules of the air in the box
(SEG)

QUESTION 7

The phrase "latent heat of fusion" is used to describe the amount of heat required to change

A A liquid into a gas without raising its temperature
B A liquid into a gas with a rise in temperature
C A solid into a liquid without raising its temperature
D A solid into a liquid with a rise in temperature.

QUESTION 8

In a room at 20 °C, liquid naphthalene (melting at 80 °C) is allowed to cool from 100 °C. Which one of the graphs (Fig. 10.27) best shows the cooling?

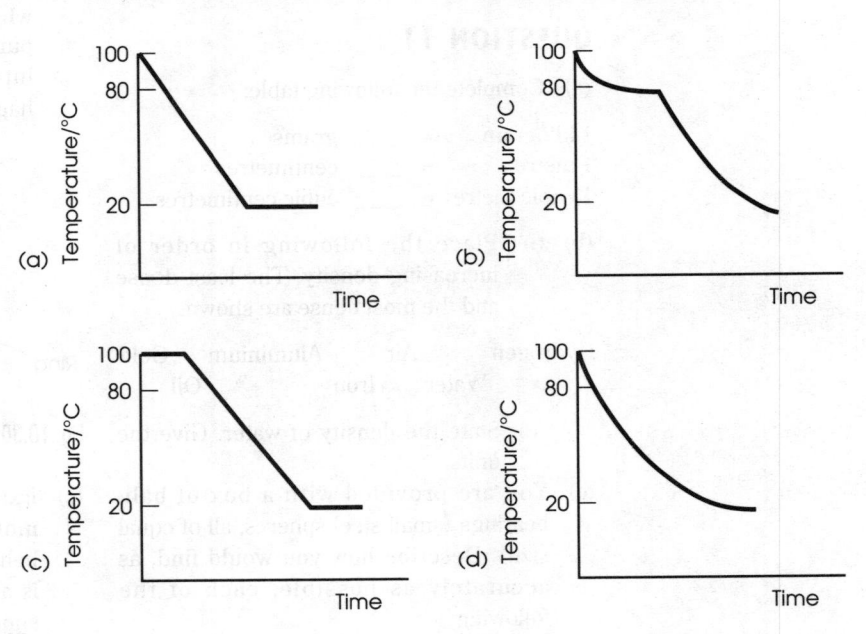

Fig. 10.27

STRUCTURED QUESTIONS

QUESTION 9

(a) In the diagram (Fig. 10.28), the bottom circle represents the molecules in a liquid. Complete the top circle to represent the molecules in a gas.
(b) With reference to the diagram, explain why gases can be compressed easily but liquids cannot. (2 lines)
(c) Brownian motion is usually shown in a school laboratory by looking at smoke specks under a microscope.
  (i) Describe the motion of the smoke specks. (1 line)

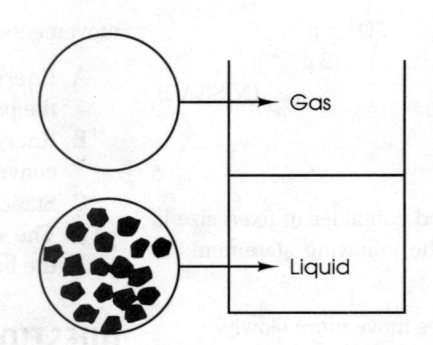

CHAPTER 10 STRUCTURE OF MATTER AND KINETIC THEORY

Fig. 10.28

(ii) What causes this motion? (2 lines)
(NEAB)

QUESTION 10

(a) Assuming air is made up of molecules, which are always moving, how do we explain why the pressure of the air increases as its volume decreases. (2 lines)
(b) (i) How could you increase the pressure of air in a sealed container without changing its volume? (1 line)
(ii) Explain your answer to (i) in terms of the motion of the molecules. (2 lines)

QUESTION 11

(a) Complete the following table:

1 kilogram = ____ grams
1 metre = ____ centimetres
1 cubic metre = ____ cubic centimetres

(b) (i) Place the following in order of increasing density. The least dense and the most dense are shown.

Hydrogen   Air   Aluminium   Gold
      Water   Iron   Oil

(ii) State the density of water. Give the units.

(c) You are provided with a box of ball-bearings (small steel spheres, all of equal size). Describe how you would find, as accurately as possible, each of the following:

(i) The mass of one sphere;
(ii) The volume of one sphere;
(iii) The density of steel. (ULEAC)

QUESTION 12

(a) A light cotton loop can rest on a soap film which has been formed on a metal ring.

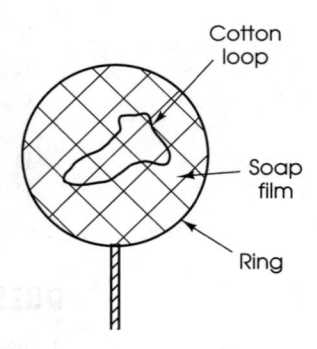

Fig. 10.29

(i) Draw arrows on the diagram to show the forces acting on the thread.
(ii) What name is given to the forces acting on the cotton thread?
(iii) Why do these forces seem to have no effect on the surface of the soap film?

(b) The diagram below shows what happens when the soap film inside the thread is punctured and the thread is drawn out into a circle. Explain why this should happen.

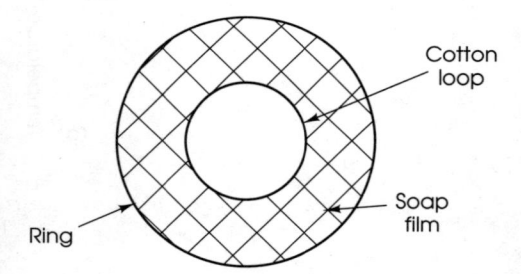

Fig. 10.30

(c) Explain in terms of the forces between molecules why the surface of a liquid behaves like a stretched elastic skin that is always trying to shrink. Your answer should include a diagram. (SEG)

CHAPTER 10 ANSWERS TO EXAMINATION QUESTIONS

ANSWERS TO EXAMINATION QUESTIONS

MULTIPLE CHOICE QUESTIONS

Question	1	2	3	4	5	6	7	8
Answer	D	B	E	B	D	D	C	B

STRUCTURED QUESTIONS

ANSWER 9

(a) See Fig. 10.24. Gas particles are about 10 × further apart than particles in a liquid.

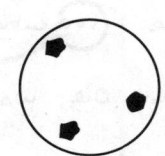

Fig. 10.31

(b) There are no gaps between the particles of a liquid even though they are free to move. The liquid cannot be compressed as the particles themselves cannot be squashed smaller and there are no spaces to push them into. A gas has lots of space between the particles and can therefore be compressed easily. As the volume is reduced the particles will hit the walls more often and the resulting increase in pressure makes further compression harder.

(c) (i) Smoke specks move continuously in a random way in three dimensions.
(ii) Motion is caused by collisions of air molecules. Enough collisions in a particular direction exert a resultant force on the smoke particle.

ANSWER 10

(a) Decreased volume means smaller distances moved between collisions with the walls of a container. Each collision exerts a force so more collisions per second gives a greater force on the container and therefore greater pressure.

(b) (i) Increase the temperature.
(ii) Increased temperature raises kinetic energy of the molecules. Therefore more collisions per second and greater pressure.

ANSWER 11

(a) 1 kilogram = 1000 grams
1 metre = 100 centimetres
1 cubic metre = 10^6 cubic centimetres
(1 000 000 cm³)

(b) (i) Hydrogen, Air, Oil, Water, Aluminium, Iron, Gold.

(ii) Density of water is 1000 kg/m³ or 1 g/cm³.

(c) (i) Count out a known number of ball-bearings (say 20). Find the mass of 20 spheres using a top-pan electronic balance. Divide the mass by 20 to find the mass of one sphere.

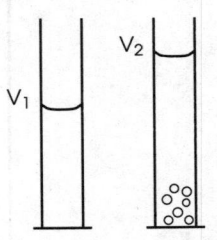

Fig. 10.32

(ii) Several possibilities: (a) Lay 20 spheres in a line. Measure total length. Divide by 20 to find average diameter and therefore average radius. Volume is $\frac{4}{3}\pi r^3$. (b) Measure a known volume of water with a measuring cylinder. Record its volume V_1. Drop in 20 spheres, displacing some water. Record the new volume V_2. Here $(V_2 - V_1)$ is the volume of 20 spheres. $(V_2 - V_1) \div 20$ is the volume of one sphere. (Fig. 10.32.)

(iii) Density = mass of one sphere ÷ volume of one sphere.

ANSWER 12

This is a higher level question.

(a) (i) Show a pair of equal and opposite forces acting perpendicular to the thread.
(ii) Surface tension.
(iii) The forces will act equally on both sides of any line in the surface.

(b) The forces pulling the thread outwards are no longer counterbalanced and the film tries to reach a minimum area.

(c) Your diagram and explanation should show that the forces on the molecules in the liquid are balanced but those at the surface are not. The attractive forces between the molecules are greater than the repulsive ones. This will mean that the attractive forces from neighbouring molecules will put the surface into a state of tension.

STUDENT'S ANSWER – EXAMINER'S COMMENTS

STUDENT ANSWER TO QUESTION 11

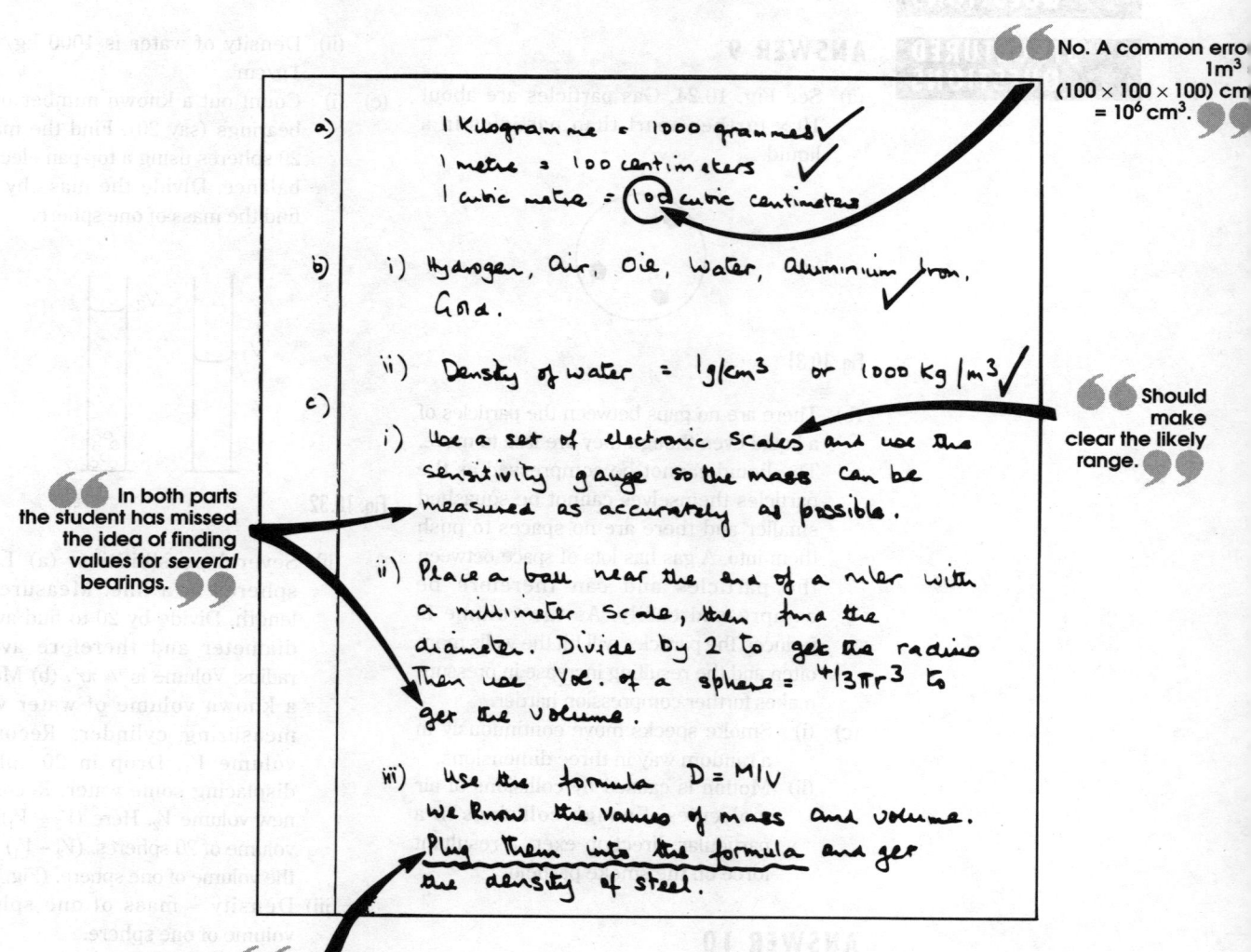

a)
1 Kilogramme = 1000 grammes ✓
1 metre = 100 centimeters ✓
1 cubic metre = 100 cubic centimeters

> No. A common error. 1m³ (100 × 100 × 100) cm = 10⁶ cm³.

b)
i) Hydrogen, Air, Oil, Water, Aluminium, Iron, Gold. ✓

ii) Density of water = 1g/cm³ or 1000 kg/m³ ✓

> Should make clear the likely range.

c)
i) Use a set of electronic scales and use the sensitivity gauge so the mass can be measured as accurately as possible.

ii) Place a ball near the end of a ruler with a millimeter scale, then find the diameter. Divide by 2 to get the radius. Then use Vol. of a sphere = 4/3πr³ to get the volume.

> In both parts the student has missed the idea of finding values for *several* bearings.

iii) Use the formula D = M/V
We know the values of mass and volume. Plug them into the formula and get the density of steel.

> Not a very good statement

REVIEW SHEET

- The three states of matter are _____, _____ and _____.

- _____ and _____ are both called fluids because they can flow.

- Write down the equation for density and state suitable units for the density of a liquid.

- Four steel balls displace 25 cm³ of water and have a mass of 210 g. Their average density is _____.

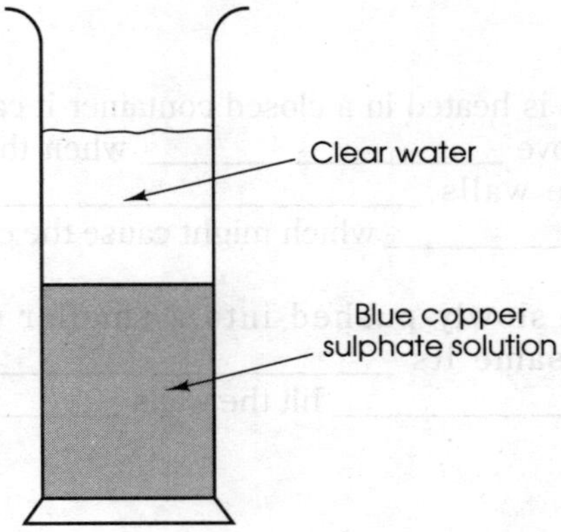

Fig. 10.33

- The diagram (Fig. 10.33) shows water which has been carefully floated on top of some blue copper sulphate solution.

    1. What will you see happen? _____

    2. How long do you think this will take? _____

    3. What does this tell you about particles in a liquid?
       _____

    4. Why would the process be much faster in a gas mixture?
       _____
       _____

- The energy taken in at constant temperature to change the state of a material is called _____.

- When two solids are pushed tightly together there is no diffusion because the particles _____.

- Write down four factors that can increase the rate of evaporation of a liquid.

    1. _____   2. _____

    3. _____   4. _____

- Explain briefly how a gas produces a pressure on the walls of its container.
  _____
  _____

- Put the following in order of increasing density.

  | ice   water   petrol   wood   aluminium   concrete |

- When a liquid evaporates it is the _____ particles that escape. Separating the particles uses _____ heat so the liquid that is left is _____.

- To make a liquid boil at a higher temperature you could _____ the pressure on it.

- When a gas is heated in a closed container it can be very dangerous because the particles move _____ when they are given more kinetic energy and hit the walls _____ often. This is an increase in _____ which might cause the container to _____.

- If a gas is slowly pushed into a smaller space so that its temperature stays the same its _____ will increase because the _____ hit the walls _____ often.

CHAPTER 11

PRESSURE AND HYDRAULICS

FORCE AND PRESSURE

PRESSURE IN LIQUIDS

MEASUREMENT OF PRESSURE

ATMOSPHERIC PRESSURE

HYDRAULIC MACHINES

PRESSURE AND UPTHRUST

BOYLE'S LAW

ANEROID BAROMETER AND ALTIMETER

WEATHER MAPS

ARCHIMEDES PRINCIPLE

FLUID FLOW AND PRESSURE

PRINCIPLES OF FLIGHT

GETTING STARTED

Pressure and force are ideas which are often confused. A **force** is applied at a particular point, and causes a change of some sort; **pressure** is the result of the force acting on an area. Pressure effects are noticeable when a solid rests on a surface, when a liquid is compressed, or when a gas changes its volume or its temperature. The air around us exerts a large pressure on our bodies, and the fluids in our bodies are able to withstand this pressure. Weather forecasts depend on the ability of a meteorologist to predict how pressure changes will affect patterns in the atmosphere, and many technological applications depend on pressure changes in gases and liquids. This chapter will try to explain some of these ideas.

ESSENTIAL PRINCIPLES

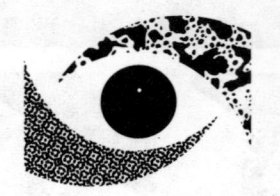

1 > FORCE AND PRESSURE

> **Force and pressure are often confused. Make sure that you clearly understand the difference between the terms and can use them correctly. (What are their units?)**

(a) FORCE

A *force* is only definable in terms of its effects. It is anything which changes or tends to change the motion of an object (see Ch. 3). The same force can cause different effects if it acts on different areas.

In Fig. 11.1 a 1 kg mass is placed above a wood block resting on Plasticine. The force on each block is 10 N. The Plasticine will be more deformed in (a) than (b) because in (a) the force is exerted on a smaller area; another way of saying this is that "the pressure in (a) is greater".

Fig. 11.2

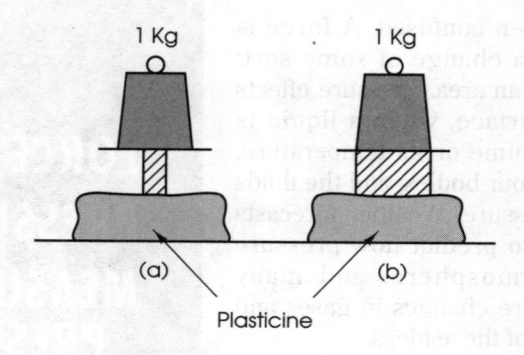

Fig. 11.1 Pressure depends on area.

(b) PRESSURE

Pressure is the effect of a force on an area. The same force acting on a small and a large area will give a larger pressure for the smaller area. Simple examples of this are:

1. There is a greater pressure under the point of a drawing pin than under the head, when the same force is applied (Fig. 11.2).
2. Animals with a large weight tend to have feet with a large surface area, reducing the pressure they exert on the ground (e.g. elephants, camels; Fig. 11.3).

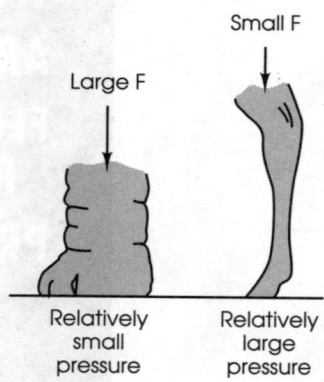

Fig. 11.3

3. Knives, saws, chisels, etc., have a small area of cross-section so that the application of a small force gives a large pressure (Fig. 11.4).

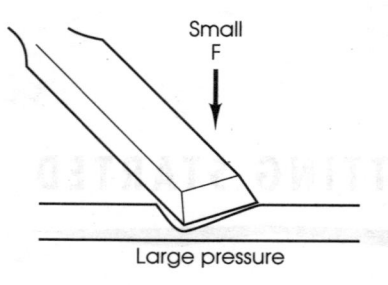

Fig. 11.4

These and many other examples suggest that when a force is applied, the pressure which results from it depends on the area over which it is acting, i.e.

$$\text{Pressure} = \frac{\text{Force}}{\text{Area}}$$

The units are therefore N/m² or N/cm²; 1 newton per square metre (1 N/m²) is called 1 Pascal (1 Pa). This enables us to calculate how much pressure is exerted, and to compare pressure effects if forces and areas are known.

EXAMPLE 1

An average grown person weighs about 650 N (has a mass of 65 kg). A typical area below one shoe would be about 170 cm². To calculate the pressure on the ground, we need to convert the units.

$$1 \text{ cm}^2 = (10^{-2} \times 10^{-2}) \text{ m}^2$$
$$= 10^{-4} \text{ m}^2$$
$$170 \text{ cm}^2 = 170 \times 10^{-4} \text{ m}^2$$
$$= 1.7 \times 10^{-2} \text{ m}^2$$

Then

$$\text{Pressure} = \frac{\text{Force}}{\text{Area}} = \frac{650}{3.4 \times 10^{-2}}$$
$$= 1.9 \times 10^4 \text{ Pa}$$

If the same person stood on one foot, the force exerted would be the same (650 N) but the area would be halved, so the pressure is doubled. The same person standing on stilts, where the area is even smaller, would exert an even bigger pressure. Clearly pressure increases as the area over which the force is acting becomes smaller.

2 PRESSURE IN LIQUIDS – THEORY

We have defined pressure as force ÷ area. It is clearly more difficult to define this for a liquid where forces and areas are not as obvious as in the case of a solid. A little thought and some theory helps solve the problem.

Imagine an object below the surface of a liquid. All the liquid above it has a weight and will exert a force, since weight is itself a force caused by the pull of a planet. If the object has an area, A, and is h metres below the surface, the situation is rather like that of Fig. 11.5.

The object is lying under a weight of liquid, which is exerting a force on its area. Then

$$\text{Pressure} = \frac{\text{Force (weight)}}{\text{Area}}$$

Weight of the object = (Mass) × g
(g = gravitational field strength)

but

$$\text{Mass} = \text{Volume} \times \text{Density}$$
$$= \text{Height} \times \text{Area} \times \text{Density}$$

$$\text{Pressure} = \frac{g \times \text{Height} \times \text{Density} \times \text{Area}}{\text{Area}}$$

$$= \text{Height} \times \text{Density} \times g$$

or in **symbols**

▶ Pressure = $\rho g h$

where ρ = density, g = gravitational field strength and h = depth of liquid. This means that:

1. Pressure increases with fluid depth.
2. Pressure increases with fluid density.

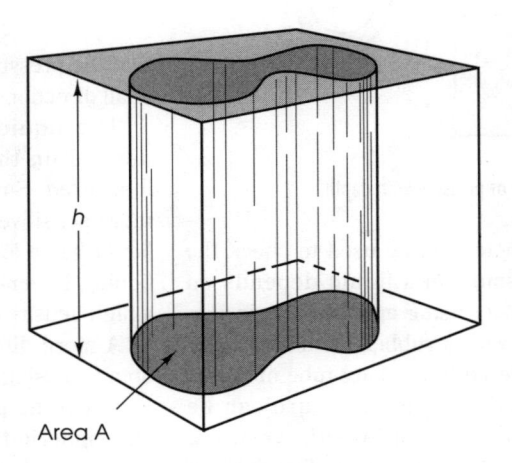

Fig. 11.5 Pressure below a liquid column.

3 MEASUREMENT OF PRESSURE

While pressure below a solid or a liquid is easily determined, a gas presents more of a problem. Gas pressure in a laboratory is usually measured with a manometer (Fig. 11.6). This is a U-tube containing a suitable liquid.

Before connecting to the gas supply the level of liquid in each tube is the same. The pressure along a horizontal line below the liquid is the same, since pressure is proportional to depth. Above the surface of the liquid, the pressure is that of the atmosphere, P_A.

So the pressure at X or Y = P_A + pressure due to height of liquid above X or Y. On connecting to a gas supply (e.g. the outlet of the mains gas supply in a lab) the manometer liquid levels change (Fig. 11.7). Since the gas pressure is greater than atmospheric pressure, the liquid in the right-hand column of the manometer is pushed upwards. The pressure on X is now the pressure of the gas supply. This is the same as the pressure at Z (same level).

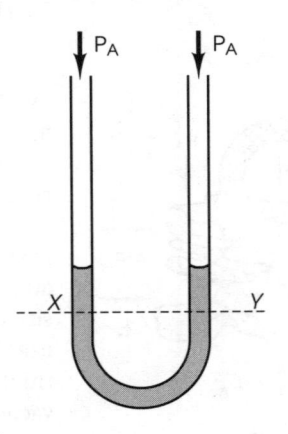

Fig. 11.6 Manometer.

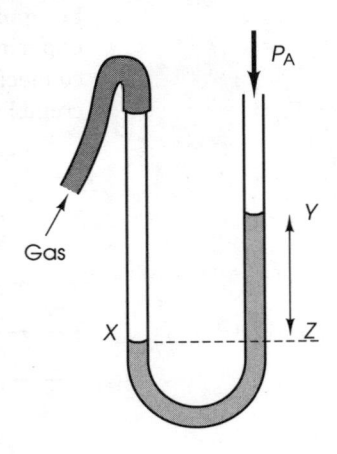

Fig. 11.7 Manometer used to measure gas pressure.

Pressure at Z = P_A + Pressure due to liquid column YZ
(h centimetres)

Gas pressure = P_A + h centimetres of liquid

It is common for pressures to be expressed in liquid column equivalents, but they can be converted to pascals using $P = \rho g h$.

190 CHAPTER 11 **PRESSURE AND HYDRAULICS**

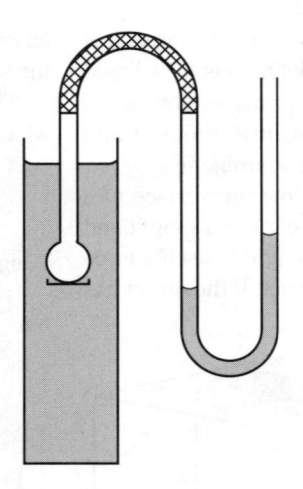

Fig. 11.8 Variation of pressure with depth.

The manometer can be used to check the idea that pressure in a liquid depends on depth and density using apparatus as in Fig. 11.8. A funnel with a rubber membrane over one end is lowered into a long tube of liquid. The depth of liquid and pressure can be measured and the relationship verified. Similarly, using different density liquids, with the funnel at a fixed depth, proves that pressure is proportional to density.

If the funnel is arranged as in Fig. 11.9 and lowered to a fixed depth it can also be shown

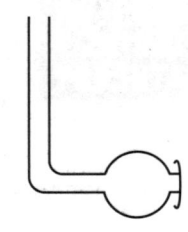

Fig. 11.9

that the pressure at a given depth is the same in all directions.

The liquid used in a manometer will depend on the pressure difference to be measured. Small values of pressure will be more sensitively measured if the manometer liquid has a low density (water or an organic liquid); larger values of pressure may require a high-density oil or even mercury.

A more direct reading of pressure can be obtained using a Bourdon pressure gauge.

When the pressure of the gas is *less* than atmospheric the liquid will move the other way so that it is higher in the arm of the manometer that is connected to the gas. Measure the height difference h as before and the gas pressure is $P_A - h$ cm of liquid.

4 ATMOSPHERIC PRESSURE

This has already been mentioned in connection with the measurements using a manometer. We live underneath a large air mass (the atmosphere) and it exerts pressures on us. The size of this pressure can be gauged from the "collapsing can" experiment (Fig. 11.10), where a tin can connected to a vacuum pump collapses and crumbles as air is removed from it.

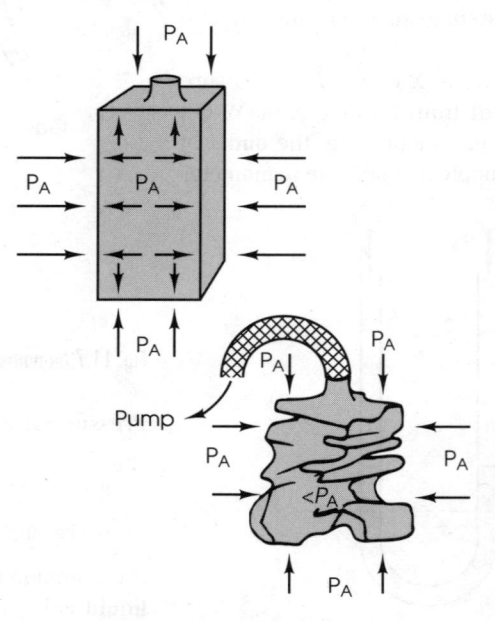

Fig. 11.10 The "collapsing can" experiment.

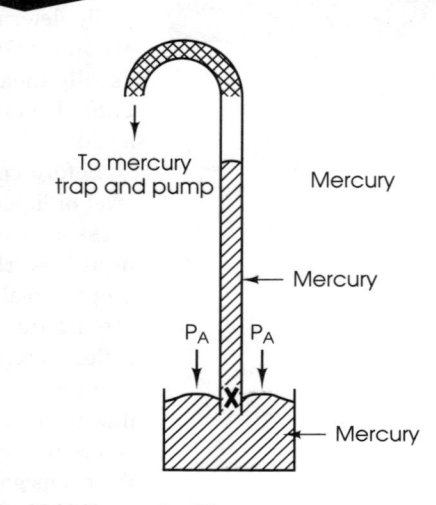

Fig. 11.11 Mercury rises 76 cm.

Under ordinary conditions the atmosphere exerts pressure on the can from all directions and the air inside also exerts an equal pressure on all walls of the can. The pump removes air from the can, and the pressure inside it is reduced. The can's walls are pushed in on all sides by the pressure of the atmosphere. To obtain a clearer idea of the size of the pressure of the atmosphere we can use the apparatus of Fig. 11.11. A long (1 m) thick-walled glass tube is connected to a vacuum pump with a mercury trap to prevent mercury entering the pump, and is then maximum height the mercury rises is about 76 cm. Therefore atmospheric pressure is equivalent to the pressure below a column of mercury 76 cm high.

The mercury barometer uses the same principle. A 1 m long tube, closed at one end, is filled with mercury. Holding a finger over the open end, the tube is inverted into a mercury trough (gloves should be worn!). The mercury level falls to about 76 cm (Fig. 11.12). Above the mercury there is now a vacuum. Again it is seen that the atmosphere can support a column of mercury 76 cm high. The pressure at X below the column is equal to the atmospheric pressure, P_A. The pressure below this column is given by

$$P_A = \rho g h$$
$$= 13\,600 \times 10 \times 0.76$$
$$(\rho_{mercury} = 13\,600 \text{ kg/m}^3)$$
$$= \underline{103\,360 \text{ Pa}}$$

The figure 76 cm varies from time to time as the atmospheric pressure varies, and this gives an indication of prevailing weather conditions.

A more common barometer is an aneroid barometer (see "Extension Materials").

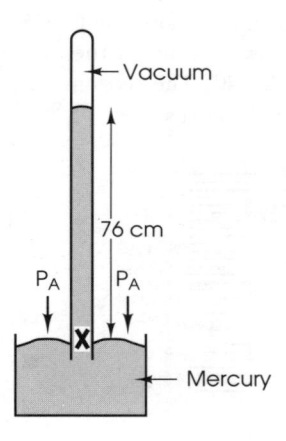

Fig. 11.12 A mercury barometer.

placed in a trough of mercury (Fig. 11.11). The pump is turned on and mercury rises up the tube. It rises because the pump removes air, reducing the pressure in the tube. The atmosphere pushes on the surface of the mercury in the trough, forcing it up the tube until the pressure at X is equal to the atmospheric pressure. It is found that the

5 HYDRAULIC MACHINES

Hydraulic machines use liquid pressure to transfer a force from one place to another, using the following properties of liquids:

1. They are incompressible.
2. At the same depth, liquid pressure is the same in all directions.
3. Any change in liquid pressure is transmitted instantly to all parts of the liquid

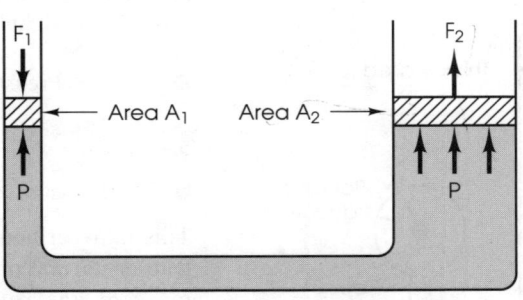

Fig. 11.13 Principle of hydraulic systems.

The basic idea is shown in Fig. 11.13. If a force F_1 is applied to the smaller piston whose area is A_1 the pressure below the surface is $P = F_1/A_1$. This pressure is transmitted through the liquid and is now applied at the larger piston, area A_2,

$$\text{Pressure} = \frac{\text{Force}}{\text{Area}}$$

$$\text{Force} = \text{Pressure} \times \text{area}$$

Force applied at the larger cylinder

$$F_2 = P \times A_2 = \frac{F_1 \times A_2}{A_1}$$

Since A_2 is greater than A_1, a small force applied at the smaller cylinder is multiplied to become a large force applied at the larger cylinder. Although the force is made greater, energy is still conserved and at best work done by F_1 = work done by F_2. In Fig. 11.14

$$F_1 \times d_1 = F_2 \times d_2$$

So if the force is increased 10 times, the distance moved is decreased in the same proportion.

This is the basic principle behind hydraulic jacks and hydraulic brakes. Obviously if air entered the hydraulic fluid, the system would not work well since gases can be compressed and pressure would not be transmitted instantly from one side of the system to the other.

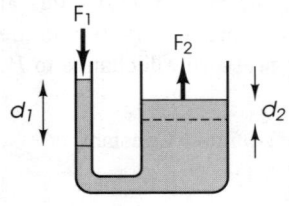

Fig. 11.14

6 ▶ PRESSURE AND UPTHRUST IN A LIQUID

An object immersed in a fluid has a force on it which tends to push it upwards out of the liquid. This is called "upthrust". The reason for it is based on pressure differences.

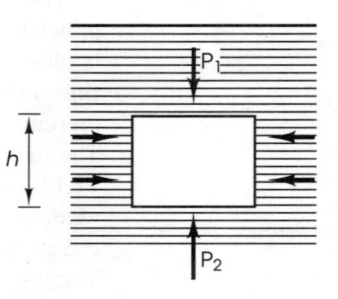

Fig. 11.15 Pressure is greater below the block than above it.

Pressure increases with depth, so for an object below a liquid surface (Fig. 11.15), the forces on the sides will balance out, since pressure is the same at any horizontal level. The pressure P_2 below the object must, however, be greater than the pressure P_1 above it.

For an object height h in a liquid of density ρ, the pressure difference

■ $\qquad P_2 - P_1 = \rho g h$

The upthrust force is equal to the pressure difference multiplied by the base area of the object (Force = Pressure × Area)

$$\text{Force} = (P_2 - P_1)A = A(\rho g h)$$

but $A \times h$ is the volume of the object

$$\text{Force} = \rho g \text{ (Volume)}$$

and since Volume × Density = Mass of liquid

■ $\qquad$ Force = Mass × g

■ $\qquad$ Force = Weight of liquid equivalent to the volume of the object immersed

i.e.

Upthrust force =
$\qquad$ Weight of liquid displaced by the object

This is known as **Archimedes principle**. See also "Extension materials".
An object will float if the upthrust force is equal to its own weight. This means that if a large enough weight of liquid can be displaced (e.g. by a liner) then an object will float.

7 ▶ PRESSURE AND VOLUME OF GASES – BOYLE'S LAW

❝ This idea is often used in experimental work with fluids. Volume = Area × length of tube ∴ If area is constant Volume ∝ length of tube. Make sure you understand this use of proportionality in drawing graphs. ❞

The molecular explanation of pressure and volume changes in a gas is discussed in Chapter 10. This section is concerned with the large-scale behaviour of a gas. One laboratory version of an apparatus to investigate pressure and volume changes is shown in Fig. 11.16. Air is enclosed in a thick-walled tube by a light oil. The tube is attached to a centimetre scale. By pumping air above the oil in the reservoir, pressure is transmitted through the oil and the air in the tube can be compressed. The pressure is recorded on the Bourdon pressure gauge.

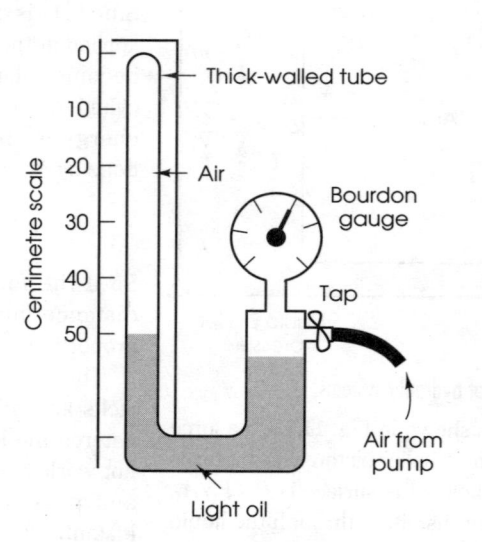

Fig. 11.16 Boyle's law apparatus.

Since the tube is of uniform cross-section the volume of gas trapped in the tube is proportional to the length of gas read from the scale.

The pressure is increased in stages and the length of gas (proportional to volume) is recorded. The tap on the reservoir enables the pressure to be reduced and a "check" set of readings can be taken as the pressure is reduced.

A graph of pressure against "volume" (or length of air) shows the pattern of Fig. 11.17, i.e. volume decreases as pressure increases. This is an inverse relationship. If now the pressure is plotted against inverse volume (1/volume) the graph is a straight line (Fig. 11.18), i.e.

■ $\qquad \text{Pressure} \propto \dfrac{1}{\text{Volume}}$

or

■ $\qquad$ Pressure × Volume = Constant

This is described as "Boyle's law". It holds true at normal pressures provided that the mass of gas remains constant, and the temperature remains constant. If a gas at pressure P_1 and volume V_1 has its volume changed to V_2, the pressure will change to P_2. Since

$$\text{Pressure} \times \text{Volume} = \text{Constant}$$

Then

■ $\qquad P_1 V_1 = P_2 V_2$

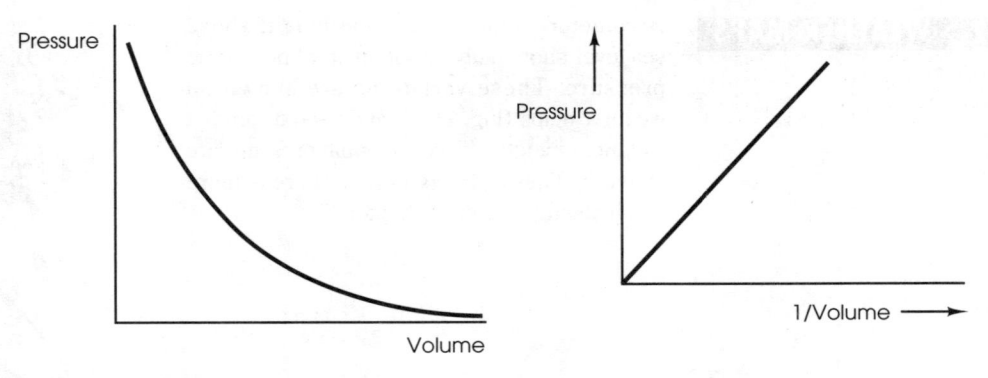

Fig. 11.17 Variation of pressure and volume.

Fig. 11.18 Pressure ∝ 1/volume.

EXAMPLE 2

A gas at 76 cm of mercury pressure occupies a volume of 2 litres. What pressure is required to reduce the volume to 0.25 litres?
Using

$$P_1 V_1 = P_2 V_2$$

$$76 \times 2 = P_2 \times 0.25$$

$$P_2 = 608 \text{ cm mercury}$$

(Notice that provided the units are consistent on both sides of the equation there is no need to convert to the SI system.)

EXTENSION MATERIALS

1> ANEROID BAROMETER AND ALTIMETER

This consists of a thin-walled metal box, the air inside of which has been partly removed, leaving low-pressure gas inside it (Fig. 11.19). It is prevented from collapsing by a strong spring. Changes in atmospheric pressure will compress the box slightly, and if the pressure is reduced the box will recover its shape. The small movements are amplified by a lever system which moves a pointer over a scale, calibrated against a mercury barometer.

The same device can be used as an altimeter in an aircraft. The pressure of the atmosphere changes with height above sea-level and the scale can be calibrated to read height rather than pressure.

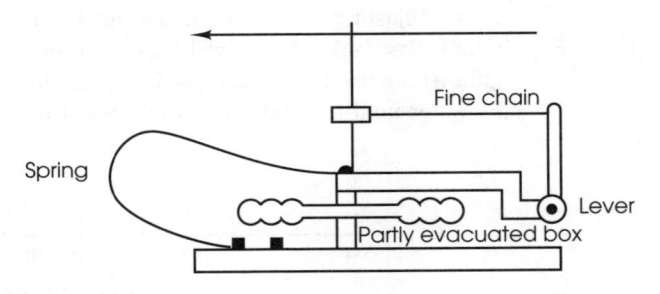

Fig. 11.19 Aneroid barometer.

2 > WEATHER MAPS

Barometers kept at the same height above sea-level show daily variation in atmospheric pressure. These variations are shown on weather maps (Fig. 11.20) and used to predict weather changes. Places of equal pressure are joined by lines called **isobars**. There is more detail about weather in chapter 17.

Fig. 11.20 Isobars on a weather map.

3 > ARCHIMEDES PRINCIPLE

Upthrust = weight of fluid displaced

This relationship was shown in section 6 and is equally true for both liquids and gases.

In many cases the weight displaced is *less* than the weight of the object and the upthrust is less than the weight of the object.

The object then moves *downwards*, e.g. a stone in water. The apparent weight of the object is still less than the real weight and when objects are recovered from underwater they seem to become much heavier as they leave the water and the upthrust is removed. You might notice this if you lift up another person in the swimming baths.

If an object displaces a weight of fluid that is *greater* than the weight of the object then the upthrust is greater than the weight of the object and it moves *upwards*. This would be the case for a cork in water or a balloon filled with hydrogen or hot air. In a few cases the weight of fluid displaced is *equal* to the weight of the object so that there is no overall force acting up or down and the object *floats* or *hovers* at the same level. A submarine can do this by adjusting the amount of air and water in its ballast tanks. A ship will float when the upthrust is equal to its weight, so it settles into the water until it displaces its own weight of water. When the ship takes on cargo it gets heavier and settles further into the water to restore the balance.

The principle is also used in a **hydrometer**. This is a small weighted float with a density scale on its side. When it is floating in a liquid it must displace its own weight of the liquid. It will sink to different depths in liquids of different density in order to do this and the density can be read from the liquid level on its scale. The scale is not uniform (i.e. not equally spaced) and will have smaller values at the top.

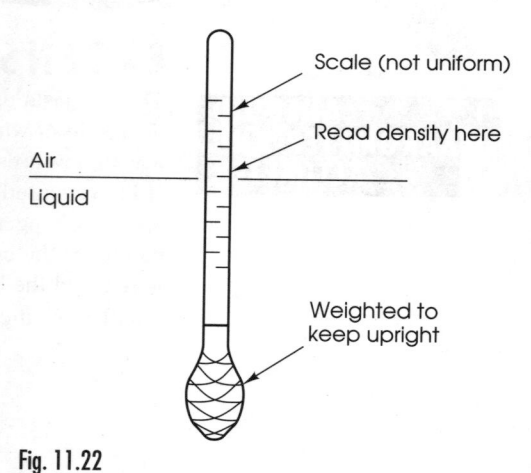

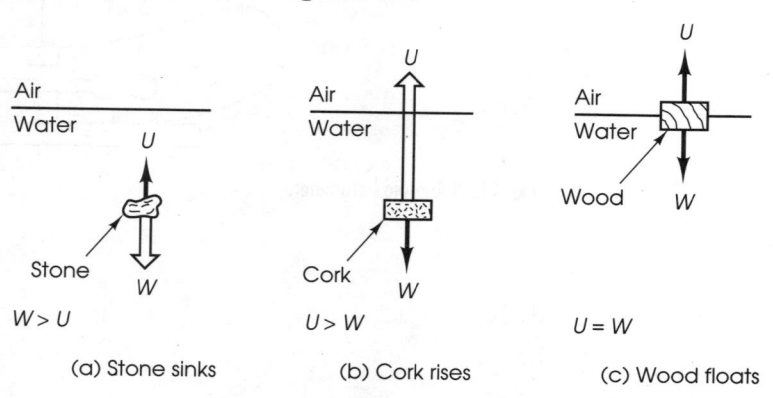

Fig. 11.22

Fig. 11.21

(a) Stone sinks W > U
(b) Cork rises U > W
(c) Wood floats U = W

4 FLUID FLOW AND PRESSURE

When a fluid passes through a narrower tube its velocity increases and its pressure gets smaller.

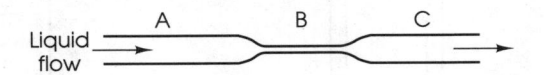

Fig. 11.23

The pressure at B in the diagram will be less than that at A or C.

If you blow between the two sheets of paper in Fig. 11.24 they move towards each other because of the reduced pressure between them. The idea that the faster flowing stream of fluid has a lower pressure is called **Bernoulli's Principle**.

Fig. 11.24

Paper strips in still air

Paper strips with air flow between them

5 PRINCIPLES OF FLIGHT

An aeroplane will be subject to four basic forces: **thrust** (T), **drag** (D), **lift** (L) and **weight** (W).

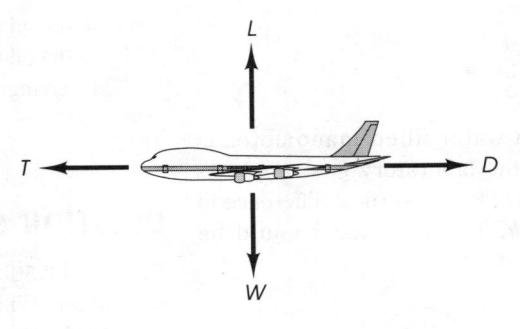

Fig. 11.25

For level flight at constant velocity the forces must be in equilibrium so that thrust = drag and lift = weight. Forward acceleration will happen when thrust > drag and the aeroplane will rise when lift > weight.

The forward thrust will usually be obtained from the engines and drag is the result of the air resistance and **turbulence** in the air behind. Streamlining reduces the drag by making the turbulence less. The weight is caused, as always, by the pull of gravity on the mass of the plane.

Lift is produced by the shape of the wing and its angle into the air (called the **angle of attack**). The shape of the wing causes the air flow above the wing to be faster than that below so that the pressure is less above the wing obeying Bernoulli's principle. If the wing has a large enough surface area the pressure difference will produce the required lift.

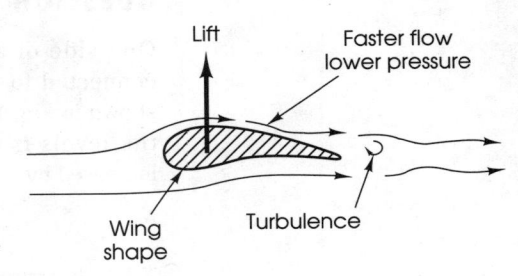

Fig. 11.26

Increasing the angle of attack increases lift until it reaches about 15° when the pressure lowering effect suddenly starts to disappear. This is called **stalling** and is caused by a sudden increase in turbulence.

A glider will normally get its thrust by falling fast enough to overcome drag. A glider can also get lift by being in a rising current of warm air (a **thermal**). It can then also get thrust by falling forward *relative to the rising air* so that drag is overcome without a loss of height.

EXAMINATION QUESTIONS

MULTIPLE CHOICE QUESTIONS

QUESTION 1

The instrument shown in Fig. 11.27 is used to measure gas pressure. It is called a

A Barometer
B Bourdon gauge
C Manometer
D Thermometer

(SEG)

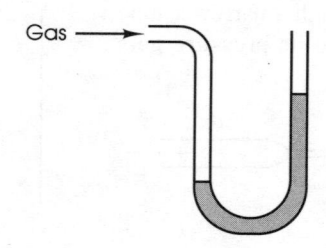

Fig. 11.27

QUESTION 2

Pressure can be calculated from

A $\dfrac{\text{Mass}}{\text{Area}}$ D $\dfrac{\text{Force}}{\text{Volume}}$

B $\dfrac{\text{Force}}{\text{Area}}$ E $\dfrac{\text{Force}}{\text{Density}}$

C $\dfrac{\text{Mass}}{\text{Volume}}$ (ULEAC)

QUESTION 3

One side of a water-filled manometer is connected to the laboratory gas supply as shown in Fig. 11.28. The vertical difference in the levels is h. The distance h could be increased by

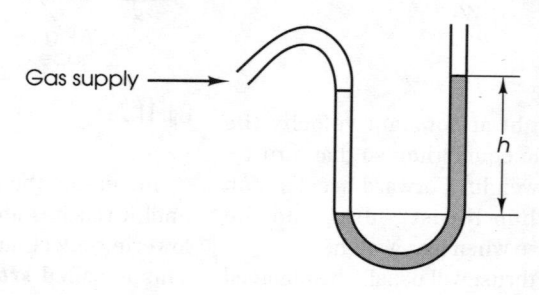

Fig. 11.28

A Use of an oil of lower density than water
B Use of mercury instead of water
C Tilting the tube clockwise
D Tilting the tube anticlockwise.
E Increasing the cross-sectional area of the tube.   (ULEAC)

QUESTION 4

If a mercury barometer is taken to the top of a mountain the level of mercury in the tube will fall provided that the temperature remains constant. This is because the

A Tube expands
B Tube contracts
C Mercury weighs more
D Air pressure decreases
E Force of gravity increases   (ULEAC)

QUESTION 5

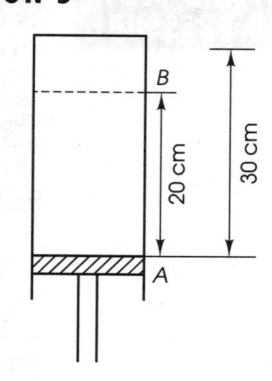

Fig. 11.29

Figure 11.29 shows a piston and a cylinder, of such a design that trapped air cannot pass the piston. The top of the piston moves from A to B, without affecting the temperature of the enclosed air. As a result of this, the air pressure is

A Reduced to a third   D Doubled
B Reduced to a half   E Trebled
C Unchanged   (ULEAC)

QUESTION 6

Figure 11.30 shows a simple mercury barometer. Which one of the distances A–E should be measured to determine the atmospheric pressure?

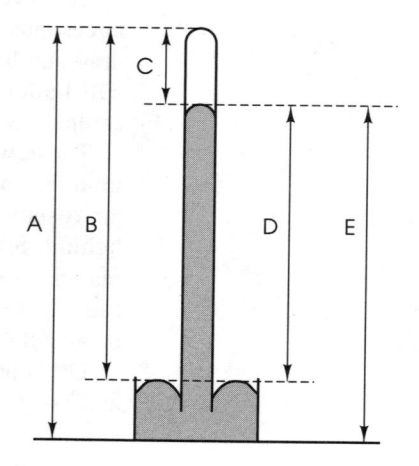

Fig. 11.30

QUESTION 7

An empty aerosol can may "explode" if left in strong sunlight, because the molecules inside

A Are attracted towards each other
B Collide more frequently with each other
C Collide more frequently with the walls
D Completely fill the can   (ULEAC)

STRUCTURED QUESTIONS

QUESTION 8

(a) Figure 11.31(a) shows a mercury barometer.
  (i) What is the average value of the height H above sea-level? (1 line)
  (ii) Why is it important that the space above the mercury contains no air? (2 lines)
  (iii) Explain why the diameter of the tube does not affect H. (3 lines)

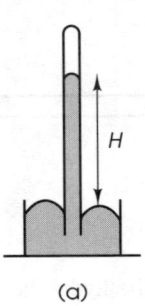

Fig. 11.31

(b) Figure 11.31(b) shows an aneroid barometer.
  (i) What is part Z? (1 line)
  (ii) What is the purpose of part Z? (2 lines)

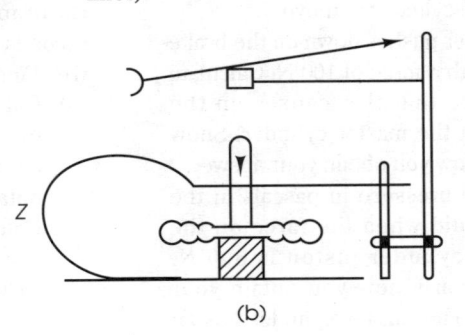

(c) While washing up, a boy lifted a tumbler full of water to the position shown in Fig. 11.31(c). Explain why the water stayed in the glass. (2 lines)

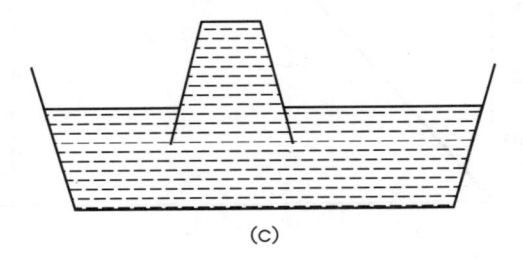

(d) A motorist attached her wing-mirror to the windscreen of her car with a suction disc as shown in Fig. 11.31(d).
  (i) Explain what holds the disc to the body of the car. (1 line)
  (ii) In hot sunshine the car was parked in the sun. The mirror and disc fell from the screen. Suggest two reasons for this. (4 lines) (ULEAC)

QUESTION 9

(a) (i) Draw a labelled diagram of the apparatus you would use to show that the atmosphere exerts a pressure.
  (ii) Explain how you would carry out the experiment.
  (iii) Explain carefully how the experiment shows that the atmosphere exerts a pressure.

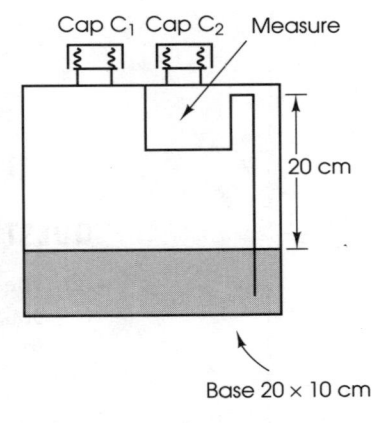

Fig. 11.32

(b) Figure 11.32 shows a plastic container for liquid fertiliser as used by gardeners. The container has a built-in measure so that the liquid can easily be used in the correct amount. (Throughout the question you are to assume that the density of the liquid is the same as that of water.) In order to fill the measure, the sides of the container are squeezed.
  (i) State which of C_1 and C_2 should be tightly closed at this stage. (1 line)
  (ii) Explain why. (2 lines)
  (iii) Calculate how much extra pressure, measured in pascals (over and above atmospheric), will be needed in the container in order to fill it with liquid. (3 lines)
  (Use $g = 10$ m/s^2 and density of water = 1000 kg/m^3.)
  (iv) Name the type of energy the liquid would gain by being pushed up into the measure. (1 line)
  (v) In fact the person squeezing the container in order to fill the measure would probably have to supply more energy than that accounted for in (iv) above. Give a reason for this. (3 lines)

(c) Suppose the container shown in Fig. 11.32 has a negligible weight and contains 2 litres of liquid. Given the dimension of the container as shown in Fig. 11.32, calculate the pressure which it exerts on the ground. (4 lines)
(Use $g = 10$ m/s^2 and density of water = 1000 kg/m^3 or 1 kg/l.) (ULEAC)

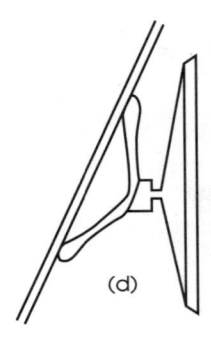

CHAPTER 11 PRESSURE AND HYDRAULICS

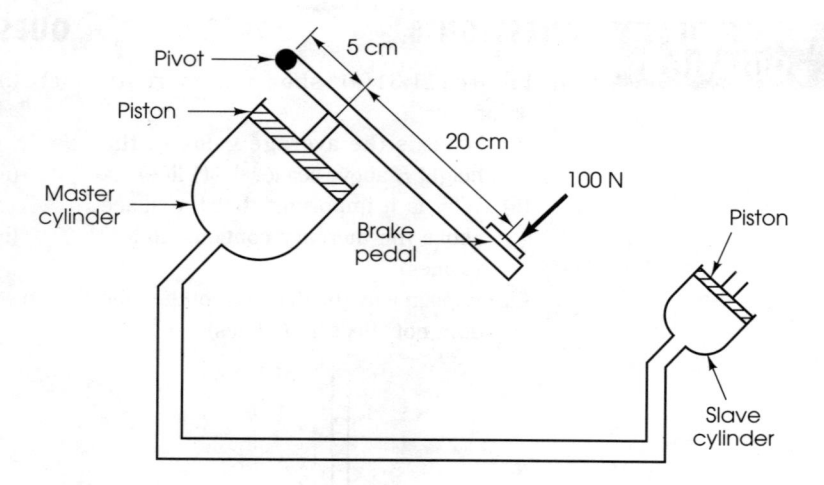

Fig. 11.33

QUESTION 10

(a) The diagram shows part of the hydraulic braking system of a motor car.
   (i) Mark with an arrow, on the diagram, the direction in which the piston in the slave cylinder moves when the driver presses down on the brake pedal.
   (ii) Explain why the downward force on the brake pedal causes the piston in the slave cylinder to move.
   (iii) The driver pushes down on the brake pedal with a force of 100 N. Calculate the force that this causes on the piston in the master cylinder. Show clearly how you obtain your answer.
   (iv) Find the pressure in pascals in the brake fluid when the force on the master cylinder piston is 300 N. Show clearly how you obtain your answer. The master cylinder has an area of 20 cm².
   (v) The piston in the master cylinder has an area 10 times that of the piston in the slave cylinder. What is the force on the slave cylinder piston when the force on the master cylinder piston is 300 N? Show clearly how you obtain your answer.

(b) The graph below shows the motion of a car of mass 1000 kg over a period of 30 seconds.
   (i) Find the acceleration of the car.
   (ii) Calculate the resultant force acting on this car to produce this acceleration. Show clearly how you obtain your answer.
   (iii) Calculate the average speed of the car over the 30 seconds. Show clearly how you obtain your answer.
                                                       (NICCEA)

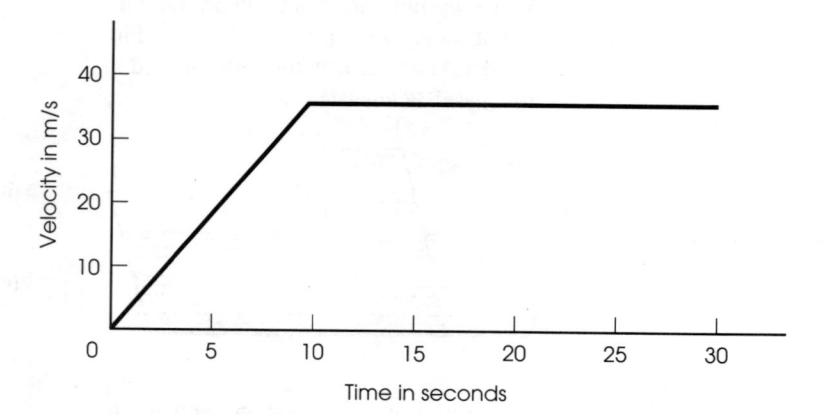

Fig. 11.34

ANSWERS TO EXAMINATION QUESTIONS

MULTIPLE CHOICE QUESTIONS

Question	1	2	3	4	5	6	7
Answer	C	B	A	D	E	D	C

STRUCTURED QUESTIONS

ANSWER 8

(a) (i) The average height H = 76 cm (0.76 m).
    (ii) If air is present, pressure will be exerted on the top of the mercury column, which will reduce the height which can be supported by the atmospheric pressure and give a reading which is too small.
    (iii) Pressure is the same at all points on the same horizontal level. The mercury in the tube is balancing the pressure of the atmosphere on the top of the mercury in the trough. The area does not matter. (Or pressure = $\rho g h$ – does not concern area.)

(b) (i) Z is a strong spring.
    (ii) It prevents the can from collapsing and restores it to its original shape if pressure falls.

(c) Atmospheric pressure pushing on the water surface is greater than the pressure below the column of water in the tumbler.

(d) (i) When the suction disc is pressed on to the car body some air escapes below the pad. Under the pad the air pressure is therefore reduced, so atmospheric pressure outside the pad holds it to the body of the car.
    (ii) Air under the pad gains kinetic energy. The volume is restricted so the pressure rises until it is equal to or above atmospheric pressure. The car body expands, allowing air under the rubber pad, and restoring pressure.

ANSWER 9

(a) This part will depend on your choice of experiment. There is no one correct answer, but parts (ii) and (iii) must refer to the diagram in part (i).

(b) (i) C_1 must be closed.
    (ii) Otherwise squeezing the can will simply expel air from C_1 and have no effect on the liquid.
    (iii) Pressure = Height × density × g

$$= 0.2 \times 1000 \times 10$$
$$(0.2 \text{ m} = 20 \text{ cm})$$
$$= \underline{2000 \text{ Pa}}$$

    (iv) (Gravitational) Potential energy.
    (v) Energy will be needed to deform the plastic can.

(c)
$$\text{Pressure} = \frac{\text{Force}}{\text{Area}} = \frac{\text{Weight of liquid}}{\text{Area}}$$

$$= \frac{2 \times 10}{0.2 \times 0.1} = \underline{1000 \text{ Pa}}$$

ANSWER 10

This is a further level question.

(a) (i) An arrow on the diagram near the slave cylinder pointing outwards.
    (ii) The liquid transmits pressure from master cylinder to slave cylinder because the liquid cannot be compressed.
    (iii) Take moments about the pivot (see chapter 3)

$$25 \times 100 = 5 \times F$$
$$F = \underline{500 \text{ N}}$$

    (iv) $\text{Pressure} = \dfrac{\text{Force}}{\text{Area}} = \dfrac{300}{20}$

$$= \underline{15 \text{ N/cm}^2}$$
$$(= 15 \times 10\,000 = 150\,000 \text{ Pa})$$

    (v) Force = Pressure × Area
$$= 15 \times 2 = \underline{30 \text{ N}}$$

(b) (i) $\text{Acceleration} = \dfrac{\text{Change in velocity}}{\text{Time taken}}$

$$= \frac{35}{10} = \underline{3.5 \text{ m/s}^2}$$

    (ii) Force = Mass × Acceleration (See chapter 5)
$$= 1000 \times 3.5 = \underline{3500 \text{ N}}$$

    (iii) Distance moved
$$= 0.5 \times 10 \times 35 + 20 \times 35$$
$$= \underline{875 \text{ m}}$$

$$\text{Average speed} = \frac{\text{Distance travelled}}{\text{Time}}$$

$$= \frac{875}{30} = \underline{29.2 \text{ m/s.}}$$

Note how some questions can include work from several topics.

STUDENT'S ANSWER WITH THE EXAMINER'S COMMENTS

STUDENT ANSWER TO QUESTION 9

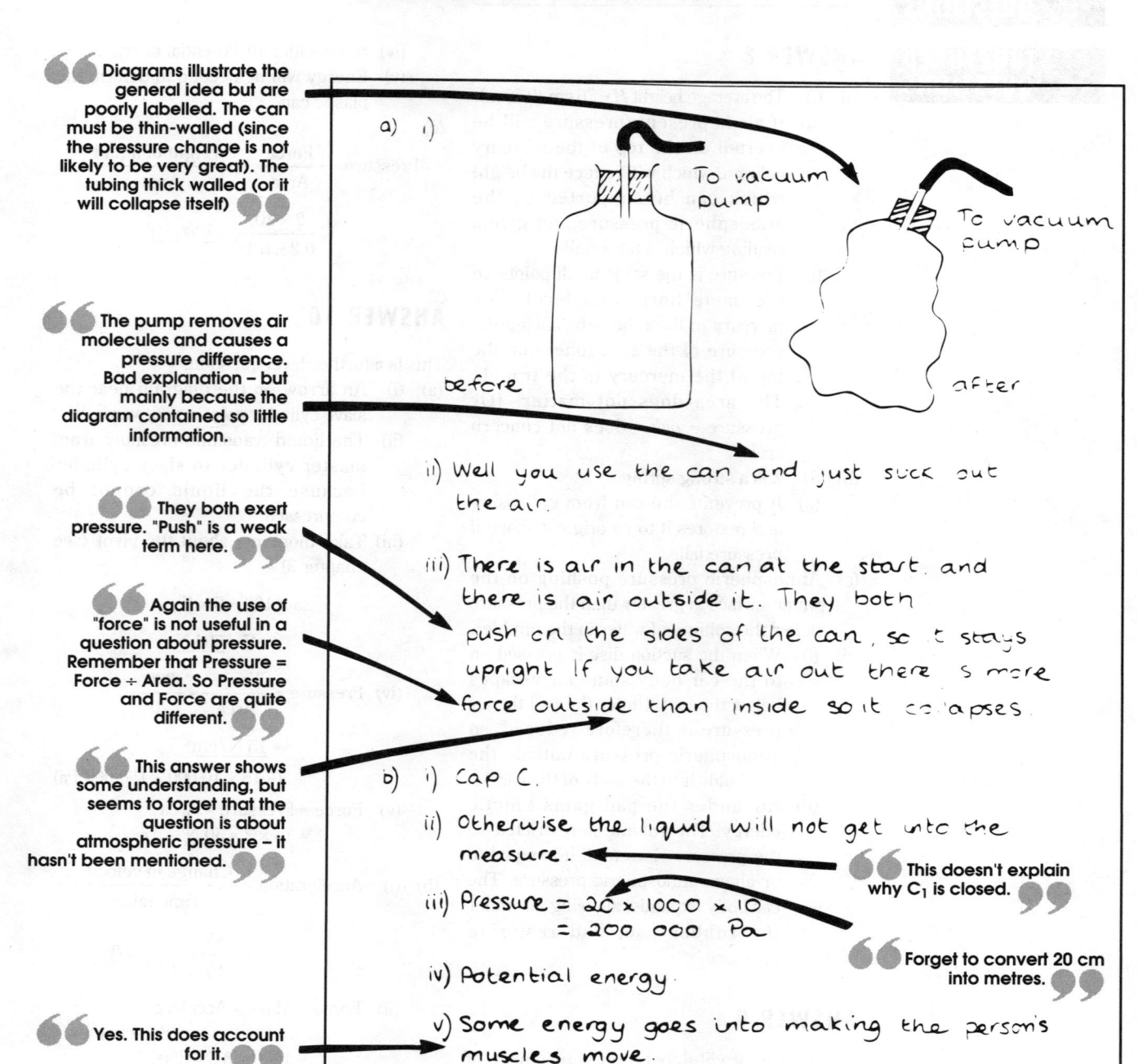

> **Diagrams illustrate the general idea but are poorly labelled. The can must be thin-walled (since the pressure change is not likely to be very great). The tubing thick walled (or it will collapse itself)**

a) i) [Diagram: "before" shows an upright can with tubing labelled "To vacuum pump"; "after" shows a crumpled can with tubing labelled "To vacuum pump"]

> **The pump removes air molecules and causes a pressure difference. Bad explanation – but mainly because the diagram contained so little information.**

ii) Well you use the can and just suck out the air.

> **They both exert pressure. "Push" is a weak term here.**

> **Again the use of "force" is not useful in a question about pressure. Remember that Pressure = Force ÷ Area. So Pressure and Force are quite different.**

iii) There is air in the can at the start, and there is air outside it. They both push on the sides of the can, so it stays upright. If you take air out there's more force outside than inside so it collapses.

> **This answer shows some understanding, but seems to forget that the question is about atmospheric pressure – it hasn't been mentioned.**

b) i) Cap C.

ii) Otherwise the liquid will not get into the measure.

> **This doesn't explain why C₁ is closed.**

iii) Pressure = 20 × 1000 × 10
           = 200 000 Pa

> **Forget to convert 20 cm into metres.**

iv) Potential energy.

> **Yes. This does account for it.**

v) Some energy goes into making the person's muscles move.

> **Lucky to get the right answer. Wiser to show the steps in a calculation.**

c) Pressure = force ÷ area
           = 1000 Pa

REVIEW SHEET

- Complete the equations

    Pressure =   Pressure in a liquid =

- The pressure of the gas supply can be measured with a _____.

- Atmospheric pressure can be measured using a _____.

- Boyle's law states that _____
  _____
  _____

- In a hydraulic system the pressure is the _____ under each piston. If the areas are different then the _____ will be different on each piston. The piston that has the largest _____ on it will also have the largest _____ but will move through a smaller distance so that the work done at each piston is the same.

- When a bubble expands to twice its original volume the pressure inside it will _____ provided that the _____ stays the same.

- A stone will sink in water because its weight is greater than _____.

- When a hot air balloon stays at a constant height its weight will be equal to the _____.

- Pressure in a fluid acts in all _____.

- A standard atmosphere pressure is the same as _____ mm of mercury.

- A pressure of 1 N/m² is called 1 _____.

- A man who weighs 700 N stands on an area of 200 cm². The pressure caused is _____ N/cm² or _____ Pa.

- What depth of water will have the same pressure as one atmosphere? (*Hints* – remember the depth of mercury that has the same pressure as one atmosphere and that mercury is 13.6 times as dense as water.)

- Briefly explain why ladies with high-heeled shoes are sometimes banned from rooms with wooden floors.
  _____
  _____
  _____

- An isobar is a line which joins _____
  _____.

- Describe an experiment which will show that the pressure of the atmosphere is large.
  _____
  _____
  _____
  _____

- Name the four forces that act on an aeroplane

    1. _____   2. _____
    3. _____   4. _____

- What do you understand by "Boyle's Law"?
  _____
  _____
  _____
  _____

- Draw a graph to show how pressure varies with volume

- Upthrust = _____.

- Using the idea of "upthrust" explain why each of the following occurs, using a diagram in each case

  a) A stone sinks

  b) A cork rises

  c) Wood floats

- Explain the workings of a *hydrometer*, using a diagram

- What must be true to achieve level flight at constant velocity?
  _____
  _____

CHAPTER 17

HEAT ENERGY

GETTING STARTED

Changes of temperature have a considerable effect on the behaviour of materials, and many aspects of design have to take account of fluctuations in temperature. A temperature change indicates that heat energy has either flowed into or out of a material. There is a clear distinction between the ideas of heat and temperature. Heat is an *energy form*, like kinetic and potential energy, or electricity. Temperature is a measure of the kinetic energy of the particles of the material and gives an indication of the direction in which heat energy will flow – usually from high temperature to low temperature. This section deals with the distinction between heat and temperature, and with the ways in which the properties of solids, liquids and gases are changed by heating.

TEMPERATURE SCALES

EFFECTS OF HEAT ON SOLIDS AND LIQUIDS

EFFECTS OF TEMPERATURE CHANGE ON GASES

SPECIFIC HEAT CAPACITY

LATENT HEAT

CONVECTION, CONDUCTION AND RADIATION

THE GREENHOUSE EFFECT

THE GENERAL GAS EQUATION

HEAT INSULATION

EXPANSION OF LIQUIDS

U – VALUES

EXPANSIVITY

ESSENTIAL PRINCIPLES

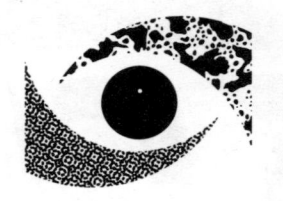

1. TEMPERATURE SCALES

> *A common error is to suggest that the particles themselves expand. This of course is silly. They take up more space because they are moving faster.*

Any property of a material can be used as a thermometric property, provided that it varies in a ***uniform*** way. The most common property used is the ***expansion of a liquid***, like mercury or alcohol, in a uniform glass tube. However, the ***pressure changes of a gas***, the ***resistance changes of a metal*** and ***thermoelectric EMF in a thermocouple***, are all suitable changes for measuring temperature. Apart from a property which is temperature-dependent, two fixed points are required in defining a temperature scale. The most common are:

1. The freezing-point of pure water, 0 °C.
2. The boiling-point of pure water, 100 °C, at a fixed pressure (76 cm mercury).

The values 0 °C and 100 °C are arbitrary. It is convenient to adopt a scale of 100 intervals. To calibrate a thermometer, the lower fixed point 0 °C is marked when the thermometer is placed in pure melting ice; the ice must be pure since impurities lower its melting-point (Fig. 12.1). The upper fixed point, which is correctly called the steam point, is the temperature of steam ***just above*** the surface of boiling water. The thermometer bulb is not placed in the water because impurities raise the boiling-point. Equally the pressure above the water must be 76 cm of mercury since pressure changes affect the temperature at which water boils (Fig. 12.2). The interval between the fixed points is then divided into 100 equal parts (degrees).

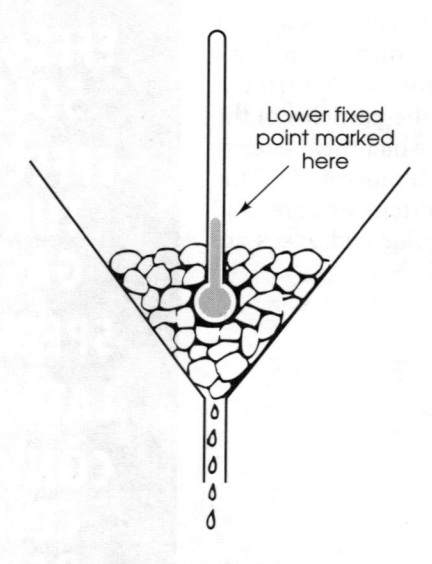

Fig. 12.1 Determining the lower fixed point.

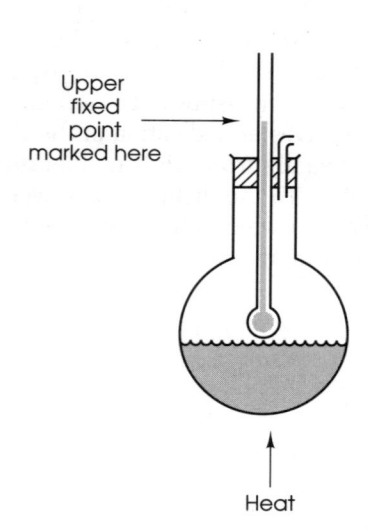

Fig. 12.2 Determining the upper fixed point.

2. EFFECTS OF HEAT ON SOLIDS AND LIQUIDS

The most obvious effect is ***expansion***. Solids and liquids expand on heating because more energy is applied to their particles, which in turn respond by increasing their kinetic energy. This results in the bulk of the solid or liquid taking up a ***larger volume***. (The particles themselves do not expand, but since they are moving faster they occupy more space.)

Solids only expand a little with each °C temperature increase, and liquids expand rather more than solids. A useful application of ***solid*** expansion is a ***bimetal strip***. This consists of two metals welded together, which have different expansions for a given rise in temperature. Copper and iron are often used. Copper expands more for a given temperature

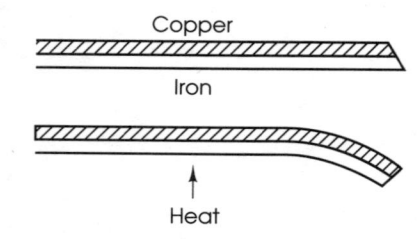

Fig. 12.3 A bimetallic strip.

rise than does iron. On heating, the strip therefore curves, as shown in Fig. 12.3. This property can be used to make or break a contact in an electrical circuit.

The circuit in Fig. 12.4 would act as a fire alarm, the bimetal strip bending to complete the circuit when the temperature rises. Similarly, bimetal strips can "break" a circuit, and as such are used in thermostats.

Melting and *evaporation* are also associated with the heating of solids and liquids. These are dealt with in Chapter 10 when considering kinetic theory.

Liquids expand much more than solids for similar temperature rises.

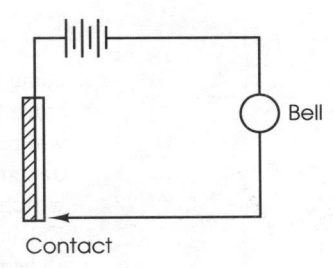

Fig. 12.4 Bimetallic strip as a fire alarm.

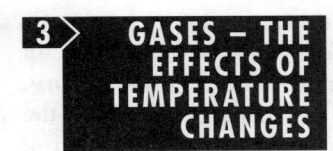

3 > GASES – THE EFFECTS OF TEMPERATURE CHANGES

Temperature changes cause larger effects in gases than in solids or liquids because the particles are so mobile. Heat energy applied to a gas sample will always change the kinetic energy of the particles, but the effect of this change will depend on the conditions which apply to the gas. Assuming that the mass of gas is constant, there are two *extreme* situations:

1. Keeping the *volume fixed* – in which case the pressure of the gas will increase as the temperature rises.
2. Keeping the *pressure fixed* – in which case the volume of gas will increase as the temperature rises.

The molecular explanation of these effects is again dealt with in Chapter 10.

(a) WITH A FIXED VOLUME OF GAS

Here there will be a change in *pressure* if the *temperature* rises. A suitable apparatus to investigate this is shown in Fig. 12.5. A water bath is used to heat a flask of air. The temperature of the water bath is the same as the air in the flask, and is recorded on a thermometer. Pressure changes of the gas are recorded on the Bourdon gauge. The temperature can be raised in suitable steps, about 10–20 °C, and the pressure recorded. When the water reaches boiling-point, allow the apparatus to cool and during cooling take a second set of readings of pressure at each temperature selected. A mean value of pressure can be found from these two sets of readings. A graph can be drawn of *pressure* against *temperature*. It will look like that in Fig. 12.6. The graph shows that there is a numerical relationship between the pressure and the temperature of the gas at constant

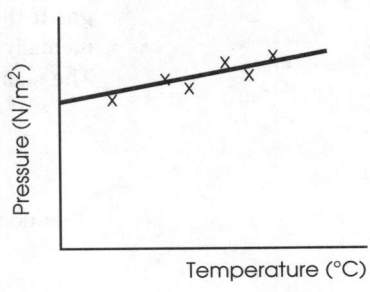

Fig. 12.6 Variation of gas pressure with temperature.

volume. This relationship is *not* a proportional one – the graph does not pass through point (0, 0) – and this means that a doubled temperature change will *not* give a doubled pressure change. "Proportion" means that when one quantity changes in a particular way, another quantity changes in the same way (doubling one thing causes the doubling of another). This would also mean that a graph of the two quantities must pass through (0, 0). Of course temperature, on the Celsius scale, is a number chosen in an arbitrary manner, assigning 0 °C as the temperature at which pure ice melts. Since the value is assigned in this manner it is little wonder that other materials behave in rather different ways.

The axis of the pressure and temperature graph is placed where it is because the zero of temperature is taken as the melting-point of ice. However, a more rational "zero" for temperature in this context is where the *pressure of a gas is zero*, and where the molecules stop moving. If the experimental

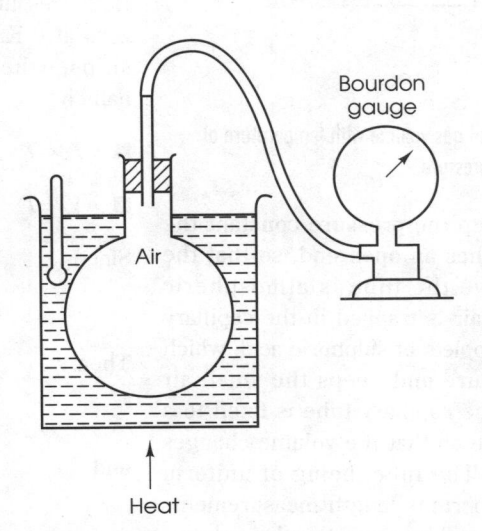

Fig. 12.5 Variation of gas pressure with temperature at constant volume.

graph is taken to *this* point it is found to be at −273 °C. This is called absolute zero – there being no movement of particles at this temperature (Fig. 12.7). This temperature – the point where particles have no kinetic energy – is designated the zero of the "Absolute scale" which is named after its discoverer, Lord Kelvin. The point −273 °C is called 0 K (zero Kelvin): the ° sign is left out because there is no decision to be made about where "zero" is, since it is the same for *all* materials.

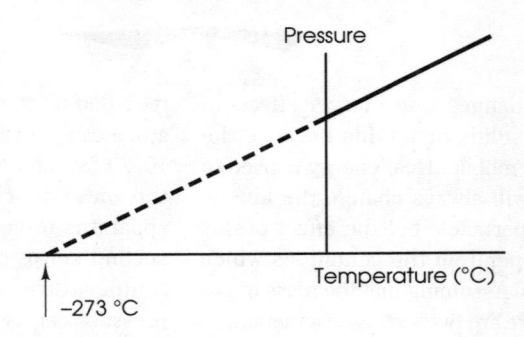

Fig. 12.7

(b) WITH A FIXED PRESSURE

Here there will be a change in *volume* of the gas if the temperature rises. This is experimentally much more difficult to demonstrate. The standard apparatus is shown in Fig. 12.8.

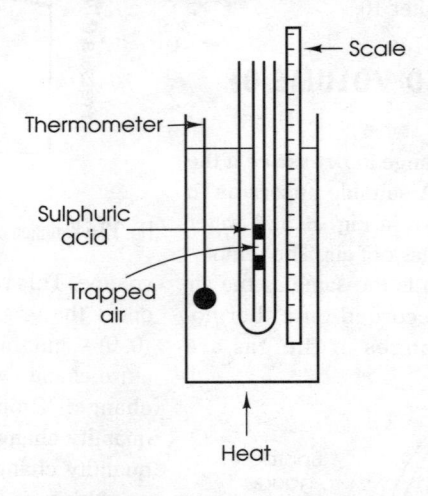

Fig. 12.8 Variation of gas volume with temperature at constant pressure.

In order to keep the pressure constant the capillary tube has an open end, so that the pressure above the tube is atmospheric pressure. The air is trapped in the capillary tube by two droplets of sulphuric acid, which absorbs moisture and keeps the small air sample dry. The capillary tube is fixed to a millimetre scale so that the volume changes can be noted. The tube, being of uniform cross-section, permits length measurements to be made that will be proportional to volume.

The *temperature* is raised by heating the water bath and the corresponding change in length (and therefore volume) of the air column is noted. This is done both on *raising* the temperature, and on *cooling*, giving two sets of readings from which the *mean* value is taken. A graph plotted of *volume* against *temperature* gives the pattern of Fig. 12.9. This is similar to the pressure and temperature graph and it would again cut the temperature axis at −273 °C if it were extrapolated (taken further back), as in Fig. 12.10. The absolute zero of temperature is −273 °C or 0 K.

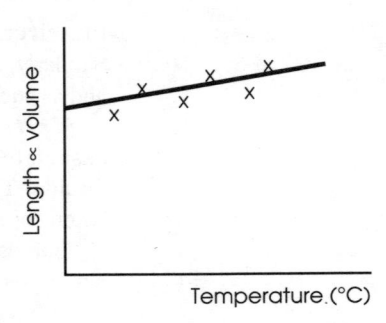

Fig. 12.9

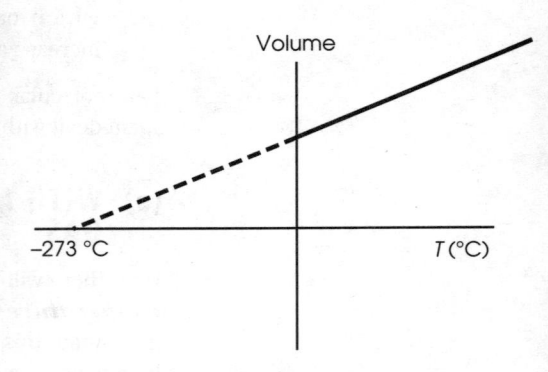

Fig. 12.10

Both pressure and volume of an ideal gas are zero at 0 K. This leads to the two relationships, where ∝ means *proportional*, namely:

- $P \propto T$ (measured in kelvins)
- $V \propto T$ (measured in kelvins)

Since

$$0 \text{ K} = -273 \text{ °C}$$

Then

$$0 \text{ °C} = +273 \text{ K}$$

and

$$100 \text{ °C} = +373 \text{ K}$$

The volume/temperature and pressure/temperature relationships can also be expressed as

Charles' Law

$$\frac{V_1}{V_2} = \frac{T_1}{T_2}$$

(if mass and pressure constant and temperature is in kelvins)

The Pressure Law

$$\frac{P_1}{P_2} = \frac{T_1}{T_2}$$

(if mass and volume constant and temperature is in kelvins)

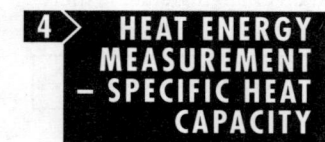

4 HEAT ENERGY MEASUREMENT – SPECIFIC HEAT CAPACITY

The difference between "heat" and "temperature" has already been discussed. It is clear that if 100 W of power (energy per second) is applied to a small mass and to a large mass, then the *smaller mass* will show a *larger temperature* change, although the heat energy applied to both masses will be the same (Fig. 12.11).

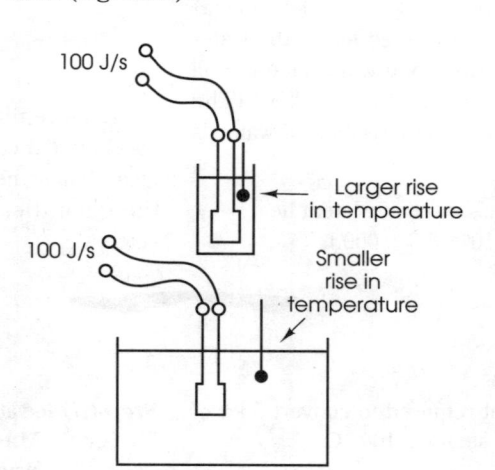

Fig. 12.11 Heat energy depends on mass.

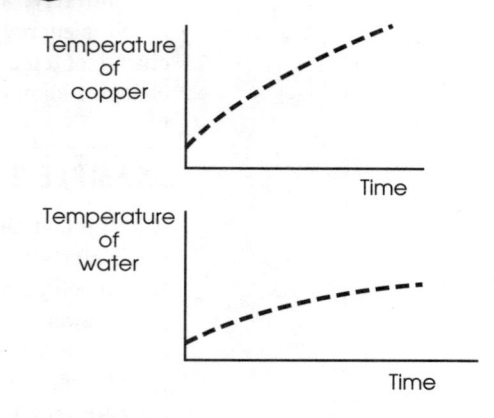

Fig. 12.12

Apart from the effect of mass, the *material* also affects the way in which added joules of heat energy change the temperature of an object. If 1 kg of *copper*, in the form of a solid block, and 1 kg of *water* are both heated with the same immersion heater, supplying the same power over the same time, then the temperature changes will work rather like those in Fig. 12.12. The two materials have *different* heat capacities – the same energy supply causes a different temperature change. This suggests that a change in heat energy depends on the *mass* of material heated, the *temperature* rise produced and a factor which depends on the *type of material*. This factor is called the **specific heat capacity** of the material. It is defined as **the heat energy required to raise the temperature of 1 kg of the material by 1 °C or 1 K**.

The specific heat capacity of *water* is 4200 joules per kilogram per kelvin (J/kg K). This means that 4200 J of energy are needed to raise the temperature of 1 kg of water by 1 degree (Celsius or Kelvin). The specific heat capacity of *copper* is 380 J/kg K. This means that only 380 J of energy are needed to raise the temperature of 1 kg of copper by 1 degree (Celsius or Kelvin).

The *measurement* of specific heat capacity is dealt with in "Extension Materials". However, a few sample calculations should illustrate the idea.

EXAMPLE 1

A tank contains 160 kg of cold water at 20 °C. Calculate (a) the energy needed to raise the temperature of the water to 60 °C, and (b) the time this will take using a 5 kW electric immersion heater.

(a) The specific heat capacity of water is 4200 J/kg K.

To raise 1 kg by 1 °C needs 4200 J

To raise 160 kg by 40 °C needs 160 × 4200 × 40

Energy required = 26 880 000 J

This part of the example introduces a simple equation for finding heat energy changes:

Heat energy = Mass × specific heat capacity × change in temperature

(It applies to heat gained by a mass, or to heat lost from it.)

(b) A 5 kW heater provides 5000 J/s. Since 26 880 000 J are needed, then

$$\text{Time} = \frac{26\,880\,000}{5000} = 5376 \text{ s}$$

(which is about 1½ h).

5 > LATENT HEAT

When a solid melts to form a liquid, it undergoes the change of state *without* any temperature change. All the energy supplied goes to breaking bonds in the solid. The energy required to convert 1 kg of a solid at its melting-point into liquid, without any change of temperature, is called the ***specific latent heat of fusion*** of the solid.

Similarly, a liquid at its boiling-point requires energy to change to a gas, without a change of temperature. The energy needed to change 1 kg of liquid at its boiling-point to gas without any temperature change is called the ***specific latent heat of vaporisation*** of the liquid. When a liquid cools and solidifies the latent heat of fusion is released as bonds re-form, which maintains the liquid–solid medium at its melting-point until all has solidified. Similarly a gas condensing gives out its latent heat of vaporisation. The energy supplied or evolved on changing state is therefore simply given by:

> **Energy = Mass × specific latent heat**

EXAMPLE 2

A kettle contains 1.6 kg of water. After the water starts to boil, the kettle is left on. (a) How much energy is needed for all the water to boil away? (b) How long will it take to boil dry if the kettle is rated as 2.5 kW. (The specific latent heat of vaporisation of water is 2.3×10^6 J/kg.)

(a) Energy = Mass × specific latent heat
= $1.6 \times 2.3 \times 10^6$ = 3 680 000 J.

(b) The kettle provides 2500 J/s. Therefore

$$\text{Time needed} = \frac{3\,680\,000}{2500} = 1472 \text{ s}$$

Some more difficult examples use both the specific heat capacity and specific latent heat ideas. These need step-by-step calculations of the quantities of energy involved at each stage.

EXAMPLE 3

Calculate the heat required to convert 5 kg of ice at –20 °C into steam at 100 °C.

Specific heat capacities: Water 4200 J/kg K
Ice 2100 J/kg K

Specific latent heat of
fusion of ice = 340 000 J/kg

Specific latent heat of
vaporisation of water = 2.3×10^6 J/kg

Step (i) Ice at –20 °C heating to 0 °C:
Energy = Mass × specific heat capacity × temperature rise
= $5 \times 2100 \times 20$ = 210 000 J

Step (ii) Ice at 0 °C turning to water at 0 °C:
Energy = Mass × specific latent heat of fusion
= $5 \times 340\,000$ = 1 700 000 J

Step (iii) Water at 0 °C heating to 100 °C:
Energy = Mass × specific heat capacity × temperature rise
= $5 \times 4200 \times 100$ = 2 100 000 J

Step (iv) Water at 100 °C changing to steam at 100 °C:
Energy = Mass × specific latent heat of vaporisation
= $5 \times 2.3 \times 10^6$ = 11 500 000 J

The total energy is the ***sum*** of steps (i)–(iv), i.e. 15 510 000 J.

6 > CONVECTION IN LIQUIDS AND GASES

This is the main method of ***transfer of heat energy*** in a fluid. A heated liquid or gas expands, so its particles occupy a greater volume than when it was cold. This in turn means that there is a ***decrease*** in density.

The effect can be seen by filling gas jars with hot and cold water, and adding a drop of dye to the hot one. With care the hot liquid can be inverted over the cold. The hot, less dense, liquid floats above the cold, denser liquid (Fig. 12.13).

If the ***reverse*** is tried, the hot, less dense liquid travels upwards, warming the cold

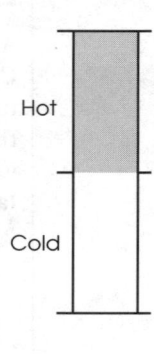

Fig. 12.13 Hot liquids are less dense than cold liquids.

liquid and giving an even temperature distribution (Fig. 12.14). This is the principle of *convection*. Hotter, less dense liquids and gases move **upwards** through colder denser fluids.

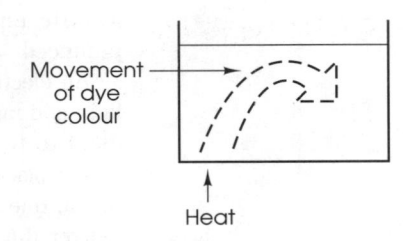

Fig. 12.15 Convection.

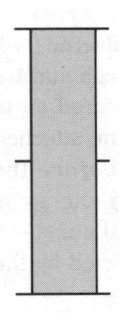

Fig. 12.14 Hot liquid floats upwards giving an even temperature distribution.

A ***convection current*** is the continuous movement of the fluids; this is usually studied by tracking the liquid movement with a few crystals of dye (Fig. 12.15). The dye shows the path of warm, less dense liquid. At the same time cooler liquid is taking its place, and the whole mass of the liquid is warmed (Fig. 12.16).

The use of a so-called "radiator" to warm a room is an example of a large-scale convection

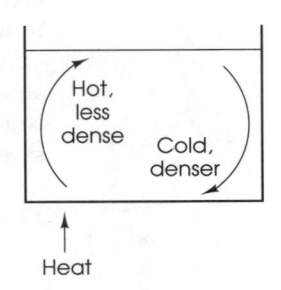

Fig. 12.16 Convection currents.

current. Near the heater, warm, less dense air rises, colder air takes its place and this is heated in turn. The heat energy is transferred ***throughout*** the room by the movement of the whole mass of air. This happens on a large scale over land masses, giving rise to convection currents called thermals, which are made use of by glider pilots.

> It is useful to be able to state typical schemes for insulating a home and the reasons why a particular method is effective.

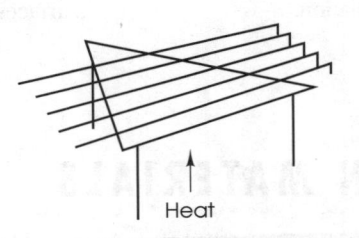

7 > CONDUCTION IN SOLIDS

Fig. 12.17 Comparison of conductivity.

Rods of different materials, heated as shown, can illustrate the idea of rates of ***conduction*** (Fig. 12.17). The rods have a matchstick sealed to one end with wax. If they are equally heated, the matchsticks fall at different times. Heat is flowing along the rods ***without the material itself moving***. This is an example of conduction. Generally, metals are good conductors, and non-metallic solids tend to ***conduct badly***, and are called ***insulators***.

The mechanism of conduction relies on the passing of kinetic energy from one vibrating particle to another, so a good conductor will have strong linkages between particles. Since the inter-particle linkages are ***not*** as strong in liquids as in solids, and are almost non-existent in gases, liquids and especially gases are very poor conductors. These properties are put to good use in house insulation – cavity walls and window double glazing make use of the insulating properties of air. The types of solid material used in loft insulation are those which are both poor conductors and which help trap a still layer of air which acts as a very effective insulating layer.

Metals have a lot of electrons which can move quite freely from one atom to another throughout the piece of material. These electrons can carry the energy quite rapidly through a metal and are the main reason why all metals are good conductors. Solids such as plastics have none of these "free" electrons and also have long molecules which are difficult to vibrate. They may be such poor conductors that the plastic will melt and burn because the heat remains concentrated in one place.

8 > HEAT RADIATION

This important mechanism of ***heat energy transfer*** does not rely on particles at all. It is the means by which we receive heat energy from the sun, across space, by means of electromagnetic waves in the infra-red region of the spectrum. The waves are ***not*** heat carriers, but their ***absorption*** by matter causes an increase in molecular kinetic energy, and a heating effect is produced.

An electric fire filament emits both visible light and invisible infra-red waves, and can be used to test two important properties. A heater placed midway between two sheets of metal, one blackened and one silvered, will deliver the same energy on to each surface (Fig. 12.18). If a metal disc is secured on to each metal sheet with wax, the one attached to the blackened sheet falls off *before* the other. This is because radiated energy is absorbed better by the blackened sheet – a large proportion of energy is reflected by the silvered one.

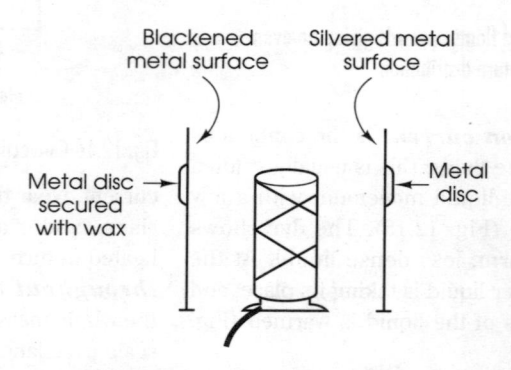

Fig. 12.18 Blackened surfaces are good absorbers of radiation.

Black and roughened surfaces are good **absorbers** of heat radiation.

Another metal sheet, but with one side silvered and the other blackened (Fig. 12.19), can be used to show another property if initially heated with Bunsen burners. The two surfaces must be at the same temperature, but the black surface emits more radiation than the silvered one.

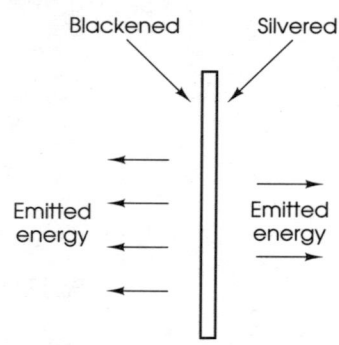

Fig. 12.19 Blackened surfaces are good emitters of radiation.

This can be simply felt by holding the hand near each surface in turn, or more precisely observed using a thermopile. Aluminium beakers filled with the same quantity of hot water from a kettle will also show this if one has been polished and the other painted dull black. The temperature of the water in the dull black container falls faster.

Black and roughened surfaces are better *emitters* of heat radiation than are silvered surfaces.

EXTENSION MATERIALS

1 MEASUREMENT OF SPECIFIC HEAT CAPACITY

The apparatus used for this determination is often a solid block of the material, drilled with holes into which can be fitted a small electrical immersion heater and a thermometer. In the case of a liquid, the liquid is placed in a well-insulated container.

METHOD

The mass of the block is found, and its initial temperature noted. The circuit is set up as shown (Fig. 12.20) and values are adjusted with the rheostat to give suitable current and PD. (The rheostat also enables these values to be held steady during the experiment.) A stop-clock is started and the current turned on for a given time – enough to give about 20 °C temperature increase. At the end of this time the current is switched off and the final temperature taken.

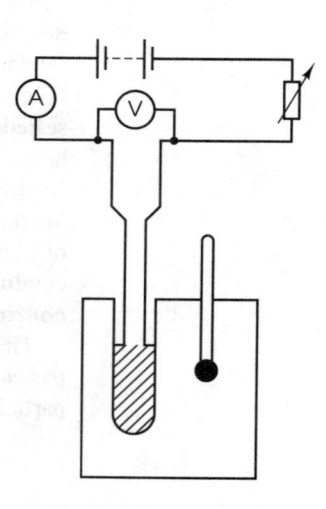

Fig. 12.20 Determining specific heat capacity.

READINGS TAKEN

Mass of block = M kilograms

Starting temperature = T_1 °C

Final temperature = T_2 °C

Current = I amps

PD = V volts

Time = t seconds

CALCULATION

Energy supplied electrically = IVt (joules)

= Mass × specific heat capacity × temperature rise

Therefore

$$\text{Specific heat capacity} = \frac{IVt}{M(T_2 - T_1)}$$

2 "GREENHOUSE EFFECT"

Radiation from the sun contains a mixture of wavelengths, including visible, ultra-violet and infra-red. Just as visible light is a band of wavelengths and not a single one, so too infra-red is a band containing many wavelengths. The wavelengths of infra-red emitted by a hot object depend on its temperature – hotter objects emit smaller wavelength, high-frequency waves, which penetrate glass in the same way that visible light passes through glass (Fig. 12.21). Infra-red from the **sun** has both small and large wavelengths present, and the larger wavelengths cannot pass through glass. The inside of a greenhouse therefore becomes heated by these low-wavelength rays when they are absorbed. The temperature of **objects** inside the greenhouse rises and **they also** emit infra-red radiation. However, as these rays have a longer wavelength, they are trapped **inside** the glass and the temperature rises even more. This principle is used in the case of **solar panels** for heating. A glass or transparent cover traps heat by the "greenhouse" effect. The absorber is blackened to assist absorption of thermal radiation. Water circulated through the panels is therefore heated and pumped to the domestic supply (Fig. 12.22).

The Earth's atmosphere has some gases which behave in a similar manner to the greenhouse glass. They allow through the shorter wavelengths from the Sun that heat the surface of the Earth but absorb and radiate back the longer wavelengths that the Earth's cooler surface emits. The heat energy is therefore trapped and the average temperature of the outer surface of the Earth and the atmosphere is raised. These gases (such as carbon dioxide from the burning of fuels) could upset the delicate temperature system which controls the weather. Note that this is NOT the same effect as either holes in the ozone layer or acid rain.

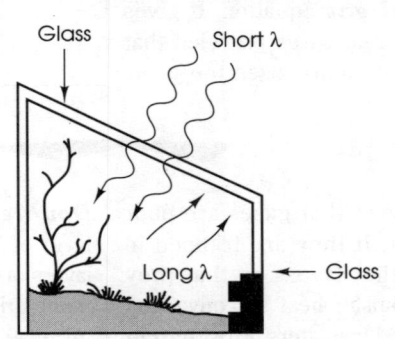

Fig. 12.21 The "greenhouse effect".

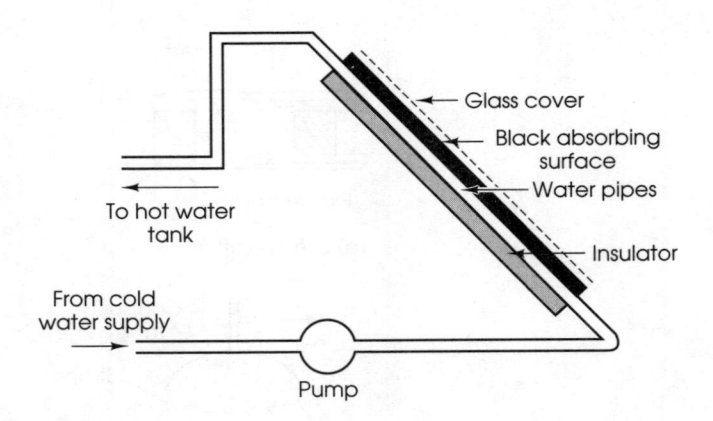

Fig. 12.22 Solar heating panel.

3. THE GENERAL GAS EQUATION

Provided that the mass of gas remains the same there are three main factors that can change: pressure, volume and temperature. In this chapter and the previous one you will have met the three gas laws that tell you what happens when each of these is kept constant and the connection between the other two is determined. The laws are for a constant mass of gas.

Boyle's law at constant temperature

$$P_1 V_1 = P_2 V_2$$

Charles' law at constant pressure

$$\frac{V_1}{V_2} = \frac{T_1}{T_2}$$

The pressure law at constant volume

$$\frac{P_1}{P_2} = \frac{T_1}{T_2}$$

We can combine all three of these together into one equation to see what happens when all three factors are changed. The law is only really true for a perfect gas and is sometimes known as the *ideal gas* equation. It gives correct answers for real gases provided that the particles are not compressed too close together that the forces between the particles becomes significant.

$$\frac{P_1 V_1}{T_1} = \frac{P_2 V_2}{T_2}$$

Where P_1 = first pressure, V_1 = first volume and T_1 = first temperature. P_2 = second pressure, V_2 = second volume and T_2 = second temperature. The temperatures MUST be in kelvin.

EXAMPLE

A gas has a volume of 300 ml at 6 atmospheres pressure and 327 °C. What will its volume become at 1 atmosphere pressure and 27 °C?

$$T_1 = 273 + 327 = 600 \text{ K}$$
$$T_2 = 273 + 27 = 300 \text{ K}$$

$$\frac{P_1 V_1}{T_1} = \frac{P_2 V_2}{T_2}$$

$$\frac{6 \times 300}{600} = \frac{1 \times V_2}{300}$$

$$V_2 = \frac{6 \times 300 \times 300}{600} = \underline{900 \text{ ml}}$$

4. HEAT INSULATION

We have already seen that gases are poor conductors of heat. If they are trapped in small bubbles or thin layers so that they cannot move and transfer heat by convection then they will be good insulators. Most **warm clothing** works on this principle, trapping layers of warm air between layers of clothing and pockets of air between the fibres of the material. Several layers of clothing will be warmer than one thick layer.

House insulation uses similar principles. **Double glazing** works because an extra layer of insulating air is trapped between the layers of glass. **Roof/loft insulation** is made from thick layers of fibreglass matting or mineral wool and **hot water tanks** are covered with a fibreglass blanket or have about 25 mm of rigid plastic foam bonded to the outside. **Cavity walls** can be filled with mineral wool and **water pipes** covered with plastic foam. The gas bubbles trapped in closed cells of plastic foam make it a good insulator.

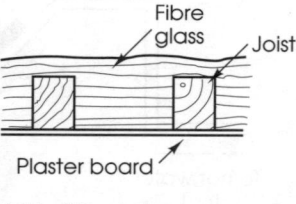

Fig. 12.23

(a) Loft insulation

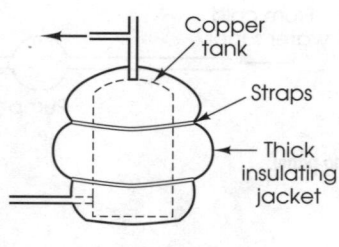

(b) Cavity wall insulation

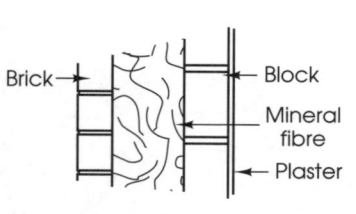

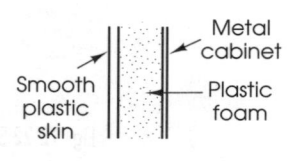

(c) Hot water storage

(d) Wall of refrigerator

5 > EXPANSION OF LIQUIDS

Most liquids expand steadily as temperature rises. If you investigate this remember that the container will also be expanding. Water is unusual in that it contracts from 0°C to 4°C and then expands. This means that the water has its minimum volume and maximum density at 4°C. When pond water cools below 4°C in the winter the water becomes less dense and floats above the water at 4°C which sinks to the bottom. Ice will therefore form from the top downwards and plants and animals in the water can survive.

6 > U-VALUES

This is a practical way to determine the heat loss through the walls, windows, roof and doors of a building.

A *U-value* is the power loss through a square metre of the material when the temperature difference across it is 1 °C (or 1 K) The U-values can be obtained from standard tables and have been determined by experiment in real situations. If you find the total power loss from a room or building you will know the power of the heating system needed to maintain the temperature.

Power loss = U-value × area × temperature difference.

Some U-values are given in the table.

Material	U-value in W/m² °C
Double brick cavity wall	1.7
Double brick wall with cavity insulation	0.6
Single glazed window	5.6
Double glazed window	3
Tiled roof	2.2
Insulated roof	0.5

EXAMPLE

Find the power loss through a double glazed patio door that measures 2.2 m by 3 m if the room temperature is 20 °C when the temperature outside is –2 °C.

Area = 2.2 × 3 = 6.6m²
Temperature difference = 22°C
U-value = 3W/m²°C

Power loss = U-value × area × temperature difference.
= 3 × 6.6 × 22 = <u>436 W.</u>

(So almost 0.5 kW is being lost through this window alone!)

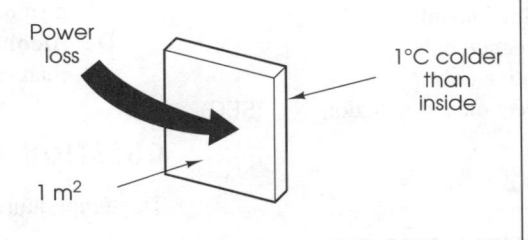

Fig. 12.24

7 > EXPANSIVITY

When solids expand they do so by a small amount but with a very large force. This expansion must be allowed for in many engineering designs or there will be severe damage. A steam pipe for example may change considerably in length when turned off and a desert oil pipeline may have considerable temperature changes from midday to the middle of the night.

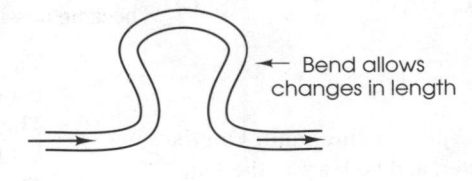

Fig. 12.25

For the same reason gaps must be left at the ends of bridges and railway lines to allow for expansion and contraction.

Metal parts can be permanently fitted together by machining the outer piece very slightly too small. If the inner is then cooled (liquid nitrogen), or the outer heated, they will fit and then cannot be parted when allowed to return to normal temperature.

A metal bottle top may be unscrewed more easily after being put in running hot water for a short time so that it expands. A glass may break when suddenly put into very hot water. It is a poor conductor and the outside is expanding faster than the inside! Rivets may be put in hot so that they pull the materials together when they contract on cooling.

The *linear expansivity* of a solid is the expansion of 1 m of the solid when its temperature rises by 1 °C. It is sometimes given the symbol α and the units will be /°C. The value will be small some examples are as follows:

Material	Expansivity/°C	Material	Expansivity/°C
steel	0.0000150	aluminium	0.0000230
copper	0.0000170	invar*	0.0000009
brick	0.0000090	concrete	0.0000120
glass	0.0000080	PVC	0.0001500

EXAMPLE

A concrete bridge is 80 m long at −10 °C on a cold night. How much will it have expanded on a hot day when its temperature is 30 °C? Using the value of expansivity from the table,

$$\text{Expansion} = \text{linear expansivity} \times \text{orig. length} \times \text{temp. change}$$
$$= 0.000012 \times 80 \times 40$$
$$= \underline{38 \text{ mm}}$$

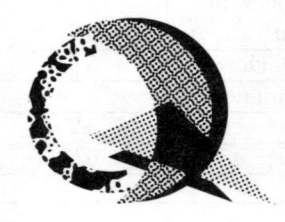

EXAMINATION QUESTIONS

MULTIPLE CHOICE QUESTIONS

QUESTION 1

Energy may be transmitted through a vacuum by

- A Conduction only
- B Convection only
- C Radiation only
- D Convection and radiation   (SEG)

QUESTION 2

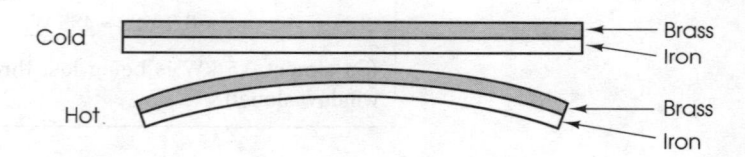

Fig. 12.26

The strips of brass and iron are firmly fixed together as shown in Fig. 12.26. The bar is straight when cold. When heated the bar bends as in the diagram. This is because

- A The brass has expanded more than the iron.
- B Iron is a poor conductor of heat.
- C The iron has expanded more than the brass.
- D Both metals have expanded by equal amounts.   (SEG)

QUESTION 3

Two liquids are spilt on the hand. One is alcohol, one is water, and both are at the same temperature. The alcohol feels colder than the water, because

- A Alcohol has a higher boiling-point than water.
- B Alcohol is a worse conductor of heat than water.
- C Alcohol has a higher specific latent heat of vaporisation than water.
- D Alcohol evaporates more readily than water.   (ULEAC)

QUESTION 4

The temperature of pure melting ice is

- A −273 K
- B 0 K
- C 100 K
- D 273 K   (SEG)

QUESTION 5

Which of the following does *not* work by expansion?

- A Mercury thermometer
- B Bimetallic strip fire alarm
- C Vacuum flask
- D Cut-out on automatic kettle (ULEAC)

QUESTION 6

A metal cap was found to be so tight that it could not be unscrewed from its bottle. After directing a stream of hot water on to the cap, it became possible to remove it. This is because

- A The hot water acted as a lubricant between the glass and the bottle.
- B The increased air pressure in the bottle caused the cap to expand.
- C The glass in the neck of the bottle contracted.
- D The pressure of the air trapped in the screw threads caused the cap to expand.

E The metal cap expanded more than the glass. (ULEAC)

QUESTION 7

In cold weather, the metal handlebars of a bicycle feel colder to the hands than the plastic handgrips. This is because

A The metal is at a lower temperature than the plastic.
B The plastic material contains more heat energy than the metal.
C The metal is a better conductor of heat than plastic.
D The shining metal does not reflect radiated heat well.
E The plastic material is a good radiator of heat. (ULEAC)

QUESTION 8

Which of the following is *not* due in some way to the movement of molecules?

A Convection of heat
B Pressure of a gas
C Transfer of heat by radiation
D Thermal conduction
E Transmission of sound

QUESTION 9

A beaker contains water, initially at room temperature. It is continuously stirred while a hot object is immersed in it. Which one of the graphs (Fig. 12.27) best shows the temperature changes which follow?

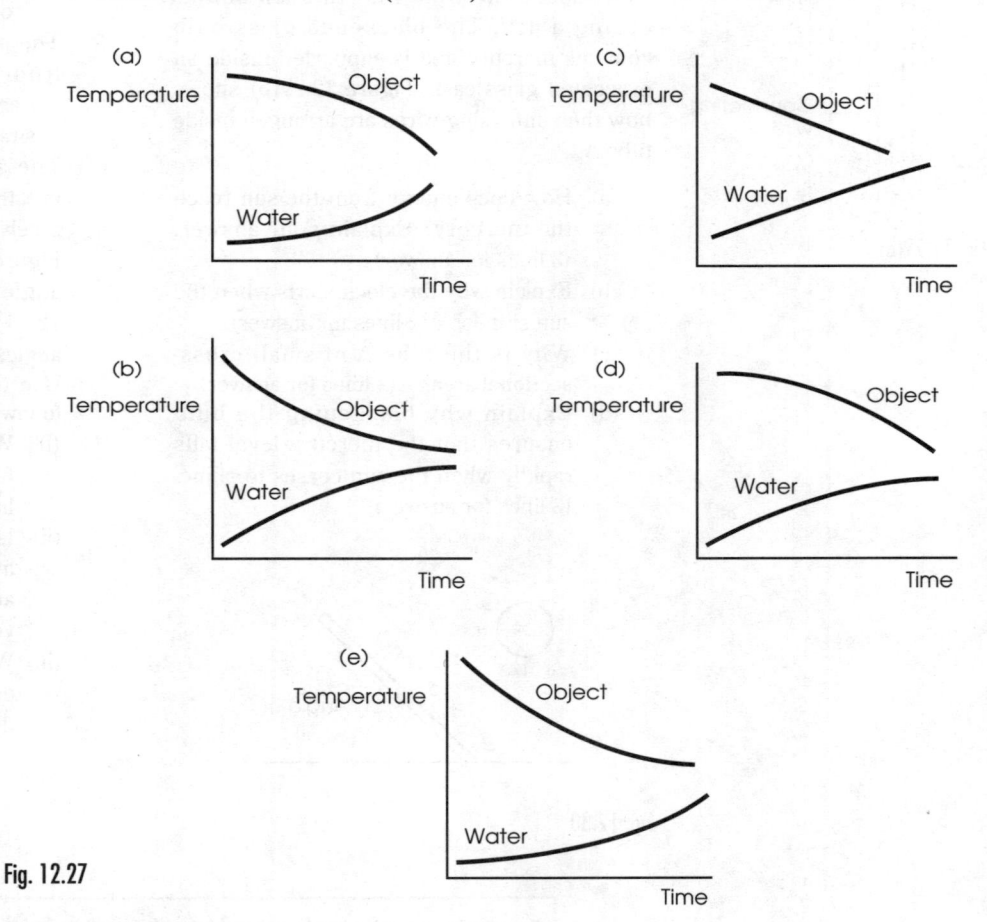

Fig. 12.27

QUESTION 10

Figure 12.28 shows a section through a particular type of building board. Which line in the following table shows why such boards provide good heat insulation?

	Aluminium foil is	Expanded polystyrene is
A	A poor conductor	A good reflector
B	A poor reflector	A poor conductor
C	A good reflector	A poor conductor
D	A good conductor	A good reflector

Fig. 12.28

STRUCTURED QUESTIONS

QUESTION 11

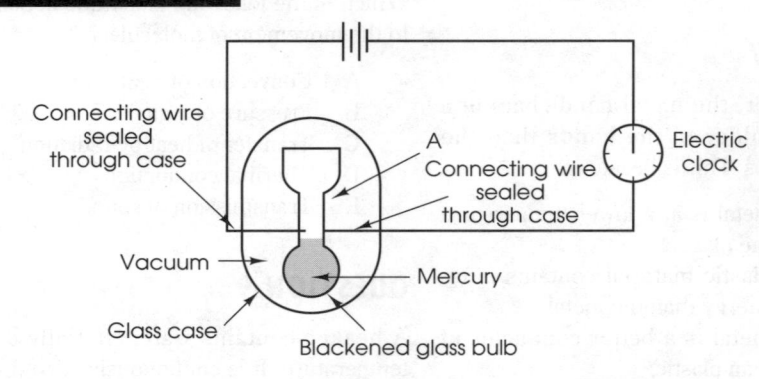

Fig. 12.29(a)

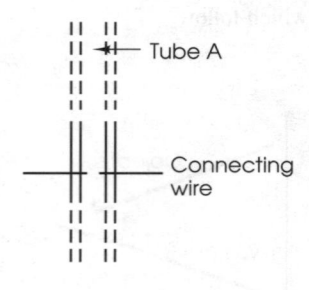

Fig. 12.29(b)

Figure 12.29(a) illustrates an instrument used to measure the time that the sun shines during a day. The blackened glass bulb contains mercury and is supported inside an evacuated glass case. Figure 12.29(b) shows how the connecting wires are arranged inside tube A.

(a) How does energy from the sun reach the mercury? Explain your answer. (3 lines for answer)
(b) Explain why the clock starts when the sun shines? (2 lines for answer)
(c) Why is the tube A of small cross-sectional area? (2 lines for answer)
(d) Explain why blackening the bulb ensures that the mercury level falls rapidly when the sun ceases to shine. (3 lines for answer).

Fig. 12.30

QUESTION 12

This question is about solar panels, devices that are sometimes seen on the roofs of houses and are used to provide hot water. An example is shown in Fig. 12.30.

(a) State the purpose of the following:
  (i) The insulation behind the absorber panel. (1 line)
  (ii) Having the absorber painted black. (1 line)
  (iii) Having a glass cover on top of the panel. (3 lines)
(b) (i) Name suitable materials for making the absorber panel and waterways (do not use brand names). (1 line)
  (ii) Give your reasons for the choice of such materials. (4 lines)
(c) The pipe connecting the water outlet from the panel to the hot water storage pipe is kept short. Why is this desirable? (2 lines)
(d) The angle of tilt of the solar panel greatly affects the amount of energy it receives at different times of the year. Figure 12.30 shows what is meant by angle of tilt. The table of data (Fig. 12.31) shows the effect of different angles of tilt for the summer months. Use the table of data to answer the following questions:
  (i) What angle of tilt would be ideal for a solar panel in April? (1 line)
  (ii) Is it better to have the panel tilted at 40 all the summer, or at an angle of 50 all the summer? Show your working. (3 lines)
  (iii) What is the maximum amount of energy a 4 m² panel could receive during a day in July? (2 lines)

(ULEAC)

Energy in Megajoules to a 1 m² panel										
Month	Angle of tilt									
	0°	10°	20°	30°	40°	50°	60°	70°	80°	90°
Apr.	20.5	22.3	23.8	24.9	24.8	24.1	22.7	20.5	18.4	15.1
May	26.3	27.7	28.4	28.8	27.4	25.2	23.0	19.8	16.6	13.0
June	28.4	28.8	29.2	29.2	27.4	25.2	22.3	19.1	15.1	11.2
July	28.1	28.4	28.8	29.2	27.4	25.6	23.0	20.2	16.2	12.2
Aug.	23.0	24.8	25.6	25.9	26.3	24.8	22.7	20.5	17.3	13.7
Sept.	16.2	18.7	20.5	21.6	22.3	22.7	21.6	20.5	18.7	16.2

Fig. 12.31

QUESTION 13

A saucepan of water is put on the hotplate of an electric cooker. The hotplate is *then* switched on and the temperature of the water is recorded every minute until the water boils. The temperature each minute is shown in the table.

Time (min)	0	1	2	3	4	5	6	7	8
Temperature (°C)	15	20	33	49	64	79	93	100	100

(a) Plot a graph of the temperature (vertical axis) against time (horizontal axis) on the graph paper. Join the points by a smooth line.
(b) Explain why the rise in temperature of the water is slower at first. (2 lines)
(c) What is the boiling-point of water? (1 line)
(d) From your graph, determine how many seconds it takes for the water to boil. (1 line)
(e) If the power of the hotplate is 1000 W, how much energy is used to bring the water just to the boil? (3 lines)
(f) Some energy is lost from the sides of the saucepan to the surrounding air. What is the best type of surface for the outside of the saucepan if it is to lose the least amount of heat? Give a reason for your choice. (2 lines)
(g) In a similar experiment with a second saucepan of water it took twice as long for the water to boil. Suggest possible reasons for this. (2 lines)

(NICCEA)

QUESTION 14

(a) To compare the rate at which two different types of surface absorb radiant heat, the apparatus shown below was set up. Can X has a polished surface and can Y has a dull black surface. The starting temperature of the water in each can was 20 °C.

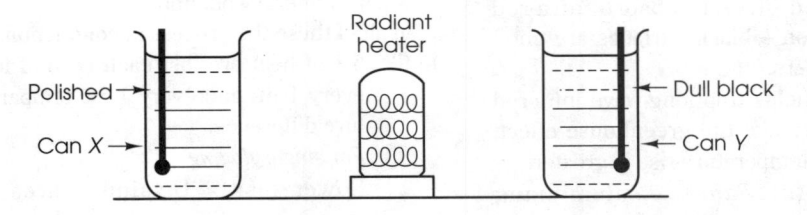

Fig. 12.32

(i) To make this a fair comparison state *two* things that should be the same for each can.
(ii) Which can will show a greater rise in temperature? Explain your answer.

(b) The loss of heat from a house can take place through the roof, through the floor and through the walls. For each of these ways suggest how the heat loss can be reduced.
In each case name the method of heat loss that is being reduced.

(c) (i) A single glazed window has a U value of 5.0 W/m² °C. Explain in detail what this means.
(ii) A house has a total window area of 15 m². Calculate the heat energy, in megajoules, saved in one hour if the owner replaced all the single glazed windows with double glazing of U value 2.8 W/m² °C. The temperature inside the house is 20 °C and the outside temperature is 10 °C. Show clearly how you obtain your answer.
(iii) The house is heated by electricity. One unit of electricity costs 7.5p and is equivalent to 3.6 MJ. Calculate the saving per day of installing the double glazing.

(d) In a steel rolling mill, hot steel comes out of a set of rollers and is cooled under jets of water before being formed into a coil as in the diagram.
(i) Give ONE reason why water is suitable as a coolant in this case.
The mass of steel passing out from the rollers per second is 380 kg. The steel leaves the rollers at a temperature of 1250 °C and it is coiled at a temperature of 600 °C.
(ii) Calculate the heat lost by the steel each second. Give your answer in kilojoules (specific heat capacity of steel = 500 J/kg °C).

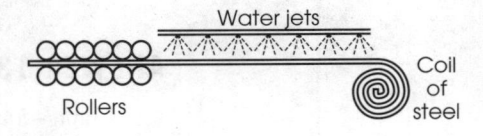

Fig. 12.33

ANSWERS TO EXAMINATION QUESTIONS

1. MULTIPLE CHOICE QUESTIONS

Question	1	2	3	4	5	6	7	8	9	10
Answer	C	A	D	D	C	E	C	C	B	C

2. STRUCTURED QUESTIONS

ANSWER 11

(a) The mechanism is radiation. The tube is enclosed in a vacuum. No other mechanism transmits across a vacuum (i.e. conduction and convection require a material).

(b) Heat energy is transferred to the mercury. Its temperature rises and it expands up tube A. Since it is a metal it is an electrical conductor, and makes connection with the wires, completing the circuit.

(c) Small cross-section means large change in length for a small volume change. The device is therefore sensitive to small changes in temperature.

(d) Black surfaces are good emitters of heat radiation so the temperature of the mercury will fall more rapidly.

ANSWER 12

(a) (i) Insulation to prevent heat loss through the back of the panel.
 (ii) Painted black to absorb infra-red radiation – black surfaces are good absorbers.
 (iii) Glass helps trap long-wave infra-red – rather like the greenhouse effect, so the temperature rise is greater.

(b) (i) and (ii) *Panel* – aluminium; aluminium – light, cheap, good conductor. *Waterways* – copper; copper – good conductor.

(c) Shorter pipe reduces surface area for heat loss by conduction through the pipe and convection in the air around the pipe.

(d) (i) 30°
 (ii) At 40° total energy received all summer = 155.6 MJ.
 At 50° total energy received all summer = 147.6 MJ.
 Therefore 40° is better.
 (iii) Maximum July value is 29.2 MJ (for 1 m² panel). Therefore (4 × 29.2) = 116.8 MJ.

ANSWER 13

(a) Graph – four points to note:
 1. Label axes correctly;
 2. Units on axes;
 3. Points plotted correctly;
 4. Points joined with a smooth curve.

(b) At first the electricity supply has to heat the hotplate to the required temperature, so less energy is transferred to the water. Equally conduction through the base of the saucepan takes time.

(c) 100 °C.

(d) 400 seconds (from graph).

(e) 1000 × 400 = 400 000 J.

(f) Shining outside – poor radiation emitter.

(g) Possibly twice the mass of water used or half the power of the hotplate.

ANSWER 14

This is a further level question.

(a) (i) Same distance from heater, same volume/mass of in each can, same metal for each can etc.
 (ii) Can Y because dull surfaces are better absorbers of radiant heat.

(b) roof – fibreglass matting or mineral wool
 floor – carpet and foam underlay
 walls – mineral wool fibre.
 in all of these the process in conduction.

(c) (i) 5 J of heat are lost each second for every 1 m² and every 1 °C temperature difference.
 (ii) *For single glazing*
 Power loss = U-value × area × temperature difference.
 Power loss = 5 × 15 × 10 = 750 W.

 For double glazing
 Power loss = U-value × area × temperature difference.
 Power loss = 2.8 × 15 × 10 = 420 W
 Energy saved per second = power saved = 750 – 420 = 330 J
 Energy saved per hour = 330 × 60 × 60 = 1 188 000 J = 1.2 MJ
 (iii) Energy saved in one day = 1.2 × 24 = 28.8 MJ.
 Number of units saved = 28.8/3.6 = 8
 Saving = 8 × 7.5 = 0.60

(d) (i) Water has a high specific heat capacity and a high specific latent heat capacity.
 (ii) Heat = mass × specific heat capacity × temperature change
 = 380 × 500 × 650 = 123 500 000 J
 = 123 500 kJ

TUTOR'S QUESTION AND ANSWER

QUESTION

(a) Many domestic oil-fired central heating systems operate by pumping water through a boiler, and circulating the heated water through pipes to radiators. The same water is recirculated continuously through the system. In one such system, water flows at a rate of 0.6 kg/s. Water enters the boiler at a temperature of 35 °C and leaves the boiler at a temperature of 75 °C. Each kilogram of oil provides 3×10^7 J to heat the water. The density of oil is 850 kg/m^3. The specific heat capacity of water is 4200 J/kg K.
Calculate:
  (i) The energy absorbed by the water per second as it passes through the boiler.
  (ii) The mass of oil which would provide this energy.
  (iii) The time required to consume 1 m^3 of oil if the system runs continuously.

(b) In practice the action of the boiler is a little more complicated. The water inlet and outlet temperatures are not constant, and when the outlet temperature exceeds a given pre-set value, the burner is switched OFF. The burner is switched ON again when the outlet temperature falls below a second, and lower, pre-set value.
  (i) State and explain the factors which would determine the fraction of the time in which the oil would be burned.
  (ii) State and explain the steps a householder might take to keep this fraction to a minimum.
  (iii) Outline the principle of operation of a device which might be used to turn the burner ON or OFF. (SEG)

ANSWER

(a) (i) Energy per second
= Mass per second × specific heat capacity × temperature rise
= 0.6 × 4200 × 40 = <u>100 800 J</u>

(ii) Mass of oil = $\dfrac{100\ 800}{3 \times 10^7}$ = <u>0.003 kg</u>

(iii) Mass of 1 m^3 of oil = 850 kg. 0.003 kg are burnt per second. Therefore,

Time required = $\dfrac{850}{0.003}$ s

= 283 333 s = 78 h

(b) (i) Obviously the pre-set temperatures determine how much energy is needed to produce a given energy change in the water (and therefore a rise in temperature). The number of radiators used will affect the overall house temperature, as will the surface are of the radiators. The time for the fuel burning to be OFF will depend on how quickly the rooms cool. A large heat loss through an uninsulated ceiling will give a larger fraction of time when the boiler is operating.

(ii) Insulation of loft, walls, windows. Draught exclusion, double glazing, etc.

(iii) The device used might operate rather like a bimetallic strip, or something similar, which uses expansion to control switching. There would need to be a valve or switch to provide ON/OFF control.

STUDENT'S ANSWER WITH THE EXAMINER'S COMMENTS

STUDENT ANSWER TO QUESTION 13

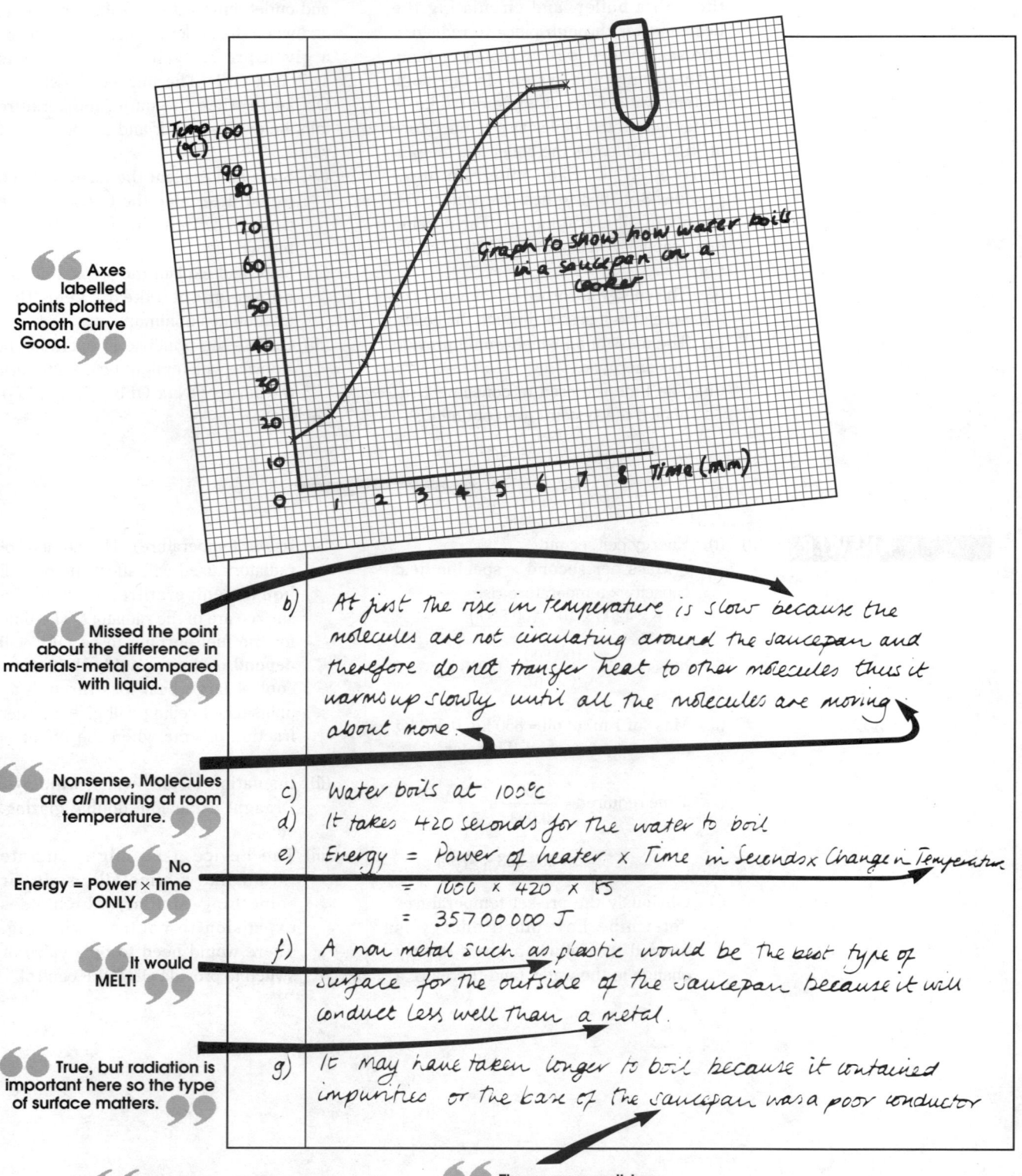

Graph to show how water boils in a saucepan on a cooker

(Temp °C vs Time (min), curve rising from ~15°C to ~100°C)

> **Axes labelled points plotted Smooth Curve Good.**

> **Missed the point about the difference in materials-metal compared with liquid.**

b) At first the rise in temperature is slow because the molecules are not circulating around the saucepan and therefore do not transfer heat to other molecules thus it warms up slowly until all the molecules are moving about more.

> **Nonsense, Molecules are *all* moving at room temperature.**

c) Water boils at 100°C

d) It takes 420 seconds for the water to boil

e) Energy = Power of heater × Time in Seconds × Change in Temperature
   = 1000 × 420 × 85
   = 35 700 000 J

> **No Energy = Power × Time ONLY**

f) A non metal such as plastic would be the best type of surface for the outside of the saucepan because it will conduct less well than a metal.

> **It would MELT!**

g) It may have taken longer to boil because it contained impurities or the base of the saucepan was a poor conductor

> **True, but radiation is important here so the type of surface matters.**

> **The graph is well done, as is the information obtained from it. The other parts are weak, suggesting poor understanding of the topic, and not enough practice in answering questions.**

> **These are possible, but unlikely to result in a *doubled* time to boil.**

REVIEW SHEET

- Write down briefly how the upper and lower fixed points are determined on a Celsius thermometer.

    Upper fixed point

    _____

    _____

    Lower fixed point _____

    _____.

- Which will expand most when heated at constant pressure: solid, liquid or gas?
    _____

- Name the three ways in which heat can be transmitted from one place to another.

    1. _____ 2. _____ 3. _____

- Write down the following equations

    1. Boyle's law   2. Charles' law

    _____   _____

    3. The pressure law   4. The ideal gas equation

    _____   _____.

- In the gas laws the temperature MUST be in _____.

- 20 °C is the same as _____ K,   400 K is the same as _____ °C.

- Heat energy gained or lost when a material changes temperature is found by using the specific heat of the material. Complete the equation:

    Energy gained or lost = specific heat capacity × _____ × _____

- The greenhouse effect in the atmosphere depends on the fact that cooler objects radiate at _____ wavelengths which are absorbed and radiated back by gases in the air but the gases will transmit the _____ wavelengths from the hot Sun.

Complete the following table

Object to be insulated	Insulating material
Hot water tank	
Cold water pipe	
Cavity wall	
	Layers of clothing

- To keep heat in, the outside of a pan should be _____ but to release heat quickly a car radiator should be _____.

- The U-value of a double glazed panel will be _____ than the value for a single glazed panel.

- Convection cannot occur in a _____. The only way the energy can reach us from the sun is by _____.

- How much heat is needed to raise the temperature of 1 kg of water from 20 °C to 100 °C ? (specific heat capacity of water is 4200 J/kg K).
  _____
  _____
  _____

- Two metals such as _____ and _____ can be bonded together to make a _____ strip which will bend when its temperature changes.

- Describe an experiment you might use to help you measure *specific heat capacity*.
  _____
  _____
  _____
  _____
  _____
  _____
  _____
  _____
  _____
  _____
  _____

- What is meant by "linear expansivity".
  _____
  _____
  _____

CHAPTER 13

MAGNETISM AND ELECTRO-MAGNETISM

GETTING STARTED

Magnetic effects have been known and used for centuries, particularly in navigation. However, it is the link between electric currents and magnetic effects which is important both in theory and in practical application. Magnetic sensing devices such as relays make circuit switching possible by remote control. Microphones and loudspeakers also use magnetic effects and, perhaps most importantly, so does the electric motor.

PERMANENT MAGNETS

MAGNETISING AND DEMAGNETISING

ELECTROMAGNETISM

FORCES ON CURRENTS

THE "CATAPULT" FORCE

d.c. ELECTRIC MOTOR

THE LOUDSPEAKER

RELAY CIRCUITS

MAKE AND BREAK CIRCUITS

THE ELECTRIC BELL

TAPE RECORDINGS

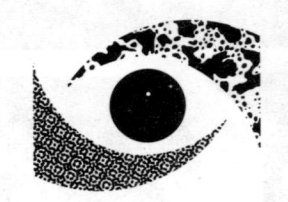

ESSENTIAL PRINCIPLES

1 > PERMANENT MAGNETS

A *magnetic material* is one which can be attracted to a permanent magnet, and which could *itself be magnetised*. Iron, nickel and cobalt are metals which show this behaviour, and so do alloys of them, like steel.

A single, freely suspended, permanent magnet will line itself up in the magnetic field of the earth, so that one particular end of it points towards the earth's magnetic north pole. This end is called the **north-seeking (N-seeking) pole** of the magnet. The other end is the **south-seeking pole** (Fig. 13.1).

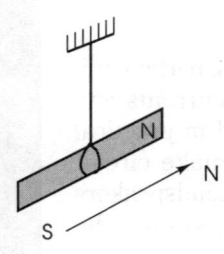

Fig. 13.1 Establishing the polarity of a magnet.

If two N-seeking poles of magnets are brought together they *repel* each other, as will two S-seeking poles. But a N-seeking pole *attracts* a S-seeking pole. The rule is:

▶ Unlike poles attract.
▶ Similar poles repel.

But note that either type of pole will attract a piece of magnetic material (which has no poles). *Repulsion* only takes place between *similar poles of magnetised materials*.

A magnetic compass is itself a small horizontally mounted magnet. Its N-seeking end can be identified by holding it well away from magnetic materials and noticing which end points to the north of the earth (Fig. 13.2). In future diagrams the **N-seeking end of a compass** will be drawn as the **head of an arrow**.

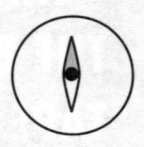

Fig. 13.2

If a compass is brought near a permanent magnet, the N-end of the needle is *repelled* from the N-seeking end of the magnet. The pattern, as the compass is moved around the magnet, is shown in Fig. 13.3. The force on the N-seeking end of the compass is away from the north pole of the magnet and

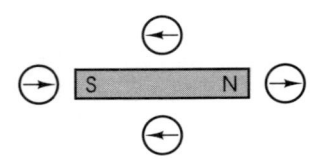

Fig. 13.3 The N-seeking end of a compass used to establish a pattern.

towards its south pole. The region around a magnet where a force is experienced can be shown using iron filings or by careful plotting with compasses. The region is called the **magnetic field** of the magnet.

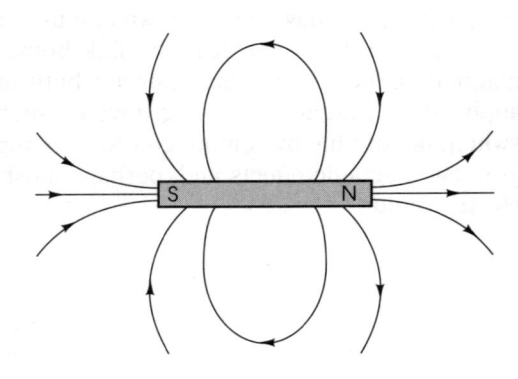

Fig. 13.4 The pattern of flux for a bar magnet.

The *pattern* revealed by filings or compass plotting shows *lines* along which a compass needle would line up. These are called **lines of magnetic force** or **lines of magnetic flux**. The lines of a flux for a single bar magnet are shown in Fig. 13.4. The **direction** is the way an N-seeking pole would point in the field, i.e. **away from the north pole** of the magnet and **towards its south pole**.

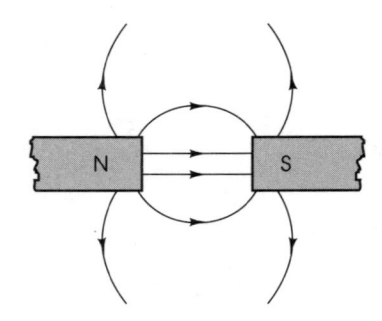

Fig. 13.5 Flux pattern between attracting magnetic poles.

Other typical patterns are also shown. Figure 13.5 is the **field between attracting poles**. This gives a fairly uniform (steady strength) field in the region between the two poles. Figure 13.6 is the **field for**

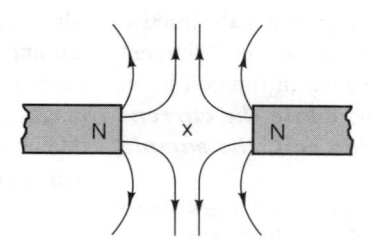

Fig. 13.6 Flux pattern for repelling poles.

repelling north poles. There is no field at point X (sometimes called a *neutral* point). A *horseshoe magnet* is like a bar magnet bent at the centre. It gives a field *between its poles*, as in Fig. 13.7. Notice that *field lines do not cross*, and that they *begin or end on the magnet*.

Magnets with curved pole pieces are sometimes used to give a very uniform field (Fig. 13.8) when used with a soft iron armature.

Magnetic materials which are difficult to magnetise but are also difficult to demagnetise are suitable for making permanent magnets. Such materials are called *hard* magnetic materials. Some uses, such as

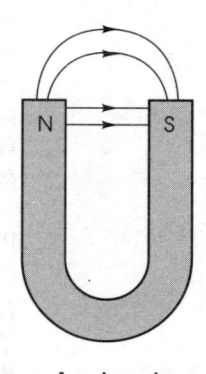

Fig. 13.7 Flux pattern for a horseshoe magnet.

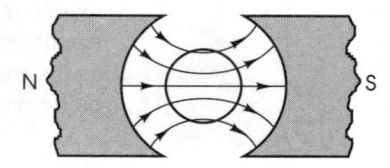

Fig. 13.8

electromagnets, the centre cores of relay coils and transformer cores must magnetise and demagnetise quickly and easily. The materials to do this are called *soft* magnetic materials.

2 > MAGNETISING AND DEMAGNETISING

A piece of iron placed in contact with a permanent magnet will, for the time they are in contact, produce magnetic poles and can then itself attract magnetic materials (Fig. 13.9). This is described as *induced magnetism*, and is the reason why iron filings can be used to reveal the lines of flux in a magnetic field. Each filing becomes temporarily an induced magnet.

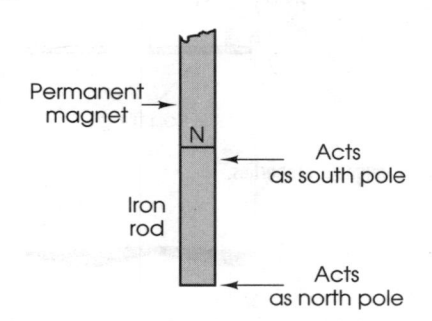

Fig. 13.9 Induced magnetic poles.

Fig. 13.10(a)   Fig. 13.10(b)

(a) DIRECTION OF MAGNETISM

The *direction* of induced magnetism follows the usual rules. The end closest to the north pole of the magnet becomes a south pole. A sample can be permanently magnetised by induction if a permanent magnet is repeatedly stroked over the sample from one end to the other, and lifted clear of the sample before the next move along it. The directions of magnetism are shown in Figs 13.10(a) and (b).

(b) ELECTRICAL METHODS OF MAGNETISING

A more effective method of magnetising is an *electrical* one.

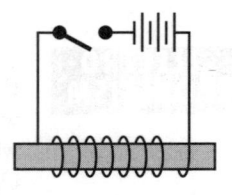

Fig. 13.11 d.c. method of magnetising.

(c) DEMAGNETISING

Demagnetising can occur if a sample is *heated above a critical temperature*, called the *curie temperature*, and *then rapidly cooled. Repeated hammering*

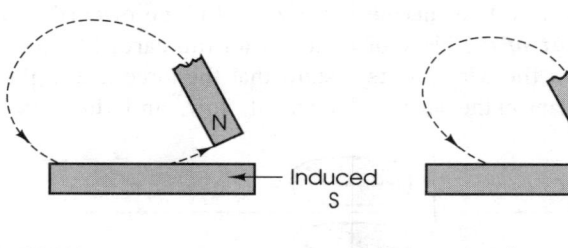

also causes demagnetising. A non-destructive demagnetising method uses a.c. in a different way. The sample is placed in the coil in an east–west direction, and *while the current is still flowing in the coil, the sample is rapidly removed*.

If this procedure is repeated a few times the sample is demagnetised (Fig. 13.12).

(d) MAGNETIC MATERIALS SHOW VARIATIONS IN MAGNETIC PROPERTIES

Soft iron is easily magnetised, but it loses its magnetism easily as well. It is called a soft magnetic material. This makes it very suitable as the core of an electromagnet, in a relay or bell circuit or in the core of a transformer, where rapid magnetising and demagnetising are important (Fig. 13.13). However, **steel**, a hard magnetic material, is more difficult to magnetise, though once it is magnetised it retains it. It is therefore ideal as a permanent magnet or a compass needle (Fig. 13.14).

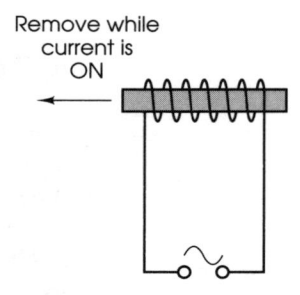

Fig. 13.12 a.c. method of demagnetising.

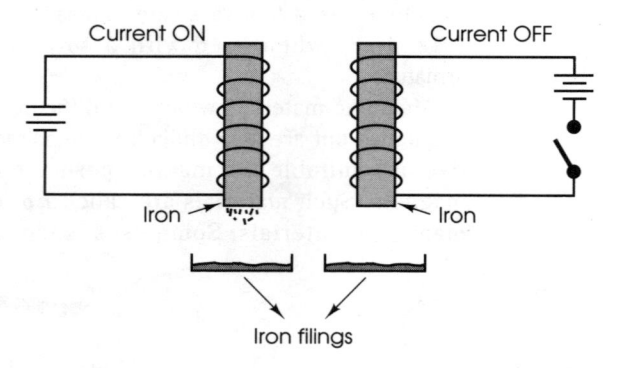

Fig. 13.13 Soft iron gains and loses magnetism easily.

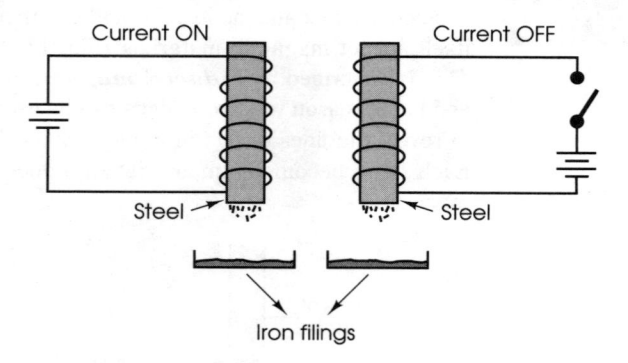

Fig. 13.14 Steel retains some magnetic properties.

3 ELECTRO-MAGNETISM

Whenever an electric current flows in a wire, there is a magnetic field produced around the wire. A single straight wire carrying a current will affect a compass needle. If the compass is placed *below* the wire (Fig. 13.15), the needle points *across* the wire, *out of* the plane of the page. A needle *above* the wire points *across* the wire *into* the plane of the page.

If the current direction is *reversed*, the compass needle directions also reverse. The pattern of the magnetic flux can be seen more easily if the current flows up a wire through a horizontal piece of card. If a compass is moved on the card, the needle directions show that the force is at right angles to the current flow, and the flux lines form a

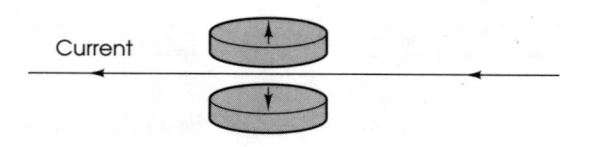

Fig. 13.15

circular pattern around the wire (Fig. 13.16). Again reversing the current reverses the field direction.

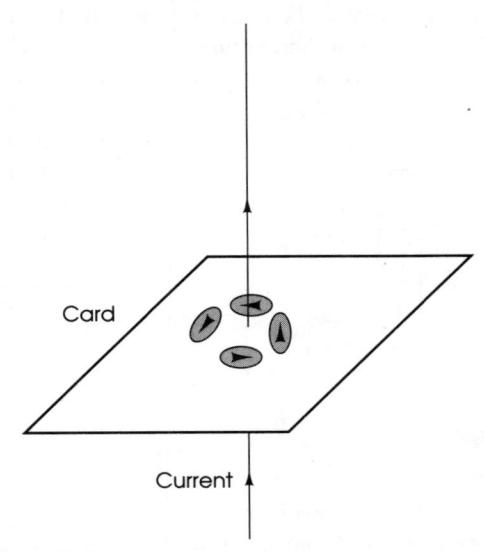

Fig. 13.16

The pattern is usually illustrated as if the card were viewed from above. The *dot* in the centre of Fig. 13.17 represents a current in a wire moving **upwards, *out of*** the plane of the page. The *cross* in Fig. 13.18 represents a current moving **downwards, *into*** the plane of the page.

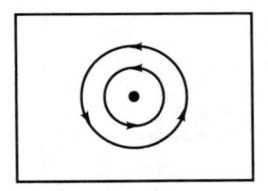

Fig. 13.17 Flux patterns for a single wire carrying current.

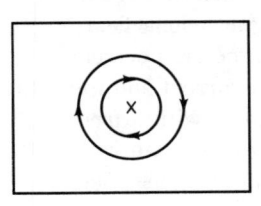

Fig. 13.18 Flux patterns for a single wire carrying current.

> Another way of finding the direction is to use the 'Maxwell Corkscrew Rule'

The further away from the wire, the weaker the magnetic force. This is represented by drawing flux lines further apart.

The directions can be worked out using the *right-hand grip rule*. Point your thumb (right hand) in the direction of the current. Curl your fingers. Your fingers give the direction of the lines of flux.

The magnetic effect of a current in a single wire is weak. Stronger fields can be obtained using a coil of wire (a solenoid). This gives the same field pattern as a single bar magnet, and it is very uniform along the centre of the coil (Fig. 13.19).

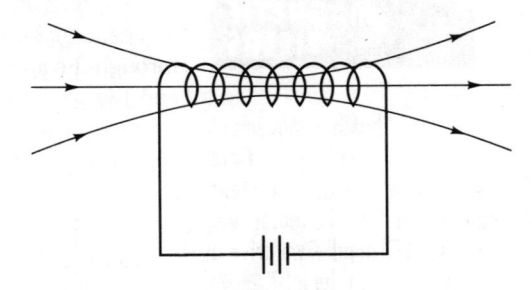

Fig. 13.19 Flux through a solenoid.

The *strength* of the field is increased if:

1. The current is increased;
2. The number of turns of the coil is increased;
3. A soft iron core is placed in the coil.

The *direction* of the field depends on two factors:

1. The direction of the current flow;
2. The direction in which the wire is coiled.

Figure 13.20 shows current flowing in a *clockwise direction* around end X of the core. This makes this end a *south pole*. (A letter S with clockwise arrows helps in remembering this.)

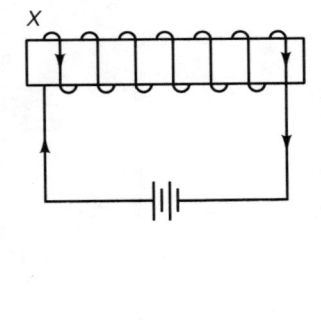

Fig. 13.20 South pole for a clockwise current.

In Fig. 13.21 the current flow at end X is *anticlockwise*, giving a *north pole*. Once again, having fixed the winding of the coil, the polarity can be changed simply by reversing the current direction.

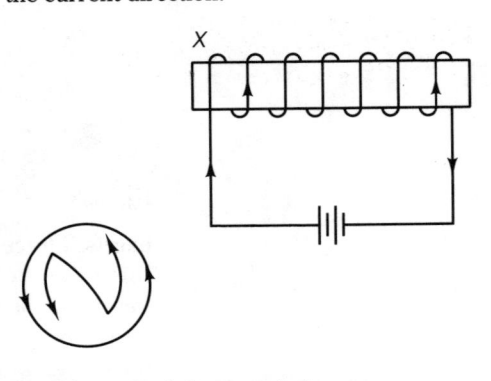

Fig. 13.21 North pole for an anticlockwise current.

4 FORCES ON CURRENTS IN MAGNETIC FIELDS

> ThuMb = Movement
> First finger = Field
> SeCond Finger = Current
> and remember it's the motor rule
> – so LEFT hand – we drive a
> motor car on the left!

A long strip of aluminium foil placed in the field of a strong permanent magnet has no force acting on it, since aluminium is not a magnetic material. If a current is then passed through the aluminium, there is a larger force and the strip moves upwards, at 90° to the magnetic field direction (Fig. 13.22).

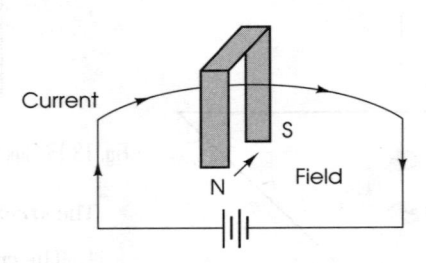

Fig. 13.22 A catapult field.

If the current direction is reversed, the force on the current is reversed, and so therefore is the movement direction (Fig. 13.23).

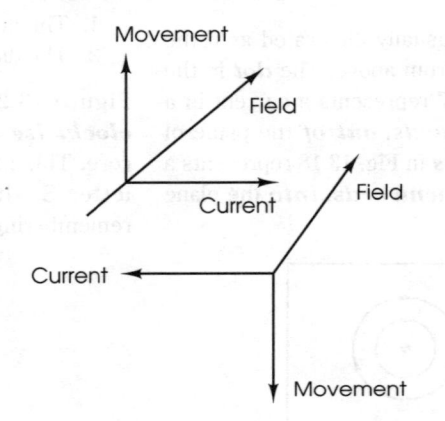

Fig. 13.23

The movement direction can also be changed by *changing the field direction*. Unlike effects in electric or gravitational fields, a magnetic field exerts a force on a current which is at 90° to both the current and the field. This can also be shown with a free-moving piece of copper wire on two rails carrying current (Fig. 13.24). A magnetic field

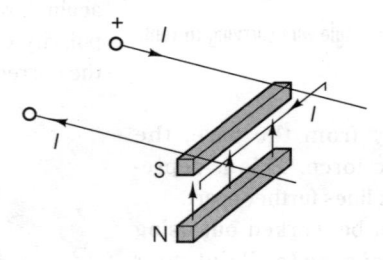

Fig. 13.24

exerts a force on the current at 90° to it. In this case the wire moves along the track. Reversing the field would make the wire shoot off the end of the track. The easiest way to remember which way the force acts is to use **Fleming's left-hand rule** (Fig. 13.25):

- If the thumb, first finger and second finger of the left hand are held at 90° to each other, and
- the first finger is pointed in the direction of the field, and
- the second finger is pointed in the direction of the current, then
- the thumb indicates the direction of movement. (This does require a certain amount of contortion for some arrangements!)

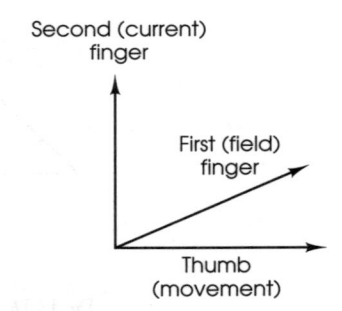

Fig. 13.25

The reason for this movement comes from the interaction of two magnetic fields, that of the permanent magnet and that due to the current. In the arrangement shown in Fig. 13.26, Fleming's rule predicts that the wire will move inwards.

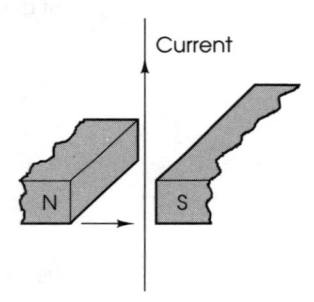

Fig. 13.26

Now think about the **fields**. The field of the magnet is shown (from above) in Fig. 13.27(a) and that of the current in Fig. 13.27(b).

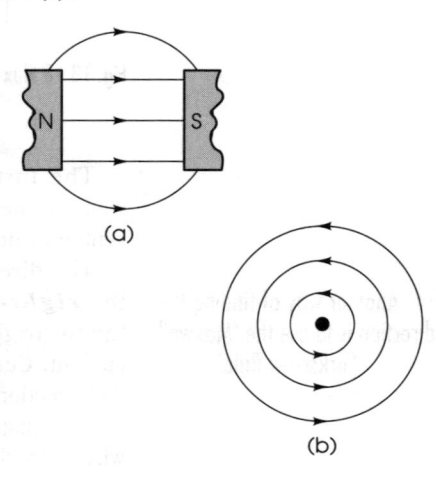

Fig. 13.27(a) and (b) Components of a catapult field.

If the two fields are superimposed on each other, the result is that **below** the wire the two sets of flux **combine** in the **same direction**, whereas **above** the wire they are **opposing**. This result is shown in Fig. 13.28.

In consequence the wire moves from the stronger field to the weaker field – or referring back to Fig. 13.26, **into** the plane of the paper as predicted by Fleming's rule. This combined field is sometimes referred to as a *catapult field*.

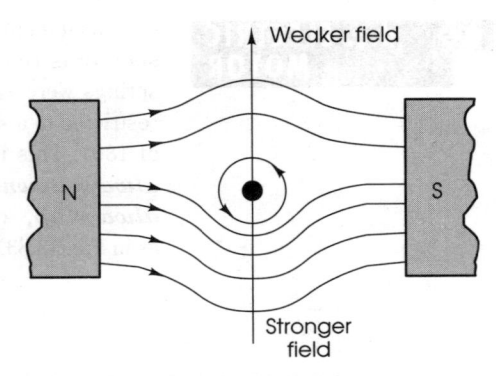

Fig. 13.28 Effect of the combined fields.

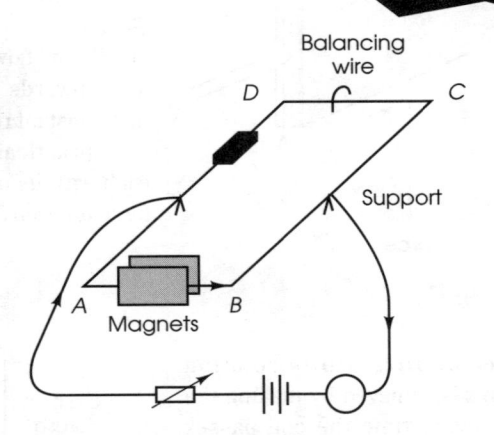

5 > THE SIZE OF THE "CATAPULT" FORCE

Fig. 13.29 A current balance.

This can be investigated using a *current balance*. This is a wire frame with an insulating portion fixed in it and balanced on two conducting supports. Current can therefore be passed around the frame, *in at one support* and *out at the other* (Fig. 13.29). If the current flow is along AB, and the magnetic field is out of the plane of the paper, then the force on AB is *downwards* (Fig. 13.30).

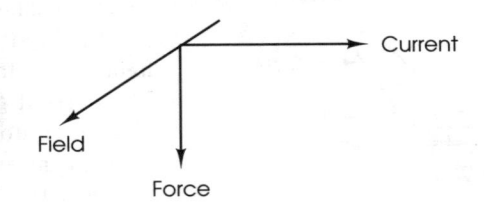

Fig. 13.30

Small lengths of wire placed on arm CD can be used to restore the balance. Since the weight of the wires is equal to the magnetic force, the size of the force is found.

If the current is varied using the variable resistor it can be shown how the force depends on the current. The magnetic field can also be changed if electromagnets are used in place of permanent magnets. It is found that the force depends on:

1. The size of the current;
2. The size of the field;
3. The length of the wire in the field.

In practice the length of wire is increased by having several turns of wire in the field. A coil carrying current in a field is a good way of illustrating this. A wood frame, free to move about on an axle, can be wound with insulated wire to form a coil. Current is then let in and out of the coil through wires wound like loose springs at each end of the axle (Fig. 13.31).

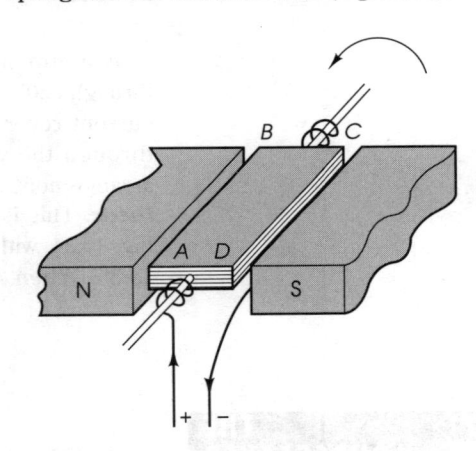

Fig. 13.31 Rotation of a coil in a uniform field.

Current flows in the direction ABCD. The direction of force on AB is downwards and the force on CD is upwards, so an *anticlockwise* rotation is produced, which is *opposed* by the forces produced in the springs (Fig. 13.32). The effect of changing the number of turns, the current and the field can be shown by the change in the angle of rotation produced.

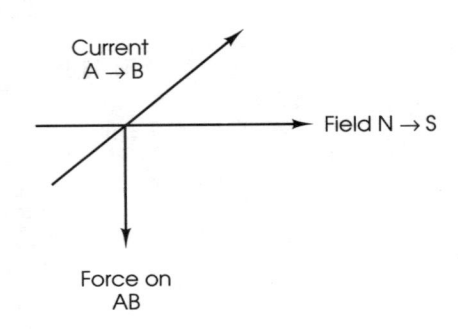

Fig. 13.32

6 d.c. ELECTRIC MOTOR

The movement of the coil described in the last section is restricted by the springs. If the springs were **removed**, the movement is still restricted to a single turn through a maximum of 180°. This is because the force on AB is **always downwards** and the force on CD is **always up**, so that when the coil is vertical, as in Fig. 13.33, the forces will keep it there.

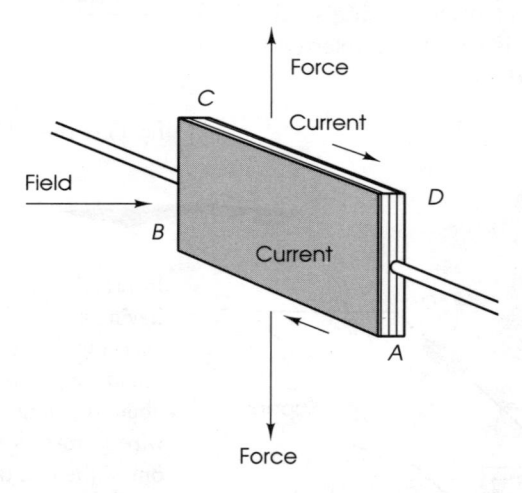

Fig. 13.33

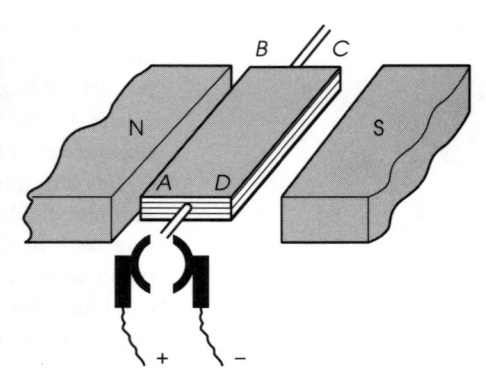

Fig. 13.34 d.c. motor arrangement.

A motor needs **continuous** rotation through 360°. This is achieved by making the current reverse every time the coil passes through the vertical position, by using an arrangement called a **split-ring commutator**. This is shown attached to the coil in Fig. 13.34, with an end-on view shown in Fig. 13.35. When AB reaches the bottom of its rotation the two half-rings reverse the ⊕ and ⊖ sides of the circuit. As a result the current in AB now flows from B to A and the force on it is upwards. Similarly, BC moves down so that constant rotation is achieved.

A practical motor may have many coils each with its own commutator to increase the force on each 360° turn.

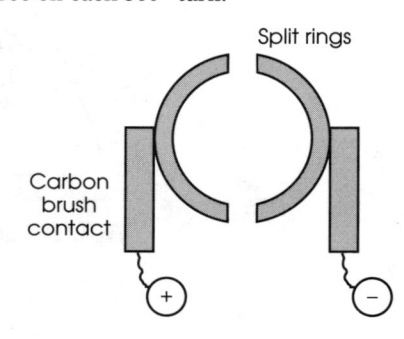

Fig. 13.35 Commutator with contacts.

7 THE LOUDSPEAKER

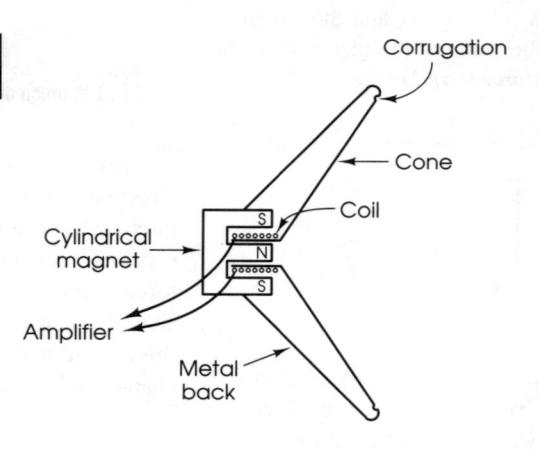

Fig. 13.36

The coil is attached to the centre of the cone and is in the field between the poles of a circular magnet.

The input is a current of the same frequency as the sound that is to be produced. The current goes through the coil and an electric motor effect is produced. As the current alternates the coil is pushed backwards and forwards at the same frequency and the card cone sends out the soundwaves. The edge of the cone is corrugated so that it can flex many times per second without cracking and splitting. Strong permanent magnets are needed to produce loud clear sound with little distortion.

EXTENSION MATERIALS

1. RELAYS AND RELAY CIRCUITS

❝ Relays are often used in transistor circuits. A small current flows in the transistor circuit but it is enough to switch the relay and operate a second circuit. ❞

A **relay** is an electromagnetic switch. In its simplest form it has two circuits. The ***input circuit*** supplies current to a coil. Only a small current is needed for the electromagnet in this circuit to become magnetised. The electromagnet then attracts a soft iron rocking armature which closes the contacts connected to the ***output circuit***, where a high current may flow (Fig. 13.37). A small input current controls a larger output current. The circuit symbol for a relay is shown in Fig. 13.38.

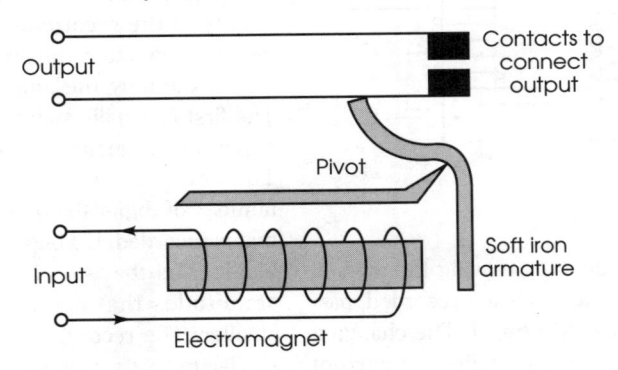

Fig. 13.37 Magnetic relay.

There is a certain ***minimum current*** needed to make the relay ***switch***, and this can be used to make the relay act as a ***sensor***.

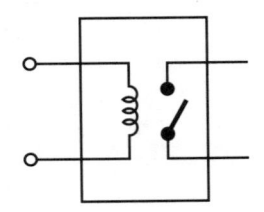

Fig. 13.38 Circuit symbol for a relay.

If the thermistor in circuit (Fig. 13.39) has a large enough resistance when it is cold, then the current in the coil will be ***less than*** that needed to switch the relay. If the temperature rises, the thermistor resistance falls, the current rises, thereby switching the relay and operating the bell.

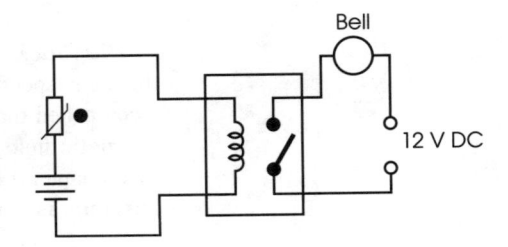

Fig. 13.39 Thermistor to control relay switching.

2. MAKE AND BREAK CIRCUITS – THE ELECTRIC BELL

This circuit causes the bell to ring continuously by automatically switching the current ON and OFF (making and breaking the circuit). When the switch is closed, current flows, and the electromagnet is magnetised. The soft iron armature is attracted to the electromagnet and the hammer hits the bell gong (Fig. 13.40). This breaks contact with the contact screw and the current stops flowing. The electromagnet loses its magnetism. The springy metal pulls the armature back and contact is made again, so the process repeats as long as the switch is closed. (*NB*. If the electromagnet core and armature were made of steel they would ***not*** lose their magnetism and the hammer would stay in contact with the gong after only one ring of the bell.)

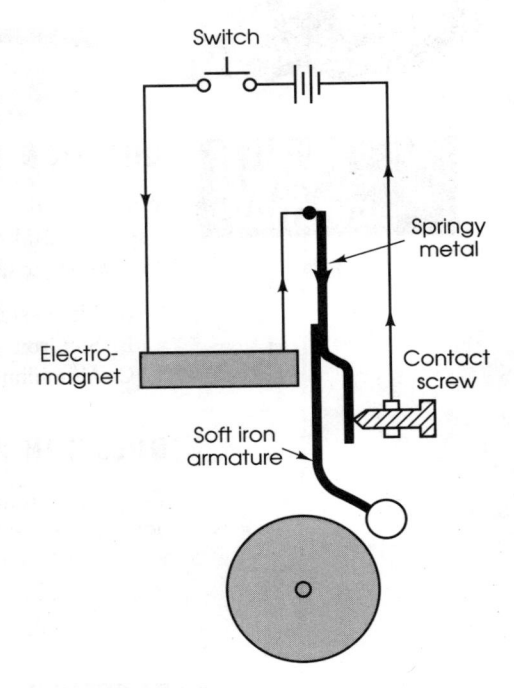

Fig. 13.40 Electric bell circuit.

3. TAPE RECORDERS

The sound is recorded on a narrow strip of plastic tape which has a thin coating of magnetic material bonded to its surface.

Recording is carried out by changing the sound wave into an electric current of the same frequency using a microphone. This is made stronger by an amplifier and then sent into a small but powerful electromagnet called the **record head**. As the current changes the field of the magnet also reverses at the same frequency and records the changing pattern on the tape which is moving past the head.

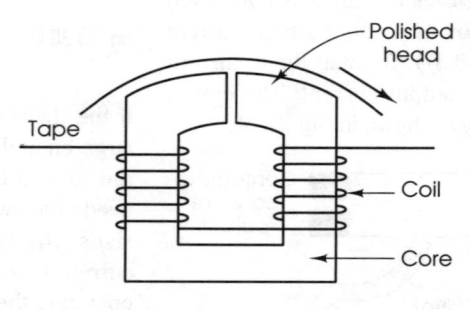

Fig. 13.41

Playback is done by moving the tape, at the same speed as it was when recorded, past a coil called the **replay head**. The changing magnetic field in the coil induces a current (see chapter 14) of the same frequency. This current is amplified and sent to the loudspeaker which produces sound of the same frequency as the original sound wave. On some recorders the same coil is used as the replay head and record head.

Erasing is done by passing the tape by an electromagnet called an **erase head** that has a high frequency alternating current in it. The magnetic field from this is changing so rapidly that the original pattern on the tape is removed.

This process will given an **analogue** recording which may become distorted after a time and is difficult to transmit (see chapter 16).

A **digital recording** is obtained by turning the analogue signal into a series of numbers that represent its amplitude. The numbers are then recorded onto the tape. The quality of the recording will depend on two factors: how often the sound is sampled and how accurately the amplitude is measured. The first is usually stated as a frequency. The bigger the frequency the better the recording. The second is decided by the maximum number of digits (bits) in the binary number that is recorded. If a bigger number with more bits is used the "steps" between the possible amplitudes that can be recorded become smaller. The recording on a compact disc is similar in that a number is recorded but it is as a series of small dents that reflect a laser beam instead of being magnetic.

EXAMINATION QUESTIONS

MULTIPLE CHOICE QUESTIONS

QUESTION 1

Which of the following materials could be used to make the needle of a pocket navigating compass?

A Magnesium
B Soft iron
C Aluminium
D Steel
E Brass

(ULEAC)

QUESTION 2

Two bar magnets are placed so that their north poles are 2 cm apart. Which diagram in Fig. 13.42 best represents the resulting magnetic field?

(ULEAC)

QUESTION 3

Which one of the following must be made from a material which maintains its magnetism?

A The commutator for a d.c. motor
B The magnet in a moving coil meter
C The core of a transformer
D The core of an electromagnet
E The slip rings of an a.c. generator

QUESTION 4

In Fig. 13.43, the two rectangles represent two light, cylindrical iron cores, about 1 cm apart. The two circuits are identical except that the left-hand one contains a switch. When the switch is closed, the gap labelled X

A Tends to increase
B Remains the same
C Tends to decrease
D Increases then decreases
E Decreases then increases

(ULEAC)

(a)
(b)
(c)
(d)
(e)

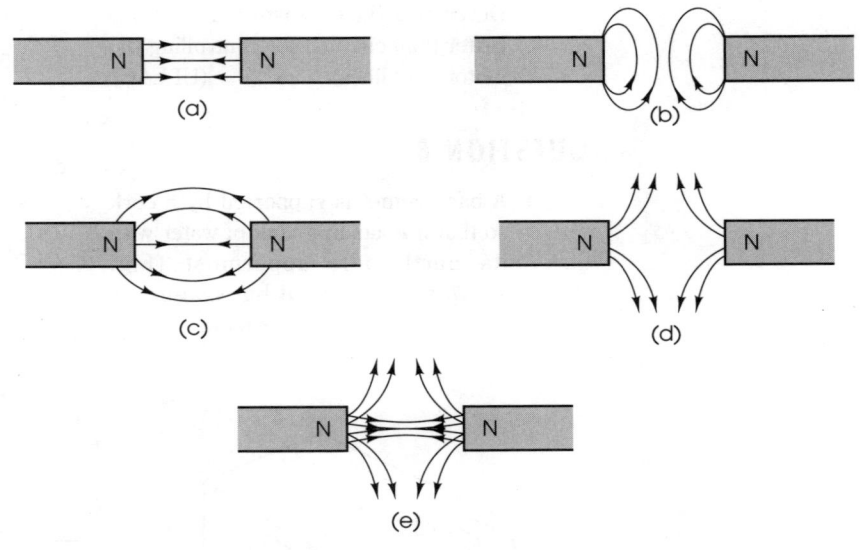

Fig. 13.42

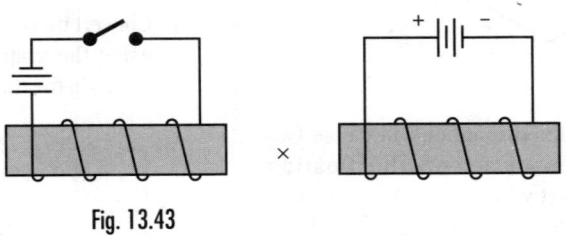

Fig. 13.43

QUESTION 5

A horizontal wire carries a current in the direction shown in Fig. 13.44 between the magnetic poles N and S of two magnets. The direction of the force on the wire is

A From N to S
B From S to N
C In the direction of the current
D Vertically upwards   (SEG)

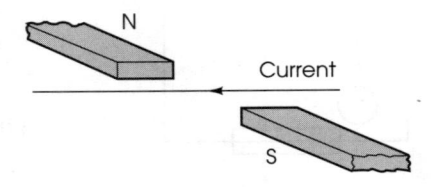

Fig. 13.44

Explain your answer.   (NICCEA)

STRUCTURED QUESTIONS

QUESTION 6

Two metal rods are placed in a long coil as shown in Fig. 13.45. When a direct current flows through the coil the rods move apart. When the current is switched OFF the rods return to their original positions.

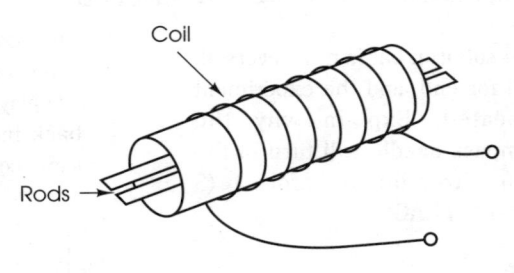

Fig. 13.45

(a) Why did the rods move apart?
(b) From what metal are the rods likely to be made? Give a reason for your answer.
(c) If alternating current from a mains transformer is passed through the coil, what effect, if any, will it have on the rods?

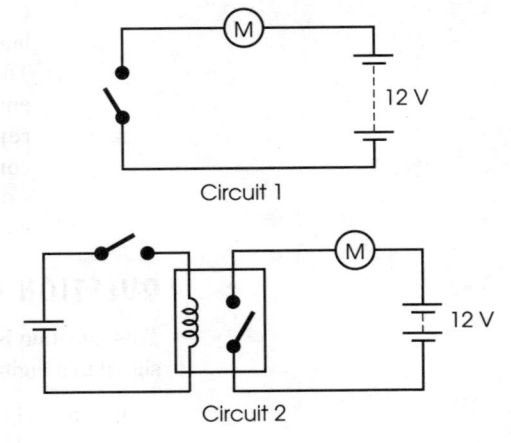

Fig. 13.46

QUESTION 7

The circuits in Fig. 13.46 show two ways of

(b) Describe a situation where circuit 2 is better than circuit 1 for controlling the motor. (3 lines) (ULEAC)

QUESTION 8

(a) A bar magnet is supported by a cork so that it floats in a tank of water with its north pole uppermost (Fig. 13.47(a)). A second bar magnet is placed on the side of the tank.

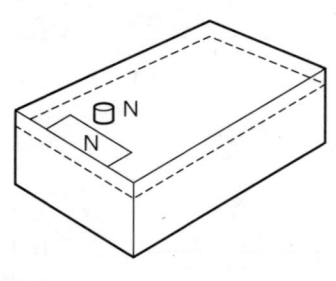

Fig. 13.47(a)

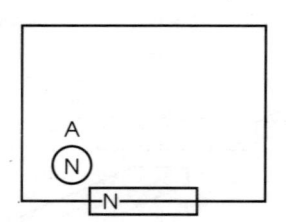

Fig. 13.47(b)

(i) The fixed magnet will cause two forces to act on the floating magnet when it is held in position A. Add arrows to Fig. 13.47(b) to show the directions of these two forces.
(ii) The floating magnet is now released. Show on the plan view (Fig. 13.47(b)) the subsequent movement of the magnet.

(b) A bar magnet, a piece of soft iron and a compass are all placed on a horizontal bench as shown in Fig. 13.48.

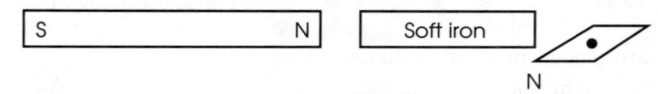

Fig. 13.48

(i) State and explain which way the compass needle will turn. (2 lines)
(ii) The soft iron bar is now reversed, end for end, and the experiment repeated. Explain why the compass needle will turn in the same direction as before. (3 lines) (ULEAC)

QUESTION 9

This question is about converting an analogue signal to a digital signal.

(a) Explain how you know that the signal is analogue.
(b) A digitiser records the voltage every 0.4 ms. Write down the first five voltages in the second column of the table.

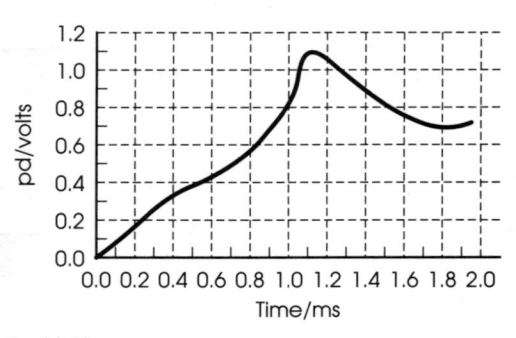

Fig. 13.49

Time	Voltage	Code
0		
0.4 ms		
0.8 ms		
1.2 ms		
1.6 ms		

(c) Convert these voltages into integer codes using the graph (Fig. 13.50). Enter the values in the third column of the table.

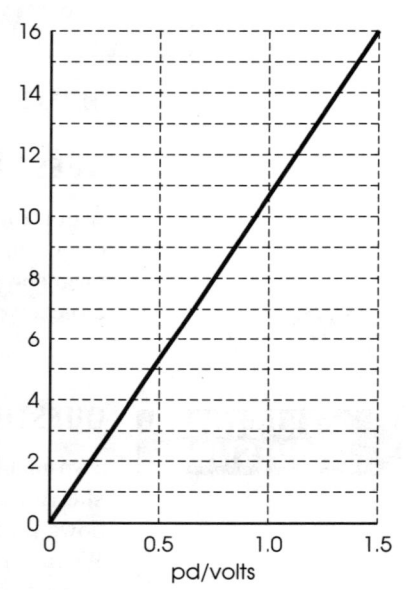

Fig. 13.50

(d) This code is then recorded onto a compact disc. Draw the output of the CD player when the code is converted back into a voltage signal using the same code again. (MEG)

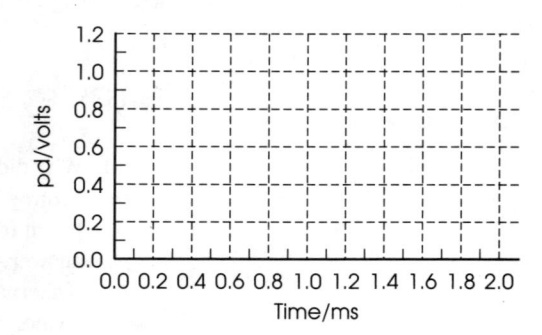

Fig. 13.51

ANSWERS TO EXAMINATION QUESTIONS

MULTIPLE CHOICE QUESTIONS

Question	1	2	3	4	5
Answer	D	D	B	C	D

STRUCTURED QUESTIONS

ANSWER 6

(a) The rods move apart because each has been magnetised in the same direction by the current in the coil. The polarity of a given end is the same for each rod and they repel.

(b) The rods are likely to be made of soft iron. One reason is that when the current is turned off, the rods quickly lose their magnetism and return to their original positions. They must be made of a "soft" magnetic material.

(c) The rods will vibrate, moving away and returning at the frequency of the supply. On each part of the a.c. cycle the rods repel. As the current passes through zero the rods come together again.

ANSWER 7

(a) When current flows in the relay coil the electromagnet in it becomes magnetic. This attracts the metal in the switch which, in moving, closes the contacts to the second circuit, and turns the second circuit on.

(b) If the motor ran on a high voltage or required a large starting current, the relay would isolate the "used" side of the circuit from the dangerously high value side. Only a small current is needed to activate the relay coil.

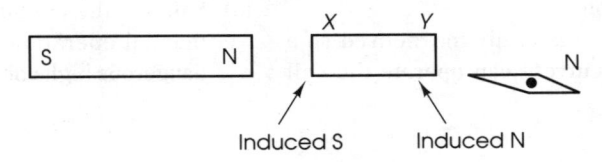

Fig. 13.53

ANSWER 8

(a) (i) and (ii) Two forces – repelled by N, attracted by S. Pole moves along resultant force direction. See Fig. 13.52.

Two forces– repelled by N attracted by S

Pole moves along resultant force direction

Fig. 13.52

(b) (i) The needle turns as shown in Fig. 13.53. The soft iron becomes an induced magnet as indicated. The N-seeking end of the compass is repelled.

(ii) The soft iron will not retain this polarity. When it is reversed end Y becomes induced south and X induced north – so no change in the compass needle.

ANSWER 9

This is a further level short question.

(a) The signal is smooth and continuous.
(b) 0, 0.3, 0.55, 1.05, 0.75.
(c) 0, 3, 6, 11, 8.
(d) Points (not a line) marked correctly with the same values as in (a).

CHAPTER 13 MAGNETISM AND ELECTROMAGNETISM

TUTOR'S QUESTION AND ANSWER

QUESTION

Figure 13.54 shows the switching of a high-voltage circuit by a relay operated by a 12 V supply.

(a) Calculate the current flowing in the relay coil if its resistance is 48 Ω.
(b) Calculate the energy transformed in the coil in 2 min.
(c) The relay is wound on a metal core.
  (i) State a suitable metal for the core.
  (ii) Explain why you think this metal suitable.
  (iii) What would happen if the core was made of copper?
(d) Give a reason why the high voltage is switched in this way rather than by inserting a switch directly into the high-voltage circuit. (MEG)

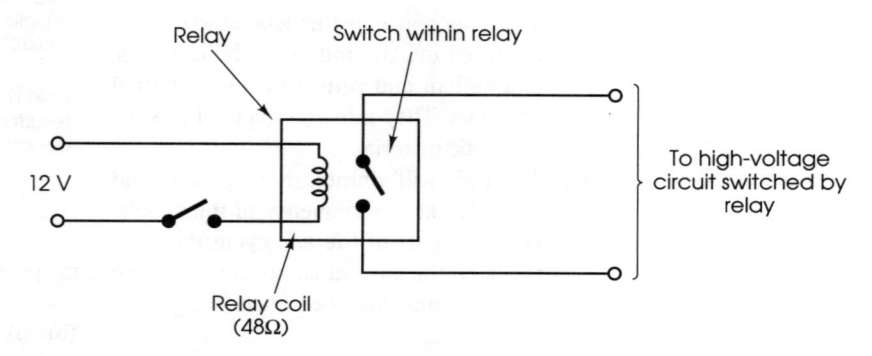

Fig. 13.54

ANSWER

(a) $V = IR$, therefore

$$I = \frac{V}{R} = \frac{12}{48} = \underline{0.25 \text{ A}}$$

(b) Energy = $IVt = 0.25 \times 12 \times 2 \times 60$

$$= \underline{360 \text{ J}}.$$

(c) (i) Soft iron.
  (ii) Soft iron is easily magnetised so a small current can operate the coil and switch the relay on. It easily loses its magnetism so the relay can also switch off.
  (iii) Copper is **not** a magnetic material so the only field would be that of the coil itself which would not be enough to attract the switch armature.

(d) Safety – the circuit to be switched by a manual operation is isolated from the dangerous high-voltage system.

CHAPTER 13 STUDENT'S ANSWER WITH THE EXAMINER'S COMMENTS 237

STUDENT'S ANSWER WITH THE EXAMINER'S COMMENTS

STUDENT ANSWER TO QUESTION 7

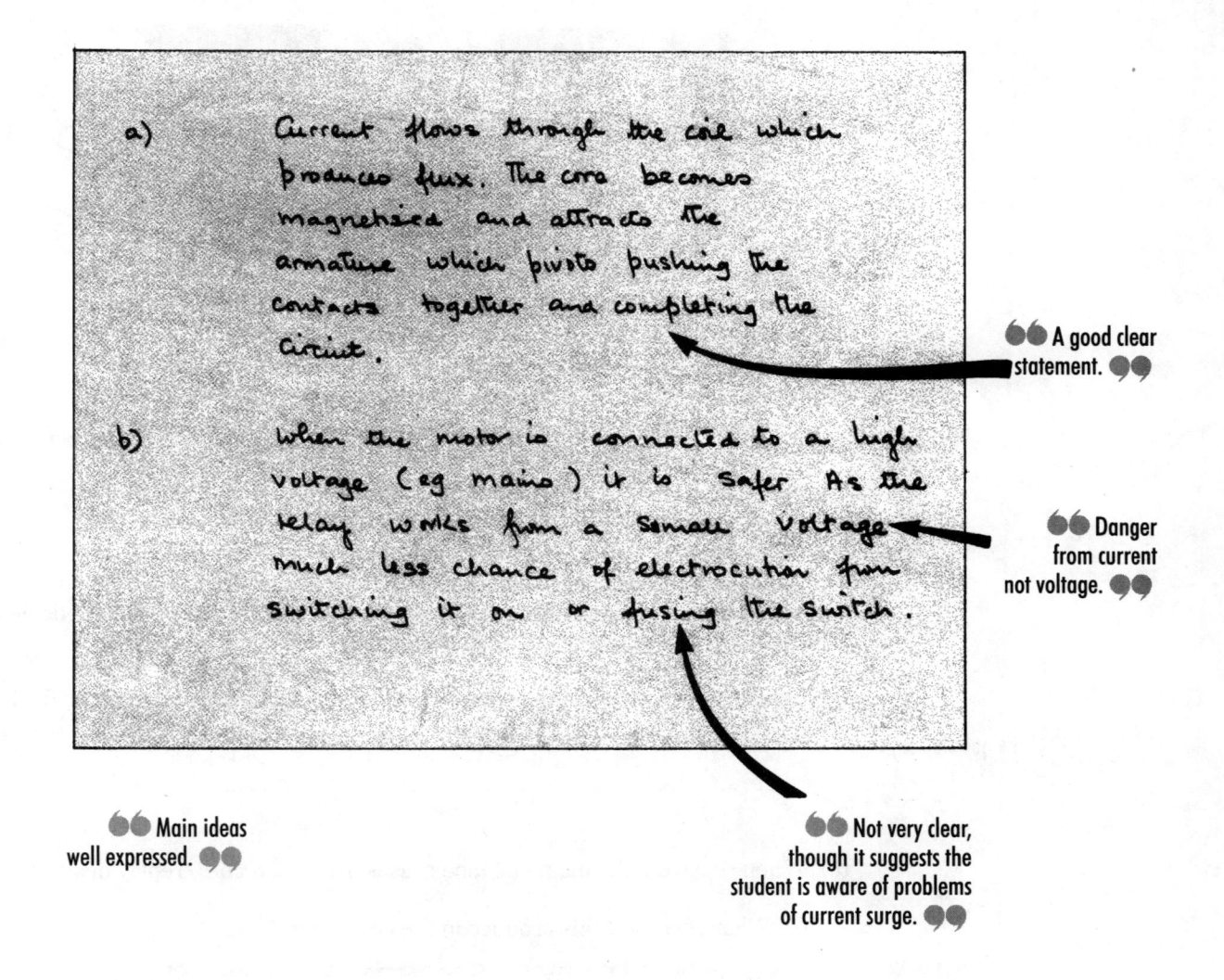

a) Current flows through the coil which produces flux. The core becomes magnetised and attracts the armature which pivots pushing the contacts together and completing the circuit.

66 A good clear statement. **99**

b) When the motor is connected to a high voltage (eg mains) it is safer. As the relay works from a small voltage much less chance of electrocution from switching it on or fusing the switch.

66 Danger from current not voltage. **99**

66 Main ideas well expressed. **99**

66 Not very clear, though it suggests the student is aware of problems of current surge. **99**

MORE EXAMINER'S COMMENTS CENTRAL/HIGHER LEVEL

The diagram shows some of the parts in a cassette tape recorder.

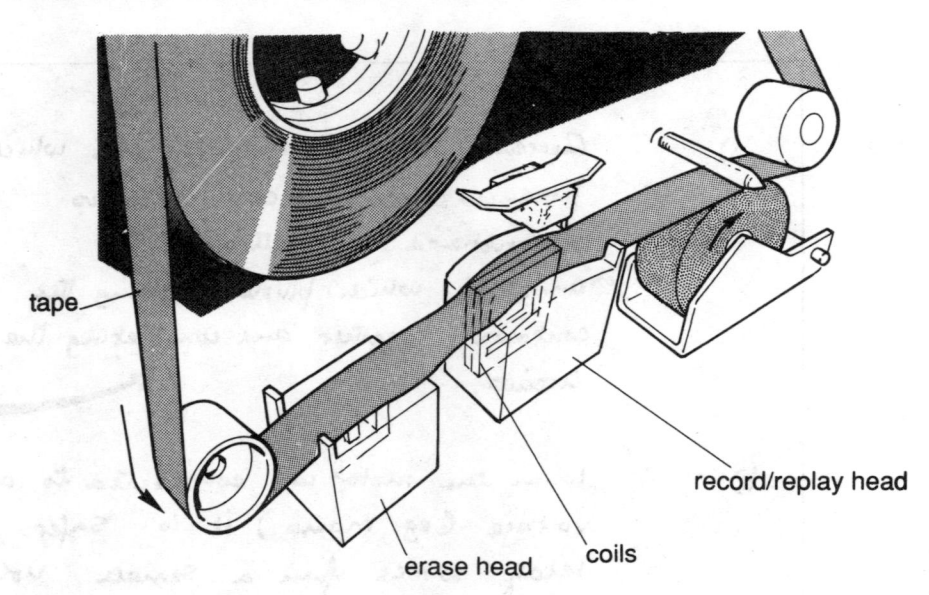

[Diagram labels: tape, record/replay head, coils, erase head]

The record/play head consists of a coil of wire wound around a core. When making a recording, an electrical signal passes through the coil to produce a magnetic field. This field leaves a magnetic pattern on the tape.

(a) Explain why recorded tapes should not be stored in a strong magnetic field.

> 🗨 The question says *explain* 🗨

The tapes get wiped ....(1)

(b) When replayed, the magnetic tape passes over the record/replay head.

  (i) What effect will this produce in the coil of wire?

> 🗨 Correct 🗨

A changing current is produced ....(1)

  (ii) The signal from the coil of wire is amplified and passes to the loudspeaker. Why does the signal need to be amplified to make the loudspeaker work?

> 🗨 Correct 🗨

So that it has enough energy to drive the loudspeaker ...(1)

(c) The pattern on the tape can be destroyed by passing the tape over the erase head. An alternating current passes through a coil around the erase head.

  (i) What is an alternating current?

> 🗨 Very vague! The current flows first in one direction and then the other. This is then repeated. 🗨

It goes to and fro ....(1)

  (ii) How does an alternating current destroy the recording on the tape?

> 🗨 The a.c. makes it a changing magnetic field. This new, high frequency pattern is recorded on the tape instead of the original magnetic pattern 🗨

It makes a magnet ....(1)

REVIEW SHEET

- All magnets have _____ poles.

- Name the three magnetic metal elements.
   1. _____.   2. _____.   3. _____.

- Lines of force are also called _____.

- Lines of force show the direction that would be taken by a __ pole and therefore often go from a __ pole to a __ pole. The lines will be _____ when the field is stronger.

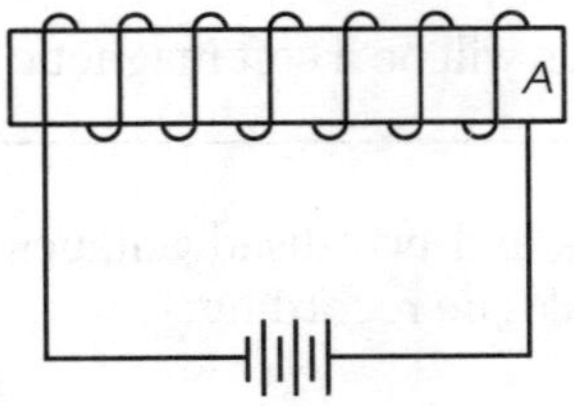

Fig. 13.55

- The end A of the iron bar in the diagram will be a _____ pole.

- Name a use for a relay. _____.

- The wire in the diagram carries a current as shown by the arrow.

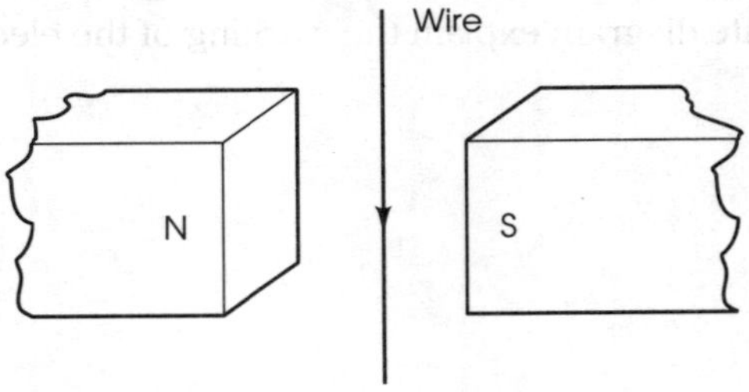

Fig. 13.56

What is the direction of the force on the wire? _____.

What is the name for the sort of magnetic field that produces this force?
_____.

State two things that you could do to make the force on the wire greater.
_____.

- A d.c. motor must have a split ring commutator. Explain *why* the split ring commutator is needed.

_____

_____.

- Draw a diagram of the split ring commutator.

CHAPTER 13 MAGNETISM AND ELECTROMAGNETISM

- Name three things that you could increase in order to change the design of an electric motor and make it turn faster.

    1. _____. 2. _____. 3. _____.

- Name suitable materials for

    1. The coil of a motor. _____

    2. The brushes of a motor. _____

    3. The permanent magnet of a motor. _____

    4. The core of the coil for a relay. _____

    5. The armature of an electric bell. _____

    6. The core of an electromagnet for lifting ferrous scrap. _____

    7. The core of a tape recorder read/write head. _____

- Which of the above materials will be a soft magnetic material.
  _____

- Write down two advantages and two disadvantages of a digitally recorded signal when compared with an analogue recording.

    Advantages: 1. _____

                   2. _____

    Disadvantages: 1. _____

                   2. _____

- Using an appropriate diagram explain the working of the electric bell

  _____
  _____
  _____
  _____
  _____
  _____
  _____

CHAPTER 14

INDUCED EMF & AC

- INDUCED e.m.f. AND FARADAY'S LAW
- LENZ'S LAW
- THE DYNAMO
- DYNAMOS AND MOTORS
- THE TRANSFORMER
- TRANSFORMER EFFICIENCY
- POWER TRANSMISSION
- POWER STATIONS
- THE NATIONAL GRID SYSTEM
- DIODE PROTECTION

GETTING STARTED

Electricity and magnetism are closely linked. An electric current gives rise to a magnetic field, and current flowing in a magnetic field is acted upon by a force. This can be put to useful effect in the d.c. motor, converting electrical energy to kinetic energy. This section explores the *reverse effect*, obtaining electrical energy from kinetic energy using magnetic flux changes. This has application in various devices including dynamos and transformers. Many such effects rely on a changing or alternating current, and some properties of alternating currents will also be considered.

CHAPTER 14 INDUCED EMF & AC

ESSENTIAL PRINCIPLES

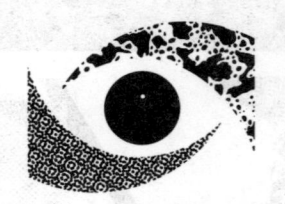

1 > INDUCED e.m.f. AND CHANGING FLUX

❝❝ Be careful of using the expression induced CURRENT. Induced currents can occur *as a result of* an induced e.m.f. if a circuit is complete – but the e.m.f. comes FIRST. ❞❞

A single wire connected to a sensitive galvanometer, and moved in a magnetic field as shown (in Fig. 14.1), causes a movement on the galvanometer. This means that a small current flows. The flow occurs *only* when the wire moves, and only then if it *moves across* the magnetic field, *not* when it moves in the same direction as the field.

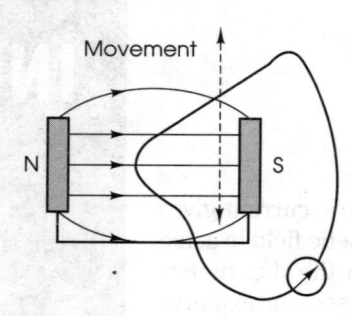

Fig. 14.1 Moving a wire in a field induces an e.m.f.

For current to flow, there must be a source of e.m.f. The e.m.f. is induced in the wire. Current then flows because there is a complete circuit. The e.m.f. can also be induced if a magnet moves relative to a stationary wire. However, the effect is more noticeable if the wire is in the form of a coil or solenoid (Fig. 14.2). Again the e.m.f. only occurs when the magnet moves.

It can be shown, by adapting the experimental arrangement that the *greatest deflection* occurs when:

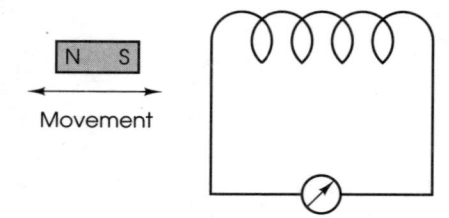

Fig. 14.2 A magnet moving relative to a coil induces an e.m.f.

1. A large number of turns of coil is used;
2. The magnet is very strong;
3. The magnet moves very quickly.

A **magnetic field** can be pictured as consisting of *lines of magnetic flux*. Figure 14.3 shows the relation between the coil and the magnetic flux of the magnet as the magnet moves towards the coil. The flux linking the coils is changing. The e.m.f. induced is **greatest** when the "flux linkages" are **changing fastest**. The same applies on withdrawing the magnet.

The rule can therefore be simply stated as the **induced e.m.f. is proportional to the rate of change of magnetic flux linking the coil.** In other words, the *more flux* (stronger magnet), the *more links* (more coils) and the *faster speed* (bigger change), the *greater the e.m.f.* This is called *Faraday's Law*. An e.m.f. is induced, whether or not a current flows – current *will* flow if the circuit is complete.

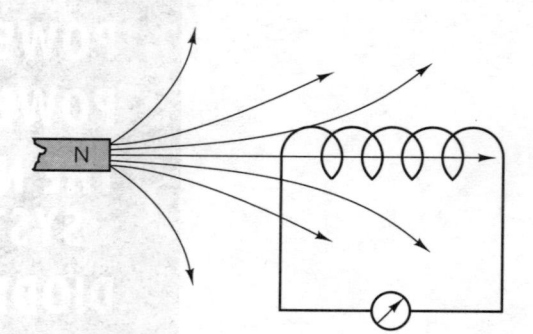

Fig. 14.3 Changing flux "linking" a coil.

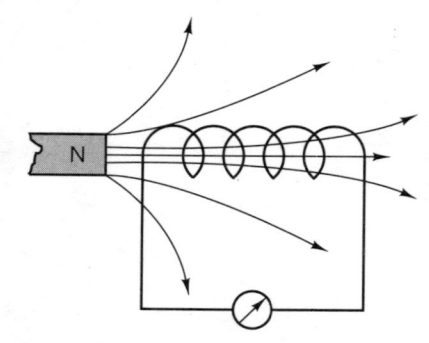

2 > DIRECTION OF INDUCED e.m.f.

In moving a magnet towards or away from a coil, the *direction* of the galvanometer deflection will depend on which way the movement occurs. Consider Fig. 14.4. As the north pole of this magnet moves *towards* the coil, the current flow and therefore the direction of induced e.m.f. are noted to be as

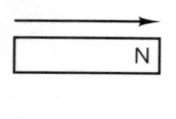

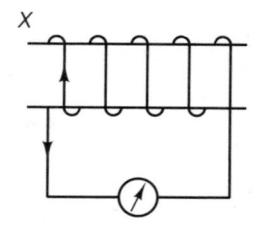

Fig. 14.4

shown, namely *anticlockwise* at end X of the coil. This means that the magnetic field produced by the *induced current* has made end X like a north pole itself – *opposing* the approach of the magnet.

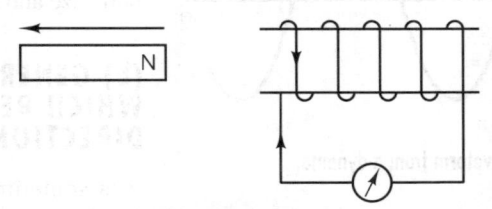

Fig. 14.5 Direction of induced e.m.f.

If the north end moves *away*, the current is *reversed*, and X behaves like a south pole opposing the departure of the north pole (Fig. 14.5). Similarly an approaching south pole gives rise to current making end X like a south pole itself. A south pole leaving the coil makes X like a north pole. **The direction of induced e.m.f. is such as to oppose the motion producing it.** This is called **Lenz's Law**. This sounds very odd, but imagine what

❝ The statement is also called the Lenz law of electromagnetic induction. ❞

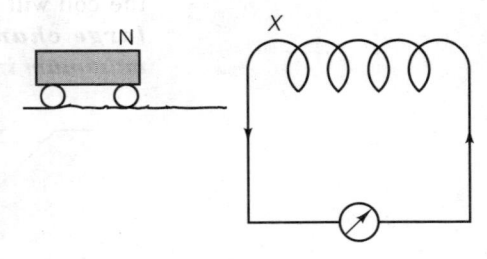

would happen if this were not so. Imagine the north pole of a magnet mounted on wheels and given a small push towards the coil (Fig. 14.6). If the current flowed to make end X a south pole, instead of as really happens, a repelling north pole, then the magnet would be attracted, and accelerate to X. The flux change would be greater, giving a greater induced e.m.f., more current, a stronger attracting field, more acceleration, etc. One small push, and a little work done would produce a huge energy conversion. Energy can only be converted if work is done, so the direction rule for e.m.f. is only a *consequence of energy conservation*.

Fig. 14.6

3 > GENERATING AN e.m.f. – THE DYNAMO

The e.m.f. induced in all previous examples have been very small, and only occur when a wire moves in a field or a magnet moves relative to a coil. To produce a *continuous source of e.m.f., continuous motion in a field* is required.

(a) GENERATING AN e.m.f. IN ALTERNATING DIRECTIONS

A coil is wound on a wooden or soft iron armature, and is rotated in a magnetic field provided by the poles of permanent magnets. As side AB moves upwards it cuts the flux of the magnet and an e.m.f. is induced (Fig. 14.7).

❝ The fact that BOTH frequency and amplitude change is often forgotten by candidates. Frequency change is easily remembered but amplitude (induced e.m.f.) depends in this case on frequency, so the two occur together. ❞

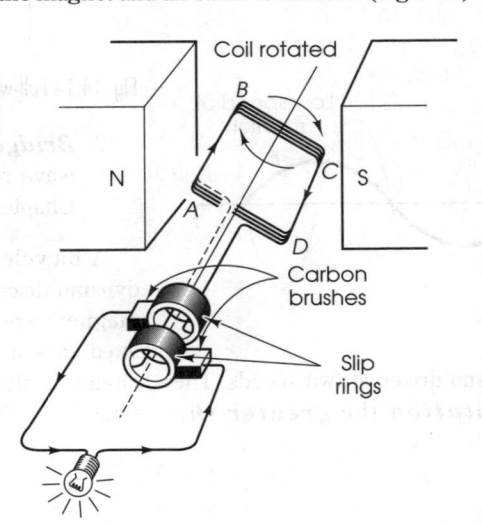

Fig. 14.7 a.c. dynamo system.

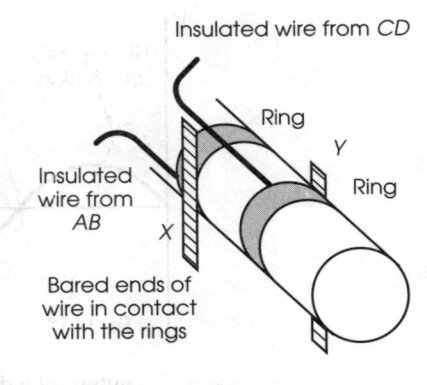

The direction of induced e.m.f. in a wire is given, as in a motor, by **Fleming's rule**, but using the **right** hand. Therefore e.m.f. induced is from A to B. Similarly there is an e.m.f. induced from C to D and, if the external circuit is complete, current flows in the direction ABCD. The ends of the coil are in contact with carbon brushes through slip rings, so that side AB of the coil is always in contact with brush X and CD is always in contact with brush Y (Fig. 14.8). When BC is vertical, side AB moves down, and the e.m.f. and current in AB are now in the *opposite direction* to when AB was moving upwards.

Fig. 14.8 A slip-ring commutator.

An oscilloscope connected across XY shows that the e.m.f. is continuously changing in size and direction (Fig. 14.9). The maximum e.m.f. occurs when there is the

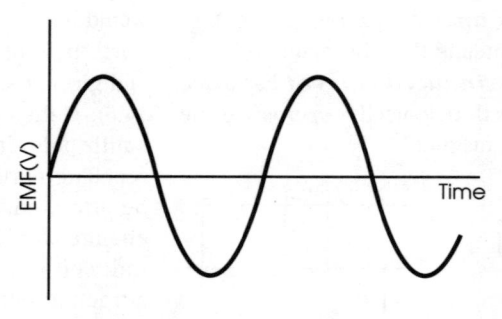

Fig. 14.9 Output waveform from a dynamo.

greatest rate of flux change. When the coil is horizontal as in Fig. 14.10 there is no flux cutting through the coil. A small movement of the coil will "capture" flux, resulting in a *large change* in the situation and the *maximum induced e.m.f.*

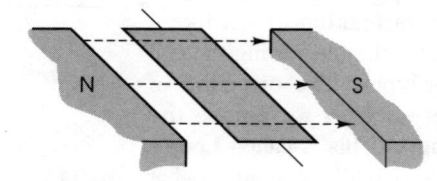

Fig. 14.10

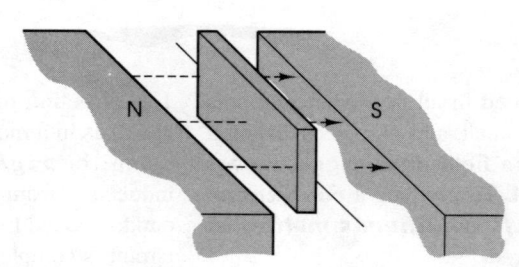

Fig. 14.11

With the coil vertical (Fig. 14.11) the maximum flux is linking the coil. However, a small movement will *not* change the linkage by a lot, if at all. There is now zero induced e.m.f.

If the dynamo is rotated more quickly, two effects are noted. Figure 14.12 shows the

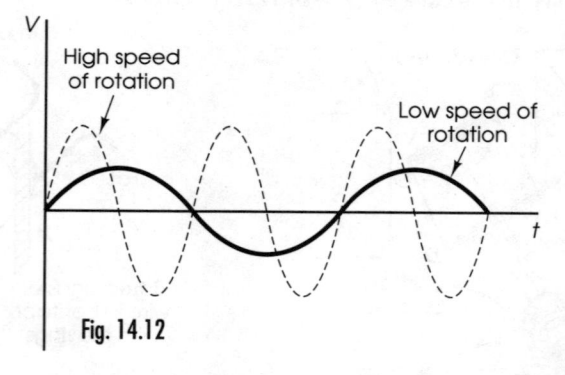

Fig. 14.12

output of a dynamo driven at two speeds. The *faster the rotation* the *greater the frequency of the voltage change*, and the *greater the amplitude of the maximum e.m.f.*, since flux is now being cut more rapidly. This form of dynamo gives an alternating output, the e.m.f. and current change both size and direction.

(b) GENERATING AN e.m.f. WHICH REMAINS IN THE SAME DIRECTION

It is sometimes convenient to generate an e.m.f. which remains in the *same* direction. There are two ways of achieving this:

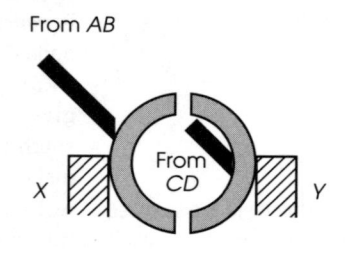

Fig. 14.13 Split-ring commutator.

1. *Use of split rings*. If split rings (Fig. 14.13) are used in place of slip rings, then when AB and CD change their direction of induced e.m.f., they also change output contacts X and Y. In this way the output from X and Y are always in the same direction, though the e.m.f. will still vary in size. The waveform of the output is shown in Fig. 14.14. This is called a *full-wave rectified output*.

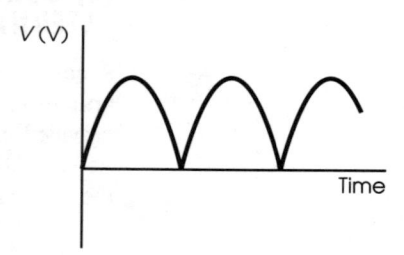

Fig. 14.14 Full-wave rectification.

2. *Bridge rectifier.* This also gives full-wave rectification and is discussed in Chapter 8.

A bicycle dynamo is similar to the a.c. dynamo discussed in this section, except that magnets are usually made to rotate within fixed coils in order to produce the necessary changing flux. The output is, however, the same.

4 DYNAMOS AND MOTORS

> This is again a consequence of conservation of energy.

A dynamo is designed to convert kinetic energy into electrical energy, and a motor converts electrical energy into kinetic energy. The same design applies in each case – both have a coil, magnets and a commutator of some sort contacting carbon brushes. When a dynamo is turned by hand with no external circuit (i.e. no current is drawn) it can be turned easily. However, if it is required to light a bulb, and therefore to supply current, it is much harder to turn. In lighting a bulb, current is flowing in the coil. The force on the current is **opposed** to the original force turning the dynamo, so more **work** must be done to overcome this force.

Similarly when a motor is running, the coil is turning in a magnetic field and flux is being cut. The motor has an e.m.f. induced in its coil which *opposes* the original supply. This is called a **back e.m.f.** and it limits the current flow in the motor.

5 A DIFFERENT WAY OF CHANGING FLUX

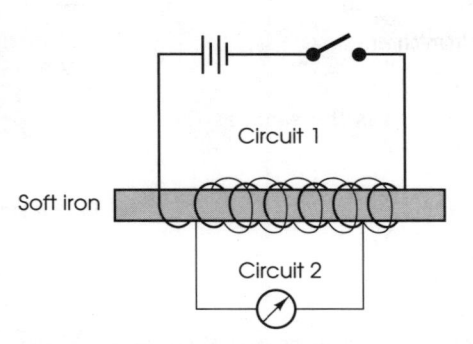

Fig. 14.15 "Mutual" change of flux.

Figure 14.15 shows two separate circuits containing coils, and wound on to the same piece of soft iron rod. If the switch in circuit 1 is closed, there is a momentary current flow in circuit 2. The same thing happens when circuit 1 is switched OFF, but the flow in circuit 2 is in the *opposite* direction to the way it flowed before. There is no current in circuit 2 except on switching circuit 1 ON or OFF.

This is a **different** way of inducing an e.m.f. Originally there is no magnetic flux in the soft iron. When the current first flows in circuit 1 flux builds up in the iron, to a steady value. This means that flux is changing in the other circuit, so an e.m.f. is induced while the change is taking place. When the current flow is steady and the flux remains constant there is no induced e.m.f.

On switching circuit 1 OFF, the flux in the iron collapses, again causing a flux change, but in the opposite direction, in circuit 2. If the flux in the first circuit could change continuously, then there would be a continuous e.m.f. induced in the other circuit. This can be achieved using alternating current, and is the principle behind the **transformer**.

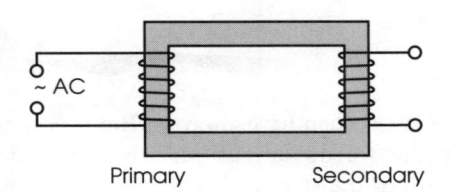

6 THE TRANSFORMER

Fig. 14.16 Simple transformer.

The circuit is shown in Fig. 14.16. It consists of a central closed soft iron core, which itself is made of laminations, rather than one solid piece of iron. Two coils of insulated copper wire, called the **primary coil** and the **secondary coil**, are wound on the core as shown. If an alternating e.m.f. is applied to the primary coil, an oscilloscope across the secondary shows an alternating e.m.f. across the secondary. If the secondary circuit is completed with a bulb, it will light continuously.

The explanation for transformer action is best split into a **sequence** of **statements**, explaining what is happening at each stage:

1. The applied alternating e.m.f. drives alternating current through the primary.
2. The alternating current in the primary causes alternating magnetic flux in the core.
3. Changing flux in the core links with the secondary coil and induces an alternating e.m.f.
4. The secondary e.m.f. drives alternating current in a completed secondary circuit.

The size of the induced e.m.f. in the secondary depends on the primary e.m.f., and also on the relative number of turns of wire in the primary and secondary coils.

With 120 turns on the primary side and 240 turns on the secondary side, 6 V a.c. applied to the primary gives about 12 V a.c. at the secondary output (Fig. 14.17). This is called a **step-up transformer**.

CHAPTER 14 INDUCED EMF & AC

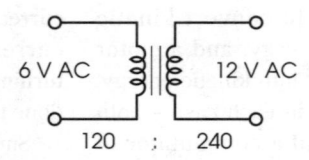

Fig. 14.17 Step-up transformer; circuit symbol.

With 240 turns (primary) and 120 turns (secondary) at 6 V input gives about 3 V output; a **step-down transformer** (Fig. 14.18).

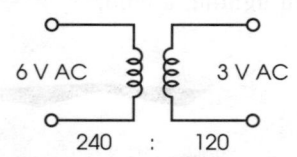

Fig. 14.18 Step-down transformer.

The ratio of voltages is the same as the turns ratio, or

$$\frac{V_p}{V_s} = \frac{N_p}{N_s}$$

where V_p = primary voltage;
V_s = secondary voltage;
N_p = number of primary turns;
N_s = number of secondary turns.

However, the **actual** number of turns must be enough to prevent a coil burning out; 20 on the primary and just 2 on a secondary would result in too much heat generated. There must be enough turns to give reasonable resistance of a few ohms. Although a step-up transformer will give a greater output voltage than its supplied input, it does not multiply energy. **Energy is still conserved** as the following circuit shows.

In order to measure the energy supplied to the primary and secondary circuits, readings of current and voltage are required. This means that **a.c. meters** are necessary, or in the case of voltage measurements a calibrated oscilloscope could be used.

A resistor, or a lamp, is used as a "load" in the secondary to complete the circuit (Fig. 14.19). If the input voltage is 6 V a.c., and the turns ratio is 120 : 240, the output will be near 12 V. If the current in the primary is 0.5 A, then it is found that the secondary current will be about 0.25 A.

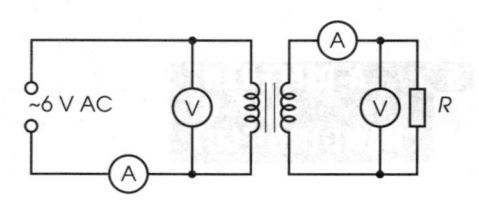

Fig. 14.19 Measurement of power in a transformer circuit.

- Power is energy per second.
- Power in primary = $I_p V_p$.
- Power in secondary = $I_s V_s$.
- It is found that **approximately** $I_p V_p = I_s V_s$.
- **Always** $I_p V_p \geq I_s V_s$.

So energy is conserved. If the voltage rises, the current **falls** in the same proportion. Stepping down the voltage **increases** the current.

7 TRANSFORMER EFFICIENCY

Values quoted in the last section have always been qualified by the words "about" or "approximately". An **ideal** transformer would be one for which

$$\frac{V_p}{V_s} = \frac{N_p}{N_s}$$

and

$$V_p I_p = V_s I_s$$

However in reality, while transformers tend to be very efficient indeed, there are ways in which the energy supplied is converted into other unwanted forms, which leads to **less than** 100 per cent efficiency of conversion. These "losses" can be reduced by good design.

WAYS OF REDUCING LOSSES IN EFFICIENCY

1 ENERGY CONVERTED TO HEAT IN THE COILS

Whenever a current flows, heat is produced, given by I^2R. The use of **low-resistance wire** helps minimise this wasted energy.

2 HEATING OF THE CORE-EDDY CURRENTS

The core is a magnetic conductor, but also a conductor of electric current. Changing flux in the core induces e.m.f. in the core itself which causes surges (eddies) of current in the core, and produces heat. This is reduced by **laminating the core**.

3 FLUX LOSS

The transformer depends, for efficient action, on all flux produced in the primary arriving at the secondary. A square core with sharp edges leads to flux leakage to the air. A **good core design** (e.g. a circle with the secondary wound on top of the primary) can eliminate the source of inefficiency.

4 HYSTERESIS

During a cycle of magnetic reversal there is a loss of energy to the magnetic material. **Soft iron** suffers less from this than steel, and is therefore more appropriate as a core material.

8 POWER TRANSMISSION

Energy converted at a power station from chemical or nuclear energy to electrical (in most cases) has to be transmitted over long distances through the National Grid system. This means that it has to be transmitted through wires, which have resistance, and which cause wasteful energy conversion into heat.

The fact of energy conversion into heat during transmission is easily illustrated in a laboratory, if a short length of high-resistance wire is used to model the large resistance of many kilometres of wire used in transmission.

The 12 V lamp connected in parallel across the supply glows brightly, indicating that there is a large energy conversion. The lamp at the right-hand side of the high-resistance line only glows dimly. Energy is "lost" from electrical energy to heat and is not available to the lamp (Fig. 14.20). Since energy = power × time the total energy can be found by considering the power at the input and output ends of the line:

$$\text{Power} = IV$$

Therefore

$$P_{IN} = P_{OUT} + P_{LOSS}$$

and

$$IV_{OUT} = IV_{IN} - IV_{LOSS}$$

The circuit is a series circuit so the current is the same throughout. This suggests that losses can be reduced by using low currents, because $IV_{LOSS} = I^2R$.

The same arrangement of apparatus driven at 240 V a.c. has two lamps of the same power as before at about the same brightness, so less energy loss is occurring (Fig. 14.21).

At the higher voltage, the current is smaller, and the energy loss is smaller. However, in practice, it is not possible to use a high voltage transmitted directly to a consumer. The answer is to use an alternating

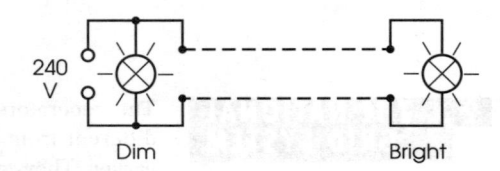

Fig. 14.21 High-voltage power line.

supply which can be transformed to give a high-voltage transmission at low current, and therefore low power loss.

At the generating end the voltage is raised by a factor of 1 : 20, so the current is reduced (Fig. 14.22). Smaller current flows in the wires to the delivery end, so there is less heat loss. Since there is less energy converted to heat, there is more energy conversion at the end of the wires.

Note: This experiment produces high voltage and should *not* be carried out by students.

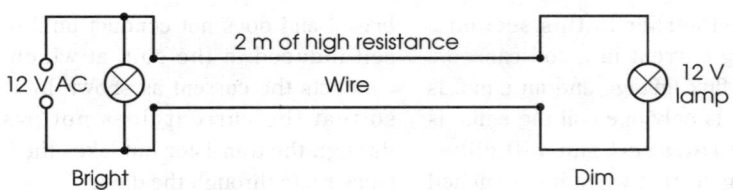

Fig. 14.20 Low-voltage power line.

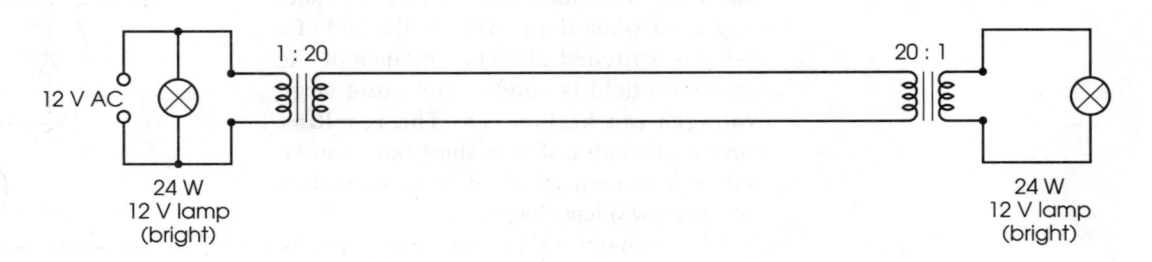

Fig. 14.22 Use of transformers to reduce power losses.

EXTENSION MATERIALS

1. POWER STATIONS

In the UK the majority of our electrical energy is generated using oil or coal as a fuel, though there is increasing use of nuclear energy and some additions to the National Grid from "alternative" sources. The sequence produced in a power station is as follows:

1. Heat energy is produced by burning coal or oil, or from fission in the core of a reactor.
2. Water is heated and converted to high-temperature steam, which is also maintained at high pressure.
3. The steam is allowed to expand into a low-pressure region and in doing so it turns the blades of a turbine, after which it is condensed back to water, for use again in the boiling. Condensing the steam requires large cooling towers, and a lot of heat is lost to the atmosphere.
4. The moving turbines rotate generators, producing electricity by electromagnetic induction. The voltage is stepped up by a transformer before transmission. The flow diagrams (Fig. 14.23) show the process, and the energy conversion.

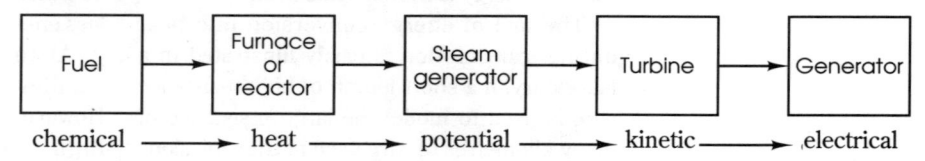

Fuel → Furnace or reactor → Steam generator → Turbine → Generator

chemical → heat → potential → kinetic → electrical

Fig. 14.23

2. THE NATIONAL GRID SYSTEM

The generators at a power station are slightly different from the simple dynamo described earlier. They are designed with a set of coils, producing three separate supplies of a.c. known as a *three-phase supply*. Each supply is out of phase with the other two, so that there is always current in two of the three wires. Heavy-duty machinery is usually run on a three-phase supply, while an ordinary household has only one phase supplied to it. The supply is generated at 25 kV and stepped up to 400 kV for transmission. A series of transformers, called substations, steps the voltage down for consumption. Industrial users receive the three-phase supply at 33 kV or 11 kV. Households receive one phase at 240 V, with one house in three receiving a particular phase from the three available.

3. DIODE PROTECTION

As we have seen earlier in this section a rapidly changing current in a coil causes a rapid change of flux linkage and an e.m.f. is induced. If there is only one coil the e.m.f. is said to be *self induced* and will either oppose a growing current when it is switched off or will help maintain a decreasing current that is being switched off. (This is another illustration of Lenz's law.) This can be quite important when the current to the coil of a relay is switched off. The collapse of the magnetic field is sudden and quite large voltages can be induced. The resulting current, though lasting a short time, can be sufficient to permanently damage transistors or other low voltage hardware.

The transistors can be protected by connecting a diode across the coil as shown in the diagram. The diode is normally reverse biased and does not conduct until the p.d. is self induced in the coil, at which point it conducts the current as shown by the arrow so that the current does not pass down through the transistor but takes the low resistance route through the diode.

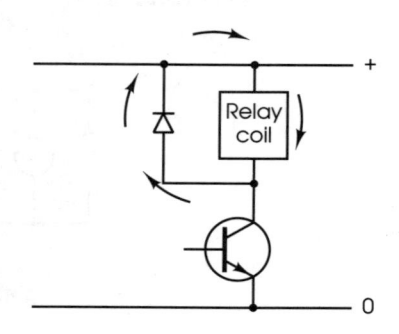

Fig. 14.24

EXAMINATION QUESTIONS

MULTIPLE CHOICE QUESTIONS

QUESTION 1

Power losses in the National Grid system are reduced by using

- A Thin cables
- B High cables
- C Underground cables
- D High voltages (SEG)

QUESTION 2

A step-down transformer changes 240 V a.c. to 48 V a.c.. There are 2000 turns on the primary coil. The number of turns on the secondary coil is

- A 40
- B 400
- C 5000
- D 10000 (SEG)

QUESTION 3

On electricity bills 5p is charged for each "unit" used. This means 5p for each unit of

- A Electric charge
- B Electric current
- C Electrical energy
- D Electrical voltage (SEG)

QUESTION 4

When 24 V is applied across the primary of a transformer, the current in the primary is 2 A. The output voltage from the secondary is 12 V. What is the ratio of the number of turns in the secondary to the number of turns in the primary?

- A 1 : 4
- B 1 : 2
- C 1 : 1
- D 2 : 1
- E 4 : 1 (ULEAC)

QUESTION 5-7

Signals are applied to the Y-plates of an oscilloscope. Which one of the diagrams in Fig. 14.25 shows the trace obtained in each case?

5. An alternating voltage with the time base switched OFF.
6. The same alternating voltage with the time base switched ON.
7. A voltage from a 1.5 V cell with the time base switched ON. (ULEAC)

QUESTION 8

In the National Grid system the transmission

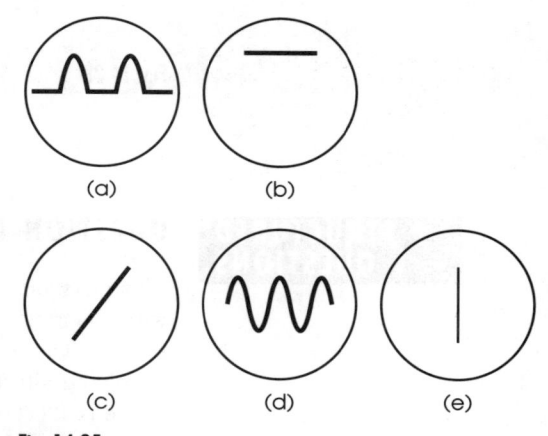

Fig. 14.25

of electrical energy is by means of overhead conductors. These conducting wires carry

- A Alternating current at high voltage
- B Alternating current at high frequency
- C Alternating current at low voltage
- D Direct current at high voltage
- E Direct current at low frequency (ULEAC)

QUESTION 9

Figure 14.26 represents a simple transformer with 20 turns on the primary coil and 80 turns on the secondary. If 4 V a.c. is supplied to the primary coil, what voltage would you expect across the secondary coil?

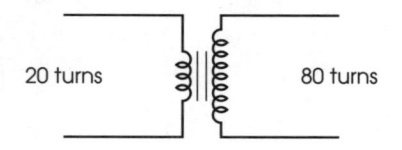

Fig. 14.26

- A 4 V
- B 16 V
- C 100 V
- D 240 V (ULEAC)

QUESTION 10

Karen sets up the circuit shown in Fig. 14.27. Which of the traces shown in Fig. 14.28 might be seen on the oscilloscope screen? (SEG)

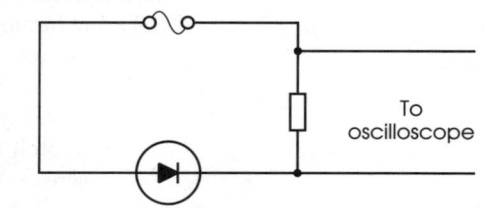

Fig. 14.27

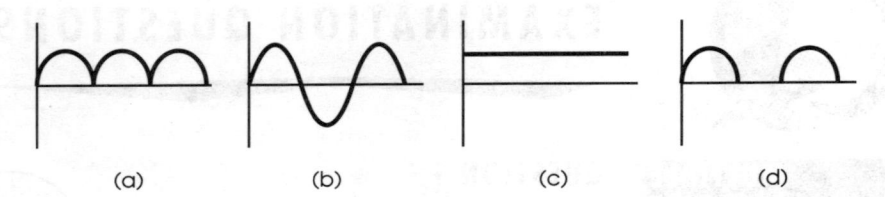

Fig. 14.28

(a) (b) (c) (d)

STRUCTURED QUESTIONS

QUESTION 11

This question is about supplying a consumer with electrical power from the National Grid system. The voltage across the power lines supplying alternating current to an isolated house is 120000 V (Fig. 14.29). The device D changes the voltage of the supply to 240 V.

(a) What do we call the device D? (1 line)
(b) Why is the supply not transmitted all the way at 240 V? (2 lines)
(c) Why cannot 120 000 V be used, unchanged, in the house? (Give two reasons)
(d) Why is alternating current used? (1 line) (ULEAC)

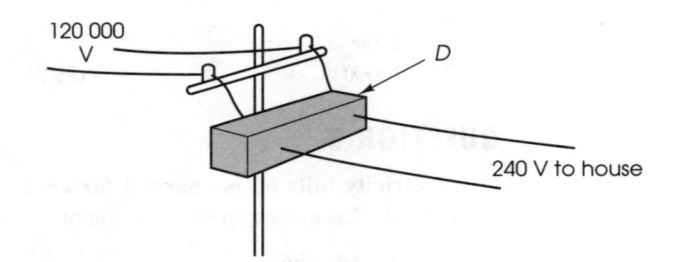

Fig. 14.29

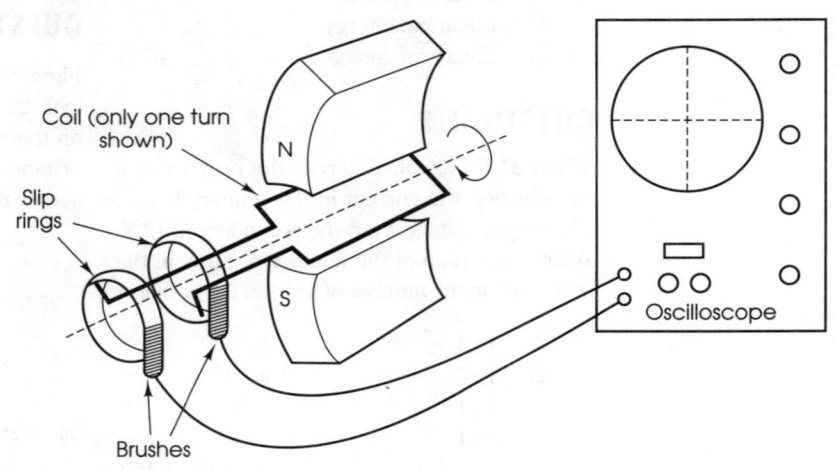

Fig. 14.30

QUESTION 12

An a.c. generator is connected to the Y-inputs of an oscilloscope, as shown in Fig. 14.30. The time base of the oscilloscope is on so that a horizontal line is seen on the screen when the coil is not turning.

(a) Sketch what might be seen on the screen (Fig. 14.31) if the coil is turned at steady speed.
(b) Sketch what you might see on the screen (Fig. 14.32) if the coil is turned at a faster speed.
(c) State two ways in which the generator could be changed so that it would produce a greater e.m.f. (voltage) (2 lines)

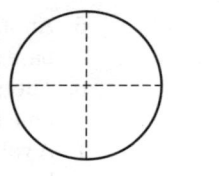

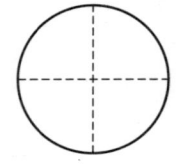

Fig. 14.31   Fig. 14.32

(d) The large a.c. generators used in power stations use electromagnets instead of permanent magnets. They are driven by turbines. Suggest reasons for these differences. (3 lines) (NEAB)

QUESTION 13

Figure 14.33 shows a power station which generates 100 MW of power. The voltage is stepped up to 400 kV and then power is transmitted by the National Grid over a large distance. The voltage is stepped down before the power is used by industry and homes in a town.

(a) Given that 100 MW is fed into the transmission line at 400 kV, calculate the current flowing in the transmission line. (3 lines)
(b) If the resistance of the transmission line is 100 Ω calculate the potential drop along the line due to the current. (1 line)
(c) Calculate the power "lost" along the transmission line. (2 lines)
(d) Calculate what fraction of the power is "lost". (2 lines)
(e) What happens to the "lost" power? (2 lines)
(f) Explain why less power is "lost" when a given amount of power is transmitted at high voltage and low current, rather than high current and low voltage. (4 lines)
(g) Why is there a saving on the cables when the current is low? (2 lines)
(h) The Electricity Board normally transmits power over long distances using overhead power lines, but the general public would often prefer power lines to be put underground.
  (i) Give one advantage of having overhead power lines. (1 line)
  (ii) Give one advantage to the general public of having the power lines underground. (1 line)

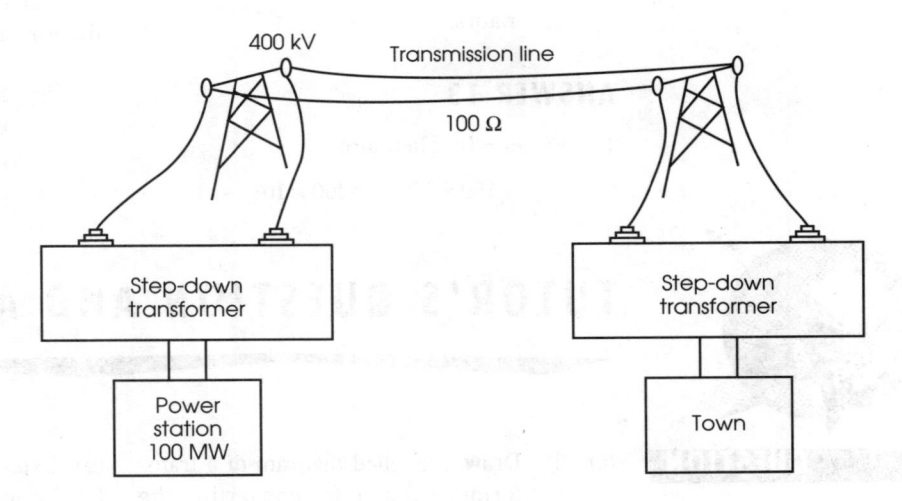

Fig. 14.33

ANSWERS TO EXAMINATION QUESTIONS

MULTIPLE CHOICE QUESTIONS

Question	1	2	3	4	5	6	7	8	9	10
Answer	D	B	C	B	E	D	B	A	B	D

STRUCTURED QUESTIONS

ANSWER 11

(a) Device D is a transformer.
(b) The current would be higher to transmit the same power. This would result in greater power losses. Equally, heavier duty cable would be needed, which would be more expensive.
(c) Voltage would be dangerously high for a person to use with safety – equally for a given power appliance the current would be very high indeed.
(d) Alternating current is used because the voltage can easily be stepped up for transmission with low power losses and stepped down for domestic uses.

Transformers do NOT work on direct current.

ANSWER 12

(a) See Fig. 14.34(a).
(b) See Fig. 14.34(b).

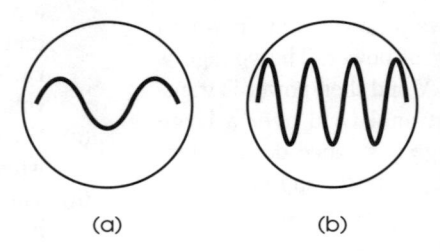

(a) (b)

Fig. 14.34

(c) Possible changes: more turns of wire, stronger magnets, larger area of coil.
(d) Electromagnets are stronger and more easily constructed than large permanent magnets. Turbines are needed because a lot of energy is required to turn the generators.

ANSWER 13

(a) Power = IV. Therefore

$$100 \times 10^6 = I \times 400 \times 10^3$$

Therefore

$$I = \frac{100 \times 10^6}{400 \times 10^3} = \underline{250 \text{ A}}$$

(b) $V = IR$. Therefore

$$V = 250 \times 100 = \underline{25 \text{ kV}}$$

(c) Power = IV. Therefore

$$\text{Power} = 25\,000 \times 250 = \underline{6.25 \text{ MW}}$$

(d) Fraction is

$$\frac{6.25}{100} = \underline{0.0625} \text{ or } \underline{6.25\%}$$

(e) Power "loss" is through heat developed in the transmission lines.
(f) For a given amount of power to be transmitted, the higher the voltage the smaller the current. Power losses are given by I^2R, so small current results in smaller power loss.
(g) Low current can be transmitted using thin cables thus causing a saving in outlay cost.
(h) (i) Easier repair and maintenance if calbes are overhead.
    (ii) More attractive and unspoiled environment if cables are underground.

TUTOR'S QUESTION AND ANSWER

QUESTION

(a) (i) Draw a labelled diagram of a transformer suitable for converting the 240 V main supply to 12 V a.c.
    (ii) If the transformer is ideal and has 80 turns on its secondary (12 V) winding, how many turns should it have on its primary winding?

(b) Explain how the transformer works.
(c) Transformers are not usually 100 per cent efficient. Give a full explanation of two ways in which energy losses occur.
(d) Explain the part played by transformers in the distribution of electrical energy around the country. (UCLES)

ANSWER

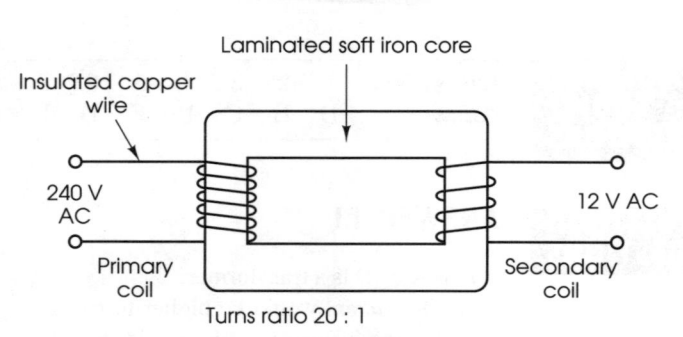

Fig. 14.35

(a) (i) See Fig. 14.35.
    (ii) With a turns ratio of 20 : 1, the primary needs $20 \times 80 = \underline{1600 \text{ turns.}}$

(b) The alternating supply drives alternating current through the primary coil. This produces alternating magnetic flux. The flux passes through the soft iron core, and links with the secondary coil. Since the flux is continuously changing there is an induced e.m.f. in the secondary (alternating) coil which can drive alternating current in a load in the secondary circuit.

(c) The current in the coils will cause a heating effect, which causes the "loss" of some energy. Heating depends on I^2R so low currents and low-resistance wire help eliminate this. Flux changing in the core will induce e.m.f.s in the core itself, so currents, called eddy currents, flow in the core and cause core heating. This is reduced by laminating the core – preventing currents from having a path to flow throughout the core.

(d) Transmission over long distances uses high voltage and low current to prevent excessive power losses (loss through heating proportional to I^2). A transformer at the power station is used to give the high voltage (step-up) and at a substation a step-down transformer converts the high voltage to a suitable safe value for household or industrial use.

STUDENT'S ANSWER WITH THE EXAMINER'S COMMENTS

STUDENT ANSWER TO QUESTION 13

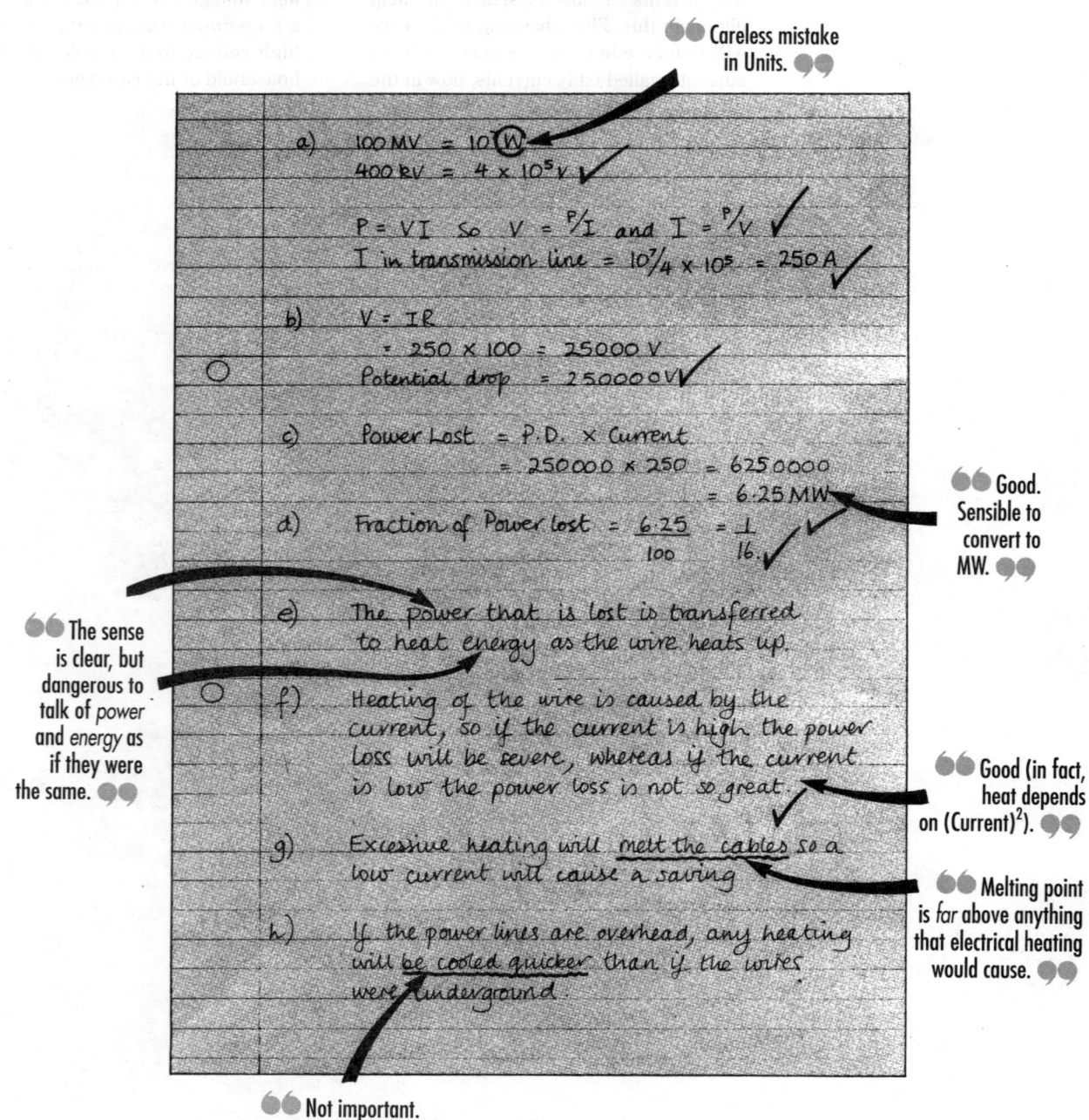

Careless mistake in Units.

a) 100 MV = 10⁸ W ←
   400 kV = 4 × 10⁵ V ✓

   P = VI so V = P/I and I = P/V ✓
   I in transmission line = 10⁸ / 4 × 10⁵ = 250 A ✓

b) V = IR
   = 250 × 100 = 25000 V
   Potential drop = 250000 V ✓

c) Power Lost = P.D. × Current
   = 250000 × 250 = 6250000
   = 6.25 MW

Good. Sensible to convert to MW.

d) Fraction of Power lost = 6.25 / 100 = 1/16 ✓

e) The power that is lost is transferred to heat energy as the wire heats up.

The sense is clear, but dangerous to talk of *power* and *energy* as if they were the same.

f) Heating of the wire is caused by the current, so if the current is high the power loss will be severe, whereas if the current is low the power loss is not so great.

Good (in fact, heat depends on (Current)²).

g) Excessive heating will <u>melt the cables</u> so a low current will cause a saving

Melting point is *far* above anything that electrical heating would cause.

h) If the power lines are overhead, any heating will <u>be cooled quicker</u> than if the wires were <u>underground</u>.

Not important. Environmental issues more vital.

REVIEW SHEET

- State Faraday's law: _____
  _____.

- State Lenz's law: _____
  _____.

- Complete the following equations for an ideal transformer.

  $V_p I_p =$ $\dfrac{V_s}{V_p} =$

- Power is transmitted at _____ voltage on the National Grid system to avoid _____ _____.

- The core of a transformer will be _____ to avoid heat losses.

- A transformer that increases voltage is a Step _____ transformer.

- A transformer with 2000 turns on the primary coil and 200 turns on the secondary coil will be a _____ transformer.

- Name three ways to increase the output voltage from a generator
  1. _____.   2. _____.
  3. _____.

- Sketch the output waveform from a simple a.c. generator

- A transformer has 240 V a.c. applied to its 1200 turn primary coil. The secondary coil consists of 5 thick turns of copper. What is the secondary voltage?
  _____
  _____
  _____.

- If the ends of the secondary coil are joined by an iron nail it becomes red hot. Explain briefly why this happens.
  _____
  _____
  _____.

- There are hints here about how electric welders work!

Complete the following table for four transformers.

Primary volts	Secondary volts	Primary turns	Secondary turns
240	12	12 000	
240	2400		1000
	24	120	240
110		200	400

■ Write under each stage the form of *energy* involved.

Fuel → Furnace or reactor → Steam generator → Turbine → Generator

■ A magnet is pushed into a coil. Write down three ways in which you could *increase* the e.m.f. produced.

1. _____.   2. _____.

3. _____.

■ A transformer is used to light a 12 V 24 W bulb. If the primary voltage is 240 V what is the current in the primary coil?

_____
_____.

■ Draw a diagram of a simple a.c. generator and label the main parts.

CHAPTER 15

ATOMIC STRUCTURE AND RADIOACTIVITY

GETTING STARTED

The model used for a "picture" of a particle of matter so far is a *submicroscopic sphere with no particular structure*. This serves to explain the packing of particles in a solid or the behaviour of gases in Brownian motion or diffusion. It does *not* explain why some materials are good conductors of electricity or of heat, and will certainly not serve to explain the strange behaviour of *radioactive materials*. A revised model is needed to cover these aspects, and to help make accurate future predictions. We need, therefore, to think how the simple "atom" model of kinetic theory should be *adapted* to account for electrical phenomena. This means that we must consider carefully the notion of "moving charges". Equally the discovery that some materials have properties described as "radioactive", means that new ideas about atoms have to be thought through. This section attempts to link the three notions – **atoms** have a substructure which can account for **electrical** properties; within that structure there are **energy** considerations which cause some atoms to be unstable; these ideas give some insight into what an atom may be like.

NO investigation of ionising materials should be carried out by students with this level of knowledge and experience. Experiments on radioactive materials may only be carried out by more experienced students and there are strict rules about supervision, safety, and disposal of waste.

- IDEAS ABOUT CHARGES
- CURRENT AND CHARGE
- THERMIONIC EMISSION
- ELECTRON DEFLECTION
- ATOMS, ELECTRONS AND IONS
- RADIOACTIVE MATERIALS
- MODEL FOR AN ATOM
- ATOM STRUCTURE
- RADIOACTIVE DECAY
- NUCLEAR CHANGES
- CLOUD CHAMBERS
- MEDICAL APPLICATIONS
- INDUSTRIAL USES
- FISSION AND NUCLEAR REACTORS

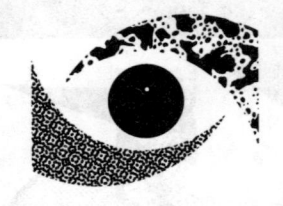

ESSENTIAL PRINCIPLES

1 › IDEAS ABOUT CHARGES

Charge, like mass, is a fundamental idea in physics, and yet it is difficult to say what it is! The only way of approaching the idea of charge is to look at what charges **can do**.

"RUBBING" EXPERIMENTS

It is well known that a piece of insulating material, such as polythene, perspex or PVC, when rubbed on a duster (also an insulator) acquires the property of attracting small objects (Fig. 15.1).

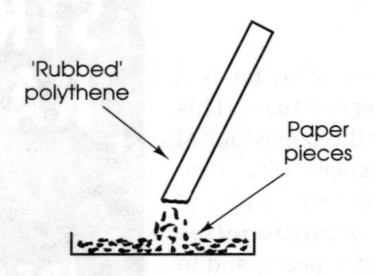

Fig. 15.1 Attraction of uncharged material to charged objects.

The nature of the "attracted" objects does not seem to matter, provided their mass is small, but only an insulating material can cause this attraction. The word "charged" is used to describe **what happens** to the polythene when it is rubbed. The results of this test on many materials suggest as a basic rule that:

- **Charged objects attract uncharged objects.**

The attraction will cause movement of the uncharged object if it has a small mass (and therefore a small weight).

Pairs of charged objects have two possible effects. A strip of charged polythene will **repel** another strip of charged polythene (Fig. 15.2). However, a piece of charged cellulose acetate is **attracted** by a piece of charged polythene (Fig. 15.3).

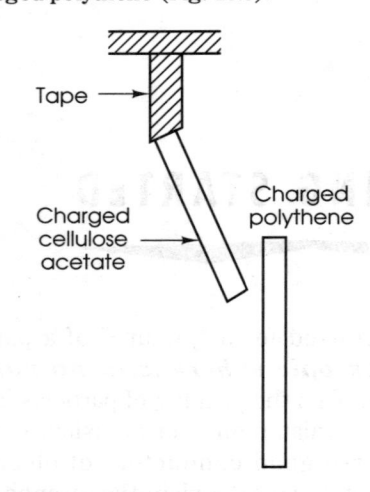

Fig. 15.3 Unlike charges attract.

This led to the idea that **two** sorts of charges can be produced, the **types which repel** and the **types which attract**. For simplicity they are called **positive** ⊕ and **negative** ⊖.

- **Similar charges** ⊕ and ⊕ **repel** or ⊖ and ⊖ **repel.**
- **Opposite charges** ⊕ and ⊖ **attract** or ⊖ and ⊕ **attract.**

The model for an atom does not contain "charge" as one of its properties, so the model needs changing to include charges. Since charging happens to a piece of polythene when it is rubbed, then **originally** it must have the charges present in **equal** quantities. Atoms do not usually show charge-like properties **unless** energy is transferred to them in some way. A strip of polythene which has not been charged would have equal ⊕ and ⊖ charges (Fig. 15.4). This seemed to be true for all large-scale pieces of matter. If the polythene is rubbed, there is a transfer of energy and charges may be enabled to move. The **charges which move** are electrons, i.e. **negative charges**. A material which ends up with an **overall negative charge** has **received electrons**; a **positively charged** material has **lost electrons**.

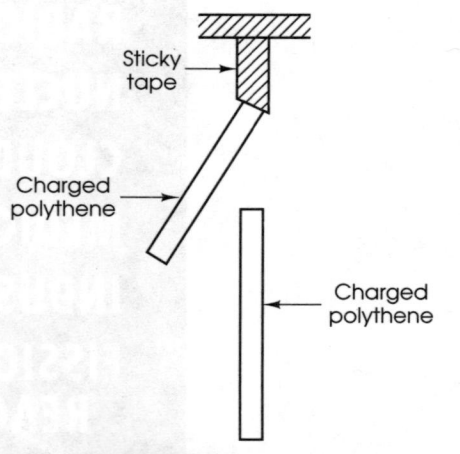

Fig. 15.2 Similar charges repel.

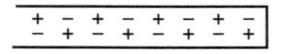

Fig. 15.4 Most objects are electrically neutral.

CHAPTER 15 **ESSENTIAL PRINCIPLES** 259

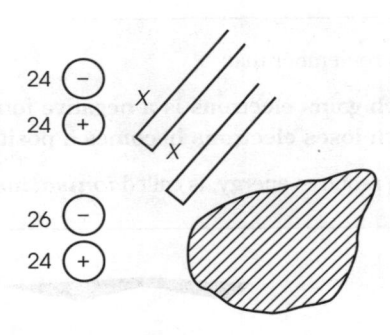

Fig. 15.5 Charge movement.

A simple diagrammatic, and unrealistic, situation is given in Fig. 15.5. Originally X had equal numbers of ⊕ and ⊖ charges. After rubbing it gains two extra ⊖ charges, so that its *overall* charge is now **negative**. The "rubber", having lost negative charge, now also has an unbalanced situation, with its *overall* charge being **positive**. Becoming positively charged means **losing electrons**. Charge can be "induced" in an uncharged object. A positively charged rod near an uncharged object attracts it because the mobile electrons redistribute in the uncharged material (Fig. 15.6).

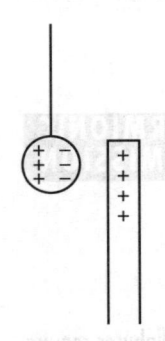

Fig. 15.6 Charge redistribution.

2 > CURRENT AND CHARGE

The unit of charge is the **coulomb** (C); 1 C is the charge associated with about 6.2×10^{18} electrons.

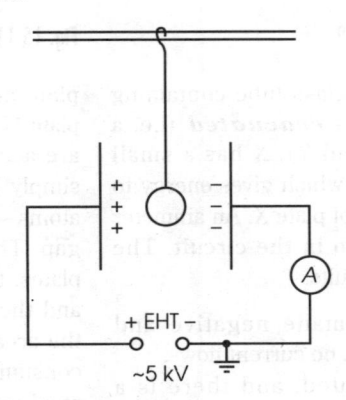

Fig. 15.7 "Shuttling ball" experiment.

Demonstrations like that illustrated in Fig. 15.7 suggest that an electric current is simply a *flow of charge*. The ball in the diagram is made of polystyrene, but painted with a carbon-based paint (or aluminium paint) to make it conduct. The high-voltage supply connected across the metal plates charges them ⊕ and ⊖ respectively. If the ball is touched on to one plate it becomes charged and is repelled, moving across to the other where the process is repeated. The ball shuttles to and fro, carrying charges across the gap, and the **ammeter** (a sensitive light-beam meter) records a small current.

A flow of 1 C/s gives a meter reading of 1 A. Therefore

$$\text{Current} = \frac{\text{Charge}}{\text{Time}} \quad \text{or} \quad I = \frac{Q}{t}$$

(See also direct currents section, Chapter 7.)

In the arrangement of Fig. 15.7 the current was a flow of both ⊕ and ⊖ charge, in opposite directions – both were contributing to the current and the meter reading was in one direction only. A similar effect occurs if a small flame, from a match or a candle, is placed in the gap between the plates (Fig. 15.8). The flame "splits", being attracted part to one plate and part to the other, and a small current is again recorded. This suggests that a flame contains charges of **both** kinds.

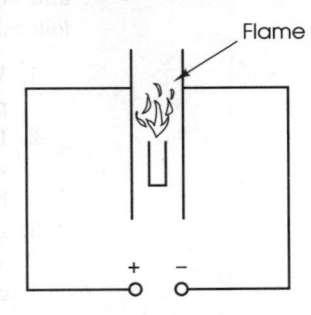

Fig. 15.8 "Flame splitting".

These charges originate in the hot gases of the flame and are called **ions** (Fig. 15.9).

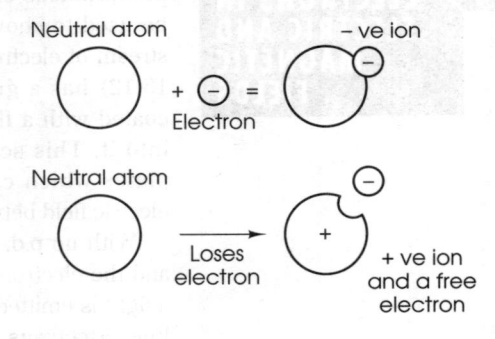

Fig. 15.9 Ionisation.

CHAPTER 15 ATOMIC STRUCTURE AND RADIOACTIVITY

> Make sure that you remember that:
>
> ■ **An atom which gains electrons is a negative ion.**
> ■ **An atom which loses electrons becomes a positive ion.**
>
> The process, which requires energy, is called *ionisation*.

3 THERMIONIC EMISSION

Energy is required to cause electrons to be removed from atoms. One way of doing this is by using heat energy. Figure 15.10 shows a suitable apparatus. A glass tube containing two plates, X and Y, is *evacuated* (i.e. a vacuum between X and Y). X has a small heater circuit behind it which gives energy to the atoms of the metal of plate X. An ammeter and voltmeter are also in the circuit. The following are typical results:

1. With X and Y made negative and positive as shown, no current flows.
2. If X is then heated, and there is a voltage between X and Y of a few hundred volts, a current will flow.
3. If X is heated, but it is made positive and Y is negative, there is again no current.

> 66 Not all syllabuses require knowledge of thermionic emission or the motion of electron streams. Check your own syllabus. 99

Fig. 15.10 Thermionic emission.

This suggests that heating X *releases negative particles* (*electrons*) which are attracted to Y, completing the circuit. The release of electrons from a metal by heating is called *thermionic emission*.

An electron "gun" is a useful way of producing a stream of electrons thermionically (Fig. 15.11). The heater and negative plate are arranged as before. The positive plate is a cylinder with a hole in it. Electrons are accelerated to the positive plate. Many simply hit the plate and are absorbed by its atoms – but some pass out through the central gap. The greater the voltage between the plates, the more the energy of the electrons, and the greater their velocity. After leaving the area between the plates they travel with constant velocity since there is no longer a resultant force acting on them.

The whole arrangement is still in an evacuated tube since an electron colliding with a gas molecule would lose energy to the molecule.

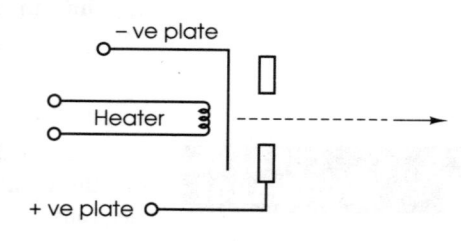

Fig. 15.11 Electron gun.

4 ELECTRONS IN ELECTRIC AND MAGNETIC FIELDS

Modifications of the "electron gun" tube can be used to show some other properties of a stream of electrons. The deflection tube (Fig. 15.12) has a gun at one end and a screen coated with a fluorescent chemical inserted into it. This screen is supported by metal plates which can be charged, creating an electric field between the plates.

With no p.d. across the "deflector" plates, and the electron gun arrangement connected, a light is emitted from the screen in a straight line. Electrons hit the screen on emerging from the gun and then kinetic energy is

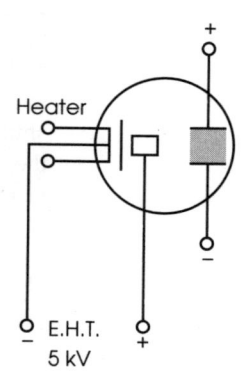

Fig. 15.12 Electron deflection tube.

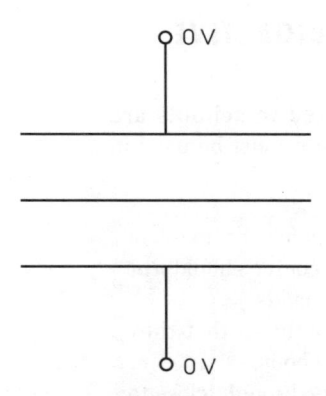

Fig. 15.13 Deflector plates with no potential difference.

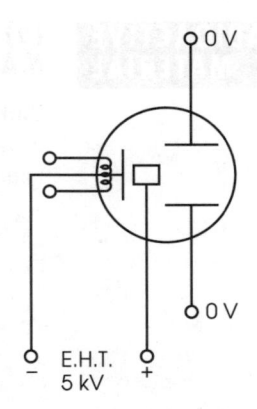

Fig 15.15 Fine-beam tube arrangement.

converted to light emitted by the fluorescent material (Fig. 15.13). If the top plate is made positive and the lower plate negative the beam curves upwards. The *amount of curvature* depends on the *voltage* between the plates (Fig. 15.14).

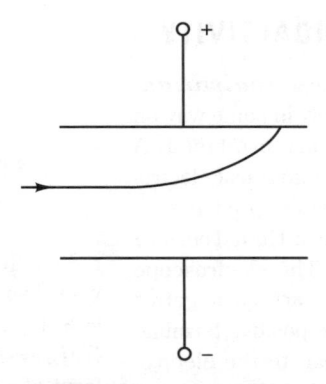

Fig. 15.14 Electrons deflected by an electric field.

Reversing the polarity of the plates reverses the force on the electrons, and the direction of movement. Electrons can be deflected by electric fields. The force on the charges acts towards the positive plate. This reinforces the idea that electrons carry negative charge. A similar arrangement, with no p.d. between the plates, can be used to show the effect of a magnetic field (Fig. 15.15). The region where the electrons hit the screen can be placed in a strong magnetic field, using either permanent magnets or a pair of coils. With the field into the plane of the page, the deflection is downwards, and with the field out, the deflection reverses, to be upwards (Fig. 15.16).

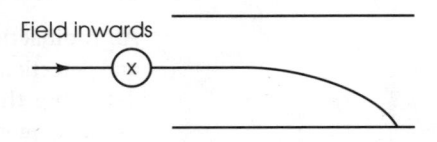

Fig. 15.16 Magnetic field deflection.

This is like the effects seen in *electromagnetism*. If the charge flow (current) and field are at right angles, the direction of the force on the charges is at 90° to both field and charge flow.

Electron streams constitute a current, and can therefore be deflected by magnetic fields.

Note: Sometimes the apparatus is slightly different to that shown. The various electrodes are the same but the screen is made by coating the end of the tube with a phosphor. With no fields applied the electron beam will make a dot at the centre of the screen. Electric fields will move the dot up or down and magnetic fields will move the spot horizontally.

5 ATOMS, ELECTRONS AND IONS

At this stage some statements about these particles may be helpful:

1. An atom is the **smallest** particle which is recognisable as having properties which are also those of larger groups of atoms. Atoms are electrically neutral.
2. Atoms must, within themselves, have **electrical charges** called ⊕ and ⊖ charges.
3. The **negative charges** are fairly mobile. They are called **electrons**.
4. To release electrons from atoms, **energy** is required.
5. A **stream of moving electrons** is the same as an **electric current**.
6. A stream of electrons is **deflected** by both **electric** and **magnetic fields** and can cause **fluorescence** of some chemical compounds.
7. An **ion** is an atom which has **either gained electrons (negative ion)** or **lost electrons (positive ion)**.

6 RADIOACTIVE MATERIAL

(a) HANDLING RADIOACTIVE MATERIALS

Radioactive sources used in schools are usually very weak, but care must be used in handling them.

1. *Forceps* should always be used in moving a source; the source should *not* be touched with bare hands.
2. Sources should be held so that they point *away from* the body.
3. Sources should *not* be brought close to the eyes.
4. When using radioactive sources, an *authorised person* must be in attendance. Sources should be stored in a locked and labelled store.
5. On handling sources, you should *wash your hands before eating*.

> Even weak sealed sources may only be handled by students who are over 16 years old (DES regulation).

(b) DETECTING RADIOACTIVITY

All radioactive sources cause *ionisation*, and detection methods all rely in some way on detecting the ions which are produced. A simple demonstration uses a gold leaf electroscope. This can be charged positive or negative using an EHT (Extra High Tension) power supply (Fig. 15.17). The electroscope casing is connected to the earthed negative terminal of the EHT and the positive terminal is touched with a flying lead to the electroscope cap. This charges the electroscope positively and the gold leaf *rises* (positive charges repelling the leaf).

> EHT stands for "Extra High Tension" meaning a power supply capable of several kilojoules of energy per coulomb!

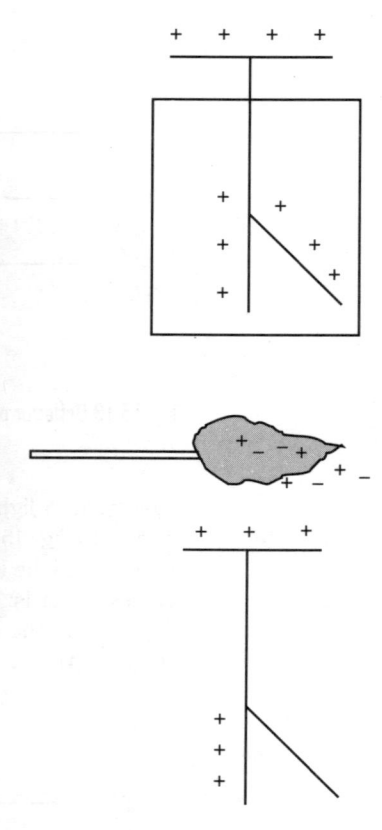

Fig. 15.18 Flames contain ions which discharge a charged electroscope.

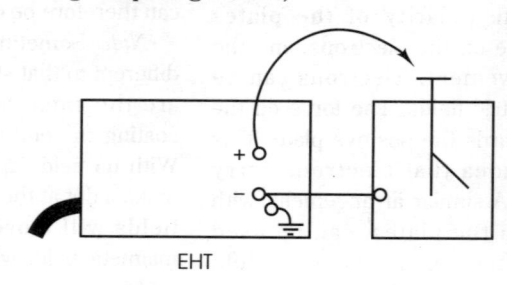

Fig. 15.17 Charging an electroscope from EHT.

A flame, which contains ions of both types, brought near the cap causes the leaf to fall rapidly, discharging the electroscope – the negative charges in the flame neutralise the positive charge (Fig. 15.18). If a *radioactive source* is brought near the charged cap, a similar effect occurs, suggesting that the source causes *ionisation* of the air near the cap.

IONISATION

All radioactive materials cause ionisation, and it is this property which enables detection of radioactivity and helps our understanding of what happens in radioactive decay. The most versatile method of detecting radiation is the *Geiger-Müller tube* connected to some form of counting device. The whole arrangement is often called a *Geiger counter*. The "count" can be a sound pulse, or a digital electronic counter. The Geiger counter only operates when there is a p.d. of about 400 V across the tube. It is measuring *ionisation caused by radioactive sources*.

MEASUREMENTS WITH A GEIGER COUNTER

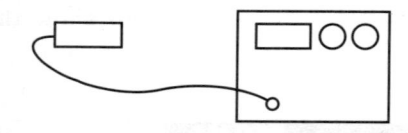

Fig. 15.19 Geiger tube and counter.

The tube and counter are arranged as shown in Fig. 15.19. With no radioactive source near the tube, a small count will be registered, about 16–30 counts per minute. This is called the *background count*. The background count is caused by radiation from space and from naturally occurring sources in the earth. Experimental measurements with radioactive sources should take account of background figures, especially if the source is weak.

Measurements are taken as ***count rates,*** meaning the number of counts in a particular period of time, for example in 1 min. An average over several time intervals should be taken.

(c) ABSORPTION OF RADIATION

Radioactive matgerials emit three recognised forms of radiation:

1. α (**alpha**)-particles;
2. β (**beta**)-particles;
3. γ (**gamma**)-waves (sometimes called γ-rays).

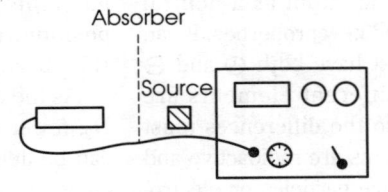

Fig. 15.20 Absorption of ionising radiation.

These behave differently when materials are placed between the source and the detector (Fig. 15.20).

- α-particles are ***absorbed*** by thin paper or card, or even by travelling through 10–20 cm of air.
- β-particles can ***penetrate*** card, but a thinsheet of aluminium foil will absorb them.
- γ-waves show a ***reduced count rate*** on passing through several centimetres thickness of lead, but the count is still above the background count.

The α and β particles hit atoms and ***knock electrons off*** them causing ***ions*** to be formed. Each collision takes some energy and the particle is slowed until it eventually doesn't have enough energy to cause any more ionisation. α *particles are relatively large* (in atomic terms) and therefore hit a lot of atoms in short distance and go out in straight lines. Their range is short but the ionisation is concentrated. β *particles are much smaller* (they are high speed electrons) and therefore travel between some of the atoms without hitting them so that the range is greatly increased. As they slow down they will be deflected more by the collisions and their tracks can show random changes in direction. The ionisation caused will be much more spread out than that caused by α.

γ radiation is quite different as each γ is a short burst of electromagnetic waves called a ***photon.*** The waves are very short wavelength, high frequency waves and they are very penetrating and carry a lot of energy. They will pass between most other particles but, when they do hit one, all the energy is used in the one ionisation releasing an electron with enough energy to behave rather like a β particle and cause more ionisation.

(d) ELECTRIC AND MAGNETIC FIELD EFFECTS

If a source which emits all three types of radiation is arranged as shown in Fig. 15.21, and if at first there is no magnetic field present, the count rate can be recorded and corrected for background count. If the field is then applied, using either a strong permanent magnet or a

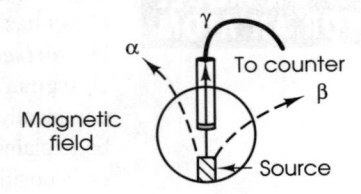

Fig. 15.21 Deflection of ionising radiation in a magnetic field.

strong electromagnet, and the position of the Geiger tube changed, it is found that the following effects occur:

1. β-particles are deflected in such a direction as to suggest that they carry negative charge.
2. α-particles are deflected by a much smaller amount, and in the opposite direction to β-particles.
3. γ-waves are not deflected at all.

The identification of α, β and γ could be achieved by noting the ***absorption properties*** in the three positions of the tube.

In a similar way, an ***electric field*** shows that:

- β have the properties of negative charge;
- α have the properties of positive charge;
- γ show no charge properties.

Since α and β show ***different amounts of deflection,*** they must also have ***different masses.***

Further experiments show that:

- α-particles are ***helium nuclei,*** consisting of two protons and two neutrons. They have two units of positive charge.
- β-particles are the same as electrons. They have negative charge and 1/1800 the mass of a proton.
- γ-waves are high-frequency eletromagnetic waves, like short-wavelength X-rays.

(e) UNITS FOR MEASUREMENT

Radioactive sources have to be measured in terms of their activity rather than their mass.

A small mass of short half life could be much more dangerous than a larger mass with a very long half life that was emitting very little radiation. An activity of one decay per second is called a **bequerel** (Bq).

Sources used to be measured in curies (Ci) where

$$1 \text{ Ci} = 3.7 \times 10^{10} \text{ Bq}.$$

This is a very large unit and sources for schools were about 5 µCi. The same source would now be simply stated as 185 kBq.

The effect of the radiations on human tissue is different for the three types. Alpha radiation is about 20 times more dangerous to us than beta or gamma. The dose received by a person is measured in units called **sieverts** (Sv) which take into account the type of radiation and the organs affected.

A dose of 10 Sv can be fatal. A year's dose from background and routine X-rays or aircraft flights (where there is less atmosphere to protect you from cosmic radiation) will be about 0.003 Sv.

7> A MODEL FOR AN ATOM

The simple model of an atom as a neutral object has now acquired new properties. It can be *ionised*, so it must have both ⊕ and ⊖ charges. Atoms of different elements are chemically different, so the differences must be explained. Some atoms are radioactive and emit positive or negative particles or electromagnetic -waves.

Part of the solution to the problem came from the experiment conducted by **Geiger and Marsden,** under the supervision of **Rutherford.** The experiment is simple: the results are surprising.

A source of α-particles is arranged to direct an α-particle beam at a thin metal foil (gold, silver and platinum are typical). The particles pass through the foil and are detected on emerging from it. The whole apparatus is in a vacuum tube, to prevent energy loss through gas ionisation. At the "straight through" position, D_1, most α-particles are detected (Fig. 15.22).

As the detector is swung through an angle, D_2, fewer and fewer are detected, but some can be detected as having moved through an angle of 90°. Most surprisingly, a few particles are detected at large angles, when the detector is in a position such as D_3. They seem to have bounced back from the foil.

α-particles from the source have large energy and positive charge. It is no surprise that most pass through the foil, losing little energy, but the few which deflect through large angles must have encountered a *large force* to stop them and to return them in their original direction. Rutherford, analysing the results, concluded the following:

1. If most α-particles can pass through atoms with no effect, then most of an atom must be *space.*
2. If a few α-particles are given large deflections, then within that space they must find a positive charge which is great enough to repel them.
3. Since few α-particles return, compared with the many which pass through the atom, the positive charge of the atom must occupy a very small volume.

He called the **positive centre** of the atom the **nucleus.**

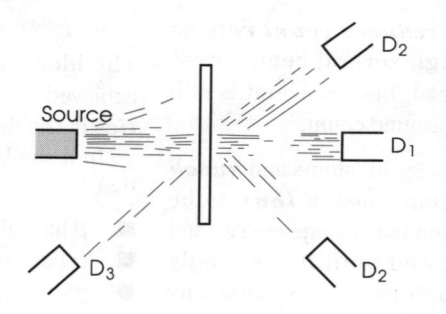

Fig. 15.22 The scattering of α-particles by thin foils.

8> ATOM STRUCTURE AND ELEMENTS

(a) NUCLEUS

Rutherford was aware that his "nucleus" had no electrons in it – since the nucleus has positive charge. An atom must, then, be a nucleus ⊕ with electrons ⊖ occupying the space around the nucleus. Electrons have a very small mass, so most of an atom's mass consists of the nucleus.

The nucleus itself is made up of two further particles: **protons,** which have one unit of ⊕ charge and one unit of mass, and **neutrons,** which have one unit of mass and no charge.

A neutral atom has the same number of **electrons** ⊖ **outside** the nucleus, as there are **protons** ⊕ **inside** it.

A simple, **but incorrect,** picture of the structure of an atom looks like a small solar system, with the nucleus at the centre and the electrons moving like planets. The more likely picture is a very **chaotic** one, but the solar system model is easier to understand (Fig. 15.23).

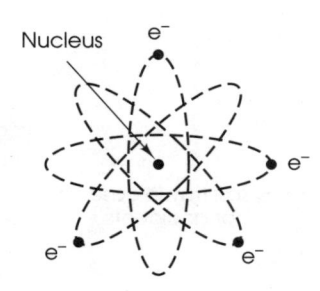

Fig. 15.23 Nuclear model of an atom.

(b) CHEMIST'S TABLE OF MASS ORDER

The simplest atom of all is the **hydrogen atom**. It has a nucleus with one mass unit and one unit of positive charge (i.e. a proton). It must also have one electron to balance the charge of the proton (Fig. 15.24).

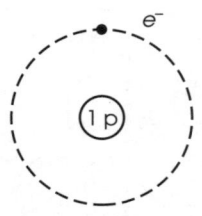

Fig. 15.24 A model for the hydrogen atom.

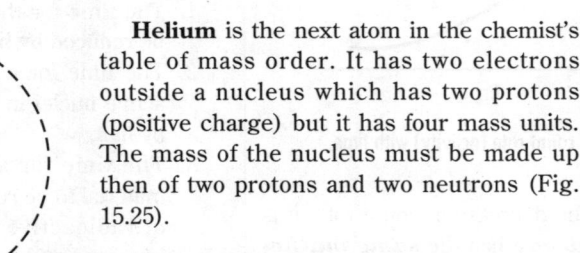

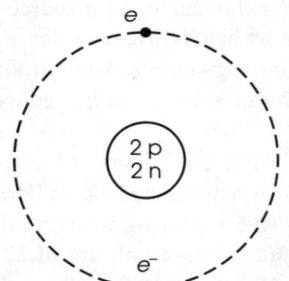

Helium is the next atom in the chemist's table of mass order. It has two electrons outside a nucleus which has two protons (positive charge) but it has four mass units. The mass of the nucleus must be made up then of two protons and two neutrons (Fig. 15.25).

Fig. 15.25 A model for the helium atom.

All atoms are made up in the same way:

- The total mass is all in the nucleus which is made up of protons ⊕ and neutrons (no charge).
- The proton ⊕ charge is balanced by the electrons ⊖ charge.
- Electrons have very small mass, and can be discounted for their mass contribution.

Uranium and **thorium** are both naturally occurring radioactive materials. They have an excess of neutrons in their nuclei and this may be a clue to the reason for their radioactive nature.

(c) SYMBOLS

Chemists use **symbols** to write down the names of atoms, H for hydrogen. O for oxygen, Cu for copper and so on. A physicist uses these to write out what a nucleus is like, and **adds numbers to the symbol** to say how much charge and how much **mass** is present:

- $^{1}_{1}H$ is a **hydrogen** nucleus;
- $^{4}_{2}He$ is a **helium** nucleus;
- $^{16}_{8}O$ is an **oxygen** nucleus.

The **top number** is called the **nucleon number**. It is the **total number of protons and neutrons in the nucleus** (i.e. the total particles making up the nuclear mass). The **lower number** is called the **proton number**. It is the **total positive charge in the nucleus** and is therefore the same as the total number of electrons in a neutral atom.

(d) ISOTOPES

Sometimes atoms occur which are identical except for the number of neutrons in the nucleus. Such atoms are **isotopes**. They will belong to the same element because they have the same number of protons and they will have identical chemistry. One will be slightly more massive than the other. Some elements have several stable isotopes.

$^{1}_{1}H$ and $^{2}_{1}H$ are isotopes of hydrogen. $^{2}_{1}H$ is called Deuterium and is sometimes known as "heavy hydrogen".

$^{35}_{17}Cl$ and $^{37}_{17}Cl$ are isotopes of chlorine. There is about three times as much of the first isotope as the second in natural chlorine so that its average mass is 35.5. Sometimes an isotope has a nucleus with a number of neutrons that is not quite stable. It will then throw out a piece of the nucleus – it will be radioactive, and is called a radioisotope.

9 > RADIOACTIVE DECAY

Nuclei do not emit radiation for ever. Eventually they become stable and behave like ordinary atoms with no excess of energy. The process is called **decay**. This can be investigated in a laboratory using a source which decays (becomes stable) quickly.

A sealed source called a **protactinium generator** can be used to demonstrate radioactive decay. When the generator is shaken and inverted the liquid in it chemically separates a small quantity of a radioactive material. Place a Geiger tube above and close to the source and record the count rate after each half minute. Plotting a graph of count rate against time produces the sort of graph shown in Fig. 15.26 (called an exponential curve) and enables the **half life** to be determined.

266 CHAPTER 15 **ATOMIC STRUCTURE AND RADIOACTIVITY**

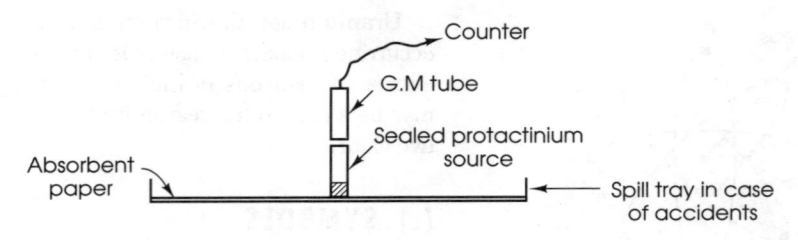

Fig. 15.26

Similar experiments can be carried out with appropriate sources and a Geiger counter. The results always show the same pattern, though the time-scale will be different for different sources.

1. The decay is **random.** You cannot exactly predict what the count will be at any time. (This is particularly noticeable in recording background counts.)
2. The overall pattern is one of **decreasing activity** (Fig. 15.27).

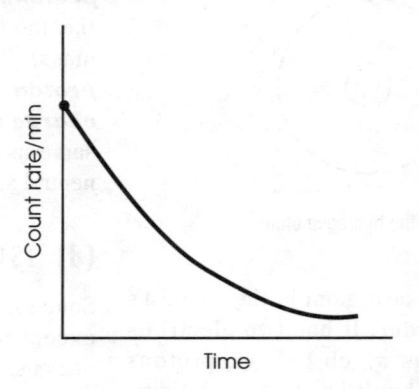

Fig. 15.27 Decay of count rate (activity) with time.

Apart from the decrease in count rate, it is found that the **decay** has the **same mathematical pattern** for **all** sources.

This is illustrated in Fig. 15.28. The time taken for the count rate to fall from 5000 counts per minute to 2500 counts per minute

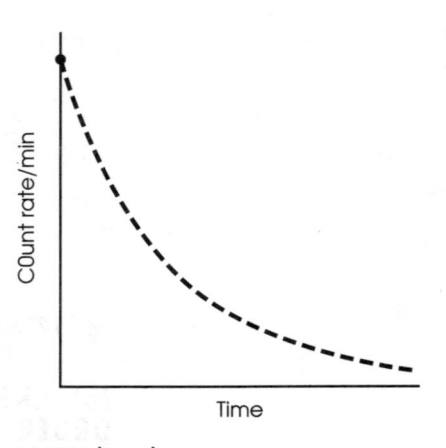

Fig. 15.28 Radiator decay.

(i.e. to reduce the activity by a half), is the **same** as the time to fall from 3000 counts per minute to 1500 counts per minute. In fact the time for a radioactive source to decay in activity from any value to half that value is the same for that particular source, and cannot be altered by external changes of temperature, pressure, etc. This time is called the **half-life** of the source, and it can vary from source to source from fractions of a second to millions of years.

Half-life can be defined in a number of ways:

1. The time for the activity of a source to be reduced by half its original value.
2. The time for a given number of radioactive nuclei in a source to be reduced by half.
3. The time for a given mass of active material to be reduced by half. So if 68 g of radioactive material is originally present, and it has a half-life of 12 h then after 12 h there will be 34 g still active; after 24 h, 17 g is still active; after 36 h, 8.5 g is still active . . .

---

10 NUCLEAR CHANGES AND RADIOACTIVE DECAY

While a nucleis is emitting radiation it is removing particles or changing its energy by emitting γ-waves. Each α-particle emitted consists of a helium nucleus $^4_2$He, which means two protons and two neutrons. Each β-particle means emitting an electron. If a nucleus emits particles it becomes a different chemical element, since each element has its own pattern of protons, neutrons and electrons. **α-particle decay** is shown by a particular uranium nucleus, $^{238}_{92}$U. This has 92 protons and 146 neutrons in its nucleus. Removal of an α-particle means removing 2 neutrons and 2 protons. This changes the nucleus to a new material, thorium. The following equation shows the effect:

$$^{238}_{92}U \xrightarrow{\alpha} {}^{234}_{90}Th + {}^4_2He$$

(γ-waves are also emitted. These do **not** change the type of nucleus, but help stabilise its energy.)

▶ In **general** if a nucleus of an element X is ^A_ZX where A = nucleon number and Z = proton number, then α-particle decay gives a new material Y where

$$^A_Z X \xrightarrow{\alpha} {}^{A-4}_{Z-2}Y + {}^4_2He$$

β-particle decay is a little harder to understand, since β-particles are the same as electrons, and the nucleus does **not** contain electrons. However, the neutron in the nucleus is itself unstable and can at times behave like a proton–electron combination:

$$_0^1n \rightarrow {_1^1}p + {_{-1}^0}e \text{ emitted as } \beta\text{-particle}$$

If a β-particle is emitted then the **mass of the nucleus is not changed** but the **proton number** (number of positive charges) *is increased by one*, and **again the nucleus** *is changed*. A typical β-particle decay is shown by strontium:

$$_{38}^{90}Sr \xrightarrow{\beta} {_{39}^{90}}Y + {_{-1}^0}e$$

(again energy is also emitted in the form of γ-waves).

The general equation is

$$_Z^A X \xrightarrow{\beta} {_{Z+1}^A}Y + {_{-1}^0}e$$

EXTENSION MATERIALS

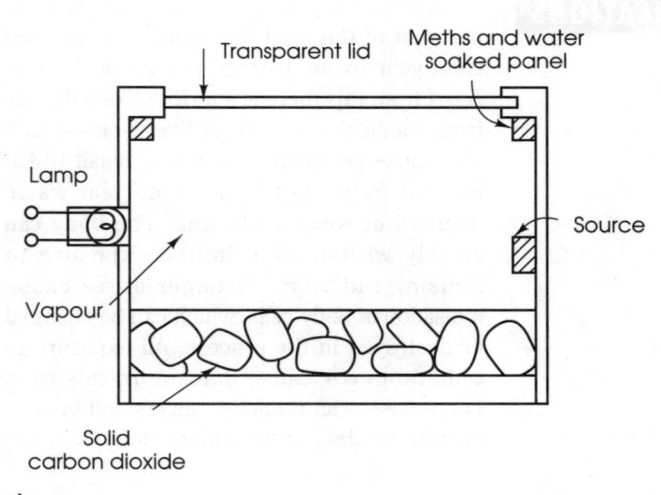

1 CLOUD CHAMBERS

Fig. 15.29 Cloud chamber.

This is another method by which the effects of a radioactive source can be noted. It again relies on ionisation but the effects are *visible*. The principle is simple. A mixture of air and water vapour is cooled to the point where the water molecules are about to condense. The presence of charged particles, like ions, enables **condensation** to take place, and a trail of condensing liquid droplets forms along the path of any such ions.

The saturated vapour is contained in a "cloud chamber" (Fig. 15.29) and is cooled by using solid carbon dioxide. A radioactive source inserted in the chamber emits particles (α or β) or ionising γ-waves. Water droplets condense around the ions leaving *visible tracks*, illuminated by a light source. The tracks differ, depending on how heavily the original radiation caused ionisation of the air. Typical tracks are shown in Fig. 15.30.

- α-tracks are straight and easily seen, because α-particles cause a lot of ionisation. They are about the same length, showing that each α has about the same energy.
- β-tracks are less clear since they cause less ionisation. They show straight tracks for high kinetic energy particles, but a slower-travelling β-particle is easily deflected by electrons of the atoms in the chamber and gives rise to sudden direction changes.
- γ-waves leave no direct tracks, but are able to eject electrons from atoms and these low-energy electrons leave faint patterns.

In the particular case of α-sources, the tracks occasionally show an additional interesting piece of behaviour. The tracks caused by ionisation are typically thick and straight and can be seen to be **randomly** produced. Very infrequently, tracks show a **fork** (Fig.

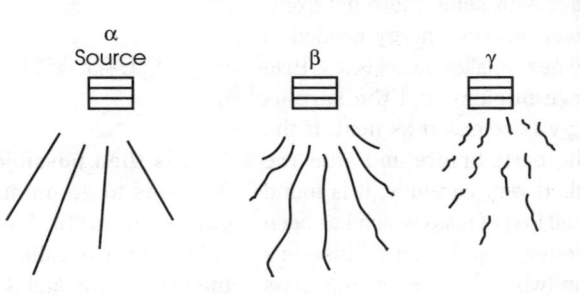

Fig. 15.30 Particle tracks in a cloud chamber.

15.31), resulting from the approach of a positively charged ∝-particle to a nucleus. The α and the nucleus **repel** each other and the angle of the fork depends on the relative masses of the α-particle and nucleus. In the particular case where the cloud chamber is filled with helium gas, the fork is a right angle. This follows since α-particles and helium nuclei are identical, and since collision between identical masses gives rise to this particular behaviour.

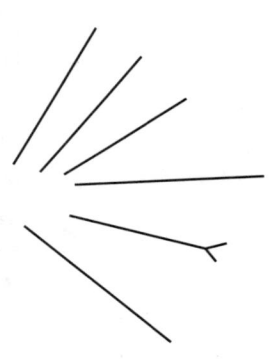

Fig. 15.31 The rare occurrence of a nuclear collision.

2 MEDICAL APPLICATIONS

All radioactive sources cause ionisation; background radiation accounts for about 78 per cent of the total radiation dose received each year by an average person in the UK. Apart from this there is a further likely dosage from medical applications like X-rays which also cause ionisation, and a very small (0.4%) amount from the fall-out of nuclear waste disposal or weapons testing. The body can clearly withstand a limited exposure to ionising radiation. Stronger doses cause ionisation of body cells, which can be changed or destroyed in the process. All exposure to radiation *can* cause damage in this way. Large doses can produce cancers and genetic change producing hereditary defects in the children of people exposed to radiation.

On the positive side, carefully controlled radiation doses can be used to kill cancer cells, and there is widespread use of γ-radiation to kill bacteria, as in the sterilisation of medical instruments where heat would damage the material (e.g. plastic replacement joints).

Radio-isotopes can also be given internally to patients for diagnostic tests, typically to produce images of parts of the body, like the lungs or kidneys, which are transparent to X-rays. The source is usually a γ-wave emitter which causes little ionisation inside the body, but which will affect a photographic plate giving an image of the organ to be examined.

3 INDUSTRIAL USES

A radioactive substance added to a liquid or gas in a pipeline in an industrial plant can be used to measure flow rate and to detect leakage. γ-radiation can pass out of pipes so that a Geiger counter or other detector will reveal the rate of flow of the fluid, or the position of any leaks in a building complex or in an underground system of pipes.

Control of the thickness of metal sheets, or of paint layers, can be achieved by sending radiation through the material on a production line. A radiation detector measures the intensity of (usually) β-radiation; *variations* in intensity can be fed back to the machinery to cause standardisation of sheet thickness.

4 FISSION AND NUCLEAR REACTORS

When the nucleus of some large atoms is hit by a neutron the neutron is absorbed for a very short time and then the new nucleus splits into two parts together with some more neutrons. This is called **fission**. The energy needed to hold together the new smaller nuclei is less than the original large nucleus and the surplus **binding energy** is released as heat. If the masses of all the parts before and after the fission are checked very carefully, it is found that there is a small loss of mass which has been converted into energy and obeys Einstein's $E = mc^2$ equation (where E = energy, m = mass and c = the velocity of light). Only certain nuclei will produce this effect and the best known ones are the nuclides ^{235}U and ^{239}Pu.

e.g. Fission of uranium-235.

$$^{235}_{92}U + ^{1}_{0}n \rightarrow ^{236}_{92}U \rightarrow \begin{array}{l} \text{2 or 3 neutrons} \\ + \\ \text{2 nuclei} \\ + \\ \text{ENERGY} \end{array}$$

It is then possible for some of the new neutrons to go on and hit other nuclei and cause them to fission. If this process continues it is called a **chain reaction.** If the mass of the fuel is very small the neutrons leave it without hitting another nucleus and

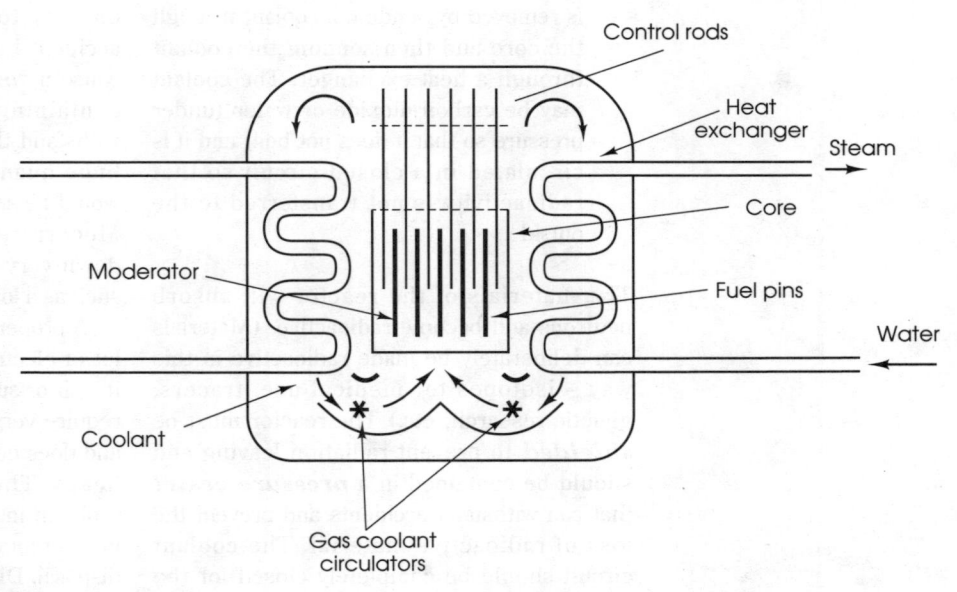

Fig. 15.32

the reaction stops. If the mass is big enough, one neutron (on average) will hit another nucleus and cause it to fission so that the chain reaction carries on. This mass, where the chain reaction is just maintained, is called the **critical mass**. If the mass is bigger than the critical mass, then more than one neutron hits another nucleus and the chain reaction starts to grow. Since the atoms are very close together this will happen very rapidly and in a very short time millions of atoms are splitting at the same time releasing huge amounts of energy in a nuclear explosion. This is the basis of atomic weapons.

In a **nuclear reactor** the chain reaction is controlled by removing some of the neutrons. The energy appears as heat which is steadily removed from the reactor core and used to boil water to make steam. The steam is then used in the same way as in other types of power station (i.e. it drives turbines which in turn drive generators to produce the electricity). The main parts of the reactor are shown in Fig. 15.32.

The main parts of the reactor have the following purposes:

- **fuel pins:** The fuel pins or rods are made from stainless steel and contain the **uranium** or **plutonium** fuel. They are lowered into the centre of the reactor (the reactor core) and can be taken out again when the fuel in them is used up ("spent"). The rods will then contain the **"fission products"** which include the new nuclei produced when the fuel atoms split. These new isotopes will include many dangerously radioactive ones and the spent fuel needs careful treatment. The rods are first put into a large pool of water and left there until the short half-life nuclides have decayed. Water is used because it is quite good at absorbing the neutrons that are being produced. The rods are then stripped open by remote control in a sealed workshop and the remaining chemicals dissolved in acid so that they can be chemically separated. The long half-life isotopes that are still dangerous are then stored until they can be safely disposed of. One way of doing this is to seal the radioactive material in glass or ceramic bricks so that it cannot leak away and then bury the bricks in caves in a stable rock.

- **Moderator:** The neutrons that are produced in the fission have too much kinetic energy for them to be easily absorbed and produce another fission. The moderator, which is usually made of graphite or water, slows down the neutrons so that they are more likely to be captured by a ^{235}U nucleus. A reactor that operates using these slower neutrons is a **thermal reactor.**

- **Control rods:** The chain reaction has to be controlled so that the reaction is just "critical"; i.e., it is just keeping itself going. The control rods are made from cadmium or boron steel which are good at absorbing neutrons. If the reaction goes too fast the rods are lowered further into the reactor so that they absorb neutrons and the reaction is slowed down. The reactor will have a lot of this type of rod so that they can all be put into the core and shut the reactor down quickly in any sort of emergency.

- **Coolant:** The purpose of the reactor is to produce heat and this heat must be steadily removed from the core as it is produced by the chain reaction. The heat is removed by sending a coolant through the core and then sending the coolant through a heat exchanger. The coolant may be carbon dioxide or water (under pressure so that it does not boil) and it is circulated in a closed circuit so that radioactivity is not transferred to the outside.

The materials of the reactor will absorb neutrons and become radioactive. (Materials can deliberately be made radioactive in this way – isotopes for medical use, tracers, genetic research, etc.) The reactor must be **shielded** to prevent radiation leaving and should be contained in a **pressure vessel** that can withstand accidents and prevent the loss of radioactive material. The coolant circuit should be completely closed for the same reason. The proportion of fissionable material in the core of a reactor is not large enough to cause an explosion after an accident but it can produce enough heat to cause a **"melt-down"**. The pressure vessel containing the core should be able to withstand this for a while but, because of the huge quantities of energy available, there would be serious consequences. (Chernobyl.) Modern reactors are designed to be shut down very quickly in the case of accidents such as a loss of coolant.

A properly managed reactor can produce a lot of electricity with little or no pollution to the air or surrounding countryside. It does not require very large quantities of chemical fuel and does not produce large waste tips or spoil heaps. The waste products are the main problem in that they have long half-lives and present long term problems in safe storage or disposal. Dismantling the power station at the end of its life may be very difficult and expensive.

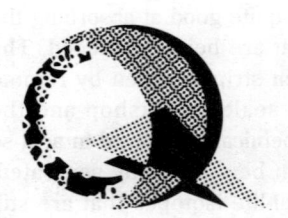

EXAMINATION QUESTIONS

MULTIPLE CHOICE QUESTIONS

QUESTION 1

The name of one type of particle found in the nucleus of an atom is

A An ion
B An electron
C A molecule
D A proton
E An isotope
(NISEAC)

QUESTION 2

When a polythene rod is rubbed with a duster, the rod becomes negatively charged. This charge is caused by the transfer of

A Electrons from the duster to the rod
B Atoms from the duster to the rod
C Protons from the duster to the rod
D Electrons from the rod to the duster
(SEG)

QUESTION 3

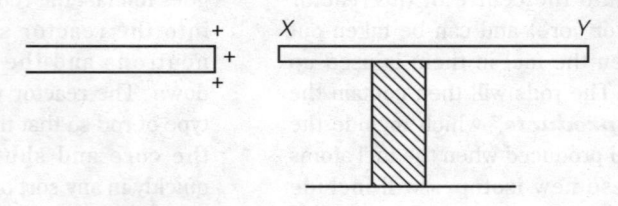

Fig. 15.33

In Fig. 15.33 a positively charged plastic rod is brought close to a metal rod XY on an insulated stand. How are the charges redistributed in the rod?

A Negative charges at both ends of the rod
B Positive charges at both ends of the rod
C Negative charges at end X and positive charges at end Y
D Positive charges at end X and negative charges at end Y (ULEAC)

QUESTION 4

A mercury atom contains 80 protons, 80 electrons and 120 neutrons. How many particles are there in its nucleus?

A 80
B 120
C 200
D 280
(ULEAC)

QUESTION 5

Which of the following statements about nuclear fission is true?

A Atoms gain electrons to form ions.
B Several atoms combine to form a molecule.
C A nucleus splits into smaller nuclei.
D The materials used must be in a strong magnetic field.
E The atom loses all its electrons.

QUESTION 6

The half-life of radioactive carbon is 5600 years. What will be the time after which the activity has reduced to one-quarter?

A 1400 years   D 11 200 years
B 2800 years   E 22 400 years
C 8400 years   (NICCEA)

QUESTION 7

Which statement about the half-life of a radioactive substance is true?

A It always remains the same.
B It increases with pressure.
C It is affected by chemical reactions.
D It becomes less as time goes on.
E It varies with the temperature of the substance.

QUESTION 8

A nucleus contains 12 protons and 15 neutrons. Which one of the following gives the proton number and nucleon number?

	Proton number	Nucleon number
A	12	15
B	12	27
C	12	12
D	15	27
E	27	12

QUESTION 9

Which one of the following best describes beta particles emitted by a radioactive substance?

A Atoms   D electromagnetic energy
B Electrons
C Ions   E Neutrons

QUESTION 10

Count rate per second	55	35	15	5	6	5
Thickness of aluminium (mm)	0	2	4	6	8	10

The table shows how the count rate varied as the thickness of an aluminium absorber was increased between a beta source and a detector. The count rate does not fall to zero because

A The thickness of aluminium is not great enough.
B Aluminium cannot absorb beta radiation completely.
C There is background radiation of about 5 counts per second.
D The beta particles are deflected by the aluminium.
E The energy of the beta particles is too great.   (NICCEA)

STRUCTURED QUESTIONS

QUESTION 11

(a) State the nature of each of the following radiations (1 line for each):
    (i) Gamma radiation;
    (ii) Ultraviolet radiation;
    (iii) Beta radiation;
    (iv) Infra-red radiation;
    (v) Alpha radiation.

(b) Which, if any, of the radiations listed in (a)
    (i) does not travel at the same speed in a vacuum as visible light (1 line);
    (ii) are not emitted from the nucleus of an atom. (1 line)

(c) When radiation passes through matter, it may cause ionisation.
    (i) Explain briefly what is meant by ionisation. (1 line)
    (ii) Which of the radiations listed in (a) will produce the greatest amount of ionisation per centimetre of path length? (1 line)

(d) An isotope of uranium $^{235}_{92}U$ decays with the emission of alpha radiation to give an isotope of thorium (Th).
    (i) Name the particles which make up the nucleus of $^{235}_{92}U$ stating clearly how many there are of each in the nucleus. (2 lines)
    (ii) State the atomic number and mass number of the isotope of thorium which is formed.
    Atomic number
        (Proton number) ....
    Mass number
        (Nucleon number) ....
    (iii) The isotope of thorium which is formed has a half-life of 25 hours. What is meant by the half-life of a radioactive element? (2 lines)
    (iv) If 0.64 mg of the thorium is isolated and placed in a lead container, after how long will the mass of thorium have dropped to 0.04 mg?

(e) Is $^{238}_{92}X$, where X represents the symbol of the element, an isotope of uranium? Give a reason for your answer. (2 lines)
    (NICCEA)

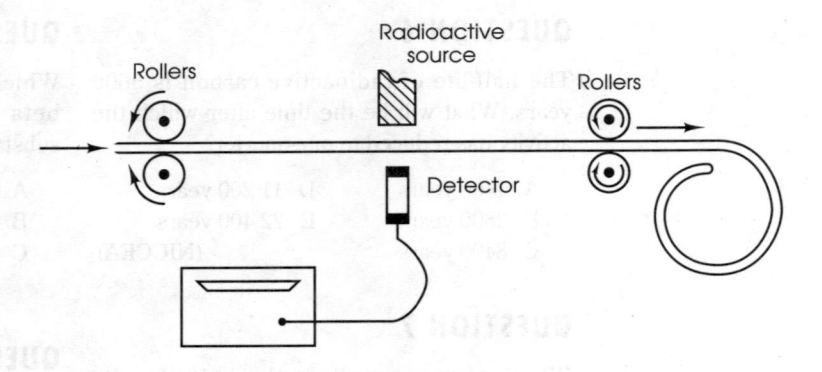

Fig. 15.34

QUESTION 12

In a factory which makes baking foil changes in the thickness of the foil are detected using a radioactive source and a detector (Fig. 15.34). The source emits β-particles.

(a) Explain how changes in the thickness of the foil covering are detected. (3 lines)

(b) Explain why neither alpha nor gamma sources would be suitable for this application. (3 lines) (NEAB)

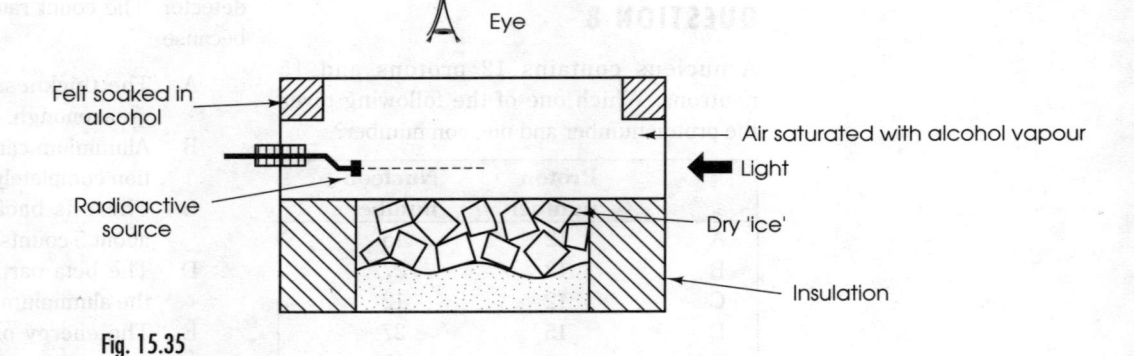

Fig. 15.35

QUESTION 13

(a) Figure 15.35 represents a diffusion cloud chamber. The top half is transparent, so that light may be shone in, and particle tracks may be seen from the top. Alpha particles emitted from the radioactive source form ions.

(i) What are ions?
(ii) To achieve the correct conditions the cloud chamber base must be cooled. How is this done?
(iii) The tracks are formed by alcohol condensing along the paths followed by the alpha particles. On what does the alcohol vapour condense? (2 lines)
(iv) Looking down on the cloud chamber, the alpha particle tracks appear as in Fig. 15.36. The tracks are about equal in length. What does this suggest about the energies of the α-particles? (4 lines)
(v) Imagine that an alpha particle from the source were to collide with a stationary particle of equal mass within the cloud chamber. Give a labelled sketch to show what the cloud chamber track would look like.

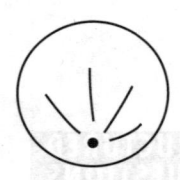

Fig. 15.36

(b) The count rate near a radioactive source was measured over a period of time using a Geiger counter. After subtracting the "background" radiation count rate the following graph was plotted (Fig. 15.37).

(i) Describe how you would measure the background radiation count rate. (3 lines)
(ii) Use the graph to find the half-life of the radioactive source. (1 line)

(c) (i) What type of charge is carried by α-particles? (1 line)
(ii) What type of charge is carried by β-particles? (1 line)
(iii) Which is more easily absorbed. α-particles or β-particles? (1 line)
(iv) How would you distinguish between α-particles and β-particles? Describe tests you would carry out to identify each source. (4 lines) (ULEAC)

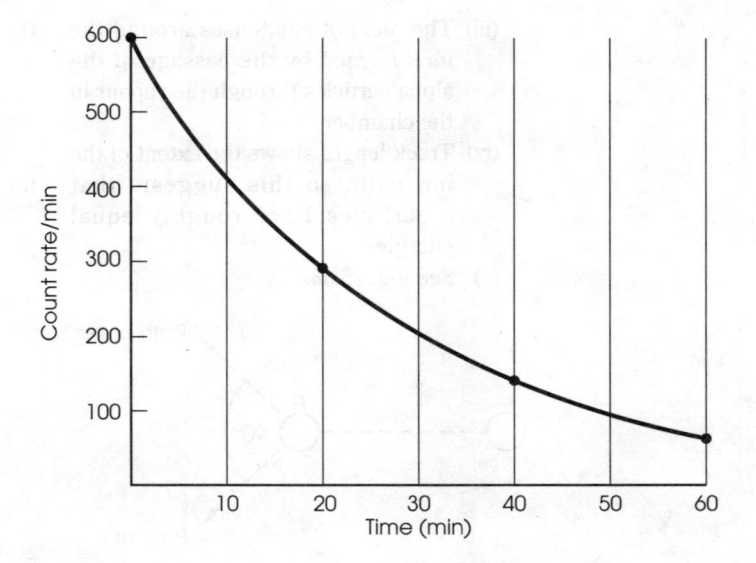

Fig. 15.37

ANSWERS TO EXAMINATION QUESTIONS

MULTIPLE CHOICE QUESTIONS

Question	1	2	3	4	5	6	7	8	9	10
Answer	D	A	C	C	C	D	A	B	B	C

STRUCTURED QUESTIONS

ANSWER 11

(a) (i) Gamma radiation is short-wavelength, high-frequency, electromagnetic radiation.
 (ii) Ultraviolet radiation is electromagnetic radiation with a wavelength longer than gamma but smaller than visible light (see Ch. 9).
 (iii) Beta radiation consists of a stream of fast-moving electrons.
 (iv) Infra-red radiation is electromagnetic radiation with a longer wavelength than visible light (see Ch. 9).
 (v) Alpha radiation is a stream of high-energy helium nuclei.

(b) (i) Alpha and beta radiation.
 (ii) Ultraviolet and infra-red radiation.

(c) (i) Ionisation is the process by which a neutral atom loses electrons to become a positive ion or gains electrons to become a negative ion.
 (ii) Alpha radiation causes the heaviest ionisation.

(d) (i) 92 protons, 143 neutrons.
 (ii) Atomic number 90; mass number 231.
 (iii) Half-life is the time for the original number of radioactive nuclei to be reduced by half.
 (iv) 100 hours.

(e) Yes. Isotopes are chemically identical (same proton number) but have different numbers of neutrons. Proton number of uranium given in the question is 92.

ANSWER 12

(a) The beta source emits beta particles most of which can penetrate the baking foil. Beta particles are not very penetrating and any change in thickness of the foil will result in a greater or smaller number arriving at the detector.

(b) Alpha particles would be totally absorbed by the foil and the air between the source and the top surface of the covering. Gamma waves would hardly be absorbed at all, so small variations in thickness would not be registered by the detector.

ANSWER 13

(a) (i) Ions are the result of atoms either losing electrons or gaining electrons. If they lose electrons they become positive ions and if they gain electrons they become negative ions.
 (ii) The cloud chamber is cooled by using solid carbon dioxide (dry ice) in the base.

(iii) The alcohol condenses around the ions formed by the passage of the alpha particles through the vapour in the chamber.
(iv) Track length shows the extent of the ion path, so this suggests that α-particles have roughly equal energies.
(v) See Fig. 15.38.

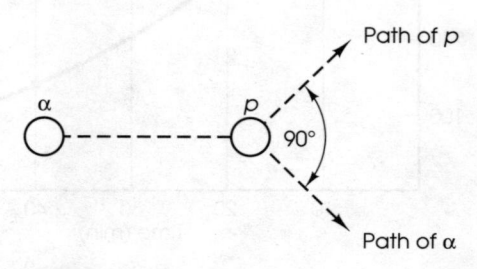

Fig. 15.38

(b) (i) Turn the Geiger counter voltage to its operating value. Record the count over several minutes. Take a mean value of counts per minute.
(ii) Half-life is 20 min.
(c) (i) Positive charge.
(ii) Negative charge.
(iii) α-particles.
(iv) Either absorption (α easily absorbed by paper, β absorbed by aluminum) or by magnetic deflection.

STUDENT'S ANSWER WITH THE EXAMINER'S COMMENTS

STUDENT ANSWER TO QUESTION 13

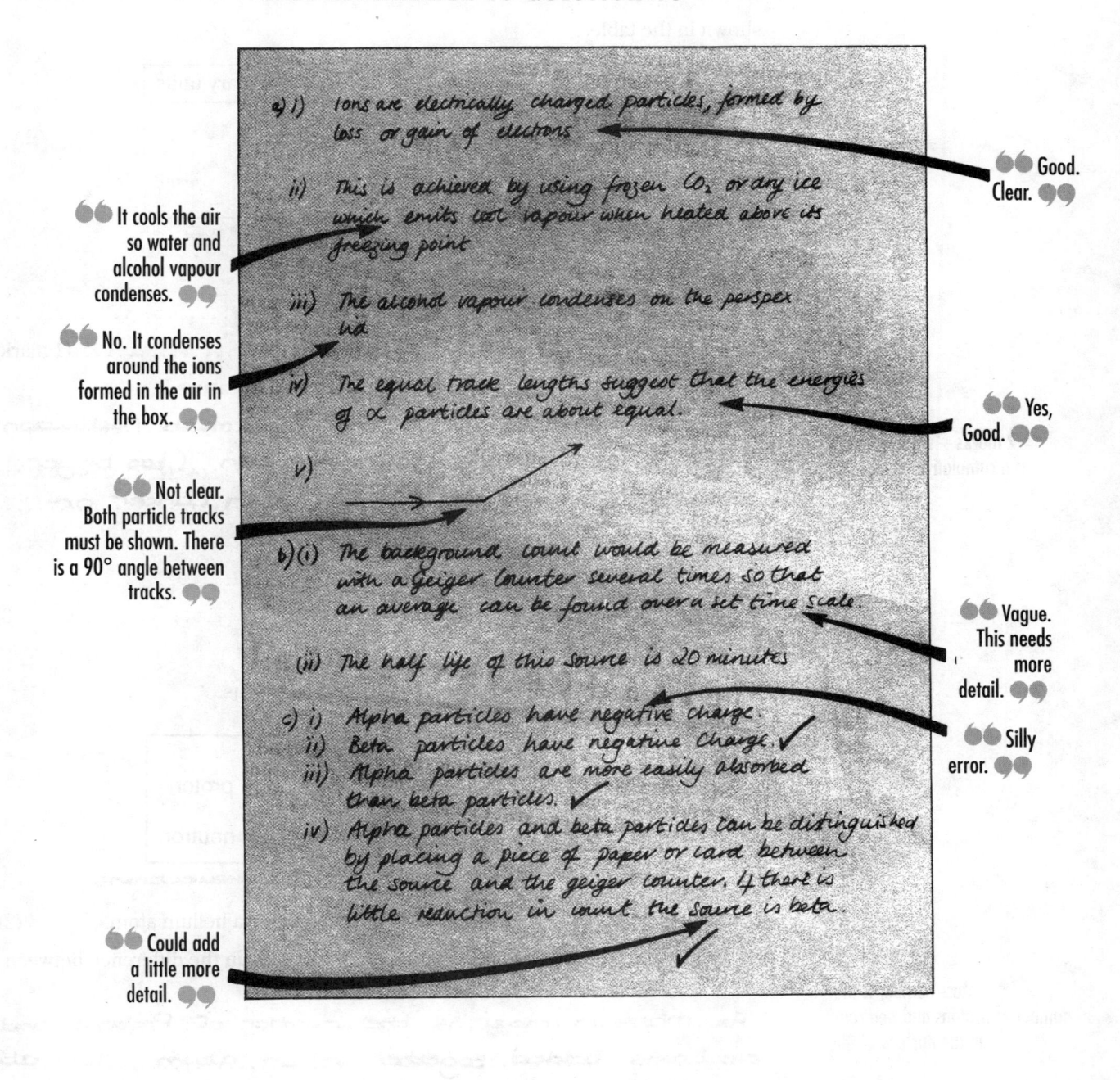

a) i) Ions are electrically charged particles, formed by loss or gain of electrons.

> **Good. Clear.**

ii) This is achieved by using frozen CO_2 or dry ice which emits cool vapour when heated above its freezing point.

> **It cools the air so water and alcohol vapour condenses.**

iii) The alcohol vapour condenses on the perspex lid.

> **No. It condenses around the ions formed in the air in the box.**

iv) The equal track lengths suggest that the energies of α particles are about equal.

> **Yes, Good.**

v)

> **Not clear. Both particle tracks must be shown. There is a 90° angle between tracks.**

b) (i) The background count would be measured with a Geiger counter several times so that an average can be found over a set time scale.

> **Vague. This needs more detail.**

(ii) The half life of this source is 20 minutes.

c) i) Alpha particles have negative charge.

> **Silly error.**

ii) Beta particles have negative charge. ✓

iii) Alpha particles are more easily absorbed than beta particles. ✓

iv) Alpha particles and beta particles can be distinguished by placing a piece of paper or card between the source and the geiger counter. If there is little reduction in count the source is beta. ✓

> **Could add a little more detail.**

MORE EXAMINER'S COMMENTS
CENTRAL/HIGHER LEVEL

(a) Information on the average amount of radiation received by a person in a year is shown in the table.

source	amount/arbitrary units
natural background	125.0
medical sources	55.2
occupational hazards	1.7
other radiation	2.0

(i) Give one cause of natural background radiation.

Cosmic Radiation ....(1 mark)

(ii) Explain why the dose of X-rays you receive should be measured.

So that you don't receive too much radiation from it, as too much radiation (too bigger dosage of it) can lead to skin cancer or other cancers. ....(3)

> **66** 2 marks – stress the idea of a cumulative dose **99**

(b) The diagram represents the structure of a helium nucleus.

[diagram: circle labelled "outer shell" containing smaller circle labelled "nucleus" with 3 protons inside; two X marks added on outer shell]

key:
● = proton
○ = neutron
X = electrons

(i) Add information to the diagram so that it represents a helium atom. (2)

(ii) Use the information in the diagram to help you explain the difference between mass number and atomic number.

The mass number is the number of protons and electrons added together in an atom, the atomic number is the number of protons in an atom ....(2)

> **66** Mass number is the number of protons and *neutrons* in the nucleus **99**
>
> **66** 1 mark **99**

REVIEW SHEET

- A hot wire can emit _____. This is called _____.

- The two types of particle that are found in the nucleus are _____ and _____.

- In a neutral atom the number of electrons will be the same as the number of _____.

- Two atoms are isotopes of the same element. They will have the same number of _____ but a different number of _____.

- The half-life of a radioisotope is the time taken for _____.

- There are three types of radioactivity. Name them in order of their penetrating power: _____.

- Which of the three types of radioactivity is not a particle? _____.

- Name three sources of background radiation.

    1. _____   2. _____.
    3. _____.

- The number of protons in the nucleus is called the _____ or the _____.

- The type of radioactivity deflected easily by a magnetic field is _____.

- For each of the following parts of a nuclear reactor state what the part is for and name a suitable material.

Part	Function	Material
Fuel pin		
Coolant		
Moderator		
Control rod		

- Complete the following table

	Mass	Charge
proton		
neutron		
electron		
α particle		
β particle		
γ photon		

- An isotope has a half-life of 10 mins. If you had 0.08 g of it, how much would be left after half an hour? _____.

- Name two uses for β sources.

    _____ _____.

- Name a medical use for γ radiation. _____.

- α particles consist of _____ so they are the same as the nucleus of a _____ atom.

- Briefly explain what is meant by a *chain reaction*.
  _____
  _____
  _____.

- $^{226}_{88}$Ra is an isotope of radium which emits α particles.
  What is its nucleon number? _____ .
  What is its proton number? _____ .
  How many neutrons are there in its nucleus? _____ .

- Write an equation for the α emission if the new atom is an isotope of radon (Rn)

- Ions are formed when atoms _____ .

- Two charges that are _____ will repel each other.

- State a method of disposing of long half-life nuclear waste. _____
  _____ .

- A worker wears a badge to detect exposure to radiation. It contains a piece of photographic film which is half covered by aluminium foil. Which types of radiation can each half of the film detect?
  Foil covered half _____ . Other half _____ .

- Name the following units:
  Dose of radiation _____ . Activity of a source _____ .

CHAPTER 16

ELECTRONICS: SYSTEMS

- ON–OFF LOGIC SWITCHES
- LOGIC GATES
- COMBINING LOGIC GATES
- PRACTICAL USE OF LOGIC GATES
- INFORMATION AND BINARY NUMBERS
- BISTABLE MULTIVIBRATORS
- ANALOGUE AND DIGITAL SIGNALS
- MOTOR – CONTROL SYSTEM
- THE LATCH
- ANALOGUE SYSTEMS AND OP-AMPS
- INVERTING AMPLIFIER
- A VOLTAGE COMPARATOR

GETTING STARTED

The earlier electronics section dealt with some of the individual *components* which are found in a simple electronics circuit. The use of *integrated circuits* means that many such components can be connected in a single miniature "chip" which can do the job of many larger-scale pieces of equipment. The technology of this branch of physics is moving fast, and it is more useful to analyse the behaviour of a circuit in terms of the way the output and input voltages are related, rather than by looking in detail at what goes on inside the circuit. This means treating each electronics block as a building brick, which can link with others to give a useful result; the method of analysis is called a "systems" approach, and is the way in which a professional engineer would be likely to solve problems.

Voltage signals applied to a system are described as *analogue* or *digital*. An **analogue** system has an input and output voltage which may have any value. **Digital** systems respond only to one of two signals, high or low, which are described commonly as logic level 1 or logic level 0. We will deal with digital systems first.

There has been some confusion over standard symbols for logic gates. Some boards simply draw a square box and write the name of the gate in it whilst others use "standard" symbols. The only one likely to cause any confusion is that for the AND gate (and therefore for the NAND gate).

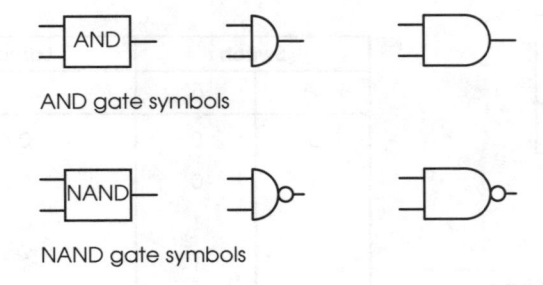

AND gate symbols

NAND gate symbols

Fig. 16.1

The symbols on the right are the more commonly accepted ones. Check with your teacher to see which you should use.

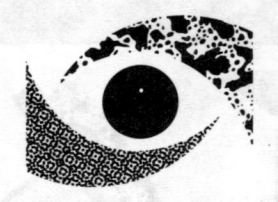

ESSENTIAL PRINCIPLES

1 > ON–OFF LOGIC SWITCHES

Digital systems only show two states, ON and OFF. These two states are described as *logic 1* and *logic 0*. A simple way of illustrating the idea would be to use ordinary switches, as shown in Fig. 16.2.

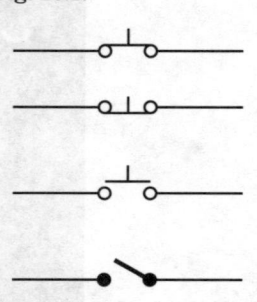

Fig. 16.2 Closed and open switches.

One way of showing how some circuits behave is by using a *truth table*. This summarises what is possible for a circuit. The circuit in Fig. 16.3(a) can only have its switch ON or OFF and the lamp is also either ON or OFF. Representing ON = 1 and OFF = 0 gives the table in Fig. 16.3(b).

Switch	Lamp
0	0
1	1

Fig. 16.3(b)

A more complicated example is shown in the circuit of Fig. 16.4(a). Switches are labelled S and lamps labelled L (truth table, Fig. 16.4(b)).

Fig. 16.3(a) ON/OFF logic.

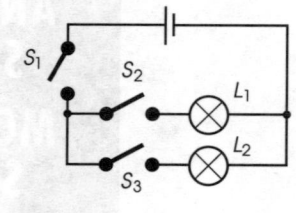

Fig. 16.4(a) Parallel ON/OFF logic.

Switch			Lamp	
S_1	S_2	S_3	L_1	L_2
0	0	0	0	0
1	0	0	0	0
1	1	0	1	0
1	0	1	0	1
1	1	1	1	1

Fig 16.4(b)

Many systems are complicated. To simplify the circuit diagram, the supply is often removed, and a "line" is drawn to represent the positive (+) side of the circuit. Another line represents the (–) side, which is usually written as 0 V. The circuit of Fig. 16.3(a) would then be represented as in Fig. 16.5.

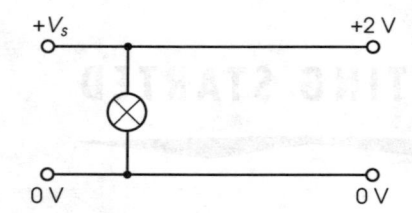

Fig. 16.5 Representing a logic circuit.

The switch can also be left ON, suggesting that it is possible to make all possible connections.

Another system, with its corresponding truth table, helps to illustrate this point (Figs. 16.6(a) and (b)).

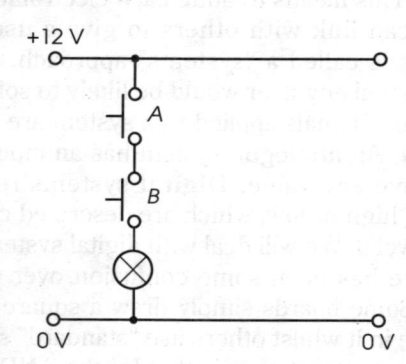

Fig. 16.6(a) Series logic with such switches.

Switch		Lamp
A	B	
0	0	0
1	0	0
0	1	0
1	1	1

Fig. 16.6(b)

These circuits are quite easy to work out, with more practice being given in the examination questions at the end of the chapter.

2> LOGIC GATES

An electronic "gate" is a circuit which will only allow an output signal under particular input situations. The word "gate" is used because the circuitry can effectively only be either open (logic 1) or shut (logic 0), and different combinations are needed to achieve opening and shutting.

Each gate is a piece of electronic circuitry and it is described by the way in which its output will become logic **high** = 1 when its input is changed.

AND-GATE

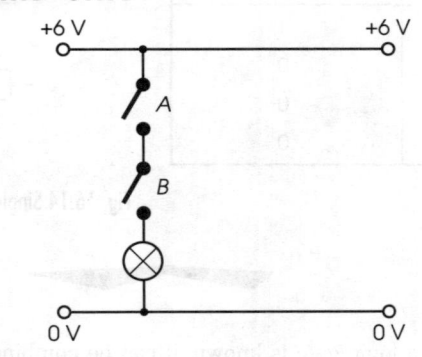

Fig. 16.7

A gate description called AND simply means that the output will go high if *both* of two inputs are also high. In simple switch terms this could be a circuit of the type shown in Fig. 16.7, where the lamp only lights if both A *and* B are on. Any version of an AND-gate can be shown as in the circuit of Fig. 16.8(a). If the out terminal is connected to a lamp or a voltmeter between the out terminal and 0 V, it will give the truth table (Fig. 16.8(b)) as A and B inputs are moved between input high = 1 and low = 0.

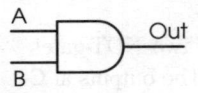

Fig. 16.8(a) AND-gate.

Input		Output
A	B	
0	0	0
1	0	0
0	1	0
1	1	1

Fig. 16.8(b)

Any system giving this output is called AND. The output is high if both one input AND the other is at logic high.

All of the circuits will always need a positive and negative supply connection. This is left off the diagrams to make them simpler but it is really there to give the "complete circuits" that you read about in chapter 7.

OR-GATE

OR-gates work differently. The output goes high if either one *or* the other or both inputs go high. The symbol is shown in Fig. 16.9(a), with the corresponding truth table (Fig. 16.9(b)).

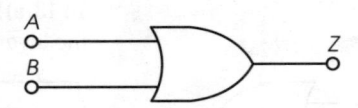

Fig. 16.9(a) OR-gate.

Input		Output
A	B	Z
0	0	0
1	0	1
0	1	1
1	1	1

Fig. 16.9(b)

NOT-GATE

A NOT-gate is also called an inverter. A high = 1 input causes a low = 0 output, and vice versa. The symbol is given in Fig. 16.10(a), and here the truth table (Fig. 16.10(b)) simply says that the output is the inverse of the input.

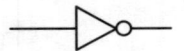

Fig. 16.10(a) Inverter.

Input	Output
0	1
1	0

Fig. 16.10(b)

NAND-GATE

The NOT-gate can reverse the behaviour of another gate. So AND followed by NOT gives NOT-AND, written as NAND (Fig. 16.11(a)). The truth table (Fig. 16.11(b)) is the inverse of that for AND.

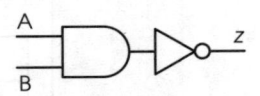

Fig. 16.11(a) AND + inverter.

Input		Output
A	B	
0	0	1
1	0	1
0	1	1
1	1	0

Fig. 16.11(b)

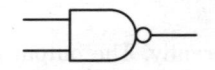

Fig. 16.12 NAND-gate.

The NAND-gate function is represented by Fig. 16.12. The circle following the gate implies a negative gate "instruction".

NOR-GATE

In a similar way, NOR means NOT-OR (Fig. 16.13(a)) and the truth table (Fig. 16.13(b)) is the inverse of OR.

Fig. 16.13(a) NOR-gate.

Input		Output
A	B	
0	0	1
1	0	0
0	1	0
1	1	0

Fig. 16.13(b)

If the two inputs of NAND are connected together, the gate behaves as an inverter (NOT). The same is true if the two inputs of a NOR are connected together (Fig. 16.14).

In all logic gate circuits you should make sure that all the inputs are connected to either high or low. If you leave inputs not connected some gates will not behave properly.

Fig. 16.14 Single input NOR or single input NAND inverts.

3 COMBINING LOGIC GATES

Once the function of a logic gate is known, it can be combined with others to give a required output behaviour. Some examples are given below.

EXAMPLE 1

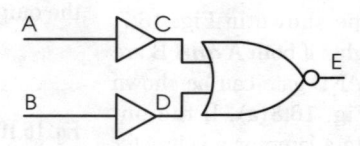

Fig. 16.15(a)

Figure 16.15(a) represents a two-input system. Construct its truth table and suggest a use for it.

The system is made up of two NOT-gates (inverters) followed by NOR. The outputs at C and D are therefore the inverse of the inputs at A and B. Output E will be high when **neither** one, **nor** the other, **nor** both its inputs is high. This gives us the truth table in Fig. 16.15(b). The combination can therefore be used as an AND-gate, passing a signal only when both inputs go to logic 1.

Inputs		Outputs		
A	B	C	D	E
0	0	1	1	0
1	0	0	1	0
0	1	1	0	0
1	1	0	0	1

Fig. 16.15(b)

EXAMPLE 2

Complete the truth table for the system shown in Fig. 16.16(a).

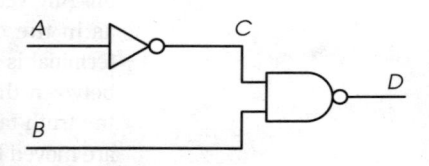

Fig. 16.16(a)

This is a NOT-gate leading to one input of a NAND-gate. The other NAND input may go either to logic 1 or logic 0 (Fig. 16.16(b)).

Inputs		Outputs	
A	B	C	D
0	0	1	1
0	1	1	0
1	0	0	1
1	1	0	1

Fig. 16.16(b)

4 > PRACTICAL USE OF LOGIC GATES

The input to a logic gate is a voltage applied between a gate terminal and the 0 V line of the system. Inputs are typically close to 0 V (certainly below 0.7 V) or close to 5 V, giving the two states logic 0 and logic 1.

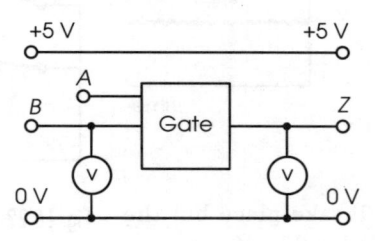

Fig. 16.17

Figure 16.17 shows that both input and output voltages are read between a terminal and the 0 V line. A lead from terminal B could connect the gate to the 5 V line or the 0 V line.

Often the voltage is caused by a current through a resistive component, such as a thermistor or LDR, in a similar way to the earlier electronics applications. An example is shown in Fig. 16.18, where the input is applied to a NOT-gate. The output will be high if the input is near 0 V; this will happen if resistor R has a low voltage across it compared with the thermistor.

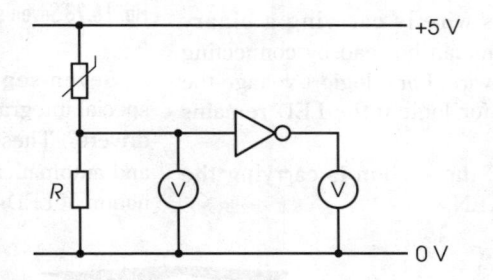

> **Voltages are proportional to resistance values.**

Fig. 16.18

If the minimum required voltage is 0.7 V then the values of the resistances must be in the ratio

$$\frac{R_{thermistor}}{R} = \frac{4.3}{0.7}$$

since there is a total of 5 V across the two of them.

Usually a light emitting diode (LED) is used as an output indicator in place of a voltmeter. The voltage required to operate it is about 2 V and the current through it should not exceed about 10 mA. In practice a series resistor is also connected into the circuit to prevent an overlarge current flowing in the LED (Fig. 16.19).

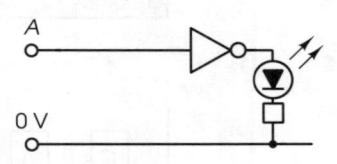

Fig. 16.19

Since the output of a gate is typically 5 V, the resistor must have a voltage of 3 V across it, so its values will be about

$$\frac{3}{10 \times 10^{-3}} = 300 \, \Omega$$

The maximum current output of a gate is only a few milliamps. A LED can be driven directly but a more powerful device, such as a headlamp bulb or motor, would need indirect switching. The gate output could be fed to a transistor which could in turn switch a *relay*.

5 > INFORMATION AND BINARY NUMBERS

Gates are used extensively in information and data processing. Much of this information is numerical and can be handled by the use of **binary** arithmetic.

We are used to counting in a scale of 10 using 1 2 3 4 5 6 7 8 9 0. Digital system outputs can only use the *two* states of logic high = 1 and logic low = 0. However, the two symbols are enough to encode numerical information. If only 1 and 0 are available, then numbers become

Scale of 10	Binary
0	0
1	1
2	10
3	11
4	100
5	101
6	110
7	111
8	1000 etc.

There is an advantage in doing this as compared to transmitting information with a voltage of precise value to represent a number. Namely that when a voltage is transmitted between parts of a system, its value can be modified by electronic disturbances called "noise" which are picked up from signals in the environment. As a result the voltage value will not remain totally the same. This is illustrated in Fig. 16.20.

In a similar way music is not faithfully reproduced on older records because of variations in the electrical signal to the sound centre.

However, if the signal representing a number is transmitted digitally, using a "bus" of wires, the signal fluctuations are small and the output is still accepted as logic 0 or logic 1.

Sending the number 5 would need three wires carrying a 0 or 1 value. Digitally 5 = 101.

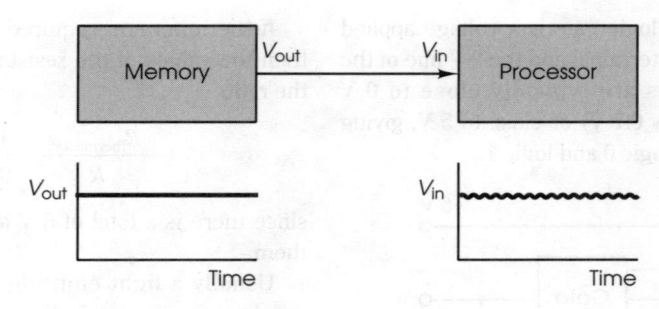

Fig. 16.20

The fluctuations still take place but the number is still recognisable (Fig. 16.21).

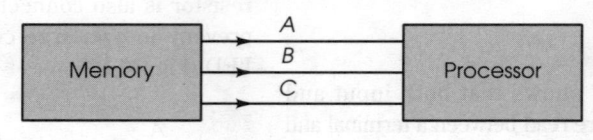

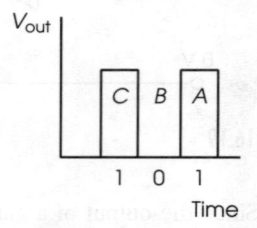

Fig. 16.21

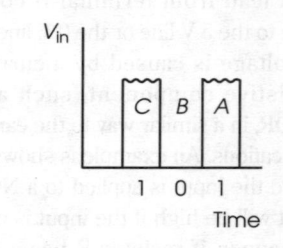

If a four-bus wire is carrying a binary number, its value can be read by connecting an LED to each wire. For a logic 1 voltage the LED will glow, for logic 0 the LED remains OFF.

In Fig. 16.22 the system is carrying the number 1010 = TEN.

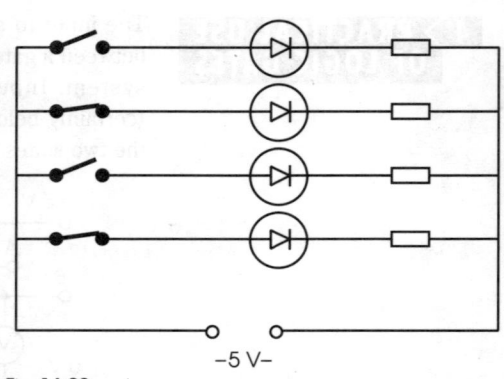

Fig. 16.22

A seven-segment display consists of seven separate LEDs arranged in a single unit to "decode" a binary number into a decimal number. The diodes are arranged as in Fig. 16.23. To make number 3, the diodes which are lit would be A, B, G, C, D.

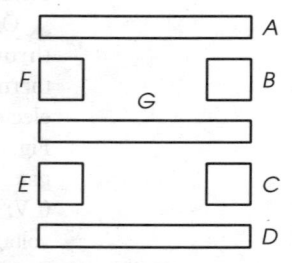

Fig. 16.23 Seven-segment display.

Seven-segment displays are driven by special integrated circuits known as "decoder-drivers". These have an input in binary form, and automatically illuminate to correct combination of LEDs to give the decimal equivalent.

6 BISTABLE MULTIVIBRATOR SYSTEM

This may be constructed in a number of ways. The important thing is that whatever happens to the input, the output has only one of two stable states. These are achieved by **feedback**. A connection between output and input **reinforces** information.

In Fig. 16.24 if input A is high and input B is not connected, then indicator A is off and the B input is at logic 0.

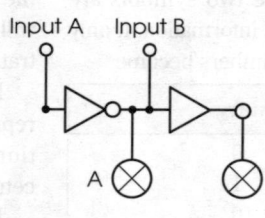

Fig. 16.24

Similarly if input A is not connected and B is at logic 1, the output of B is at logic 0 and of A is at logic 1.

Now if the output of B is fed back to the input of A a **bistable system** is obtained (Fig. 16.25). Input A goes high, input B is not yet connected, output A goes low, output B goes high and reinforces the high input to A. The original connection to A can be removed and the message is retained. The system has a **memory**.

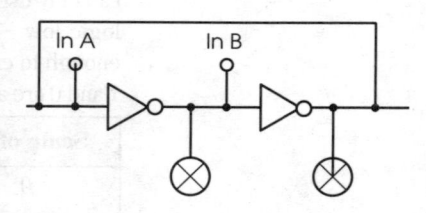

Fig. 16.25 Bistable system

The same sequence is obtained using two linked NOR-gates (Fig. 16.26). NOR gives a logic 1 output if neither one NOR another NOR both inputs is high (i.e. only when **both** are at logic 0).

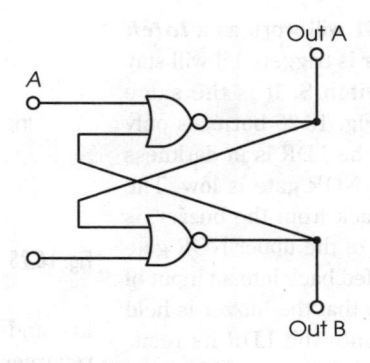

Fig. 16.26 Bistable system.

Here, if A input is at logic 1, A output is logic 0 and the feedback to the other NOR gate is logic 0. If input B is also at logic 0 then output B will be at logic 1 and will stay like that (because it is fed back to NOR gate A). The only way to change the system is to let input A go to logic 0 and then make input B go to logic 1. This will "reset" the circuit so that output A is logic 1 and output B is logic 0. If you make A logic 1 for a short time the circuit can be "set" again. This *latch* is used in section 2 of the "Extension materials".

7 ANALOGUE AND DIGITAL SIGNALS

An analogue signal can vary smoothly and continuously. Most natural changes are like this; e.g. temperature, time, the brightness of the light from the Sun.

A digital signal changes in small steps and cannot have values that fall between the steps. Most computers accept signals of this type because the size of each step is easily represented by a number. The digital signal will be accurate enough if you keep the steps small.

Watches can be analogue (with motor driven hands that rotate smoothly through all the times) or digital (so that they go up in small steps of either a second or a minute). Natural analogue measurements can be turned into digital ones by an analogue to digital converter (ADC) in a computer.

EXTENSION MATERIALS

The circuits discussed in this section use other components with logic gates in order to achieve a useful end product. The LED indicators normally used to show output voltages require little current, and to control more powerful apparatus, relays are often needed.

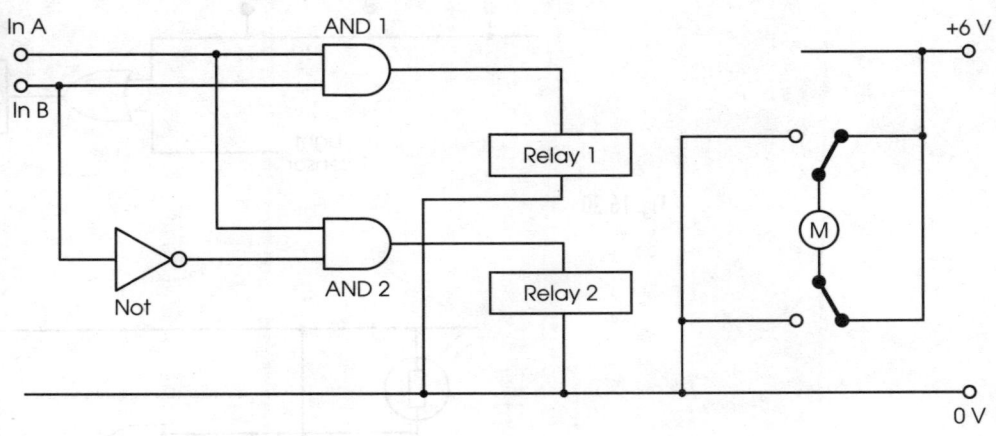

1 A MOTOR-CONTROL SYSTEM

Fig. 16.27

If input A and B (Fig. 16.27) are at logic 1, AND-gate 1 is open but 2 is closed. Relay 1 drives the motor circuit switch and the motor rotates in a particular direction.

If B is now made logic 0, AND-gate 1 closes, 2 opens. Relay 2 now switches and the motor rotates in the opposite direction.

2 A BISTABLE LATCH

The circuit in Fig 16.31 will work as a *latch* so that once the buzzer is triggered it will stay on until *reset* by switch S. It is the same bistable as shown in Fig. 16.26 but uses only one of the outputs. If the LDR is in darkness its input to the upper NOR gate is low. The other input, the feedback from the buzzer, is also low so the output of the upper NOR gate is high. This logic 1 is fed back into an input of the lower NOR gate so that the buzzer is held off. If a light shines onto the LDR its resistance falls, the input to the upper NOR gate goes high, and the output of the gate goes low. Both inputs to the lower NOR gate are now low so the buzzer is switched on. The circuit is latched in this state by the feedback from the buzzer to the upper NOR gate so that the buzzer continues to sound even though the LDR is no longer illuminated.

If the LDR is no longer illuminated the circuit can be reset by switching S up and then back down again. The high input to the lower NOR gate will have put the buzzer back to off and the circuit is back in its original state.

The whole circuit can be obtained in a "chip" called a RS flip-flop. (The RS stands for Reset Set. In some syllabuses it is called a SR flip-flop) (Fig 16.28).

When both inputs are low the output Q stays in its previous state. Pulsing (sending high for short time) the S (set) input sends Q low and $\bar{Q}$ high. Pulsing the R (reset) input reverses this. If both inputs go high at the same time the result is unpredictable.

When this is used as a latch the circuit is often drawn as a labelled box (Fig 16.29).

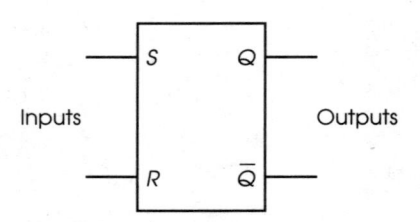

Fig. 16.28

Fig. 16.29

This can be the basis of a burglar alarm where the reset is usually a key (or number pad) controlled switch. The sensor could be inside a cupboard where it is normally dark. Exchanging the LDR and its resistor would give a sensor that was switched on by a short period of darkness. Simple switches in door frames or under carpets could also connect the upper NOR gate to a high input and trigger the system (Fig 16.30).

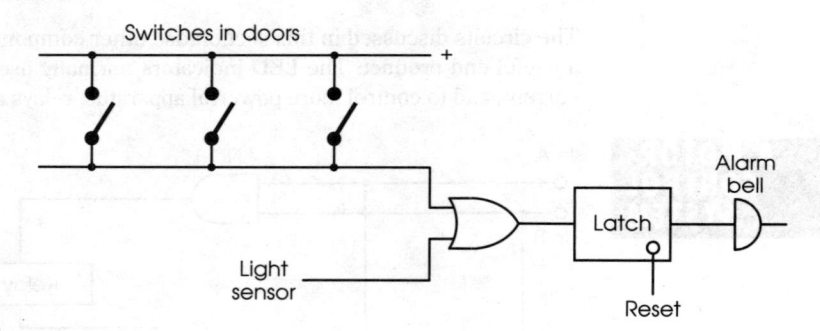

Fig. 16.30

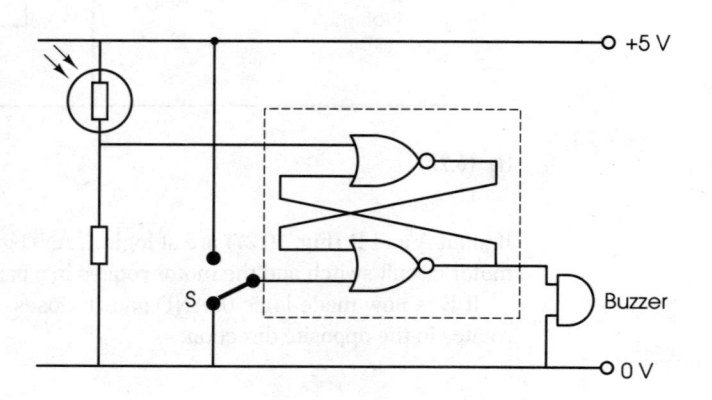

Fig. 16.31

3. ANALOGUE SYSTEMS – THE OP-AMP, BASIC CONNECTIONS

The systems dealt with before have only two states (logic 1 and logic 0). The OP-AMP (operational amplifier) is an *analogue* system. It can *follow changes as time goes on* and this represents them directly, not just as high and low.

The amplifier has five connections and is represented in Fig. 16.32. The connections to the supply are labelled $+V_s$ and $-V_s$. The supply is connected differently from most systems.

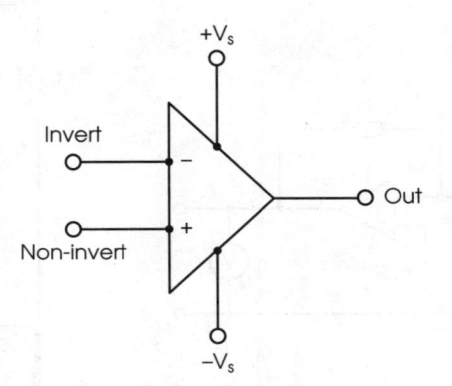

Fig. 16.32 Operational amplifier.

It is usual to describe a circuit as having a ⊕ and ⊖ line (+5 V and 0 V in an electronics system).

Here the connections are such as to give the variation of voltage in both a positive and a negative direction. This is done by dictating the 0 V of potential, by earthing a terminal (Fig. 16.33).

A *potentiometer* connected between $+V_s$ and $-V_s$ will give an input between the maximum positive and negative values: typically +15 V to −15 V and +5 V to − 5 V. But to do this there must always be one voltmeter terminal which is connected to the reference value of 0 V (Fig. 16.34).

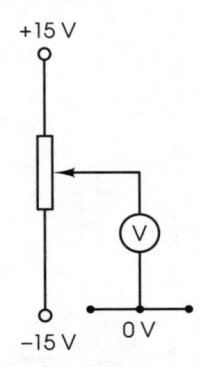

Fig. 16.34 Potentiometer control of OP-AMP supply.

The connections required to power an OP-AMP are not often shown in circuit diagrams. The behaviour of the OP-AMP depends on the way in which the remaining connections are made. The output value is, as in gate circuits, taken as the voltage between the output terminal and the 0 V line (Fig. 16.35). The other two connections are called the *inverting input* (denoted ⊖) and the *non-inverting input* (denoted ⊕). These, and a feedback connection, dictate how the system behaves.

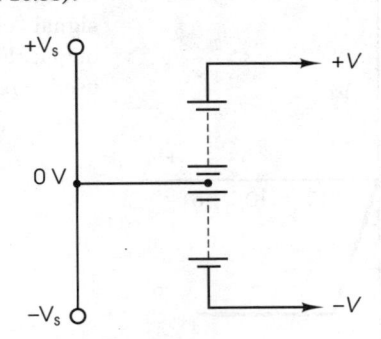

Fig. 16.33 OP-AMP supply connections.

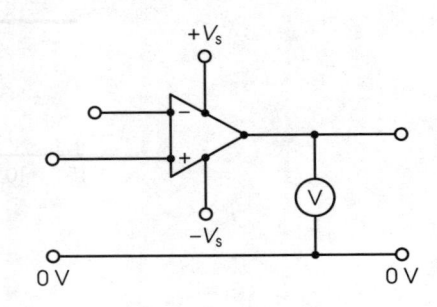

Fig. 16.35 OP-AMP connections.

4. BEHAVIOUR OF THE OP-AMP INVERTING INPUT

If a voltage is applied between the inverting input and the 0 V rail, and the non-inverting input is connected also to 0 V, the output is very large. The amplifier gives the same large output regardless of the input. A more controlled system is obtained if a further feedback resistor is connected, as in Fig. 16.36. If $R_f = R_i$ the output voltage is the same as the input, but its direction is reversed:

$$V_{in} = -V_{out}$$

When R_f is greater than R_i, the output

Fig. 16.36 OP-AMP with feedback.

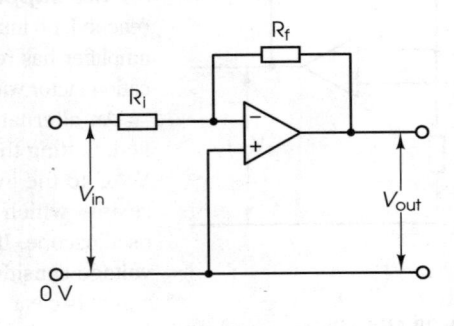

voltage is greater in value than the input, and again its direction is reversed. Now

$$V_{out} = -\frac{R_f}{R_i} V_{in}$$

and the device amplifies. Careful measurements of the behaviour can be made by varying V_{in} slowly with a potentiometer (Fig. 16.37). Suppose that R_f = 10 kΩ and R_i = 1 kΩ. Then $V_{out} = -10\, V_{in}$.

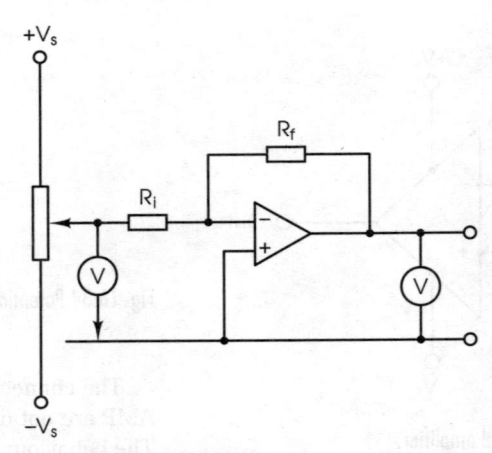

Fig. 16.37 Inverting amplifier.

A graph showing how V_{in} and V_{out} behave may look like that of Fig. 16.38. It is seen that amplification is limited. The voltage of the supply in this case was + 5 V to 0 V to –15 V, and this is the maximum output.

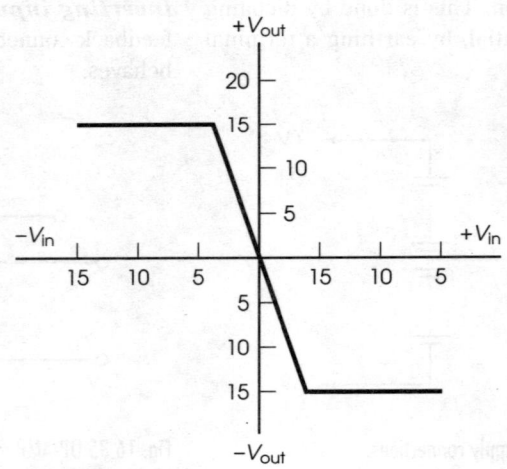

Fig. 16.38

The **range of amplification depends on the supply voltage**. When this value is reached, no further amplification is possible. The amplifier has reached **saturation**. The amplification factor within this limitation is $-R_f/R_i$.

An alternating voltage may also be amplified. Setting the value R_f/R_i = 5 and applying 1 V AC to the input resistor gives the following results which may be seen on a dual beam oscilloscope. If the two beams have the same voltage sensitivity setting, amplification of the signal is clear. If the time bases are connected to a common earth, the inverting of the output can be seen (Fig. 16.39).

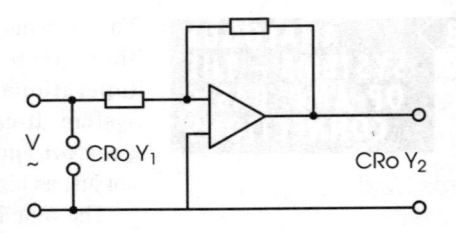

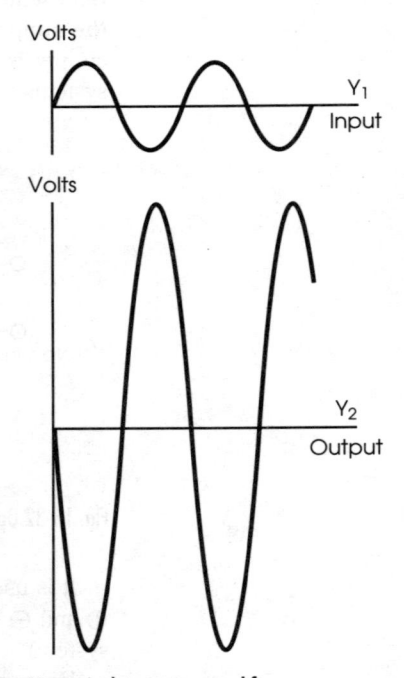

Fig. 16.39 a.c. with inverting amplifier.

However, the amplifier is still limited by the supply. If a larger input is applied, say 4 V a.c. with the same (5) amplification factor, the signal "clips" at 15 V leading to a distorted output (Fig. 16.40). In the extreme this can be used to provide a square-wave output.

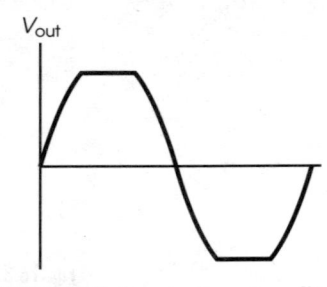

Fig. 16.40 Output with distortion due to "cut-off".

Within the limitation set by the supply, the voltage gain with a.c. is fairly constant regardless of the frequency of the signal. However, it does tend to fall off with high frequencies, i.e. those above about 10^4 Hz.

The non-inverting input may also be used with connections as in Fig. 16.41. The output is now in the same direction as the input, but the gain is now given by

$$V_{out} = V_{in}\left(1 + \frac{R_2}{R_1}\right)$$

which is smaller than in the inverting amplifier case.

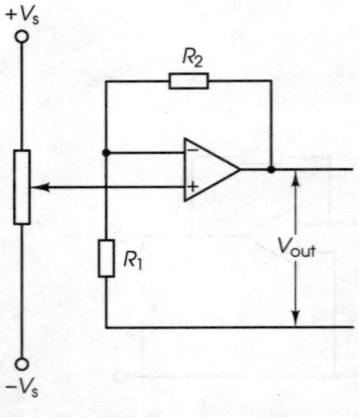

Fig. 16.41 OP-AMP with non-invert-ing input.

5 THE VOLTAGE COMPARATOR

The op-amp can also be used as a voltage comparator.

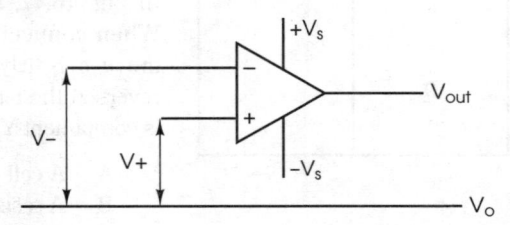

Fig. 16.42

The gain of the amplifier without the feedback resistors is *very* large. If two voltages are connected to the inverting and non-inverting inputs the amplifier will saturate and its output will go to either $+V_s$ or $-V_s$.

If $V+ > V-$ then the output becomes $+V_s$.

If $V+ < V-$ then the output becomes $-V_s$.

This can be used in circuits such as that of Fig. 16.43.

When the LDR is in the light it will have a low resistance and a low voltage across it so that the non-inverting input is higher than that set by the variable resistor R. The output is therefore high $(+V_s)$. When the LDR is in the dark the non-inverting input goes lower than that at the inverting input and the final output is low $(-V_s)$. The level of light at which the op-amp switches can be set by the variable resistor R. This effect can be useful when the next stage is a digital circuit such as a logic gate as the output is always high or low and not slowly changing.

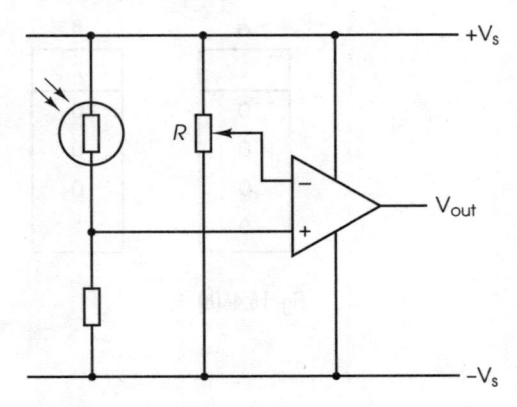

Fig. 16.43

EXAMINATION QUESTIONS

MULTIPLE CHOICE QUESTIONS

QUESTION 1

Which one in Fig. 16.44 is the circuit symbol for a NAND gate? (NISEAC)

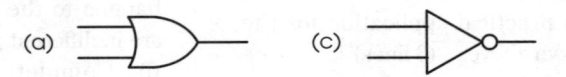

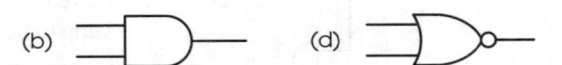

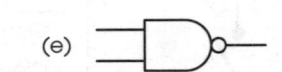

Fig. 16.44

QUESTION 2

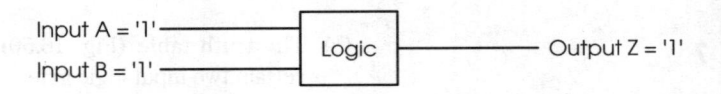

Fig. 16.45

On testing a logic gate with the conditions shown in Fig. 16.45, a student found the output Z to be a logic level "1". The gate could be

A   A NOR gate or an AND gate
B   An AND gate or an OR gate
C   An OR gate or a NOR gate
D   A NAND gate or an OR gate
E   An AND gate or a NAND gate
(NICCEA)

QUESTION 3

Which one of the following conducts electricity in one direction only?

A   Diode   C   Lamp
B   Fuse   D   Thermistor

QUESTION 4

Figure 16.46(a) shows an incomplete truth table for an AND gate which has inputs X and Y and output Z. Which of the following in Fig. 16.46(b) is the correct version of the last column of the truth table? (ULEAC)

X	Y	Z
0	0	
0	1	
1	0	
1	1	

Fig. 16.46(a)

A	B	C	D
Z	Z	Z	Z
0	0	0	1
0	0	1	0
0	0	1	0
0	1	1	1

Fig. 16.46(b)

QUESTION 5

In Fig. 16.47, box Y contains a component. When connected as shown the lamp lights more brightly than normal. If the cell is reversed the lamp does not light at all. Which is component Y most likely to be?

- A A cell
- B A resistor of large resistance
- C A coil of copper wire
- D A diode rectifier
- E A capacitor

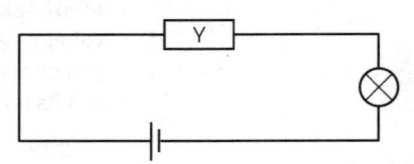

Fig. 16.47

STRUCTURED QUESTIONS

QUESTION 6

In the circuit in Fig. 16.48, the relay coil is energised and can close switch S if the **output** of the NOT gate is high. When a bright light is shone on the light-dependent resistor the input to the NOT gate falls.

(i) Why does this happen? (2 lines)
(ii) What happens to the rest of the circuit because of this? (2 lines)
(iii) Suggest a practical application for the circuit shown above. (3 lines)

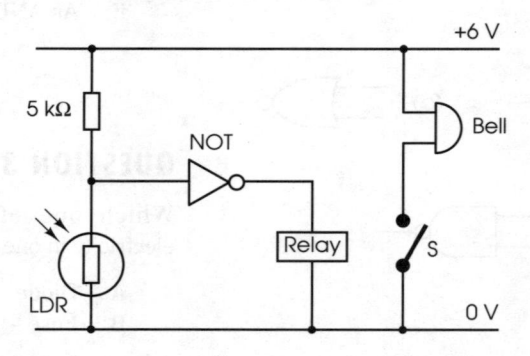

Fig. 16.48

QUESTION 7

(a) The circuit in Fig. 16.49(a) contains two switches A and B which can either be open or closed. Figure 16.49(b) is a truth table for the circuit. It shows what will

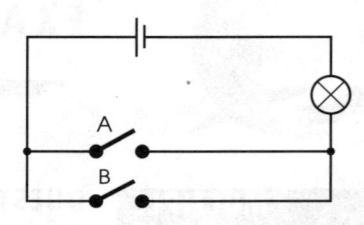

Fig. 16.49(a)

happen to the lamp when the switches are in different positions.

(i) Complete the truth table for the circuit.
(ii) State in words the condition for the lamp to be lit. (1 line)

Switch A	Switch B	Lamp ON or OFF
Open	Open	
Closed	Open	
Open	Closed	
Closed	Closed	

Fig. 16.49(b)

(b) The truth table (Fig. 16.50) refers to a certain two-input logic gate.
(i) What logic gate is indicated by this table?
(ii) Draw a symbol representing this logic gate.

Input		Output
A	B	
0	0	0
0	1	1
1	0	1
1	1	1

Fig. 16.50

(c) A circuit is to be designed so that a bell will ring if a push switch is operated, but only if there is also an input from a light (or heat) sensor or both. These requirements can be summarised in the table (Fig. 16.51).
  (i) Complete the table.
  (ii) This result can be achieved by using two 2-input logic gates between the switch and sensors and the bell. Show how this can be done completing the lines below.

Push switch _____
Light sensor _____ to bell.
Heat sensor _____

(NISEAC)

Push switch	Light sensor	Heat sensor	Output
0	0	0	0
0			0
0			0
0			0
1	0	0	0
1			
1			
1			

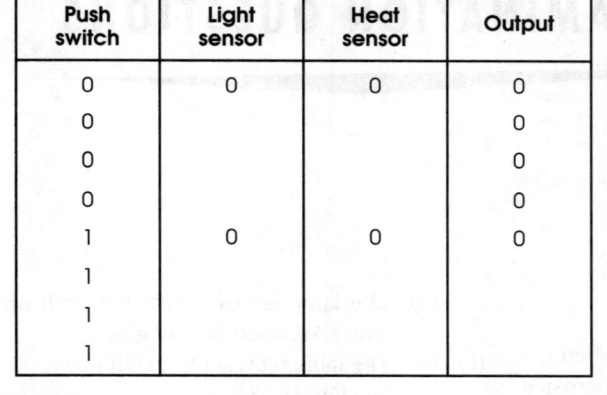

Fig. 16.51

NOT

A	P
0	1
1	0

Fig. 16.52(a)

QUESTION 8

(a) A NOT gate can be added to the output of a two-input OR logic gate to produce a two-input NOR (NOT OR) logic gate. The completed truth tables for a NOT and an OR gate are given in Fig. 16.52(a) and (b). A and B are inputs. P is the output. Complete the truth table for a two-input NOR gate (Fig. 16.52(c)).

OR

A	B	P
0	0	0
0	1	1
1	0	1
1	1	1

Fig. 16.52(b)

A	B	P
0	0	
0	1	
1	0	
1	1	

Fig. 16.52(c)

(b) The circuit symbol for a two-input NAND (NOT AND) gate is shown in Fig. 16.53(a). Also given is the truth table for a two-input NAND gate (Fig. 16.53(b)). In the design of logic systems, a NAND gate is a basic "building block" as in the circuit shown in Fig. 16.54(a).

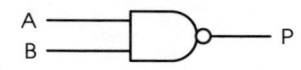

Fig. 16.53(a)

A	B	P
0	0	1
0	1	1
1	0	1
1	1	0

Fig. 16.53(b)

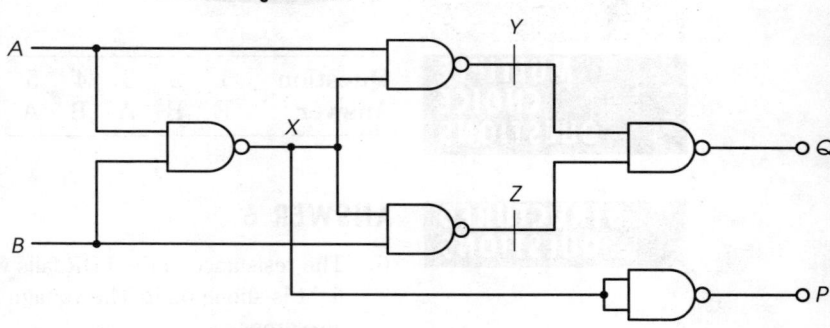

Fig. 16.54(a)

  (i) Complete the truth table for this circuit (Fig. 16.54(b)).
  (ii) What arithmetic function does this circuit perform?
(c) The output of a logic circuit can be displayed using an LED and associated series resistor as shown in Fig. 16.55.
  (i) When the LED is lit, what is the logic state at A?

A	B	X	Y	Z	P	Q
0	0	1				
0	1	1				
1	0	1				
1	1	0				

Fig. 16.54(b)

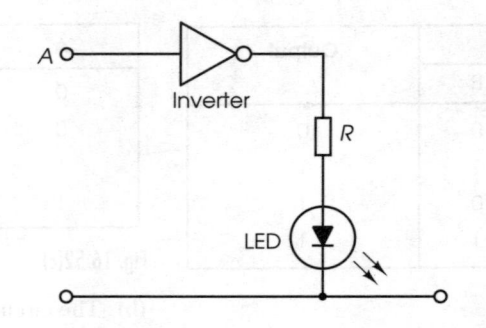

Fig. 16.55

(ii) The LED has a potential difference of 2 V across it and a current of 10 mA flowing through it when it is lit. What is the potential difference across resistor R when the LED is lit?
(iii) Calculate the resistance of R.
(iv) Why is resistor R needed?

(d) In a factory a particular piece of machinery has an alarm button to warn the operator of a fault. The system has a blue lamp (alight when the machine is operating normally), a red warning lamp and a buzzer. There is a fault detection system and an "operator acknowledge" button. If a fault is detected the blue lamp goes out, the red lamp comes on and a buzzer sounds. When the operator acknowledges the fault, by pressing the button, the buzzer stops but the red light stays on. Complete the output columns of the truth table (Fig. 16.56) to show what states are wanted. (NEAB)

Input		Output		
Fault	Operator acknowledge	Red	Buzzer	Blue
0	0			
0	1			
1	0			
1	1			

Fig. 16.56

ANSWERS TO EXAMINATION QUESTIONS

MULTIPLE CHOICE QUESTIONS

Question	1	2	3	4	5
Answer	E	B	A	B	A

STRUCTURED QUESTIONS

ANSWER 6
(i) The resistance of the LDR falls when the light is shone on it. The voltage across it also drops.
(ii) The NOT input falls, so its output becomes high, energising the relay coil and switching the bell circuit.
(iii) The system could act as a warning against excessive light levels or to control lighting conditions.

ANSWER 7
(a) (i) See Fig. 16.57.

Switch A	Switch B	Lamp
Open	Open	Off
Closed	Open	On
Open	Closed	On
Closed	Closed	On

Fig. 16.57

(ii) The lamp is ON if either A or B or both are closed (an OR gate).

(b) (i) The table represents an OR gate.
(ii) See Fig. 16.58.

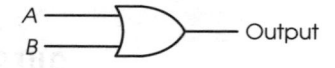

Fig. 16.58

(c) (i) See Fig. 16.59(a).
(ii) See Fig. 16.59(b). The system needs to link the heat and light sensors with an OR gate. The output combines with the push through an AND gate.

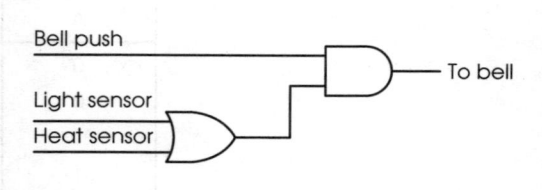

Fig. 16.59(a)

Push switch	Light sensor	Heat sensor	Output
0	0	0	0
0	1	0	0
0	0	1	0
0	1	1	0
1	0	0	0
1	1	0	1
1	0	1	1
1	1	1	1

Fig. 16.59(b)

ANSWER 8

(a) See Fig. 16.60.
(b) (i) See Fig. 16.61.
    (ii) Addition.

A	B	P
0	0	1
0	1	0
1	0	0
1	1	0

Fig. 16.60

A	B	X	Y	Z	P	Q
0	0	1	1	1	0	0
0	1	1	1	0	0	1
1	0	1	0	1	0	1
1	1	0	1	1	1	0

Fig. 16.61

(c) (i) Logic state of A is level 0.
    (ii) p.d. across $R = (5 - 2) = 3$ V.
    (iii)
$$R = \frac{V}{I} = \frac{3}{10 \times 10^{-3}} = 300 \, \Omega$$
    (iv) R protects the LED from high currents.
(d) See Fig. 16.62.

Input		Output		
Fault	Operator acknowledge	Red	Buzzer	Blue
0	0	0	0	1
0	1	0	0	1
1	0	1	1	0
1	1	1	0	0

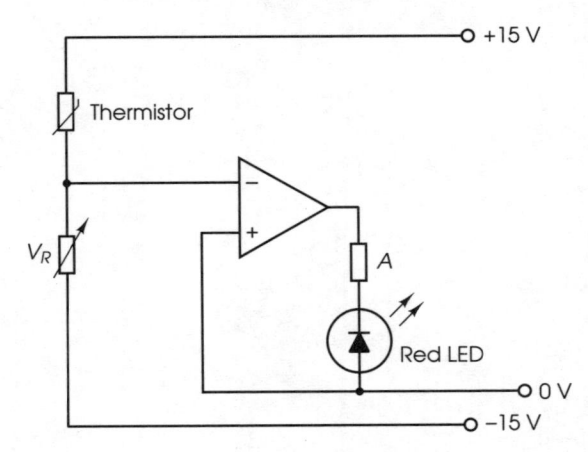

Fig. 16.62

TUTOR'S QUESTION AND ANSWER

QUESTION

This question is about a freezer alarm. Figure 16.63 shows a freezer alarm system which uses an operational amplifier.

Fig. 16.63

(a) The two inputs of the operational amplifier are called inverting and non-inverting.
    (i) State which of the inputs is connected to the 0 V line.
    (ii) What is meant by the term inverting input of the operational amplifier?
(b) When the freezer warms up above its working temperature of –20 °C a red LED comes ON to give a warning.
    (i) Explain why a resistor is placed in series with the LED at the output of the operational amplifier.
    (ii) When lit, the LED has a forward voltage drop at 2 V at a current of 10 mA. Calculate the value of the output resistor A.
(c) It is required to add a second, green LED to the output of the system, such that it will go OFF when the red LED comes ON.
    (i) Complete Fig. 16.63 showing the correction position of the green LED.
    (ii) What advantage is there in adding the green LED to the system?
(d) Explain carefully the action of the operational amplifier when the temperature of the freezer increases. (MEG)

ANSWER

(a) (i) Non-inverting.
(ii) The output is in the opposite direction to the input. An increasing input gives a decreasing output and vice versa.

(b) (i) The resistor limits the current through the LED to avoid damage.
(ii) Voltage across $R = 15 - 2 = 13$ V. Therefore

$$R = \frac{13}{10 \times 10^{-3}} = 1300 \, \Omega$$

(c) (i) See Fig. 16.64.
(ii) It shows if the temperature of freezing is correct, or if the green LED goes OFF and the red LED does not come ON, the battery supplying the system is low.

(d) The voltage across the thermistor decreases so the voltage across V_R increases. The voltage across V_R is greater than 0 V, so since the input is inverting the output voltage goes below 0 V and the red LED lights.

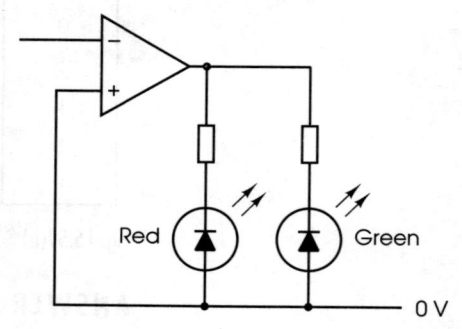

Fig. 16.64

STUDENT'S ANSWER WITH THE EXAMINER'S COMMENTS

STUDENT ANSWER TO QUESTION 8

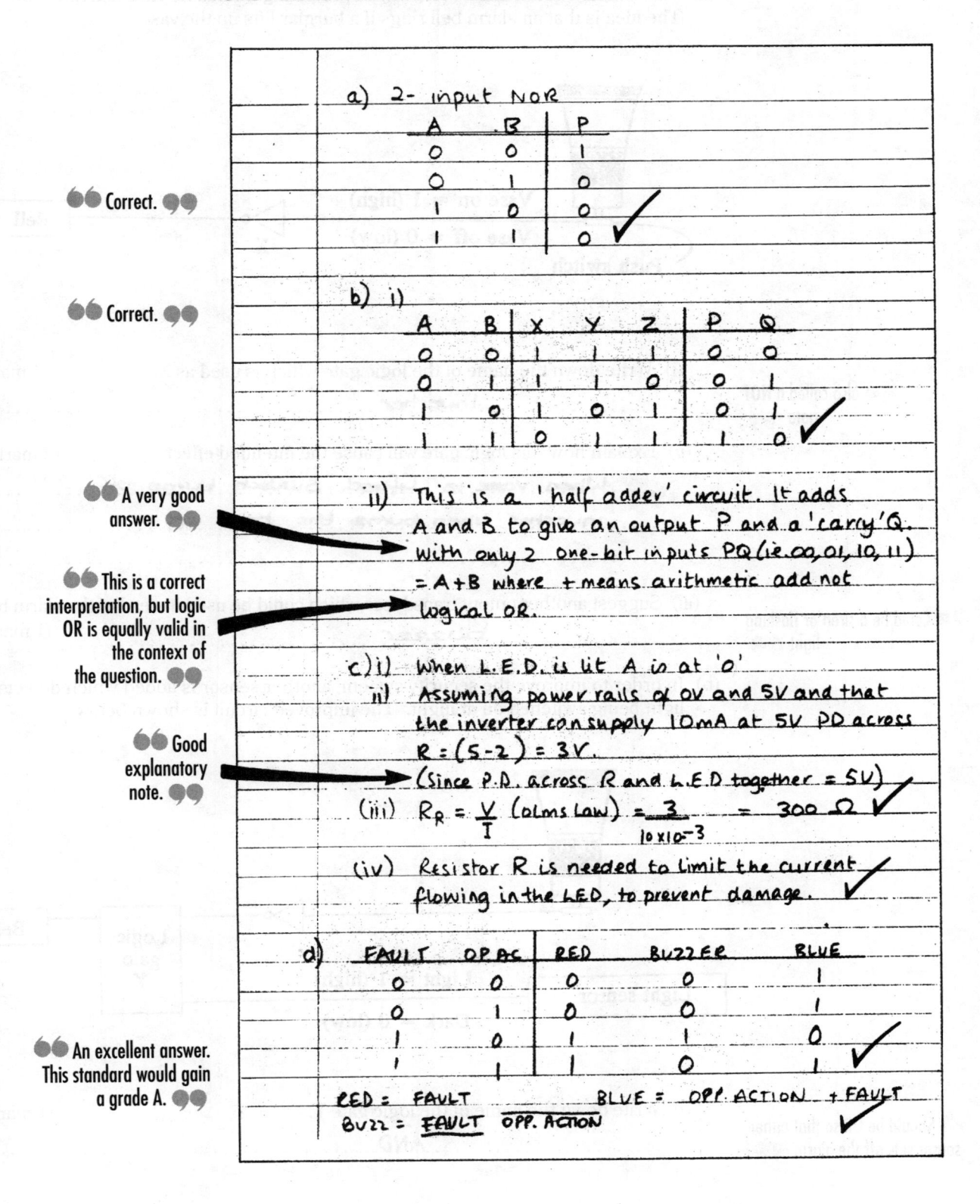

a) 2-input NOR

A	B	P
0	0	1
0	1	0
1	0	0
1	1	0

> Correct.

b) i)

A	B	X	Y	Z	P	Q
0	0	1	1	0	0	0
0	1	1	1	0	0	1
1	0	1	0	1	0	1
1	1	0	1	1	1	0

> Correct.

ii) This is a 'half adder' circuit. It adds A and B to give an output P and a 'carry' Q. With only 2 one-bit inputs PQ (i.e. 00, 01, 10, 11) = A+B where + means arithmetic add not logical OR.

> A very good answer.
>
> This is a correct interpretation, but logic OR is equally valid in the context of the question.

c) i) When L.E.D. is lit A is at '0'

ii) Assuming power rails of 0V and 5V and that the inverter can supply 10mA at 5V PD across R = (5-2) = 3V.
(Since P.D. across R and L.E.D together = 5V)

> Good explanatory note.

(iii) $R_R = \frac{V}{I}$ (Ohms Law) $= \frac{3}{10 \times 10^{-3}} = 300\,\Omega$

(iv) Resistor R is needed to limit the current flowing in the LED, to prevent damage.

d)

FAULT	OP AC	RED	BUZZER	BLUE
0	0	0	0	1
0	1	0	0	1
1	0	1	1	0
1	1	1	0	1

RED = FAULT   BLUE = OPP. ACTION + FAULT
BUZZ = FAULT · OPP. ACTION

> An excellent answer. This standard would gain a grade A.

MORE EXAMINERS COMMENTS
CENTRAL/HIGHER LEVEL

(a) The diagram below shows one way of protecting a valuable vase in a museum. The idea is that an alarm bell rings if a burglar lifts up the vase.

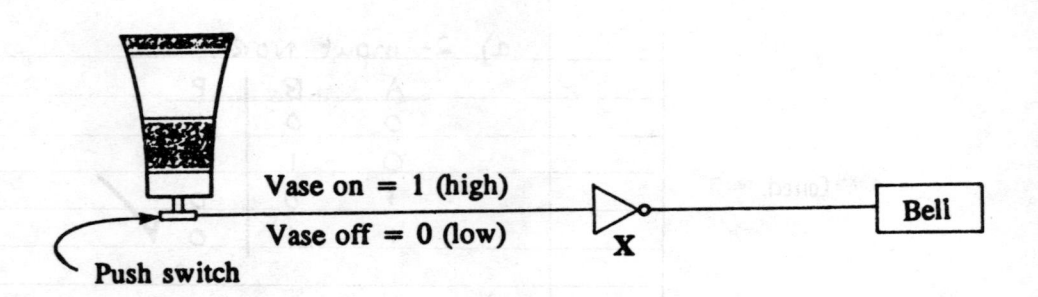

Vase on = 1 (high)
Vase off = 0 (low)
Push switch
X → Bell

(i) Write down the name of the logic gate which is used as X. (1 mark)

Inverter

> 66 also called a NOT gate 99

(ii) Explain how this logic gate will cause the intended effect. (2 marks)

When vase is lifted switch turns off inverter then turns the bell on

(iii) Suggest another output transducer which could be used instead of the alarm bell. (1 mark)

buzzer

> 66 Could be a siren or flashing light 99

(b) In order to improve the security system, another sensor is added which detects a light being switched on at night. The improved circuit is shown below.

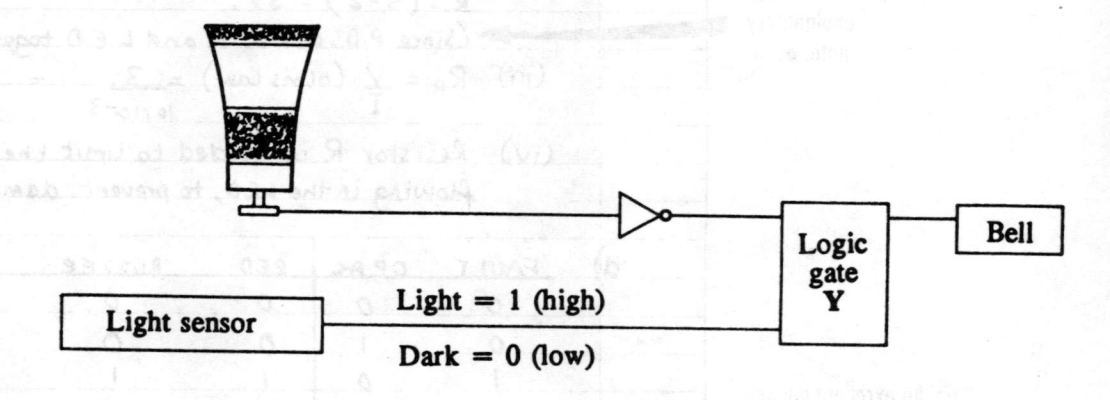

Light sensor
Light = 1 (high)
Dark = 0 (low)
Logic gate Y → Bell

(i) Write down the name of the logic gate Y. (1 mark)

AND

> 66 Should be OR so that either sensor sets off the alarm 99

(ii) Besides the two sensors already used, suggest one other sensor which could be used to detect the presence of a burglar. (1 mark)

Pressure mat switch

> 66 Could be a magnetic switch in the door 99

REVIEW SHEET

- Draw the symbols for each of the following logic gates:

    NOT   AND   OR

    NOR   NAND

- Complete each of the following truth tables:

NOT

Input	Output
1	
0	

AND

Input		Output
0	0	
0	1	
1	0	
1	1	

OR

Input		Output
0	0	
0	1	
1	0	
1	1	

NAND

Input		Output
0	0	
0	1	
1	0	
1	1	

NOR

Input		Output
0	0	
0	1	
1	0	
1	1	

- How can a NAND gate be connected so that it behaves as a NOT gate? _____

- Write the following numbers in binary:

    ten _____   seven _____   five _____

- When there is feedback in a circuit the _____ is connected to the _____.

- The two inputs of an op-amp are called the _____ and the _____.

- When the output voltage of an op-amp reaches the supply voltage it has reached _____. This will cause the output to be _____ as the waveform is cut off (clipped).

CHAPTER 16 **ELECTRONICS: SYSTEMS**

- Draw a circuit diagram to show how two NOT gates can be connected to make a simple latch circuit.

- Why is it more reliable to transmit digital data than analogue data? _____
_____
_____

CHAPTER 17

EARTH, SPACE AND WEATHER

THE UNIVERSE
THE SOLAR SYSTEM
AN EXPANDING UNIVERSE
GRAVITY AND FIELD STRENGTH
PLANET AND STAR FORMATION
CREATION – THE "BIG BANG"
THE LIFE CYCLE OF A STAR
DAYS AND SEASONS
INSIDE THE EARTH
EARTHQUAKES AND WAVES
TECTONIC PLATES
PHASES OF THE MOON
TIDES
ATMOSPHERE AND WEATHER
CLOUDS AND FOG
STAR GAZING
ROCKS, FOSSILS AND THE ROCK CYCLE
NEWTON'S LAW
THE UPPER ATMOSPHERE
ECLIPSES
POWERING THE SUN – FUSION
INSIDE THE EARTH

GETTING STARTED

This chapter is about the planet that we live on and its place in the universe. We will look at how the Earth and the other planets were created, and what they are made from. We will look at why we divide our time into night and day and the reason for the seasons. In many countries earthquakes are important events and we will study their cause and try to understand why the Earth's surface has the structure that it does. Finally we will have a look at the complicated system in the atmosphere that we call weather.

- In this chapter you should remember that a billion = 1000 million and that distances in astronomy are measured in light years. One *light year* is the distance travelled by light in a year (at 300 000 km per second).

ESSENTIAL PRINCIPLES

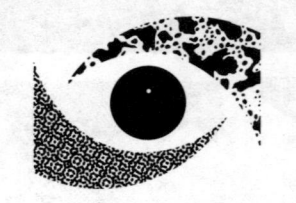

1 > THE ORDER OF THINGS

We live on a **planet**, the Earth, that is a satellite of a star that we call the **Sun**.

Our **Sun** is an ordinary star. It is about 1 392 000 km across and the temperature at its centre is about 13 million °C. At this temperature electrons are separated from their atoms and form a **plasma**. (A plasma is not solid, liquid or gas and is really a fourth state of matter with its own special properties.) The sun is mostly made of hydrogen and at such a temperature the hydrogen nuclei hit each other hard enough to join together in a fusion reaction. This releases heat energy and fuels the Sun. The Sun then radiates energy at 4×10^{26} W.

The **universe** is made up of lots of **galaxies**, about a hundred billion of them. Each galaxy is a collection of a huge number of stars. Some of the galaxies are close to each other and such a group is called a **cluster**. Each galaxy will contain dust and clouds of gas as well as stars. It is possible that lots of stars have planets round them but even the nearest stars in our galaxy are too far away for us to be sure. (The brightest, Sirius, is about 8.6 light years away. The nearest, apart from the Sun, is Proxima Centauri about 4.2 light years away).

Our star, the Sun, belongs to a galaxy called the **Milky Way**. We are on the edge of the galaxy and you can see it at night looking like a bright band of stars across the sky. It looks like this because we are looking at it edge on. If you could see it from a distance it would look like a giant flat spiral with several arms. Many other galaxies have this shape but some are just elliptical (oval). The Milky Way contains about 100 billion stars and is about 100 thousand light years across. Its spiral shape spins round once in 250 million years.

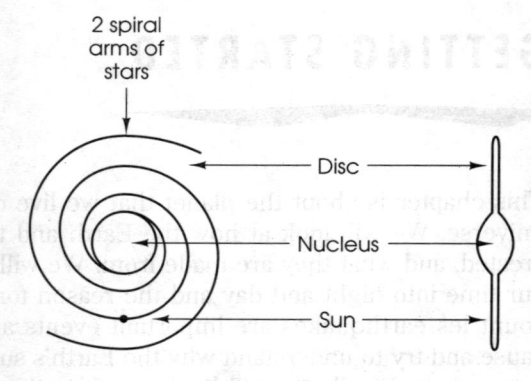

Fig. 17.1

It is part of a small cluster called the *"Local Group"*. The other big galaxy in the Local Group is called M31 but is better known as the Andromeda galaxy. The numbers involved in this sort of science are extremely large and show us to inhabit a rather small planet orbiting an ordinary star that is one of a huge number of similar stars arranged in galaxies.

2 > THE SOLAR SYSTEM

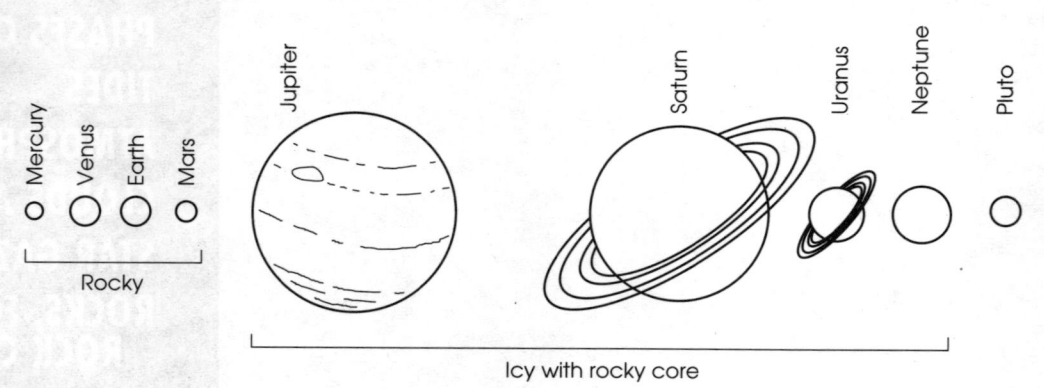

Fig. 17.2

The nine planets that orbit the Sun form our **solar system**. As the distance from the Sun increases the radiation that reaches each planet from the Sun becomes much less and the planets become colder. The temperatures range from the day side of Mercury at about 450 °C to Neptune at −228 °C with the Earth at a comfortable (for us) 17 °C. Of our near neighbours, Venus has a thick atmosphere with a lot of CO_2 that creates a strong greenhouse effect and raises its surface temperature to about 475 °C. Mars has a number of Earthlike features such as mountains, polar icecaps and volcanoes but is colder and its thin atmosphere has a pressure only about 1/100 of that on Earth. When Viking 1 landed on Mars in 1976 the temperature at midday was only −31 °C

The planets are of two types. The **rocky** (terrestrial) planets are the four closest to the Sun and are small and dense with a rocky surface. They mostly have cores of iron and nickel surrounded by rock. The **icy** planets further out are large low density worlds with a thick atmosphere. They seem to be mostly made of hydrogen and helium turned liquid by the huge pressure with a rocky core of some sort at the centre. Most simple chemicals such as water or ammonia or our atmospheric gases would be liquid or solid on such a world. Pluto does not fit either type very well. It is small, like the rocky planets, but is so far from the Sun that it is very cold and has a low density like the icy planets.

Many of the planets are large enough to have captured passing objects which now orbit them as moons. Most moons are small but four of those round Jupiter are as big, or bigger than, our moon.

In the table mass, diameter and gravity are related to that of Earth which is taken as 1. Density is relative density (i.e. number of times the density of water). Average distance to Sun is in millions of km.

> Mass, diameter and gravity are relative to earth (=1). Density is relative to water (=1).

	Mercury	Venus	Earth	Mars	Jupiter	Saturn	Uranus	Neptune	Pluto
Mass	0.06	0.81	1	0.11	318	95	14.5	17.2	0.1
Diameter	0.38	0.95	1	0.53	11	9	4	4	0.2
Gravity	0.38	0.9	1	0.38	2.6	1.2	0.9	1.2	0.1
Density	5.4	5.2	5.5	3.9	1.3	0.69	1.2	1.7	1.8
Rocky/icy	rocky	rocky	rocky	rocky	icy	icy	icy	icy	icy
Moons	0	0	1	2	16	17	10	8	1
Orbit time	88d	225d	1y	1.9y	11.9y	29.5y	84y	165y	248y
Average dist. to Sun (mn km)	58	108	150	228	778	1,427	2,870	4,500	5,900

3 > AN EXPANDING UNIVERSE

When materials are at high temperatures they radiate light. The exact spectrum that is produced depends on the type of atoms that are present. If we look at the spectrum from a low density gas such as that in a sodium lamp it will be made up of exact lines in a pattern that is special to the sodium atoms that they come from. When atoms are more closely packed they give out a more continuous spectrum like the spectrum from a bulb and the hotter the atoms are the shorter the wavelength of the light will become. (You can see this when you slowly increase the current through a bulb. At first it glows dull red, then more orange and eventually the shorter green and blue waves are emitted as well so that the mixture of waves appears white.) Stars will emit this sort of continuous spectrum of light. As the light leaves the star it passes through more of the atoms that make the star and these will **absorb** their own special pattern of light waves so that the continuous spectrum that comes to us is crossed by dark lines. The lines are called Fraunhoffer lines after their discoverer. The pattern of these lines tells us what the stars are made from. We know that most of the Sun is hydrogen with about 25% helium and only about 2% heavier elements.

When astronomers looked at the lines in the spectrums of stars they found that the patterns were as they expected but they were moved more towards the red, longer wave, end of the spectrum than they should be. This effect is called **red shift**. It is caused by the star that you are looking at moving away from you as it gives out the light. This spreads out the waves more so that they have a longer wavelength and are moved towards the red end of the spectrum. The faster the star moves away from you the bigger the red shift of its spectrum. (This an example of the ***Doppler effect.***) Astronomers were surprised to find that **all** the other galaxies were moving away from us and that more distant ones were moving away faster. The explanation seems to be that the entire universe is getting bigger and bigger as the galaxies spread out. We live in an ***expanding universe***. Astronomers think that the force of gravity is attracting all the material back towards the centre and that this is slowing down the expansion so that it will eventually stop and the universe might begin to collapse back again.

Activity

One problem is that you cannot tell where the centre of the universe is. Wherever you are it will still appear that all the stars are moving away from you.

In Fig. 17.3(a) you are near to the Sun S and looking at stars A and B. These move

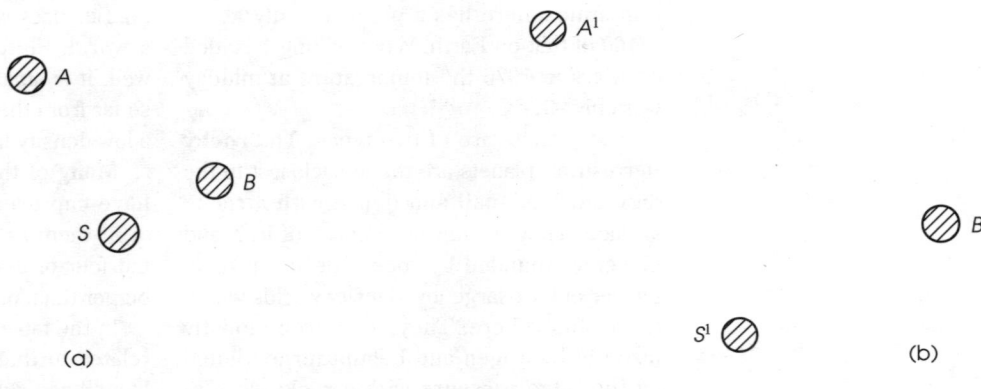

Fig. 17.3

away from you until they look like Fig. 17.3(b). Make a tracing of Fig. 17.3(b) using thin paper. You don't think that you have moved so put the tracing on top of Fig. 17.3(a) with S' on top of S to show stars A and B leaving you along straight lines. If an alien living near star B has also been star-gazing it will think B has not moved. Slide the tracing across until B¹ is on top of B and you will see that he also thinks that all the stars are moving away from him! The fact is that all the stars are separating as the universe gets bigger and we are not in the centre.

4 > GRAVITY AND FIELD STRENGTH

Any two masses will attract each other with the force that we say is caused by *gravity*. The force gets bigger as the masses get bigger and rapidly gets smaller as the distance between them increases. The force is only significant when one of the masses is very large – as it would be for a planet or a star.

A large object such as a planet or a star will make a force on any object in the space around it. This is called a gravitational field. The strength of the field at a particular place is the force that is exerted on a 1 kg mass at that place. The field strength is given the symbol g and will also be the same as the acceleration of a mass released at that place. The weight of an object near to a star or planet is given by

$$\text{weight} = \text{mass} \times g$$

At the surface of the Earth $g = 10$ N/kg, so a man of mass 70 kg will weigh 700 N.

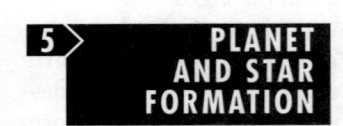

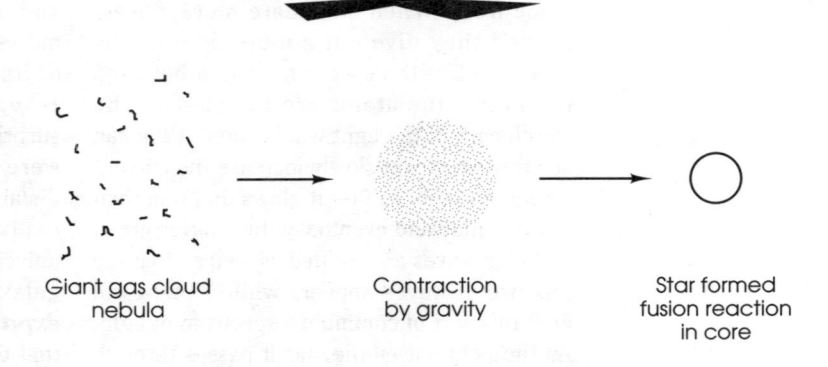

5 > PLANET AND STAR FORMATION

Giant gas cloud nebula → Contraction by gravity → Star formed fusion reaction in core

Fig. 17.4

The space between stars is filled with a very thinly scattered gas. Most of this is hydrogen gas with a few other atoms and occasional specks of dust. In some places in the sky we can see giant clouds of this gas and dust and we call such a cloud in space a *nebula*. Dark nebulas block our views of the stars beyond them and contain dust about the same size as the dust in cigarette smoke.

In some cases a giant cloud of gas will be pulled together by gravity and start to collapse towards its centre.

As more material is drawn in and the centre becomes more dense the arriving atoms are attracted more and are travelling faster and therefore have more energy. The energy increases the temperature of the material and a *star* begins to grow. When the temperature is great enough some of the atoms are travelling so fast inside the star that their nuclei are forced together and they form a new larger atom. This is called a *fusion reaction* and releases energy to power the star. Eventually the outward pressure of the fast-moving particles inside the star is balanced by the inward force of gravity and the star becomes stable, emitting radiation and powered by the fusion reaction in its core. Really big clouds of gas can form clusters of stars.

As the star is being formed some of the gas and dust can form a spinning disc that surrounds the star. Some of the material in the disc round our Sun condensed together and formed lumps that could then attract other material and slowly grow into the planets which still spin round in the plane where the disc of gas used to be. Close to the Sun it would be hotter and at first only those materials that had higher melting points would be able to condense out of the gas and form the basis of the *rocky planets*. Farther away from the Sun it was cooler and other materials with lower melting points could condense to form the *icy planets*. The planets are trapped in their orbits by gravity which provides the centripetal force that is needed (see chapter 5.) The Earth appears to be about 4600 million years old so our solar system probably began about 5 billion years ago.

6 CREATION

(i) Old ideas

There have been many theories to explain how the universe started and most ancient civilisations and religions had their own to explain the facts as they were known. Many included a flat surface for the Earth with the sky somehow held above it and stars moving on the surface of the sky. Most had a god that created the system at some time in the distant past. Since, to men at the time, the Earth was clearly the largest and most important object it was placed at the centre of most models of the universe. After discovering that the Earth was round, western civilisation believed that the Earth was at the centre and that the other planets rotated round it. A sun-centred (heliocentric) theory was strongly resisted.

(ii) The "Big Bang"

We now accept the idea of a solar system and our place in a galaxy and the universe as we have already described it. Scientists now try to explain how it all began. The universe is still expanding, all the galaxies moving apart so they may have all come from one central place. Tracing the movements back would suggest that all the material in the universe might have been in one place about 15 billion years ago. Then there was a gigantic explosion called the *"big bang"* that threw all the matter outwards. As it moved outwards gravity would have pulled some of it together to form the stars and galaxies.

(iii) The steady state theory

Another theory was that matter was always being created in the space between galaxies as they moved apart. This would then form new galaxies so that the universe remained in a "steady state" overall. This was a commonly accepted idea in the 1950s and 1960s but then microwave radiation was discovered that appears to have originated in the big bang and the big bang theory became more widely accepted. In the 1990s the data collected by special satellites such as COBE has confirmed this radiation is real and even that it is not quite evenly distributed where the first galaxies began to form not long after the big bang.

(iv) A repeating universe

The big bang theory does not explain how all the matter came to be in one place to begin with. There are a number of possibilities but one is that gravity will eventually cause the universe to collapse back inwards to its original place and size in a "big crunch" and the whole cycle will begin again with another big bang.

This cycle could then keep on repeating.

7 THE LIFE CYCLE OF A STAR

Stars don't remain the same for ever. A star like the Sun is called a *main sequence* star and is stable as we found in section 5.

A star the size of the Sun will eventually start to run out of nuclear fuel (hydrogen) for fusion and grow a lot bigger. It will also be cooler at its surface and become a *red giant*. The red giant may be hundreds of times bigger than the Sun, overcoming some of the inner planets, and last for millions of years.

Our Sun is expected to last for about 10 billion years as a "normal" star and then another billion as a giant. We are about halfway through the "normal" stage. Inside the giant, near its core, the helium formed by the fusion process will be fused to make

CHAPTER 17 EARTH, SPACE AND WEATHER

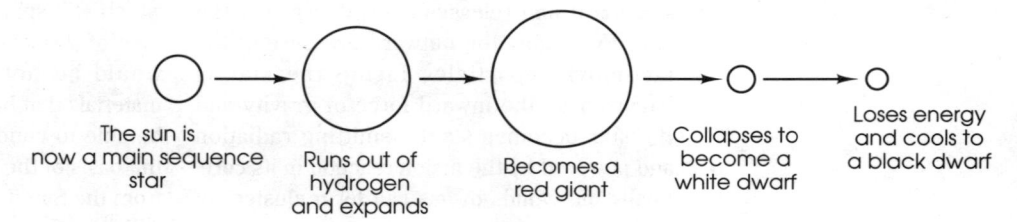

```
The sun is          Runs out of       Becomes a      Collapses to      Loses energy
now a main sequence hydrogen          red giant      become a          and cools to
star                and expands                      white dwarf       a black dwarf
```

Fig. 17.5

larger nuclei. As it eventually dies the giant will send some of its matter out into the galaxy as glowing gas and what is left will contract smaller and smaller until it becomes a *white dwarf*. This will be very dense (more than a ton per teaspoonful) and gives out a lot of radiation. This will again last for millions of years but is continuously losing energy and eventually cools and becomes a cold and dark *black dwarf* (sometimes called a dark body).

A star bigger than the Sun will probably make an even more dense core that will explode and be seen from other stars as a *supernova* as the light and dust is thrown outwards. A smaller piece of the centre will probably be left behind and become a *neutron star*, small but almost unbelievably heavy – about the weight of a mountain per teaspoonful and perhaps only a few tens of km across.

Stars that are even bigger can end in another different way. They are so big that gravity keeps on pulling the matter together until the star, perhaps 20 times the size of the Sun, has become about the size of a city. It is so dense that the force of gravity has become enormous and nothing, not even light, can escape. It has become a *black hole*.

When stars explode or throw out part of their matter into space it is eventually captured in a gas cloud and becomes a part of a new star or planet. We think that a lot of the heavier, more complicated elements were made by fusion reactions inside stars and then thrown out as a sort of dust into space. Planets like ours contain material that was formed in other suns billions of years ago, thrown out into space and eventually collected together near our Sun. There is some evidence that a lot of it came from a supernova that exploded just before our Sun evolved. We think that our Sun is therefore made from the remains of others – it is a second or third generation star. Without the bits left from earlier stars we wouldn't exist because there wouldn't be any of the larger atoms such as oxygen, iron, etc.

8 > DAYS AND SEASONS

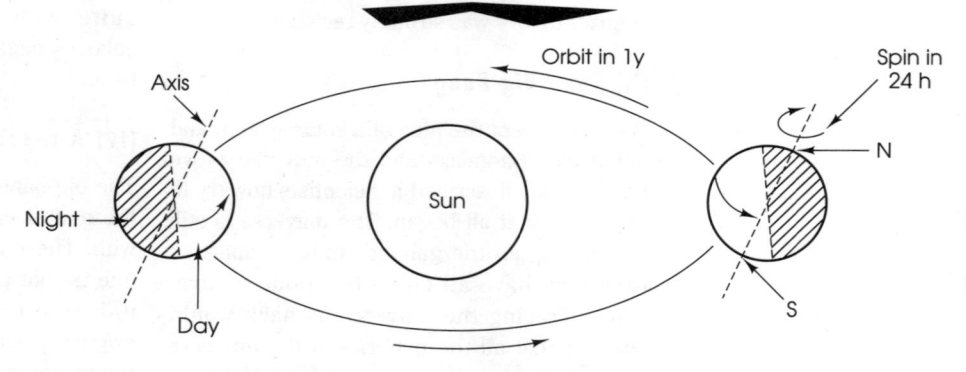

Fig. 17.6

The Earth rotates on an axis through the N and S poles once every 24 hours. Only the side of the Earth facing the Sun is lit by it and in daylight whilst that part of the Earth facing away from the Sun has night. At the same time the Earth is moving in its orbit round the Sun, which takes one year.

The N–S axis that the Earth is rotating round is tilted by about 23° so that the radiation from the Sun is not evenly spread over its surface. At one time in its orbit the N pole is tilted away from the Sun and the S pole towards it (the right hand side of Fig. 17.6). The result is that the northern half of the Earth is getting less heat and the southern half is getting more. The northern hemisphere is in winter and the southern hemisphere is in summer. At places tilted towards the Sun the period of daylight is longer than the night and the Sun rises higher in the sky. The pole tilted towards the Sun will get 24 hours of daylight in the middle of its summer. At the same time the pole tilted away from the Sun remains in darkness for the whole day. Six months later, on the opposite side of the orbit, the reverse will be true as the northern hemisphere gets more energy and is in summer (the left hand side of Fig. 17.6).

9> INSIDE THE EARTH

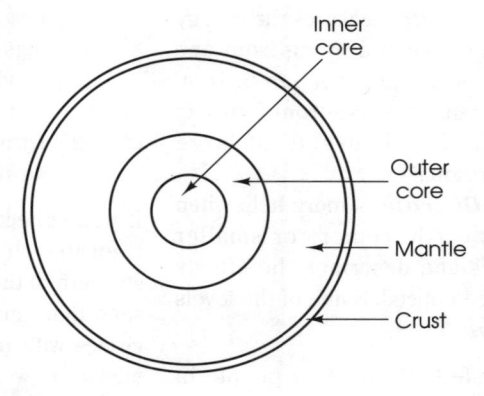

Fig. 17.7

The Earth is almost spherical and about 12 800 km in diameter. It is made up of a number of layers as seen in Fig. 17.7. The outer layer is the *crust* and it is quite thin varying from about 70km under the continents to about 10 km under the oceans. The *continental crust* is mostly granite and floats on top of the more dense *oceanic crust* which is mostly basalt.

The *mantle* is a dense layer of rock and metal oxides between the crust and the core. It is not melted but is "plastic" which means that it can flow. (The bitumen used to make roads is this sort of a plastic – it seems solid but can be squashed by a big truck and slowly flows downhill, especially when it is warm.) As you go towards the centre the temperature increases and the *outer core* is hot enough to be made from molten iron and nickel. The outer core is about 2200 km thick. Currents moving round in this liquid outer core are believed to produce the Earth's magnetic field rather like a giant electromagnet. Farther in the pressure becomes so great that the metals cannot remain melted and there is a solid *inner core* that is about 2600 km in diameter. These facts are known because of the way that earthquakes travel through the earth.

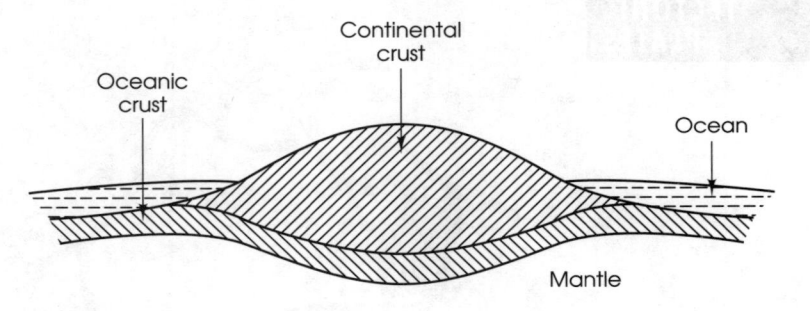

Fig. 17.8

10> EARTHQUAKES AND WAVES

The place where an earthquake occurs in the rocks of the Earth's crust is called the *focus*. The place directly above this on the surface of the Earth is called the *epicentre*. The waves generated by an earthquake will travel through the Earth and be detected at other places by a *seismometer*. An earthquake will send out three types of wave:

- ■ *P waves* (Pressure waves) are longitudinal waves and therefore travel as a series of compressions in the same way as a sound wave. These waves can move through both solids and liquids and can therefore travel through both the mantle and the core to reach the opposite side of the Earth. The changing density of the mantle may cause the path of the P waves to bend (as they are steadily *refracted,* see chapter 6).

- ■ *S waves* (Shear or Shake waves) are transverse waves and they can travel through the solid of the mantle but not the liquid of the outer core. Some of the S waves may be *reflected* from the surface of the liquid core and a shadow is left at the other side of the Earth that the S waves cannot reach. This proves that the core does exist and helps scientists to work out its size.

- ■ *L waves* (Long waves) are the waves that travel round the crust on the surface. They will arrive last but do the most damage.

The strength of earthquakes is measured on two scales:

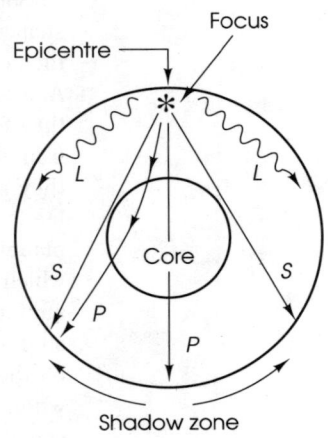

Fig. 17.9

- The **Richter scale** measures the energy of the earthquake and going from one point to the next (e.g. from 5 to 6) is an increase of ten times (so from 5 to 7 is 100 times!). This is useful for large powerful earthquakes.
- The **Mercalli scale** is more help when describing earth tremors or smaller earthquakes and describes the effects that would be noticed. Some of the levels are as follows:

  2   Hardly felt. Noticed by people in bed.
  4   Hanging objects swing. Doors and windows rattle.
  6   People frightened, run outdoors. Felt by all. Some damage.
  8   Cracks open in ground. Some buildings collapse.
  10   Landslides. Most buildings damaged badly.
  12   Large areas of ground moved up and down. Total damage.

If you collect evidence from witnesses and then use the Mercalli scale to mark the strength of the earthquake on a map, it can be seen that equal levels can be joined forming circles with the epicentre at the middle. The effects get weaker as the circles get wider.

Information about earthquakes is called *seismic*; e.g. seismic waves are measured by a *seismometer* in which a pen plots the waves on a chart as they arrive. This would then be examined by a seismologist.

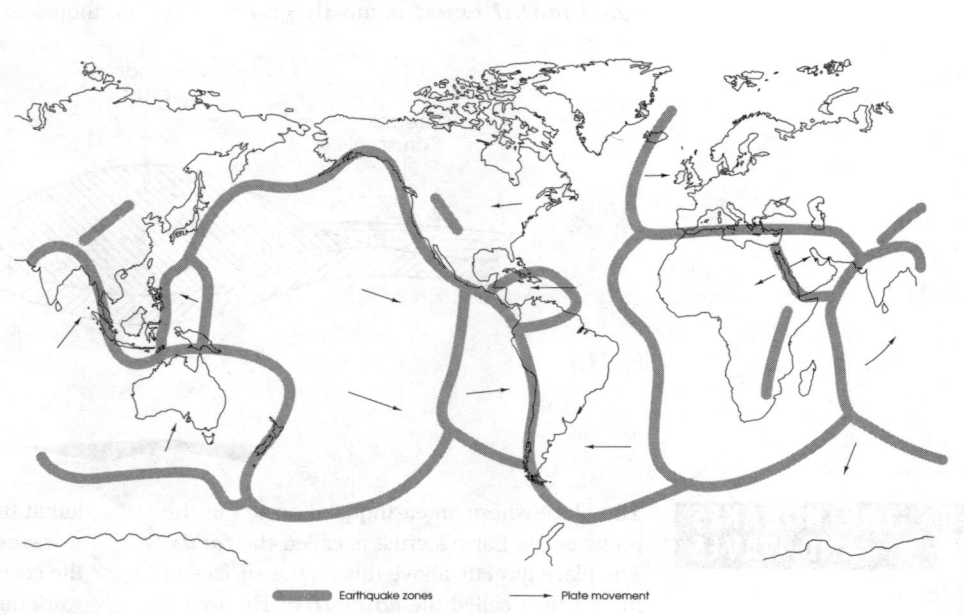

11 TECTONIC PLATES

Fig. 17.10   — Earthquake zones   → Plate movement

Plotting where earthquakes occur in the Earth's crust shows that they are not randomly spread but are in a pattern as shown in Fig. 17.10.

Some of the continents also seem to have shapes that fit together. If you trace a map and then cut out the three shapes of Africa, South America and North America you can see that they fit together quite well. If the older rocks from the edges of these shapes are compared they are also a good geological match. This leads us to believe that the surface of the planet is made up of a set of large **plates** which are slowly moving about on the planet surface. Further evidence is found by studying the evolution of plants and animals on the separated continents. These show us when the continents were joined (common evolution) and when they separated (after this the evolution was different on each continent – e.g. marsupials in Australia have only a few close relatives in South America). Movements of the plates cause the major earthquakes. The movement may be caused by convection currents in the mantle that the plates rest on.

- The plates can be sliding sideways past each other. This may happen in sudden "jerks" when the energy has built up enough to force the plates along. This happens along vertical **transform faults** in the crust like the one in California called the San Andreas fault. Satellite pictures show how features like river beds can be suddenly re-routed by the surface movement.
- The plates can move apart from each other at **constructive plate boundaries**. This leaves a gap and **magma** (melted rock) comes up from below,

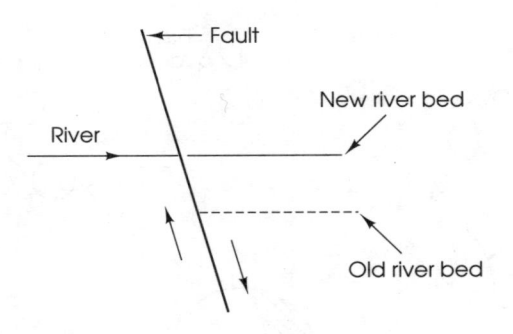

Fig. 17.11

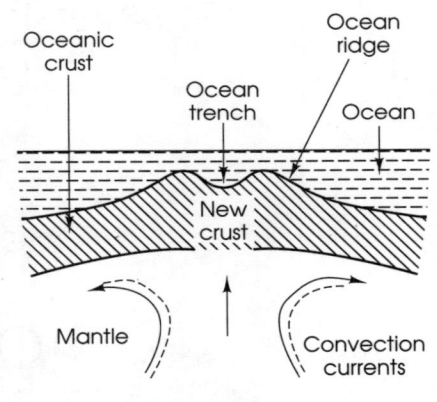

Fig. 17.12
(a) Plates moving apart
(b) Oceanic plates moving together 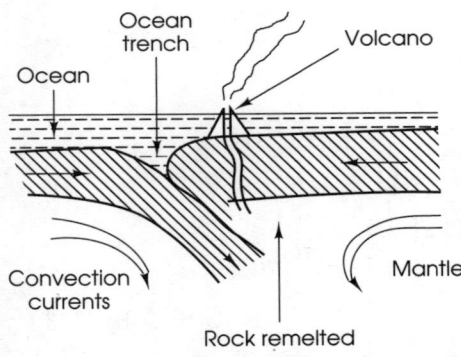

solidifies and forms new crust. The earthquakes are not as strong as in the other cases. The new rock is basalt and forms an *oceanic ridge*. This happens in the "mid-Atlantic ridge" where Africa and South America are moving apart. In the Atlantic this movement is about 2 cm per year and about 9 cm per year in the Pacific. If plates move apart under continents instead of the ocean then a *rift valley* is formed on the surface. As Africa moved away from Arabia a rift valley was formed which is now filled by the Red Sea.

- The plates can slide towards each other at *destructive plate boundaries*. The thinner but denser ocean plate gets pushed under the continental plate where it eventually melts. This is called *subduction*. The continental plates are forced upwards and there will be a lot of violent earthquakes and volcanoes. This happens along the western coast of South America and in Japan. If two continental plates collide, the rocks from the ocean that was between the two continents gets squashed together and pushed upwards to form *fold mountains*. This produced the Himalayas where the Indian plate and the Eurasian plate are moving towards each other. The rock that is pushed downwards may gain so much energy that it is remelted and finds its way back to the surface to form volcanoes.

12> PHASES OF THE MOON

We only see the moon by the sunlight that is reflected from it. Since only the half of the moon that is facing the sun get light from it, we see different phases of the moon as it orbits round the Earth.

When the moon is between us and the Sun (1 in the diagram) the illuminated side is away from us and we have a dark "*new*" moon. By position 2 we can see some of the side of the moon facing the Sun as a bright *crescent*. By 3 we can see half of the moon and it is a quarter of the way round its orbit. The bright part that we can see increases through the *gibbous* stage (4), where more than half of the moon can be seen, to the *full* moon (5) where we can see all of the side that is facing the Sun. For this half of the orbit where the lit area that we can see is increasing, the moon is *waxing*. The reverse then happens in the other half of the orbit and the moon is said to be *waning*. The whole orbit takes 28 days. Since the moon also rotates once on its own axis in the same time, it always has the same side facing the Earth.

308 CHAPTER 17 **EARTH, SPACE AND WEATHER**

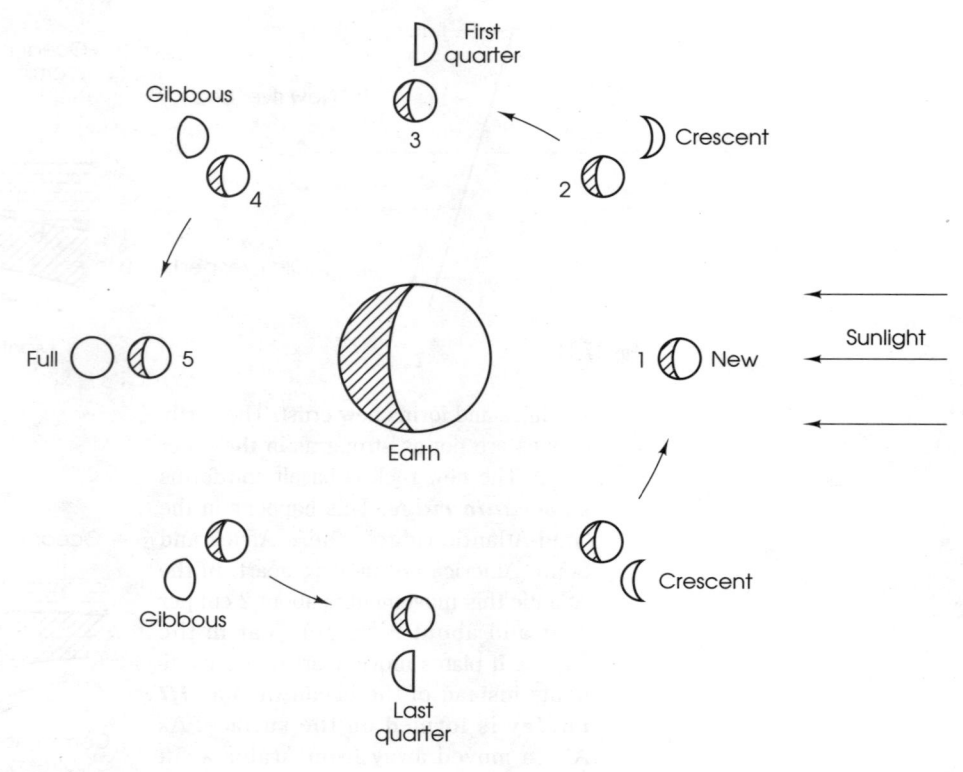

Fig. 17.13

13> TIDES

On the side of the Earth nearest to the moon the water in the seas will be attracted to the moon by gravitational attraction and will bulge out slightly. On the other side of the Earth, opposite to the moon, there is another bulge of approximately the same size where the moon has least attraction. As the Earth rotates once per day, any place where you observe the sea level will pass through each of these bulges and the water level will rise (**high tide**) and fall (**low tide**) twice each day. (Fig 17.14)

Even though it is a lot farther away the Sun also has an effect on the tides. When the Earth, the moon and the Sun are all in a straight line the Sun increases the effect and the tides are bigger than usual and are called **spring tides**. (Fig 17.15)

When the Sun is at right angles to the Earth and moon it will cancel the effect of the moon a little and smaller tides are produced. These are called **neap tides**. (Fig 17.16)

Spring and neap tides will occur about twice each month.

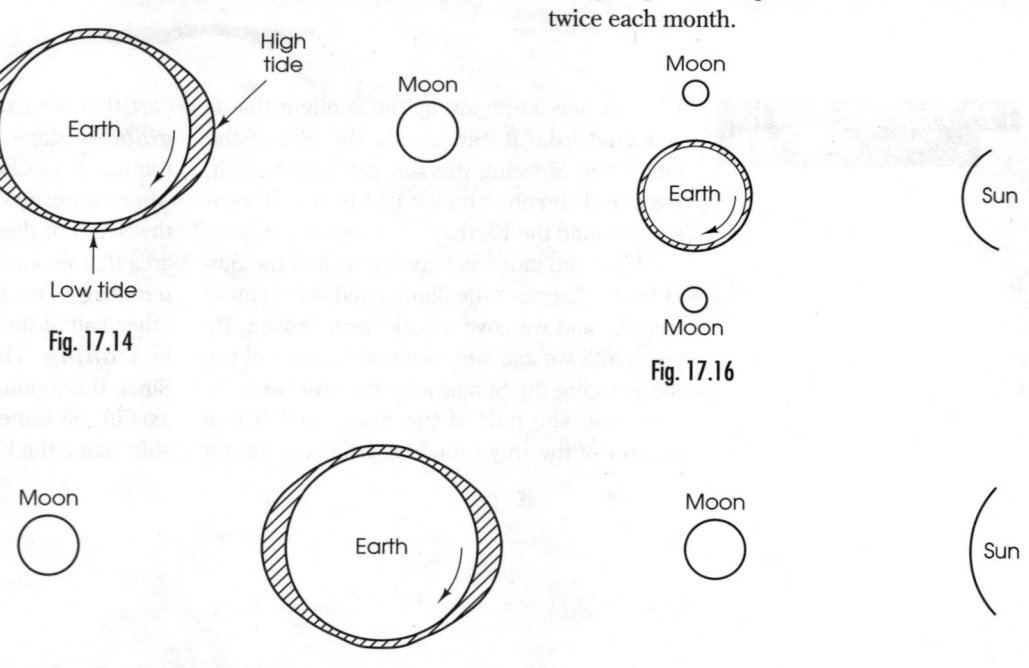

Fig. 17.14

Fig. 17.16

Fig. 17.15

14> ATMOSPHERE

An atmosphere will be created round a planet from the gases that condense as it is made and from volcanic gases released by the hot rocks afterwards. If the planet is small or hot the molecules of gas will be going fast enough to escape into space and the atmosphere is lost (e.g. mercury). A large cold planet will attract the molecules in its atmosphere a lot and they will move more slowly at the lower temperature so they cannot escape. The Earth is massive enough and its atmosphere is cool enough for it to keep all but the very lightest gases from escaping. The atmosphere of the Earth was probably first made of carbon dioxide, water vapour, methane and ammonia.

The carbon dioxide would be reduced and the oxygen increased as plants developed.

More carbon dioxide became trapped in coal, oil and gas deposits and in sedimentary rocks that are carbonates (limestones and chalks).

The methane and ammonia reacted with the new oxygen until they were eliminated. Nitrogen was put into the air by bacteria. Some of the oxygen became ozone in the upper atmosphere and this protected the plants and animals, speeding up the process of creating our present atmosphere.

Our atmosphere is now made up of:

- nitrogen about 78%
- oxygen about 20%
- carbon dioxide about 0.03%
- inert gases less than 1%
- water vapour varies a lot from nil to about 5%
- dust and other particles.

The atmosphere has been very similar to this for the last 200 million years. The average pressure exerted at sea level by the atmosphere in Britain is 101 300 Pa. This pressure will fall rapidly as you go upwards so that it is halved when you are about 6000 m above sea level. (See chapter 11 for more about Pa and about barometers to measure pressure.)

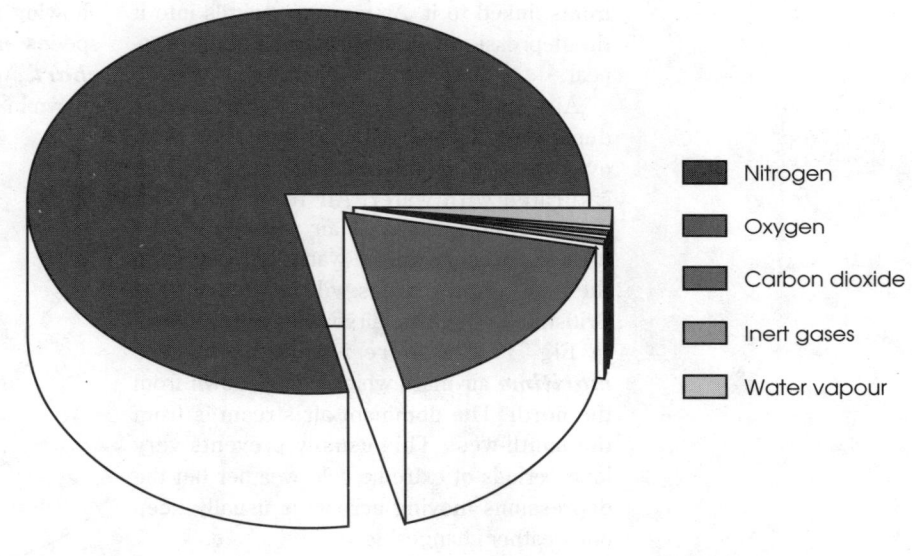

Fig. 17.17

15> WEATHER

As the Earth spins on its axis it causes some of its atmosphere to swirl into eddies rather than being uniform. These areas can have pressure above or below the average. Energy from water vapour condensing in colder air and from convection currents can increase these effects and they move through the atmosphere changing our weather. So that we can see the pattern of the pressure changes we join all places on our map that have equal air pressure by lines called *isobars*. A pressure of 100 000 Pa (the same as 10 N/cm²) is called 1 *bar* and the isobars usually have their pressure marked in *millibars*. Winds will be stronger where the isobars are closer together.

Regions of high pressure are called **anticyclones**. The wind will spiral outwards in a clockwise direction (in the Northern hemisphere), the air being replaced by air from much higher in the atmosphere falling into the centre of the system. The winds are usually light and the anticyclone is slow moving. The weather produced is usually bright and clear with little cloud. This can be warm in summer but the lack of cloud gives low temperatures, especially at night, in winter. The weather close to a high pressure tends to be calm and settled.

Regions of low pressure are called **depressions** (or cyclones). The weather close to a depression is usually wetter and unsettled.

(a) Anticyclone

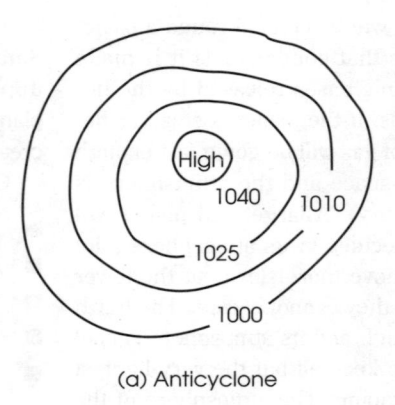

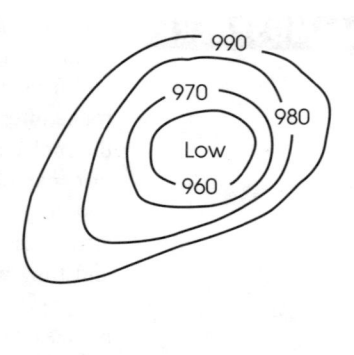

(b) Depression or cyclone

Fig. 17.18

The wind will spiral inwards in an anticlockwise direction (in the Northern hemisphere) and can be much stronger than that from a high pressure. If you stand with the wind on your back the centre of the depression will be on your left. Depressions will move quite rapidly and cause the weather to change often in Britain as they move, usually from west to east. A depression will usually have weather fronts linked to it. As more air spirals into it the depression will eventually fill and disappear.

Air can have different properties depending on where it has been. Air from over the ocean – *maritime* air – will be saturated with water. Air from over land masses – *continental* air will be dry. Air from the tropics will be warm but that from the polar, Arctic areas will be cold. In the British Isles the main airstreams are as shown in Fig. 17.19. There is also an *arctic maritime* air mass which comes down from the north. The dominant air stream is from the south-west. This usually prevents very long periods of extreme cold weather but the depressions moving across us usually keep our weather changeable.

When cold and warm air masses meet they form a *front*. Depressions often develop a warm front and a cold front. In a *warm front* the warm moist air rises over the cold dry air and it is shown on a map as a line with semicircles. In a *cold front* the cold dry air is pushing under the warm moist air and it is shown on the map as a line with triangles on it. Between the two fronts there will be a wedge of warmer moist air and the weather will change as the two fronts pass over. A map showing all of this information and the wind speeds and directions is called a *synoptic chart*. An example of this for a depression is shown in Fig. 17.20.

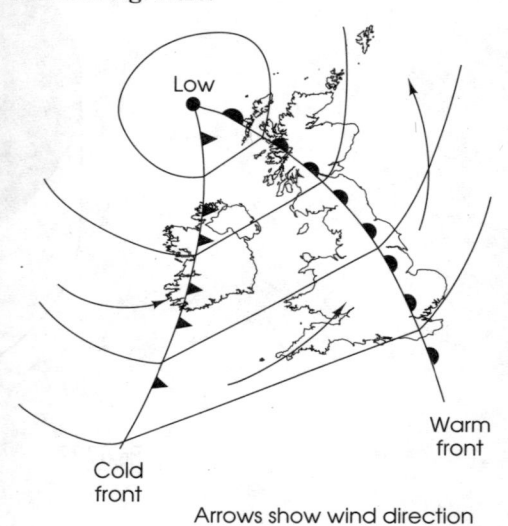

Fig. 17.20

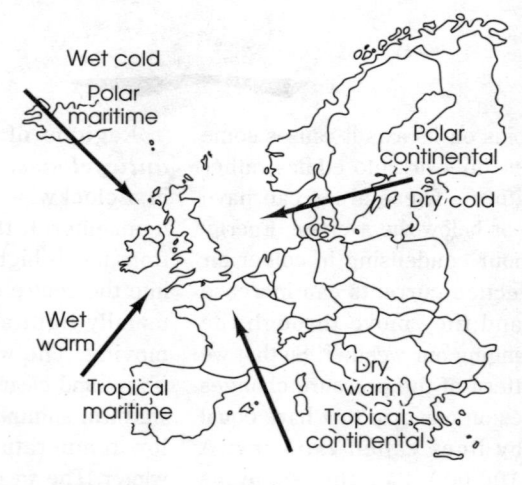

Fig. 17.19

The two fronts and the clouds that usually go with them are shown in Fig. 17.22. There will be a change of wind direction and air temperature as each front passes. The depression will move approximately in the direction of the isobars between the fronts (WNW in Fig. 17.20). Sometimes the cold front will catch up with the warm front pushing it upwards. This is called an occluded front and is shown as a line marked with alternate triangles and semicircles. (Fig 17.21)

All of these things cause the weather and help us to try and predict it. Satellite pictures now show us the weather systems and we can

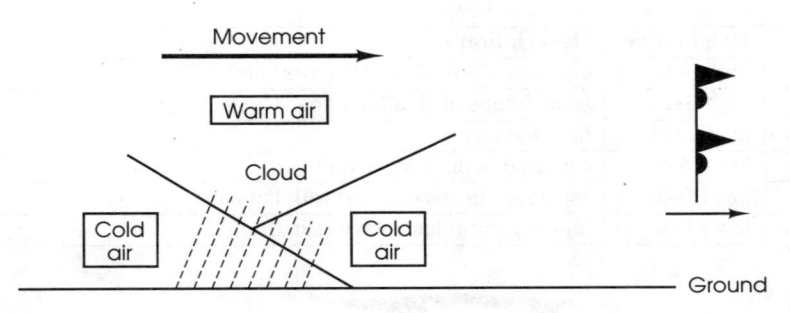

Fig. 17.21

Fig. 17.22 shows what will happen when the fronts from a depression pass.

- At A high cirrus cloud is seen. The weather is fine but the pressure starts to fall.
- At B the pressure is still falling, the cloud thickens and it starts to rain.
- At C the pressure steadies, the air temperature rises and the wind turns more westerly. The warm front passes.
- At D it is dull with low cloud and some drizzle.
- At E there will be heavy rain, the pressure starts to rise and the wind turns more northwesterly. The cold front has passed and the temperature will fall again. Clouds gradually become more scattered and the wind dies away.

track their movement. In Britain a radar system also tracks the rainfall. To describe the weather you would need to take measurements of temperature, atmospheric pressure, mm of rainfall, amount of cloud cover, wind direction and speed at regular intervals together with the hours of sunshine each day.

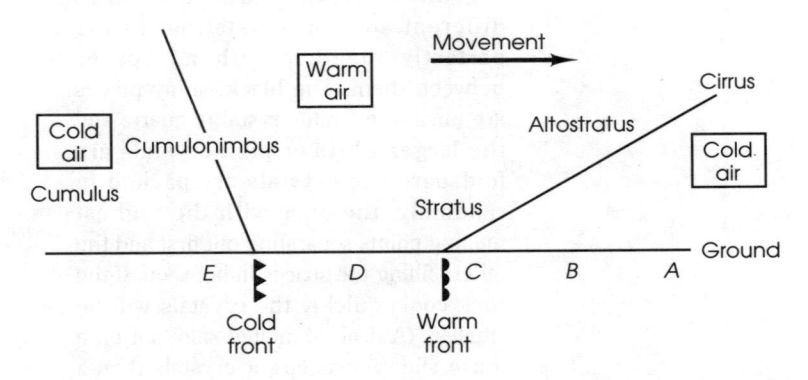

Fig. 17.22

16. CLOUDS AND FOG

Water can be held in the air as *vapour*. The amount that can be held by the air depends on temperature. If the air holds as much water as possible it is *saturated*. If air is cooled it will eventually become saturated and if cooled further some of the water has to *condense* as small droplets. This may happen on summer nights causing *dew*.

In autumn the ground is often wet and the air becomes saturated. If the night sky has little cloud the ground will cool quickly by radiating heat and the air near the ground will become colder. The water vapour will condense in lots of droplets forming *fog*. In industrial areas with dust in the air the water condenses on the dust particles forming smog.

In a similar way air that is pushed upwards will become colder and the water will start to condense forming *clouds* of small droplets. If the cloud is cooled more these drops grow in size until the drops become too heavy to stay in the air and fall as rain. This can happen on the western side of our hills as the westerly wind from over the Atlantic is pushed upwards. Clouds at different heights look different and have different names. The names can help you remember their features:

cumulus	fluffy or lumpy
stratus	flat layers
cirrus	high and made of ice crystals
nimbo-	giving rain
alto-	medium height

Fig. 17.23

Name	Height/km	Description
cirrus	high 6–12	delicate, wispy. Called "mares tails"
cirrocumulus	high 6–10	small lumps of cloud in lines
altostratus	medium 4–5	high flat layers
stratus	low 0.5–2	continuous thick low cloud
cumulus	low 1.0–2	separated heaps of cloud with flat base
cumulonimbus	low 1.0–6	high big cumulus, heavy rain, thunder.

17> ROCKS

There are three types of rock depending on how they were formed.

- *Igneous rock* is rock that has been formed by the cooling of molten rock (magma) that has been forced up from under the crust. It will then turn solid as a mass of crystals. If you examine a piece of *granite* you will be able to see three different sorts of crystal, all fitting perfectly together with no spaces between them. The black, shiny pieces are mica, the white crystal is quartz and the larger white or pink crystals are feldspar. The crystals are packed in randomly, the ones with the highest melting points separating out first and the others filling the spaces in between. If the rock cools quickly the crystals will be smaller. (A drop of melted salol put on a warm slide forms larger crystals than a drop put onto a cold slide from a fridge.) Lava will often have cooled very quickly and the crystals will be too small to see. The lava may seem very light because volcanic gases that were bubbling through it when it left the volcano are trapped inside it.

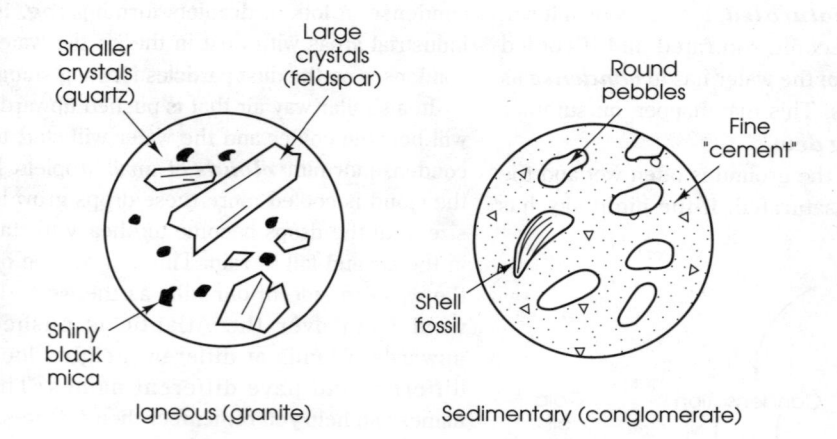

Fig. 17.24

- *Sedimentary rock* will have been formed from smaller particles of rock that have settled to the bottom of water. As water flows down rivers it carries small pieces of rock that have been broken away from the higher ground (see weathering). These pieces will wear away the river bed producing more pieces and the grinding of the pieces against each other makes them rounded in the same way as pebbles on a beach. The faster the water flows the larger the pieces of rock it can carry. A big river in flood from a storm or melting snow can move large boulders.

When the river reaches a lake or the sea the water slows down and the particles sink to the bottom forming layers. The tiny particles form layers of mud. Bigger ones, sand and pebbles can be mixed with the mud or put in separate layers. As the layers build up the water is squeezed out and the weight slowly cements the pieces together making a solid rock. *Sandstones* and *limestones* are sedimentary rocks. Sedimentary rocks, especially limestone, may contain *fossils*. The most common are sea shells that have fallen to the bottom and become trapped in the sediment. Remember that younger sedimentary rocks will be on top of older ones. The type of fossil preserved in the rock may help to identify rocks of the same age as the rock will usually contain fossils of the particular plants and animals from the time when the sediment was laid down.

The rocks will not always appear in flat horizontal layers as they were first formed. Movements in the Earth's crust since may cause the rock to be tilted, folded or even turned upside down.

- *Metamorphic rocks* are rocks that have been changed by heat and pressure. They may have been pushed deep underground, crushed by mountain folding or they may have been close to hot magma that has pushed up close to the surface. Examples are *marble,* which was originally limestone, and *slate,* which was originally mudstone.

Minerals are the crystal materials from which rocks are made. Each different mineral is a single chemical compound. The exact proportions of minerals in a particular type of rock will vary in different specimens. Some minerals may be metal ores that are worth mining for the metal or chemicals with other uses, e.g. galena is a lead ore found in veins in the rock in Derbyshire that was mined for its lead content. Fluorspar is quarried for use in the iron and chemical industries.

Weathering breaks rocks into smaller pieces. ***Erosion*** carries away the pieces. There are a number of processes that all help to weather and erode rocks and which eventually wear away even the biggest mountains.

Rain can dissolve some minerals and wash away smaller pieces.

Ice has a bigger volume than the water that it is formed from. When water freezes in cracks in the rock the forces can be big enough to split pieces off.

Glaciers grind rocks away as they slowly move downwards. Glaciers can transport much larger pieces than rivers.

Wind will carry away small pieces and can rapidly erode soft rock if the wind has grit in it (a sort of natural sand-blasting process).

Hot ***sunshine*** will raise the temperature of the surface of a rock so that it expands more than the rock underneath and the outer layer is split off.

Tree ***roots*** and plant roots grow down into cracks, gradually pushing them apart.

Acid rain and other atmospheric pollution may react with the rock and greatly speed up the weathering process. This is seen clearly in industrial areas where gravestones of marble will be much more eroded than those in cleaner air or those, like granite, that resist acids.

Soil is made from small pieces of rock mixed with the dead remains of plants and animals (called ***humus***). The type of rock, the amount of humus, and the depth of the soil will alter how fertile it is.

EXTENSION MATERIALS

1> STAR GAZING

Looking at the sky at night with a telescope or binoculars will enable you to see many stars and some nebula as well as getting a clear view of the moon. (Checking that you understand and can follow the phases of the moon is easy if you observe it regularly.) Some of the stars appear in recognisable patterns even though they may actually be great distances apart. These patterns are called *constellations* and can be useful in identifying which particular part of the sky you are observing.

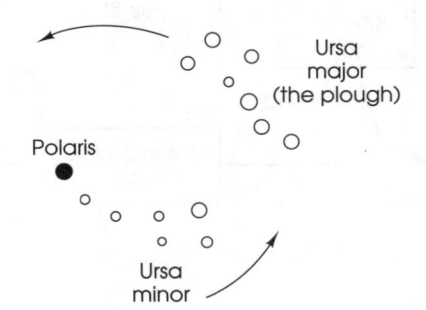

Fig. 17.25

The exact view of the stars that you get depends on where we are along the Earth's orbit (time of year) and how the Earth has rotated on its axis (time of day). You can find out what you can expect to see, or identify particular stars, by using a planisphere. Only the pole star (Polaris) will appear to be stationary because it is along the line of the Earth's axis. As the Earth rotates the other stars seem to go in an arc around the pole star as can be seen on photographs with a long time exposure.

You may see ***shooting stars*** which are properly called ***meteors***. They are really small bits of rock in space that hit the atmosphere and burn up, producing the bright streak that we see. If a small bit survives to reach the surface of the Earth it is called a ***meteorite***.

The ***planets*** will move across our sky as they travel in their orbit round the Sun. You would need tables of dates and times to know when to see them best. Don't confuse them with the more rapid passage of a satellite across the sky which is much more easy and common to see on a clear night. Venus is closer to the Sun and can only be seen clearly at dusk or dawn.

Comets also orbit the Sun in long elliptical orbits that sometimes swing close enough to the Sun for them to be seen for a few weeks before moving away again. The head of the comet is probably mostly carbon dioxide and ice and a few tens of km across. The tail is gas and dust released from the comet by the heat of the Sun. The tail always faces away from the Sun.

2 FOSSILS

Spiral shape

Legs and antenna rare

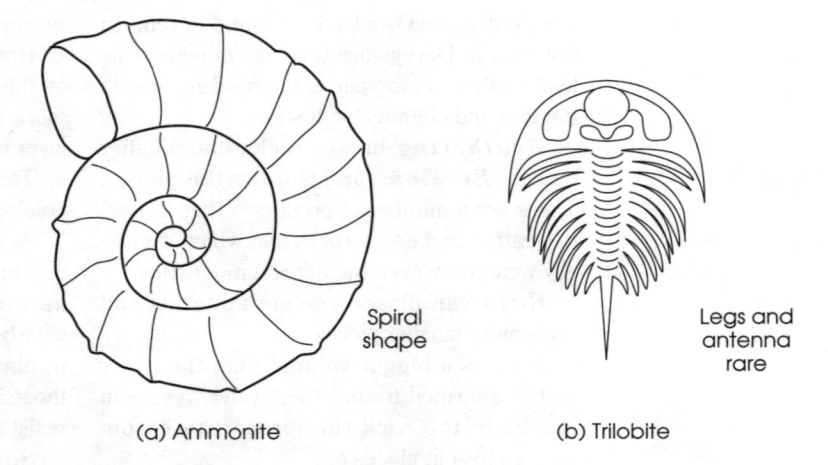

(a) Ammonite (b) Trilobite

Fig. 17.26

Fossils are the remains of plants and animals that have been preserved in the rock. Common ones are **sea shells** and **corals** in limestone and **ferns** and **club mosses** in coal and shale. **Ammonites** are spiral shells that once contained an animal rather like the nautilus with its head and tentacles out of the opening. They can be cut in half to show chambers inside the shell where the animal produced larger chambers as it grew bigger.

Trilobites were rather like large water-dwelling woodlice with lots of legs and an armoured three piece shell. They are sometimes found curled up, presumably for defence, and the tracks of their feet have been found in soft sedimentary rock from the ocean bottom. Fossils give us a lot of evidence for our modern theories about rocks. For example sea shells are common in the limestones high in the Alps giving more evidence of the mountain folding and uplifting process.

3 THE ROCK CYCLE

The three types of rock do not stay in the same form forever. They are steadily cycled through the different forms as summarised in the diagram. Some parts of the cycle may take millions of years to complete.

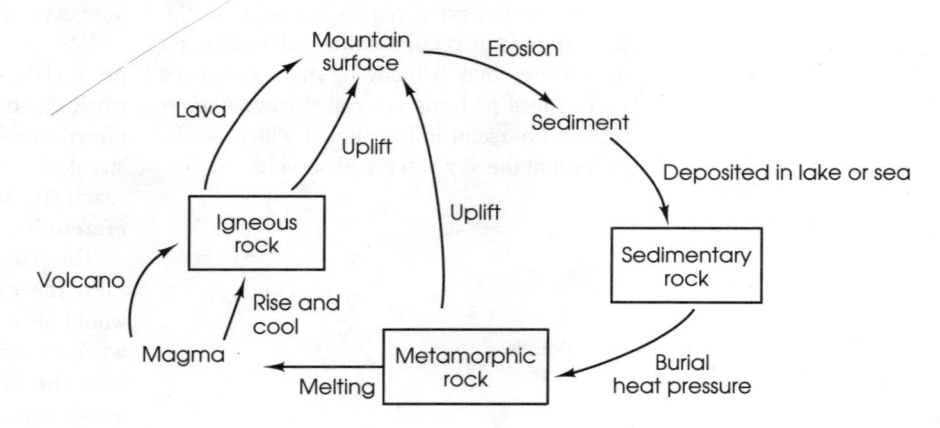

Fig. 17.27

4 NEWTON'S LAW OF GRAVITATION

The gravitational force between any two objects of mass m_1 and m_2 that are a distance d apart is given by

$$F = \frac{Gm_1m_2}{d^2}$$

where G is the universal constant of gravitation and has a value of 6.67×10^{-11} Nm²/kg². Note that the force depends inversely on the square of the distance between the masses which is why it seems to reduce so quickly. If you ever use this equation you can measure d between the centres of mass – for many common shapes such as spheres for planets this is at the centre of each mass. This is the attractive force that usually provides the centripetal force needed to keep a satellite (or planet or moon) in its orbit.

5 THE UPPER ATMOSPHERE

The air thins rapidly as you go upwards. 50% of it is below 6 km and 99% of it below 40 km. Various levels of the atmosphere have special properties and names.

- **Troposphere** Up to about 12 km. Contains all Earth's climate and weather. Temperature falls by about 6 °C for each 1000 m.
- **Stratosphere** From 12 km to about 46 km. Temperature rises again because of a layer of ozone that absorbs incoming ultraviolet radiation.
- **Mesosphere** From 46 km to about 80 km. Temperature falls rapidly to about −90 °C. No water, dust or ozone.
- **Thermosphere** Above 80 km. Virtually no atmosphere at all above 100 km. Small amount of atomic oxygen at high temperature.
- **Exosphere** Above 600 km. Merges with interplanetary medium. About equal proportions of hydrogen and helium up to 2400 km and then mainly hydrogen.
- **Ionosphere** Charged particles between about 65 and 800 km. The particles form layers that can reflect radio waves and cause the **auroras** (northern lights, southern lights).

6 ECLIPSES

A *lunar eclipse* will occur when the moon orbits into the shadow of the Earth. Remember that the moon, like all other objects in space except stars, is only seen by reflected light. This is NOT the same effect as that which causes the phases of the moon.

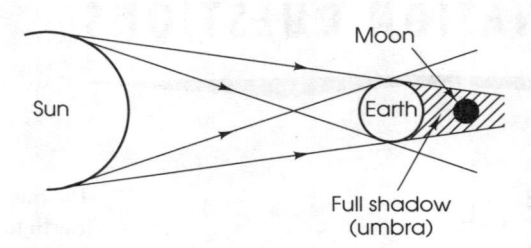

Fig. 17.28

A *solar eclipse* will occur when the moon orbits between the Sun and the Earth so that a shadow is cast onto the Earth's surface. Scientists will try to observe the Sun in a total eclipse so that its bright disc is covered and solar flares can be seen more clearly.

The shadow of the moon will cross the Earth's surface as the moon moves in its orbit. At a place in the path of the middle of the shadow the area of the Sun that appears to be covered increases (partial eclipse) until it is all covered (total eclipse) and then decreases again. Only a narrow strip of the Earth's surface will get a total eclipse but a wider area on each side will see a partial eclipse.

Total eclipse at A.   Partial eclipse at B or C.

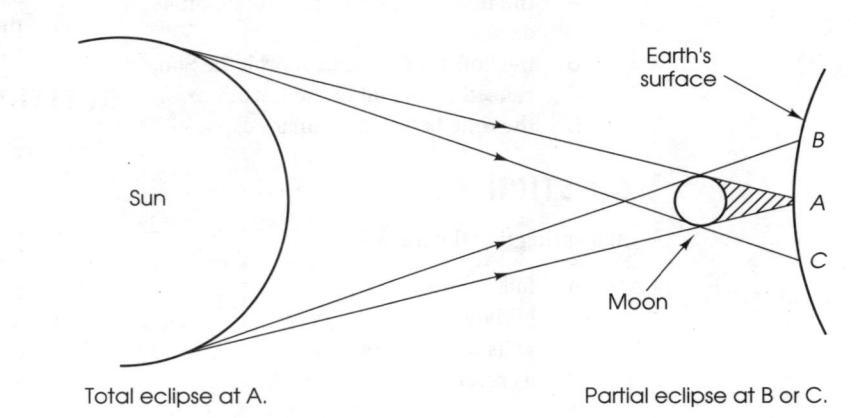

Fig. 17.29

7 POWERING THE SUN – FUSION

We know the mass of the Sun and the rate at which it radiates energy. If it produced the energy by burning its mass in some sort of a combustion reaction it would have used up all its fuel in a few thousand years. Since this is not true the reaction must be of a different type. We believe the reaction to be a **fusion reaction** in which hydrogen nuclei collide and join to form helium nuclei which can then fuse with other nuclei to produce larger nuclei. Each fusion releases some energy because the energy needed to bind together the particles in the larger nucleus is slightly less than the sum of the separate energies. The reaction will only happen at the high temperatures and pressures at the centre of a star because the particles are both positive in charge and will strongly repel when pushed closer together. The masses needed to produce energy by this reaction are relatively small compared with combustion. The heavier isotopes of hydrogen used in the reaction are called deuterium and tritium.

$$_1^1H + {}_1^1H \rightarrow {}_1^2H + e^+ + v$$

$$_1^1H + {}_1^2H \rightarrow {}_2^3He + \gamma$$

$$_2^3He + {}_2^3He \rightarrow {}_2^4He + {}_1^1H + {}_1^1H$$

Overall this is the same as

$$4\,{}_1^1H \rightarrow {}_2^4He + energy$$

The new particles e+ and v are called a positron (like an electron but positively charged) and a neutrino.

8 INSIDE THE EARTH AGAIN

Some courses look at the structure of the Earth in more detail and use the following terms:

- **Lithosphere** [10–50 km]   The layer containing the tectonic plates. Made from continental crust, oceanic crust and mantle rock, all solid.
- **Asthenosphere** [50–250 km]   The layer containing the convection currents that move the plates. Viscous liquid mantle rock.
- **Mesosphere** [250–2900 km]   Solid mantle rock.
- **Outer core** [2900–5200 km]   Liquid mixture of nickel and iron.
- **Inner core** [5200–6371 km]   Solid mixture of nickel and iron.

EXAMINATION QUESTIONS

MULTIPLE CHOICE QUESTIONS

QUESTION 1

A year is

- A the time for the Earth to rotate on its axis.
- B the time for the Earth to orbit the Sun.
- C caused by the tilt of the Earth's axis.
- D the time between annular eclipses.

QUESTION 2

At a spring tide the moon is

- A full.
- B gibbous.
- C at its first quarter.
- D a crescent.

QUESTION 3

A star much larger than the Sun will eventually become

- A a black hole.
- B a supernova.
- C a red giant.
- D a white dwarf.

QUESTION 4

In a total lunar eclipse

- A the moon is on the opposite side of the Sun to the Earth.
- B the Sun is on the opposite side of the Earth to the moon.
- C the Sun and the moon are on the same side of the Earth.
- D the Earth is in the moon's shadow.

QUESTION 5

Metamorphic rocks

- A come from volcanoes.
- B always contain large crystals.
- C have been reformed under heat and pressure.
- D are formed from solids that settle out of water.

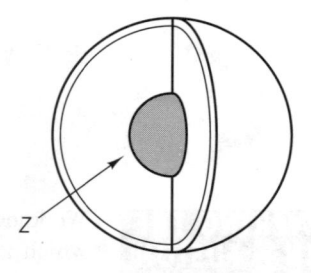

Fig. 17.30

QUESTION 6

The part of the Earth lettered Z is called the

- A crust.

B   outer core.
C   inner core.
D   mantle.

QUESTION 7

Our galaxy is

A   at the centre of the universe.
B   a spiral nebula.
C   the local group.
D   the Milky Way.

QUESTION 8

At a warm front

A   warm air is riding over cold air.
B   cold air is pushing under warm air.
C   the pressure suddenly falls.
D   the clouds will be very high.

QUESTION 9

Low flat clouds producing a lot of rain are

A   cirrus.
B   altostratus.
C   stratus.
D   cumulus.

QUESTION 10

In an earthquake

A   only the P waves can reach the opposite side of the Earth through its centre.
B   L waves go into the Earth and reflect from the core.
C   S waves are the slowest of the waves produced.
D   it is the P waves that do the most surface damage.

QUESTION 11

Isobars join places with the same

A   temperature.
B   humidity.
C   pressure.
D   height.

QUESTION 12

Which of the following lists some planets in order of their distance from the Sun?

A   Earth, Saturn, Pluto.
B   Mercury, Mars, Earth.
C   Earth, Venus, Jupiter.
D   Mars, Venus, Saturn.

STRUCTURED QUESTIONS

QUESTION 13

(a) The average surface temperature on the Earth is about 10 °C. Suggest a value for the average surface temperature of the planet Mercury.
(b) Explain why the surface temperature of a planet depends on its position in the Solar System.
(c) Explain how each of the following affects the surface temperature of the Earth.
   (i) The Sun.
   (ii) The Earth's atmosphere.
   (iii) The rotation of the Earth.
(d) There is evidence that planets other than the Earth have turbulent atmospheres.
   (i) Name ONE planet which we know to have an atmosphere.
   (ii) What evidence is there to suggest that this planet has an atmosphere?
(e) The moon has no atmosphere. How has this affected the surface features of the moon?

(ULEAC)

QUESTION 14

The diagram (Fig 17.31) shows the different air streams (air masses) that can affect the British weather. Use the diagram to help you answer the questions that follow it.

(a) In the summer of 1989, there were long periods of hot, dry weather. People noticed that their cars were often covered with a fine dry, red dust.
   (i) Which *one* of the five airstreams dominated the weather during the summer of 1989?
   (ii) Mark on the map with an X where the dust is likely to have come from.
   (iii) How did the red dust get to Britain?
(b) The weather in the south-west of Britain is usually warm and humid (damp).
   (i) Which *two* airstreams are most likely to bring damp weather to Britain?
       Give a reason for your answer.

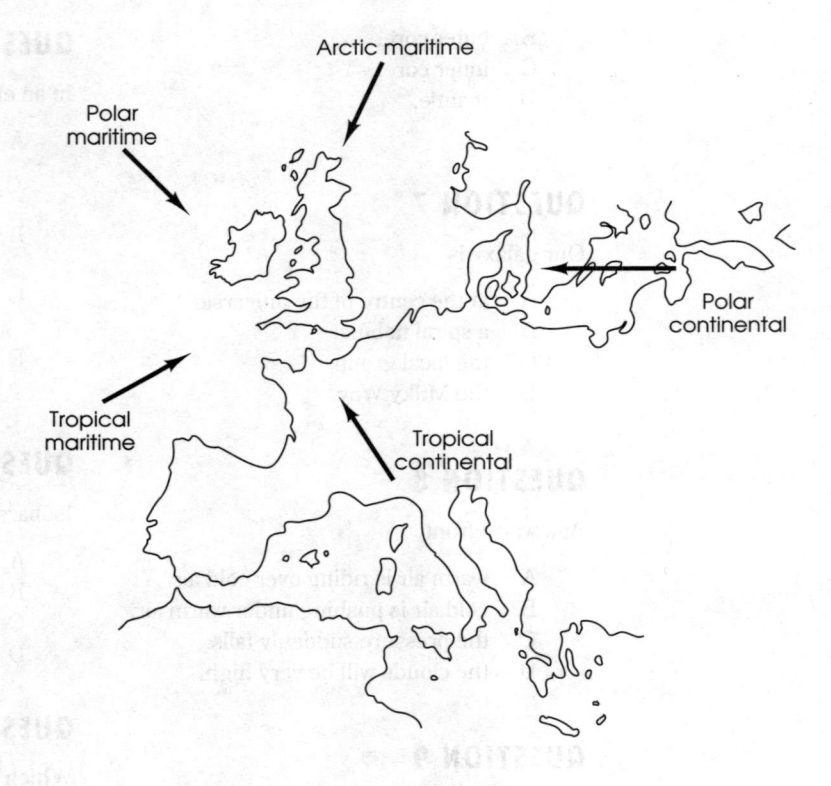

318 CHAPTER 17 **EARTH, SPACE AND WEATHER**

Fig. 17.31

(ii) Which *one* of the airstreams gives the south-west of Britain its usual weather conditions? Give a reason for your answer.

(c) Which *one* of the air streams would cause the weather conditions described below?

Very dry, cool in summer, very cold in winter.

(SEG)

QUESTION 15

In an earthquake the sudden movement of the rocks produces 3 types of seismic waves known as P, S and L waves.

The diagram below illustrates how these waves travel away from the epicentre of the earthquake.

(a) Explain in detail how the movement of the P and S waves through the Earth provides evidence to support the layered structure of the Earth shown in the diagram.

(b) Why do the L waves provide no evidence to support the layered structure of the Earth?

(c) What evidence is there to support the idea that the liquid in the outer core is moving?

(SEG)

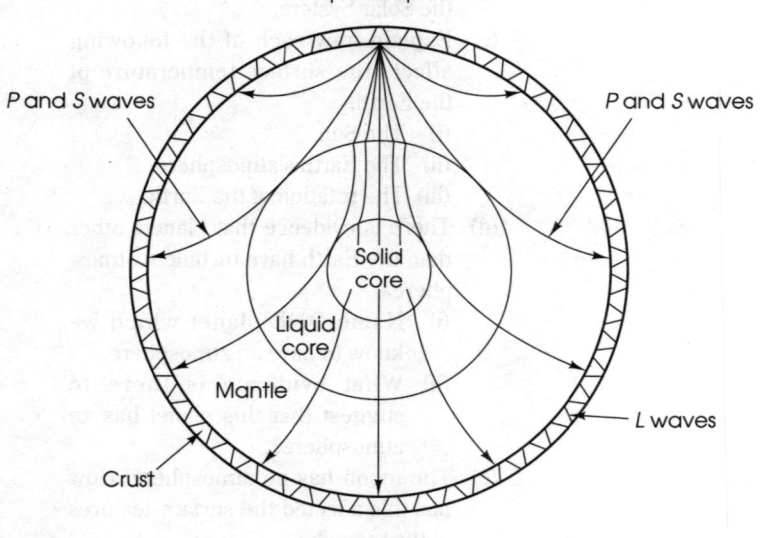

Fig. 17.32

OUTLINE ANSWERS

1. MULTIPLE CHOICE QUESTIONS

Question	1	2	3	4	5	6	7	8	9	10	11	12
Answer	B	A	A	B	C	D	D	A	C	A	C	A

2. STRUCTURED QUESTIONS

ANSWER 13

This is an intermediate/higher level question.

(a) The temperature must be greater than 10 °C. (The actual figure is in the table earlier in this chapter. 1 mark

(b) A planet that is closer to the Sun will receive a greater amount of energy per square metre on its surface. 4 marks

(c) (i) The Sun radiates energy which is received by the Earth.
(ii) The Earth's atmosphere traps the energy. Some heat is retained in the water vapour and heat radiated back out by the Earth is absorbed or reflected back by the cloud layer (greenhouse effect).
(iii) The rotation of the Earth ensures that the energy received is spread more evenly over the whole surface. 2 marks each part

(d) (i) Venus or Mars, etc. 1 mark
(ii) Evidence depends on the planet chosen, e.g. Venus has dense clouds that stop us seeing the surface and we can see storms in these clouds. 2 marks

(e) The surface is more cratered because meteorites are not burned up before hitting the surface.
The surface is not eroded away by winds and rain.
The temperature difference between night and day is greater than if there was an atmosphere and climate. 1 mark each.

ANSWER 14

This is a foundation/intermediate level question.

(a) (i) Tropical continental. 1 mark
(ii) X at North Africa/southern Europe. 1 mark
(iii) Picked up and carried by the air mass.

(b) (i) Polar maritime, tropical maritime. 1 mark
The air masses spend a lot of time passing over the sea so that they pick up moisture. 1 mark
(ii) Tropical maritime. 1 mark
The air is both wet and warm 1 mark

(c) Polar continental 1 mark

ANSWER 15

This is a higher tier question.

(a) The following facts would each be given 1 mark as they are stated in your answer. A second mark is given for what is inferred.

Waves refract as they travel inwards (1) suggesting a change in rock density (1).
S waves cannot pass through a liquid (1) and cannot pass through the centre of the Earth which must be liquid (1).

The shadow zone (1) and the reflection of some P waves shows that there must be a solid core (1).

(b) The L waves provide no evidence because they only travel in the Earth's crust. 1 mark

(c) The Earth has a magnetic field which is explained by the movement of the liquid outer core. 1 mark (SEG)

STUDENT'S ANSWER WITH THE EXAMINER'S COMMENTS

STUDENT ANSWER ON AN EXAMINATION QUESTION

> 66 Direction should be more SE. 99

> 66 Good answers at first. 99

> 66 Easy mark missed C is low. 99

> 66 Also light winds and clear sky. 99

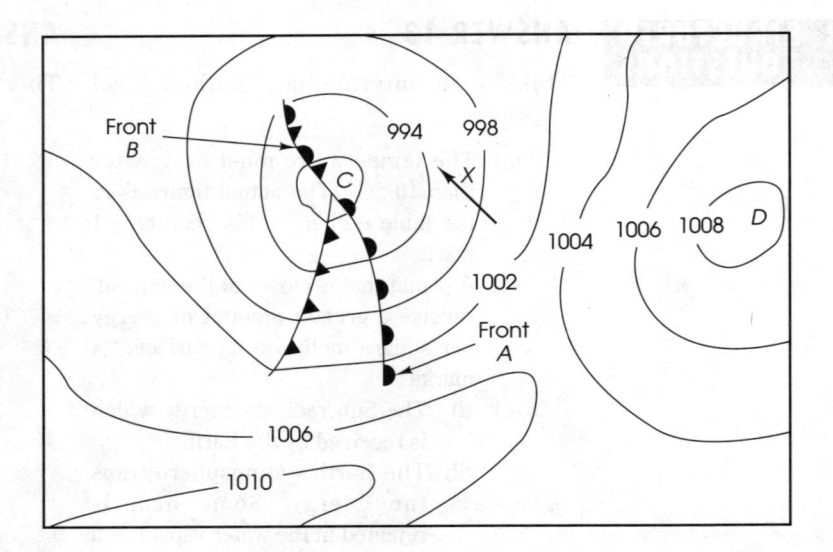

a) What is a *front?* The line where two air masses meet.

b) What sort of front is front A? Warm

c) What sort of front is front B? Occluded

d) What sort of pressure centre is C? →

e) Mark on the diagram the wind direction at X.

f) If it is summer what do you think the weather will be like at D?
→ Hot and Sunny

g) Explain why fog might be formed above wet ground on a clear night in winter.

When it gets cold the water in the air condenses and forms fog because cold air can't hold as much water as warm air. It will be cold because the skies are clear.

> 66 Good answer but order a bit muddled. Water evaporates into air in warmer daytime. 99

REVIEW SHEET

- The nearest star to earth is the _____. The next nearest is _____.

- The name of our galaxy is _____.

- Our galaxy is part of a cluster called the _____.

- What will the next two stages be in the life of the Sun?
  1. _____.   2. _____.

- Name the planets in the solar system starting nearest to the Sun.

- Which planet is
  a) largest? _____.
  b) smallest? _____.
  c) hottest? _____.
  d) coldest? _____.
  e) the one with most moons? _____.

- What is the name of the theory for the creation of the universe that most scientists believe in? _____ _____.

- A cloud of dust and gas in space that could form stars is called a _____.

- The reaction that powers a star is a _____.

- The three types of rock are
  1. _____   2. _____   3. _____

- The outer layer of the Earth is called the _____.

- In the northern hemisphere the star that does not appear to move is _____.

- The moon orbits the Earth in _____ days.

- There will be higher tides called _____ _____ when the _____ is also in line with the moon and the Earth.

- Granite that contains large crystals will have been cooled _____.

- Name an example of a plant fossil and an animal fossil.
  Plant fossil _____.   Animal fossil _____.

- Winds in the northern hemisphere will rotate _____-wise into a depression.

- High wispy clouds are called _____.

- Low flat rain clouds are called _____.

- The three types of earthquake wave are _____.

- The type of earthquake wave that only travels in the crust is _____.

- A _____ tide is lower than a normal tide. At such a tide the phase of the moon will be _____.

- Name five ways in which rocks can be broken down or eroded.
  1. _____.   2. _____.   3. _____.
  4. _____.   5. _____.

- Between Africa and South America at the mid-Atlantic _____ the plates are moving _____.

- The Earth orbits the _____ in 1 _____ . Its axis is tilted at about _____° so that more heat reaches the northern hemisphere in _____ but less in the _____ hemisphere at the same time so it is in winter. The Earth spins on its axis once each _____ which gives us one period of dark and one of light each _____.

- The layer of the Earth that is liquid is the _____ and it is made from _____.

- A man who has a mass of 75 kg will weigh _____ on Earth and _____ on the moon where the gravitational field strength is about one sixth of that at the Earth's surface.

- The highest layer of the atmosphere merges with "space" and is called the _____.

- In a fusion reaction _____ nuclei join to make a _____ nucleus and release energy.

- The biggest stars will eventually become _____.

- Mountains like the Alps are produced by _____ when the crust is pushed together between two _____ that are moving towards each other.

- A rift valley occurs when _____.

- Make a list of some of the evidence for tectonic plates.
  _____
  _____
  _____
  _____

APPENDIX 1: EQUATIONS

From the examination year of 1994 the government has decided that there are certain equations that you may not be given in National Curriculum Science examinations. Since your examination will be fulfilling part of these regulations you will have to learn them too. The order is alphabetical so that you can find the one that you need more quickly. They are:

Acceleration = $\dfrac{\text{change in velocity}}{\text{time taken}}$ $\qquad a = \dfrac{v-u}{t}$

Boyle's Law:
 Pressure × volume = constant $\qquad P_1V_1 = P_2V_2$

Charge stored = capacitance × p.d. $\qquad Q = CV$

Charge transferred = current × time $\qquad Q = It$

Charles' Law:
 $\dfrac{\text{Volume}}{\text{Temperature}}$ = constant $\qquad \dfrac{V_1}{T_1} = \dfrac{V_2}{T_2}$

Density = $\dfrac{\text{mass}}{\text{volume}}$ $\qquad D = \dfrac{m}{v}$

Energy = mass × specific heat capacity × change in temperature $\qquad W = msT$

Energy changed = p.d. × current × time $\qquad W = VIt$

Energy changed = current^2 × resistance × time $\qquad W = I^2Rt$

Efficiency = $\dfrac{\text{energy output}}{\text{energy input}} = \dfrac{\text{work output}}{\text{work input}}$

Efficiency = $\dfrac{MA}{VR} \times 100\%$

Expansion = linear expansivity × original length × rise in temperature.

Force = mass × acceleration $\qquad F = ma$

General Gas Equation:
 $\dfrac{\text{Pressure} \times \text{volume}}{\text{Temperature}}$ = constant $\qquad \dfrac{P_1V_1}{T_1} = \dfrac{P_2V_2}{T_2}$

Gravitational PE = weight × height $\qquad PE = mgh$

Heat loss per sec (power loss) = U - value × area × temperature difference

Heat of fusion = mass × specific latent heat of vapourisation

Heat of vapourisation = mass × specific latent heat of vapourisation

Kinetic Energy = $\tfrac{1}{2}$ × mass × velocity^2 $\qquad KE = \dfrac{m \times v^2}{2}$

Mechanical advantage = $\dfrac{\text{load}}{\text{effort}}$

Moment = force × perpendicular distance to pivot

Momentum = mass × velocity

Potential difference = $\dfrac{\text{work done}}{\text{charge moved}}$

Potential divider equation: $\qquad V_{out} = \dfrac{V_{in} \times R_1}{(R_1 + R_2)}$

Power = $\dfrac{\text{energy changed}}{\text{time taken}} = \dfrac{\text{work done}}{\text{time taken}} =$ $\qquad P = \dfrac{W}{t}$

Power = p.d. × current $\qquad P = VI$

Power = current² × resistence $\qquad P = I^2 R$

Pressure = $\dfrac{\text{normal force}}{\text{area}}$ $\qquad P = \dfrac{F}{A}$

Pressure of a liquid = depth × density × g $\qquad P = h\rho g$

Pressure law:
Pressure = $\dfrac{\text{constant}}{\text{temperature}}$ $\qquad \dfrac{P_1}{T_1} = \dfrac{P_2}{T_2}$

Ohm's Law:
Resistance = $\dfrac{\text{potential difference}}{\text{current}}$ $\qquad R = \dfrac{V}{I}$

Resistors in series: $\qquad R_{TOTAL} = R_1 + R_2 + \ldots$

Resistors in parallel: $\qquad \dfrac{1}{R_{TOTAL}} = \dfrac{1}{R_1} + \dfrac{1}{R_2} + \ldots$

Speed = $\dfrac{\text{distance moved}}{\text{time taken}}$ $\qquad V = \dfrac{S}{t}$

Transformer equation: $\qquad \dfrac{V_{out}}{V_{in}} = \dfrac{N_{secondary}}{N_{primary}}$

Velocity = $\dfrac{\text{change in displacement}}{\text{time taken}}$ $\qquad V = \dfrac{S}{t}$

Velocity ratio = $\dfrac{\text{distance moved by effort}}{\text{distance moved by load}}$

Voltage gain = $\dfrac{\text{voltage output}}{\text{voltage input}}$ $\qquad A = \dfrac{V_{out}}{V_{in}}$

Wave velocity = frequency × wavelength $\qquad v = f\lambda$

Work done = force × distance moved in direction of force $\qquad W = Fs$

Weight = mass × gravitational field strength $\qquad \text{Weight} = mg$

APPENDIX 2: THE PROGRAMME OF STUDY

These are the sections of the Programme of Study for Science that apply to the majority of the syllabuses for Science: Physics.

Attainment target 3: Materials and their properties

(ii) Pupils should investigate the quantitative relationships between the volume, pressure and temperature of a gas and use the kinetic theory to explain changes of state and other phenomena.
They should use their knowledge of the structure of the atom to explain the existence of isotopes and radioactivity. Through demonstration experiments pupils should become aware of the characteristics of radioactive emissions and determine the half-life of a nuclide. Pupils should study the different methods of detecting ionising radiation and its effects on matter and living organisms, developing an understanding of the beneficial and harmful effects.

(iv) Pupils should study, through measurement and by other means, the principles which govern the behaviour of gases in the atmosphere, and the nature of the energy transfer which drive their motion. They should study atmospheric circulation, including the qualitative relationship between pressure, winds and weather patterns. They should study the origins of the atmosphere and the oceans, and be aware of the chemical and biological factors which maintain atmospheric composition. Pupils should study, through laboratory and fieldwork, the evidence which reveals the mode of formation of later deformation of rocks, and the sources of energy that drive such processes. Pupils should study the scientific processes involved in the weathering of rocks, transport of sediments and soil formation. Pupils should understand how geological time scales are measured. They should examine data which suggests that the Earth has a layered structure, including contrasting densities between surface rocks and the whole Earth, transmission of earthquake waves and magnetic evidence. They should investigate the evidence that favours the theory of plate tectonics including the nature of rock record. They should consider how plate movements are involved in the recycling of rocks and the global distribution of the Earth's resources. They should consider theories from earlier times concerning movements of the Earth's crust, and how these were changed through advances in several fields of science and technology.

Attainment target 4: Physical processes

(i) Pupils should study the use of electricity for the transfer of energy, the measurement of energy transferred, and its relation to the costs of using common domestic devices. Such work should also develop an understanding of the dangers of electricity and the standard features and procedures which protect users of electrical equipment. They should develop an understanding of unbalanced charges involving the movement of electrons to interpret common electrostatic phenomena and should consider the dangers and use of electrostatic charge generated in everyday situations. Pupils should study electromagnetic effects in common devices. Pupils should investigate principles of electromagnetic induction as applied to the generation and transmission of electricity and devices such as dynamos and transformers. Pupils should be given opportunities to extend their quantitative study of electrical circuits. They should use measurements of voltage and current to derive measurements of electrical resistance, charge, energy transferred and electrical power. Pupils should continue to investigate the properties of components in controlling simple circuits using switches and relays, variable resistors, capacitors, diodes, transistors and logic gates. They should investigate the behaviour of bistable circuits made from two logic gates. They should consider the role of bistables in simple memory circuits to perform useful tasks. They should investigate the effects of feedback in a control system and consider the implications of information and control technology for everyday life. They should use knowledge of electronic systems, both analogue and digital, to solve problems. Pupils should develop an understanding of common electrical phenomena in conductors in terms of charge flow, including electrons and ions, and extend this to the study of thermionic emission and the production of X-rays.

(ii) Pupils should investigate the ways in which energy is transferred in a variety of personal and practical situations, including combustion of fuels. These investigations should include transfer by conduction, convection and radiation, partly in domestic contexts, including the effects of insulation. They should further develop ideas of energy conservation and efficiency of energy transfer. They should investigate the relationship between potential and kinetic energy and link these to the concept of work. They should be introduced to the idea of power as rate of energy transfer or doing work. The study should include the idea that although energy is always conserved, it may be dissipated and so it becomes harder to arrange for useful transfers of energy. They should be introduced to the ways electricity is generated in power stations from a range of resources, both renewable and non-renewable. By analysis of data, pupils should understand that some energy resources are limited and consider the longer term implications of the world-wide patterns of distribution and use of energy resources, including the "greenhouse effect'. They should be given opportunities to discuss how society makes decisions about energy resources.

(iii) Pupils should investigate the effects of forces on movement and the relationships between force, mass and acceleration. They should explore examples of motion including free-fall, circular motion and the movement of projectiles and be aware of the effect of friction. They should consider the use of ideas of momentum and energy in relation to motion in systems, for example in collisions, rockets and jet propulsion. They should investigate pressure and everyday applications of hydraulics. Pupils should investigate the relationship between forces and their effects in relation to the properties of common materials and how these determine the design, testing and strength of relevant artefacts and structures. They should apply their knowledge of the turning effect of forces and develop their understanding of centre of mass.

(iv) Pupils should explore the fundamental characteristics of sound, including loudness, amplitude, pitch and frequency. They should have opportunities to improve their understanding of the properties and behaviour of sound by developing a wave model, for example though observation of waves in ropes, in springs and on water. This should be related to pupils' experience of sounds and musical instruments, acoustics, electronic instruments and recording. They should be given the opportunity to investigate devices, for example microphones and loudspeakers, which act as transducers. They should understand the importance of noise control in the environment. Pupils should investigate the characteristics and effects of vibration, including resonance, in a range of mechanical systems. They should extend this study to include some uses of electronic sound technology in, for example, industry (cleaning and quality control), medicine (prenatal scanning) and social contexts (musical instruments). Pupils should investigate the fundamental characteristics of light, such as reflection, refraction, diffraction, interference and polarisation. They should relate these characteristics to the wave model. They should investigate the types of electromagnetic radiation, their uses and their potential dangers in: domestic situations (microwaves, infra-red, ultra-violet); communication (radio, microwaves, light); and medicine (X-rays, gamma rays). They should study the process of transmission of waves through different media, including the relationship between speed, frequency and wavelength. They should understand the working of a range of optical devices.

(v) Pupils should have opportunities to use the idea of gravitational force to explain the movement and positions of the Earth, Moon, Sun, planets and other bodies in the Universe. The idea of gravitational force should also be applied to tides, comets and satellites. Pupils should consider the possibilities and limitations of space travel and the use of the data gained. Pupils should know that other planets are geologically active and that their present composition is related to their distance from the Sun. Pupils should understand that the Sun is powered by nuclear fusion processes. Pupils should examine ideas that have been used in the past and more recently, to explain the character and origin of the Earth, other planets, stars and the Universe. They should study the life cycle of stars.

APPENDIX 3

There are quite a lot of special symbols that you should know for components in electrical circuits. The common ones are on this page.

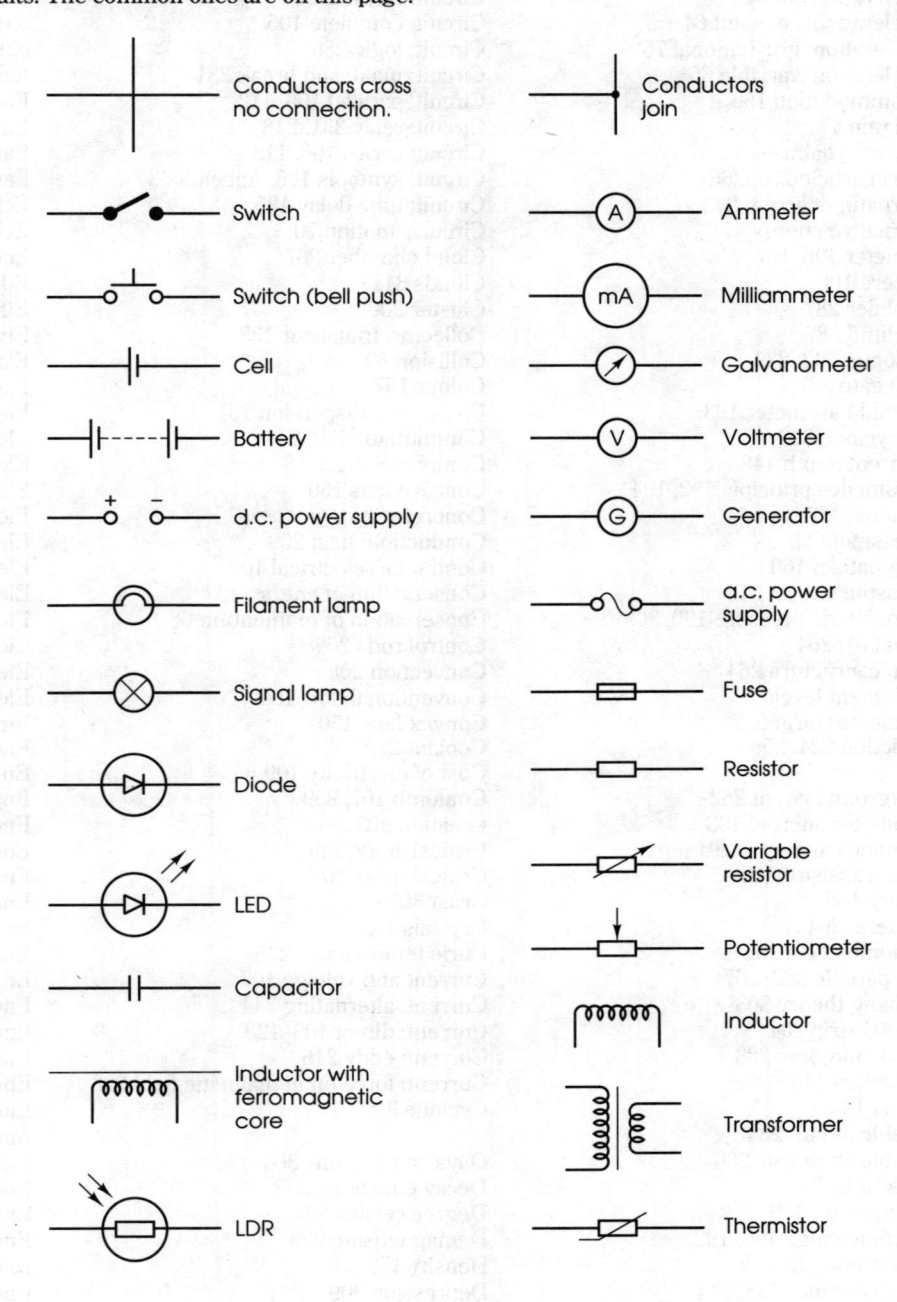

Symbol	Name	Symbol	Name
	Conductors cross no connection.		Conductors join
	Switch	A	Ammeter
	Switch (bell push)	mA	Milliammeter
	Cell		Galvanometer
	Battery	V	Voltmeter
	d.c. power supply	G	Generator
	Filament lamp		a.c. power supply
	Signal lamp		Fuse
	Diode		Resistor
	LED		Variable resistor
	Capacitor		Potentiometer
	Inductor with ferromagnetic core		Inductor
	LDR		Transformer
			Thermistor

INDEX

Absolute zero 206
Absorber 210, 263
Acceleration 28, 64
Acceleration: constant 64
Acceleration: gravitational 76
Acceleration: variable 65
Accommodation 156
Acid rain 47
Aims of syllabuses 4
Alpha particle 263, 266
Alternating current 243
Alternative energy 47
Ammeter 106, 107
Ampere 106
Amplifier 287
Amplitude 87
Analogue 232, 279
AND gate 281
Aneroid barometer 193
Anticyclone 309
Apparent depth 148
Archimedes principle 192, 194
Armature 231
Assessment 59
Astigmatism 160
Atmosphere 309, 315
Atmospheric pressure 190, 309
Atom 261, 264
Atomic structure 264
Attainment levels 7
Attainment targets 2
Attraction 224, 258

Background count 262
Barometer aneroid 193
Barometer mercury 191
Base: transistor 133
Battery 106
Bequerel 264
Bernoulli effect 195
Beta particle 263, 267
Big bang theory 303
Bimetal strip 204
Binary numbers 283
Binoculars 149
Biogas 48
Bistable circuit 284
Bistable latch 285, 286
Black hole 304
Boiling point 179
Bourdon gauge 190, 192
Boyle's law 192, 212
Bridge rectifier 135, 244
Brownian motion 175

Camera 156
Camera lens 156
Camera: pin hole 146
Capacitance 132
Capacitor 132
Capacitor: smoothing 136
Capillary action 179
Catapult field 229
Cell 106
Celsius 204
Centre of mass 27
Centripetal force 70, 76, 314
Chain reactions 268

Charge 107, 259
Charles' law 207, 212
Circuit: bistable 284
Circuit: complete 106
Circuit: logic 280
Circuit: make and break 231
Circuit: parallel 106, 112
Circuit: relay 231, 248
Circuit: series 106, 112
Circuit: symbols 106, Appendix 3
Circuit: time delay 135
Circular motion 70
Cloud chamber 267
Clouds 311
Cluster 300
Collector: transistor 133
Collision 69
Colour 157
Colour and dispersion 151
Commutator 230, 244
Compression 23, 88
Concave lens 150
Concrete 23
Conduction: heat 209
Conductor: electrical 106
Conservation of energy 43
Conservation of momentum 68
Control rods 269
Convection 208
Conventional flow 106
Convex lens 150
Coolant 269
Cost of electricity 109
Coulomb 107, 259
Creation 303
Critical angle 149
Critical mass 269
Crust 305
Crystals 173
Curie temperature 225
Current and voltage 107
Current: alternating 244
Current: direct 105–128
Current: eddy 246
Current: force on in magnetic field 228
Cyclone 309

Days and seasons 304
Decay equations 266
Degree celsius 204
Demagnetising 225
Density 172
Depression 309
Diagrams 15
Diffraction 93
Diffusion 174
Digital 232, 279, 285
Digital transmission 283
Diode 131, 248
Diode protection 248
Diode: light emitting 133, 137
Dispersion 151
Displacement 62, 72
Distance 62
Distance multiplier 50
Doppler effect 301
Double insulation 118
Drag 195

Dynamo 243, 245

e.m.f. 112, 242
e.m.f. Back 245
e.m.f. induced 242
Ear 94
Earth 109
Earth: atmosphere 309, 315
Earth: structure 305, 316
Earthquakes 305
Echo 89
Echo sounding 89
Eclipses 315
Eddy current 246
Efficiency 46, 52, 246
Einstein's equation 268
Elastic limit 28
Elastic material 28
Electric bell 231
Electric field 261, 263
Electric motor 230
Electromagnetic spectrum 153
Electromagnetic wave 94, 153
Electromagnetism 226
Electron 106, 259
Electron gun 260
Electronic systems 279–298
Electronics 129–144
Electroscope 262
Element 264
Emitter: transistor 133
Endoscope 150
Energy 41
Energy and charge 107
Energy and matter 268
Energy arrows 52
Energy binding 268
Energy degradation 44
Energy electrical 108
Energy renewable/non-renewable 47
Energy: alternative 47
Energy: biomass 48
Energy: chemical 47
Energy: conservation of 43
Energy: fossil fuels 47
Energy: geothermal 49
Energy: heat 44
Energy: hydroelectric 48
Energy: kinetic 43
Energy: nuclear 47
Energy: potential 43
Energy: solar 47
Energy: tidal 49
Energy: wavepower 48
Energy: windpower 48
Equations of motion 73
Equations: decay 266
Equations: list of, Appendix 1
Equilibrium 25
Evaporation 176
Examination boards 12
Expansion 204
Expansivity 213
Eye 156

Farad 132
Faraday's law 242
Fault 306

INDEX

Feedback 284, 287
Fibre optics 149
Field 224, 260, 302
Filters 158
Fission 268
Fission products 269
Fleming's left hand rule 228
Fleming's right hand rule 243
Flight: principles of 195
Fluid 172
Fluid flow 195
Fluid friction 23
Flux 242
Focal length 150
Focus: principal 150, 154
Fog 311
Food 42
Force 22
Force multiplier 50
Force on a current carrier 228
Force: centripetal 70, 314
Force: normal 25
Force: reaction 25
Force: resultant 29, 67
Forcemeter 22
Forces and particles 173
Fossil fuel 42
Fossils 314
Fraunhoffer lines 301
Frequency 87
Friction 23, 46
Front 210
Fuel 42, 47
Fuel pins 269
Fuse 109, 115
Fusion reaction 315

Galaxy 300
Galvanometer 117
Gamma wave 263, 266
Gas behaviour 173, 177, 205
Gas diffusion 174
Gas laws 192, 205, 207, 212
Gas model 174
Gates 281
Gears 46
Geiger and Marsden experiment 264
Geiger-Muller tube 262
General gas equation 212
Generator 243
Geothermal energy 49
Gradient 64, 111, 113
Graphs 15
Gravitation 314
Gravitation: Newton's law 314
Gravitational acceleration 66
Gravitational field strength 302
Greenhouse effect 211

Half life 265, 266
Harmonics 94
Hearing 94
Heat 203
Heat: conduction 209
Heat: convection 208
Heat: latent 208
Heat: measurements 210
Heat: radiation 209
Heat: specific heat capacity 207, 210
Helium 263, 265
Hertz 87
Hooke's law 28, 29
Hydraulics 191
Hydroelectric power 48

Hydrometer 194
Hysteresis 247

Icy planet 301
Igneous rock 312
Image 147, 154, 155
Impulse 68, 75
Inertia 76
Infra red 153
Insulation: heat 212
Insulator: electrical 106
Insulator: heat 209
Interference 92, 151
Internal reflection 148
Internal resistance 117
Inverter 281, 288
Investigation 16
Ion 261
Ionisation 262
Isobar 309
Isotope 265

Jet engine 71
Joule 44

Kelvin temperature scale 206
Kinetic energy 42, 75
Kinetic theory 173, 175

Lamina 28, 246
Laminated core 245, 247
Latch 286
Latent heat 176, 208
Lens 150
Lens equation 159
Lenz's law 242
Levers 46, 50
Lift 195
Light Dependent Resistor (LDR) 130, 286
Light Emitting Diode (LED) 133, 137, 283
Light year 299
Liquid 172
Liquid expansion 204, 213
Loading effects 46
Local group 300
Logic 280
Logic gate 281
Long sight 160
Longitudinal wave 87, 305
Loudspeaker 230

Machines 45
Magnetic field 224, 242, 263
Magnetic materials 224
Magnetising 225
Magnetism 223–240
Magnification 155, 159
Mains electricity 109, 248
Manometer 189
Mantle 305
Mass 24
Materials 28, 106
Matter 172
Mechanical Advantage 46, 50
Melt-down 270
Meniscus 179
Mercalli scale 306
Mercury barometer 191
Metamorphic rock 312
Milky way 300
Mineral 312
Mirror 147

Moderator 269
Moment 26
Momentum 68
Momentum: conservation of 68
Moon: phases of 307
Motion 61
Motion in a circle 70
Motion: equations of 73
Motion: Newton's laws 66
Motor 230, 245
Motor: control system 285
Multiple Choice 14

NAND gate 281
National Curriculum 2
National grid 248
Natural frequency 86
Neutron 264
Neutron star 304
Newton 67
Newton's laws of motion 66
NOR gate 282
Normal force 24
NOT gate 281
Nuclear energy 47, 268
Nuclear reactor 268
Nucleus 264

Ohm's law 110
Operational amplifier 287
Optical fibre 149
Optics 145–170
OR gate 281
Oscillations 86
Oscilloscope (CRO) 114
Overtones 94

Parallax 29
Parallelogram of forces 29
Particle 173
Pascal 188
Pendulum 86
Period 86, 95
Periscope 149
Phase 151, 248
Phases of moon 307
Photoelectric effect 158
Photon 263
Photosynthesis 42, 48
Pinhole camera 146
Pitch 89
Planck's constant 158
Planet 300
Planet formation 302
Plug: mains 109
Polarisation 152
Potential difference (p.d.) 108, 112
Potential divider 130, 137
Potential energy 43
Power 41, 45
Power station 248
Power: electrical 108
Power: pack circuit 136
Power: transmission 247
Pressure 188
Pressure law 207, 212
Pressure vessel 270
Primary colours 158
Principal focus 150, 154
Principle of Moments 26
Prism 148
Projectiles 69
Projector 156
Protactiniuum 265

INDEX

Proton 264
Proton number 265
Pulleys 45, 51

Quality of sound 88, 94

Radiation: absorption 263
Radiation: heat 209
Radio waves 153
Radioactive decay 265, 266
Radioactivity 262
Radioactivity: uses 268
Randomness 266
Rarefaction 88
Ray diagrams 154
Ray of light 146
RCCB 115
Reaction force 24
Rectifier 135
Rectifier 131, 135
Red giant 303
Red shift 301
Reflection 91, 147
Refraction 91, 147
Refractive index 148
Refrigerator 178
Relay 231, 248
Repulsion 224, 258
Resistance 110, 112
Resistance of themistor 130
Resistivity 116
Resistor 106, 130
Resistor: light dependent 130
Resistor: variable 130
Resistors in parallel 112
Resistors in series 112
Resonance 86
Resultant force 29, 67
Rheostat 130
Richter scale 306
Ring main 115
Ripple tank 90
Rock cycle 314
Rockets 71
Rocky planet 301, 303

Safety: electrical 115
Sagety: radioactivity 262
Satellites 75
Satellites: geostationary 75
Satellites: polar 75
Saturation 288
Scalar 25
Seasons 304
Secondary colours 158
Sedimentary rock 312

Seismometer 305, 306
Short sight 160
Sievert 264
Slip ring commutator 243
Smoke cell 175
Smoothing circuit 136
Solar panel 211
Solar system 300
Solid 173
Sound 88
Sound: speed of 89
SPAG 6
Specific heat capacity 207, 210
Speed 62
Speed of light 94, 299
Speed of sound 89
Split ring commutator 230, 244
Spring 95
SR latch 286
Stability 27
Stalling 195
Star: life cycle 303
Star formation 302
State: change of 176
States of matter 172
Static electricity 258
Static friction 23
Stroboscope 90
Structured questions 14
Subduction 307
Supernova 304
Surface tension 178
Switch 106
Switch: two way 118
Switching circuits 134
Syllabus coverage 3
Symbols: chemical 265
Symbols: electrical 106, Appendix 3
Synoptic chart 310
Systems: analogue 279, 285
Systems: digital 279, 285

Tacoma Narrows bridge 87
Tape recorder 232
Techtonic plates 306
Temperature 204
Temperature and gases 205
Temperature scales 204
Tension 23
Terminal velocity 30, 67
Thermal air current 209
Thermionic emission 260
Thermistor 111, 114
Thrust 195
Ticker tape 62
Tides 308

Tiers 5
Time delay circuit 134
Total internal reflection 148
Transducers 137
Transformer 245
Transistor 133
Transmission of power 247
Transverse wave 87
Truth table 280
Turns ratio 246
Two way switches 118

U-values 213
Ultra violet 153
Unit: cost of electrical energy 109
Universe 300
Universe: expansion of 301
Upthrust 192, 194

Vector 25
Velocity 62
Velocity ratio 46, 51
Velocity: constant, uniform 62, 64
Velocity: terminal 30, 67
Virtual image 147
Viscosity 30
Vision: defects 160
Volt 107
Voltage comparator 289
Voltmeter 107, 117

Watt 45
Wave 87
Wave equation 92
Wave front 89
Wave: P.S.L. 305
Wave: behaviour 87, 89
Wave: electromagnetic 94
Wave: gamma 263
Wave: light 151
Wave: longitudinal 87
Wave: sound 88
Wave: transverse 87
Wavelength 87
Weather 309
Weather: fronts 310
Weather: maps 193, 310
Weathering 313
Weight 3, 195
White dwarf 304
Wind energy 48
Work 41, 44

X-rays 94

Young's double slit experiment 152, 157